American Government and Politics Today

2023–2024 Brief, Enhanced, Eleventh Edition

Steffen W. Schmidt
Iowa State University

Mack C. Shelley II
Iowa State University

Barbara A. Bardes
University of Cincinnati

 Cengage

Australia • Brazil • Canada • Mexico • Singapore • United Kingdom • United States

American Government and Politics Today Brief, Enhanced, Eleventh Edition

Steffen W. Schmidt, Mack C. Shelley II, Barbara A. Bardes

SVP, Product: Erin Joyner

VP, Product: Thais Alencar

Portfolio Product Director: Laura Ross

Associate Portfolio Product Manager: Kristin Cole

Product Assistant: Danny Radar

Learning Designer: Rebecca Shuman

Content Manager: Dan Saabye

Senior In-House Subject Matter Expert, Political Science: Emily Hickey

Senior Digital Project Manager: Dana Edmunds

Director, Product Marketing: Neena Bali

Executive Marketing Manager: Valerie Hartman

Content Acquisition Analyst: Deanna Ettinger

Compositor: Straive

Art Director: Sarah Cole

Cover Image Source: Jeremy Hogan/ SOPA Images/Damian Dovarganes

For product information and technology assistance, contact us at **Cengage Customer & Sales Support, 1-800-354-9706 or support.cengage.com.**

For permission to use material from this text or product, submit all requests online at **www.copyright.com.**

Library of Congress Control Number: 2022946546

Student Edition:
ISBN: 978-0-357-79538-5

Loose-leaf Edition:
ISBN: 978-0-357-79539-2

Cengage
200 Pier 4 Boulevard
Boston, MA 02210
USA

Cengage is a leading provider of customized learning solutions. Our employees reside in nearly 40 different countries and serve digital learners in 165 countries around the world. Find your local representative at **www.cengage.com.**

To learn more about Cengage platforms and services, register or access your online learning solution, or purchase materials for your course, visit **www.cengage.com.**

Printed in the United States of America
Print Number: 01   Print Year: 2022

Contents in Brief

Preface xvii

About the Authors xxii

Part I: The American System

Chapter 1   The Democratic Republic 1

Chapter 2   Forging a New Government: The Constitution 22

Chapter 3   Federalism 46

Chapter 4   Civil Liberties 68

Chapter 5   Civil Rights 95

Part II: The Politics of American Democracy

Chapter 6   Public Opinion, Political Socialization, and the Media 122

Chapter 7   Interest Groups and Political Parties 151

Chapter 8   Campaigns and Elections 180

Part III: Institutions of American Government

Chapter 9   Congress 207

Chapter 10   The President 235

Chapter 11   The Executive Branch 259

Chapter 12   The Courts 282

Part IV: Policymaking

Chapter 13   Domestic and Economic Policy 308

Chapter 14   Foreign Policy 332

Appendix A   The Declaration of Independence 359

Appendix B   The Constitution of the United States 361

Appendix C   *Federalist Papers* No. 10 and No. 51 381

Appendix D   Government Spending and Revenue Charts 389

Glossary 391

Index 403

Contents

Preface xvii

About the Authors xxii

Part I: The American System

Chapter 1   The Democratic Republic   1

Politics and Government 2

    Why Is Government Necessary? 2

    Limiting Government Power 3

    Authority and Legitimacy 3

Democracy and Other Forms of Government 4

    Types of Government 4

    Direct Democracy as a Model 4

    The Dangers of Direct Democracy 5

    A Democratic Republic 5

What Kind of Democracy Do We Have? 6

    Democracy for Everyone 7

    Democracy for the Few 7

    Democracy for Groups 8

Which Side Are You On?: Will the U.S. Ever Get Back to the Way It Was Before COVID-19? 8

Fundamental Values 9

    Liberty Versus Order 10

    Liberty Versus Equality 11

    The Proper Role and Size of Government 12

    The 2020 Election 14

2022 Elections: Predictions and Results 15

Political Ideologies 15

    Conservatism 15

    Liberalism 16

    The Traditional Political Spectrum 17

    Problems With the Traditional Political Spectrum 18

    A Four-Cornered Ideological Grid 18

Making A Difference: Seeing Democracy in Action 19

Key Terms • Chapter Summary • Test Yourself

SOPA Images Limited/Alamy Stock Photo

Chapter 2   Forging a New Government: The Constitution   22

Garen Meguerian/Moment/Getty Images

The Colonial Background   23

Separatists, the *Mayflower*, and the Compact   23
More Colonies, More Government   24

Which Side Are You On?: Is America a Christian Nation?   25

British Restrictions and Colonial Grievances   26
The First Continental Congress   26
The Second Continental Congress   26

An Independent Confederation   27

The Resolution for Independence   28
July 4, 1776—The Declaration of Independence   28
The Rise of Republicanism   29
The Articles of Confederation: Our First Form of Government   30

The Constitutional Convention   32

Factions Among the Delegates   32
Politicking and Compromises   33
Working Toward Final Agreement   35
The Final Document   37

The Difficult Road to Ratification   37

The Federalists Push for Ratification   37
The March to the Finish   38
The Bill of Rights   39

Altering the Constitution   39

The Formal Amendment Process   40
Informal Methods of Constitutional Change   41

Making A Difference: How Can You Affect the U.S. Constitution?   43

Key Terms • Chapter Summary • Test Yourself

Chapter 3   Federalism   46

Federalism and Its Alternatives   47

A Unitary System   47
A Confederal System   47
A Federal System   48
Why Federalism?   48
Arguments Against Federalism   50

NICK ADAMS/REUTERS/Newscom

The Constitutional Basis for American Federalism 50

Powers of the National Government 50

Powers of the State Governments 51

Prohibited Powers 52

Concurrent Powers 52

The Supremacy Clause 53

Interstate Relations 53

Defining Constitutional Powers—The Early Years 54

McCulloch v. Maryland (1819) 54

Gibbons v. Ogden (1824) 55

States' Rights and the Resort to Civil War 55

The Continuing Dispute Over the Division of Power 57

Dual Federalism 57

The New Deal and Cooperative Federalism 58

The Politics of Federalism 58

Which Side Are You On?: The Federal Government Has Unconstitutionally Usurped Too Much Power From the States 59

Methods of Implementing Cooperative Federalism 60

Federalism and Today's Supreme Court 62

A Trend Toward States' Rights 63

Recent Decisions 63

Making A Difference: Writing E-mails and Texting to the Editor 65

Key Terms • Chapter Summary • Test Yourself

Chapter 4   Civil Liberties   68

The Constitutional Bases of Our Liberties 69

Protections Listed in the Original Constitution 69

Extending the Bill of Rights to State Governments 70

Incorporation Under the Fourteenth Amendment 70

Freedom of Religion 71

The Separation of Church and State—The Establishment Clause 71

The Free Exercise Clause 74

Freedom of Expression 75

No Prior Restraint 75

The Protection of Symbolic Speech 75

The Protection of Commercial Speech 76

Gregory Rec/Portland Press Herald/Getty Images

Attempts to Ban Subversive or Advocacy Speech 76

The Eclipse of Obscenity as a Legal Category 77

Unprotected Speech: Slander 78

Student Speech 79

Freedom of the Press 80

Today, Large Tech Companies Dominate the Media 81

The Right to Privacy 81

Which Side Are You On?: Do Big Tech Media Companies Have the Right to Censor Content? 82

Privacy Rights and Abortion 82

Privacy Rights and the "Right to Die" 85

The Great Balancing Act: The Rights of the Accused Versus the Rights of Society 86

Rights of the Accused 87

Extending the Rights of the Accused 88

The Exclusionary Rule 88

Civil Liberties Versus Security Issues 90

Subsequent Revelations of NSA Activity 90

Making A Difference: Your Civil Liberties: Searches and Seizures 92

Key Terms • Chapter Summary • Test Yourself

Chapter 5 Civil Rights 95

Samuel Corum/Getty Images News/Getty Images

The African American Experience and the Civil Rights Movement 96

Ending Servitude 96

The Ineffectiveness of the Early Civil Rights Laws 97

The End of the Separate-but-Equal Doctrine 98

De Jure and *De Facto* Segregation 99

The Civil Rights Movement 99

Modern Civil Rights Legislation 100

Civil Rights and the Courts 104

Standards for Judicial Review 104

The Supreme Court Addresses Affirmative Action 105

Experiences of Other Underrepresented Groups 107

Latinos and the Immigration Issue 107

National Security and the Rights of Immigrants 109

Which Side Are You On?: Should We Close Off Our Southern Border Again? 110

The Trauma of Native Americans 111

Women's Struggle for Equal Rights 112

　　Early Women's Political Movements 112

　　The Modern Women's Movement 112

　　Women in Politics Today 114

　　Gender-Based Discrimination in the Workplace 114

The Rights and Status of LGBTQ+ Americans 116

　　Growth in the LGBTQ+ Rights Movement 116

　　State and Local Laws Targeting LGBTQ+ Persons 116

　　"Don't Ask, Don't Tell" 117

　　Same-Sex Marriage 117

　　The Rights of Transgender Individuals 118

Making A Difference: Dealing with Discrimination 119

Key Terms • Chapter Summary • Test Yourself

Part II: The Politics of American Democracy

michael melia/Alamy Stock Photo

Chapter 6 Public Opinion, Political Socialization, and the Media 122

Public Opinion and Political Socialization 123

　　Consensus and Divided Opinion 123

　　Forming Public Opinion: Political Socialization 123

　　The Media and Public Opinion 125

Which Side Are You On?: Should the Federal Communications Commission Reinstate the Fairness Doctrine? 126

　　Political Events and Public Opinion 126

The Influence of Demographic Factors 127

　　Educational Achievement 127

　　Economic Status 129

　　Religious Denomination 129

　　Religious Commitment and Beliefs 129

　　Race and Ethnicity 130

　　The Latino Vote 130

　　The Gender Gap 131

　　Geographic Region 131

Measuring Public Opinion 132

The History of Opinion Polls 132

Sampling Techniques 133

The Difficulty of Obtaining Accurate Results 134

Additional Problems With Polls 135

Public Opinion and the Political Process 136

Political Culture and Public Opinion 136

Policymaking and Public Opinion 137

The Media in the United States 137

The Roles of the Media 137

Television Versus the Newer Media 140

Challenges Facing the Media 141

The Media and Political Campaigns 142

Political Advertising 143

Management of News Coverage 143

Going for the Knockout Punch—Presidential Debates 144

Political Campaigns and the Internet 144

Blogosphere Politics 145

Bias in the Media 146

Making A Difference: Being a Critical Consumer of the News 148

Key Terms • Chapter Summary • Test Yourself

Chapter 7 Interest Groups and Political Parties 151

A Nation of Joiners 152

Thousands of Groups 152

Interest Groups and Social Movements 153

Reasons to Join—or Not Join 153

Types of Interest Groups 153

Economic Interest Groups 154

Which Side Are You On?: Should States Raise the Minimum Wage? 156

Environmental Interest Groups 158

Public-Interest Groups 158

Additional Types of Interest Groups 159

Interest Group Strategies 160

Direct Techniques 160

Indirect Techniques 161

Regulating Lobbyists 162

MedSci/Alamy Stock Photo

Political Parties in the United States 163

Functions of Political Parties in the United States 163
The Party Organization 164
The Party-in-the-Electorate 165
The Party-in-Government 166

A History of Political Parties in the United States 167

The Formative Years: Federalists and Anti-Federalists 167
Democrats and Whigs 168
The Civil War Crisis 168
The Post–Civil War Period 168
The Progressive Interlude 169
The New Deal Era 170
An Era of Divided Government 170
The Parties Today 171

2022 Elections: Partisan Trends in the 2022 Elections 172

Why Has the Two-Party System Endured? 172

The Historical Foundations of the Two-Party System 172
Political Socialization and Practical Considerations 173
The Winner-Take-All Electoral System 173
State and Federal Laws Favoring the Two Parties 174
The Role of Minor Parties in U.S. Politics 174
The Rise of the Independents 176

Making A Difference: You Can Be a Convention Delegate 177

Key Terms • Chapter Summary • Test Yourself

Chapter 8   Campaigns and Elections   180

The Twenty-First-Century Campaign 181

Who Is Eligible? 181
Who Runs? 181
Managing the Campaign 182

Financing the Campaign 184

The Evolution of the Campaign Finance System 185
The Current Campaign Finance Environment 186

2022 Elections: Financing the Congressional Races 189

Running for President: The Longest Campaign 189

Reforming the Presidential Primaries 189

Vince360/Shutterstock.com

The Invisible Primary 190

The Party Decides 191

Primaries and Caucuses 191

Front-Loading the Primaries 192

On to the National Convention 193

The Electoral College 194

The 2020 Election and the January 6, 2021 Demonstrations at the Capitol 195

How Are Elections Conducted? 196

Voting by Mail 196

Voting Fraud and Voter ID Laws 196

Turning Out to Vote 198

Legal Restrictions on Voting 199

Is the Franchise Still Too Restrictive? 199

Which Side Are You On?: Should Noncitizens Be Able to Vote in the United States? 200

How Do Voters Decide? 201

Party Identification 201

Other Political Factors 202

Demographic Characteristics 202

Making A Difference: Registering and Voting 203

Key Terms • Chapter Summary • Test Yourself

Part III: Institutions of American Government

Chapter 9 Congress 207

The Nature and Functions of Congress 208

Bicameralism 208

The Lawmaking Function 209

The Representation Function 209

Service to Constituents 210

The Oversight Function 210

The Second Impeachment Investigation 211

Oversight of the Biden Administration 211

The Public-Education Function 211

The Conflict-Resolution Function 211

The Powers of Congress 211

AP Images/J. Scott Applewhite

House–Senate Differences and Congressional Perks 213

Size and Rules 213
Debate and Filibustering 213

Which Side Are You On?: Is It Time to Get Rid of the Filibuster? 214

Congresspersons and the Citizenry: A Comparison 215
Perks and Privileges 216

Congressional Elections and Apportionment 216

Candidates for Congressional Elections 217
Apportionment of the House 217
Gerrymandering 218
"Minority-Majority" Districts 220

How Congress Is Organized 221

2022 Elections: Party Control After the 2022 Midterm Elections 222

The Power of Committees 222
Committees Versus the Leadership 222
Types of Congressional Committees 223
The Selection of Committee Members 224
Leadership in the House 225
Leadership in the Senate 227

Lawmaking and Budgeting 228

How Much Will the Government Spend? 228
Preparing the Budget 230
Congress Faces the Budget 231
Budget Resolutions and Crises 231

Making A Difference: Learning About Your Representatives 232

Key Terms • Chapter Summary • Test Yourself

Chapter 10 The President 235

Who Can Become President? 236

Birthplace and Age 236
The Process of Becoming President 236

The Many Roles of the President 237

Head of State 237

Which Side Are You On?: Should We Elect the President by
Popular Vote? 238

Chief Executive 239

Geopix/Alamy Stock Photo

Commander in Chief 240

Chief Diplomat 241

Chief Legislator 242

Party Chief and Politician 244

Presidential Powers 245

Emergency Powers 246

Executive Orders 247

Executive Privilege 247

Signing Statements 248

Abuses of Executive Power and Impeachment 248

The Executive Organization 250

The Cabinet 250

The Executive Office of the President 251

The Vice President 253

The Vice President's Job 253

Presidential Succession 254

Making A Difference: Communicating With the White House 256

Key Terms • Chapter Summary • Test Yourself

Chapter 11   The Executive Branch   259

The Nature and Scope of the Federal Bureaucracy 260

Public and Private Bureaucracies 260

The Size of the Bureaucracy 260

The Federal Budget 262

The Organization of the Executive Branch 263

Which Side Are You On?: We Have to Stop Overspending by the Federal Government 264

Cabinet Departments 264

Independent Executive Agencies 266

Government and Government-Controlled Corporations 268

Staffing the Bureaucracy 270

Political Appointees 270

History of the Federal Civil Service 270

Modern Attempts at Bureaucratic Reform 272

Sunshine Laws Before and After 9/11 273

Privatization, or Contracting Out 273

The Issue of Whistleblowers 274

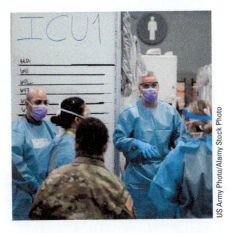

US Army Photo/Alamy Stock Photo

Bureaucrats as Politicians and Policymakers 275

The Rulemaking Environment 276

Negotiated Rulemaking 277

Bureaucrats as Policymakers 278

Congressional Control of the Bureaucracy 278

Making A Difference: What the Government Knows About You 279

Key Terms • Chapter Summary • Test Yourself

Chapter 12 The Courts 282

Sources of American Law 283

The Common Law Tradition 283

Constitutions 284

Statutes and Administrative Regulations 284

Case Law 284

The Federal Court System 285

Basic Judicial Requirements 285

Parties to Lawsuits 285

Procedural Rules 286

Types of Federal Courts 286

Federal Courts and the War on Terrorism 289

The Supreme Court at Work 290

Which Cases Reach the Supreme Court? 291

Court Procedures 292

Decisions and Opinions 292

The Selection of Federal Judges 293

Judicial Appointments 293

Which Side Are You On?: Should State Judges Be Elected? 294

Partisanship and Judicial Appointments 295

The Senate's Role 296

Policymaking and the Courts 298

Judicial Review 298

Judicial Activism and Judicial Restraint 299

The Roberts Court 299

What Checks Our Courts? 302

Making A Difference: Changing the Legal System 305

Key Terms • Chapter Summary • Test Yourself

Part IV: Policymaking

Chapter 13   Domestic and Economic Policy   308

Which Side Are You On?: Does Entitlement Spending Corrupt Us? 309

The Policy-Making Process: The CARES Act 310

The CARES Act: Agenda Building 310
The CARES Act: Policy Formulation 311
The CARES Act: Policy Adoption 311
The CARES Act: Policy Implementation 311
The CARES Act: Policy Evaluation 312

Health Care in the Twenty-first Century 312

Health Care's Role in the American Economy 312
The Affordable Care Act—Obamacare 314

Energy and the Environment 316

Energy Independence—A Strategic Issue 316
Climate Change 318

The Politics of Economic Decision Making 320

Good Times, Bad Times 320
Fiscal Policy 321
The Public Debt and Deficit Spending 322
Monetary Policy 324

The Politics of Taxation 327

Federal Income Tax Rates 327
Income Tax Loopholes and Other Types of Taxes 328

Making A Difference: Learning About Entitlement Reform 329

Key Terms • Chapter Summary • Test Yourself

Chapter 14   Foreign Policy   332

Facing the World: Foreign and Defense Policies 333

Aspects of Foreign Policy 333
Idealism Versus Realism in Foreign Policy 334

Terrorism and Warfare 335

The Emergence of Terrorism 335
Wars in Iraq 337

ZUMA Press/ZUMA Press, Inc./Alamy Stock Photo

Planetpix/Alamy Stock Photo

Afghanistan 337
The Civil War in Syria and the Rise of ISIS 338

U.S. Diplomatic Efforts 339

Nuclear Weapons 340
Israel and the Palestinians 342
The New Power: China 343
Economic Troubles in Europe 345

Who Makes Foreign Policy? 346

Constitutional Powers of the President 346
The Executive Branch and Foreign Policy Making 348
Congress Balances the Presidency 349

The Major Foreign Policy Themes 350

The Formative Years: Avoiding Entanglements 350
The Era of Internationalism 350
Superpower Relations 351

Which Side Are You On?: How Dangerous Is Putin's Russia for the World? 354

Making A Difference: Working for Human Rights 355

Key Terms • Chapter Summary • Test Yourself

Appendix A   The Declaration of Independence   359

Appendix B   The Constitution of the United States   361

Appendix C   *Federalist Papers* No. 10 and No. 51   381

Appendix D   Government Spending and Revenue Charts   389

Glossary   391
Index   403

Preface for the Instructor

Some believe that the 2020 elections were among the most consequential ever. In that year, Americans appeared to pass judgment on Donald Trump, whom they had elected in 2016. In November 2018, the public had already made an initial assessment of Trump's record by handing the U.S. House of Representatives to the Democrats—a net 41 seats switched from Republican to Democrat. The dramatic contest between Trump and Joe Biden in 2020 completed this popular reassessment. The 2020 elections must be viewed in the context of the Coronavirus pandemic which was raging then, the resulting economic collapse, and many demonstrations against perceived police violence.

The first two years of the Biden administration saw many, if not most, of Trump's policies reversed. Did Biden and his supporters in Congress go too far? If one looks at his popularity rating from the polls, the answer appeared to be yes. For much of his first two years, Biden's approval rating was less than 40 percent. The 2022 mid-term elections confirmed the public's non-acceptance of many of Biden's policies. Facing historically high inflation rates did not help the Democrats. The Republicans picked up enough seats in the House to take the majority. At least a two-year period of divided government will ensue, thus preventing most, if not all, major legislation from being passed.

One thing was and continues to be certain: American politics today will never be without tension, drama, and conflict. Throughout this Enhanced Brief Edition of *American Government and Politics Today*, you will read about how our government has responded to past issues and how it is responding to current conflicts.

This enhanced edition is a condensed and updated version of the larger editions of *American Government and Politics Today*. It has been created specifically for those instructors who want a text that presents the fundamental components of the American political system while retaining the quality and readability of the larger editions. You will find that this enhanced edition is up to date in every respect. The text, figures, tables, and all pedagogical features reflect the latest available data. We have also included coverage of all recently issued laws, regulations, and court decisions that have—or will have—a significant impact on American society and our political system.

Like the larger editions, this volume places a major emphasis on political participation and involvement. This brief, fourteen-chapter text has been heralded by reviewers as the best essentials text for its affordability, conciseness, clarity, and readability.

New to the Enhanced Eleventh Edition

Much of the text was thoroughly updated for the Eleventh Edition. This is an enhanced edition, meaning that key changes in the American political landscape have been inserted throughout every single chapter.

- Insights on the outcome and impact of the 2022 midterm elections are integrated throughout.
- Providing the most current coverage available, all charts and graphs are updated to 2022 and 2023, when possible.

- New coverage includes highlights of key 2021 and 2022 Supreme Court cases.

- The authors offer insightful coverage and analysis of the Biden administration's actions during his first two years as president.

- Careful attention is given to diversity, equity and inclusiveness (DEI) throughout.

Special Pedagogical Features

- *Making a Difference* At the end of every chapter, a feature entitled *Making a Difference* enhances our emphasis on student participation. These features provide newly updated, useful information for active citizenship. We offer tips on how to find information on issues, how to learn about your elected representatives, how to join and participate in advocacy organizations, how to protect your civil rights and liberties, and more.

- *Which Side Are You On?* Every chapter includes this debate-style feature, which concludes with a *For Critical Analysis* question to invite critical thinking.

- **"At Issue"** boxes turn the spotlight on current events and controversies and then conclude with "For Critical Analysis" questions that spark lively discussion and deeper reflection on the material.

- **Learning outcomes** open every chapter and correlate with each major section, giving students a road map to the book's key concepts.

- **Quizzes at the end of each chapter**—also correlated to the learning outcomes—reinforce concepts, helping students maximize their study time and course success.

- **Key Terms**—Important terms that are boldfaced and defined in the text when they are first used. These terms are defined in the text margins, listed at the end of the chapter with the page numbers on which they appear, and included in the Glossary at the back of the book.

- **InterAct**—A mini-feature that directs students to selected websites and encourages them to take one or more actions when they get there.

- **Chapter Summary**—A point-by-point summary of the chapter text.

Appendices

The Brief Edition of *American Government and Politics Today* includes, as appendices, both the Declaration of Independence (Appendix A) and the U.S. Constitution (Appendix B). The text of the Constitution has been annotated to help students understand the meaning of the various provisions in this important document. Appendix C presents *Federalist Papers* No. 10 and No. 51. These selections are also annotated to help students grasp their importance in understanding the American philosophy of government. Appendix D contains pie charts that explain the expenditures and revenues of the federal government.

MindTap for *American Government and Politics Today,* Enhanced Brief Edition

Printed Access Card ISBN: 9780357795453
Instant Access Code ISBN: 9780357795446

MindTap for *American Government and Politics Today:* Enhanced Brief Eleventh Edition is an immersive, outcomes-driven online learning experience built upon Cengage content and correlated to a core set of learning outcomes. MindTap is the platform that gives you complete control of your course to craft unique learning experiences that challenge students, build confidence, and elevate performance.

MindTap introduces students to core concepts from the beginning of your course using a simplified learning path that progresses from understanding to application. Built upon proven learning research and theory, auto-graded assessments and content are paired in a visually captivating side-by-side format.

A variety of activity types enable students to flex their critical thinking muscles while soaking in key concepts. Use MindTap for *American Government and Politics Today,* Enhanced Brief Edition as-is, or personalize it to meet your specific course needs. You can also easily integrate MindTap into your Learning Management System (LMS).

Cengage Infuse for *American Government and Politics Today:* Brief Eleventh Edition

Printed Access Card ISBN: 9780357795484
Instant Access Code ISBN: 9780357795477

Cengage Infuse is an embedded course kit that lives inside your Learning Management System (LMS). Set up your course in 15 minutes or less—complete with an eTextbook and auto-graded assessments—all within a system you and your students already know.

For Your Students

Access *American Government and Politics Today:* Enhanced Brief Eleventh Edition resources by visiting **www.cengage.com**. If you purchased MindTap access with your book, click on "**Register a Product**" and then enter your access code.

Cengage Read

Cengage Read, the new mobile app, enables students to study on the go. Students can read and listen to Cengage eTextbooks, and highlight and take notes when and where it's most convenient, both online and off. Best of all, it's free to download on any smartphone or tablet.

Your Instructor Supplements

This Instructor Companion Website is an all-in-one resource for class preparation, presentation, and testing. Accessible through Cengage.com/login with your faculty account, you will find available for download: book-specific Microsoft® PowerPoint® presentations, a Test Bank compatible with multiple learning management systems (LMSs), an Instructor Manual, and more.

The Test Bank, offered in Blackboard, Moodle, Desire2Learn, and Canvas formats, contains learning objective-specific multiple-choice and essay questions for each chapter. Import the test bank into your LMS to edit and manage questions, and to create tests.

The Instructor's Manual includes information about all of the activities and assessments available for each chapter and their correlation to specific learning objectives, an outline, key terms with definitions, a chapter summary, and several ideas for engaging with students with discussion questions, ice breakers, case studies, and social learning activities that may be conducted in an on-ground, hybrid, or online modality.

The Microsoft® PowerPoint® presentations are closely tied to the Instructor Manual, providing ample opportunities for generating classroom discussion and interaction. They offer ready-to-use, visual outlines of each chapter, which may be easily customized for your lectures. A guide to teaching online presents technological and pedagogical considerations and suggestions for teaching the Introduction to American Government course when you can't be in the same room with students. Access the Instructor Companion Website for these resources and more at www.cengage.com/login.

Acknowledgments

In preparing *American Government and Politics Today:* Brief Enhanced Eleventh Edition, we were the beneficiaries of the expert guidance of a skilled and dedicated team of publishers and editors. We have benefited greatly from the supervision and encouragement provided by our Portfolio Product Director, Laura Ross.

We are grateful to our Content Manager, Daniel Saabye, for his ability to make this project as smooth-running and as perfect as is humanly possible. We are indebted to the staff at Straive. Their ability to generate the pages for this text quickly and accurately made it possible for us to meet our ambitious printing schedule. We also thank Emily Hickey, Senior Subject Matter Expert; and Rebecca Schuman, Learning Designer. In addition, our gratitude goes to all those who worked on the various supplements offered with this text. We would also like to thank Valerie Hartman, Executive Marketing Manager, for her tremendous efforts in marketing the book.

Many other people helped during the research and editorial stages of this edition. Gregory Scott coordinated the authors' efforts and provided editorial and research assistance. Maureen Johnson's copyediting abilities contributed greatly to the book. We also thank Roxie Lee for her assistance, and Sue Jasin of K&M Consulting for her contributions to the smooth running of the project. Finally, we are grateful for the proofreading services provided by Sheila Joyce.

We are also very thankful for the constructive comments and advice provided by our colleagues and peers, especially those whose thoughtful insights helped us shape this new edition:

David W. Gethings, Kennesaw State University
Timothy W. Kneeland, Nazareth College

We would also like to thank the following instructors whose feedback was instrumental in shaping recent prior editions:

Paul Blakelock, Lone Star College–Kingwood
Justin Deplato, Florida State College at Jacksonville
David Goldberg, College of DuPage
Tonya Gray, Central Carolina Community College
Robert L. Hall, Jr., Florida State College at Jacksonville
La Della Levy, College of Southern Nevada, Charleston
Charlotte Meador, Lone Star College–Kingwood
Don Mirjanian, College of Southern Nevada, Charleston
Jennifer Morrison, Murray State University
Azubike Kalu-Nwiwu, Erie Community College
Charles Scruggs, Genesee Community College
Gwyn Sutherland, Elizabethtown Community and Technical College

Any errors, of course, remain our own. We welcome comments from instructors and students alike. Suggestions that we received on previous editions have helped us to improve this text and to adapt it to the changing needs of instructors and students.

S.W.S.
M.C.S.
B.A.B.

About the Authors

Steffen W. Schmidt

Steffen W. Schmidt is professor emeritus of political science at Iowa State University. He grew up in Colombia, South America, and has studied in Colombia, Switzerland, the United States, and France. He has a B.A. from Rollins College and obtained his Ph.D. from Columbia University, in public law and government.

Dr. Schmidt has published 14 books and more than 130 articles in scholarly journals and major newspapers.

He is the recipient of numerous prestigious teaching prizes, including the Amoco Award for Lifetime Career Achievement in Teaching and the Teacher of the Year award.

Schmidt is a pioneer in the use of web-based and real-time video courses and is a founding member of the American Political Science Association's section on Computers and Multimedia.

He is known as "Dr. Politics" for his extensive commentary on U.S. politics and cyber threats in U.S. and international media. He comments on CNN en Español, Fox, Telemundo, Univision, and public radio, as well as CTV (Canada Cable TV) and the BBC. He has been quoted in every major news source in the world including *The Economist*, the *New York Times*, the *Washington Times, Kyodo News* of Japan, *Agence France-Presse*, Latin American news media, and others. He is the guest of two weekly radio shows on KASI Clear Channel and on Concord, New Hampshire, radio with Deborah "Arnie" Arnesen.

Dr. Schmidt is a founding member of the Department of Defense U.S. Strategic Command Academic Alliance, which focuses on cybersecurity policy.

He is on Facebook (SteffenWSchmidt) and Twitter (DrPolitics).

Mack C. Shelley II

Mack C. Shelley II is professor of political science and statistics at Iowa State University. After receiving his bachelor's degree from American University in Washington, D.C., he completed graduate studies at the University of Wisconsin at Madison, where he received a master's degree in economics and a Ph.D. in political science. He taught for two years at Mississippi State University before arriving at Iowa State in 1979.

Shelley has published numerous articles, books, and monographs on public policy. From 1993 to 2002, he served as elected coeditor of the Policy Studies Journal. His published books include *The Permanent Majority: The Conservative Coalition in the United States Congress; Biotechnology and the Research Enterprise* (with William F. Woodman and Brian J. Reichel); *American Public Policy: The Contemporary Agenda* (with Steven G. Koven and Bert E. Swanson); *Redefining Family Policy: Implications for the 21st Century* (with Joyce M. Mercier and Steven Garasky); and

Quality Research in Literacy and Science Education: International Perspectives and Gold Standards (with Larry Yore and Brian Hand).

His leisure time includes traveling, working with students, and playing with the family dog and cats.

Barbara A. Bardes

Barbara A. Bardes is professor emerita of political science and former dean of Raymond Walters College at the University of Cincinnati. She received her B.A. and M.A. from Kent State University. After completing her Ph.D. at the University of Cincinnati, she held faculty positions at Mississippi State University and Loyola University in Chicago. She returned to Cincinnati, her hometown, as a college administrator. She has also worked as a political consultant and directed polling for a research center.

Bardes has written articles on public opinion and foreign policy, and on women and politics. She has authored *Thinking about Public Policy; Declarations of Independence: Women and Political Power in Nineteenth-Century American Fiction;* and *Public Opinion: Measuring the American Mind* (with Robert W. Oldendick).

Bardes's home is located in a very small hamlet in Kentucky called Rabbit Hash, famous for its 150-year-old general store. Her hobbies include traveling, gardening, needlework, and antique collecting.

The Democratic Republic

SOPA Images Limited/Alamy Stock Photo

A crowd at the National Mall in Washington D.C. on July 4. ▶ **What do people mean when they wave the American flag?**

The five **Learning Outcomes (LOs)** below are designed to help improve your understanding of this chapter. After reading this chapter, you should be able to:

≫ **LO 1-1** Define the terms politics, government, order, liberty, authority, and legitimacy.

≫ **LO 1-2** Distinguish the major features of direct democracy and representative democracy.

≫ **LO 1-3** Explain why majoritarianism as a theory of how democratic systems work doesn't really apply to the U.S.

≫ **LO 1-4** Summarize the conflicts that can occur between the values of liberty and order, and between those of liberty and equality.

≫ **LO 1-5** Discuss conservatism, liberalism, and other popular American ideological positions.

Check your understanding of the material with the Test Yourself section at the end of the chapter.

Politics, for many people, is the "great game," and it is played for high stakes. After all, the game involves vast sums and the very security of the nation. In the last few years, the stakes have grown higher still.

In 2020, American voters picked former vice president Joseph Biden to be the next president of the United States. Senator Kamala Harris (D-CA), daughter of immigrants from India and Jamaica, was the new vice president. The elections were hard fought. Allegations of election fraud by the outgoing Donald Trump administration were not successful. Biden's popular vote margin was large. As we explain in this text, however,

Americans choose their president through the Electoral College, not the popular vote. There, the margin between the candidates was closer.

The Senate ended up being equally divided between Republicans and Democrats. Because the vice president can cast a tie-breaking vote, the Senate became controlled by the Democrats. Democrats also continued to hold the House, although they lost quite a few seats. From the first day in office, Biden rescinded many changes Trump had made while president. Biden also issued numerous executive orders, such as discontinuing the building of the Keystone XL pipeline from Canada. By the time the 2022 midterms occurred, enough voters had soured on Biden's policies to allow the Republicans to take control of the House by a narrow margin. The Democrats retained a similarly slim majority in the Senate.

Politics and Government

> **» LO 1-1:** Define the terms politics, government, order, liberty, authority, and legitimacy.

Politics
The struggle over power or influence within organizations or informal groups that can grant or withhold benefits or privileges.

What is politics? **Politics** can be understood as the process of resolving conflicts and deciding "who gets what, when, and how."[1] More specifically, politics is the struggle over power or influence within organizations or informal groups that can grant or withhold benefits or privileges.

We can identify many such groups and organizations. In every community that makes decisions through formal or informal rules, politics exists. For example, when a church decides to construct a new building or hire a new minister, the decision is made politically. Politics can be found in schools, social groups, and any other organized collection of individuals. Of all the organizations that are controlled by political activity, however, the most important is the government.

Institution
An ongoing organization that performs certain functions for society.

Government
The institution that has the ultimate authority for making decisions that resolve conflicts and allocate benefits and privileges within a society.

What is the government? Certainly, it is an **institution**—that is, an ongoing organization that performs certain functions for society. An institution has a life separate from the lives of the individuals who are part of it at any given moment in time. The **government** is an institution within which decisions are made that resolve conflicts and allocate benefits and privileges. The government is also the preeminent institution within society because it has the ultimate authority for making these decisions.

Why Is Government Necessary?

Perhaps the best way to assess the need for government is to examine circumstances in which government, as we normally understand it, does not exist. What happens when multiple groups compete violently with one another for power within a society? There are places around the world where such circumstances exist. A current example is the Middle Eastern nation of Syria, run by the dictator Bashar al-Assad.

In 2011, the government of Syria killed peaceful protesters, which led to an armed rebellion. The government lost control of much of the country, and its forces repeatedly massacred civilians in contested areas. Some rebels, such as the so-called Islamic State (ISIS), were extreme Islamists. Others were more moderate. By 2013, rebels were fighting each other as well as the government. In much of Syria, law and order had broken down completely. By 2020, when the government forces had regained control of most of the country, almost 500,000 people had been killed, and more than half of the country's people had been driven from their homes. The fighting was not quite over as of 2023. The Northwestern IDLIB region remained outside of government control.

---

1. Harold Lasswell, *Politics: Who Gets What, When, and How* (Gloucester, Mass.: Peter Smith Publisher, 1990). Originally published in 1936.

As the example of Syria shows, one of the foundational purposes of government is the maintenance of security, or **order**. By keeping the peace, a government protects its people from violence at the hands of private or foreign armies and criminals. If order is not present, it is not possible for the government to provide any of the other benefits that people expect from it. Order is a political value to which we will return later in this chapter.

Limiting Government Power

A complete collapse of order and security, as was seen in Syria, actually is an uncommon event. Much more common is the reverse—too much government control. In January 2022, the human rights organization Freedom House judged that 56 of the world's countries were "not free." This term is defined by the level of political rights and civil liberties in each area. These nations contain 29 percent of the world's population. Such countries may be controlled by individual kings or dictators. Saudi Arabia's king, Salman bin Abdulaziz Al Saud, and North Korea's dictator Kim Jong-un are obvious examples. Alternatively, a political party, such as the Communist Party of China, may monopolize all the levels of power. The military may rule, as in Thailand since 2014.

Rouzbeh Fouladi/ZUMA Press/Newscom

Image 1.1 Hard-line Iranian women protest against the U.S. killing of Iranian general Qassem Soleimani. He was believed to be preparing an attack against U.S. forces in Iraq. The photos show Soleimani with Iran's supreme leader Ali Khamenei (left). ▶ Does the government of Iran have legitimacy? Why or why not?

In all of these examples, the individual or group running the country cannot be removed by legal means. Freedom of speech and the right to a fair trial are typically absent. Dictatorial governments often torture or execute their opponents. Such regimes may also suppress freedom of religion. Revolution, whether violent or nonviolent, is often the only way to change the government.

In short, protection from the violence of domestic criminals or foreign armies is not enough. Citizens also need protection from abuses of power by their own government. To protect the liberties of the people, it is necessary to limit the powers of the government.

Liberty—the greatest freedom of the individual consistent with the freedom of other individuals—is a second major political value, along with order. We discuss this value in more detail later in this chapter.

Authority and Legitimacy

Every government must have **authority**—that is, the right and power to enforce its decisions. Ultimately, the government's authority rests on its control of the armed forces and the police. In normal times, few people in the United States, however, base their day-to-day activities on fear of the government's enforcement powers. Most people, most of the time, obey the law because this is what they have always done. Also, if they did not obey the law, they would face the disapproval of friends and family. Consider an example: Do you avoid injuring your friends or stealing their possessions because you are afraid of the police—or because if you undertook these actions, you no longer would have friends?

Under normal circumstances, the government's authority has broad popular support. People accept the government's right to establish rules and laws. When authority is broadly accepted, we say that it has **legitimacy**. Authority without legitimacy is a recipe for trouble.

Order
A state of peace and security. Maintaining order by protecting members of society from violence and criminal activity is one of the oldest purposes of government.

Liberty
The greatest freedom of the individual that is consistent with the freedom of other individuals in the society.

Authority
The right and power of a government or other entity to enforce its decisions.

Legitimacy
Popular acceptance of the right and power of a government or other entity to exercise authority.

Events in several Arab nations since 2011 can serve as an example. The dictators who ruled Egypt, Libya, and Tunisia had been in power for decades. None of these nations had a tradition of democracy, and so it was possible for undemocratic rulers to enjoy a degree of legitimacy. After years of oppressive behavior, these regimes slowly lost that legitimacy. The rulers survived only because they were willing to employ violence against any opposition. In Egypt and Tunisia, the end came when soldiers refused to use force against massive demonstrations. Having lost all legitimacy, the rulers of these two countries then lost their authority as well. In Libya, the downfall and death of the dictator Muammar Gaddafi came only after a seven-month civil war. (Egypt's shaky new democracy collapsed in 2013, however, when the army seized power.)

Democracy and Other Forms of Government

≫ **LO 1-2:** Distinguish the major features of direct democracy and representative democracy.

The different types of government can be classified according to which person or group of people controls society through the government.

Types of Government

Totalitarian Regime
A form of government that controls all aspects of the political, social, and economic life of a nation.

At one extreme is a society governed by a **totalitarian regime**. In such a political system, a small group of leaders or a single individual—a dictator—has ultimate control over all decisions for the society. Every aspect of political, social, and economic life is controlled by the government. The power of the ruler is total (thus, the term totalitarianism). Examples of such regimes include Germany under Adolf Hitler and the former Soviet Union under Joseph Stalin.

Authoritarianism
A type of regime in which only the government itself is fully controlled by the ruler. Social and economic institutions exist that are not under the government's control.

A second type of system is authoritarian government. **Authoritarianism** differs from totalitarianism in that only the government itself is fully controlled by the ruler. Social and economic institutions, such as churches, businesses, and labor unions, exist that are not under the government's control.

Many of our terms for describing the distribution of political power are derived from the ancient Greeks, who were the first Western people to study politics systematically. One form of rule was known as aristocracy, literally meaning "rule by the best." In practice, this meant rule by wealthy members of ancient families. Another term from the Greeks is theocracy, which literally means "rule by God" (or the gods). In practice, theocracy means rule by self-appointed religious leaders. Iran is a rare example of a country in which supreme power is in the hands of a religious leader, the Grand Ayatollah Ali Khamenei. One of the most straightforward Greek terms is oligarchy, which simply means "rule by a few."

Democracy
A system of government in which political authority is vested in the people.

The Greek term for rule by the people was **democracy**. Within the limits of their culture, some of the Greek city-states operated as democracies. Today, in much of the world, the people will not grant legitimacy to a government unless it is based on democracy.

Direct Democracy as a Model

Direct Democracy
A system of government in which political decisions are made by the people directly, rather than by their elected representatives.

The Athenian system of government in ancient Greece is usually considered the purest model for **direct democracy** because the citizens of that community debated and voted directly on all laws, even those put forward by the ruling council of the city. (Women, resident foreigners, and enslaved people, however, were excluded because they were not citizens.) This form of government required a high level of participation from every citizen. The Athenians believed that although a high level of participation might lead to instability in government, citizens, if informed about the issues, could be trusted to make wise decisions.

Direct democracy also has been practiced at the local level in Switzerland and, in the United States, in New England town meetings. At these town meetings, important decisions—such as levying taxes, hiring city officials, and deciding local ordinances—are made by majority vote. Some states provide a modern adaptation of direct democracy for their citizens. In these states, representative democracy is supplemented by **initiative** or **referendum**. Both processes enable the people to vote directly on laws or constitutional amendments. The **recall** process, which is available in many states, allows the people to vote to remove an official from state office before their term has expired.

The Dangers of Direct Democracy

Although they were aware of the Athenian model, the framers of the U.S. Constitution were opposed to such a system. They considered democracy to be dangerous and a source of instability. But in the 1700s and 1800s, the idea of government based on the consent of the people gained increasing popularity. Such a government was the main aspiration of the American Revolution of 1775–83. At the time of

AP Images/Toby Talbot

Image 1.2 These Woodbury, Vermont, residents cast their ballots after a town meeting to vote on the school budget and sales taxes. ▶ What type of political system does the town meeting best represent?

the revolution, however, ordinary people were still considered to be too uneducated to govern themselves, too prone to the influence of demagogues (political leaders who manipulate popular prejudices), and too likely to subordinate non-majority rights to the tyranny of the majority.

James Madison, while defending the new scheme of government set forth in the U.S. Constitution, warned of the problems inherent in a "pure democracy:"

> *A common passion or interest will, in almost every case, be felt by a majority of the whole . . . and there is nothing to check the inducements to sacrifice the weaker party or an obnoxious individual. Hence it is that such democracies have ever been spectacles of turbulence and contention, and have ever been found incompatible with personal security or the rights of property; and have in general been as short in their lives as they have been violent in their deaths.*[2]

A Democratic Republic

The framers of the U.S. Constitution chose to craft a **republic**, meaning a government in which sovereign power rests with the people, rather than with a king or a monarch. A republic is based on **popular sovereignty**. To Americans of the 1700s, the idea of a republic also meant a government based on common beliefs and virtues that would be fostered within small communities.

The U.S. Constitution created a form of republican government that we now call a **democratic republic**. The people hold the ultimate power over the government through elections, but all national policy decisions are made by elected officials. For the founders, even this distance between the people and the government was not sufficient. The Constitution made sure that the Senate and the president would not be elected by a direct vote

Initiative
A procedure by which voters can petition to vote on a law or a constitutional amendment.

Referendum
An electoral device whereby legislative or constitutional measures are referred by the legislature to the voters for approval or disapproval.

Recall
A procedure allowing the people to vote to dismiss an elected official from office before their term has expired.

Republic
A form of government in which sovereign power rests with the people, rather than with a king or a monarch.

Popular Sovereignty
The concept that ultimate political authority is based on the will of the people.

Democratic Republic
A republic in which leaders elected by the people make and enforce laws and policies.

---

2. James Madison, in Alexander Hamilton, James Madison, and John Jay, *The Federalist Papers*, No. 10 (New York: Signet, 2003), p. 71. See Appendix C of this textbook.

of the people. Senators were chosen by state legislatures (although a later constitutional amendment allowed for the direct election of senators). The founders also established an Electoral College to choose the president, in the hope that such a body would prevent voters from directly making the choice.

Despite these limits, the new American system was unique in the amount of power it granted to the ordinary citizen. Over the course of the following two centuries, democratic values became more and more popular, at first in Western nations and then throughout the rest of the world. The spread of democratic principles gave rise to another name for our system of government—**representative democracy**. The term representative democracy has almost the same meaning as democratic republic, with one exception. Recall that in a republic, not only are the people sovereign, but there is no king. What if a nation develops into a democracy but preserves the monarchy as a largely ceremonial institution? That is exactly what happened in Britain. The British, who have long cherished their kings and queens, found the term democratic republic unacceptable. A republic, after all, meant there could be no monarch. The British therefore described their system as a representative democracy instead.

Representative Democracy
A form of government in which leaders elected by the people make and enforce laws and policies, but in which the monarchy may be retained in a ceremonial role.

Principles of Democratic Government. All representative democracies rest on the rule of the people as expressed through the election of government officials. In the 1790s in the United States, only free white males were able to vote, and in some states they had to be property owners as well. Women in many states did not receive the right to vote in national elections until 1920, and the right to vote was not secured in all states by African Americans until the 1960s. Today, **universal suffrage** is the rule.

Universal Suffrage
The right of all adults to vote for their government representatives.

Because everyone's vote counts equally, the only way to make fair decisions is by some form of majority will. But to ensure that **majority rule** does not become oppressive, modern democracies also provide guarantees of minority rights. If political minorities were not protected, the majority might violate the fundamental rights of members of certain groups—especially groups that are unpopular or dissimilar to the majority population, such as racial minorities.

Majority Rule
A basic principle of democracy asserting that the greatest number of citizens in any political unit should select officials and determine policies.

To guarantee the continued existence of a representative democracy, there must be free, competitive elections. Thus, the opposition always has the opportunity to win elective office. For such elections to be totally open, freedom of the press and freedom of speech must be preserved so that opposition candidates can present their criticisms of the government to the people.

Constitutional Democracy. Another key feature of Western representative democracy is that it is based on the principle of **limited government**. Not only is the government dependent on popular sovereignty, but the powers of the government are also clearly limited, either through a written document or through widely shared beliefs. The U.S. Constitution sets down the fundamental structure of the government and the limits to its activities. Such limits are intended to prevent political decisions based on the whims or ambitions of individuals in government rather than on constitutional principles. The Constitution allows for the peaceful transfer of power as well as the acceptance of election results.

Limited Government
A government with powers that are limited either through a written document or through widely shared beliefs.

What Kind of Democracy Do We Have?

» **LO 1-3:** Explain why majoritarianism as a theory of how democratic systems work doesn't really apply to the U.S.

Political scientists have developed many theories about American democracy, including majoritarianism, elite theory, and pluralism. Advocates of these theories use them to describe American democracy either as it actually is or as they believe it should be.

Some scholars argue that none of these three theories, which we discuss next, fully describes the workings of American democracy. These experts say that each theory captures a part of the true reality but that we need all three theories to gain a full understanding of American politics.

Democracy for Everyone

Many people believe that in a democracy, the government ought to do what the majority of the people want. This simple proposition is the heart of majoritarian theory. As a theory of what democracy should be like, **majoritarianism** is popular among both political scientists and ordinary citizens. Many scholars, however, consider majoritarianism to provide a surprisingly poor description of how U.S. democracy actually works. Policies adopted by the U.S. government are often strikingly different from the ones endorsed by the public in opinion polls. One example is religion in the public schools. Solid majorities have long advocated a greater role for religion in the public schools, even to the point of teachers leading students in prayer. Most elected officials, however, have tried to uphold the constitutional principle of "separation of church and state."

Kevin Kane/Getty Images Entertainment/Getty Images

Image 1.3 Taylor Swift is shown at one of her many concerts. She's publicly supported Democratic candidates for president and Congress.
▶ How influential are pop singers?

Majoritarianism
A political theory holding that in a democracy, the government ought to do what the majority of the people want.

Elite Theory
The argument that society is ruled by a small number of people who exercise power to further their self-interest.

Democracy for the Few

If ordinary citizens are not really making policy decisions with their votes, who is? One theory suggests that elites really govern the United States. **Elite theory** holds that society is ruled by a small number of people who exercise power to further their self-interest. American democracy, in other words, is a sham democracy according to this theory. Few people today believe it is a good idea for the country to be run by a privileged minority. In the past, however, many people believed that it was appropriate for the country to be governed by an elite. Consider the words of Alexander Hamilton, one of the framers of the Constitution:

> All communities divide themselves into the few and the many. The first are the rich and the wellborn, the other the mass of the people. . . . The people are turbulent and changing; they seldom judge or determine right. Give therefore to the first class a distinct, permanent share in the government. They will check the unsteadiness of the second, and as they cannot receive any advantage by a change, they therefore will ever maintain good government.[3]

Some versions of elite theory assume that there is a small, cohesive elite class that makes almost all the important decisions for the nation,[4] whereas others suggest that voters choose among competing elites. Popular movements of varying political persuasions often advocate simple versions of elite theory.

---

3. Alexander Hamilton, "Speech in the Constitutional Convention on a Plan of Government," in Joanne B. Freeman, ed., *Alexander Hamilton: Writings* (New York: Library of America, 2001).
4. Michael Parenti, *Democracy for the Few*, 9th ed. (Belmont, Calif.: Wadsworth Publishing, 2011).

Democracy for Groups

A different school of thought holds that our form of democracy is based on group interests. Even if the average citizen cannot keep up with political issues or cast a deciding vote in any election, individuals' interests will be protected by groups that represent them.

Pluralism
A theory that views politics as a conflict among interest groups. Political decision making is characterized by bargaining and compromise.

Theorists who subscribe to **pluralism** see politics as a struggle among groups to gain benefits for their members. Given the structure of the American political system, group conflicts tend to be settled by compromise and accommodation. Because there are a multitude of interests, no one group can dominate the political process. Furthermore, because most individuals have more than one interest, conflict among groups need not divide the nation into hostile camps.

Many political scientists believe that pluralism works very well as a descriptive theory. As a theory of how democracy should function, however, pluralism has problems. Citizens with low incomes are rarely represented by interest groups. At the same time, citizens who are rich may be overrepresented. (Still, citizens with low incomes do receive useful representation from religious and liberal groups.) There are also serious doubts as to whether group decision making always reflects the best interests of the nation. Indeed, critics see a danger that groups may grow so powerful that all policies become compromises crafted to satisfy the interests of the largest groups. The interests of the public as a whole, then, are not considered. Critics of pluralism have suggested that a democratic system can be almost paralyzed by the struggle among interest groups.

The arrival of the COVID-19 pandemic in 2020 raised new questions about the ability of the nation to pull together. While there were encouraging examples of a "we're all in this together" spirit, the pandemic also appeared to have the power to pull the nation further apart. We look at the impact of the pandemic in this chapter's *Which Side Are You On?* feature.

Which Side Are You On?

Will the U.S. Ever Get Back to the Way It Was Before COVID-19?

At first, it was "a cloud as small as a man's hand." The SARS-CoV-2 virus was a new virus in the coronavirus family that humans had not previously encountered. Often referred to as simply "coronavirus," it caused the disease known as COVID-19. It was very contagious. The number of cases could double every few days which meant it was capable of exponential growth. With such rapid spread, in ten doublings, one case becomes more than a thousand. In twenty doublings, one case becomes more than a million. At first, the death rate seemed to be more than 1 percent of those infected. The disease spread through the United States, starting slowly in February 2020, but by mid-March, the nation woke up to the seriousness of the threat. State governors from coast to coast issued stay-at-home orders to stop the spread. Millions of people had already taken action. Festivals, sporting events, and theaters closed well before the official shutdowns. Restaurants, stores, and churches followed. By mid-April, at least a fifth of the workforce was out of a job.

The nation's medical system was overwhelmed in certain hot spots, such as New York City. The lockdown provided time to build up a response. Even as the country slowly reopened, facemasks were everywhere. "Social distancing" required people to stay six feet apart. Large gatherings seemed out of the question. What the world needed was a vaccine, which did arrive just after the November 2020 elections.

We Will Just Have to Adapt to a "New Normal"

Americans did not wait on the government. People everywhere did what they could. Yet only one institution existed with the power and wealth needed to truly defeat the pandemic. That institution was government. Many believed that the need for federal action to combat COVID-19 would change the way Americans view their government. Only government could fund the vast medical effort necessary to defeat the enemy. Only government had the power

(Continued)

to support those facing financial ruin. Even as the virus raged, conservative lawyers were seeking to have the Affordable Care Act ruled unconstitutional—a result that could have deprived millions of health insurance. Such an attitude was unlikely to prevail. Health care, always a key issue, was now *the* issue. Supporters of an active government were confident that regardless of how the elections turned out, the popular demand for effective, larger government would be permanent.

Let's face it, most Americans now accept the rules and regulations imposed by a larger, more intrusive government because of COVID-19. That is not about to change overnight.

In a Few Years We'll Be Right Back Where We Started

Others were not so sure. The one past event that most resembled the COVID-19 pandemic was the influenza pandemic of 1918. That virus infected about 500 million around the world and killed an estimated 50 million people. Yet by 2020, how many people remembered it? World Wars I and II, the Great Depression, Nazism, communism—these events shaped the twentieth century. Not the flu. Today's coronavirus may have more to do with the debate over "big government," because we can respond to it in ways our ancestors never could. But not everyone endorsed government action. Some responded out of the nation's tradition of radical individualism. For them, the shutdown in the spring of 2020 and the following restrictions were as bad as the disease itself. Many observers thought the politics of the pandemic would soon become invisible.

By 2022, at least one scholarly study showed that states and countries that locked down did not fare any better than those that did not impose lockdowns. Studies showed mixed effects of measures like mask-wearing (e.g., many of the studies on mask wearing found that the quality and fit of masks matter). This information supported the views of those against big government such that they will no longer submit to blanket government restrictions on their future behavior. Of course, there were others who never submitted to the governments' restrictions anyway.

■ For Critical Analysis

China, where the first known infections of COVID-19 were discovered, attempted to gain control of it through radically authoritarian measures. How does the American system prevent such a response?

Fundamental Values

>> **LO 1-4:** Summarize the conflicts that can occur between the values of liberty and order, and between those of liberty and equality.

The writers of the U.S. Constitution believed that the structures they had created would provide for both popular sovereignty and a stable political system. They also believed that the nation would be sustained by its **political culture**—the patterned set of ideas, values, and ways of thinking about government and politics that characterized its people. Even today, there is considerable consensus among American citizens about certain concepts—including the rights to liberty, equality, and property—that are deemed to be basic to the U.S. political system.

Most Americans are descendants of immigrants who came from diverse cultural and political backgrounds. You can see how immigration will continue to change the composition of the nation in future years in Figure 1.1. Given the changing nature of our population, now and in the past, how can we account for the broad consensus that exists around basic values? Primarily, it is the result of **political socialization**—the process by which political beliefs and values are transmitted to new immigrants and to our children. The two most important sources of political socialization are the family and the educational system.

The most fundamental concepts of the American political culture are those of the dominant culture. The term dominant culture refers to the values, customs, and language established by the groups that traditionally have controlled politics and government in a society. The dominant culture in the United States has its roots in Western European civilization. From that civilization, American politics inherited a bias in favor of individualism, private property, and Judeo-Christian ethics.

Political Culture
A patterned set of ideas, values, and ways of thinking about government and politics that characterizes a people.

Political Socialization
The process by which people acquire political beliefs and values.

Figure 1.1	Projected Changes in U.S. Ethnic Distribution

▶ **What political changes could result when non-Latino whites are no longer a majority of the U.S. population?**

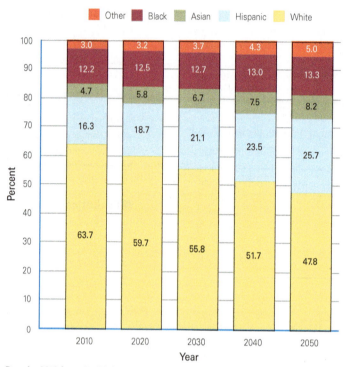

Data for 2010 from the 2010 census. Data for 2020 through 2050 are Census Bureau projections.

Latinos may be of any race. The chart categories White, Black, Asian, and Other are limited to non-Latinos. Other consists of the following non-Latino groups: Native American, Native Alaskan, Native Hawaiian, Other Pacific Islander, and two or more races.

Sources: U.S. Bureau of the Census and authors' calculations.

Liberty Versus Order

Civil Liberties
Those personal freedoms, including freedom of religion and of speech, that are protected for all individuals in a society.

Bill of Rights
The first ten amendments to the U.S. Constitution.

In the United States, our **civil liberties** include religious freedom—both the right to practice whatever religion we choose and the right to be free from any state-imposed religion. Our civil liberties also include freedom of speech—the right to express our opinions freely on all matters, including government actions. Freedom of speech is perhaps one of our most prized liberties, because a democracy could not endure without it. These and many other basic guarantees of liberty are found in the **Bill of Rights**, the first ten amendments to the Constitution.

Liberty, however, is not the only value widely held by Americans. A substantial portion of the American electorate believes that certain kinds of liberty threaten the traditional social order. The right to privacy is a particularly controversial liberty. The United States Supreme Court has held that the right to privacy can be derived from other rights that are explicitly stated in the Bill of Rights. The Supreme Court has also held that under the right to privacy, the government cannot ban private homosexual behavior by consenting adults.[5] More recently, the Court also held that the government cannot prohibit

---

5. *Lawrence v. Texas*, 539 U.S. 558 (2003).

same-sex marriage.[6] Some Americans believe that such rights threaten the sanctity of the traditional family (mother, father, and children) and the general cultural commitment to a specific ideal of moral behavior. Of course, others disagree with this point of view.

Security is another issue that follows from the principle of order. When Americans have felt particularly fearful or vulnerable, the government has emphasized national security over civil liberties. Such was the case after the Japanese attack on Pearl Harbor in 1941, which led to the U.S. entry into World War II. Thousands of Japanese Americans were held in internment camps, based on the assumption that their loyalty to this country was in question. More recently, the terrorist attacks on the Pentagon and the World Trade Center on September 11, 2001, renewed calls for greater security at the expense of some civil liberties.

Liberty Versus Equality

The Declaration of Independence states, "All men are created equal." The proper meaning of equality, however, has been disputed by Americans since the Revolution. Much of American history—and indeed, world history—is the story of how the value of **equality**, the idea that all people are of equal worth, has been extended and elaborated.

Image 1.4 Black people line up to register to vote in Selma, Alabama, following passage of the 1965 Voting Rights Act. ▶ Why is voting so important for democracy?

Equality
As a political value, the idea that all people are of equal worth.

First, the right to vote was granted to all adult white males, regardless of whether they owned property. The Civil War resulted in the end of slavery and established that, in principle at least, all citizens were equal before the law. The civil rights movement of the 1950s and 1960s sought to make that promise of equality a reality for African Americans. Other movements have sought equality for additional racial and ethnic groups, for women, for persons with disabilities, and for LGBTQ+ individuals. (This term stands for lesbian, gay, bisexual, transgender, queer [or sometime questioning], and the plus represents other relevant identities that are non-binary.)

Although many people believe that we still have a way to go in obtaining full equality for all these groups, we have come a long way already. No American in the nineteenth century could have imagined that the 2008 Democratic presidential primary elections would be closely fought contests between an African American man (Illinois senator Barack Obama) and a white woman (New York senator Hillary Rodham Clinton). The idea that same-sex marriage could even be open to debate would have been mind-boggling as well.

Promoting equality often requires limiting the right to treat people unequally. In this sense, equality and liberty can be conflicting values. Today, the right to deny equal treatment to the members of a particular race has very few defenders. Yet as recently as eighty years ago, this right was a cultural norm.

It can also be argued that liberty and equality are complementary. For example, people or groups cannot really enjoy liberty if they do not have equal rights under the law.

Economic Equality. Equal treatment regardless of race, religion, gender, gender identity, or other characteristics is a popular value today. Equal opportunity for individuals to develop their talents and skills is also a value with substantial support. Equality of economic status, however, is a controversial value.

---

6. *Obergefell v. Hodges*, 133 S.Ct. 2584 (2015).

For much of history, the idea that the government could do anything about the division of society between rich and poor was not something about which people even thought. Most people assumed that such an effort was either impossible or undesirable. This assumption began to lose its force in the 1800s. As a result of the growing wealth of the Western world and a visible increase in the ability of government to take on large projects, some people began to advocate the value of universal equality, or egalitarianism. Some radicals dreamed of a revolutionary transformation of society that would establish an egalitarian system—that is, a system in which wealth and power were redistributed more equally.

Many others rejected this vision but still came to endorse the values of eliminating poverty and at least reducing the degree of economic inequality in society. Antipoverty advocates believed then and believe now that such a program could prevent much suffering. In addition, they believed that reducing economic inequality would promote fairness and enhance the moral tone of society generally.

Property Rights and Capitalism. The value of reducing economic inequality is in conflict with the right to **property**. This is because reducing economic inequality typically involves the transfer of property (usually in the form of tax dollars) from some people to others. For many people, liberty and property are closely entwined. Our capitalist system is based on private property rights. Under **capitalism**, property consists not only of personal possessions but also of wealth-creating assets such as farms and factories. Capitalism is also typically characterized by considerable freedom to make binding contracts and by relatively unconstrained markets for goods, services, and investments.

Property—especially wealth-creating property—can be seen as giving its owners political power and the liberty to do whatever they want. At the same time, the ownership of property immediately creates inequality in society. The desire to own property, however, is so widespread among all classes of Americans that radical egalitarian movements have had a difficult time securing a wide following in this country.

Property
Anything that is or may be subject to ownership.

Capitalism
An economic system characterized by the private ownership of wealth-creating assets, free markets, and freedom of contract.

The Proper Role and Size of Government

Americans have substantial differences of opinion on the values just described—liberty, order, and equality. Americans also have a wide variety of needs and interests. From the very beginning of the republic, these opinions and interests have yielded different conceptions of what government ought to do and how large it should be. Traditionally, these varying conceptions have taken the form of arguments over the size of government.

Many Americans believe that "That government is best which governs least," a motto popularized by Henry David Thoreau.[7] The flaw in Thoreau's slogan is that opposition to "big government," taken by itself, is a somewhat empty idea. Almost invariably, those who oppose big government do so because there are things that they do not want the government to do. Thoreau, for example, was opposed to the Mexican-American War and to federal support for the institution of slavery.

Citizens often express contradictory opinions on the size of government and the role that it should play in their lives. Americans tend to oppose "big government" in principle even as they endorse its benefits. Those who complain about the amount of taxes they pay each year may also worry about the lack of funds for more teachers in the local schools. Such tensions have done much to shape American politics from the Revolutionary Era to the twenty-first century.

---

7. Thoreau, Henry David, "Resistance to Civil Government," *Aesthetic Papers*, Elizabeth Peabody, ed. (Boston and New York: The Editor and G.P. Putnam, 1849), pp. 189-211. Later reprinted under the titles "Civil Disobedience" and "On the Duty of Civil Disobedience."

| Figure 1.2 | Employment Rates for U.S. Persons Aged 25–54, 1977–2022 |

In March 2020, the pandemic suddenly put tens of millions out of work. ▶ **What problems can result if large numbers of adults leave the workforce?**

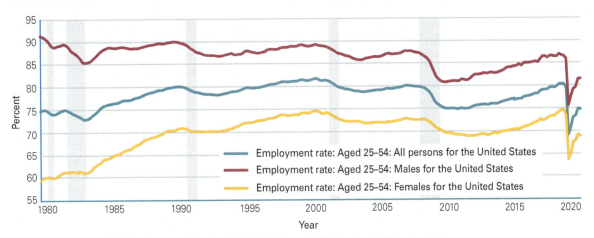

Employment rate: Aged 25–54: All persons for the United States
Employment rate: Aged 25–54: Males for the United States
Employment rate: Aged 25–54: Females for the United States

Source: Federal Reserve Economic Data (FRED); Organization for Economic Cooperation and Development.

Big Government and the Great Recession. In September 2008, a financial meltdown threatened the world economy. The impact of the Great Recession was so strong that the share of Americans with jobs did not return to the 2008 level until the beginning of 2020, just before the COVID-19 pandemic struck, as you can see in Figure 1.2. The immediate result of this disaster in the November 2008 elections was to guarantee Democrat Barack Obama the presidency and grant the Democrats unusually large margins in the U.S. Senate and House of Representatives. The newly empowered Democrats passed major spending programs aimed at saving the economy. In 2010, Congress and President Obama also approved a major health care initiative, the Affordable Care Act (ACA) (also called Obamacare), that had no direct connection to fighting the recession.

Such actions persuaded millions that big government was out of control. In 2010, voters swung heavily to the Republicans, giving them control of the House. While Obama was reelected in 2012, Republicans took control of the Senate in 2014. The result was divided government and a near-absence of new legislation, an era that came to an end in 2016 when Republican Donald Trump won the presidency. Divided government reoccurred in 2023.

Who Benefits From Government? It soon became clear that neither Trump nor his most ardent followers were particularly enamored of the traditional small-government conservatism endorsed by most Republican officeholders. This attitude had also been common among supporters of the Tea Party, an earlier conservative movement.[8] While the Tea Party built itself around rhetorical opposition to big government, most Tea Party supporters had no problems with programs such as Medicare and Social Security that benefited older voters. They did oppose programs such as Obamacare that were seen as primarily benefiting Americans with low incomes and non-majority group members. The question, in other words, was not so much the size of government but who benefits from government.

---

8. Theda Skocpol and Vanessa Williamson, *The Tea Party and the Remaking of Republican Conservatism* (New York: Oxford University Press, 2012).

Under Trump, this underlying theme became dominant. For example, after Hurricane Michael devastated the Florida Panhandle in 2018, many Floridians worried that the federal government's response was inadequate. As one Trump supporter put it, "He's not hurting the people he needs to be hurting."[9]

Trump's Supporters. Trump won the presidency in part because loyal Republicans rallied to his campaign. Still, a new block of voters—many of whom had not voted in previous elections—put him over the top. Trump's strongest support came from white voters without a college education. This group is commonly called the white **working class**. By 2016, it was clear that many members of this class were experiencing a social crisis marked by despair, falling life expectancies, and drug abuse. In fact, county by county, poor health was as much an indicator of Trump support as low levels of education.[10]

The Reaction Against Trump. Trump's election came as a surprise to most observers—apparently including Trump himself. Trump lost the popular vote by more than 2.8 million votes, a margin of more than 2 percent. He won by carrying the Electoral College, mentioned earlier. His victory was based on very narrow margins in three traditionally Democratic states—Michigan, Pennsylvania, and Wisconsin. At the same time, Democrat Hillary Clinton was piling up huge margins in states such as California, Massachusetts, and New York. Those extra popular votes won Clinton no additional Electoral College votes, however.

The day after Trump's inauguration, a women's march drew crowds of several million across the nation—the largest U.S. demonstrations seen in decades. Many were angry that Trump had won despite multiple accusations of sexual harassment. Other women demonstrated for a variety of other reasons. In 2017, Republicans in Congress passed a large tax reform law. An attempt to repeal Obamacare failed in the Senate by one vote. Repeal would have cost millions their health care insurance.

In the mid-term elections of 2018, Democrats scored a net gain of 41 seats in the U.S. House and took control of the chamber. The Republicans, however, gained two seats in the Senate, despite losing the popular vote for that chamber by 17.5 million. Republican turnout was high, but Democratic turnout was higher. The outcome was determined in part by well-educated suburbanites, especially women. Some of the white working-class voters who broke for Trump in 2016 also returned to the Democrats. In addition to the Obamacare issue, many anti-Trump voters were motivated by the harsh treatment handed out to asylum seekers, many of them from Central America.

The 2020 Election

Despite facing stiff headwinds, including numerous House attempts to impeach him (two of which succeeded), Trump was happy about how well his policies were working. There was a strong economy during the first few years of his presidency. In 2019, the American economy was booming with an historically low rate of unemployment. Unemployment rates for all groups, such as Latino and Black people, had also fallen to historic lows. Then the COVID-19 pandemic hit in early 2020, and much of the country shut down for months.

Large political rallies were cancelled. Trump could no longer campaign the way he did previously. The Democratic candidate, Joe Biden, gave some speeches from his home. The economy soon was in shambles with millions unable to work because of government-forced

Working Class
Currently, those with no college education. Traditionally, individuals or families in which the head of household was employed in manual or unskilled labor.

---

9. Patricia Mazzei, "'It's Just Too Much': A Florida Town Grapples With a Shutdown After a Hurricane," *The New York Times*, January 7, 2019, p. 1.
10. "Illness as Indicator," *The Economist* (London), November 19, 2016, p. 25.

Predictions and Results

As spring of 2022 headed to summer, the situation was looking sunny for the Republicans. The issues dominating the national political debate—high inflation, a looming recession, unnerving violent crime rates, disarray at the border with Mexico—were issues that traditionally favored their party. In addition, Democratic President Joseph Biden was suffering from anemic approval ratings and a general lack of public trust.

Then, in the fall, the midterm elections happened. The Republicans did take back control of the U.S. House of Representatives, but with a much smaller majority than predicted. The U.S. Senate, in contrast, stayed with the Democrats, by a similarly razor-thin margin. To explain these results, post-election analyses focused primarily on two circumstances that greatly benefitted Democrats. First, in late June, the United States Supreme Court overturned women's constitutional right to abortion, leaving all such decisions to the states. This decision that may have heartened the country's Republican base but gave Democrats an issue to rally around. Second, many Republican candidates endorsed Donald Trump's claims that he had been robbed of the presidency two years earlier by a crooked election process. These extreme views tended to overshadow efforts by the party leadership to focus on inflation and crime.

According to the numbers, Democrat candidates did much better than expected in states where voters perceived abortion rights to be under threat *and* Trump supporters had loudly challenged the 2020 presidential election outcome. Where these factors were not present, Republican candidates did quite well. In fact, counting only the popular vote for all the nation's House races in 2022, the Republicans won by a comfortable margin. As predicted.

---

business shutdowns. Many Americans were sick from COVID and were afraid to leave their homes. In November 2020, a record number of Americans voted. The winner was Joe Biden and his vice presidential pick, Kamala Harris (the first woman and the first Black person and Asian American to become vice president of this country).

Political Ideologies

> **LO 1-5:** Discuss conservatism, liberalism, and other popular American ideological positions.

A political **ideology** is a closely linked set of beliefs about politics. The concept of ideology is often misunderstood. Many people think that only individuals whose beliefs lie well out on one or the other end of the political spectrum have an ideology. Actually, almost everyone who has political opinions can be said to have an ideology. Indeed, many "non-ideological" people carry two or more ideologies in their heads, which is why they can hold some opinions that are conservative and others that are liberal.

Political ideologies offer people well-organized theories that propose goals for society and the means by which those goals can be achieved. At the core of every political ideology is a set of guiding values. The two ideologies most referred to in discussions of American politics are conservatism and liberalism.

Conservatism

Those who favor the ideology of **conservatism** seek to conserve traditional practices and institutions. In that sense, conservatism is as old as politics itself. Compared with

Ideology
A comprehensive set of beliefs about the nature of people and about the role of an institution or government.

Conservatism
A set of beliefs that includes a limited role for the national government in helping individuals, support for traditional values and lifestyles, and a cautious response to change.

Aspects and Angles/Shutterstock.com

Image 1.5 A supporter of President Trump waits for him to speak at rally in Des Moines, Iowa in January 2020. ▶ What were some of the concerns motivating Trump's most ardent supporters?

other political tendencies, conservatives place a high value on order, specifically in-group loyalty and respect for authority. This includes patriotism and support for a firm hand by the police. The conservative vision of the world includes a place for everyone, but also everyone in their place. Men and women have their appropriate roles. Many conservatives see members of the LGBTQ+ community as violating the natural order. The rich and people with low incomes also have their natural place: success is attributed to hard work and other virtues, while poverty is seen as the consequence of personal failings. It is appropriate for employers to exercise authority over employees.

These attitudes have major implications for economic policy. In the past, enterprises were largely free to act as they pleased in the marketplace and in managing their employees. Government regulation of business increased greatly in the 1930s, as Democratic president Franklin D. Roosevelt (1933–45) initiated a series of massive interventions in the economy in an attempt to counter the effects of the Great Depression. Many conservatives consider the Roosevelt administration to be a time when America took a wrong turn.

The Conservative Movement. It was in the 1950s, however, that American conservatism took its modern shape. The **conservative movement** that arose in that decade provided the age-old conservative impulse with a fully worked-out ideology. The new movement first demonstrated its strength in 1964, when Senator Barry Goldwater of Arizona was nominated as the Republican presidential candidate. Goldwater lost badly to Democrat Lyndon B. Johnson, but from that time forward movement conservatives have occupied a crucial position in the Republican Party.

Conservative Movement
An American movement founded in the 1950s that provides a comprehensive ideological framework for conservative politics.

Conservative Values. Modern conservatives strongly endorse liberty, but they generally define it as freedom from government imposition of nontraditional ideals such as LGBTQ+ rights or government interference in business. Conservatives believe that the private sector probably can outperform the government in almost any activity.

Conservatives place a relatively low value on equality. Believing that individuals and families are primarily responsible for their own well-being, they typically oppose high levels of antipoverty spending and government expenditures to stimulate the economy, favoring tax rate cuts instead.

Liberalism

Liberalism
A set of beliefs that includes advocacy of positive government action to improve the welfare of individuals, support for civil rights, and tolerance for political and social change.

The term **liberalism** stems from the word liberty and originally meant "free from prejudice in favor of traditional opinions and established institutions." Liberals have always been skeptical of the influence of religion in politics, but in the nineteenth century they were skeptical of government as well. From the time of Democratic presidents Woodrow Wilson (1913–21) and Franklin D. Roosevelt, however, American liberals increasingly sought to use the power of government for nontraditional ends. Their goals included support for organized labor and for people with low incomes. New programs instituted by the Roosevelt administration included Social Security and unemployment insurance.

Modern Liberalism. American liberalism took its modern form in the 1960s. Liberals rallied to the civil rights movement, which sought to obtain equal rights for African Americans. As the feminist movement grew in importance, liberals supported it as well. Liberals won new federal health care programs such as Medicare and Medicaid, and the promotion of such programs became a key component of liberal politics. Finally, liberals reacted more negatively to U.S. participation in the Vietnam War (1965–75) than did other Americans, and for years thereafter liberalism was associated with skepticism about the use of U.S. military forces abroad.

Table 1.1	The Traditional Political Spectrum

▶ What issues are not addressed by this spectrum?

	Socialism	Liberalism	Conservatism	Libertarianism
How much power should the government have over the economy?	Active government control of major economic sectors	Positive government action to control the economy	Positive government action to support capitalism	Almost no regulation of the economy
What should the government promote?	Economic equality, community	Economic security, equal opportunity, social liberty	Economic liberty, morality, social order	Total economic and social liberty

Liberal Values. Those who favor liberalism place a high value on social and economic equality. As we have seen, liberals champion the rights of minority group members and favor substantial antipoverty spending. In contrast to conservatives, liberals often support government intervention in the economy. They believe that capitalism works best when the government curbs capitalism's excesses through regulation. Like conservatives, liberals place a high value on liberty, but they tend to view it as the freedom to live one's life according to one's own values. Liberals, therefore, usually support LGBTQ+ rights, including the right to same-sex marriage. Liberals are an influential force within the Democratic Party.

The Traditional Political Spectrum

A traditional method of comparing political ideologies is to arrange them on a continuum from left to right, based primarily on how much power the government should exercise to promote economic equality. Table 1.1 shows how ideologies can be arrayed on a traditional political spectrum. In addition to liberalism and conservatism, this example includes the ideologies of socialism and libertarianism.

Socialism falls on the left side of the spectrum.[11] Socialist parties and movements have been important in other countries around the world, but socialists have usually played a minor role in the American political arena. An obvious exception has been senator and presidential candidate Bernie Sanders (D-VT), a self-proclaimed "democratic socialist." Following the 2018 midterm elections, Sanders was no longer alone—socialists had established a tiny but vocal presence on the left wing of the Democratic Party.

In the past, socialists typically advocated replacing investor ownership of major businesses with either government ownership or ownership by employee cooperatives. Socialists believed that such steps would break the power of the very rich and lead to an egalitarian society. In more recent times, socialists in western countries have advocated more limited programs that redistribute income and power.

On the right side of the spectrum is **libertarianism**, a philosophy of skepticism toward most government activities. Libertarians strongly support property rights and typically oppose regulation of the economy and redistribution of income. Libertarians support *laissez-faire* capitalism. (*Laissez faire* is French for "let it be.")[12] Libertarians also tend

Interact

The Pew Research Center asks, "Are you a Solid Liberal? A Steadfast Conservative? Or somewhere in between?" You may have a good sense of your personal political ideology. Then again, you may not. Pew has a "Political Typology Quiz" that you can locate by searching for that term in your browser. Take the quiz to find out how Pew classifies your politics. Alternatively, your instructor can set it up so that your entire class can take the quiz together (see the buttons at the bottom of the Pew webpage). If your class takes the test, responses of individual students are anonymous.

Socialism
A political ideology based on strong support for economic and social equality. Socialists traditionally envisioned a society in which major businesses were taken over by the government or by employee cooperatives.

Libertarianism
A political ideology based on skepticism or opposition toward most government activities.

---

11. The terms left and right in the traditional political spectrum originated during the French Revolution, when revolutionary deputies to the Legislative Assembly sat to the left of the assembly president and conservative deputies sat to the right.

12. For a classic and influential presentation of libertarian economics, see Milton Friedman, *Capitalism and Freedom* (1962; repr., University of Chicago Press, 2002).

Figure 1.3   A Four-Cornered Ideological Grid

▶ **Can you name some celebrities, media personalities, or politicians who fall into the conservative category? The liberal category? If so, who are they?**

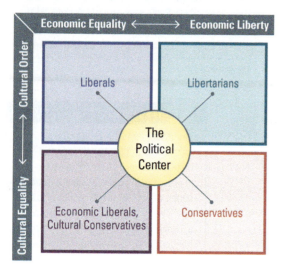

to oppose government attempts to regulate personal behavior and promote moral values. We might expect, therefore, that a consistent libertarian would support same-sex marriage. Many libertarians are also skeptical about U.S. military interventions abroad. In recent years, libertarian ideas have influenced the Republican Party.

Problems With the Traditional Political Spectrum

Many political scientists believe that the traditional left-to-right spectrum is not sufficient. Take the example of libertarians. In Table 1.1, libertarians are placed to the right of conservatives. If the only question is how much power the government should have over the economy, this is where they belong. Libertarians, however, strongly advocate freedom in social matters. They oppose government action to promote traditional moral values, although such action is often favored by other groups on the political right. Their strong support for cultural freedoms seems to align them more closely with modern liberals than with conservatives.

Liberalism is often described as an ideology that supports "big government." If the objective is to promote equality, the description has some validity. In the moral sphere, however, conservatives tend to support more government regulation of social values and moral decisions than do liberals. Thus, conservatives tend to oppose LGBTQ+ rights legislation and propose stronger curbs on pornography. Liberals usually show greater tolerance for a wide variety of life choices and oppose government attempts to regulate personal behavior and morals.

A Four-Cornered Ideological Grid

For a more sophisticated breakdown of recent American popular ideologies, many scholars use a four-cornered grid, as shown in Figure 1.3. The grid includes four possible ideologies. Each quadrant contains a substantial portion of the American electorate. Individual voters may fall anywhere on the grid, depending on the strength of their beliefs about economic and cultural issues.

Economic Liberals, Cultural Conservatives. Note that there is no generally accepted term for persons in the lower-left position, which we have labeled "economic liberals, cultural conservatives." Some scholars have used terms such as populist to describe this point of view, but these terms can be misleading. Populism more accurately refers to a hostility toward political, economic, or cultural elites, and it can be combined with a variety of political positions, both left and right.

Individuals who are economic liberals and cultural conservatives tend to support government action both to promote the values of economic equality and fairness and to defend traditional values on issues such as the nuclear family and marriage. These individuals may describe themselves as conservative or moderate. They may vote for a Republican candidate based on their conservative values. More often, they may be Democrats due to their support for economic liberalism. Many of these Democrats are African Americans or members of other minority groups.

Libertarians. The libertarian position on the four-cornered grid does not refer to the small Libertarian Party, which has only a minor role in the American political arena. Rather, libertarians typically support the Republican Party. Economically successful individuals are more likely than members of other groups to hold libertarian opinions.

Liberal Versus Progressive. Even though all four ideologies are popular, the various labels we have used in the four-cornered grid are not equally favored. Voters are much more likely to describe themselves as conservative than as liberal. In the political battles of the last several decades, the conservative movement has consistently made liberal a term of derision, and they have succeeded in devaluing the term among much of the public. Indeed, few politicians today willingly describe themselves as liberal, and many liberals prefer to describe themselves as **progressive** instead. This term dates back to the years before World War I (1914–18), when it referred to advocates of reform in both of the major political parties. Public opinion polls suggest that progressive is a relatively popular label.

Progressive
A popular alternative to the term liberal.

Making A Difference

Seeing Democracy in Action

One way to understand the American political system is to observe a legislative body in action. By "legislative body," we don't mean only the U.S. Congress and the various state legislatures—there are thousands of elected legislatures in the United States at all levels of government. You might choose to visit the meeting of a city council or a county commission.

Why Should You Care? Local legislative bodies can have a direct impact on your life. City councils or county commissions typically oversee the police or the sheriff's department, and the behavior of the police is a matter of interest even if you live on campus. If you live off campus, local authorities are responsible for an even greater number of issues that affect you directly. Are there items that the sanitation department refuses to pick up, for example? You might be able to change its policies by lobbying your councilperson.

What Can You Do? To find out when and where local legislative bodies meet, call the clerk of the council or commission. If you live in a state capital, you can view a meeting of the state legislature instead. In many communities, city council meetings and county board meetings can be seen on public-access TV channels.

While attending a business session of the legislature, keep in mind the theory of representative democracy. The commissioners or council members are elected to represent their constituents (those who voted them into office). Observe how often the members refer to their constituents or to the special needs of their district. Listen for sources of conflict within a community. If there is a debate, for example, over a zoning proposal that involves an issue of land use, try to figure out why some members oppose the proposal.

To follow up on your visit, try to get a brief interview with one of the members of the council or board. In general, legislators are very willing to talk to students, particularly students who also are voters. Ask the member how they see the job of representative. How can the wishes of the constituents be identified? How does the representative balance the needs of the particular ward or district that they represent with the good of the entire community?

Bill Clark/CQ-Roll Call Group/Getty Images

Image 1.6 Young students meet with Nancy Pelosi at the U.S. Capitol Building. Pelosi, a Democrat, was the Speaker (leader) of the U.S. House of Representatives. ▶ Why might elected officials be willing to meet with students?

///

Key Terms

authoritarianism 4
authority 3
Bill of Rights 10
capitalism 12
civil liberties 10
conservatism 15
conservative movement 16
democracy 4
democratic republic 5
direct democracy 4

elite theory 7
equality 11
government 2
ideology 15
initiative 5
institution 2
legitimacy 3
liberalism 16
libertarianism 17
liberty 3
limited government 6

majoritarianism 7
majority rule 6
order 3
pluralism 8
political culture 9
political socialization 9
politics 2
popular sovereignty 5
progressive 19
property 12
recall 5

referendum 5
representative democracy 6
republic 5
socialism 17
totalitarian regime 4
universal suffrage 6
working class 14

///

Chapter Summary

» **LO 1-1** Politics is the process by which people decide which members of society receive certain benefits or privileges and which members do not. It is the struggle over power or influence within institutions or organizations that can grant benefits or privileges. Government is an institution within which decisions are made that resolve conflicts and allocate benefits and privileges. It is the predominant institution within society because it has the ultimate decision-making authority.

Two fundamental political values are order, which includes security against violence, and liberty, the greatest freedom of the individual consistent with the freedom of other individuals. To be effective, government authority—the right and power to enforce its decisions—must be backed by legitimacy.

» **LO 1-2** Many of our terms for describing forms of government came from the ancient Greeks. In a direct democracy, such as that of ancient Athens, the people themselves make the important political decisions. The United States is a democratic republic—also called a representative democracy—in which the people elect representatives to make the decisions.

» **LO 1-3** Theories of American democracy include majoritarianism, elite theory, and pluralism. In majoritarianism, the government does what the majority wants. Under elite theory, the real power lies with one or more elites. Pluralism means that organized interest groups contend for power.

» **LO 1-4** Fundamental American values include liberty, order, equality, and property. Not all of these values are fully compatible. The value of order often competes with civil liberties, and economic equality competes with property rights, which represent liberty to many people.

» **LO 1-5** Conservatives advocate for a limited role for government, support traditional values, and are cautious about change. Liberals support government action to improve individual welfare, civil rights, and political and social change. Economic liberalism and conservatism can be analyzed separately from cultural liberalism and conservatism.

Test Yourself

1. When citizens of a nation do not enjoy liberty, the government frequently will:
   a. abolish the right to a fair trial.
   b. provide government funds to churches.
   c. engage in military aggression.

2. When authority is broadly accepted, we say it has:
   a. popularity.
   b. validity.
   c. legitimacy.

3. A principal characteristic of direct democracy is that:
   a. all lawful residents have citizenship rights.
   b. laws are made by the entire citizenry acting together.
   c. the power of the government is limited to protect minorities.

4. A democratic republic is based on all of the following principles except:
   a. popular sovereignty.
   b. majority rule.
   c. a limited monarchy.

5. A word or phrase used to describe our democratic system in terms of competition among groups is:
   a. majoritarianism.
   b. pluralism.
   c. elite theory.

6. Many of our basic guarantees of liberty are found in:
   a. the Bible.
   b. the Declaration of Independence.
   c. the Bill of Rights.

7. Our economic system, under which property consists not only of personal possessions but also of wealth-creating assets, is called:
   a. capitalism.
   b. industrialism.
   c. democracy.

8. A major theme of American politics during the twenty-first century has been:
   a. arguments over whether all citizens should have the right to vote.
   b. controversies over the proper size of government.
   c. disputes as to the role of the military.

9. Popular American ideologies include:
   a. conservatism, liberalism, and libertarianism.
   b. conservatism, liberalism, and Islamism.
   c. conservatism, liberalism, and populism.

10. Important members of the conservative movement have included:
    a. President Franklin D. Roosevelt.
    b. Senator Barry Goldwater.
    c. President Lyndon B. Johnson.

11. Since the 1960s, most liberals have strongly supported all of these except:
    a. civil rights for African Americans.
    b. federal health care programs.
    c. the use of U.S. military forces abroad.

12. A common term that has come to replace liberalism in current American politics is:
    a. populism.
    b. progressivism.
    c. libertarianism.

Essay Questions

1. In Australia and Belgium, citizens are legally required to vote in elections. Would such a requirement be a good idea in the United States? What changes might take place if such a rule were in effect?

2. In your own life, what factors have contributed to your political socialization? To what extent were your political values shaped by your family, by school experiences, by friends, and by the media?

Answers to multiple-choice questions: 1. a, 2. c, 3. b, 4. c, 5. b, 6. c, 7. a, 8. b, 9. a, 10. b, 11. c, 12. b.

2 Forging a New Government: The Constitution

Garen Meguerian/Moment/Getty Images

Independence Hall in Philadelphia. In this building, the founders signed the Declaration of Independence and wrote the Constitution. At the time, Philadelphia was the largest city in the country. ▶ **Why might the founders have placed the nation's capitol somewhere else?**

The five **Learning Outcomes (LOs)** below are designed to help improve your understanding of this chapter. After reading this chapter, you should be able to:

≫ **LO 2-1** Explain how the colonial experience prepared Americans for independence, the restrictions that Britain placed on the colonies, and the American response to those restrictions.

≫ **LO 2-2** Describe the significance of the Declaration of Independence and the Articles of Confederation, as well as the weaknesses of the Articles.

≫ **LO 2-3** Discuss the most important compromises reached at the Constitutional Convention and the basic structure of the resulting government.

≫ **LO 2-4** Summarize the arguments in favor of and the arguments against adopting the Constitution, and explain why the Bill of Rights was adopted.

≫ **LO 2-5** Explain why you think the framers made it so difficult to amend the Constitution.

Check your understanding of the material with the Test Yourself section at the end of the chapter.

We the People of the United States, in Order to form a more perfect Union, establish Justice, insure domestic Tranquility, provide for the common defence, promote the general Welfare, and secure the Blessings of Liberty to ourselves and our Posterity, do ordain and establish this Constitution for the United States of America.

Every schoolchild in America has at one time or another been exposed to these famous words from the Preamble to the U.S. Constitution. The document itself is remarkable. The U.S. Constitution, compared with others in the fifty states and in the world, is relatively short. Because amending it is difficult, it also has relatively few amendments. The Constitution has remained largely intact for more than two hundred years. To a great extent, this is because the principles set forth in the Constitution are sufficiently broad that they can be adapted to meet the needs of a changing society.

How and why the U.S. Constitution was created is a story that has been told and retold. It is worth repeating, because knowing the historical and political context in which this country's governmental machinery was formed is essential to understanding American government and politics today. The Constitution did not result just from creative thinking. Many of its provisions were grounded in the political philosophy of the time.

The delegates to the Constitutional Convention in 1787 brought with them two important sets of influences: their political culture and their political experience. In the years between the first settlements in the New World and the writing of the Constitution, Americans had developed a political philosophy about how people should be governed, and they had tried out several forms of government. These experiences gave the founders the tools with which they constructed the Constitution.

The Colonial Background

> **» LO 2-1:** Explain how the colonial experience prepared Americans for independence, the restrictions that Britain placed on the colonies, and the American response to those restrictions.

In 1607, a company chartered by the English government sent a group of settlers to establish a trading post, Jamestown, in what is now Virginia. Jamestown was the first permanent English colony in the Americas. The king of England gave the backers of this colony a charter granting them "full power and authority" to make laws "for the good and welfare" of the settlement. The colonists at Jamestown instituted a representative assembly of individuals who represented the population. This assembly functioned as the colony's lawmaking body, or **legislature**. Its establishment served as a precedent that was to be observed in later colonial adventures.

Legislature
A government body responsible for making laws.

Separatists, the *Mayflower*, and the Compact

The first New England colony was established in 1620. A group made up in large part of Separatists, who wished to break with the Church of England, came over on the ship *Mayflower* to the New World, landing at Plymouth (Massachusetts). Before going onshore, the adult males—women were not considered to have any political status—drew up the Mayflower Compact, which was signed by forty-one of the forty-four men aboard the ship on November 11, 1620.

The reason for the compact was obvious. This group had landed in a spot outside the jurisdiction of the Virginia Company of London, which had chartered its settlement.[1] The Separatist leaders feared that some of the *Mayflower* passengers might conclude that they were no longer under any obligations of civil obedience. Therefore, some form of public authority was imperative. As William Bradford (one of the Separatist leaders) later recalled, there were "discontented and mutinous speeches that some of the strangers [non-Separatists] amongst them had let fall from them in the ship; that when they came ashore they would use their own liberty; for none had power to command them."

---

1. The original plan was to land in what is now New York.

The Significance of the Compact. The compact was not a constitution. It was a political statement in which the signers agreed to create and submit to the authority of a government, pending the receipt of a royal charter. The Mayflower Compact's historical and political significance is twofold: It depended on the consent of the affected individuals (and thus served as an example of popular sovereignty), and it served as a prototype for similar compacts in American history.

By the time of the American Revolution, the compact was well on its way toward achieving mythic status. In 1802, John Quincy Adams, son of the second American president, spoke these words at a founders' day celebration in Plymouth: "This is perhaps the only instance in human history of that positive, original social compact, which speculative philosophers have imagined as the only legitimate source of government."[2]

Pilgrim Beliefs. Although the Plymouth settlers committed themselves to self-government, in other ways their political ideas were not those that are prevalent today. The new community was a religious colony. Separation of church and state and most of our modern civil liberties were alien to the settlers' thinking. By the time the U.S. Constitution was written, the nation's leaders had a very different vision of the relationship between religion and government. We look at some of the founders' beliefs in this chapter's *Which Side Are You On?* feature.

More Colonies, More Government

Another outpost in New England was set up by the Massachusetts Bay Colony in 1630. Then followed Rhode Island, Connecticut, New Hampshire, and others. By 1732, the last of the thirteen colonies, Georgia, was established. During the colonial period, Americans developed a concept of limited government, which followed from the establishment of the

Bettmann/Getty Images

Image 2.1 The signing of the Mayflower Compact, by the American painter Jean Leon Gerome Ferris. ▶ Was the compact a constitution? Why or why not?

---

2. *A General History of New England from the Discovery to MDCLXXX* by Rev. William Hubbard, 2nd edition, Boston, Little and Brown, 1815.

first colonies under Crown charters. Theoretically, Britain governed the colonies. In practice, owing partly to the colonies' distance from London, the colonists exercised a large measure of self-government.

The colonists were able to make their own laws, as in the Fundamental Orders of Connecticut in 1639. The Massachusetts Body of Liberties in 1641 supported the protection of individual rights. In 1682, the Frame of Government of Pennsylvania was passed. Along with the Pennsylvania Charter of Privileges of 1701, it foreshadowed our modern Constitution and Bill of Rights. All of this legislation enabled the colonists to acquire crucial political experience. After independence was declared in 1776, the states quickly set up their own new constitutions.

Which Side Are You On?

Is America a Christian Nation?

Christianity permeated the world of the first English settlers. North and South, church attendance was often mandatory. Nine colonies had churches that were established by law.

The Declaration of Independence, however, makes no reference to Christ. The word God does not appear in the Constitution. By 1790, officially established churches were found only in Connecticut and Massachusetts, and the Congregational Church in Massachusetts had drifted so far from its Puritan origins that many of its members no longer accepted the divinity of Jesus. That is, they belonged to Unitarian congregations. One result of this development was that in the national elections of 1796 and 1800, neither major party fielded a presidential candidate who was, by modern definition, a Christian. John Adams, Unitarian, squared off against Thomas Jefferson, freethinker.

These facts raise the question: Just how Christian were the founders? More to the point, did the founders intend the United States to be a "Christian nation"?

We Were Always a Christian Nation

Christian conservatives point out that numerous American leaders throughout history have characterized the country as a Christian nation. The revolutionaries of 1776 often viewed the struggle in religious terms. Quite a few believed that God had a special plan for America to serve as an example to the world. The great majority of the colonists considered themselves Christians. Today, 65 percent of Americans identify themselves as such. If the term "Christian nation" merely identifies the beliefs of the majority, it is undeniably an accurate label.

To Christian conservatives who would like to change what is taught in the schools, however, the term means much more.

They contend that American law is based on the laws of Moses as set down in the Bible. They also believe that America's divine mission is not just an opinion held by many people—it should be taught as literal truth. Finally, this group argues that "freedom of religion does not mean freedom from religion." The language of the First Amendment means only that the national government should not prefer one church over another.

Keeping Church and Government Apart

Many mainstream scholars disagree with the previous arguments. For example, researchers have been unable to find American court cases that reference the laws of Moses. Ultimately, these people say, to argue that the founders were not serious about the separation of church and state is to ignore the plain language of the Constitution. True, most of the authors of the Constitution were Christians, but the founders were also steeped in Enlightenment rationalism. Enlightenment figures such as England's John Locke (1632–1704), France's Voltaire (1694–1778), and Scotland's Adam Smith (1723–90) emphasized reason and individualism rather than tradition. Enlightenment thinking also rejected "enthusiasm" in religion. Enthusiasm referred to the spirit that allowed Protestant and Catholic Europeans to kill one another in the name of God over a period of two centuries. For the founders, mixing church and government was a recipe for trouble.

■ For Critical Analysis

Today, candidates for president benefit when they use religious language and when they are comfortable discussing their faith. Is this at all troubling? Why or why not?

British Restrictions and Colonial Grievances

The conflict between Britain and the American colonies, which ultimately led to the Revolutionary War, began in the 1760s when the British government decided to raise revenues by imposing taxes on the American colonies. Policy advisers to Britain's King George III, who ascended to the throne in 1760, decided that it was only logical to require the American colonists to help pay the costs of Britain's defending them during the French and Indian War (1754–63). The colonists, who had grown accustomed to a large degree of self-government and independence from the British Crown, viewed the matter differently.

In 1764, the British Parliament passed the Sugar Act, which imposed a tax that many colonists were unwilling to pay. Further legislation was to come. In 1765, Parliament passed the Stamp Act, providing for internal taxation of legal documents and even newspapers. The colonists' Stamp Act Congress, assembled in 1765, called this act "taxation without representation." The colonists boycotted the purchase of English commodities in response.

The success of the boycott (the Stamp Act was repealed a year later) generated a feeling of unity within the colonies. The British, however, continued to try to raise revenues from the colonies. When Parliament passed duties on glass, lead, paint, and other items in 1767, the colonists again boycotted British goods. The colonists' fury over taxation climaxed in the Boston Tea Party: Colonists dressed as Mohawk Native Americans dumped almost 350 chests of British tea into Boston Harbor as a gesture of tax protest. In retaliation, Parliament passed the Coercive Acts (the "Intolerable Acts") in 1774, which closed Boston Harbor and placed the government of Massachusetts under direct British control. The colonists were outraged—and they responded.

The First Continental Congress

New York, Pennsylvania, and Rhode Island proposed a colonial gathering, or congress. The Massachusetts House of Representatives requested that all colonies hold conventions to select delegates to be sent to Philadelphia for such a congress.

The First Continental Congress was held in Philadelphia at Carpenters' Hall on September 5, 1774. It was a gathering of delegates from twelve of the thirteen colonies (delegates from Georgia did not attend until 1775). At that meeting, there was little talk of independence. The congress passed a resolution requesting that the colonies send a petition to King George III expressing their grievances. Resolutions were also passed requiring that the colonies raise their own colonial militias and boycott British trade. The British government condemned the congress's actions, treating them as open acts of rebellion.

The Second Continental Congress

By the time the Second Continental Congress met in May 1775 (all of the colonies were represented this time), fighting had already broken out between the British and the colonists. One of the main actions of the Second Continental Congress was to establish an army. It did this by declaring the militia that had gathered around Boston an army and naming George Washington as commander in chief. Congressional participants still attempted to reach a peaceful settlement with the British Parliament. One declaration of the congress stated explicitly that "we have not raised armies with ambitious designs of separating from Great Britain, and establishing independent states." But by the beginning of 1776, military encounters had become increasingly frequent.

Public debate was acrimonious. Then Thomas Paine's *Common Sense* appeared in Philadelphia bookstores. The pamphlet was a colonial best seller. (To do relatively as well

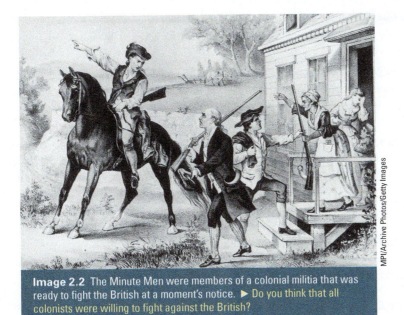

MPI/Archive Photos/Getty Images

Image 2.2 The Minute Men were members of a colonial militia that was ready to fight the British at a moment's notice. ▶ Do you think that all colonists were willing to fight against the British?

today, a book would have to sell between 10 million and 12 million copies in its first year of publication.) Many agreed that Paine did make common sense when he argued that

> *A government of our own is our natural right: And when a man seriously reflects on the precariousness [instability, unpredictability] of human affairs, he will become convinced, that it is infinitely wiser and safer, to form a constitution of our own in a cool and deliberate manner, while we have it in our power, than to trust such an interesting event to time and chance.*[3]

Paine further argued that "nothing can settle our affairs so expeditiously as an open and determined declaration for Independence."[4]

Students of Paine's pamphlet point out that his arguments were not new. They were common in tavern debates throughout the land. Rather, it was the near poetry of his words—which were at the same time as plain as the alphabet—that struck his readers.

An Independent Confederation

>> **LO 2-2:** Describe the significance of the Declaration of Independence and the Articles of Confederation, as well as the weaknesses of the Articles.

On April 6, 1776, the Second Continental Congress voted for free trade at all American ports with all countries except Britain. This act could be interpreted as an implicit declaration of independence. The next month, the congress suggested that each of the colonies establish a state government unconnected to Britain. Finally, in July, the colonists declared their independence from Britain.

---

3. Thomas Paine, *Common Sense* (Dublin, Ohio: Coventry House Publishing, 2016).
4. Ibid.

The Resolution for Independence

On July 2, the Resolution for Independence was adopted by the Second Continental Congress:

> RESOLVED, That these United Colonies are, and of right ought to be free and independent States, that they are absolved from allegiance to the British Crown, and that all political connection between them and the state of Great Britain is, and ought to be, totally dissolved.

In June 1776, Thomas Jefferson had already been writing drafts of the Declaration of Independence. When the Resolution for Independence was adopted on July 2, Jefferson argued that a declaration clearly putting forth the causes that compelled the colonies to separate from Britain was necessary. The Second Continental Congress assigned the task to him.

Natural Rights
Rights held to be inherent in natural law, not dependent on governments.

Social Contract
A voluntary agreement among individuals to secure their rights and welfare by creating a government and abiding by its rules.

July 4, 1776—The Declaration of Independence

Jefferson's version of the Declaration was amended to gain unanimous acceptance (for example, his condemnation of the trade in enslaved people was eliminated to satisfy Georgia and North Carolina), but the bulk of it was passed intact on July 4, 1776. On July 19, the modified draft became "the unanimous declaration of the thirteen United States of America." On August 2, it was signed by the members of the Second Continental Congress.

Universal Truths. The Declaration of Independence has become one of the world's most renowned and significant documents. The words opening the second paragraph of the Declaration indicate why this is so:

> We hold these Truths to be self-evident, that all Men are created equal, that they are endowed by their Creator with certain unalienable Rights, that among these are Life, Liberty, and the Pursuit of Happiness—That to secure these Rights, Governments are instituted among Men, deriving their just Powers from the Consent of the Governed, that whenever any Form of Government becomes destructive of these Ends, it is the Right of the People to alter or abolish it, and to institute new Government.

Natural Rights and Social Contracts. The statement that "all Men are created equal" and have **natural rights** ("unalienable Rights"), including the rights to "Life, Liberty, and the Pursuit of Happiness," was revolutionary at that time. Its use by Jefferson reveals the influence of the English philosopher John Locke (1632–1704), whose writings were familiar to educated American colonists, including Jefferson. In his *Two Treatises of Government*, published in 1690, Locke had argued that all people possess certain natural rights, including the rights to life, liberty, and property.

Locke went on to argue that the primary purpose of government was to protect these rights. Furthermore, government was established by the people through a **social contract**—an agreement among the people to form a government and abide by its rules. As you read earlier, such contracts, or compacts, were not new to Americans. The Mayflower Compact was the first of several documents that established governments or governing rules based on the consent of the governed.

Image 2.3 Benjamin Franklin, John Adams, and Thomas Jefferson work on the Declaration of Independence. ▶ Why was that document so important?

Archive Images/Alamy Stock Photo

After setting forth these basic principles of government, the Declaration of Independence goes on to justify the colonists' revolt against Britain. Much of the remainder of the document is a list of what "He" (King George III) had done to deprive the colonists of their rights. (See Appendix A at the end of this book for the complete text of the Declaration of Independence.)

The Significance of the Declaration. The concepts of equality, natural rights, and government established through a social contract were to have a lasting impact on American life. The Declaration of Independence set forth ideals that have since become a fundamental part of our national identity. The Declaration also became a model for use by other nations around the world.

Certainly, most Americans are familiar with the beginning words of the Declaration. Yet few Americans ponder the obvious question: What did these assertions in the Declaration have to do with independence? Clearly, independence could have been declared without these words. Even as late as 1857, Abraham Lincoln admitted, "The assertion that 'all men are created equal' was of no practical use in effecting our separation from Great Britain; and it was placed in the Declaration, not for that, but for future use."[5]

Essentially, the immediate significance of the Declaration of Independence, in 1776, was that it established the legitimacy of the new nation in the eyes of the colonists themselves. In addition, the Declaration made it possible for foreign governments to recognize the United States as an independent nation. What the new nation needed most were supplies for its armies and a commitment of foreign military aid. Unless the United States appeared to the world as a political entity separate and independent from Britain, no foreign government would enter into an agreement with its leaders. In fact, foreign support was crucial to the success of the revolution.

The Rise of Republicanism

Although the colonists had formally declared independence from Britain, the fight to gain actual independence continued for five more years, until British general Charles Cornwallis surrendered at Yorktown in 1781. In 1783, after Britain formally recognized the independence of the United States in the Treaty of Paris, George Washington disbanded the army. During these years of military struggles, the states faced the additional challenge of creating a system of self-government for an independent United States.

Some colonists wanted to form a strong central government even before independence from Britain. Others, who called themselves republicans (not to be confused with today's Republican Party), were against a strong central government. They opposed monarchy, executive authority, and virtually any form of restraint on the power of local groups.

These republicans were a major political force from 1776 to 1780. Indeed, they almost prevented victory over the British by their unwillingness to cooperate with any central authority.

During this time, all of the states adopted written constitutions. Eleven of the constitutions were completely new. Two of them—those of Connecticut and Rhode Island—were old royal charters with minor modifications. In most states, republican sentiment led to increased power for the state legislatures. In Georgia and Pennsylvania, **unicameral (one-body) legislatures** were unchecked by executive or judicial authority. In almost all states, the legislature was predominant.

Unicameral (one-body) Legislatures
A legislature with only one legislative chamber, as opposed to a bicameral (two-chamber) legislature, such as the U.S. Congress.

---

5. David Armitage, *The Declaration of Independence: A Global History* (Cambridge, Mass.: Harvard University Press, 2007), p. 26.

Confederation
A political system in which states or regional governments retain ultimate authority except for those powers they expressly delegate to a central government.

States
A group of people occupying a specific area and organized under one government. It may be either a nation or a subunit of a nation.

The Articles of Confederation: Our First Form of Government

The fear of a powerful central government led to the passage of the Articles of Confederation, which created a weak central government. The term **confederation** is important. It means a voluntary association of independent **states**, in which the member states agree to only limited restraints on their freedom of action. As a result, confederations seldom have an effective executive authority.

In June 1776, the Second Continental Congress began the process of composing what would become the Articles of Confederation and Perpetual Union, more commonly known as the Articles of Confederation. The final draft was completed by November 15, 1777, but not until March 1, 1781, did the last state, Maryland, agree to ratify the Articles. Well before the final ratification, however, many of the Articles were implemented—the Continental Congress and the thirteen states conducted American military, economic, and political affairs according to the standards and the form specified by the Articles.[6]

The Articles Establish a Government. Under the Articles, the thirteen original colonies, now states, established on March 1, 1781, a government of the states—the Congress of the Confederation. The congress was a unicameral assembly of so-called ambassadors from each state, with every state possessing a single vote. Each year, the congress would choose one of its members as its president of the congress (that is, the presiding officer), but the Articles did not provide for a president of the United States.

The congress was authorized in Article X to appoint an executive committee of the states "to execute in the recess of Congress, such of the powers of Congress as the United States, in Congress assembled, by the consent of nine [of the thirteen] states, shall from time to time think expedient to vest with them." The congress was also allowed to appoint other committees and civil officers necessary for managing the general affairs of the United States. In addition, the congress could regulate foreign affairs and establish coinage and weights and measures. But it lacked an independent, direct source of revenue and the necessary executive machinery to enforce its decisions throughout the land. Article II of the Articles of Confederation guaranteed that each state would retain its sovereignty. Table 2.1 summarizes the powers—and the lack of powers—of congress under the Articles of Confederation.

Accomplishments Under the Articles. The new government had some accomplishments during its eight years of existence under the Articles of Confederation. Certain states' claims to western lands were settled. Maryland had objected to the western land claims of Connecticut, Massachusetts, New York, and Virginia. It was only after these states consented to give up their land claims to the United States as a whole that Maryland signed the Articles of Confederation. Another accomplishment under the Articles was the passage of the Northwest Ordinance of 1787, which established a basic pattern of government for new territories north of the Ohio River. All in all, the Articles represented the first real pooling of resources by the American states.

Weaknesses of the Articles. In spite of these accomplishments, the Articles of Confederation had many defects. Although congress had the legal right to declare war and to conduct foreign policy, it did not have the right to demand revenues from the states.

---

6. Keith L. Dougherty, *Collective Action Under the Articles of Confederation* (New York: Cambridge University Press, 2006).

Table 2.1	The Confederation Congress—Powers and Limits

▶ **Why would states be reluctant to forward taxes to the Confederation?**

Congress Had Power to	Congress Lacked Power to
• Declare war and make peace.	• Provide for effective treaties and control foreign relations. It could not compel states to respect treaties.
• Enter into treaties and alliances.	• Compel states to meet military quotas. It could not draft soldiers.
• Establish and control armed forces.	
• Request soldiers and funds from states.	• Regulate interstate and foreign commerce. It left each state free to tax imports from other states.
• Regulate coinage.	
• Borrow funds and issue bills of credit.	• Collect taxes directly from the people. It had to rely on states to collect and forward taxes.
• Fix uniform standards of weight and measurement.	• Compel states to pay their share of government costs.
• Create admiralty courts.	• Provide and maintain a sound monetary system or issue paper money. This was left up to the states, and paper currencies in circulation differed tremendously in purchasing power.
• Create a postal system.	
• Regulate Indian affairs.	
• Guarantee citizens of each state the rights and privileges of citizens in the several states when in another state.	
• Adjudicate disputes between states on state petition.	

It could only ask for them. Additionally, the actions of congress required the consent of nine states. Any amendments to the Articles required the unanimous consent of the congress and confirmation by every state legislature. Furthermore, the Articles did not create a national system of courts.

Basically, the functioning of the government under the Articles depended on the goodwill of the states. Article III simply established a "league of friendship" among the states—no national government was intended.

Probably the most fundamental weakness of the Articles, and the most basic cause of their eventual replacement by the Constitution, was the lack of power to raise funds for the militia. The Articles contained no language giving congress coercive power to raise revenue (by levying taxes) to provide adequate support for the military forces controlled by congress. Due to a lack of resources, the Continental Congress was forced to disband the army after the Revolutionary War, even in the face of serious Spanish and British military threats.

Shays's Rebellion and the Need to Revise the Articles. Because of the weaknesses of the Articles of Confederation, the central government could do little to maintain peace and order in the new nation. The states bickered among themselves and increasingly taxed each other's goods. By 1784, the country faced a serious economic depression. Banks were calling in old loans and refusing to make new ones. People who could not pay their debts were often thrown into debtors' prisons.

In August 1786, musket-bearing farmers led by former revolutionary captain Daniel Shays seized county courthouses and disrupted the trials of debtors in Springfield, Massachusetts. Shays and his men then launched an attack on the federal arsenal at Springfield, but they were repulsed. Shays's Rebellion demonstrated that the central government could not protect the citizenry from armed rebellion or provide adequately for the public welfare. The rebellion spurred the nation's political leaders to action.

The Constitutional Convention

≫ LO 2-3: Discuss the most important compromises reached at the Constitutional Convention and the basic structure of the resulting government.

The Virginia legislature called for a meeting of all the states to be held at Annapolis, Maryland, on September 11, 1786—ostensibly to discuss commercial problems only. It was evident to those in attendance (including Alexander Hamilton of New York and James Madison of Virginia) that the national government had serious weaknesses that had to be addressed if it was to survive. Among the important problems to be solved were the relationship between the states and the central government, the powers of the national legislature, the need for executive leadership, and the establishment of policies for economic stability. The result of this meeting was a petition to the Continental Congress for a general convention to meet in Philadelphia in May 1787 "to consider the exigencies [needs] of the union."

The designated date for the opening of the convention at Philadelphia, now known as the Constitutional Convention, was May 14, 1787. Few of the delegates had actually arrived in Philadelphia by that time, however, so the opening was delayed. The convention formally began in the East Room of the Pennsylvania State House on May 25.[7] Fifty-five of the seventy-four delegates chosen for the convention actually attended. (Of those fifty-five, only about forty played active roles at the convention.) Rhode Island was the only state that refused to send delegates.

Factions Among the Delegates

We know much about the proceedings at the convention because James Madison kept a daily, detailed personal journal. A majority of the delegates were strong nationalists—they wanted a central government with real power, unlike the weak central government under

EDSITEment.neh.gov

Image 2.4 George Washington, who would become the nation's first president, presided over the Constitutional Convention of 1787. It formally opened in the East Room of the Pennsylvania State House (later named Independence Hall) on May 25. ▶ Why might Washington have been chosen to chair this convention?

---

7. This was the same room in which the Declaration of Independence had been signed eleven years earlier. The State House was later named Independence Hall.

the Articles of Confederation. George Washington and Benjamin Franklin were among those who sought a stronger government.

Among the nationalists, some—including Alexander Hamilton—went as far as to support monarchy. Another important group of nationalists was of a more republican stripe. Led by James Madison of Virginia and James Wilson of Pennsylvania, these republican nationalists wanted a central government founded on popular support.

Other factions included a group of delegates who were totally against a national authority. Two of the three delegates from New York quit the convention when they saw the nationalist direction of its proceedings.

Politicking and Compromises

The debates at the convention started on the first day. James Madison had spent months reviewing European political theory. When his Virginia delegation arrived ahead of most of the others, it got to work immediately. By the time George Washington opened the convention, Governor Edmund Randolph of Virginia was prepared to present fifteen resolutions proposing fundamental changes in the nation's government. In retrospect, this was a masterful stroke on the part of the Virginia delegation. It set the agenda for the remainder of the convention—even though, in principle, the delegates had been sent to Philadelphia for the sole purpose of amending the Articles of Confederation.

The Virginia Plan. Randolph's fifteen resolutions proposed an entirely new national government under a constitution. Basically, the plan called for the following:

- A **bicameral (two-chamber) legislature**, with the lower chamber chosen by the people and the smaller upper chamber chosen by the lower chamber from nominees selected by state legislatures. The number of representatives would be proportional to a state's population, thus favoring the large states. This legislature could void any state laws.
- The creation of an unspecified national executive, elected by the legislature.
- The creation of a national judiciary, appointed by the legislature.

Bicameral (two-chamber) Legislature
A legislature made up of two parts, called chambers. The U.S. Congress, composed of the House of Representatives and the Senate, is a bicameral legislature.

It did not take long for the smaller states to realize they would fare poorly under the Virginia Plan, which would enable Massachusetts, Pennsylvania, and Virginia to form a majority in the national legislature. The debate on the plan dragged on for a number of weeks. It was time for the small states to come up with their own plan.

The New Jersey Plan. On June 15, William Paterson of New Jersey offered an alternative plan. He proposed the following:

- The fundamental principle of the Articles of Confederation—one state, one vote— would be retained.
- Congress would be able to regulate trade and impose taxes.
- All acts of Congress would be the supreme law of the land.
- Several people would be elected by Congress to form an executive office.
- The executive office would appoint a Supreme Court.

Basically, the New Jersey Plan was simply an amendment of the Articles of Confederation. Its only notable feature was its reference to the **supremacy doctrine**, which was later included in the Constitution.

Supremacy Doctrine
A doctrine that asserts the priority of national law over state laws. This principle is stated in Article VI of the Constitution.

The "Great Compromise." The delegates were at an impasse. Most wanted a strong national government and were unwilling even to consider the New Jersey Plan. But when the Virginia Plan was brought up again, the small states threatened to leave. It was not until

July 16 that a compromise was achieved. Roger Sherman of Connecticut proposed the following:

- A bicameral legislature in which the lower chamber, the House of Representatives, would be apportioned according to the number of free inhabitants in each state, plus three-fifths of the enslaved persons.
- An upper chamber, the Senate, which would have two members from each state elected by the state legislatures.

Great Compromise
The compromise between the New Jersey and Virginia plans that created one chamber of the Congress based on population and one chamber representing each state equally; also called the Connecticut Compromise.

This plan, known as the **Great Compromise**, broke the deadlock. (The plan is also called the Connecticut Compromise because of the role of the Connecticut delegates in the proposal.) It did exact a political price, however, because it permitted each state to have equal representation in the Senate. Having two senators represent each state diluted the voting power of citizens living in more heavily populated states and gave the smaller states disproportionate political power. Nonetheless, the Connecticut Compromise resolved the controversy between small and large states. In addition, the Senate would act as a check on the House, which many feared would be dominated by the masses and excessively responsive to them.

The Three-Fifths Compromise. The Great Compromise also temporarily resolved another major issue—how to deal with enslaved persons in the representational scheme. Slavery was still legal in several northern states, but it was concentrated in the South. Many delegates were opposed to slavery and wanted it banned entirely in the United States. Charles Pinckney of South Carolina led strong southern opposition to a ban on slavery. Furthermore, the South wanted enslaved persons to be counted along with free persons in determining representation in Congress. Delegates from the northern states objected. Sherman's three-fifths proposal was a compromise between northerners who did not want enslaved persons counted at all and southerners who wanted them counted in the same way as free white people. Actually, Sherman's Connecticut plan spoke of three-fifths of "all other persons" (and that is the language of the Constitution itself). It is not hard to figure out, though, who those other persons were. The three-fifths compromise illustrates the power the southern states had at the convention.

The Trade in Enslaved Persons and the Future of Slavery. The three-fifths compromise did not completely settle the slavery issue. There was also the question of the trade in enslaved persons. Eventually, the delegates agreed that Congress could not ban the importation of enslaved persons until after 1808. The compromise meant that the matter of slavery itself was never addressed directly. The South won twenty years of unrestricted trade in enslaved persons and a requirement that escaped enslaved persons in free states be returned to their owners.

Many delegates, including some owners of enslaved persons such as George Washington and James Madison, had serious objections to slavery. Why, then, did they allow slavery to continue? Historians have long maintained that the framers had no choice—that without a slavery compromise, the delegates from the South would have abandoned the convention. Indeed, this was the fear of a number of antislavery delegates to the convention. Madison, for example, said, "Great as the evil is, a dismemberment of the Union would be even worse."[8]

A number of historians have made an additional point. Many American leaders believed that slavery would die out naturally. These leaders assumed that in the long run, the labor of enslaved people could not compete with the labor of free citizens. This assumption turned out to be incorrect.

---

8. Speech before the Virginia ratifying convention on June 17, 1788, as cited in Bruno Leone, ed., *The Creation of the Constitution* (San Diego: Greenhaven Press, 1995), p. 159.

Other Issues. The South also worried that the northern majority in Congress would pass legislation unfavorable to its economic interests. Because the South depended on agricultural exports, it feared the imposition of export taxes. In return for acceding to the northern demand that Congress be able to regulate commerce among the states and with other nations, the South obtained a promise that export taxes would not be imposed. As a result, the United States is among the few countries that do not tax their exports.

There were other disagreements. The delegates could not decide whether to establish only a Supreme Court or to create lower courts as well. They deferred the issue by instituting a Supreme Court and allowing Congress to establish lower courts. They also disagreed over whether the president or the Senate would choose the Supreme Court justices. A compromise was reached under which the president would nominate the justices and the Senate would confirm or reject the nominations.

These compromises, as well as others, resulted from the recognition that if one group of states refused to ratify the Constitution, it was doomed.

Working Toward Final Agreement

The Connecticut Compromise was reached by mid-July. The makeup of the executive branch and the judiciary, however, was left unsettled. The remaining work of the convention was turned over to a five-person Committee of Detail, which presented a rough draft of the Constitution on August 6. It made the executive and judicial branches subordinate to the legislative branch.

The Madisonian Model—Separation of Powers. The major issue of **separation of powers** had not yet been resolved. The delegates were concerned with structuring the government to prevent the imposition of tyranny, either by the majority or by a minority. It was Madison who proposed a governmental scheme—sometimes called the **Madisonian Model**—to achieve this: The executive, legislative, and judicial powers of government were to be separated so that no one branch had enough power to dominate the others. The separation of powers was by function, as well as by personnel, with Congress passing laws, the president enforcing and administering laws, and the courts interpreting laws in individual circumstances.

Each of the three branches of government would be independent of the others, but they would have to cooperate to govern. According to Madison, in *Federalist Paper* No. 51 (see Appendix C), "the great security against a gradual concentration of the several powers in the same department consists in giving to those who administer each department the necessary constitutional means and personal motives to resist encroachments of the others."

The Madisonian Model—Checks and Balances. The "constitutional means" Madison referred to is a system of **checks and balances** through which each branch of the government can check the actions of the others. For example, Congress can enact laws, but the president has veto power over congressional acts. That is, the president can reject the legislation. The Supreme Court has the power to declare acts of Congress and of the executive unconstitutional, but the president appoints the justices of the Supreme Court, with the advice and consent of the Senate. (The Supreme Court's power to declare acts unconstitutional was not mentioned in the Constitution, although arguably the framers assumed that the Court would have this power—see the discussion of judicial review later in this chapter.) Figure 2.1 outlines these checks and balances.

Separation of Powers
The principle of dividing governmental powers among different branches of government.

Madisonian Model
A structure of government proposed by James Madison, in which the powers of the government are separated into three branches: executive, legislative, and judicial.

Checks and Balances
A major principle of the American system of government whereby each branch of the government can check the actions of the others.

Bettmann/Getty Images

Image 2.5 James Madison (1751–1836) has been called "the master builder of the Constitution." ▶ What did he do to earn that title?

Figure 2.1 Checks and Balances

The major checks and balances among the three branches of the U.S. government are illustrated here. The Constitution does not mention some of these checks. Checks and balances can be thought of as a confrontation of powers or responsibilities. Each branch checks the actions of the others. Two branches in conflict have powers that can result in balances or stalemates, requiring one branch to give in or both to reach a compromise. ▶ **Which result is more likely?**

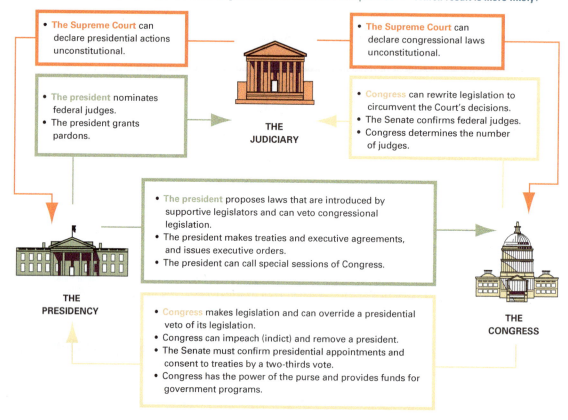

- **The Supreme Court** can declare presidential actions unconstitutional.

- **The president** nominates federal judges.
- The president grants pardons.

THE JUDICIARY

- **The Supreme Court** can declare congressional laws unconstitutional.

- Congress can rewrite legislation to circumvent the Court's decisions.
- The Senate confirms federal judges.
- Congress determines the number of judges.

- **The president** proposes laws that are introduced by supportive legislators and can veto congressional legislation.
- The president makes treaties and executive agreements, and issues executive orders.
- The president can call special sessions of Congress.

THE PRESIDENCY

- Congress makes legislation and can override a presidential veto of its legislation.
- Congress can impeach (indict) and remove a president.
- The Senate must confirm presidential appointments and consent to treaties by a two-thirds vote.
- Congress has the power of the purse and provides funds for government programs.

THE CONGRESS

In the years since the Constitution was ratified, the checks and balances built into it have evolved into a sometimes complex give-and-take among the branches of government. Generally, for nearly every check that one branch has over another, the branch that has been checked has found a way of getting around it. For example, suppose that the president checks Congress by vetoing a bill. Congress can override the presidential veto by a two-thirds vote. Additionally, Congress holds the "power of the purse." If it disagrees with a program endorsed by the executive branch, it can simply refuse to appropriate the funds necessary to operate that program.

Similarly, the president can impose a countercheck on Congress if the Senate refuses to confirm a presidential appointment, such as a judicial appointment. The president can simply wait until Congress is in recess and then make what is called a "recess appointment," which does not require the Senate's immediate approval.

The Executive. Some delegates favored a plural executive, made up of a committee. This idea was abandoned in favor of a single chief executive. Some argued that Congress should choose the executive. To make the presidency completely independent of Congress, however, an **Electoral College** was adopted. This group would be made up of electors chosen by the states, and each state would have as many electors as it had members of Congress.

The founders hoped that through this system, the president would be elected by prominent citizens, not ordinary voters. In fact, for some years after the Constitution was adopted, electors in about half the states were chosen by the state legislature, not directly by the voters. Even in those states, however, the organization of political parties from 1796 on gave ordinary voters some input into choosing the president. A vote for a party's state legislative candidate, after all, was also a way to support that party's presidential candidate. By 1832, the South Carolina legislature was the only one still choosing electors.

The Final Document

On September 17, 1787, the Constitution was approved by thirty-nine delegates. Of the fifty-five who had attended originally, only forty-two remained. Three delegates refused to sign the Constitution. Others disapproved of at least parts of it but signed anyway to begin the **ratification** debate.

The Constitution that was to be ratified established the following fundamental principles:

- Popular sovereignty, or control by the people
- A republican government in which the people choose representatives to make decisions for them
- Limited government with written laws, in contrast to the powerful British government against which the colonists had rebelled
- Separation of powers, with checks and balances among branches to prevent any one branch from gaining too much power
- A federal system that allows for states' rights because the states feared too much centralized control

The Difficult Road to Ratification

>> **LO 2-4:** Summarize the arguments in favor of and the arguments against adopting the Constitution, and explain why the Bill of Rights was adopted.

The founders knew that ratification of the Constitution was far from certain. Indeed, because it was almost guaranteed that many state legislatures would not ratify it, the delegates agreed that each state should hold a special convention. Elected delegates to these conventions would discuss and vote on the Constitution. Further departing from the Articles of Confederation, the delegates agreed that as soon as nine states (rather than all thirteen) approved the Constitution, it would take effect, and Congress could begin to organize the new government.

The Federalists Push for Ratification

The two opposing forces in the battle over ratification were the Federalists and the Anti-Federalists. The **Federalists** favored a strong central government and the new Constitution. Their opponents, the **Anti-Federalists**, wanted to prevent the Constitution as drafted from being ratified.[9]

Electoral College
A group of persons, called electors, that officially elects the president and the vice president of the United States. The electors are selected by each state and the District of Columbia.

Ratification
Formal approval.

Federalists
An individual who was in favor of the adoption of the U.S. Constitution and the creation of a federal union with a strong central government.

Anti-Federalists
An individual who opposed the ratification of the new Constitution in 1787. The Anti-Federalists were opposed to a strong central government.

---

9. There is some irony here. At the Constitutional Convention, those opposed to a strong central government pushed for a federal system because such a system would allow the states to retain some of their sovereign rights. The label Anti-Federalists thus contradicted their essential views.

Interact

Our Constitution is based on the separation of powers, but in many other democracies, the legislative and executive branches are united. The chief executive, often called the prime minister, is also the leader of parliament (the legislature). In fact, parliament elects the prime minister. Use any search engine on the internet to research the structure of the governments of Britain, Denmark, Poland, or another European country. On various sites, learn the meaning of terms that are new to you. Consider— or discuss with your classmates— which constitutional principles of the country you chose to research would be surprising or unacceptable to Americans. How would the United States be different if the founders had adopted a parliamentary system?

The *Federalist Papers*. In New York, opponents of the Constitution were quick to attack it. Alexander Hamilton answered their attacks under a pseudonym in newspaper columns and secured two collaborators—John Jay and James Madison. In a very short time, those three political figures wrote a series of eighty-five essays in defense of the Constitution and of a republican form of government.

These widely read essays, called the *Federalist Papers*, appeared in New York newspapers from October 1787 to August 1788 and were reprinted in the newspapers of other states. Although we do not know for certain who wrote every one, it is apparent that Hamilton was responsible for about two-thirds of the essays. These included the most important ones interpreting the Constitution, explaining the various powers of the three branches, and presenting the theory of judicial review. Madison's *Federalist Paper* No. 10 (see Appendix C), however, is considered a classic in political theory. It deals with the nature of groups—or factions, as he called them. In spite of the rapidity with which the *Federalist Papers* were written, they are considered by many to be perhaps the best example of political theorizing ever produced in the United States.[10]

The Anti-Federalist Response. Many of the Anti-Federalists' attacks on the Constitution were also brilliant. The Anti-Federalists claimed that the Constitution was written by aristocrats and would lead to aristocratic tyranny. More important, the Anti-Federalists believed that the Constitution would create an overbearing central government hostile to personal liberty. (The Constitution said nothing about freedom of the press, freedom of religion, or any other individual liberty.) They wanted to include a list of guaranteed liberties, or a bill of rights. Finally, the Anti-Federalists decried the weakened power of the states.[11]

The Anti-Federalists cannot be dismissed as unpatriotic extremists. They included such patriots as Patrick Henry and Samuel Adams. They were arguing what had been the most prevalent view in that era. This view derived from the French philosopher Baron de Montesquieu (1689–1755), an influential theorist. Montesquieu believed that a republic was possible only in a relatively small society governed by direct democracy or by a large legislature with small districts. The Madisonian view favoring a large republic, particularly as expressed in *Federalist Papers* No. 10 and No. 51 (see Appendix C), was actually an exceptional view in those years. Indeed, some researchers believe it was mainly the bitter experiences with the Articles of Confederation, rather than Madison's arguments, that persuaded the state conventions to ratify the Constitution.

The March to the Finish

The struggle for ratification continued. Strong majorities were procured in Connecticut, Delaware, Georgia, New Jersey, and Pennsylvania. After a fierce struggle in Massachusetts, that state ratified the Constitution by a narrow margin on February 6, 1788. By the spring, Maryland and South Carolina had ratified by sizable majorities. Then on June 21 of

---

10. Some scholars believe that the *Federalist Papers* played only a minor role in securing ratification of the Constitution. Even if this is true, these writings still have lasting value as an authoritative explanation of the Constitution.

11. Herbert J. Storing edited seven volumes of Anti-Federalist writings and released them in 1981 as *The Complete Anti-Federalist*. Political science professor Murray Dry has prepared a more manageable one-volume version of this collection: Herbert J. Storing, ed., *The Anti-Federalist* (Chicago: University of Chicago Press, 2006).

that year, New Hampshire became the ninth state to ratify the Constitution. Although the Constitution was formally in effect, this meant little without Virginia and New York. Virginia ratified it a few days later, but New York did not join in for another month.

The Bill of Rights

The U.S. Constitution would not have been ratified in several important states if the Federalists had not assured the states that amendments to the Constitution would be passed to protect individual liberties against incursions by the national government. Many members of the Constitutional Convention had not thought that a Bill of Rights was needed, or even desirable. Some argued that listing particular rights might imply the absence of rights that were not mentioned. Still, a Bill of Rights turned out to be a political necessity.

Many of the recommendations of the state ratifying conventions included specific rights that were considered later by James Madison as he labored to draft what became the Bill of Rights. Madison had to cull through more than two hundred state recommendations. It was no small task, and in retrospect he chose remarkably well. One of the rights appropriate for constitutional protection that he left out was equal protection under the laws—but that was not commonly regarded as a basic right at that time. Not until 1868 was the Constitution amended to guarantee that no state shall deny equal protection to any person.

On December 15, 1791, the national Bill of Rights was adopted when Virginia agreed to ratify the ten amendments. On ratification, the Bill of Rights became part of the U.S. Constitution. The basic structure of American government had already been established. Now the fundamental rights and liberties of individuals were protected, at least in theory, at the national level.

The proposed amendment that Madison characterized as "the most valuable amendment in the whole lot"—which would have prohibited the states from infringing on the freedoms of conscience, press, and jury trial—had been eliminated by the Senate. Thus, the Bill of Rights as adopted did not limit state power, and individual citizens had to rely on the guarantees contained in a particular state constitution or state bill of rights. The country had to wait until the violence of the Civil War before significant limitations on state power in the form of the Fourteenth Amendment became part of the national Constitution.

Theo Wargo/WireImage/Getty Images

Image 2.6 Lin-Manuel Miranda portrayed Alexander Hamilton in the smash-hit Broadway musical *Hamilton*. About two-thirds of the *Federalist Papers* were written by Hamilton.
▶ What was the impact of that writing on American political thought?

Altering the Constitution

≫ **LO 2-5:** Explain why you think the framers made it so difficult to amend the Constitution.

As amended, the U.S. Constitution consists of about seven thousand words. It is shorter than any state constitution except that of Vermont. The federal Constitution is short because the founders intended it to be only a framework for the new government, to be interpreted by succeeding generations. One of the reasons it has remained short is that the formal amending procedure does not allow for changes to be made easily. Article V of the Constitution outlines the ways in which amendments may be proposed and ratified.

The Formal Amendment Process

Two formal methods of proposing an amendment to the Constitution are available: (1) a two-thirds vote in each chamber of Congress or (2) a national convention that is called by Congress at the request of two-thirds of the state legislatures. This second method has never been used.

Ratification can occur by one of two methods: (1) by a positive vote in three-fourths of the legislatures of the various states or (2) by special conventions called in the states and a positive vote in three-fourths of them. The second method has been used only once, to repeal Prohibition (the ban on the production and sale of alcoholic beverages). That situation was exceptional—prohibitionist forces were in control of the legislatures in many states in which a majority of the population actually supported repeal.

Congress has considered more than twelve thousand amendments to the Constitution. Only thirty-three amendments have been submitted to the states after having been approved by the required two-thirds vote in each chamber of Congress, and only twenty-seven have been ratified—see Table 2.2. It should be clear that the amendment process is very difficult. Because of competing social and economic interests, the requirement that two-thirds of both the House and the Senate approve the amendments is hard to achieve.

Table 2.2	Amendments to the Constitution		
▶ Why have so few amendments been adopted?			
Amendment	**Subject**	**Year Adopted**	**Time Required for Ratification**
1st–10th	The Bill of Rights	1791	2 years, 2 months, 20 days
11th	Immunity of states from certain suits	1795	11 months, 3 days
12th	Changes in Electoral College procedure	1804	6 months, 3 days
13th	Prohibition of slavery	1865	10 months, 3 days
14th	Citizenship, due process, and equal protection	1868	2 years, 26 days
15th	No denial of vote because of race, color, or previous condition of servitude	1870	11 months, 8 days
16th	Power of Congress to tax income	1913	3 years, 6 months, 22 days
17th	Direct election of U.S. senators	1913	10 months, 26 days
18th	National (liquor) prohibition	1919	1 year, 29 days
19th	Women's right to vote	1920	1 year, 2 months, 14 days
20th	Change of dates for congressional and presidential terms	1933	10 months, 21 days
21st	Repeal of the Eighteenth Amendment	1933	9 months, 15 days
22d	Limit on presidential tenure	1951	3 years, 11 months, 3 days
23d	District of Columbia electoral vote	1961	9 months, 13 days
24th	Prohibition of tax payment as a qualification to vote in federal elections	1964	1 year, 4 months, 9 days
25th	Procedures for determining presidential disability and presidential succession and for filling a vice-presidential vacancy	1967	1 year, 7 months, 4 days
26th	Prohibition of setting the minimum voting age above eighteen in any election	1971	3 months, 7 days
27th	Prohibition of Congress's voting itself a raise or cut in pay that takes effect before the next election	1992	203 years

After an amendment has been approved by Congress, the process becomes even more arduous. Three-fourths of the state legislatures must approve the amendment. Only those amendments that have wide popular support across parties and in all regions of the country are likely to be approved.

Why was the amendment process made so difficult? The framers feared that a simple amendment process could lead to a tyranny of the majority, which could pass amendments to oppress disfavored individuals and groups. The cumbersome amendment process does not seem to stem the number of amendments that are proposed in Congress, however, particularly in recent years.

Informal Methods of Constitutional Change

Looking at the sparse number of formal constitutional amendments gives us an incomplete view of constitutional change. The brevity and ambiguity of the original document have permitted great alterations in the Constitution by way of varying interpretations over time. As the United States grew, both in population and in territory, new social and political realities emerged. Congress, presidents, and the courts found it necessary to interpret the Constitution's provisions in light of these new realities. The Constitution has proved to be a remarkably flexible document, adapting itself time and again to new events and concerns.

Congressional Legislation. The Constitution gives Congress broad powers to carry out its duties as the nation's legislative body. For example, Article I, Section 8, of the Constitution gives Congress the power to regulate foreign and interstate commerce. Although there is no clear definition of foreign commerce or interstate commerce in the Constitution, Congress has cited the commerce clause as the basis for passing thousands of laws.

Peter Steiner The New Yorker Collection/The Cartoon Bank

Image 2.7   *"Remember, gentlemen, we aren't here just to draft a constitution. We're here to draft the best damned constitution in the world."*

Presidential Actions. Even though the Constitution does not expressly authorize the president to propose bills or even budgets to Congress,[12] presidents since the time of Woodrow Wilson (1913–21) have proposed hundreds of bills to Congress each year that are introduced by the president's supporters in Congress.

Presidents have also relied on their Article II authority as commander in chief of the nation's armed forces to send American troops abroad into combat, although the Constitution provides that Congress has the power to declare war. Presidents have also conducted foreign affairs by the use of executive agreements, which are legally binding understandings reached between the president and a foreign head of state. The Constitution does not mention such agreements.

Judicial Review

The power of the Supreme Court or any court to examine and possibly declare unconstitutional federal or state laws and other acts of government.

Judicial Review. Another way that the Constitution adapts to new developments is through judicial review. **Judicial review** refers to the power of U.S. courts to examine the constitutionality of actions undertaken by the legislative and executive branches of government. A state court, for example, may rule that a statute enacted by the state legislature violates the state constitution. Federal courts (and ultimately, the United States Supreme Court) may rule unconstitutional not only acts of Congress and decisions of the national executive branch, but also state statutes, state executive actions, and even provisions of state constitutions.

The Constitution does not specifically mention the power of judicial review. In 1803, the Supreme Court claimed this power for itself in *Marbury v. Madison*, in which the Court ruled that a particular provision of an act of Congress was unconstitutional.[13]

Through the process of judicial review, the Supreme Court adapts the Constitution to modern situations and changing values. For example, it ruled in 1896 that "separate-but-equal" public facilities for African Americans were constitutional. By 1954, however, the times had changed, and the Supreme Court reversed that decision.[14] Woodrow Wilson summarized the Supreme Court's work when he described it as "a constitutional convention in continuous session." Basically, the law is what the Supreme Court says it is at any point in time.

Interpretation, Custom, and Usage. Changes in ways of doing political business have also led to reinterpretation of the Constitution. For example, the Constitution does not mention political parties, yet these informal, "extraconstitutional" organizations make the nominations for offices, run the campaigns, organize the members of Congress, and in fact change the election system from time to time.

In many ways, the Constitution has been adapted from a document serving the needs of a small, rural republic to one that provides a framework of government for an industrial giant with vast geographic, natural, and human resources.

---

12. Note, though, that the Constitution, in Article II, Section 3, does state that the president "shall from time to time … recommend to [Congress's] consideration such measures as he shall judge necessary and expedient." Some scholars interpret this phrase to mean that the president has the constitutional authority to propose bills and budgets to Congress for consideration.
13. 5 U.S. 137 (1803).
14. *Brown v. Board of Education of Topeka*, 347 U.S. 483 (1954).

Making A Difference

How Can You Affect the U.S. Constitution?

The Constitution has survived more than two hundred thirty-five years of turbulent history. It is also an evolving document, however. Twenty-seven amendments have been added to the original Constitution. How can you, as an individual, help to rewrite the Constitution?

Why Should You Care? The laws of the nation have a direct impact on your life, and none more so than the supreme law of the land. The most important issues in society are often settled by the Constitution. For example, for the first seventy-five years of the republic, the Constitution implicitly protected the institution of slavery. If the Constitution had never been changed through the amendment process, the process of abolishing slavery would have been much different and might have involved extraconstitutional measures.

What Can You Do? Various groups support or oppose a number of constitutional amendments. One proposal would create a constitutional requirement to balance the federal budget. If such an amendment sounds like a good idea to you, there are a variety of organizations you might investigate, including the Balanced Budget Amendment Task Force. You can find such groups by using Google or another search engine.

Other Americans have different concerns. In 2010, the Supreme Court struck down a wide range of campaign finance laws in *Citizens United v. Federal Election Commission*.[15] One result of this ruling is the "super PACs" that flood television networks with attack advertisements during recent elections. A proposed constitutional amendment would overturn the *Citizens United* ruling. If getting the money out of politics is of interest to you, check out Move to Amend or Free Speech for People.

---

15. 558 U.S. 310 (2010).

Image 2.8 Supporters of the Equal Rights Amendment in 1980. The amendment would have written the equality of women into the Constitution. It was not ratified by a large enough number of states, however, and so was not adopted. ▶ Why is it so hard to amend the Constitution?

Bill Pierce/The LIFE Images Collection/Getty Images

Key Terms

Anti-Federalist 37
bicameral (two-chamber)
   legislature 33
checks and balances 35
confederation 30

Electoral College 37
Federalist 37
Great Compromise 34
judicial review 42
legislature 23

Madisonian Model 35
natural rights 28
ratification 37
separation of powers 35
social contract 28

states 30
supremacy
   doctrine 33
unicameral (one-body)
   legislatures 29

Chapter Summary

» **LO 2-1** The first permanent English colonies were established at Jamestown in 1607 and Plymouth in 1620. The Mayflower Compact created the first formal government in New England.

In the 1760s, the British began to impose on their increasingly independent-minded colonies a series of taxes and legislative acts. The colonists responded with protests and boycotts of British products. Representatives of the colonies formed the First Continental Congress in 1774. The Second Continental Congress established an army in 1775 to defend colonists against attacks by British soldiers.

» **LO 2-2** On July 4, 1776, the Second Continental Congress approved the Declaration of Independence. Perhaps the most revolutionary aspects of the Declaration were its statements that people have natural rights to life, liberty, and the pursuit of happiness; that governments derive their power from the consent of the governed; and that people have a right to overthrow oppressive governments. During the Revolutionary War, the states signed the Articles of Confederation, creating a weak central government with few powers. The Articles proved to be unworkable because the national government had no way to ensure compliance by the states with such measures as securing tax revenues.

» **LO 2-3** General dissatisfaction with the Articles of Confederation prompted the call for a convention in Philadelphia in 1787. Delegates focused on creating a constitution for a new form of government. The Virginia Plan, which favored the larger states, and the New Jersey Plan, which favored small ones, did not garner sufficient support. The Great Compromise offered by Connecticut provided for a bicameral legislature and thus resolved the large-state/small-state dispute. The final version of the Constitution provided for the separation of powers, checks and balances, and a federal form of government.

» **LO 2-4** The Anti-Federalists argued against adopting the Constitution, but supporters of the document won in the end. Fears of a strong central government prompted the addition of the Bill of Rights to the Constitution. The Bill of Rights, which includes the freedoms of religion, speech, and assembly, was initially applied only to the federal government, but amendments to the Constitution following the Civil War were interpreted to ensure that the Bill of Rights would apply to the states as well.

» **LO 2-5** An amendment to the Constitution may be proposed either by a two-thirds vote in each chamber of Congress or by a national convention called by Congress at the request of two-thirds of the state legislatures. Ratification can occur either by the approval of three-fourths of the legislatures of the states or by special conventions called in the states for the purpose of ratifying the amendment and approval by three-fourths of these conventions. Informal methods of constitutional change include reinterpretation through congressional legislation, presidential actions, and judicial review.

Test Yourself

1. The Mayflower Compact, signed at Plymouth (Massachusetts) in 1620, was designed to:
   a. separate New England from the previously established colony of Virginia.
   b. require that all settlers obey the laws of the new colony.
   c. establish the Church of England in the new colony.

2. When the First Continental Congress convened in 1774, the British government:
   a. took no notice of it.
   b. agreed to allow the colonies to form a unified government.
   c. treated the meeting as an act of rebellion.

3. The Declaration of Independence established as unalienable rights those of:
   a. life, liberty, and property.
   b. life, liberty, and the pursuit of happiness.
   c. liberty, equality, and fraternity.

4. During the Revolutionary War era, those calling themselves republicans stood for:
   a. a strong central government.
   b. state legislatures unchecked by national or other authority.
   c. national unity to defeat the British.

5. A major defect in the Articles of Confederation was:
   a. the lack of power to raise funds for military forces.
   b. the lack of treaty-making power.
   c. the inability to easily communicate with citizens.

6. At the Constitutional Convention, the Great, or Connecticut, Compromise broke the deadlock between all of the following except:
   a. supporters of the Virginia and New Jersey plans.
   b. the large and small states.
   c. the northern and southern states.

7. Which of the following fundamental principles was not established by the Constitution of 1787?
   a. popular sovereignty, or control by the people.
   b. limited government with written laws.
   c. a requirement that state governments uphold the liberties listed in the Bill of Rights.

8. When no branch of government—executive, legislative, or judicial—is able to dominate the others, we call this:
   a. effective government.
   b. the separation of powers.
   c. limited government.

9. Those who opposed the ratification of the Constitution were called:
   a. Anti-Federalists.
   b. Federalists.
   c. Loyalists.

10. The major drafter of the Bill of Rights was:
    a. Washington.
    b. Jefferson.
    c. Madison.

11. The reason the U.S. Constitution has so few amendments is that:
    a. the formal amendment process is exceedingly difficult.
    b. the Constitution was written so well that it hasn't needed to be amended.
    c. Congress doesn't have time to consider new amendments.

12. When an amendment to the Constitution is sent to the state legislatures, how many must approve it if it is to be adopted?
    a. a majority of the states.
    b. two-thirds of the states.
    c. three-quarters of the states.

Essay Questions

1. Consider what might have happened if Georgia and the Carolinas had stayed out of the Union because of a desire to protect slavery. What would subsequent American history have been like? Would the eventual freedom of enslaved persons have been delayed—or advanced?

2. A result of the Great Compromise is that representation in the Senate dramatically departs from the one-person, one-vote rule. The 39.7 million people who live in California elect two senators, as do the almost 600,000 people living in Wyoming. What political results might occur when the citizens of small states are much better represented than the citizens of large ones?

Answers to multiple-choice questions: 1. b, 2. c, 3. b, 4. b, 5. a, 6. c, 7. c, 8. b, 9. a, 10. c, 11. a, 12. c.

3 Federalism

A National Park Service ranger shows damage to a thousand-year-old Redwood tree in the Redwood National and State Parks. The wood that poachers stole from the tree is highly valuable. ▶ **Is this joint state/national operation an example of federalism?**

The five **Learning Outcomes (LOs)** below are designed to help improve your understanding of this chapter. After reading this chapter, you should be able to:

》LO 3-1 Explain some of the benefits of the federal system for the United States.

》LO 3-2 Describe how the various provisions of the U.S. Constitution provide a framework for federalism.

》LO 3-3 Discuss how, in the early years of the republic, the United States Supreme Court confirmed the authority of the national government, and how that authority was ratified by the Civil War.

》LO 3-4 Define the terms dual federalism, cooperative federalism, categorical grants, block grants, and fiscal federalism.

》LO 3-5 Explain who benefits and who loses when the Supreme Court makes decisions that give the government in Washington, D.C., more power over the states.

Check your understanding of the material with the Test Yourself section at the end of the chapter.

In the United States, rights and powers are reserved to the states by the Tenth Amendment. In recent years, however, it may appear that the federal government, sometimes called the national or central government, has predominated. Nevertheless, that might be an exaggerated perception, for there are 89,526 separate governmental units in this nation. This number includes not just the national and state governments, but the governments of counties, municipalities, school districts, and a variety of special districts.

Visitors from France or Spain are often surprised by the complexity of our system of government. Consider that a criminal action can be defined by state law, by national law, or by both. Thus, a criminal suspect can be prosecuted in the state court system or in the federal court system (or both). Often, economic regulation covering exactly the same issues exists at the local level, the state level, and the national level—generating multiple forms to be completed, multiple procedures to be followed, and multiple laws to be obeyed. Many programs are funded by the national government but administered by state and local governments.

Relations between central governments and local units can be structured in various ways. Federalism is one of these ways. Understanding federalism and how it differs from other forms of government is important in understanding the American political system. Indeed, many political issues today would not arise if we did not have a federal form of government in which governmental authority is divided between the central government and various subunits.

Federalism and Its Alternatives

> **» LO 3-1:** Explain some of the benefits of the federal system for the United States.

There are almost two hundred independent nations in the world today. Each of these nations has its own system of government. Generally, though, we can describe how nations structure relations between central governments and local units in terms of three models: (1) the unitary system, (2) the confederal system, and (3) the federal system. The most popular, both historically and today, is the unitary system.

A Unitary System

A **unitary system** of government is the easiest to define. Unitary systems place ultimate governmental authority in the hands of the national, or central, government. Consider a typical unitary system—France. The regions, departments, municipalities, and communes in France have elected and appointed officials.

So far, the French system appears to be very similar to the U.S. system, but the similarity is only superficial. Under the unitary French system, the decisions of the lower levels of government can be overruled by the national government. The national government also can cut off the funding for many local government activities. Moreover, in a unitary system such as that in France, all questions of education, police, the use of land, and welfare are handled by the national government. Britain, Egypt, Ghana, Israel, Japan, the Philippines, and Sweden—in fact, a majority of all nations—have unitary systems of government.[1]

Unitary System
A centralized governmental system in which ultimate governmental authority rests in the hands of the national, or central, government.

A Confederal System

You were introduced to the elements of a **confederal system** of government earlier, when we examined the Articles of Confederation. A confederation is the opposite of a unitary governing system. It is a league of independent states in which a central government or administration handles only those matters of common concern expressly delegated to it by the member states. The central government has no ability to make laws directly applicable to member states unless the members explicitly support such laws. The United States under the Articles of Confederation was a confederal system.

Confederal System
A system consisting of a league of independent states, in which the central government created by the league has only limited powers over the states.

---

1. Recent legislation has altered somewhat the unitary character of the French political system. In Britain, the unitary nature of the government has been modified by the creation of the Scottish Parliament.

Few, if any, confederations of this kind exist today. One possible exception is the European Union (EU), a league of countries that has developed a large body of Europe-wide laws that all members must observe. Many members even share a common currency, the euro.

A Federal System

The federal system lies between the unitary and confederal forms of government. In a federal system, authority is divided, usually by a written constitution, between a central government and regional, or subdivisional, governments (often called constituent governments). The central government and the constituent governments both act directly on the people through laws and through the actions of elected and appointed governmental officials. Within each government's sphere of authority, each is supreme, in theory.

Thus, a federal system differs from a unitary one, in which the central government is supreme and the constituent governments derive their authority from it. In addition to the United States, Australia, Brazil, Canada, Germany, India, and Mexico are examples of nations with federal systems. See Figure 3.1 for a comparison of the three systems.

Why Federalism?

Why did the United States develop in a federal direction? As you have learned, the historical basis of our federal system was established in Philadelphia at the Constitutional Convention, where advocates of a strong national government opposed states' rights advocates. This conflict continued through to the ratifying conventions in the several states. The resulting federal system was a compromise. The supporters of the new Constitution were political pragmatists—they realized that without a federal arrangement, there would be no ratification of the new Constitution. The appeal of federalism was that it retained state traditions and local power while establishing a strong national government capable of handling problems common to the entire country.

Figure 3.1   **The Flow of Power in Three Systems of Government**

In a unitary system, power flows from the central government to the local and state governments. In a confederal system, power flows in the opposite direction—from the state governments to the central government. In a federal system, the flow of power, in principle, goes both ways. ▶ **Why do you think confederal systems are rare?**

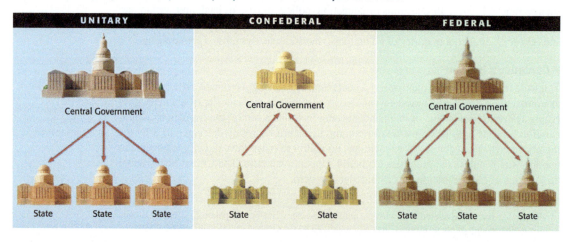

Large Geographical Areas. Even if the founders had agreed on the desirability of a unitary system, size and regional isolation would have made such a system difficult operationally. At the time of the Constitutional Convention, the thirteen states taken together were much larger geographically than England or France. Slow travel and communication, combined with geographic spread, contributed to the isolation of many regions within the states. It could take several weeks for all the states to be informed about a particular political decision.

Even with modern transportation and communications systems, the large area or population of some nations makes it impractical to locate all political authority in one place. Federalism brings government closer to the people. It allows more direct access to, and influence on, government agencies and policies, rather than leaving the population restive and dissatisfied with a remote, faceless, all-powerful central authority.

Mischa Richter/The New Yorker Collection/The Cartoon Bank

"They have very strict anti-pollution laws in this state."

Benefits for the United States. In the United States, federalism historically has yielded additional benefits. State governments have long been a training ground for future national leaders. Many presidents made their political mark as state governors. The states themselves have been testing grounds for new government initiatives. As United States Supreme Court justice Louis Brandeis once observed:

> *It is one of the happy incidents of the federal system that a single courageous state may, if its citizens choose, serve as a laboratory and try novel social and economic experiments without risk to the rest of the country.*[2]

Examples of programs pioneered at the state level include unemployment compensation, which began in Wisconsin, and air-pollution control, which was initiated in California. Same-sex marriage was first adopted in one state—Massachusetts. Recently, states have also tried new ways to manage cannabis. Many states have either explicitly or implicitly legalized the recreational use of marijuana. Other states allow it only for medicinal purposes. Yet other states still prohibit it completely. At the federal level, virtually all uses of cannabis are still considered illegal.

Allowance for Many Political Subcultures. The American way of life always has been characterized by a number of political subcultures, which divide along the lines of race and ethnic origin, region, wealth, education, and, more recently, degree of religious commitment and sexual preference. The existence of diverse political subcultures would appear to be incompatible with a political authority concentrated solely in a central government. Had the United States developed into a unitary system, various political subcultures certainly would have been less able to influence government behavior than they have been, and continue to be, in our federal system.

---

2. *New State Ice Co. v. Liebmann*, 285 U.S. 262 (1932).

Arguments Against Federalism

Not everyone thinks federalism is such a good idea. Some see it as a way for powerful state and local interests to block progress and impede national plans. Smaller political units are more likely to be dominated by a single political group. (This was essentially the argument that James Madison put forth in *Federalist Paper* No. 10, which you can read in Appendix C of this text.) In fact, the dominant groups in some cities and states resisted implementing equal rights for minority groups.

Members of various occupations have lobbied state laws that limit competition through onerous licensing requirements. Cities often adopt anti-density zoning codes that drive up the value of existing housing and can force residents with low incomes out of the area. Some argue, however, that the dominant factions in some states have been more progressive than the national government in many areas, such as environmental protection.

Critics also feel that there is too much inequity among the states, so they call for increased federal oversight of various programs. Others, however, see dangers in the expansion of national powers at the expense of the states. President Ronald Reagan (1981–89) said, "The Founding Fathers saw the federalist system as constructed something like a masonry wall. The states are the bricks, the national government is the mortar … Unfortunately, over the years, many people have increasingly come to believe that Washington is the whole wall."[3]

Enumerated Powers
Powers specifically granted to the national government by the Constitution. The first seventeen clauses of Article I, Section 8, specify most of the enumerated, or expressed, powers of the national government.

The Constitutional Basis for American Federalism

» LO 3-2: Describe how the various provisions of the U.S. Constitution provide a framework for federalism.

ZUMA Press/ ZUMA Press Inc/Alamy Stock Photo

Image 3.1 A grower in Albuquerque, New Mexico, inspects marijuana plants. ▶ Is marijuana legal everywhere?

The term federal system cannot be found in the U.S. Constitution. Nor is it possible to find a systematic division of governmental authority between the national and state governments in that document. Rather, the Constitution sets out different types of powers. These powers can be classified as (1) the powers of the national government, (2) the powers of the states, and (3) prohibited powers. The Constitution also makes it clear that if a state or local law conflicts with a national law, the national law will prevail.

Powers of the National Government

The powers delegated to the national government include both expressed and implied powers, as well as the special category of inherent powers.

Enumerated Powers. Most of the powers expressly delegated to the national government are found in the first seventeen clauses of Article I, Section 8, of the Constitution. These **enumerated powers**, also called expressed powers,

---

3. As quoted in Edward Millican, *One United People: The Federalist Papers and the National Idea* (Lexington: The University Press of Kentucky, 1990).

include coining money, setting standards for weights and measures, making uniform naturalization laws, admitting new states, establishing post offices and post roads, and declaring war. Another important enumerated power is the power to regulate commerce among the states—a topic we deal with later in this chapter.

The Necessary and Proper Clause. The implied powers of the national government are also based on Article I, Section 8, which states that the Congress shall have the power

> [t]o make all Laws which shall be necessary and proper for carrying into Execution the foregoing Powers, and all other Powers vested by this Constitution in the Government of the United States, or in any Department or Officer thereof.

This clause is sometimes called the **elastic clause**, or the **necessary and proper clause**, because it provides flexibility to our constitutional system. It gives Congress the power to do whatever is necessary to execute its specifically delegated powers. The clause was first used in the Supreme Court decision of *McCulloch v. Maryland* (discussed later in this chapter) to develop the concept of implied powers.[4] Through this concept, the national government has succeeded in strengthening the scope of its authority to meet the many problems that the framers of the Constitution did not, and could not, anticipate.

Inherent Powers. A special category of national powers that is not always implied by the necessary and proper clause consists of what have been labeled the inherent powers of the national government. These powers derive from the fact that the United States is a sovereign power among nations, and so its national government must be the only government that deals with other nations. Under international law, it is assumed that all nation-states, regardless of their size or power, have an inherent right to ensure their own survival. To do this, each nation must have the ability to act in its own interest among and with the community of nations—by, for instance, making treaties, waging war, and seeking trade.

Note that no specific clause in the Constitution says anything about the acquisition of additional land. Nonetheless, the federal government's inherent powers allowed it to make the Louisiana Purchase in 1803 and then go on to acquire Florida, Texas, Oregon, California, Alaska, Hawaii, and other lands.

Powers of the State Governments

The Tenth Amendment states that the powers not delegated (granted) to the United States by the Constitution, nor prohibited by it to the states, are reserved to the states, or to the people. These are the reserved powers that the national government cannot deny to the states. Because these powers are not expressly listed, there is sometimes a question as to whether a certain power is delegated to the national government or reserved to the states.

State powers have been held to include each state's right to regulate commerce within its borders and to provide for a state militia. States also have the reserved power to make laws on all matters not prohibited to the states by the U.S. Constitution or state constitutions and not expressly, or by implication, delegated to the national government. Furthermore, the states have **police power**—the authority to legislate for the protection of the health, morals, safety, and welfare of the people. Their police power enables states to pass laws governing such activities as crimes, marriage, contracts, education, intrastate transportation, and land use.

Elastic Clause, or Necessary and Proper Clause
The clause in Article I, Section 8, that grants Congress the power to do whatever is necessary to execute its specifically delegated powers.

Police Power
The authority to legislate for the protection of the health, morals, safety, and welfare of the people. In the United States, most police power is reserved to the states.

---

4. 17 U.S. 316 (1819).

Interact

It is also worth noting that while the United States as a whole uses a federal system of government, each state has a unitary system. Hence, it is said that county, municipal, and other local governments are "creatures of the state." In principle, a state can alter or abolish a local government (though in some instances that might require an amendment to the state constitution). Such radical measures are rare. A more common exercise of state power is to prohibit local governments from passing various laws. For example, Colorado and Ohio do not let local governments ban fracking (a method of producing oil and natural gas).

The ambiguity of the Tenth Amendment has allowed the reserved powers of the states to be defined differently at different times in our history. When there is widespread support for increased regulation by the national government, the Tenth Amendment tends to recede into the background. When the tide turns the other way (in favor of states' rights), the Tenth Amendment is resurrected to justify arguments supporting the states.

Prohibited Powers

The Constitution prohibits, or denies, a number of powers to the national government. For example, the national government has expressly been denied the power to impose taxes on goods sold to other countries (exports). Moreover, any power not granted expressly or implicitly to the federal government by the Constitution is prohibited to it. For example, many legal experts believe that, despite proposals by several Democratic presidential candidates, the national government cannot directly tax various forms of wealth without a constitutional amendment. The states are also denied certain powers. As one instance of this, no state is allowed to enter into a treaty on its own with another country.

Concurrent Powers

Concurrent Powers
Powers held jointly by the national and state governments.

In certain areas, the states share **concurrent powers** with the national government. Most concurrent powers are not specifically listed in the Constitution but are only implied. An example of a concurrent power is the power to tax. The types of taxation are divided between the levels of government. For example, states may not levy a tariff (a set of taxes on imported goods). Only the national government may do this. Many observers of today's United States Supreme Court believe that it would find a national real estate tax to be unconstitutional. In contrast, both levels of government can and do collect taxes on income. Neither government may tax the facilities of the other. If the state governments did not have the power to tax, they would not be able to function independently of the national government.

Additional concurrent powers include the power to borrow funds, to establish courts, and to charter banks and corporations. To a limited extent, the national government exercises police power, and to the extent that it does, police power is also a concurrent power. Concurrent powers exercised by the states are normally limited to the geographic area of each state and to those functions not granted by the Constitution exclusively to the national government. Examples of functions exclusive to the national government are the coinage of money and the negotiation of treaties.

One concurrent power that has been the subject of controversy is the power to establish a minimum wage. A minimum wage is the lowest wage rate that an employer can legally pay. Currently, the national minimum wage is $7.25 per hour. Many states have adopted higher minimum wages. In some localities, the minimum wage is set to rise over time to as much as $17 per hour.

The Supremacy Clause

The supremacy of the national constitution over subnational laws and actions is established in the **supremacy clause** of the Constitution. The supremacy clause (Article VI, Clause 2) states the following:

> *This Constitution, and the Laws of the United States which shall be made in Pursuance thereof; and all Treaties made ... under the Authority of the United States, shall be the supreme Law of the Land; and the Judges in every State shall be bound thereby, any Thing in the Constitution or Laws of any State to the Contrary notwithstanding.*

In other words, states cannot use their reserved or concurrent powers to thwart national policies. All national and state officers, including judges, must be bound by oath to support the Constitution. Hence, any legitimate exercise of national governmental power supersedes any conflicting state action. Of course, deciding whether a conflict actually exists is a judicial matter, as you will soon learn when we discuss the case of *McCulloch v. Maryland.*

The National Guard can serve as an example of how federal power supersedes that of the states. Normally, the National Guard functions as a state militia under the command of the governor. It is frequently called out to assist with recovery efforts after natural disasters such as hurricanes, floods, and earthquakes. The president, however, can assume command of any National Guard unit at any time. Presidents George W. Bush and Barack Obama repeatedly "federalized" such units for deployment in Afghanistan and Iraq. In the conflicts in these countries, National Guard members and reservists made up a larger percentage of the forces on combat duty than during any previous war in U.S. history.

National government legislation in a concurrent area is said to preempt (take precedence over) conflicting state or local laws or regulations in that area. One of the ways in which the national government has extended its powers, particularly since 1900, is through the preemption of state and local laws by national legislation. In the first decade of the twentieth century, fewer than twenty national laws preempted laws and regulations issued by state and local governments. By the beginning of the twenty-first century, the number had grown into the hundreds.

Interstate Relations

So far, we have examined only the relationship between central and state governmental units. The states, however, have constant commercial, social, and other dealings among themselves. The national Constitution imposes certain "rules of the road" on interstate relations. These rules have had the effect of preventing any one state from setting itself apart from the other states. The three most important clauses governing interstate relations in the Constitution, all taken from the Articles of Confederation, require each state to do the following:

- Give full faith and credit to every other state's public acts, records, and judicial proceedings (Article IV, Section 1).
- Extend to every other state's citizens the privileges and immunities of its own citizens (Article IV, Section 2).
- Agree to return persons who are fleeing from justice in another state back to that state when requested to do so (Article IV, Section 2).

Supremacy Clause
The constitutional provision that makes the Constitution and federal laws superior to all conflicting state and local laws.

Interstate Compacts
Agreements between two or more states.

Additionally, states may enter into agreements with one another called **interstate compacts**. Congressional consent is necessary if such a compact increases the power of the contracting states relative to other states (or to the national government). An example is the Port Authority of New York and New Jersey, established by an agreement between those states in 1921.

Defining Constitutional Powers—The Early Years

>> **LO 3-3:** Discuss how, in the early years of the republic, the United States Supreme Court confirmed the authority of the national government, and how that authority was ratified by the Civil War.

Although political bodies at all levels of government play important roles in the process of settling disputes over the nature of our federal system, normally it is the United States Supreme Court that casts the final vote. As might be expected, the character of the referee will have an impact on the ultimate outcome of any dispute. From 1801 to 1835, the Supreme Court was headed by Chief Justice John Marshall, a Federalist who advocated a strong central government. We look here at two cases decided by the Marshall Court: *McCulloch v. Maryland*[5] and *Gibbons v. Ogden.*[6] Both cases are considered milestones in the movement toward national government supremacy.

McCulloch v. Maryland (1819)

The U.S. Constitution says nothing about establishing a national bank. Nonetheless, at different times Congress chartered two banks—the First and Second Banks of the United States—and provided part of their initial capital. Thus, they were national banks. The government of Maryland imposed a tax on the Second Bank's Baltimore branch in an attempt to put that branch out of business. The branch's cashier, James William McCulloch, refused to pay the Maryland tax. When Maryland took McCulloch to its state court, the state of Maryland won. The national government appealed the case to the Supreme Court.

One of the issues before the Court was whether the national government had the implied power, under the necessary and proper clause, to charter a bank and contribute capital to it. The other important question before the Court was the following: If the bank was constitutional, could a state tax it? In other words, was a state action that conflicted with a national government action invalid under the supremacy clause?

Chief Justice Marshall held that if establishing a national bank aided the national government in the exercise of its designated powers, then the authority to set up such a bank could be implied. Having established this doctrine of implied powers, Marshall then answered the other question before the Court and established the doctrine of national supremacy. Marshall ruled that no state could use its taxing power to tax a part of the national government. If it could, "the declaration that the Constitution … shall be the supreme law of the land, is empty and unmeaning."

Marshall's decision enabled the national government to grow and to meet problems that the Constitution's framers were unable to foresee. Today, practically every expressed power of the national government has been expanded in one way or another by use of the necessary and proper clause.

Image 3.2 When John Marshall was chief justice of the United States Supreme Court (1801–35), he championed the power of the federal government. ▶ What are some of the most famous cases that the Marshall Court decided?

Photo Researchers/Science History Images/Alamy Stock Photo

---

5. 17 U.S. 316 (1819).
6. 22 U.S. 1 (1824).

Gibbons v. Ogden (1824)

One of the most important parts of the Constitution, included in Article I, Section 8, is the **commerce clause**, in which Congress is given the power "to regulate Commerce with foreign Nations, and among the several States, and with the Indian Tribes." The meaning of this clause was at issue in *Gibbons v. Ogden*.

The Background of the Case. Robert Fulton and Robert Livingston secured a monopoly on steam navigation on the waters in New York State from the New York legislature in 1803. They licensed Aaron Ogden to operate steam-powered ferryboats between New York and New Jersey. Thomas Gibbons, who had obtained a license from the U.S. government to operate boats in interstate waters, decided to compete with Ogden, but he did so without New York's permission. Ogden sued Gibbons. New York's state courts prohibited Gibbons from operating in New York waters. Gibbons appealed to the Supreme Court.

There were several issues before the Court in this case. The first issue was how the term commerce should be defined. New York's highest court had defined the term narrowly to mean only the shipment of goods, or the interchange of commodities, not navigation or the transport of people. The second issue was whether the national government's power to regulate interstate commerce extended to commerce within a state (intrastate commerce) or was limited strictly to commerce among the states (interstate commerce). The third issue was whether the power to regulate interstate commerce was a concurrent power (as the New York court had concluded) or an exclusive national power.

Marshall's Ruling. Marshall defined commerce as all commercial interactions—all business dealings—including navigation and the transport of people. Marshall also held that the commerce power of the national government could be exercised in state jurisdictions, even though it could not reach solely intrastate commerce. Finally, Marshall emphasized that the power to regulate interstate commerce was an exclusive national power. Marshall held that because Gibbons was duly authorized by the national government to navigate in interstate waters, he could not be prohibited from doing so by a state court.

Marshall's expansive interpretation of the commerce clause in *Gibbons v. Ogden* allowed the national government to exercise increasing authority over economic affairs throughout the land. Congress did not immediately exploit this broad grant of power. In the 1930s and subsequent decades, however, the commerce clause became the primary constitutional basis for national government regulation—as you will read later in this chapter.

States' Rights and the Resort to Civil War

The controversy over slavery that led to the Civil War took the form of a dispute over national government supremacy versus the rights of the separate states. Essentially, the Civil War brought to an ultimate and violent climax the ideological debate begun by the Federalists and Anti-Federalists even before the Constitution was ratified.

The Shift Back to States' Rights. As we have seen, while John Marshall was chief justice of the Supreme Court, he did much to increase the power of the national government and to reduce that of the states. During the administration of President Andrew Jackson (1829–37), in contrast, a shift back to states' rights began. The question of the regulation of commerce became one of the major issues in federal–state relations. When Congress passed a tariff in 1828, the state of South Carolina unsuccessfully attempted to nullify the tariff (render it void). That state claimed that in cases of conflict between a state and the national government, the state should have the ultimate authority over its citizens.

Commerce Clause
The section of the Constitution in which Congress is given the power to regulate trade among the states and with foreign countries and Native American Tribes.

During the next three decades, the North and the South became even more sharply divided—especially over the slavery issue. On December 20, 1860, South Carolina formally repealed its ratification of the Constitution and withdrew from the Union. On February 4, 1861, representatives from six southern states met at Montgomery, Alabama, to form a new government called the Confederate States of America.

War and the Growth of the National Government. The ultimate defeat of the South in 1865 permanently ended the idea that a state could successfully claim the right to secede, or withdraw, from the Union. Ironically, the Civil War—brought about in large part because of the South's desire for increased states' rights—resulted in the opposite: an increase in the political power of the national government.

Thousands of new employees were hired to run the Union war effort and to deal with the social and economic problems that had to be handled in the aftermath of the war. A billion-dollar ($1.3 billion, which is about $22 billion in today's dollars) national government budget was passed for the first time in 1865 to cover the increased government expenditures. The first (temporary) income tax was imposed on citizens to help pay for the war.

The Civil War Amendments. The expansion of the national government's authority during the Civil War was also reflected in the passage of the Civil War amendments to the Constitution. Before the war, it was a bedrock constitutional principle that the national government

Photo Researchers/Science History Images/Alamy Stock Photo

Image 3.3 John Brown (1800–59), an advocate of abolishing slavery, led an ill-fated raid on a federal arsenal at Harpers Ferry, Virginia. Brown had hoped to set off an enslaved people's uprising. He was executed on charges of treason and murder. Today, we would doubtless call him a terrorist. ▶ Why do some people nevertheless consider him a hero?

should not interfere with slavery in the states. The Thirteenth Amendment, ratified in 1865, did more than interfere with slavery—it abolished the institution altogether.

The Fourteenth Amendment, ratified in 1868, defined who was a citizen of each state. It sought to guarantee equal rights under state law with this language:

> [No] State [shall] deprive any person of life, liberty, or property, without due process of law; nor deny to any person within its jurisdiction the equal protection of the laws.

In time, the courts interpreted these words to mean that the national Bill of Rights applied to state governments, a development that we will examine later in this book. Finally, the Fifteenth Amendment (1870) gave African Americans the right to vote in all elections, including state elections—although a century would pass before that right was enforced in all states.

The Continuing Dispute Over the Division of Power

»LO 3-4: Define the terms dual federalism, cooperative federalism, categorical grants, block grants, and fiscal federalism.

Although the outcome of the Civil War firmly established the supremacy of the national government and put to rest the idea that a state could secede from the Union, the war by no means ended the debate over the division of powers between the national government and the states.

Dual Federalism

During the decades following the Civil War, the prevailing model of federalism was what political scientists have called **dual federalism**—a doctrine that emphasizes a distinction between national and state spheres of government authority. Various images have been used to describe different configurations of federalism over time. Dual federalism is commonly depicted as a layer cake, because the state governments and the national government are viewed as separate entities, like separate layers of a cake.

Under the doctrine of dual federalism, national and state governments are co-equal sovereign powers, and neither level of government should interfere in the other's sphere. The doctrine represented a revival of states' rights following the expansion of national authority during the Civil War. Many people viewed this change as a return to normal—that is, to the conditions that had existed before the war.

The Civil War crisis drastically reduced the influence of the United States Supreme Court, which had supported the institution of slavery in the years leading up to the war. Over time, however, the Court reestablished itself as the legitimate constitutional umpire. For the Court, dual federalism meant that the national government could intervene in state activities through grants and subsidies, but in most cases, it was barred from regulating matters that the Court considered to be purely local.

Dual Federalism
A model of federalism that looks on national and state governments as co-equal sovereign powers. Neither the state government nor the national government should interfere in the other's sphere.

AP Images

Image 3.4 Child labor was still common in the early 1900s. ▶ Why didn't the federal government simply ban it then?

The Court generally limited the exercise of police power to the states. For example, in 1918, the Court ruled that a 1916 national law banning child labor was unconstitutional because it attempted to regulate a local problem.[7] In effect, the Court placed severe limits on the ability of Congress to legislate under the commerce clause of the Constitution.

The New Deal and Cooperative Federalism

The doctrine of dual federalism receded into the background in the 1930s as the nation attempted to deal with the Great Depression. Franklin D. Roosevelt was inaugurated as president on March 4, 1933. In the previous year, nearly 1,500 banks had failed (and 4,000 more would fail in 1933). Thirty-two thousand businesses had closed down, and almost one-fourth of the labor force was unemployed. The public expected the national government to do something about the disastrous state of the economy. Yet for the first three years of the Great Depression (1930–32), the national government did very little.

Roosevelt, however, energetically intervened in the economy. Roosevelt's "New Deal" included large-scale emergency antipoverty programs and introduced major new laws regulating economic activity. Initially, the Supreme Court blocked many of Roosevelt's initiatives. Beginning in 1937, however, after a change in membership, the Court ceased to limit the federal government's actions. An expansive interpretation of the commerce clause became dominant.

Some political scientists have described national-state relations since 1937 as **cooperative federalism**, in which the states and the national government cooperate in solving complex common problems. Roosevelt's New Deal programs, for example, often involved joint action between the national government and the states. The pattern of national-state relationships during these years gave rise to a new metaphor for federalism—that of a marble cake. Unlike a layer cake, in a marble cake the two types of cake are intermingled, and any bite contains cake of both flavors.

The 1960s and 1970s were a time of even greater expansion of the national government's role in domestic policy. Today, few activities are beyond the reach of the regulatory arm of the national government.

The Politics of Federalism

In determining the allocation of powers between the state and national governments, conservatives traditionally have favored the states, and liberals have favored the federal government. Liberals claim that national authority has been an agent of change throughout U.S. history. The expansion of national authority during the Civil War freed enslaved persons, and beginning in the 1960s, the federal government was likewise responsible for extending civil rights such as the right to vote to African Americans.

Republicans and Democrats. For much of American history, conservative southern Democrats were the major advocates of states' rights. Then, under Republican presidents Richard Nixon (1969–74) and Ronald Reagan (1981–89), **devolution**, or the transfer of power from the national government to state governments, became a major theme for the Republican Party. In recent decades, however, competing theories of federalism often appeared

Cooperative Federalism
A model of federalism in which the states and the national government cooperate in solving problems.

Devolution
The transfer of powers from a national or central government to a state or local government.

Image 3.5 President Franklin D. Roosevelt (1933–45). Roosevelt's national approach to addressing the effects of the Great Depression was overwhelmingly popular, although many of his specific initiatives were not. ▶ How did the Great Depression change the political beliefs of many Americans?

Pictorial Press/Pictorial Press Ltd/Alamy Stock Photo

---

7. *Hammer v. Dagenhart*, 247 U.S. 251 (1918). This decision was overruled in *United States v. Darby*, 312 U.S. 100 (1940).

not to divide the two parties in practice. While the Republicans continued to advocate devolution in theory, they often did not follow it in reality.

Consider that the passage of welfare reform legislation in 1996, which involved transferring significant control over welfare programs to the states, took place under Democratic president Bill Clinton (1993–2001). In contrast, under Republican president George W. Bush (2001–2009), Congress enacted the No Child Left Behind Act of 2001. This act increased federal control over education, which had traditionally been under the purview of state governments. In another example, the Bush administration prevented California from implementing its own tough new laws to regulate air pollution. Upon taking office, Barack Obama (2009–17) reversed the Bush policies and allowed California to proceed.

Conservatives Look Again to the States. Beginning in 2009, conservative activists began to rediscover states' rights. One reason may be that from January 2009 through January 2011, the Democrats were in control of the presidency, the U.S. House, and the U.S. Senate. Republicans were shut out at the national level, and many conservatives hoped that the states would be a counterweight to the newly active national government. In fact, Republicans enjoyed considerable success in winning power at the state level in the midterm elections of 2010 and 2014. As a result of these victories, Republicans had many opportunities to implement conservative legislation at the state level.

Following the election of Republican president Donald Trump in 2016, however, Republicans tended to lose interest in states' rights. Democratic states quickly rediscovered them. States such as California and New York mounted major efforts to curtail federal authority. By 2018 and 2020, Democrats were able to recapture power in many states.

After the Republicans regained control of the House in November 2022, there have been some attempts at reducing the power of the federal government. See this chapter's *Which Side Are You On?* feature.

Which Side Are You On?

The Federal Government Has Unconstitutionally Usurped Too Much Power From the States

When comparing our federal system with a unitary system, a major difference is that if we had a unitary system, all power would emanate from Washington, D.C. That power would then be allotted to states, cities, and counties at the will of the federal (central) government. Our Constitution, though, specifies only eighteen enumerated powers for Congress. The rest of the powers granted to the federal government are either implicit or inherent.

Since the COVID-19 pandemic that started in early 2020, the federal government has attempted to impose nationwide regulations. Has the federal government gone too far?

When Faced With a Nationwide Health Crisis, Bold Nationwide Action Is Required

The last time the United States (and the world) faced a pandemic as widespread and as deadly as it did in March 2020 was during the 1917-18 Spanish flu. Over 500,000 Americans died and 50 million more died worldwide. Rather than sit back and just watch people drop like flies, in 2020, the federal government had to act. One of the first things it did was guarantee funding to private pharmaceutical companies to develop an effective vaccine. No one complained about that action.

Then the federal government passed legislation to add $600 per month to state unemployment benefits. Only a few in Congress complained about that action. Next, the federal government passed a rule that prevented property owners from evicting tenants who could not pay their rents.

Early on, the federal government passed regulations requiring that all individuals taking airplanes, working or visiting federal buildings, and those in certain occupations wear a mask. Some of those mask mandates were still in effect in the middle of 2022. Finally, federal employees for the most part were required to have at least two vaccinations. Granted, when the federal government tried

(Continued)

to mandate vaccinations by all workers in businesses with over 100 employees, the Supreme Court stepped in and said no.[8]

It's okay to take over from the states when public health is at issue.

All Actions Concerning Americans' Health Decisions Should Be Left Either to the States or to Individuals

Those who were not in agreement with federal government actions during the COVID-19 pandemic had a strong constitutional argument. There is nothing in the Constitution that gives the federal government the power to dictate individual decisions regarding the health of individuals. Therefore, forcing people to take vaccines was, and always will be, unconstitutional. At best, it is the states and the states only that should be dictating such mandates. The same is true for mask mandates. The federal government has no business telling individuals how to live their lives.

It was wrong for the federal government to tell property owners that they could not evict individuals who were unable to pay their rents. That is something that the states and cities could work out or, possibly better, that property owners and their tenants could have worked out on their own. The federal government has zero legal power to do what it did in this instance.

Surprisingly, the actual efficacy of wearing masks was never really tested. Now we know that there is little evidence that wearing masks can prevent transmission of COVID-19. After all, most masks are ill-fitting and cannot stop the microscopic viruses from either coming in or going out behind the mask.

For these and a variety of other reasons, we should not accept blanket dictums from Washington, D.C., about how to run our lives.

■ For Critical Analysis

Do you think that just because a law or regulation created by Washington, D.C., is unconstitutional, we cannot make an exception when national health is in danger?

Methods of Implementing Cooperative Federalism

One means of implementing cooperative federalism is through grants. Even before the Constitution was adopted, the national government gave grants to the states in the form of land to finance education. The national government also provided land grants for canals, railroads, and roads. In the twentieth century, federal grants increased significantly, especially during the Great Depression and again in the 1960s, when the dollar amount of these grants quadrupled. These funds were used for improvements in education, pollution control, recreation, and highways. With this increase in grants, however, came a bewildering number of restrictions and regulations.

Categorical Grants
Federal grants to a state or local government for a specific program or project.

Categorical Grants. By the 1980s, **categorical grants** were spread out across four hundred separate programs, but the largest five accounted for more than 50 percent of the revenues spent. These five programs were Medicaid (health care for people with low incomes), highway construction, unemployment benefits, housing assistance, and welfare programs to assist mothers with dependent children and people with disabilities. For fiscal year 2020, the national government gave about $740 billion to the states.

Over the decades, federal grants to the states have increased significantly. One reason is that Congress has decided to off-load some programs to the states and provide a major part of the funding for them. Also, Congress continues to use grants to persuade states and cities to operate programs devised by the federal government. Finally, states often are happy to apply for grants because they are relatively "free," requiring only that the state match a small portion of each grant.

Block Grants
Federal grants that provide funds to a state or local government for a general functional area, such as criminal justice or mental-health programs.

Block Grants. **Block grants** lessen the restrictions on federal grants given to state and local governments by grouping a number of categorical grants under one broad heading. Governors and mayors generally prefer block grants because such grants give state and local governments more flexibility in how the funds are spent. Block grants, however, make up less than 10 percent of the funds transferred to the states by the federal government.

8. *National Federation of Independent Business, et al. v. Department of Labor, Occupational Safety and Health Administration, et al.*, 595 U.S.___(2022).

Image 3.6 A teacher high-fives an elementary school student in Miami. This teacher is funded by Teach for America, a nonprofit organization that places recent college graduates in low-income community schools. The program receives federal grants. ▶ Should the national government have a role in educational policy?

An example of a block grant program is the Surface Transportation Program, sponsored by the Federal Highway Administration. This program provides state and local authorities with considerable flexibility. Funds can be used to repair highways and bridges, or to support pedestrian, bicycle, or bus projects. Still, the program only amounts to about 16 percent of all federal transportation grants.

Fiscal Federalism and State Budgets. In discussions of government policy, you may have heard the word fiscal. This word simply means "having to do with government revenues and expenditures." **Fiscal** policy, therefore, is policy concerning taxing or borrowing—and then spending the revenues. When the federal government makes grants to state and local governments, funds raised through taxation or borrowing by one level of government (the national government) are spent by another level (state and local governments). We can speak of this process as **fiscal federalism**. With almost 20 percent of state and local revenues supplied by the federal government, fiscal federalism is clearly important.

The Great Recession in the first decade of the 2000s had a devastating impact on state budgets, and in response the federal government substantially increased the amount of funding available to the states. From 2011 on, however, these extra funds were no longer available. State governments cut spending and employment substantially—so much so that total government spending as a share of the economy actually fell from 2010 through 2015. During the first year of the COVID-19 pandemic, state and local lockdowns increased unemployment dramatically. Of course, state and local revenues fell considerably during this time period. The federal government helped out state and local governments for several years. By 2022, the coffers of state and local governments were for the most part refilled and even overflowing in some jurisdictions.

Feeling the Pressure—the Strings Attached to Federal Grants. No dollars sent to the states are completely free of "strings." All funds come with requirements that must be met by the states. Often, through the use of grants, the national government has been able to

Fiscal
Having to do with government revenues and expenditures.

Fiscal Federalism
A process by which funds raised through taxation or borrowing by one level of government (usually the national government) are spent by another level (typically, state or local governments).

exercise substantial control over matters that traditionally have been under the purview of state governments. When the federal government gives federal funds for highway improvements, for example, it may condition the funds on the state's cooperation with a federal policy. This is exactly what the federal government did in the 1980s to force the states to raise their minimum alcoholic-beverage drinking age to twenty-one.

Limits on the National Government's Power to Coerce the States. The Supreme Court has generally supported the national government's attempts to pressure the states into adopting various policies through the use of grants. In the drinking-age case just mentioned, the Court held that the national government could push states to raise their drinking age by threatening to withhold 10 percent of their highway grants. A penalty of this size was not "coercive."[9] Provisions in the Affordable Care Act (Obamacare), however, penalized states that failed to expand their Medicaid programs by withholding 100 percent of their Medicaid funding. In 2015, the Court found that a penalty of that size was coercive in that it could seriously damage state budgets.[10] In other words, the Court's limit on how large a penalty the national government can impose lies somewhere between 10 and 100 percent.

The Court established another limit on national authority in 1997. The Brady Handgun Violence Prevention Act required local police officials to run background checks on persons purchasing firearms. The Court found that letting the Federal government "draft" state and local police officers into its service would be unconstitutional.[11] This ruling became relevant again in 2016 when president-elect Donald Trump threatened to revoke federal grants to "sanctuary cities." Such localities typically direct their police forces not to take down information on the immigration status of persons they stop or arrest. While Congress has passed a law that requires local law enforcement to share information with the national government, it seems likely that forcing local police to collect such information in the first place would violate the Brady Handgun ruling.

Federal Mandates

Requirements in federal legislation that forces states and municipalities to comply with certain rules.

Federal Mandates. Despite these limits, for years the federal government has passed legislation pressuring the states to improve environmental conditions or the civil rights of various groups. Since the 1970s, the national government has enacted hundreds of **federal mandates** demanding that the states take action in areas ranging from voter registration, to ocean-dumping restrictions, to the education of people with disabilities. The Unfunded Mandates Reform Act of 1995 requires the Congressional Budget Office to identify mandates that cost state and local governments more than $50 million to implement. Nonetheless, the federal government routinely continues to pass mandates for state and local governments that cost more than that to put into place.

Federalism and Today's Supreme Court

>> **LO 3-5:** Explain who benefits and who loses when the Supreme Court makes decisions that give the government in Washington, D.C., more power over the states.

The United States Supreme Court, which normally has the final say on constitutional issues, plays a major role in determining where the line is drawn between federal and state powers. Consider the decisions rendered by Chief Justice John Marshall in the cases discussed earlier in

---

9. *South Dakota v. Dole*, 483 U.S. 203 (1987).
10. *National Federation of Independent Business v. Sebelius*, 567 U.S. 519 (2012).
11. *Printz v. United States*, 521 U.S. 898 (1997).

this chapter. Since the 1930s, Marshall's broad interpretation of the commerce clause has made it possible for the national government to justify its regulation of almost any activity, even when the activity appears to be completely local in character. In the 1990s and early 2000s, however, the Court evidenced a willingness to impose some limits on the national government's authority under the commerce clause and other constitutional provisions. As a result, it is difficult to predict how today's Court might rule on a particular case involving federalism.

A Trend Toward States' Rights

Since the mid-1990s, the Supreme Court has tended to give greater weight to states' rights than it did during previous decades. In a widely publicized 1995 case, the Supreme Court held that Congress had exceeded its constitutional authority under the commerce clause when it passed the Gun-Free School Zones Act in 1990.[12] The Court stated that the act, which banned the possession of guns within one thousand feet of any school, was unconstitutional because it attempted to regulate an area that had "nothing to do with commerce, or any sort of economic enterprise." This marked the first time in sixty years that the Supreme Court had placed a limit on the national government's authority under the commerce clause.

Although the Court has tended to favor states' rights in some decisions, in other decisions it has backed the federal government's position. For example, in 2005 the Court held that the federal government's power to declare various substances to be illegal drugs superseded California's law legalizing the use of marijuana for medical treatment.[13] Yet less than a year later, the Court favored states' rights when it upheld Oregon's controversial "death with dignity" law, which allows patients with terminal illnesses to choose to end their lives early and thus avoid suffering.[14]

Recent Decisions

In recent rulings, the Supreme Court has often shown sympathy for states' rights, even while avoiding revolutionary changes in relations between the state and federal governments.

In other decisions, the Court did not seem to be in favor of states' rights. One such situation involved the Louisiana Unsafe Abortion Protection Act, which became law in 2014. In brief, the law required that physicians who performed abortions must have the right to admit patients to a hospital (so-called admitting right) within 30 miles of where the abortion would be performed. This Louisiana law was modeled after a similar Texas law, which was declared unconstitutional in 2016. Several physicians and clinics in Louisiana brought suit against the government of Louisiana. They argued, as had been argued against the Texas law, that it was unconstitutional because it imposed an undue burden on the rights of patients to obtain an abortion. The United States Court of Appeals for the Fifth Circuit upheld the Louisiana law. (That court did not examine any health-related purpose of the law.)

The Supreme Court agreed to hear the case and rendered a decision in 2020. It concluded that enforcing the hospital admitting-privileges requirement would "drastically reduce

Mark Wilson/Getty Images News/Getty Images

Image 3.7 Pro-choice supporters express their views in front of the Supreme Court. ▶ Why aren't they in front of a state capitol building?

12. *United States v. Lopez*, 514 U.S. 549 (1995).
13. *Gonzales v. Raich*, 545 U.S. 1 (2005).
14. *Gonzales v. Oregon*, 546 U.S. 243 (2006).

the number and geographic distribution of abortion providers, making it impossible for many women to obtain safe, legal abortion in the State and imposing obstacles on those who could."[15] Obviously, states' rights did not prevail in this decision.

The issue of states' rights was again addressed in 2022 when the Supreme Court overruled the 1973 *Roe v. Wade*[16] decision that had legalized abortion in all states. In its *Dobbs v. Jackson Women's Health Organization*[17] decision in 2022, the Court held that nothing in the Constitution provides a right to have an abortion. The majority in *Dobbs* ruled that the 1973 argument about a woman's right to privacy was based on an incorrect interpretation of the Constitution. The Court acknowledged that abortion "presents a profound moral issue on which Americans hold sharply conflicting views." The decision points out that it is not up to the Supreme Court to decide that moral issue. Rather, the people in each state must decide. That means that the *Dobbs* decision did not outlaw abortion. Rather, each state will decide through their legislature what state law is concerning abortion. Many states will undoubtedly keep their liberal abortion laws such as New York and California. Other states will institute restrictions or outright bans.

Gerrymandering. Members of the U.S. House and the various state legislatures are elected from districts. The Constitution assigns the power to draw the boundaries of these districts to the state legislatures. In many states, legislatures have deliberately drawn the lines to benefit one political party. This type of vote-rigging is called gerrymandering, and it is widely regarded as unfair. In 2019, however, the Court refused to find the practice to be an unconstitutional violation of voters' rights.[18] This ruling can be seen as upholding states' rights to set electoral boundaries. It also reflects the low value the Court had placed on the right to vote in recent years. The Court also displayed this attitude in 2013 when it struck down parts of the 1965 Voting Rights Act and in 2008 when it upheld strict ID requirements for voting.

Gerrymandering After the 2020 Census. After the results of the 2020 census were officially recognized, Republicans seemed confident that they were at an advantage in the redistricting of many states. Soon thereafter, Democrats realized that the redistricting process for them was going to be better than anticipated. Democrats received favorable redistricting maps in states using commissions in California, Michigan, and New Jersey. They also benefitted from states in which they were able to redraw district lines—Illinois, New Mexico, and Oregon. Ultimately, nationally, Democrats garnered over twelve more Democratic-leaning seats.

State Government Employee Unions. A decision in 2018 seemed to deal a serious blow to organized labor and demonstrated that the Court is not always deferential to states' rights when they appear to conflict with conservative principles. The Court held that state governments could not require non-members to pay fees to state government employee unions.[19] Mandatory fees are banned even when the sums are dedicated to collective bargaining and grievance procedures, rather than political activism.

Twenty-two states allowed such fees, and the decision was therefore expected to generate considerable disruption. The ruling was based on the argument, elaborated by the Court in recent years, that money can be a form of speech under the First Amendment. It overturned a forty-one-year-old precedent. A practical result of this ruling was supposed to handicap the Democratic Party, which enjoys union support. There was no evidence of this "handicap" in the 2020 elections.

---

15. *June Medical Services L.L.C. et al. v. Russo*, 591 U.S.__ (2020).
16. 410 U.S. 113 (1973).
17. 597 U.S. __ (2022).
18. *Rucho v. Common Cause*, 139 S.Ct. 2484 (2019).
19. *Janus v. AFSCME*, 138 S.Ct. 2448 (2018).

Writing E-mails and Texting to the Editor

Our federal system encourages debate over whether a particular issue should be a national, state, or local question. Many questions are, in fact, state or local ones.

Why Should You Care? Although the national government provides aid to educational programs, education is still primarily a state and local responsibility. Therefore, you can address this issue at the state or local level. Gambling laws are another state responsibility. Do you enjoy gambling—or do you believe that the effects of gambling make it a social disaster? State law—or state negotiations with Native American tribes—determines the availability of gambling.

What Can You Do? In our modern era, the number of ways in which you can communicate your opinion is vast. You can post a response on any of thousands of blogs. You could develop your own short video and post it on YouTube.

If you want to effect policy change at the state or local level, however, the local newspaper, in both its paper and online formats, continues to be essential. Blogs, YouTube, and other online venues tend to be nationally oriented. But most newspapers are resolutely local and the natural hub for discussions of local issues. Papers often allow responses and comments on their websites, and you can make a point by contributing in that fashion. Yet nothing will win you a wider audience than an old-fashioned letter to the editor, regardless of whether it appears online or is printed on paper. Use the following rules to compose an effective communication:

- Double-space the lines. Use a spelling checker and grammar checker.
- Include a lead topic sentence that is short, to the point, and powerful.
- Keep your thoughts on target—choose only one topic. Make sure it is newsworthy and timely.
- Make sure your communication is concise. Never let it exceed a page in length (double-spaced).

- If you know that facts were misstated or left out in current news stories about your topic, supply the facts. The public wants to know.
- Don't be afraid to express moral judgments. You can go a long way by appealing to the reader's sense of justice.
- Personalize the communication by bringing in your own experiences, if possible.
- If you are writing a letter, sign it and give your address (including your e-mail address) and your telephone number. Blogs and other communications may have their own rules for identifying yourself in posted comments. Follow these rules.
- If writing a letter, send or e-mail it to the editorial office of the newspaper of your choice. Their websites usually give information on where you can send mail.

Rob Bartee/Alamy Stock Photo

Image 3.8 A student reads a newspaper. ▶ Why do so few students read newspapers anymore?

///

Key Terms

block grant 60
categorical grant 60
commerce clause 55
concurrent powers 52
confederal system 47

cooperative
   federalism 58
devolution 58
dual
   federalism 57

elastic clause, or
   necessary and proper
   clause 51
enumerated powers 50
federal mandate 62
fiscal 61

fiscal federalism 61
interstate compact 54
police power 51
supremacy clause 53
unitary system 47

///

Chapter Summary

LO 3-1 There are three basic models for ordering relations between central and local governments: (a) a unitary system (in which ultimate power is held by the national government), (b) a confederal system (in which ultimate power is retained by the states), and (c) a federal system (in which governmental powers are divided between the national government and the states).

LO 3-2 The Constitution expressly grants certain powers to the national government. In addition to these enumerated powers, the national government has implied and inherent powers. Implied powers are those that are reasonably necessary to carry out the powers expressly given to the national government. Inherent powers are those that the national government holds by virtue of being a sovereign state with the right to preserve itself.

The Tenth Amendment to the Constitution states that powers not delegated (granted) to the United States by the Constitution, nor prohibited by it to the states, are reserved to the states, or to the people. In certain areas, the Constitution provides for concurrent powers (such as the power to tax), which are powers that are held jointly by the national and state governments.

The supremacy clause of the Constitution states that the Constitution, congressional laws, and national treaties are the supreme law of the land. States cannot use their reserved or concurrent powers to override national policies.

LO 3-3 Chief Justice John Marshall's expansive interpretation of the necessary and proper clause of the Constitution in *McCulloch v. Maryland* (1819),

along with his affirmation of the supremacy clause, enhanced the power of the national government. Marshall's broad interpretation of the commerce clause in *Gibbons v. Ogden* (1824) further extended the powers of the national government.

The controversy over slavery that led to the Civil War took the form of a fight over national government supremacy versus the rights of the separate states.

LO 3-4 Since the Civil War, federalism has evolved from dual federalism to cooperative federalism. In dual federalism, the states and the federal government remain supreme within their own spheres. The era since the Great Depression of the 1930s has been labeled one of cooperative federalism, in which states and the national government cooperate in solving complex problems.

Categorical grants from the federal government to state governments help finance specific projects. By attaching conditions to federal grants, the national government can affect policy changes in areas typically governed by the states. Block grants cover general functional areas and give state and local governments more flexibility. Federal mandates—laws pressuring states to implement certain policies—have generated controversy.

LO 3-5 The United States Supreme Court plays a significant role in determining the line between state and federal powers. Since the mid-1990s, there has been a trend on the part of the Court to support some states' rights. Yet the Court has also issued rulings in support of the federal government.

Test Yourself

1. The system of government in the United States that existed before the adoption of the Constitution was called a:
   a. federal system.
   b. unitary system.
   c. confederal system.

2. Reasons why the founders chose a federal system include all except:
   a. No other type of system would have been politically acceptable.
   b. The United States was large geographically, and it would have been difficult to govern just from the national capital.
   c. The thirteen states were geographically compact, so a federal system was appropriate.

3. When we say that state governments have police powers, we mean that:
   a. They have authority to legislate for the health, morals, safety, and welfare of their people.
   b. They have the right to establish law enforcement agencies.
   c. They have the right to exempt themselves from certain national laws.

4. When both the national government and the state governments share certain powers, we call them:
   a. prevailing powers.
   b. concurrent powers.
   c. constitutional powers.

5. One topic that has been addressed by both national and state legislation is:
   a. the taxation of real estate.
   b. defining who is a citizen.
   c. setting a minimum wage.

6. How must every state treat each other's public acts, records, and judicial proceedings?
   a. Accept them when they correspond to the state's own laws.
   b. Give them full faith and credit.
   c. Accept them when required to do so by the national government.

7. In the Supreme Court case of *McCulloch v. Maryland* (1819), the Court clearly established:
   a. that the Constitution is the supreme law of the land.

   b. that state governments can tax the national government.
   c. that the national government can tax the state governments.

8. The Supreme Court case of *Gibbons v. Ogden* (1824) involved regulation of:
   a. intrastate commerce.
   b. interstate commerce.
   c. foreign commerce.

9. The transfer of powers from a central or national government to a state or local one is called:
   a. devolution.
   b. cooperative federalism.
   c. states' rights.

10. When the federal (national) government sends dollars to state governments, those funds:
    a. are given without any restrictions.
    b. are to be returned to the federal government at a later date.
    c. come with many "strings" attached.

11. When funds raised by the national government are then spent by state governments, this is called:
    a. fiscal federalism.
    b. dual federalism.
    c. competitive federalism.

Essay Questions

1. Traditionally, conservatives have favored states' rights and liberals have favored national authority. Can you think of modern-day issues in which these long-standing preferences might be reversed, with conservatives favoring national authority and liberals favoring states' rights? Explain.

2. Some Tea Party activists wanted to repeal the Seventeenth Amendment. If the amendment were repealed, state legislatures would choose each state's U.S. senators. Advocates of repeal argue that it would strengthen the power of the states within the federal system. Would such a change have good or bad consequences? Explain.

Answers to multiple-choice questions: 1. c, 2. c, 3. a, 4. b, 5. c, 6. b, 7. a, 8. b, 9. a, 10. c, 11. a.

4 Civil Liberties

Gregory Rec/Portland Press Herald/Getty Images

Jewish students from Bowdoin College recite afternoon prayers before the start of a Shabbat eve service in Portland, Maine. ▶ **Do the First Amendment clauses on religion apply to private schools such as Bowdoin? Why or why not?**

The five **Learning Outcomes (LOs)** below are designed to help improve your understanding of this chapter. After reading this chapter, you should be able to:

≫ **LO 4-1** Identify the rights listed in the original Constitution, and describe the Bill of Rights.

≫ **LO 4-2** Explain how the First Amendment's establishment clause and free exercise clause guarantee our freedom of religion.

≫ **LO 4-3** Specify the limited circumstances in which the national and state governments may override the principles of free speech and freedom of the press.

≫ **LO 4-4** Determine whether the Constitution, including the Bill of Rights, explicitly gives you the right to privacy.

≫ **LO 4-5** Identify the constitutional rights of those who are accused of a crime.

Check your understanding of the material with the Test Yourself section at the end of the chapter.

"The land of the free." When asked what makes the United States distinctive, Americans will commonly say that it is a free country. Americans have long believed that limits on the power of government are an essential part of what makes this country free. Restraints on the actions of government against individuals generally are referred to as civil liberties. The first ten amendments to the U.S. Constitution—the Bill of Rights—place such restraints on the national government. Of these amendments, none is more famous than the First Amendment, which guarantees freedom of religion, speech, and the press, along with additional rights.

Most other democratic nations have laws to protect these and other civil liberties, but none of the laws is quite like the First Amendment. Take the issue of "hate speech." What if someone makes statements that stir up hatred toward a particular race or other group of people? In Germany, where memories of Nazi anti-Semitism remain alive, such speech is unquestionably illegal. In the United States, the issue is not so clear. The courts have often extended constitutional protection to this kind of speech.

In this chapter, we describe the civil liberties provided by the Bill of Rights and some of the controversies that surround them. In addition to First Amendment liberties, we look at the right to privacy and the rights of defendants in criminal prosecutions.

The Constitutional Bases of Our Liberties

>> **LO 4-1:** Identify the rights listed in the original Constitution, and describe the Bill of Rights.

As you read through this chapter, bear in mind that both the original Constitution and the Bill of Rights are relatively brief. The framers set forth broad guidelines, leaving it up to the courts to interpret these constitutional mandates and apply them to specific situations. Thus, judicial interpretations shape the true nature of the civil liberties and rights that we possess. Because judicial interpretations change over time, so do our liberties and rights. As you will read in the following pages, there have been many conflicts over the meaning of such simple phrases as freedom of religion and freedom of the press. To understand what freedoms we actually have, we need to examine how the courts—and particularly the United States Supreme Court—have resolved some of those conflicts.

Protections Listed in the Original Constitution

While Americans typically think of our civil liberties as guaranteed by the Bill of Rights, three important protections were written into the main body of the Constitution. In Article I, Section 9, we find this statement: "The privilege of the Writ of Habeas Corpus shall not be suspended, unless when in Cases of Rebellion or Invasion the public Safety may require it." The section goes on to state: "No Bill of Attainder or ex post facto Law shall be passed." What is meant by all this rather obscure legal language?

A **writ of *habeas corpus*** is a court order issued to any agency that is holding a prisoner. The writ requires the jailer to bring the prisoner before the court and explain why that person is being held. When judges find the imprisonment to be unlawful, they will order the jailer to rectify the situation. The prisoner may be brought to trial—or freed. It is *habeas corpus* that prevents the government from arbitrarily and indefinitely detaining political opponents or unpopular individuals. Following the terrorist attacks of September 11, 2001, the question of whether suspected terrorists had a right to *habeas corpus* became a major political and judicial issue.

During the early years of the republic, federal courts offered *habeas corpus* rights only to federal prisoners. Following the U.S. Civil War, however, federal courts began issuing writs on behalf of prisoners held by the states.

A **bill of attainder** is a law that inflicts punishment without a trial. An ***ex post facto* law** inflicts punishment for an act that was not illegal at the time it was committed. In Article I, Section 10 of the Constitution, the prohibition of both of these types of laws is explicitly extended to the states. In contrast, the Bill of Rights had a very different legal history.

Writ of *Habeas Corpus*
Habeas corpus means, literally, "you have the body." A writ of habeas corpus is an order that requires jailers to bring a prisoner before a court or judge and explain why the person is being held.

Bill of Attainder
A law that inflicts punishment without a trial.

***Ex Post Facto* Law**
A law that inflicts punishment for an act that was not illegal at the time it was committed.

Extending the Bill of Rights to State Governments

Many citizens do not realize that, as originally intended, the Bill of Rights limited the powers only of the national government. At the time the Bill of Rights was ratified, there was little concern over the potential of state governments to curb civil liberties. For one thing, state governments were closer to home and easier to control. For another, most state constitutions already had bills of rights. Rather, the fear was of the potential tyranny of the national government. The Bill of Rights begins with the words, "Congress shall make no law …." It says nothing about states making laws that might abridge citizens' civil liberties. In 1833, the United States Supreme Court held that the Bill of Rights did not apply to state laws.[1]

We mentioned that most states had bills of rights. These bills of rights were similar to the national one, but there were some differences. Furthermore, each state's judicial system interpreted the rights differently. Citizens in different states, therefore, effectively had different sets of civil liberties. It was not until the Fourteenth Amendment was ratified in 1868 that civil liberties guaranteed by the national Constitution began to be applied to the states. Section 1 of that amendment provides, in part, as follows:

> *No State shall ... deprive any person of life, liberty, or property, without due process of law....*

Incorporation Under the Fourteenth Amendment

There was no question that the Fourteenth Amendment applied to state governments. For decades, however, the courts were reluctant to define the liberties spelled out in the national Bill of Rights as constituting "due process of law," which was protected under the Fourteenth Amendment. Not until 1925, in *Gitlow v. New York*,[2] did the United States Supreme Court hold that the Fourteenth Amendment protected the freedom of speech guaranteed by the First Amendment to the Constitution from state infringement.

Incorporation Theory
The view that the protections of the Bill of Rights apply to state governments through the Fourteenth Amendment's due process clause.

Only gradually did the Supreme Court accept **incorporation theory**—the view that the protections of the Bill of Rights are incorporated into the Fourteenth Amendment's protection against state government actions. Table 4.1 shows the rights that the Court has incorporated into the Fourteenth Amendment and the case in which it first applied each protection. As you can see in the table, in the fifteen years following the *Gitlow* decision, the Supreme Court incorporated into the Fourteenth Amendment the other basic freedoms (of the press, assembly, the right to petition, and religion) guaranteed by the First Amendment.

It took time for the Supreme Court to require the states to accept other liberties. Only in 2010 did the Court rule that the states were obligated under the Second Amendment to recognize an individual's right to bear arms. Even with that ruling, the national and state governments retain the power to regulate the ownership of firearms. The Third Amendment bars the government from quartering soldiers in private houses during peacetime, but the Court has never imposed this obligation on the states. The reason appears to be that the Court has never heard a case in which a state allegedly violated this right. In 1982, however, a U.S. appeals court ruled to incorporate the Third Amendment.[3]

---

1. *Barron v. Baltimore*, 32 U.S. 243 (1833).
2. 268 U.S. 652 (1925).
3. *Engblom v. Carey*, 677 F.2d 957 (2d Cir. 1982).

Table 4.1	Incorporating the Bill of Rights into the Fourteenth Amendment		

▶ **Why would the Supreme Court have incorporated some of these rights many years before it incorporated others?**

Year	Issue	Amendment Involved	Court Case
1925	Freedom of speech	I	*Gitlow v. New York*, 268 U.S. 652.
1931	Freedom of the press	I	*Near v. Minnesota*, 283 U.S. 697.
1932	Right to a lawyer in capital punishment cases	VI	*Powell v. Alabama*, 287 U.S. 45.
1937	Freedom of assembly and right to petition	I	*De Jonge v. Oregon*, 299 U.S. 353.
1940	Freedom of religion	I	*Cantwell v. Connecticut*, 310 U.S. 296.
1947	Separation of church and state	I	*Everson v. Board of Education*, 330 U.S. 1.
1948	Right to a public trial	VI	*In re Oliver*, 333 U.S. 257.
1949	No unreasonable searches and seizures	IV	*Wolf v. Colorado*, 338 U.S. 25.
1961	Exclusionary rule (see "The Great Balancing Act" later in this chapter)	IV	*Mapp v. Ohio*, 367 U.S. 643.
1962	No cruel and unusual punishment	VIII	*Robinson v. California*, 370 U.S. 660.
1963	Right to a lawyer in all criminal felony cases	VI	*Gideon v. Wainwright*, 372 U.S. 335.
1964	No compulsory self-incrimination	V	*Malloy v. Hogan*, 378 U.S. 1.
1965	Right to privacy	I, III, IV, V, IX	*Griswold v. Connecticut*, 381 U.S. 479.
1966	Right to an impartial jury	VI	*Parker v. Gladden*, 385 U.S. 363.
1967	Right to a speedy trial	VI	*Klopfer v. North Carolina*, 386 U.S. 213.
1969	No double jeopardy	V	*Benton v. Maryland*, 395 U.S. 784.
2010	Right to bear arms	II	*McDonald v. Chicago*, 561 U.S. 3025.

Freedom of Religion

≫ **LO 4-2:** Explain how the First Amendment's establishment clause and free exercise clause guarantee our freedom of religion.

In the United States, freedom of religion consists of two principal rules that are presented in the First Amendment. The first rule guarantees the separation of church and state, and the second guarantees the free exercise of religion.

The Separation of Church and State—The Establishment Clause

The First Amendment to the Constitution states, in part, that "Congress shall make no law respecting an establishment of religion." In the words of Thomas Jefferson, the **establishment clause** was designed to create a "wall of separation of Church and State." As interpreted by the Supreme Court, the establishment clause in the First Amendment means at least the following:

> *Neither a state nor the federal government can set up a church. Neither can pass laws which aid one religion, aid all religions, or prefer one religion over another. Neither can force nor influence a person to go to or to remain away from church against his will or force him to profess a belief or disbelief in any religion. No person can be punished for entertaining or professing religious beliefs or disbeliefs, for church attendance or nonattendance. No tax in*

Establishment Clause
The part of the First Amendment prohibiting the establishment of a church officially supported by the national government.

any amount, large or small, can be levied to support any religious activities or institutions, whatever they may be called, or whatever form they may adopt to teach or practice religion. Neither a state nor the federal government can, openly or secretly, participate in the affairs of any religious organizations or groups and vice versa.[4]

The establishment clause covers such matters as the legality of giving state and local government aid to religious organizations and schools, allowing or requiring school prayers, teaching evolution versus creationist theories that reject evolution, placing religious displays in schools or public places, and discriminating against religious groups in publicly operated institutions.

Aid to Church-Related Schools. In the United States, about 10 percent of school-age children attend private schools. About four-fifths of these students attend a school with a religious affiliation. (In addition, more than 3 percent of all students are homeschooled.) The Supreme Court has tried to draw a fine line between permissible public aid to students in church-related schools and impermissible public aid to religion.

In 1971, in *Lemon v. Kurtzman*,[5] the Court ruled that direct state aid could not be used to subsidize religious instruction. The Court in the *Lemon* case gave its most general pronouncement on the constitutionality of government aid to religious schools, stating that (1) the aid had to be secular (nonreligious) in aim, (2) it could not have the primary effect of advancing or inhibiting religion, and (3) the government must avoid "an excessive government entanglement with religion." All laws that raise issues under the establishment clause are now subject to the three-part *Lemon* test. How the test is applied, however, has varied over the years.

In a number of cases, the Supreme Court has held that state programs helping church-related schools are unconstitutional. In other cases, in contrast, the Supreme Court has allowed states to use tax funds for lunches, textbooks, diagnostic services for speech and hearing problems, standardized tests, and special educational services for disadvantaged students attending religious schools.

School Vouchers. An ongoing controversy concerning the establishment clause has to do with school vouchers. Some people believe that the public schools are failing to educate children adequately. One proposed solution to the problem has been for state and local governments to issue school vouchers. These vouchers represent state-issued funds that can be used to purchase education at any school, public or private. At issue is whether voucher programs violate the establishment clause.

In 2002, the Supreme Court held that a voucher program in Cleveland, Ohio, did not violate the establishment clause. The Court concluded that because the vouchers could be used for public as well as private schools, the program did not unconstitutionally entangle church and state.[6] The Court's 2002 decision was encouraging to those who support school choice, whether it takes the form of school vouchers or tuition tax credits to offset educational expenses in private schools.

Today, a variety of states allow public funds to be used for private school expenses. Some have small-scale voucher or scholarship programs for a limited number of students, frequently special-needs students. A growing number of states provide tax deductions for private school expenses. Arizona passed a law in 2022 allowing all students to use vouchers.

---

4. *Everson v. Board of Education*, 330 U.S. 1 (1947).
5. 403 U.S. 602 (1971).
6. *Zelman v. Simmons-Harris*, 536 U.S. 639 (2002).

The Issue of School Prayer—*Engel v. Vitale*. Do the states have the right to promote religion in general, without making any attempt to establish a particular religion? That is the question raised in 1962 in *Engel v. Vitale*,[7] the so-called Regents' Prayer case in New York. The State Board of Regents of New York had suggested that a prayer be spoken aloud in the public schools at the beginning of each day. The recommended prayer was as follows:

> *Almighty God, we acknowledge our dependence upon Thee,*
> *And we beg Thy blessings upon us, our parents, our teachers, and our Country.*

Such a prayer was implemented in many New York public schools.

The parents of a number of students challenged the action of the regents, maintaining that it violated the establishment clause of the First Amendment. At trial, the parents lost. On appeal, however, the Supreme Court ruled that the regents' action was unconstitutional because "the constitutional prohibition against laws respecting an establishment of a religion must mean at least that in this country it is no part of the business of government to compose official prayers for any group of the American people to recite as part of a religious program carried on by any government."

Image 4.1 Public school students praying in the school library. ▶ Do their actions violate the separation of church and state?

Forbidding the Teaching of Evolution. For many decades, certain religious groups have opposed the teaching of evolution in the schools. To these groups, evolutionary theory directly counters their religious belief that human beings did not evolve but were created fully formed, as described in the biblical stories of the creation. State and local attempts to forbid the teaching of evolution, however, have not passed constitutional muster in the eyes of the Supreme Court. For example, in 1968 the Supreme Court held that an Arkansas law prohibiting the teaching of evolution violated the establishment clause because it imposed religious beliefs on students.[8] Nonetheless, state and local groups around the country continue their efforts against the teaching of evolution.

The Issue of Intelligent Design. Some school districts have considered teaching the creationist theory of "intelligent design" as an alternative explanation of the origin of life. Proponents of intelligent design contend that evolutionary theory has "gaps" that can be explained only by the existence of an intelligent creative force (God).

The federal courts took up the issue of intelligent design in 2005. The previous year, the Dover Area Board of Education in Pennsylvania had voted to require the presentation of intelligent design as an explanation of the origin of life. In 2005, a U.S. district court ruled that the Dover mandate was unconstitutional.[9] All of the school board members who endorsed the teaching of intelligent design were voted out of office.

Since 2005, advocates of intelligent design have made continued attempts to introduce their doctrine into the public schools. Intelligent design advocates have adopted the slogan

7. 370 U.S. 421 (1962).
8. *Epperson v. Arkansas*, 393 U.S. 97 (1968).
9. *Kitzmiller v. Dover Area School District*, 400 F.Supp.2d 707 (M.D.Pa. 2005).

"teach the controversy" as a way of introducing creationism alongside evolution. Opponents argue, however, that there is no controversy among biologists. Rather, the controversy is political and religious, and if it is taught at all, it should be covered in social science or politics classes.

Religious Displays on Public Property. On a regular basis, the courts are asked to determine whether religious symbols placed on public property violate the establishment clause. A frequent source of controversy is the placement of a crèche, or nativity scene, on public property during the Christmas season. The Supreme Court has allowed some displays but prohibited others. In general, a nativity scene is acceptable if it is part of a broader display that contains secular objects such as lights, Christmas trees, Santa Claus figures, and reindeer. A stand-alone crèche is not acceptable.[10]

The Free Exercise Clause

The First Amendment constrains Congress from prohibiting the free exercise of religion. Does this **free exercise clause** mean that no type of religious practice can be prohibited or restricted by government? Certainly, persons can hold any religious belief that they want, or persons can have no religious beliefs. When, however, religious practices work against public policy and the public welfare, the government can act.

For example, regardless of a child's or parent's religious beliefs, the government can require childhood vaccinations. Some states, such as Texas, allow philosophical exemption from vaccination requirements—but others, such as California, allow documented medical exemptions only. Vaccinations, of course, became a major flashpoint during the COVID-19 pandemic. Many institutions, including private businesses, required vaccinations. Some individuals refused such COVID vaccinations on religious grounds. For a while, in many instances, no exemptions were allowed. Individuals lost their jobs as a result and some students were not allowed to return to in-class learning.

Image 4.2 This nativity scene in front of the United States Supreme Court was part of a campaign to display nativity scenes on public property. ▶ What rules govern such displays?

Alex Wong/Getty Images News/Getty Images

Free Exercise Clause
The provision of the First Amendment guaranteeing the free exercise of religion.

Tax-Exempt Status and Politics. Churches and other religious organizations are tax-exempt bodies, and as a result they are not allowed to endorse candidates for office or make contributions to candidates' campaigns. Tax-exempt churches are allowed to take positions on ballot proposals, however, and may contribute to referendum campaigns. For example, both the Latter-Day Saints (the Mormons) and the Roman Catholic Church were able to fund the campaign for California's 2008 Proposition 8, a measure to ban same-sex marriage.

The Internal Revenue Service (IRS) rarely bothers to threaten the tax-exempt status of a church based on simple candidate endorsements, however. In October 2012, about 1,400 ministers collectively endorsed Republican presidential candidate Mitt Romney in a deliberate challenge to the 1954 law that prohibits such endorsements. The IRS did not respond. In 1995, though, the IRS did revoke the tax-exempt status of Branch Ministries, Inc., and in 2000 a federal district court supported the revocation.[11] Branch Ministries went far beyond simply endorsing a candidate from the pulpit. The church had used tax-exempt income to buy newspaper advertisements denouncing Democratic presidential candidate Bill Clinton.

10. *Lynch v. Donnelly*, 465 U.S. 668 (1984).
11. *Branch Ministries v. Rossetti*, 211 F.3d 137 (D.C.Cir. 2000).

Construction of Religious Buildings. In the United States, regulations on land use are typically set by local governments. Such regulations take the form of zoning ordinances (laws), which may restrict which parts of a city can be used for commercial or industrial activity. Can zoning be used to limit the size and location of churches and other religious buildings? Within limits, it can. Some communities have sought to ban new Christian church buildings in certain locations. Given that Christianity is popular, such attempts are relatively rare and have often led to negotiated settlements.

If a local government tries to use zoning to completely ban a religious denomination from constructing a house of worship anywhere, however, that can be a violation of the free exercise clause. In recent years, several local governments have tried to use zoning to impose a total ban on the construction of Islamic mosques. In general, the courts will not support such attempts.

Freedom of Expression

> **LO 4-3:** Specify the limited circumstances in which the national and state governments may override the principles of free speech and freedom of the press.

Perhaps the most frequently invoked freedom that Americans have is the right to free speech and a free press. For the most part, Americans can criticize public officials and their actions without fear of reprisal by any branch of our government.

No Prior Restraint

Restraining an activity before it has actually occurred is called **prior restraint**. When expression is involved, prior restraint means censorship, as opposed to subsequent punishment. Prior restraint of expression would require, for example, that a permit be obtained before a speech could be made, a newspaper published, or a movie or TV show exhibited. Most, if not all, Supreme Court justices have been very critical of any governmental action that imposes prior restraint on expression.

One of the most famous cases concerning prior restraint was *New York Times v. United States*[12] (1971), the so-called Pentagon Papers case. The *Times* and the *Washington Post* were about to publish the Pentagon Papers, a secret history of the U.S. government's involvement in the Vietnam War (1965–75). The documents had been obtained illegally by a disillusioned former Pentagon official. The government wanted a court order to bar publication of the papers, arguing that national security was threatened and that the documents had been stolen. The newspapers argued that the public had a right to know the information contained in the papers and that the press had the right to inform the public. The Supreme Court ruled six to three in favor of the newspapers' right to publish the information. This case affirmed the no-prior-restraint doctrine.

The Protection of Symbolic Speech

Not all expression is in words or in writing. Articles of clothing, gestures, and other forms of nonverbal expressive conduct are considered **symbolic speech**. Such speech is given substantial protection today by our courts. For example, in a landmark decision issued in 1969, *Tinker v. Des Moines School District*, the Supreme Court held that the wearing of black

Prior Restraint
Restraining an activity before it has actually occurred. When expression is involved, this means censorship.

Symbolic Speech
Expression made through articles of clothing, gestures, and other forms of nonverbal conduct.

---

12. 403 U.S. 713 (1971).

armbands by students in protest against the Vietnam War was a form of speech protected by the First Amendment.[13]

Flag Burning. In 1989, the Supreme Court ruled that state laws that prohibited the burning of the American flag as part of a peaceful protest also violated the freedom of expression protected by the First Amendment.[14] Congress responded by passing the Flag Protection Act of 1989, which was ruled unconstitutional by the Supreme Court in 1990. Congress and President George H. W. Bush immediately pledged to work for a constitutional amendment to "protect our flag"—an effort that has yet to be successful.

Cross Burning. In 2003, the Supreme Court concluded in a Virginia case that a state, consistent with the First Amendment, may ban cross burnings carried out with the intent to intimidate. The Court reasoned that historically, cross burning was a sign of impending violence, and a state has the right to ban threats of violence. The Court also ruled, however, that the state must prove intimidation and cannot infer it from the cross burnings themselves. In an impassioned dissent, Justice Clarence Thomas, who is African American and usually one of the Court's most conservative members, argued that cross burnings should be automatic evidence of intent to intimidate.[15]

The Protection of Commercial Speech

Commercial Speech
Advertising statements, which increasingly have been given First Amendment protection.

Commercial speech usually is defined as advertising statements. Can advertisers use their First Amendment rights to prevent restrictions on the content of commercial advertising? Until the 1970s, the Supreme Court held that such speech was not protected at all by the First Amendment. By the mid-1970s, however, more and more commercial speech had been brought under First Amendment protection. According to Justice Harry A. Blackmun, "Advertising, however tasteless and excessive it sometimes may seem, is nonetheless dissemination of information as to who is producing and selling what product for what reason and at what price."[16] Nevertheless, the Supreme Court will consider a restriction on commercial speech valid as long as it (1) seeks to implement a substantial government interest, (2) directly advances that interest, and (3) goes no further than necessary to accomplish its objective. In particular, a business engaging in commercial speech can be subject to liability for factual inaccuracies in ways that do not apply to noncommercial speech.

Attempts to Ban Subversive or Advocacy Speech

Over the past hundred years, the Supreme Court has established, in succession, a number of doctrines regarding language allegedly subversive to the public order.

The Clear and Present Danger Test. In 1919, the Supreme Court ruled that when a person's remarks present a clear and present danger to the peace or public order, they can be curtailed constitutionally. Justice Oliver Wendell Holmes used this reasoning when ratifying the conviction of a socialist who had been charged with violating the Espionage Act by distributing a leaflet that opposed the military draft. According to the clear and present danger test, expression may be restricted if evidence exists that such expression would cause a dangerous condition, actual or imminent, that Congress has the power to prevent.[17]

---

13. 393 U.S. 503 (1969).
14. *Texas v. Johnson,* 488 U.S. 884 (1989).
15. *Virginia v. Black,* 538 U.S. 343 (2003).
16. *Virginia State Board of Pharmacy v. Virginia Citizens Consumer Council, Inc.,* 425 U.S. 748 (1976).
17. *Schenck v. United States,* 249 U.S. 47 (1919).

The Bad Tendency Rule. Over the course of the twentieth century, the Supreme Court modified the clear and present danger rule, limiting the constitutional protection of free speech in 1925 and 1951, and then broadening it substantially in 1969.

In *Gitlow v. New York*, the Court reintroduced an earlier bad tendency rule, which placed greater restrictions on speech than are found in Justice Holmes's 1919 formulation.[18] According to this rule, speech may be curtailed if there is a possibility that such expression might lead to some "evil."

In the *Gitlow* case, a member of a left-wing group was convicted of violating New York State's criminal anarchy statute when he published and distributed a pamphlet urging the violent overthrow of the U.S. government. In its majority opinion, the Supreme Court held that the First Amendment afforded protection against state incursions on freedom of expression—the first time that the First Amendment was ever invoked against a state government. Nevertheless, Gitlow could be punished legally because his expression would tend to bring about evils that the state had a right to prevent.

The Imminent Lawless Action Test. Some claim that the United States did not achieve true freedom of political speech until 1969. In that year, in *Brandenburg v. Ohio*, the Supreme Court overturned the conviction of a Ku Klux Klan leader for violating a state statute.[19] The statute prohibited anyone from advocating "the duty, necessity, or propriety of sabotage, violence, or unlawful methods of terrorism as a means of accomplishing industrial or political reform." The Court held that the guarantee of free speech does not permit a state "to forbid or proscribe [disallow] advocacy of the use of force or of law violation except where such advocacy is directed to inciting or producing imminent [immediate] lawless actions and is likely to incite or produce such action." The **imminent lawless action test** enunciated by the Court is a difficult one for prosecutors to meet. As a result, the Court's decision significantly broadened the protection given to advocacy speech.

Image 4.3 An advertisement for Captain Morgan Long Island Iced Tea, an alcoholic beverage allegedly aimed at the college student market. ▶ What rights do alcohol marketers have under the First Amendment?

Imminent Lawless Action Test
The current standard established by the Supreme Court for evaluating the legality of advocacy speech. Such speech can be forbidden only when it is "directed to inciting … imminent lawless actions."

The Eclipse of Obscenity as a Legal Category

Traditionally, state and federal statutes made it a crime to disseminate obscene materials. But what is obscenity? Justice Potter Stewart once stated that even though he could not define obscenity, "I know it when I see it." The legal system needs a more precise definition than that, however.

The Rise and Fall of *Miller v. California*. In 1973, in *Miller v. California*, Chief Justice Warren Burger created a list of requirements that must be met for material to be legally obscene.[20] Material is obscene if (1) the average person finds that it violates contemporary community standards, (2) the work taken as a whole appeals to a prurient interest in sex, (3) the work shows patently offensive sexual conduct, and (4) the work lacks serious redeeming literary, artistic, political, or scientific merit. The definition of prurient interest would be determined by "community standards," thus leaving the definition to local and state authorities.

18. 268 U.S. 652 (1925).
19. 395 U.S. 444 (1969).
20. 413 U.S. 5 (1973).

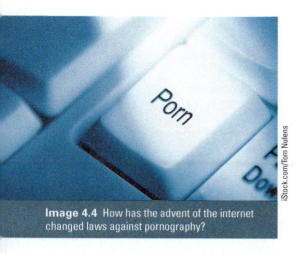

iStock.com/Tom Nulens

Image 4.4 How has the advent of the internet changed laws against pornography?

The Court's ruling came at a time when popular attitudes toward obscenity were undergoing a revolution. A few years earlier, literary works regarded as masterpieces by critics could be banned from the U.S. mail, from import, and from sale. Such works included *Lady Chatterley's Lover* by D. H. Lawrence and *Ulysses* by James Joyce. By the 1980s, however, it was possible in almost every corner of the country to buy or rent pornographic videotapes that left nothing to the imagination.

Internet Pornography. The rise of the internet in the 1990s sealed the fate of obscenity as a useful legal category. Conventional pornography on the internet was essentially impossible to police. Congress attempted to spare children from exposure to internet pornography by laws passed in 1996 and 1998, but the Court found this legislation to be unconstitutional.[21] In 2000, Congress was more successful with the Children's Internet Protection Act, which penalizes public schools and libraries if they do not install filtering software to prevent children from viewing websites with "adult" content. This law was upheld.[22] Young people today, however, are not dependent on libraries for internet access. Free Wi-Fi, for use by laptops, tablets, and smart phones, is available almost everywhere.

Remaining Restrictions. Pornography can still be limited by the private sector—for example, most mainstream movie theaters will not show a film that has received a "no [child] 17 and under admitted" (NC-17) rating from the Motion Picture Association of America. The government also retains the right to place restrictions on media that it controls, such as the broadcast spectrum. Therefore, restrictions on broadcast radio and television remain.

Pornography That Exploits Minors. The government has also successfully outlawed materials that show sexual performance by minors. In 1990, the Court ruled that states can criminalize the possession of child pornography. The Court reasoned that the ban on private possession is justified because owning the material constitutes a form of child abuse.[23] This legal reasoning, however, reveals just how barren the concept of obscenity had become. Child abuse was the crime—not obscenity. As a result, the law makes no attempt to ban depictions of sexual performance by children in literary works such as Vladimir Nabokov's *Lolita* or in obvious cartoons such as Japanese *hentai*. Novels and cartoons do not involve the exploitation of actual, identifiable children.

Unprotected Speech: Slander

Defamation of Character
Wrongfully hurting a person's good reputation.

Slander
The public uttering of a false statement that harms the good reputation of another. The statement must be made to, or within the hearing of, someone other than the defamed party.

Can you say anything you want about someone else? Not really. Individuals are protected from **defamation of character**, which is defined as wrongfully hurting a person's good reputation. The law imposes a general duty on all persons to refrain from making false, defamatory statements about others. Breaching this duty orally is the wrongdoing called **slander**. Breaching it in writing is the wrongdoing called libel, which we discuss later. The government itself does not bring charges of slander or libel. Rather, the defamed person may bring a civil suit (as opposed to a criminal action) for damages. In almost all cases, such suits are brought in state courts.

---

21. *Reno v. American Civil Liberties Union,* 521 U.S. 844 (1997); *American Civil Liberties Union v. Ashcroft,* 543 U.S. 646 (2004).
22. *United States v. American Library Association,* 539 U.S. 194 (2003).
23. *Osborne v. Ohio,* 495 U.S. 103 (1990).

Legally, slander is the public uttering of a false statement that harms the good reputation of another. Public uttering means that the defamatory statement is made to, or within the hearing of, a person other than the defamed party. If one person calls another dishonest, manipulative, and incompetent to their face when no one else is around, that does not constitute slander. If, however, a third party accidentally overhears defamatory statements, the courts have generally held that this constitutes a public uttering and may therefore be slander.

Student Speech

In recent years, high school and university students at public institutions have faced a variety of free speech challenges. Court rulings on these issues have varied by the level of school involved. Elementary schools, in particular, have great latitude in determining what kinds of speech are appropriate for their students. High school students have more free speech rights than do elementary students, and college students have the most speech rights of all.

Rights of Public School Students. High schools can impose restrictions on speech that would not be allowed in a college setting or in the general society. For example, high school officials may censor publications such as newspapers and yearbooks produced by the school's students. Courts have argued that a school newspaper is an extension of the school's educational mission and thus subject to control by the school administration.

Campus Speech and Behavior Codes. Another free speech issue is the legitimacy of campus speech and behavior codes at some state universities. These codes prohibit so-called hate speech—abusive speech attacking persons on the basis of their ethnicity, race, or other criteria. For example, a University of Michigan code banned "any behavior, verbal or physical, that stigmatizes or victimizes an individual on the basis of race, ethnicity, religion, sex, sexual orientation, creed, national origin, ancestry, age, marital status, handicap," or Vietnam-veteran status. A federal court found that the code violated students' First Amendment rights.[24] Although the courts generally have held that campus speech codes are unconstitutional restrictions on the right to free speech, such codes continue to exist.

"Political Correctness" on Campus. Free speech on campus becomes a somewhat more complicated issue when students, as opposed to the school administration, undertake controversial actions. Students have also been accused of political correctness when they condemn language that may be insensitive or even racist. Of course, criticizing other people's speech is also a way to exercise one's own freedom of speech. Given the strength of our First Amendment protections, political correctness by itself is almost never a violation of the law. To be actionable, the speech would also have to constitute slander or some other offense that inflicts a measurable injury. Hurt feelings are not enough.

Michael Stuparyk/Toronto Star/Getty Images

Image 4.5 A student at the University of Texas is part of a project to track internet censorship around the world. He and other concerned students then help people in various countries to bypass the censors. ▶ What protections does our Constitution provide for free speech on the internet?

---

24. *Doe v. University of Michigan*, 721 F.Supp. 852 (1989).

Richard Bord/WireImage/Getty Images

Image 4.6 Rapper Cardi B sued YouTube vlogger Latasha Kebe for defamation. An Atlanta jury awarded the rapper $4 million. ▶ Was that amount of money too much or too little?

Freedom of the Press

Freedom of the press can be regarded as a special instance of freedom of speech. Of course, at the time of the framing of the Constitution, the press meant only newspapers, pamphlets, magazines, and books. As technology has modified the ways in which we disseminate information, the laws touching on freedom of the press have been modified. What can and cannot be printed still occupies an important place in constitutional law, nonetheless.

Defamation in Writing. **Libel** is defamation in writing or in pictures, signs, films, or any other communication. As with slander, libel occurs only if the defamatory statements are observed by a third party. If Jane Garcia sends a private communication to John Jones wrongfully accusing him of embezzling funds, that does not constitute libel.

The case of *New York Times Co. v. Sullivan* (1964) explored an important question regarding libelous statements made about public officials.[25] The Supreme Court held that only when a statement against a public official is made with **actual malice**—that is, with either knowledge of its falsity or a reckless disregard for the truth—can damages be obtained.

The standard set by the Court in the *New York Times* case has since been applied to **public figures** generally. Public figures include not only public officials but also any persons, such as movie stars, who are generally in the public limelight. Statements made about public figures usually are related to matters of general public interest. They are made about people who substantially affect all of us. Furthermore, public figures generally have some access to a public medium for answering disparaging falsehoods about themselves, whereas private individuals do not. For these reasons, public figures have a greater burden of proof in defamation cases than do private individuals.

Libel on the Internet. The internet has vastly expanded the number of published statements by the general citizenry, including anonymous comments. Today, as a result, libelous statements can be hard even to track down, much less prosecute. Even when the identity of the person committing libel is not in doubt, it can be difficult to win a defamation suit. Lawyers are expensive, and it can be hard to show that a victim's reputation suffered actual harm. For a libel suit to succeed, defamation must often be extreme.

Consider Alex Jones, whose Infowars website deals in conspiracy theories. In 2012, a shooter murdered twenty-seven people, twenty of them small children, at the Sandy Hook Elementary School in Newtown, Connecticut. Over a period of several years, Jones claimed that the account of the shooting was a hoax, that no one died, that the parents of the children were hired actors, and that the whole incident was a scheme by activists to promote anti-gun

Libel
A written defamation of a person's character or reputation. The defamatory statement must be observed by a third party.

Public Figures
A public official, movie star, or other person known to the public because of their positions or activities.

Actual Malice
Either knowledge of a defamatory statement's falsity or a reckless disregard for the truth.

---

25. 376 U.S. 254 (1964).

legislation. Jones' campaign led to harassment and death threats for the grieving parents. Several families were forced into hiding. A judge in the case went so far as to require Jones to pay the court costs of the parents. Such rulings are rare in the United States.

Films, Radio, and TV. As we have noted, in only a few cases has the Supreme Court upheld prior restraint of published materials. The Court's reluctance to accept prior restraint is less evident with respect to motion pictures. In the first half of the twentieth century, films were routinely submitted to local censorship boards. Only in 1952 did the Court find that motion pictures were covered by the First Amendment.[26] In contrast, the Court extended full protection to the internet almost immediately by striking down provisions of the 1996 Telecommunications Act.[27] Cable TV received broad protection in 2000.[28]

While the Court has held that the First Amendment is relevant to broadcast radio and television, it has never extended full protection to these media. The Court has used a number of arguments to justify this stand—initially, the scarcity of broadcast frequencies. The Court later held that the government could restrict "indecent" programming based on the "pervasive" presence of broadcasting in the home.[29] On this basis, the Federal Communications Commission (FCC) has the authority to fine broadcasters for indecency or profanity.

Today, Large Tech Companies Dominate the Media

To be sure, standard old-fashioned TV and radio stations are almost all owned by large media companies—the giant tech conglomerates. Whether you receive your news and entertainment via cable, TV antennas, or streaming on the internet, chances are that a big tech company is the provider. How do the rules of censorship established over the past decades apply? Do private big tech companies have the right to censor what you post? Do these same media companies have the right to restrict your statements in videos, tweets, photos, etc.? Some say yes, others say no. See this chapter's *Which Side Are You On?* feature to read about two sides of this issue.

The Right to Privacy

>> **LO 4-4:** Determine whether the Constitution, including the Bill of Rights, explicitly gives you the right to privacy.

No explicit reference is made anywhere in the Constitution to a person's right to privacy. For many years, the courts did not take a very positive approach toward this right. In 1965, however, in *Griswold v. Connecticut*, the Supreme Court overthrew a Connecticut law that effectively prohibited the use of contraceptives, holding that the law violated the right to privacy.[30] Justice William O. Douglas formulated a unique way of reading this right into the Bill of Rights. He claimed that the First, Third, Fourth, Fifth, and Ninth Amendments created "penumbras formed by emanations [shadows, formed by the light], from those guarantees that help give them life and substance," and he went on to describe zones of privacy that are guaranteed by these rights.

---

26. *Joseph Burstyn, Inc. v. Wilson,* 343 U.S. 495 (1952).
27. *Reno v. American Civil Liberties Union,* 521 U.S. 844 (1997).
28. *United States v. Playboy Entertainment Group,* 529 U.S. 803 (2000).
29. *FCC v. Pacifica Foundation,* 438 U.S. 726 (1978). In this case, the Court banned seven swear words (famously used by the late comedian George Carlin) during hours when children could hear them.
30. 381 U.S. 479 (1965).

Which Side Are You On?

Do Big Tech Media Companies Have the Right to Censor Content?

We know that speech has never been one hundred percent free. That is to say, it has never been legal to say just about anything in a public forum no matter what. Private individuals have not been able to go on TV or the radio and accuse other private citizens of heinous acts, particularly when the accusations were false. But what about today? Private citizens, government officials, politicians, scientists, and others express their views not only on TV and in newspapers and magazines, but also on Twitter, Facebook, Instagram, and elsewhere. All of those platforms are privately owned. Does that mean the heads of these companies can effectively censor speech on their own platforms?

When the public good is involved, private media platforms have the right (and the duty) to prevent misinformation.

Supporters of private platform censorship argue that free speech is not at issue here. The right to free speech means that government cannot abridge free speech. But these private companies can do whatever they want. And that is what they have been doing.

Take the COVID-19 pandemic. Many anti-vaxxers started spewing fallacious information about the vaccines. In so doing, they caused perhaps millions of people to not become vaccinated. The result was more infections and more deaths. It is normal that the heads of media platforms should attempt to reduce the amount of false information available for public viewing or reading. It may be quite cute that there is a Flat-Earth Society, but it is quite another thing to allow non-scientific information about medicine to be listened to, read about, or viewed by all. Moreover, we are seeing many more competitors to the standard big-tech media platforms. They include Parler and Truth Social. Competition will cure any problems with big tech censorship.

Big Tech Is Using Its Monopoly Position to Suppress Free Speech

During the early years of the internet, everyone viewed it as a medium through which anyone could express whatever ideas they wanted to express. Gradually, certain social media platforms began to dominate. Facebook became ubiquitous. Then Twitter, then Instagram, then YouTube. Through astute purchases, Apple, Alphabet (formally just Google), and Facebook (now renamed Meta) dominate discourse on social media. These companies were never put in the same position as newspapers and television stations. They have never been considered creators of content, but rather simply transmitters of others' content. Currently, they are protected from lawsuits for defamation so long as they do not create the content. This has allowed them to become giant monopolies.

And what have they used their monopoly power to do—control speech. Anytime anyone has put something on Facebook or Twitter that countered the government's dogmatic positions concerning COVID-19, vaccinations, mask wearing, and the like, there has been censorship. Well-known and respected scientists have been deplatformed—taken off social media. Such deplatforming actions have deprived the American public of hearing, seeing, and reading alternative points of view. Even private companies should not have these sweeping powers to regulate speech.

It is time that the federal government start regulating hi-tech.

■ For Critical Analysis

While start-up alternatives to giant social media companies are being created, will that be enough to counter hi-tech's influence over public issue discourse? Why or why not?

When we read the Ninth Amendment, we can see the foundation for his reasoning: "The enumeration in the Constitution, of certain rights, shall not be construed to deny or disparage others retained by the people." In other words, the fact that the Constitution, including its amendments, does not specifically talk about the right to privacy does not mean that this right is denied to the people.

Privacy Rights and Abortion

Historically, abortion was not a criminal offense before the "quickening" of the fetus (the first movement of the fetus in the uterus, usually between the sixteenth and eighteenth weeks of pregnancy). During the last half of the nineteenth century, however, state laws became more severe. By 1973, performing an abortion at any time during pregnancy was a criminal offense in many of the states.

Image 4.7 Anti-abortion demonstrators in San Francisco in January 2020. Many devout Catholics oppose both abortion and the death penalty. ▶ What arguments might others offer to distinguish between these two issues?

Roe v. Wade. In *Roe v. Wade* (1973), the Supreme Court accepted the argument that the laws against abortion violated "Jane Roe's" right to privacy under the Constitution.[31] The Court held that during the first trimester (three months) of pregnancy, abortion was an issue solely between a woman and her physician. The state could not limit abortions except to require that they be performed by licensed physicians. During the second trimester, to protect the health of the mother, the state was allowed to specify the conditions under which an abortion could be performed. During the final trimester, the state could regulate or even outlaw abortions except when they were necessary to preserve the life or health of the mother.

After the *Roe* case, the Supreme Court issued decisions in several cases defining and redefining the boundaries of state regulation of abortion. During the 1980s, the Court twice struck down laws that required a woman who wished to have an abortion to undergo counseling designed to discourage abortions. In the late 1980s and early 1990s, however, the Court took a more conservative approach. For example, in 1989 the Court upheld a Missouri statute that, among other things, banned the use of public hospitals or other taxpayer-supported facilities for performing abortions.[32] In 1992, the Court upheld a Pennsylvania law that required preabortion counseling, a waiting period of twenty-four hours, and for girls under the age of eighteen, parental or judicial permission.[33] As a result, abortions were more difficult to obtain in some states than in others.

---

31. 410 U.S. 113 (1973). Jane Roe was not the real name of the woman in this case. It is a common legal pseudonym used to protect a person's privacy.
32. *Webster v. Reproductive Health Services,* 492 U.S. 490 (1989).
33. *Planned Parenthood v. Casey,* 505 U.S. 833 (1992).

It is worth noting that while the Court placed limits on what the national and state governments could do to restrict the availability of abortions, governments retained the right to discourage the procedure. Governments as well as individuals enjoy freedom of speech and have the right to condemn abortion. A state can issue "right-to-life" license plates without offering ones that support "freedom of choice." No level of government is required to fund abortions, and such government funding is in fact banned by the federal government and a majority of the states.

"Partial-Birth" Abortion. In 2000, the Supreme Court again addressed the abortion issue directly when it reviewed a Nebraska law banning "partial-birth" abortions. A partial-birth abortion, which physicians call intact dilation and extraction, is a procedure that can be used during the second trimester of pregnancy. Abortion rights advocates claim that in limited circumstances the procedure is the safest way to perform an abortion and that the government should never outlaw specific medical procedures. Opponents argue that the procedure has no medical merit and that it ends the life of a fetus that might be able to live outside the womb. The Supreme Court invalidated the Nebraska law on the grounds that the law could be used to ban other abortion procedures and contained no provisions for protecting the health of the pregnant woman.[34]

In 2003, legislation similar to the Nebraska statute was passed by the U.S. Congress and signed into law by President George W. Bush. In 2007, the Supreme Court, with several changes in membership since the 2000 ruling, upheld the federal law in a five-to-four vote, effectively reversing its position on partial-birth abortions.[35]

The Controversy Continued. Groups opposed to abortion continued to push for laws restricting abortion, to endorse political candidates who supported their views, and to organize protests. Because of several episodes of violence during protests at abortion clinics, in 1994 Congress passed the Freedom of Access to Clinic Entrances Act. The act prohibits protesters from blocking entrances to such clinics. The Supreme Court upheld laws requiring "buffer zones" around abortion clinics. In 2014, however, the Court ruled that a thirty-five-foot buffer zone established by Massachusetts was excessive.[36]

In recent years, abortion opponents concentrated—often unsuccessfully—on state ballot proposals that could lay the groundwork for an eventual challenge to *Roe*. Abortion opponents were successful in winning new restrictions on abortion clinics. New state laws became especially common after the 2010 elections, when Republicans took over many state legislative chambers. From 2010 to January 2022, states passed almost 500 such laws.

Subsequently, new laws restricting abortion in several states were struck down by federal district courts. In 2013, a new law in Texas required that physicians performing abortions have admitting privileges with a local hospital. (Hospitals are under no obligation to provide such privileges.) Further, abortion clinics had to follow extremely strict rules on their facilities, which in many cases would have required them to construct new (and expensive) buildings. The Texas law would have cut the number of abortion clinics in the state from an earlier forty-one to about ten.

In June 2016, the Supreme Court struck down both the admitting privileges and the facilities provisions of the law.[37] This ruling effectively overturned laws in several other states. Since that time, however, the membership of the Supreme Court has changed. Justice

34. *Stenberg v. Carhart,* 530 U.S. 914 (2000).
35. *Gonzales v. Carhart,* 550 U.S. 124 (2007).
36. *McCullen v. Coakley,* 134 S.Ct. 2518 (2014).
37. *Whole Woman's Health v. Hellerstedt,* 136 S.Ct. 1001 (2016).

Anthony Kennedy, often a supporter of abortion rights, was replaced by Brett Kavanaugh, considered a right-to-life supporter. In 2020, the Court heard a new case from Louisiana that was almost identical to the earlier Texas case. The Court ruled in *June Medical Services, L.L.C. et al. v. Russo*[38] that Louisiana cannot require that those physicians performing abortions have hospital-admission privileges at local hospitals. The Court reasoned that, otherwise, women in Louisiana would face a substantial obstacle in seeking an abortion.

The Texas legislature passed a law essentially outlawing abortions after six weeks of pregnancy. Within the law there is a provision that allows private citizens to sue those who help others get an abortion after the six-week maximum. That legislation was signed into law in September 2021 by Texas Governor Greg Abbott. In December, a state judge declared the law unconstitutional but did not stop it from being enforced. The Supreme Court, while expressing concern with the law's unique enforcement mechanism, refused to block its implementation.[39]

In December 2021, the Supreme Court heard a Mississippi case that banned most abortions after the first fifteen weeks of pregnancy. In May 2022, a draft decision was leaked to the press. Finally, in *Dobbs v. Jackson Women's Health Organization*, the Court reversed *Roe v. Wade*.[40] The situation with respect to abortion reverted to where it was prior to 1973. All legislation concerning abortions would henceforth be in the hands of each state.

Contrary to some analyses, the *Dobbs* decision did not outlaw abortion. Liberal states such as New York and California will probably keep in place their laws that currently allow abortion without many restrictions. Some more conservative states will place many restrictions on abortion or outlaw it outright except for medical emergencies. After *Dobbs*, some conservative justices faced demonstrations in front of their private residences.

Privacy Rights and the "Right to Die"

A 1976 case involving Karen Ann Quinlan was one of the first publicized right-to-die cases. The parents of Quinlan, a young woman who had been in a coma for nearly a year and who had been kept alive during that time by a respirator, wanted her respirator removed. The ruling of the New Jersey Supreme Court, *In re Quinlan*, stated that the right to privacy includes the right of a patient to refuse treatment and that patients unable to speak can exercise that right through a family member or guardian.[41] In 1990, the Supreme Court took up the issue, ruling that a patient's life-sustaining treatment can be withdrawn at the request of a family member only if there is "clear and convincing evidence" that the patient did not want such treatment.[42]

What If There Is No Living Will? Since the 1976 *Quinlan* decision, most states have enacted laws permitting people to clarify their wishes on life-sustaining procedures in "living wills." These laws have resolved the right-to-die controversy for cases in which someone has drafted a living will. Disputes are still possible if there is no living will.

An example is the case of Terri Schiavo. After the Florida woman had been in a persistent vegetative state for over a decade, her husband sought to have her feeding tube removed on the basis of oral statements that she would not want her life prolonged in such circumstances. Schiavo's parents fought this move in court but lost on the ground that a

---

38. 591 U.S. ___ (2020).
39. This was not a case per se, but a ruling that allowed this case to move forward. See *Whole Women's Health et al. v. Jackson, Judge, District Court of Texas, 114 District et al.*, December 10, 2021.
40. *Dobbs v. Jackson Women's Health Organization*, 597 U.S. __ (2022).
41. 70 N.J. 10 (1976).
42. *Cruzan v. Director, Missouri Department of Health*, 497 U.S. 261 (1990).

spouse, not a parent, is the appropriate legal guardian for a married person. Although the Florida legislature passed a law allowing then-governor Jeb Bush to overrule the courts, the state supreme court held that the law violated the state constitution.[43] The federal courts agreed with the Florida state courts, and Schiavo died shortly thereafter.

Physician-Assisted Suicide. In the 1990s, another issue surfaced: Do privacy rights include the right of terminally ill people to end their lives through physician-assisted suicide? Courts had consistently upheld state laws that prohibited this practice. Finally, the issue reached the Supreme Court.

In 1997, the Court stated that the right to privacy does not include a right to commit suicide, with or without assistance.[44] In effect, the Court left the decision on whether to permit the practice in the hands of the states. Since then, assisted suicide has been allowed in nine states plus the District of Columbia.[45] In 2006, the Supreme Court upheld Oregon's physician-assisted suicide law against a challenge from the George W. Bush administration.[46]

The Great Balancing Act: The Rights of the Accused Versus the Rights of Society

» LO 4-5: Identify the constitutional rights of those who are accused of a crime.

The United States has one of the highest murder rates in the industrialized world. It is also true that the murder rate—like the rates of other major crimes—had fallen substantially over the last two decades until 2020, as shown in Figure 4.1. In contrast, in 2020, 2021, and 2022, the murder rate in many cities in America rose. Not surprisingly, some Americans have strong opinions of the rights of those accused of violent crimes.

Sometimes an accused person, even one who has confessed to some criminal act, is set free because of an apparent legal "technicality." In such cases, many people believe that the rights of the accused are being given more weight than the rights of potential or actual victims. Why, then, give criminal suspects rights? The answer is partly to avoid convicting innocent people, but mostly because due process of law and fair treatment benefit everyone who comes into contact with law enforcement or the courts.

The courts and the police must constantly engage in a balancing act of competing rights. The basis of all discussions about the appropriate balance is, of course, the U.S. Bill of Rights. The Fourth, Fifth, Sixth, and Eighth Amendments deal specifically with the rights of criminal defendants. Some people believe that despite the Constitution, minority group members often do not receive fair treatment from law enforcement. Several well-publicized and high-profile confrontations between Black Americans and the police greatly contributed to nationwide protests against the police. The most well-known involved George Floyd, a Black man in Minneapolis. He was killed in May 2020 at the hands of a police officer who kept his knee on Floyd's neck for about nine minutes. The event was digitally recorded on a spectator's phone. The video went viral and millions viewed it worldwide. Peaceful protests

---

43. *Bush v. Schiavo,* 885 So.2d 321 (Fla. 2004).
44. *Washington v. Glucksberg,* 521 U.S. 702 (1997).
45. The states are California, Colorado, Hawaii, Maine, Montana, New Mexico, Oregon, Vermont, and Washington.
46. *Gonzales v. Oregon*, 546 U.S. 243 (2006).

Figure 4.1	**Homicide Rates**

Despite an uptick in 2016–17, homicide rates declined thereafter for a while. (The 2001 rate does not include deaths attributed to the 9/11 terrorist attacks.) Murder rates did start rising in 2020. ▶ **What are some of the reasons that murder rates sometimes go down and sometimes go up?**

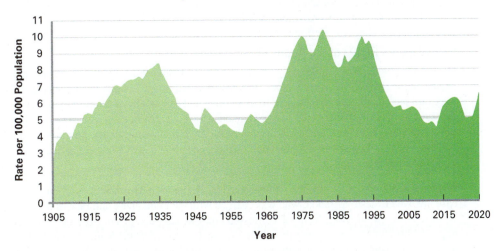

Sources: U.S. Department of Justice; and National Center for Health Statistics, Vital Statistics.

occurred throughout the nation in response, but some of the protests turned into violent riots. The protests, both peaceful and violent, lasted for months.

Rights of the Accused

The basic rights of criminal defendants are outlined below. When appropriate, the specific constitutional provision or amendment on which a right is based is also given.

Limits on the Conduct of Police Officers and Prosecutors

- No unreasonable or unwarranted searches and seizures (Amendment IV).
- No arrest except on probable cause (Amendment IV).
- No coerced confessions or illegal interrogation (Amendment V).
- No entrapment.
- On questioning, following an arrest, suspects must be informed of their rights.

Defendant's Pretrial Rights

- Writ of *habeas corpus* (Article I, Section 9).
- Prompt **arraignment** (Amendment VI).
- Legal counsel (Amendment VI).
- Reasonable bail (Amendment VIII).
- To be informed of charges (Amendment VI).
- To remain silent (Amendment V).

Arraignment
The first act in a criminal proceeding, in which the defendant is brought before a court to hear the charges against them and enter a plea of guilty or not guilty.

Trial Rights

- Speedy and public trial before a jury (Amendment VI).
- Impartial jury selected from a cross section of the community (Amendment VI).

- Trial atmosphere free of prejudice, fear, and outside interference.
- No compulsory self-incrimination (Amendment V).
- Adequate counsel (Amendment VI).
- No cruel and unusual punishment (Amendment VIII).
- Appeal of convictions.
- No double jeopardy (Amendment V).

Extending the Rights of the Accused

During the 1960s, the Supreme Court, under Chief Justice Earl Warren, significantly expanded the rights of accused persons. In a case decided in 1963, *Gideon v. Wainwright*,[47] the Court held that if a person is accused of a felony and cannot afford an attorney, an attorney must be made available to the accused person at the government's expense. Although the Sixth Amendment to the Constitution provides for the right to counsel, the Supreme Court had previously held that only criminal defendants in death-penalty cases automatically had a right to free legal counsel.

Miranda v. Arizona. In 1966, the Court issued its decision in *Miranda v. Arizona*.[48] The case involved Ernesto Miranda, who was charged with the kidnapping and rape of a young woman. After questioning, Miranda confessed and was later convicted. Miranda's lawyer appealed his conviction, arguing that the police had never informed Miranda that he had a right to remain silent and a right to be represented by counsel. The Court, in ruling in Miranda's favor, enunciated the now-familiar *Miranda* rights. Today, *Miranda* rights statements typically take the following form:

> *You have the right to remain silent. Anything you say can and will be used against you in a court of law. You have the right to speak to an attorney. If you cannot afford an attorney, one will be appointed for you. Do you understand these rights as they have been read to you?*

Exceptions to the *Miranda* Rule. As part of a continuing attempt to balance the rights of accused persons against the rights of society, the Supreme Court has made a number of exceptions to the *Miranda* rule. As one example, in an important 1991 decision, the Court stated that a suspect's conviction will not be automatically overturned if the suspect was coerced into making a confession. If the other evidence admitted at trial is strong enough to justify the conviction without the confession, then the fact that the confession was obtained illegally can be effectively ignored.[49]

The Exclusionary Rule

Exclusionary Rule
A judicial policy prohibiting the admission at trial of illegally seized evidence.

At least since 1914, judicial policy has prohibited the admission of illegally seized evidence at trials in federal courts. This is the so-called **exclusionary rule**. Improperly obtained evidence, no matter how telling, cannot be used by prosecutors. This includes evidence obtained by police in violation of a suspect's *Miranda* rights or of the Fourth Amendment. The Fourth Amendment protects against unreasonable searches and seizures and provides that a judge may issue a search warrant to a police officer only on probable cause (a demonstration of

---

47. 372 U.S. 335 (1963).
48. 384 U.S. 436 (1966).
49. *Arizona v. Fulminante*, 499 U.S. 279 (1991).

facts that permit a reasonable belief that a crime has been committed). The courts must determine what constitutes an "unreasonable" search and seizure.

The reasoning behind the exclusionary rule is that it forces police officers to gather evidence properly, in which case their due diligence will be rewarded by a conviction. Nevertheless, the exclusionary rule has always had critics who argue that it permits guilty persons to be freed because of innocent procedural errors by the police.

Adjustments to the Exclusionary Rule. This rule was first extended to state court proceedings in a 1961 Supreme Court decision, *Mapp v. Ohio*.[50] In this case, the Court overturned the conviction of Dollree Mapp for the possession of obscene materials. Police found pornographic books in her apartment after searching it without a search warrant and despite her refusal to let them in. Under the Fourth Amendment, search warrants must describe the persons or things to be seized. Officers are entitled, however, to seize items not mentioned in the search warrant if the materials are in "plain view" and reasonably appear to be contraband or evidence of a crime.[51]

Additional Court Rulings. During the past several decades, the Supreme Court has diminished the scope of the exclusionary rule by creating exceptions to its applicability. For example, the Court has created a "good faith" exception to the exclusionary rule. In 2009, the Court found that the good faith exception applies when an officer makes an arrest based on an outstanding warrant in another jurisdiction, even if the warrant in question was based on a clerical error.[52]

Not all Supreme Court cases have diminished the scope of the exclusionary rule. For example, in *Lange v. California*, the Supreme Court did not accept a challenge against Lange's arrest for driving under the influence.[53] A police officer observed Arthur Lange driving erratically, playing loud music, and honking his horn. The officer followed Lange and put on his car's overhead lights to signal that Lange should pull over. Rather than stopping, Lange drove to his driveway and entered his attached garage. The officer followed him, questioned him, and enacted a field sobriety test which was later confirmed by a blood test that showed that Lange's blood alcohol content was three times the legal limit. Lange moved to suppress the evidence of what happened after the officer entered the garage, arguing that the warrantless entry violated the Fourth Amendment. The United States Supreme Court did not agree.

The Supreme Court has also attempted to update the exclusionary rule to make it compatible with the latest technology. In 2014, for example, a unanimous Court found it unconstitutional for officers to search and seize the digital contents of a cell phone without a search warrant. According to the Court, smart phones now contain such vast quantities of private data that they are "worthy of the protection for which the Founders fought."[54] A topic that is sure to reach the Court in the future is the use of drones for surveillance by law enforcement. Under what circumstances does the use of drones violate our Fourth Amendment protections?

---

50. 367 U.S. 643 (1961).
51. *Texas v. Brown*, 460 U.S. 730 (1983); and *Horton v. California*, 496 U.S. 128 (1990).
52. *Herring v. United States*, 555 U.S. 135 (2009).
53. 594 U.S. __ (2021).
54. *Riley v. California,* 134 S.Ct. 999 (2014).

Civil Liberties Versus Security Issues

As former Supreme Court justice Thurgood Marshall once said, "Grave threats to liberty often come in times of urgency, when constitutional rights seem too extravagant to endure." Not surprisingly, antiterrorist legislation since the attacks on September 11, 2001, has eroded certain basic rights, in particular the Fourth Amendment protections against unreasonable searches and seizures.

The USA Patriot Act. The most significant piece of antiterrorism legislation, the USA Patriot Act, was passed in 2001 and renewed in 2006. Many in government believed that a lack of cooperation among government agencies was a major reason for the failure to anticipate the 9/11 attacks. One goal of the Patriot Act was to lift such barriers to cooperation. Under the Patriot Act, law enforcement officials can also secretly search a suspect's home and monitor a suspect's internet activities, phone conversations, and financial records. The government can even open a suspect's mail. While many believe that the Patriot Act is a necessary safety measure to prevent future terrorist attacks, others argue that it endangers civil liberties.

"Roving" Wiretaps. One civil liberties issue involves "roving" wiretaps. Previously, only specific telephone numbers, cell phone numbers, or computers could be tapped. Now a person under suspicion can be monitored electronically regardless of location or the technology in use. Such roving wiretaps appear to be inconsistent with the Fourth Amendment, which requires a judicial warrant to describe the place to be searched, not just the person. As an unavoidable side effect, the government has access to the conversations, text messages, and e-mail of many innocent people.

National Security Agency Surveillance. Shortly after September 11, 2001, President George W. Bush authorized the National Security Agency (NSA) to conduct secret surveillance without court warrants, even warrants from special security courts. The NSA was to monitor phone calls and other communications between foreign parties and persons within the United States when one of the parties had suspected links to terrorist organizations. When news of the program came out in 2005, it was criticized by civil liberties groups. In 2007, Congress passed a law to authorize the warrantless NSA wiretaps. The law was reauthorized in 2008.

Subsequent Revelations of NSA Activity

In June 2013, leaks provided by Edward Snowden, a federal contractor, revealed that NSA surveillance was far more extensive than previously assumed. Among the most striking revelations was that the NSA was gathering information on every domestic landline phone call made in the United States and certain other countries. The NSA did not record the contents of the calls but collected the call metadata, which includes time of call, the number of the caller, and the number of the phone that was called.

Collecting Actual Data. Under a second program, PRISM, the NSA collected information from the websites of corporations, including Apple, Google, Facebook (now Meta), Microsoft, Skype, and others. A third revelation was of NSA espionage actions against European countries. These included bugging the offices of the European Union in advance of trade talks between the United States and that organization. The NSA also bugged the cell phones of a wide variety of world leaders, including Germany's then-chancellor Angela Merkel.

Consequences of the Revelations. Snowden fled to Russia. Meanwhile, the reports resulted in an outcry by U.S. civil libertarians and by European leaders. The Obama administration defended the programs, however, noting—correctly—that they had been authorized by secret courts. In addition, former NSA director Michael Hayden bluntly stated that the Fourth Amendment, which prohibits unreasonable searches, "is not an international treaty." Foreigners, in other words, had no privacy rights that the U.S. government was bound to respect.

As you might imagine, citizens of foreign countries, especially in Europe, found such statements to be alarming. Several nations announced initiatives aimed at protecting the privacy of data belonging to their own citizens. Such steps could cut into the sales of American high-tech firms.

Apple and Microsoft Versus Government Surveillance. The question of whether government surveillance threatened high-tech businesses led to several confrontations. In 2015, domestic Islamist terrorists killed fourteen people in an attack in San Bernardino, California. The terrorists then died in a shootout with police, leaving behind a locked iPhone that the FBI sought to crack. In 2016, it obtained a court order demanding that Apple create a special version of the iPhone operating system that would bypass security controls. Apple refused, arguing that such a step would undermine the privacy of all iPhone users. Later, however, the FBI found a way to crack the iPhone without Apple's help. In January 2020, however, the FBI again demanded that Apple write new software to unlock an iPhone. This demand followed the murder of three U.S. sailors by a Saudi Arabian air force officer at a training facility in Pensacola, Florida. The Saudi officer died in a shoot-out at the scene. Again, Apple refused.

One tool used by the government in the years since 9/11 has been national security orders (NSOs), subpoenas issued by the FBI without judicial oversight. Individuals, financial institutions, and internet service providers are banned from speaking about NSOs with anyone. Other than constitutional issues, this practice raises the concern that no one would be allowed to blow the whistle on abuses of the government's powers. A U.S. district court has found NSOs to be unconstitutional, but thousands are still issued every year. In 2016, Microsoft sued the government, claiming that NSO "gag orders" violated the First and Fourth Amendments. Microsoft dropped the suit in 2017 after receiving government reassurances. In 2018, however, the company was back in court over a similar case. In the Apple and Microsoft cases, a serious concern existed that government powers first exercised in the war against terror would quickly be employed in general law enforcement.

Sergey Kohl/Shutterstock.com

Image 4.8 A demonstrator holds a picture of Edward Snowden, the former NSA contractor who released vast amounts of information about the agency's surveillance activities. ► Should Snowden have been tried or pardoned? In either case, why?

Your Civil Liberties: Searches and Seizures

Our civil liberties include numerous protections of persons who are suspected of criminal activity. Among these are limits on how the police can conduct searches and seizures.

Why Should You Care? You may be the most law-abiding person in the world, but that does not guarantee that you will never be stopped, arrested, or searched by the police. Sooner or later, most citizens have some kind of interaction with the police. People who do not understand their rights or how to behave toward law enforcement officers can find themselves in serious trouble.

What Are Your Rights? How should you behave if you are stopped by police officers? Your civil liberties protect you from having to provide information other than your name and address. Normally, even if you have not been placed under arrest, the officers have the right to frisk you for weapons, and you must let them proceed. The officers cannot, however, lawfully check your person or your clothing further if, in their judgment, no weaponlike object is produced.

Image 4.9 This man was arrested on suspicion of shooting his estranged wife and his mother-in-law. ▶ Can the police legally search him without a search warrant?

AP Images/Sharon Cekada/Post-Crescent

The officers may search you only if they have a search warrant or probable cause to believe that a search will likely produce incriminating evidence. What if the officers do not have probable cause or a warrant? Physically resisting their attempt to search you can lead to disastrous results. You can simply refuse orally to give permission for the search, if possible in the presence of a witness. Being polite is much better than acting out of anger and making the officers irritable.

If you are in your car and are stopped by the police, the same fundamental rules apply. Always be ready to show your driver's license and car registration. You may be asked to get out of the car. The officers may use a flashlight to peer inside if it is too dark to see otherwise. None of this constitutes a search. A true search requires either a warrant or a probable cause. No officer has the legal right to search your car simply to find out if you may have committed a crime.

If you are in your home and a police officer with a search warrant appears, you can ask to examine the warrant before granting entry. A warrant that is correctly made out will state the place or persons to be searched, the object sought, and the date of the warrant (which should be no more than ten days old). It will also bear the signature of a judge. If you believe the warrant to be invalid, or if no warrant is produced, you should make it clear orally that you have not consented to the search, if possible in the presence of a witness.

Officers who attempt to enter your home without a search warrant can lawfully do so only if they are pursuing a suspected felon into the house. Rarely is it advisable to give permission for a warrantless search. You, as the resident, must be the one to give permission if any evidence obtained is to be considered legal. A landlord, manager, or head of a college dormitory cannot give legal permission. A roommate, however, can give permission for a search of their room, which may allow the police to search areas where you have belongings.

To find out more about your rights and obligations under the laws of searches and seizures, you can contact the American Civil Liberties Union. Find its website by searching for "aclu."

Key Terms

actual malice 80	establishment clause 71	incorporation	symbolic speech 75
arraignment 87	exclusionary rule 88	theory 70	writ of *habeas*
bill of attainder 69	*ex post facto* law 69	libel 80	*corpus* 69
commercial speech 76	free exercise clause 74	prior restraint 75	
defamation of	imminent lawless	public figure 80	
character 78	action test 77	slander 78	

Chapter Summary

» LO 4-1 Protections included in the original Constitution include the right to a writ of *habeas corpus*, plus bans on bills of attainder and *ex post facto* laws. Originally, the Bill of Rights limited only the power of the national government, not that of the states. Gradually, however, the Supreme Court accepted incorporation theory, under which no state can violate most provisions of the Bill of Rights.

» LO 4-2 The First Amendment protects against government interference with freedom of religion by requiring a separation of church and state (under the establishment clause) and by guaranteeing the free exercise of religion. Controversial issues that arise under the establishment clause include aid to church-related schools, school vouchers, school prayer, the teaching of evolution, and religious displays on public property. The government can interfere with the free exercise of religion only when religious practices work against public policy or the public welfare.

» LO 4-3 The First Amendment protects against government interference with freedom of speech, which includes symbolic speech (expressive conduct). The Supreme Court has been especially critical of government actions that impose prior restraint on expression. Commercial speech (advertising) by businesses has received limited First Amendment protection. Restrictions on expression are permitted when the expression may incite imminent lawless action. Other speech that has not received First Amendment protection includes expression judged to be slanderous.

The First Amendment protects against government interference with the freedom of the press, which can be regarded as a special instance of freedom of speech. Speech by the press that does not receive protection includes libelous statements.

» LO 4-4 Under the Ninth Amendment, people's rights are not limited to those specifically mentioned in the Constitution. Among the unspecified rights protected by the courts is a right to privacy, which has been inferred from the First, Third, Fourth, Fifth, and Ninth Amendments. Whether an individual's privacy rights include a right to an abortion or a "right to die" continues to provoke controversy.

» LO 4-5 The Constitution includes protections for the rights of persons accused of crimes. Under the Fourth Amendment, no one may be subject to an unreasonable search or seizure or be arrested except on probable cause. Under the Fifth Amendment, an accused person has the right to remain silent. Under the Sixth Amendment, an accused person must be informed of the reason for their arrest. The accused also has the right to adequate counsel, even if they cannot afford an attorney, and the right to a prompt arraignment and a speedy and public trial before an impartial jury selected from a cross section of the community.

In *Miranda v. Arizona* (1966), the Supreme Court held that those arrested, before questioning by law enforcement personnel, must be informed of the right to remain silent and the right to counsel. The exclusionary rule forbids the admission in court of illegally obtained evidence.

Another major challenge concerns the extent to which we must forfeit civil liberties to control terrorism. Recent revelations of surveillance by the National Security Agency have fueled this debate.

Test Yourself

1. Since 1925, the Supreme Court, under the Fourteenth Amendment's due process clause, has gradually extended the Bill of Rights to cover state governments by using:
   a. incorporation theory.
   b. the establishment clause.
   c. the supremacy principle.

2. Only in this century have state governments been required to observe the right:
   a. to a writ of *habeas corpus*.
   b. to privacy.
   c. to bear arms.

3. The Supreme Court has held that any law prohibiting the teaching of evolution:
   a. violates the establishment clause because it imposes religious beliefs on students.
   b. violates the free exercise clause of the First Amendment because it bars the beliefs of religious persons.
   c. violates both the establishment clause and the free exercise clause.

4. Religious displays on public property are:
   a. always acceptable.
   b. never acceptable.
   c. acceptable as part of a broader display that contains nonreligious elements.

5. Endorsements of candidates by a minister, priest, or rabbi:
   a. are protected under the First Amendment.
   b. could threaten a congregation's tax-exempt status, but the law is not enforced.
   c. automatically result in a loss of tax-exempt status by the congregation.

6. Clothing, gestures, and other forms of expressive conduct may be considered to be:
   a. symbolic speech.
   b. subversive speech.
   c. unprotected by the First Amendment.

7. If you utter a false statement that harms the good reputation of another, it is called slander, and such expression is:
   a. always protected under the First Amendment.
   b. unprotected speech and a potential basis for a lawsuit.
   c. prosecuted as a felony in most states.

8. The right to privacy:
   a. is explicitly guaranteed by the original text of the Constitution.
   b. is explicitly guaranteed by the Fifth Amendment to the Constitution.
   c. has been inferred from other rights by the Supreme Court.

9. The Supreme Court overturned *Roe v. Wade* in:
   a. *In re Quinlan*.
   b. *Dobbs v. Jackson Women's Health Organization*.
   c. *Planned Parenthood v. Casey*.

10. The Supreme Court has ruled that the practice of assisted suicide is:
    a. constitutional.
    b. unconstitutional.
    c. an issue for the states to decide.

11. Illegally seized evidence is not admissible at trial because of the:
    a. exclusionary rule.
    b. *Miranda* rule.
    c. writ of *habeas corpus*.

12. A former head of the National Security Agency (NSA) has said that:
    a. the United States does not tap the phones of allied leaders.
    b. NSA surveillance should be exempt from judicial oversight.
    c. the Fourth Amendment, which prohibits unreasonable searches, "is not an international treaty."

Essay Questions

1. The courts have never held that the provision of military chaplains by the armed forces is unconstitutional, despite the fact that chaplains are religious leaders who are employed by and under the authority of the U.S. government. What arguments might the courts use to defend the military chaplain system?

2. In a surprisingly large number of cases, arrested individuals do not choose to exercise their right to remain silent. Why might persons not exercise their *Miranda* rights?

Answers to multiple-choice questions: 1. a, 2. c, 3. a, 4. c, 5. b, 6. a, 7. b, 8. c, 9. b, 10. c, 11. a, 12. c.

5 Civil Rights

Samuel Corum/Getty Images News/Getty Images

Protesters gather in front of the White House on June 3, 2020, to demand justice following George Floyd's death. Floyd, a Black man, was killed by Minneapolis police on May 25. ▶ **What does it mean that so many of the protesters were white?**

The five **Learning Outcomes (LOs)** below are designed to help improve your understanding of this chapter. After reading this chapter, you should be able to:

≫ **LO 5-1** Summarize the historical experience of African Americans.

≫ **LO 5-2** Define the different levels of scrutiny used by the Supreme Court in civil rights cases.

≫ **LO 5-3** Discuss the history and current status of Latinos and Native Americans.

≫ **LO 5-4** Contrast the goals of the women's suffrage movement with the goals of modern feminism.

≫ **LO 5-5** Discuss how federal legislation and public opinion about LGBTQ+ rights have evolved in recent years.

Check your understanding of the material with the Test Yourself section at the end of the chapter.

E quality is at the heart of the concept of civil rights. Generally, the term **civil rights** refers to the rights of all Americans to equal protection under the law, as provided by the Fourteenth Amendment to the Constitution. Although the terms civil rights and civil liberties are sometimes used interchangeably, scholars make a distinction between the two. Civil liberties are basically limitations on government. They specify what the government cannot do. Civil rights, in contrast, specify what the government must do to ensure equal protection and freedom from discrimination.

The history of civil rights in America is the story of the struggle of various groups to be free from discriminatory treatment. In this chapter, we look at several movements that

Civil Rights
Generally, all rights rooted in the Fourteenth Amendment's guarantee of equal protection under the law.

had significant consequences for civil rights in America: the civil rights movement of the 1950s and 1960s, the women's movement, and the movement to gain equal rights for LGBTQ+ people. Each of these movements resulted in legislation and court rulings that secured important basic rights for all Americans.

Note that most underrepresented groups in this nation have suffered—and some continue to suffer—from discrimination. These include such groups as Asian Americans, Muslim Americans, older Americans, and persons with disabilities. The fact that some groups are not singled out for special attention in the following pages should not be construed to mean that their struggle for equality is any less significant than the struggles of those groups that we do discuss.

One of the most obvious consequences of discrimination is high rates of poverty, as you can see in Figure 5.1 later in this chapter.

The African American Experience and the Civil Rights Movement

» **LO 5-1:** Summarize the historical experience of African Americans.

Before 1863, the Constitution protected slavery and made equality impossible in the sense in which we use the word today. The system of slavery, however, did not survive the American Civil War (1861–65).

Ending Servitude

With the emancipation of the enslaved people by President Lincoln's Emancipation Proclamation in 1863 and the passage of the Thirteenth, Fourteenth, and Fifteenth Amendments during the Reconstruction period (1865–77) following the Civil War, constitutional inequality was ended. (Note, though, that because women could not vote until the passage of the Nineteenth Amendment in 1920, full equality for all American citizens was not really complete.)

Constitutional Amendments. The Thirteenth Amendment (1865) states that neither slavery nor involuntary servitude shall exist within the United States. The Fourteenth Amendment (1868) tells us that all persons born or naturalized in the United States are citizens of the United States. It states, furthermore, that "[n]o State shall make or enforce any law which shall abridge the privileges or immunities of citizens of the United States; nor shall any State deprive any person of life, liberty, or property, without due process of law; nor deny to any person within its jurisdiction the equal protection of the laws." Note the use of the terms citizen and person in this amendment. Citizens have political rights, such as the right to vote and run for political office. Citizens also have certain privileges or immunities. All persons, however, including noncitizen immigrants, have a right to due process of law and equal protection under the law.

Finally, the Fifteenth Amendment (1870) reads as follows: "The right of citizens of the United States to vote shall not be denied or abridged by the United States or by any State on account of race, color, or previous condition of servitude." The right to vote is also known as **suffrage**, or the franchise. Another term is enfranchisement, which means "granting the right to vote."

The Civil Rights Acts of 1865 to 1875. From 1865 to 1875, Congress passed a series of civil rights acts to enforce the Thirteenth, Fourteenth, and Fifteenth Amendments. The

Image 5.1 Harriet Tubman was a leader of the Underground Railroad that smuggled enslaved persons to freedom. During the Civil War, she served as a nurse, spy, and scout for the Union army. ► How did slavery come to an end?

Library of Congress Prints and Photographs Division Washington, D.C. [LC-USZ62-7816]

Suffrage
The right to vote; the franchise.

Civil Rights Act of 1866 implemented the extension of citizenship to anyone born in the United States and gave African Americans full equality under the law. The Enforcement Act of 1870 set out specific criminal penalties for interfering with the right to vote as protected by the Fifteenth Amendment and by the Civil Rights Act of 1866.

Equally important was the Civil Rights Act of 1872, known as the Anti–Ku Klux Klan Act. This act made it a federal crime for anyone to use law or custom to deprive an individual of rights, privileges, and immunities secured by the Constitution or by any federal law. The Second Civil Rights Act, passed in 1875, declared that everyone is entitled to full and equal enjoyment of public accommodations, theaters, and other places of public amusement, and it imposed penalties on violators.

The Ineffectiveness of the Early Civil Rights Laws

The civil rights acts ultimately did little to secure equality for African Americans. Both the *Civil Rights Cases* and the case of *Plessy v. Ferguson* (discussed next) effectively nullified these acts. Additionally, various barriers were erected that prevented African Americans from exercising their right to vote.

The *Civil Rights Cases*. The United States Supreme Court invalidated the 1875 Second Civil Rights Act when it held, in the *Civil Rights Cases* of 1883, that the enforcement clause of the Fourteenth Amendment (which states that "[n]o State shall make or enforce any law which shall abridge the privileges or immunities of citizens") was limited to correcting official actions taken by states. Thus, the discriminatory acts of private citizens were not illegal. ("Individual invasion of individual rights is not the subject matter of the Amendment.")[1]

The 1883 Supreme Court decision met with widespread approval by white people throughout most of the United States. Twenty years after the Civil War, the white majority was all too willing to forget about the Civil War amendments to the Constitution and the civil rights legislation of the 1860s and 1870s. The other civil rights laws that the Court did not specifically invalidate became dead letters in the statute books, although they were never officially repealed by Congress.

***Plessy v. Ferguson*: Separate but Equal.** A key decision during this period concerned Homer Plessy, who was one-eighth African American. In 1892, he boarded a train in New Orleans. The conductor made him leave the car, which was restricted to white riders, and directed him to a car for nonwhites. At that time, Louisiana had a statute providing for separate railway cars for white people and African Americans.

Plessy went to court, claiming that such a statute was contrary to the Fourteenth Amendment's equal protection clause. In 1896, the Supreme Court rejected Plessy's contention in *Plessy v. Ferguson*.[2] The Court concluded that the Fourteenth Amendment "could not have been intended to abolish distinctions based upon color, or to enforce social … equality." The Court stated that segregation alone did not violate the Constitution: "Laws permitting, and even requiring, their separation in places where they are liable to be brought into contact do not necessarily imply the inferiority of either race to the other." So was born the **separate-but-equal doctrine**.

Plessy v. Ferguson became the judicial cornerstone of racial discrimination throughout the United States. The result was a system of racial segregation, particularly in the South,

Separate-But-Equal Doctrine
The doctrine holding that separate-but-equal facilities do not violate the equal protection clause of the Fourteenth Amendment to the U.S. Constitution.

---

1. 109 U.S. 3 (1883).
2. 163 U.S. 537 (1896).

supported by state and local "Jim Crow" laws. (Jim Crow was an insulting term for African Americans derived from a song-and-dance show.) These laws required separate drinking fountains; separate seats in theaters, restaurants, and hotels; separate public toilets; and separate waiting rooms for the two races. "Separate" was indeed the rule, but "equal" was never enforced, nor was it a reality.

Voting Barriers.   The brief voting enfranchisement of African Americans ended after 1877, when the federal troops that occupied the South during the Reconstruction era were withdrawn. White supremacist politicians regained control of state governments and, using everything except race as a formal criterion, passed laws that effectively deprived African Americans of the right to vote. By using the ruse that political parties were private entities, the Democratic Party managed to keep African American voters from its primaries. The **white primary** was upheld by the Supreme Court until 1944, when the Court ruled it a violation of the Fifteenth Amendment.[3]

Another barrier to African American voting was the **grandfather clause**, which restricted voting to those who could prove that their ancestors had voted before 1867. A **poll tax** required the payment of a fee to vote. Thus, African Americans with low incomes—as well as low-income white people—who could not afford to pay the tax were excluded from voting. Not until the Twenty-fourth Amendment to the Constitution was ratified in 1964 was the poll tax eliminated as a precondition to voting. **Literacy tests** were also used to deny the vote to African Americans. Such tests asked potential voters to read, recite, or interpret complicated texts, such as a section of the state constitution, to the satisfaction of local registrars—who were, of course, almost never satisfied with the responses of African Americans.

Extralegal Methods of Enforcing White Supremacy.   The second-class status of African Americans was also a matter of social custom, especially in the South. In their interactions with southern white people, African Americans were expected to observe an informal but detailed code of behavior that confirmed their inferiority. The code was backed up by the practice of lynching—mob action to murder an accused individual, usually by hanging and sometimes accompanied by torture. Of course, lynching was illegal, but southern authorities rarely prosecuted these cases, and white juries would not convict.

The End of the Separate-but-Equal Doctrine

As early as the 1930s, several court rulings began to chip away at the separate-but-equal doctrine. The Supreme Court did not explicitly overturn *Plessy v. Ferguson* until 1954, however, when it issued one of the most famous judicial decisions in U.S. history.

In 1951, Oliver Brown decided that his eight-year-old daughter, Linda Carol Brown, should not have to go to an all-nonwhite elementary school twenty-one blocks from her home, when there was a white school only seven blocks away. The National Association for the Advancement of Colored People (NAACP), formed in 1909, decided to support Oliver Brown.[4] The outcome would have a monumental impact on American society.

Brown v. Board of Education of Topeka.   The 1954 unanimous decision of the Supreme Court in *Brown v. Board of Education of Topeka* established that the segregation of races in the public schools violated the equal protection clause of the Fourteenth Amendment.[5]

White Primary
A state primary election that restricted voting to white people only. Outlawed by the Supreme Court in 1944.

Grandfather Clause
A device used by southern states to disenfranchise African Americans. It restricted voting to those whose ancestors had voted before 1867.

Poll Tax
A special tax that had to be paid as a qualification for voting. The Twenty-fourth Amendment to the Constitution outlawed the poll tax in national elections, and in 1966, the Supreme Court declared it unconstitutional in state elections as well.

Literacy Tests
A test administered as a precondition for voting, often used to prevent African Americans from exercising their right to vote.

---

3. *Smith v. Allwright*, 321 U.S. 649 (1944).
4. *NAACP* is pronounced "N-double A-C-P."
5. 347 U.S. 483 (1954).

Chief Justice Earl Warren said that separation implied inferiority, whereas the majority opinion in *Plessy v. Ferguson* had said the opposite.

The following year, in *Brown v. Board of Education* (sometimes called the second *Brown* decision), the Court declared that the lower courts needed to ensure that African Americans would be admitted to schools on a nondiscriminatory basis "with all deliberate speed."[6]

Reactions to School Integration. The white South did not let the Supreme Court ruling go unchallenged. Governor Orval Faubus of Arkansas used the state's National Guard to block the integration of Central High School in Little Rock in September 1957. President Dwight Eisenhower had to federalize the Arkansas National Guard and send in the Army's 101st Airborne Division to quell violent resistance. Central High became integrated.

Universities in the South remained segregated. When James Meredith, an African American student, attempted to enroll at the University of Mississippi in 1962, violence flared as it had in Little Rock. The riot by white people opposed to integration was so intense that President John Kennedy was forced to send in thirty thousand U.S. combat troops. Ultimately, peace was restored, and Meredith began attending classes.

De Jure and De Facto Segregation

The kind of segregation faced by Linda Carol Brown and James Meredith is called **de jure segregation**, because it is the result of discriminatory laws or government actions. (*De jure* is Latin for "by law.") A second kind of public school segregation was common in many northern communities—**de facto segregation**. This term refers to segregation that is not due to an explicit law but results from other causes, such as residential patterns. Neighborhoods inhabited almost entirely by African Americans naturally led to *de facto* segregation of the public schools.

Discrimination was still a cause of the problem, however. In many communities, landlords would only rent to African Americans in specific districts, and realtors would not allow them to view houses for sale outside of these zones. In other words, nongovernmental discrimination confined African Americans to all-Black districts, which became known as ghettos.[7]

The Civil Rights Movement

The *Brown* decisions applied only to public schools. Not much else in the structure of existing segregation was affected. In December 1955, an African American woman, Rosa Parks, boarded a public bus in Montgomery, Alabama. When the bus became crowded, Parks was asked to move to the rear of the bus, the "colored" section. She refused and was arrested. For an entire year, African Americans boycotted the Montgomery bus system. The protest was headed by a young Baptist minister, Dr. Martin Luther King, Jr. In 1956, a federal

Carl Iwasaki/The LIFE Images Collection/Getty Images

Image 5.2 Sisters Linda and Terry Lynn Brown sit on a fence outside of their racially segregated elementary school in Topeka, Kansas, in 1953. At that time, the Supreme Court had yet to decide *Brown v. Board of Education*, the landmark civil rights case that banned segregation in public schools.
▶ What were the immediate results of this decision?

De Jure Segregation
Racial segregation that occurs because of laws or administrative decisions by public agencies.

De Facto Segregation
Racial segregation that occurs because of patterns of racial residence and similar social conditions.

---

6. 349 U.S. 294 (1955).
7. Ghetto was originally the name of a district in Venice, Italy, in which Venetian Jews were required to live. Note that the U.S. government often supported residential segregation. See Richard Rothstein, *The Color of Law: A Forgotten History of How Our Government Segregated America* (New York: Liveright, 2017).

district court issued an injunction prohibiting the segregation of buses in Montgomery. The era of civil rights protests had begun.

King's Philosophy of Nonviolence. In the following year, 1957, King formed the Southern Christian Leadership Conference (SCLC). King advocated nonviolent **civil disobedience** as a means to achieve racial justice. The SCLC used tactics such as demonstrations and marches, as well as nonviolent, public disobedience of unjust laws. King's followers successfully used these methods to gain wider public acceptance of their cause.

For the next decade, African Americans and sympathetic white Americans engaged in sit-ins, freedom rides, and freedom marches. In the beginning, such demonstrations were often met with violence, and the contrasting image of nonviolent African Americans and violent, hostile white people created strong public support for the civil rights movement.

The March on Washington. In August 1963, African American leaders A. Philip Randolph and Bayard Rustin organized the massive March on Washington for Jobs and Freedom. Before nearly a quarter-million white and African American spectators and millions watching on television, Martin Luther King told the world: "I have a dream that my four little children will one day live in a nation where they will not be judged by the color of their skin but by the content of their character."

Modern Civil Rights Legislation

Attacks on demonstrators across the country using police dogs, cattle prods, high-pressure water hoses, beatings, and bombings—plus the March on Washington—all led to an environment in which Congress felt compelled to act on behalf of African Americans. The second era of civil rights acts, sometimes referred to as the second Reconstruction period, was under way.

The Civil Rights Act of 1964. The Civil Rights Act of 1964, the most far-reaching bill on civil rights in modern times, banned discrimination on the basis of race, color, religion, gender, or national origin. The act's major provisions were as follows:

- It outlawed arbitrary discrimination in voter registration.
- It barred discrimination in public accommodations, such as hotels and restaurants, that have operations that affect interstate commerce.
- It authorized the federal government to sue to desegregate public schools and facilities.
- It expanded the power of the Civil Rights Commission, which had been created in 1957, and extended its life.
- It provided for the withholding of federal funds from programs administered in a discriminatory manner.
- It established the right to equality of opportunity in employment.

Title VII of the Civil Rights Act of 1964 is the cornerstone of employment-discrimination law. It prohibits discrimination in employment based on race, color, religion, gender, or national origin. (In 2020, the Supreme Court extended this ban to gender identity.) Under Title VII, executive orders were issued that banned employment discrimination by firms that received federal funding. The 1964 Civil Rights Act created the Equal Employment Opportunity Commission (EEOC) to administer Title VII. It was not until 1972, however, that Congress gave the EEOC the right to sue employers, unions, and employment agencies. Litigation then became an important EEOC activity.

Civil Disobedience
A nonviolent, public refusal to obey allegedly unjust laws.

The Voting Rights Act of 1965. As late as 1960, only 29 percent of African Americans of voting age were registered in the southern states, in stark contrast to 61 percent of white people. The Voting Rights Act of 1965 addressed this issue. The act had two major provisions. The first outlawed discriminatory voter-registration tests. The second authorized federal registration of voters and federally administered voting procedures in any political subdivision or state that discriminated electorally against a particular group.

The act targeted counties, mostly in the South, in which fewer than 50 percent of the eligible population were registered to vote. Federal voter registrars were sent to those areas to register African Americans who had been kept from voting by local registrars. Within one week after the act was passed, forty-five federal examiners were sent to the South. A massive voter-registration drive covered the region.

The Civil Rights Act of 1968 and Other Housing Reform Legislation. The Civil Rights Act of 1968 banned discrimination in most housing and provided penalties for those attempting to interfere with individual civil rights (giving protection to civil rights workers, among others). Subsequent legislation added enforcement provisions to the federal government's rules against discriminatory mortgage-lending practices.

Consequences of Civil Rights Legislation. As a result of the Voting Rights Act of 1965 and its amendments, and the large-scale voter-registration drives in the South, the number of African Americans registered to vote climbed dramatically. By 1980, 55.8 percent of African

AFP/Stringer/Getty Images

Image 5.3 Martin Luther King, Jr.'s, speech at the Washington Monument in 1963 was watched by millions of Americans on television. ▶ What were his most famous words?

Americans of voting age in the South were registered. In recent national elections, turnout by African American voters has come very close to the white turnout. In 2008, with an African American on the presidential ballot, African American turnout exceeded that of white people for the first time in history.[8] Black voter turnout for the 2020 presidential election was 58.7 percent. White voter turnout was 63.7 percent.

Political Participation by African Americans. Today, there are more than ten thousand African American elected officials in the United States. After the 2022 elections, the U.S. Congress included at least sixty-three African Americans. The movement of African American citizens into high elected office has been sure, if exceedingly slow. Notably, recent polling data show that most Americans do not consider race a significant factor in choosing a president. In 1958, when a Gallup poll first asked whether respondents would be willing to vote for an African American as president, only 38 percent of the public said yes. By 2008, this number had reached 94 percent.

Of course, Barack Obama, first elected president in 2008 on the Democratic ticket, is African American. In addition, Obama's reelection in 2012 confirmed his place in history.

Another historical event occurred eight years later when Senator Kamala Harris (D-CA) became the first woman of color to be elected as vice president. Democratic presidential candidate Joe Biden asked her to be his running mate in August 2020. Harris had aggressively sparred with Biden in the Democratic primary debates in 2019, so many were surprised at Biden's decision. In early 2022, Biden nominated the first Black female justice, Ketanji Brown Jackson, to the Supreme Court. The Senate easily confirmed her.

Lingering Social and Economic Disparities. Social and economic disparities between white people, Black people, and other racial and ethnic minorities persist. The median household wealth for Black families in 2019 was only $24,100, while median white family wealth was $189,100. For middle-class families, wealth consists mostly of home equity, so the drastic disparity between Black and white reflects the difficulties Black people have faced difficulties establishing themselves in the housing market. The collapse in the housing market in 2008–11 also hit households of people of color much harder than white ones. Black and Latino households lost more than half of their net assets. Consider also that the poverty rate for non-Latino whites in 2019 was 7.3 percent, compared with 18.8 percent for African Americans and 15.7 percent for Latinos, as shown in Figure 5.1.

Finally, race consciousness continues to divide Black and white Americans. Whether we are talking about media stereotyping, racial profiling, or academic achievement, the Black experience is different from the white one. One of the most troubling contrasts between the races is their differing experiences with the criminal justice system. African Americans, especially men, are far more likely to be arrested and imprisoned than white people, as you can see in Figure 5.2.

---

8. A widely reported study claimed that African American turnout did not quite match that of white turnout, but this conclusion was based on an overestimate of the number of African Americans eligible to vote.

Figure 5.1   Persons in Poverty in the United States by Race and Hispanic Origin

▶ Why are children more likely to be poor?

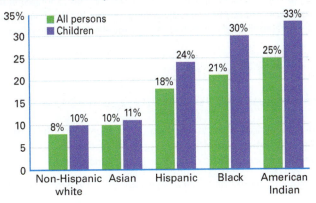

Source: Bureau of the Census, "Historical Poverty Tables: People and Families—1959 to 2018" and authors' calculations.

It is true that African Americans, young men especially, are disproportionately involved in violent crime. But they are also far more likely than white people to be arrested and convicted even when they do not commit a particular offense. About the same percentage of both Black and white people admit to using illegal drugs. Yet African Americans are three times more

Figure 5.2   Imprisonment Rates per 100,000 Persons for Selected U.S. Population Groups

▶ Why might the government want to report lower numbers?

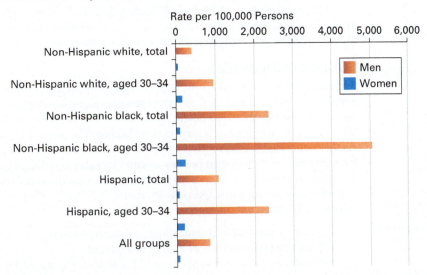

Source: Jennifer Bronson and E. Ann Carson, "Prisoners in 2017," *Bureau of Justice Statistics Bulletin*, U.S. Department of Justice (2019).

Note: The imprisonment rate measures only persons convicted of a crime and serving a sentence of at least one year. Through 2009, the government used the internationally recognized incarceration rate, which measures all persons held in custody, regardless of conviction status or period of confinement. Inevitably, the imprisonment rate yields smaller numbers—the total U.S. imprisonment rate was 440 per 100,000 persons in 2017, while the incarceration rate was 669.

likely than white people to be arrested on drug charges, and they wind up in prison far more frequently. Black youth in some urban neighborhoods report that they are stopped by police—for no particular reason—as often as once a month. Despite these long-standing problems, there is some good news. In recent years, the conviction rate for Black and Latino youth has declined sharply. (In contrast, the conviction rate for middle-aged white people has gone up.)

Civil Rights and the Courts

>> **LO 5-2:** Define the different levels of scrutiny used by the Supreme Court in civil rights cases.

The Fourteenth Amendment to the U.S. Constitution, adopted in 1869 following the Civil War, is the main constitutional basis for civil rights legislation and court decisions. Earlier we discussed the due process clause of the Fourteenth Amendment:

> *"No State shall . . . deprive any person of life, liberty, or property, without due process of law . . . ."*

This language mirrors that of the Fifth Amendment, which binds the federal government:

> *"No person shall . . . be deprived of life, liberty, or property, without due process of law . . . ."*

The due process clause was crucial to extending the civil liberties contained in the Bill of Rights to cover the actions of the individual states. The courts have made use of this clause in civil rights cases as well.

As a guarantee of civil rights, however, the next clause in the Fourteenth Amendment is at least as important:

> *". . . nor deny to any person within its jurisdiction the equal protection of the laws."*

The principal effect of *Plessy v. Ferguson*, described earlier, was to make this equal protection clause almost a dead letter in cases involving discrimination against individuals. Today, in contrast, the equal protection clause serves as the foundation of a sizable body of law.

Standards for Judicial Review

Strict Scrutiny
A judicial standard for assessing the constitutionality of a law or government action when the law or action threatens to interfere with a fundamental right or potentially discriminates against members of a suspect classification.

Suspect Classification
A classification, such as race, religion, or national origin, that triggers strict scrutiny by the courts when a law or government action potentially discriminates against members of the class.

Federal courts use three standards when engaging in judicial review of laws or executive actions. The most exacting of these, **strict scrutiny**, is employed when fundamental rights are at stake, such as those guaranteed by the Bill of Rights. Strict scrutiny also comes into play when laws are based on a **suspect classification**. The original suspect class was race. As these terms suggest, the courts are suspicious of, and will strictly scrutinize, any attempt by a government body to treat persons of different races in different ways. The Supreme Court has used this standard as a major tool in outlawing racial discrimination. Religion and national origin are also suspect classifications. To be acceptable under the strict scrutiny standard, a law must pass three tests:

- It must be justified by a compelling government interest.
- It must be narrowly tailored to meet that interest.
- It must be the least restrictive means of accomplishing the goal in question.

Intermediate, or Exacting, Scrutiny. The women's movement that arose in the 1960s led to suits claiming that various laws and government actions improperly discriminated against women. The courts were often sympathetic to such arguments. Still, the Supreme Court was reluctant to define gender as a suspect classification equivalent to race. The Court therefore established a new standard—**intermediate, or exacting, scrutiny**. To pass the intermediate scrutiny test, a law or government action "must further an important government interest by means that are substantially related to that interest." This standard is easier to meet than the standard established for strict scrutiny. In later years, the Court tightened the test by requiring an "exceedingly persuasive justification" for gender-based discrimination.

Intermediate, or Exacting, Scrutiny
A judicial standard used to determine whether a law or government action unconstitutionally discriminates against women.

Rational Basis Review. In cases in which neither strict scrutiny nor intermediate scrutiny are appropriate, the courts use **rational basis review** as a standard. This test requires that an action or law be "rationally related" to a "legitimate government interest." The legitimate interest does not have to be an interest cited by the government. If the courts can imagine a possible legitimate interest, the law stands. Rational basis review does not involve assessing the usefulness of laws. As Justice Thurgood Marshall observed on several occasions, "The Constitution does not prohibit legislatures from enacting stupid laws."[9] If a court can find no legitimate interest at all, however, a law or action can fail even this test. The courts have used rational basis review to strike down laws that discriminate against LGBTQ+ persons.

Rational Basis Review
A judicial standard for assessing a law or government action that is employed when neither strict nor intermediate scrutiny apply.

The Supreme Court Addresses Affirmative Action

As noted earlier in this chapter, the Civil Rights Act of 1964 prohibited discrimination against any person on the basis of race, color, national origin, religion, or gender. The act also established the right to equal opportunity in employment. A basic problem remained, however: underrepresented groups and women, because of past discrimination, often lacked the education and skills to compete effectively in the marketplace. In 1965, the federal government attempted to remedy this problem by implementing the concept of affirmative action. **Affirmative action** policies attempt to "level the playing field" by giving special preferences in educational admissions and employment decisions to groups that have been discriminated against in the past.

Affirmative Action
A policy in educational admissions or job hiring that gives special attention or compensatory treatment to traditionally disadvantaged groups in an effort to overcome present effects of past discrimination.

Implementing Affirmative Action. In 1965, President Lyndon Johnson issued an executive order mandating affirmative action policies to remedy the effects of past discrimination. All government agencies, including those of state and local governments, were required to implement such policies. Additionally, affirmative action requirements were imposed on companies that sell goods or services to the federal government and on institutions that receive federal funds, such as universities. Affirmative action policies were also required whenever an employer had been ordered to develop such a plan by a court or by the Equal Employment Opportunity Commission because of evidence of past discrimination. Finally, labor unions that had been found to discriminate against women or people of color in the past were required to establish and follow affirmative action plans.

Affirmative action programs have been controversial because they allegedly result in discrimination against "majority" groups, such as white males (or discrimination against other underrepresented groups that may not be given preferential treatment under a particular affirmative action program). At issue in the current debate over affirmative action programs is whether such programs, because of their discriminatory nature, violate the equal protection clause of the Fourteenth Amendment to the Constitution.

The *Bakke* Case. The first Supreme Court case addressing the constitutionality of affirmative action examined a program at the University of California, Davis. Allan Bakke, a white student who had been turned down for medical school at the Davis campus, discovered that

---

9. As quoted in Justice John Paul Stevens's concurrence to *New York State Board of Elections v. Lopez Torres*, 552 U.S. 196 (2008).

Reverse Discrimination
Discrimination against individuals who are not members of an underrepresented group.

his academic record was better than those of some of the non-majority applicants who had been admitted to the program. He sued the University of California, alleging **reverse discrimination**. The UC Davis School of Medicine had held sixteen places out of one hundred for educationally "disadvantaged students" each year, and administrators admitted to using race as a criterion for admission for these particular slots.

In 1978, the Supreme Court handed down its decision in *Regents of the University of California v. Bakke*.[10] The Court did not rule against affirmative action programs. Rather, it held that Bakke had to be admitted to the UC Davis School of Medicine because its admissions policy had used race as the sole criterion for the sixteen "minority" positions. Justice Lewis Powell, speaking for the Court, indicated that while race can be considered "as a factor" among others in admissions (and presumably hiring) decisions, race cannot be the sole factor. So affirmative action programs, but not specific quota systems, were upheld as constitutional.

Additional Limits on Affirmative Action. A number of cases decided during the 1980s and 1990s placed further limits on affirmative action programs. In a landmark decision in 1995, *Adarand Constructors, Inc. v. Peña*, the Supreme Court held that any federal, state, or local affirmative action program that uses racial or ethnic classifications as the basis for making decisions is subject to the strict scrutiny standard.[11] The Court's opinion in *Adarand* means that an affirmative action program cannot make use of quotas or preferences for unqualified persons. In addition, once the program has succeeded in achieving the purpose it was tailored to meet, the program must be changed or dropped.

In 2003, in two cases involving the University of Michigan, the Supreme Court indicated that limited affirmative action programs continued to be acceptable and that diversity was a legitimate goal. The Court struck down the affirmative action plan used for undergraduate admissions at the university, which automatically awarded a substantial number of points to applicants based on non-majority status.[12] At the same time, it approved the admissions plan used by the law school, which took race into consideration as part of a complete examination of each applicant's background.[13]

The End of Affirmative Action? Despite the position taken by the Supreme Court in the University of Michigan Law School case, affirmative action is subject to serious threats. In 2007, the Supreme Court tightened the guidelines for permissible affirmative action programs. In rejecting school integration plans in Seattle, Washington, and Louisville, Kentucky, the Court found that race could not be used as a "tiebreaker" when granting admission to a school.[14] Many observers thought that the Supreme Court might end affirmative action programs altogether in *Fisher v. University of Texas*, two cases with the same name heard in 2013 and 2016. In deciding the *Fisher* cases, however, the Court made no significant alterations to the law.[15]

Affirmative action may face a greater danger from the states. Eight states have now banned state-level affirmative action programs. In 2014, the Supreme

Jim West/Alamy Stock Photo

Image 5.4 Demonstrators march in Detroit, Michigan, in support of affirmative action programs at the state's universities. The United States Supreme Court later ruled that the state had the power to ban such programs.
► How does the government define "affirmative action"?

10. 438 U.S. 265 (1978).
11. 515 U.S. 200 (1995).
12. *Gratz v. Bollinger*, 539 U.S. 244 (2003).
13. *Grutter v. Bollinger*, 539 U.S. 306 (2003).
14. *Parents Involved in Community Schools v. Seattle School District No. 1*, 551 U.S. 701 (2007).
15. 570 U.S. 297 (2013) and 579 U.S. 365, 136 S.Ct. 2198 (2016).

Court ruled in favor of Michigan's affirmative action ban, effectively upholding the law in six other states.[16]

Experiences of Other Underrepresented Groups

» LO 5-3: Discuss the history and current status of Latinos and Native Americans.

In a brief textbook edition such as this one, it is not possible to describe the experiences of all groups of Americans who have had to struggle for civil rights. Still, two groups deserve mention: Latinos are now the nation's largest ethnic minority by population. Native Americans are notable for their unusual and troubled history, and of course, because they were here first.

Latinos and the Immigration Issue

The law recognizes that Latinos have been subjected to many of the same forms of ill treatment as African Americans. Therefore, Latinos are usually grouped with African Americans and Native Americans in laws and programs that seek to protect ethnic and racial minorities from discrimination or to address the results of past discrimination.

Immigration. The most striking characteristic of Latinos is that many of them are relatively recent immigrants. A century ago, most immigrants to the United States came from Europe. Today, most come from Latin America and Asia. At times, immigrants from Asian nations have outnumbered Latino immigrants. This change is largely due to a drop in the number of Latinos rather than an increase in the number of Asians. Table 5.1 shows the leading countries of origin for the foreign-born population in the United States.

Table 5.1	**Top Ten Countries of Origin for the Foreign-Born U.S. Population**

Hispanic countries are shown in red. ▶ Why might citizens of Mexico be especially likely to come to the United States?

Mexico	11,270,000
India	2,611,000
China (mainland)	2,217,000
Philippines	2,008,000
El Salvador	1,402,000
Vietnam	1,343,000
Cuba	1,312,000
Dominican Republic	1,163,000
Korea (North included)	1,063,000
Guatemala	959,000
ALL COUNTRIES	44,292,000

Figures are for 2017.

Source: Migration Policy Institute, "Largest U.S. Immigrant Groups over Time, 1960-Present" [www.migrationpolicy.org/programs/data-hub/charts/largest-immigrant-groups-over-time].

16. *Schuette v. Coalition to Defend Affirmative Action*, 572 U.S. 291 (2014).

The Changing Face of America. As a result of immigration, the ethnic makeup of the United States is changing. Yet immigration is not the only factor contributing to changes in the American ethnic mosaic. Another factor is ethnic differences in the total fertility rate. This rate measures the average number of children that women in a given group are expected to have over the course of a lifetime. A rate of 2.1 is the "long-term replacement rate." In other words, if a nation or group maintains a rate of 2.1, its population will eventually stabilize. This can take many years, however. On average, U.S. Latinos have a higher total fertility rate than non-Latinos, which adds to their future numbers.

Unauthorized Immigration. Unauthorized immigration—to use the language of the Department of Homeland Security—has been a major national issue for a long time. Naturally, the unauthorized population is hard to count. Some research centers use a 10-12 million number for unauthorized immigrants. Other researchers have claimed that the unauthorized population in the U.S. is closer to 20 million.[17]

We list the top ten countries of birth for unauthorized immigrants in the United States in Table 5.2.

Unauthorized immigrants typically come to the United States to work. Before the Immigration Reform and Control Act of 1986, there was no law against hiring foreign citizens who lacked proper papers. Until recently, laws penalizing employers were infrequently enforced.

Unauthorized immigrants often live in mixed households, in which one or more members of a family have lawful resident status, but others do not. Often, the parents in a family are unauthorized, while the children, who were born in the United States, possess American

Table 5.2	**Top Ten Countries of Birth for Unauthorized Immigrants**

Of necessity, these figures are rough estimates. Latino countries are shown in red. ▶ **Given high rates of poverty in Africa, why don't more Africans come to the United States?**

Mexico	4,950,000
El Salvador	750,000
Guatemala	600,000
India	525,000
Honduras	400,000
China (mainland)	375,000
Dominican Republic	240,000
Brazil	160,000
Philippines	160,000
Korea	150,000
ALL COUNTRIES	10,500,000

Numbers are for 2017.
Source: Jeffrey S. Passel and D'Vera Cohn, "Mexicans Decline to Less Than Half the U.S. Unauthorized Immigrant Population for the First Time," Pew Research Center [www.pewresearch.org/fact-tank/2019/06/12/us-unauthorized-immigrant-population-2017].

17. Mohammad M. Fazel-Zarandi, Jonathan S. Feinstein, Edward H. Kaplan, "The Number of Undocumented Immigrants in the United States: Estimates Based on Demographic Modeling with Data from 1990 to 2016," https://doi.org/10.1371/journal.pone.0201193, September 21, 2018.

citizenship. Mixed families mean that deporting unauthorized immigrants may either break up a family or force one or more American citizens into exile.

In some circumstances, though, immigrants actually choose to separate their families. Beginning in 2014, large numbers of unaccompanied children from violence-torn Central American countries turned themselves in to U.S. authorities at the Mexican border. Because these children claimed the internationally recognized right of asylum, they could not be immediately deported.

Exemptions From Deportation. Contrary to the wishes of many of his supporters, President Obama tightened the enforcement of immigration laws and deported more individuals than any previous president. In June 2012, however, Obama issued an executive order—Deferred Action for Childhood Arrivals (DACA)—providing relief to many young immigrants. Most unauthorized immigrants who came to the United States under the age of sixteen could apply for an indefinite deportation deferral and obtain work permits. These persons are popularly known as "DREAMers," after earlier legislation called the DREAM Act that failed. Many could remember no other country than the United States.

In November 2014, Obama issued another executive order extending protection to the parents of children who were citizens or legal residents. A circuit court ruled against this second order. In June 2016, the Supreme Court upheld the circuit court's decision in a four-to-four ruling that did not establish a precedent.[18]

In September 2017, President Trump announced plans to abolish the DACA program, and participants began to lose their eligibility. At that time, almost 700,000 persons were enrolled in the program, out of a possible 1.8 million. (In early 2018, however, district courts forced the government to temporarily resume accepting DACA renewals.) As a price for saving the program, Trump demanded both funding for his border wall with Mexico and also large cuts to legal immigration. Congress was unable to agree on DACA legislation that Trump was prepared to sign.

Even after Joe Biden became president in 2021, there was no clear answer to the fate of the DACA program. The only certainty was that more unauthorized immigrants were entering the United States at its southern border. We examine this issue in this chapter's *Which Side Are You On?* feature.

Political Participation by Latinos. Political participation by Latinos has increased in recent years, and they have gained political power in several states. Latinos do not vote at the same rate as African Americans, in large part because many Latinos are immigrants who are not yet citizens. Still, there are now about 6,600 Latino elected officials in the United States. Latinos have recently voted Democratic by a ratio of about two to one, and in the 2020 elections appeared to have helped tip Arizona into the Democratic column. Many Latinos are politically conservative, however. Cubans in Florida helped win that state for Trump. Mexican Americans in Texas have long shown themselves to be more conservative than they are in California. In 2022, more than 100 Republican congressional candidates were Latinos.

National Security and the Rights of Immigrants

Legal immigrants who are not citizens have certain rights. The Fourteenth Amendment states that all persons (as opposed to all citizens) shall enjoy "due process of law." Individuals who are undocumented are subject to deportation. In 1903, however, the Supreme Court ruled that

---

18. *United States v. Texas*, 136 S.Ct. 2271 (2016).

Should We Close Off Our Southern Border Again?

Throughout its history, the U.S. has had periods during which we accepted few immigrants and periods when we accepted many immigrants. In the twentieth and twenty-first centuries, we have had periods when there were great waves of unauthorized immigrants crossing our southern border and other periods when we went to great efforts to reduce those flows. During the Trump administration, hundreds of miles of barriers were erected at the southern border. We also had a "remain in Mexico" policy that required those seeking asylum to remain in Mexico while their cases were prepared for judication.

For at least the first two years of the Biden administration, the southern border was relatively open. Should we attempt again to reduce unauthorized immigration there?

The U.S. Should Show the World Its Humanitarian Credentials

Those in favor of maintaining a relatively open border in the south look to the reasons that unauthorized immigrants seek to enter the U.S. Many of them are fleeing extreme poverty and violence in the countries in which they live. Some of them are fleeing political repression. In any event, those who seek to come to this country typically want to work and are willing to work hard.

Why should we want to reduce the flow of these people when they benefit not only themselves but America, too? Whether immigrants are authorized or unauthorized does not matter in the sense that they work, create demand for goods and services, and ultimately cause average incomes to rise in the U.S. because of increased economic growth.

Authorized Immigration to Be Sure, But Not Unauthorized

Those who would prefer to go back to a more closed southern border argue that unlimited unauthorized immigration does not help the United States either in the short run or the long run. Right now, large illegal cartels control the flow of unauthorized immigrants into this country through Mexico. They charge outrageous fees for transportation. They use the chaos at the border to send illegal drugs, such as fentanyl, into this country. While unauthorized immigrants may be seeking work in the U.S., some of them are not able to find work and therefore become public charges.

Those crossing the southern border illegally are not just from Mexico. Many of them are from Central and South American countries. Why does the U.S. have to be the sole destination for these people escaping poverty and violence in their own countries? U.S. taxpayers are not required to help everybody on this globe.

For Critical Analysis

What prevents tens of millions of citizens from other countries from attempting to cross our southern border illegally?

---

the government could not deport someone without a hearing that meets constitutional due process standards.[19] Today, most people facing deportation are entitled to a hearing before an immigration judge, to representation by a lawyer, and to the right to see the evidence presented against them. The government must prove that its grounds for deportation are valid.

Limits to the Rights of Deportees: Due Process. Despite the Fourteenth Amendment, the courts have often deferred to government assertions that noncitizens cannot make constitutional claims. The Antiterrorism and Effective Death Penalty Act of 1996 was especially restrictive. The government was given the right to deport noncitizens for alleged terrorism without any court review of the deportation order. Further, the government can deport noncitizens based on secret evidence that the deportee is not allowed to see.

Limits to the Rights of Deportees: Freedom of Association. A 1999 case involved a group of noncitizens associated with the Popular Front for the Liberation of Palestine (PFLP). PFLP members had carried out terrorist acts in Israel, but there was no evidence of criminal conduct

---

19. *Yamataya v. Fisher*, 189 U.S. 86 (1903).

by the group arrested in the United States. In this case, the Supreme Court ruled that noncitizens have no First Amendment rights to object to deportation, even if the deportation is based on their political associations.[20] This ruling also covers permanent residents—noncitizens with "green cards" that allow them to live and work in the United States on a long-term basis.

Limits to the Rights of Deportees: *Ex Post Facto* Laws. As you learned earlier, the Constitution prohibits *ex post facto* laws—laws that inflict punishments for acts that were not illegal when they were committed. This provision may not apply in deportation cases, however. The 1996 Antiterrorism and Effective Death Penalty Act, mentioned earlier, provided mandatory deportation for noncitizens convicted of an aggravated felony, even if the crime took place before 1996. In some jurisdictions, marijuana possession can be an aggravated felony. Under the 1996 law, permanent residents have been deported to nations that they left when they were small children. In some cases, deported persons did not speak the language of the country to which they were deported.

The Trauma of Native Americans

Whether living on rural reservations or in urban neighborhoods, Native Americans have long experienced high rates of poverty. There is much history behind this problem.

The Demographic Collapse. During the years after Columbus arrived in America, native population numbers—both in the future United States and in the Americas generally—experienced one of the most catastrophic collapses in human history. The Europeans brought with them Old World diseases to which Native Americans had no immunity. A person who was able to resist one disease might die from another. By one estimate, 90 percent of the inhabitants of the New World died.

For their part, the Europeans had no idea what caused diseases and did not understand what was happening. When the Pilgrims landed at Plymouth in 1620, the coast of New England was lined with empty Indian village sites. The villages had been abandoned because of an epidemic touched off by shipwrecked French sailors in 1616.

Native Americans in the Nineteenth and Twentieth Centuries. In the United States, the Native American population continued to decrease through the nineteenth century—a time when the European American and African American populations were experiencing explosive growth. This decline in population was due, in part, to geographical removal and relocation that caused the destruction of the Native American way of life. The U.S. Native American population bottomed out at 250,000 at the end of the nineteenth century. Since that time, however, it has recovered substantially. The number today is about 6.79 million, people of whole or partial Native American ancestry. The total may exceed the number living here before Columbus.

Native Americans faced additional challenges. A federal policy of "assimilation" adopted in the late 1880s resulted in further loss of territory and the suppression of traditional cultures. Despite assimilation policies, Native Americans were not considered U.S. citizens. The Fourteenth Amendment states: "All persons born or naturalized in the United States,

AP Photo/Rick Browne

Image 5.5 This member of the Ute tribe attends a ceremony for Ute and Comanche leaders. ▶ What is the current population of Native Americans today?

---

20. *Reno v. American-Arab Anti-Discrimination Committee*, 525 U.S. 471 (1999).

and subject to the jurisdiction thereof, are citizens ..." The language concerning jurisdiction was inserted precisely to deny citizenship to Native Americans living as members of tribal nations. Native Americans did not become U.S. citizens until 1924.

In the late twentieth century, some Native American communities hit upon a new strategy for economic development—gambling casinos on reservation lands. This strategy was possible because the U.S. Constitution grants the responsibility for Native American relations to the national government. As a result, reservations are not subject to the full authority of the states in which they are located. Many Native Americans have improved their standards of living because of casinos on reservation lands.

Currently, there is an organized effort by Native Americans to reacquire reservation lands. Some groups are negotiating for the transfer of federal, state, and municipal property to Native American ownership and control. For example, the Kashia Band of Pomo Indians in Sonoma County, California, obtained access in 2016 to the Pacific Ocean. They recovered 700 acres with the help of the Indian Land Tenure Foundation and the Indian Land Capital Company. Other Native American nations are currently attempting similar reacquisitions.

Women's Struggle for Equal Rights

>> **LO 5-4:** Contrast the goals of the women's suffrage movement with the goals of modern feminism.

Like African Americans and other underrepresented groups, women have had to struggle for equality. During the first phase of this struggle, the primary goal of women was to obtain suffrage, or the right to vote.

Early Women's Political Movements

In 1848, Lucretia Mott and Elizabeth Cady Stanton organized the first women's rights convention in Seneca Falls, New York. The three hundred people who attended approved a Declaration of Sentiments: "We hold these truths to be self-evident: that all men *and women* are created equal."

In 1869, after the Civil War, Susan B. Anthony and Stanton formed the National Woman Suffrage Association. In their view, women's suffrage was a means to achieve major improvements in the economic and social situation of women in the United States. In other words, the vote was to be used to seek broader goals.

Lucy Stone, however, a key founder of the rival American Woman Suffrage Association, believed that the vote was the only major issue. In 1880, the two organizations joined forces. The resulting National American Woman Suffrage Association had just one goal— the enfranchisement of women—but it made little progress.

The Congressional Union for Woman Suffrage, founded in the early 1900s by Alice Paul, adopted a national strategy of obtaining an amendment to the U.S. Constitution. The Union sponsored large-scale marches and civil disobedience—which resulted in hunger strikes, arrests, and jailings. Finally, in 1920, the Nineteenth Amendment was passed: "The right of citizens of the United States to vote shall not be denied or abridged by the United States or by any State on account of sex."

The Modern Women's Movement

After gaining the right to vote in 1920, women engaged various independent political activities until the 1960s when they, once again, pushed forward a national agenda. The civil rights movement of that decade resulted in a growing awareness of rights for all groups, including women. Increased participation in the workforce gave many women a larger voice in current affairs. Additionally, the publication of Betty Friedan's *The Feminine Mystique* in 1963 focused national attention on the unequal status of women in American life.

In 1966, Friedan and others formed the National Organization for Women (NOW). Many observers consider the founding of NOW to be the beginning of the modern women's movement—the feminist movement, which renewed the call for complete political, social, and economic equality for women that began in Seneca Falls in 1848.

Feminism gained additional impetus from young women who entered politics to support the civil rights movement or to oppose the Vietnam War (1965–75). In the late 1960s, women's liberation organizations began to spring up on college campuses. Women also began organizing independent "consciousness-raising groups," in which they discussed how gender issues affected their lives. The new women's movement experienced explosive growth, and by 1970 it had emerged as a major social force.

Feminism
The movement that supports political, economic, and social equality for women.

The Equal Rights Amendment. The initial focus of the modern women's movement was to eradicate gender inequality through a constitutional amendment. The Equal Rights Amendment (ERA), which was first proposed by the National Women's political party in 1923, states as follows: "Equality of rights under the law shall not be denied or abridged by the United States or by any state on account of sex." For years, the amendment was not even given a hearing in Congress, but finally it was approved by both chambers and sent to the state legislatures for ratification in 1972.

The necessary thirty-eight states failed to ratify the ERA within the time specified by Congress, even after an extension of the deadline. To date, efforts to reintroduce the amendment have not succeeded. Since that time, three additional states have ratified the amendment—Virginia, in 2020, brought the total to the necessary thirty-eight. (Several states have also tried to repeal their ratification, a move that is probably unconstitutional.) For the ERA to take effect, Congress would have to extend the deadline once again.

Challenging Gender Discrimination in the Courts. When ratification of the ERA failed, women's rights organizations began a campaign to establish national and state laws that would guarantee the equality of women. This more limited campaign met with much success. Women's rights organizations also challenged discriminatory statutes and policies in the federal courts, contending that **gender discrimination** violated the Fourteenth Amendment's equal protection clause. Employing the intermediate scrutiny standard, the Supreme Court has invalidated many such statutes and policies. For example, in 1977 the Court held that police and firefighting units cannot establish arbitrary rules, such as height and weight requirements, that tend to keep women from participating in those occupations.[21] In 1983, the Court ruled that life insurance companies cannot charge different rates for women and men.[22]

Gender Discrimination
Any practice, policy, or procedure that denies equality of treatment to an individual or to a group because of gender.

Gender Equality on Campus. Congress sought to guarantee equality of treatment in education by passing Title IX of the Education Amendments of 1972, which states: "No person in the United States shall, on the basis of sex, be excluded from participation in, be denied the benefits of, or be subjected to discrimination under any education program or activity receiving Federal financial assistance." Title IX's best-known and most controversial impact has been on high school and collegiate athletics, although the original statute made no reference to sports.

---

21. *Dothard v. Rawlinson*, 433 U.S. 321 (1977).
22. *Arizona v. Norris*, 463 U.S. 1073 (1983).

In 2011, the Department of Education issued a statement clarifying that sexual harassment on campus, including rape, violated Title IX. Investigations by the Obama administration suggested that many schools were not taking such violations seriously. Dozens of schools were potentially subject to penalties. As a result, many colleges and universities launched efforts to address the issue.

Women in the Military. One of the most controversial issues involving women's rights has been the role of women in the armed forces. Some believed that the ERA failed because of the fear that women might be drafted (forced) into military service. Currently, no draft exists, but to this day young American men must register for it. Women do not face such a requirement.

One issue has been whether women should be allowed to serve in military combat units. In the past, women were not allowed to join such units. Due to the fluid nature of modern combat, however, women in support positions have often found themselves in firefights anyway. In January 2013, the Department of Defense lifted the Combat Exclusion Policy, and women are now able to compete for assignment to combat units. Participation in such units is usually a requirement for promotion to top military positions.

Women in Politics Today

Although a "men's club" atmosphere still prevails in Congress, the number of women holding congressional seats has increased significantly in recent years. In 2001, for the first time, a woman was elected to a leadership post in Congress—Nancy Pelosi of California became the Democrats' minority whip in the U.S. House of Representatives. In 2002, Pelosi was elected minority leader. In 2006, she became the first woman to be Speaker of the House in U.S. history. She was forced to drop back to minority leader in 2010 when the Republicans won a majority in the House, but she regained the Speakership in 2019 after the Democrats again took control.

Recent Gallup polls show that close to 90 percent of Americans said they would vote for a qualified woman for president if she was nominated by their party. Increasing numbers of women are also being appointed to cabinet posts. More women are also sitting on federal judicial benches. In 2020, Senator Kamala Harris (D-CA) was elected as the first female vice president—and the first woman of color. More women than ever now serve in Congress. Among white voters, well-educated suburban women form a growing part of the Democratic coalition, while rural, working-class women are increasingly drawn to the Republicans.

Gender-Based Discrimination in the Workplace

Traditional cultural beliefs concerning the proper role of women in society continue to be evident not only in the political arena but also in the workplace. Since the 1960s, however, women have gained substantial protection against discrimination through laws that require equal employment opportunities and equal pay.

Maximum Exposure PR/Shutterstock.com

Image 5.6 This woman, a senior airperson in the U.S. Air Force, was stationed at a base used by the United States to resupply its forces in Afghanistan. Since 2013, women have been able to serve in combat units. ▶ Why would women soldiers value the right to serve in such units?

Title VII of the Civil Rights Act of 1964. Title VII of the Civil Rights Act of 1964 prohibits gender discrimination in employment and has been used to strike down employment policies that discriminate against employees on the basis of gender. In 1978, Congress amended Title VII to expand the definition of gender discrimination to include discrimination based on pregnancy. In 2020, the Supreme Court ruled that Title VII also extended to discrimination based on sexual orientation (discussed later).

Sexual Harassment. The United States Supreme Court has also held that Title VII's prohibition of gender-based discrimination extends to **sexual harassment** in the workplace. One form of sexual harassment occurs when job opportunities, promotions, salary increases, and other benefits are given in return for sexual favors. Another form of sexual harassment is called hostile-environment harassment. It occurs when an employee is subjected to sexual conduct or comments that interfere with the employee's job performance or are so pervasive or severe as to create an intimidating, hostile, or offensive environment.

Despite laws against sexual harassment, victims often find it impossible to obtain justice even in cases of outright rape. Incidents of harassment may occur in a one-on-one setting, making them difficult to prove. Perpetrators are typically more powerful than victims. Those who complain are often fired without redress. In October 2017, however, the barriers protecting perpetrators began to break down. Dozens of women came forward to accuse Hollywood producer Harvey Weinstein of sexual abuse. The many accusations served to protect the women involved. Similar accusations spread like wildfire, first through the world of entertainment and then in other industries as well. Hundreds of powerful and famous men lost their positions. The new movement, often known by the Twitter hashtag #MeToo, had become a major source of women's empowerment.

The #MeToo movement has produced an astonishing statistic: In 2018 the number of reported rape cases was 2.5 times the number reported in 2016. It is unlikely that the 2018 report reflected an increase in the actual number of rapes. Sexual assault has always been one of the most underreported major crimes, and it appears that #MeToo led hundreds of thousands of women to come forward who would not have done so in the past.

Wage Discrimination. Although Title VII and other legislation have mandated equal employment opportunities for men and women, women continue to earn less, on average, than men do. The Equal Pay Act, which was enacted in 1963, basically requires employers to provide equal pay for substantially equal work. In other words, males cannot legally be paid more than females who perform essentially the same job.

In 2009, Congress passed the Lilly Ledbetter Fair Pay Act. This federal statute allows individuals who face pay discrimination to seek rectification using federal anti-discrimination laws. The act asks employers to promote voluntary compliance with the principle of equal pay for equal work.

Sheila Fitzgerald/Shutterstock.com

Image 5.7 The annual Women's March in cities across the nation took place on January 18, 2020. The first march, held the day after President Trump's inauguration in 2017, may have been the largest one-day demonstration in U.S. history. ▶ What grievances might women have had against Trump?

Sexual Harassment
Unwanted physical or verbal conduct or abuse of a sexual nature that interferes with a recipient's job performance, creates a hostile work environment, or carries with it an implicit or explicit threat of adverse employment consequences.

The Rights and Status of LGBTQ+ Americans

>> **LO 5-5:** Discuss how federal legislation and public opinion about LGBTQ+ rights have evolved in recent years.

On June 27, 1969, patrons of the Stonewall Inn, a New York City bar popular with the LGBTQ+ community, reacted to a police raid. They threw beer cans and bottles because they were angry at what they felt was unrelenting police harassment. In the ensuing riot, which lasted two nights, hundreds of LGBTQ+ individuals fought with police. Before Stonewall, the stigma attached to the LGBTQ+ community and the resulting fear of exposure had tended to prevent most LGBTQ+ community members from engaging in activism. In the months after Stonewall, however, the Gay Liberation Front and the Gay Activist Alliance were formed, and similar groups sprang up in other parts of the country.

Growth in the LGBTQ+ Rights Movement

The Stonewall incident marked the beginning of the movement for LGBTQ+ rights. Since then, LGBTQ+ people have formed thousands of organizations to exert pressure on legislatures, the media, schools, churches, and other organizations to recognize their right to equal treatment.

To a great extent, LGBTQ+ groups have succeeded in changing public opinion—and state and local laws that pertain to their status and rights. Nevertheless, they continue to struggle against age-old biases against homosexuality, often rooted in deeply held religious beliefs.

State and Local Laws Targeting LGBTQ+ Persons

Before the Stonewall incident, forty-nine states had sodomy laws that made various kinds of sexual acts illegal. (Illinois, which had repealed its sodomy law in 1962, was the only exception.) During the 1970s and 1980s, about half of these laws were either repealed or struck down by the courts.

Lawrence v. Texas. The states—mostly in the South—that resisted the movement to abolish sodomy laws received a boost in 1986 with the Supreme Court's decision in *Bowers v. Hardwick*.[23] In that case, the Court upheld, by a five-to-four vote, a Georgia law that made homosexual conduct between two adults a crime. But in 2003, the Court reversed its earlier position on sodomy with its decision in *Lawrence v. Texas*.[24] In this case, the Court held that laws against sodomy violate the due process clause of the Fourteenth Amendment. The Court stated: "The liberty protected by the Constitution allows homosexual persons the right to choose to enter upon relationships in the confines of their homes and their own private lives and still retain their dignity as free persons." As a result, *Lawrence v. Texas* invalidated the sodomy laws that remained on the books in fourteen states.

State Actions. Today, thirty-four states, the District of Columbia, and more than 180 cities and counties have enacted laws protecting LGBTQ+ people from discrimination in employment in at least some workplaces. Many of these laws also ban discrimination in housing, in public accommodation, and in other contexts. Finally, in 2020, Title VII of the 1964 Civil

---

23. 478 U.S. 186 (1986).
24. 539 U.S. 558 (2003).

Rights Act was expanded by the Supreme Court. In *Bostock v. Clayton County, Georgia*, the justices ruled that no person can be discriminated against because of that person's gender identification. Thus, transgender individuals are now fully covered by anti-discrimination legislation.[25]

"Don't Ask, Don't Tell"

Until recently, the armed forces have viewed homosexuality as incompatible with military service. In 1993, however, President Bill Clinton announced a new policy, described as "don't ask, don't tell." Enlistees would not be asked about their sexual orientation, and gay men and lesbians would be allowed to serve in the military so long as they did not declare that they were gay men or lesbians or engage in same-sex acts. Despite the new policy, large numbers of gay men and lesbians were expelled from the military in subsequent years.

Barack Obama promised to repeal "don't ask, don't tell" and allow lesbians and gay men to serve openly, but Congress failed to act on legislation. Still, by December 2010, respondents in a public opinion poll supported the right of gay men and lesbians to serve openly by a margin of 77 to 21 percent. In September 2010, a U.S. district court judge ruled that the ban on open military service by gay men and lesbians was unconstitutional.[26] In December Congress finally passed repeal legislation. "Don't ask, don't tell" was phased out in 2011.

Same-Sex Marriage

Given the rampant hostility toward LGBTQ+ people that existed throughout most of American history, legal same-sex marriage was beyond imagination for most Americans. Still, some same-sex couples celebrated their unions with private, unofficial ceremonies.

In 2015, however, the Supreme Court endorsed nationwide recognition of same-sex marriage. This landmark decision was part of one of the most rapid and profound extensions of civil rights in history—the recognition of equal rights regardless of sexual orientation.

The Defense of Marriage Act (DOMA). Controversy over this issue first flared up in 1993 when the Hawaii Supreme Court ruled that denying marriage licenses to same-sex couples might violate the equal protection clause of the Hawaii constitution.[27] In response, the U.S. Congress passed the Defense of Marriage Act of 1996, which banned federal recognition of same-sex couples and allowed state governments to ignore same-sex marriages performed in other states.

Recognition of Same-Sex Marriages. Massachusetts was the first state to recognize same-sex marriage. In November 2003, the Massachusetts Supreme Judicial Court ruled that same-sex couples have a right to civil marriage under the Massachusetts state constitution.[28] For four years, Massachusetts stood alone in approving such marriages. From 2008 on, however, more and more states began to accept same-sex marriage.

In June 2013, the Supreme Court found, in *United States v. Windsor*, that the provision of the Defense of Marriage Act that banned federal recognition of same-sex marriages performed by the states was unconstitutional.[29] Ever-larger numbers of state and federal judges

25. *Bostock v. Clayton County, Georgia*, 140 S.Ct. 1731 (2020)
26. *Log Cabin Republicans v. United States*, 716 F.Supp.2d 884 (C.D.Cal. 2010).
27. *Baehr v. Lewin*, 852 P.2d 44 (Hawaii 1993).
28. *Goodridge v. Department of Public Health*, 798 N.E.2d 941 (Mass. 2003).
29. 570 U.S. 744 (2013).

Image 5.8 Air Force Lieutenant Colonel Sean Hackbart (left) and his partner, Mike Culver, celebrate the official end of the military's "don't ask, don't tell" policy.
▶ How did the "don't ask, don't tell" policy come to an end?

Transgender persons
Persons whose gender identity, expression, and/or role does not conform to what is culturally associated with their sex assignment at birth.

used the arguments in *United States v. Windsor* to overturn same-sex marriage bans. Finally, in June 2015, the Supreme Court overturned the remaining state-level prohibitions in *Obergefell v. Hodges.*[30]

The Rights of Transgender Individuals

The question of who is a woman and who is a man is not as open-and-shut as many people once assumed. Thousands of people grow up convinced that their bodies are lying to them. They may have been born with the physical characteristics of one sex, but in their hearts, they know they belong to the other. The existence of such **transgender persons** has been known for many years and has led to the practice of reassigning gender through surgery. Not all transgender persons undergo such an invasive process, however. Indeed, some transgender persons find that they cannot identify as either men or women.

Forty-eight states allow birth certificates to be amended to change a person's recorded sex. Twenty-two states, however, allow such a change only following surgery. Discrimination against transgender individuals is widespread, and in recent years, such persons have increasingly come out into the open and demanded equal rights.

The Bathroom Bill Issue. In 2015 and 2016, however, various states and localities passed laws banning transgender persons from using public restrooms that did not accord with the sex listed on their birth certificates. A common argument was that trans women would use their access to women's restrooms to sexually harass women. In response to North Carolina legislation, in 2016 the Obama administration announced that any such ban in a public school would threaten the school's access to federal funding. Eleven states sued the administration in an attempt to reverse this decision.

Military Service. In June 2016, the Department of Defense ruled that members of the military could no longer be discharged because of their transgender status. President Trump, however, sought to reverse Obama's transgender policies. Obama's public school restroom ruling was overturned. Trump also sought to prevent transgender persons from serving in the military. He feared that the armed forces might be required to pay for sex-reassignment surgery. Still, top military officials were reluctant to reinstate the transgender ban, and several lawsuits were launched opposing such an action. In March 2019, the Trump administration finally imposed a ban on military service by transgender persons.

Under the Biden administration, the military's policy toward transgender individuals changed again. Transgender personnel and individuals with gender dysphoria can now serve openly in their self-identified gender. Of course, they still must meet the army's standards for military service.

30. 135 S.Ct. 2584 (2015).

Making A Difference

Dealing with Discrimination

Anyone applying for a job may be subjected to a variety of potentially discriminatory practices. The government continues to monitor the fairness and validity of criteria used in job applicant screening, and as a result, there are ways of addressing the problem of discrimination.

Why Should You Care? Some people may think that discrimination is a problem only for members of racial or ethnic minority groups. Actually, in some instances, white men have experienced "reverse discrimination"—and have obtained redress for it. Also, discrimination against women is common. Even if you are male,

Image 5.9 Members of the Council on American-Islamic Relations outside the Supreme Court building during oral arguments on *EEOC v. Abercrombie and Fitch*. The Court later ruled that the clothing retailer violated antidiscrimination laws when it refused to hire a young woman who wore a headscarf for religious reasons. ▶ What limits, if any, may be placed on religious dress?

Chip Somodevilla/Getty Images

you probably have female friends and relatives whose well-being is of interest to you.

What Can You Do? If you believe that you have been discriminated against by a potential employer, consider the following steps:

1. Evaluate your own capabilities and determine if you are truly qualified for the position.
2. Analyze the reasons why you were turned down. Would others agree with you that you have been the object of discrimination?
3. If you still believe that you have been treated unfairly, you have recourse to several agencies and services.

You should first speak to the human resources director of the company and explain politely that you believe you have not been evaluated adequately. Explain your concerns clearly. If necessary, go into detail, and say that you may have been discriminated against.

If a second evaluation is not forthcoming, contact your local state employment agency. If you still do not obtain adequate help, contact one or more of the following state officials or agencies:

- If a government entity is involved, a state ombudsperson or citizen aide may be available to mediate.
- You can contact the state civil rights or human rights commission, which should at least give you advice, even if it does not wish to take up your case.
- The state attorney general's office may have a division dealing with discrimination and civil rights.
- There may be a special commission or department, such as a women's status commission or a commission on Hispanics or Asian Americans. If so, contact this commission.
- Finally, at the national level, you can contact the Equal Employment Opportunity Commission at www.eeoc.gov.

Key Terms

affirmative action 105
civil disobedience 100
civil rights 95
de facto segregation 99
de jure segregation 99
feminism 113

gender discrimination 113
grandfather clause 98
intermediate, or exacting, scrutiny 105
literacy test 98
poll tax 98

rational basis review 105
reverse discrimination 106
separate-but-equal doctrine 97
sexual harassment 115
strict scrutiny 104

suffrage 96
suspect classification 104
transgender persons 118
white primary 98

Chapter Summary

» **LO 5-1** Before the Civil War, slavery was protected by the Constitution. Constitutional amendments after the Civil War ended slavery, and African Americans gained citizenship, the right to vote, and other rights. This protection was largely a dead letter by the 1880s, however.

Segregation was declared unconstitutional by the Supreme Court in *Brown v. Board of Education of Topeka* (1954), in which the Court stated that separation implied inferiority. In 1955, the modern civil rights movement began. The Civil Rights Act of 1964 (and its subsequent amendments) bans discrimination in employment and public accommodations on the basis of race, color, religion, gender, gender identity, or national origin. The Voting Rights Act of 1965 outlawed discriminatory voter-registration tests and authorized federal voter registration.

» **LO 5-2** The Supreme Court uses various standards when assessing the constitutionality of laws and government actions. Strict scrutiny applies to basic civil liberties and to the rights of racial, religious, and ethnic minorities. Intermediate, or exacting, scrutiny is used to consider claims of discrimination against women. Rational basis review is the easiest standard for the government to meet, but it has been used to protect LGBTQ+ persons.

Affirmative action programs are controversial because they could lead to reverse discrimination against majority groups or even other underrepresented groups. Supreme Court decisions have limited affirmative action programs, and several states now ban state-sponsored affirmative action.

» **LO 5-3** Today, most immigrants come from Asia and Latin America, especially Mexico. Many are unauthorized (or undocumented) immigrants. Most came to find jobs, but their status is a major political issue. The percentage of Latinos in the population is growing rapidly. While Latinos who are citizens benefit from the same antidiscrimination protections as African Americans, immigrants who are not citizens have few civil rights.

Unique among minority groups, Native Americans experienced demographic collapse upon the arrival of the Europeans in the New World. They continue to face high levels of poverty.

» **LO 5-4** In the early history of the United States, women had no political rights. The first women's rights convention was held in 1848. Not until 1920, with the passage of the Nineteenth Amendment, did women finally obtain the right to vote in all states. The modern women's movement began in the 1960s in the wake of the civil rights and anti–Vietnam War movements. Efforts to secure the ratification of the Equal Rights Amendment have failed so far, but the women's movement was successful in obtaining new laws, changes in social customs, and increased political representation.

Federal government efforts to eliminate gender discrimination in the workplace include Title VII of the Civil Rights Act of 1964, which prohibits gender-based discrimination, including sexual harassment on the job.

» **LO 5-5** In 2003, a Supreme Court decision effectively invalidated all remaining sodomy laws which criminalized specific sexual practices. Many states, cities, and counties now have laws prohibiting at least some types of discrimination based on sexual orientation. Gay men and lesbians gained the right to serve openly in the military in 2011 as did transgender individuals in 2021. In 2015, the Supreme Court established a constitutional right to same-sex marriage. Recently, the rights of transgender persons have become a major issue.

Test Yourself

1. The separate-but-equal doctrine was:
   a. addressed by the Supreme Court in *Plessy v. Ferguson*.
   b. addressed by the Supreme Court in *Roe v. Wade*.
   c. never addressed by the Supreme Court.

2. **Barriers to African American voting established between the Civil War and the civil rights movement included all except:**
   a. grandfather clauses.
   b. poll taxes.
   c. property qualifications.

3. **Segregation that does not follow from discriminatory laws or government actions, but from other causes, is called:**
   a. *de jure* segregation.
   b. *de facto* segregation.
   c. extralegal discrimination.

4. **The Fourteenth Amendment requires that no state shall deprive any person of life, liberty, or property, without:**
   a. due process of law.
   b. rational basis review.
   c. compensation.

5. **The federal courts employ the following standard when evaluating differential treatment by race:**
   a. rational basis review.
   b. intermediate, or exacting, scrutiny.
   c. strict scrutiny.

6. **In educational admissions and employment, affirmative action programs have:**
   a. awarded preferences to underrepresented group members.
   b. relied on numerical quotas to improve outcomes.
   c. involved federal grants to complying institutions.

7. **Currently, the largest immigrant group living in the United States comes from:**
   a. China.
   b. Mexico.
   c. India.

8. **The courts have placed serious restrictions on the rights of persons who are:**
   a. living on Native American reservations.
   b. not fluent in English.
   c. subject to deportation.

9. **In the years following the European discovery of America, the number of Native Americans:**
   a. rose because of the introduction of new foodstuffs.
   b. fell because of the introduction of new diseases.
   c. remained about the same for many years.

10. **The Equal Rights Amendment today requires:**
    a. that women be treated equally to men.
    b. that women be treated equally in the labor market.
    c. nothing at all, because the Equal Rights Amendment never passed.

11. **Sexual harassment in the workplace can involve all except:**
    a. rules that provide unequal pay for women.
    b. giving benefits in return for sexual favors.
    c. sexual conduct or comments that create a seriously hostile environment.

12. **The Defense of Marriage Act (DOMA) provided for all of the following except:**
    a. states were not required to recognize same-sex marriages conducted in other states.
    b. states were not required to recognize divorces obtained in other states.
    c. the federal government was barred from recognizing same-sex marriages when awarding benefits or collecting taxes.

Essay Questions

1. Not all African Americans agreed with the philosophy of nonviolence espoused by Dr. Martin Luther King, Jr. Advocates of Black power called for a more militant approach. Can militancy make a movement more effective, or is it typically counterproductive? Either way, why?

2. The prevention of terrorist acts committed by adherents of radical Islamism is a major policy objective today. Can we defend ourselves against such acts without abridging the civil rights and liberties of American Muslims? Explain your reasoning.

Answers to multiple-choice questions: 1. a, 2. c, 3. b, 4. a, 5. c, 6. a, 7. b, 8. c, 9. b, 10. c, 11. a, 12. b.

6 Public Opinion, Political Socialization, and the Media

michael melia/Alamy Stock Photo

WikiLeaks founder, Julian Assange, was indicted on 17 counts of violating the Espionage Act, all linked to his obtaining and publishing U.S. military and diplomatic documents that were deemed "secret." The materials were provided to him by a former Army intelligence analyst, who spent years in jail. Public opinion was mixed when the U.S. government attempted to extradite Assange from England to face trial. ▶ Why would some Americans not want Assange to face trial in the U.S.?

The six **Learning Outcomes (LOs)** below are designed to help improve your understanding of this chapter. After reading this chapter, you should be able to:

≫ **LO 6-1** Discuss major sources of political socialization, including the family, the schools, the media, and political events.

≫ **LO 6-2** Identify the effects of various influences on opinion, including education, income, religion, race, ethnicity, gender, and geography.

≫ **LO 6-3** Describe the characteristics of a scientific opinion poll, and list some of the problems pollsters face in obtaining accurate results.

≫ **LO 6-4** Analyze the effect that public opinion may have on the political process.

≫ **LO 6-5** Describe the different types of media and the changing roles they play in American society.

≫ **LO 6-6** Indicate the ways in which political bias manifests itself in the mass media.

Check your understanding of the material with the Test Yourself section at the end of the chapter.

In a democracy, the ability of the people to freely express their opinions is fundamental. Americans can express their opinions in many ways. They can e-mail newspapers. They can send text messages to their members of Congress. They can share their ideas in online forums. They can post comments on numerous social media platforms. They can organize politically. They can vote. They can respond to opinion polls.

Public Opinion and Political Socialization

» **LO 6-1:** Discuss major sources of political socialization, including the family, the schools, the media, and political events.

There is no single public opinion, because there are many different "publics." In a nation of over 335 million people, there may be innumerable gradations of opinion on an issue. What we do is describe the distribution of opinions about a particular question. Thus, we define **public opinion** as the aggregate of individual attitudes or beliefs shared by some portion of the adult population.

Public Opinion
The aggregate of individual attitudes or beliefs shared by some portion of the population.

Consensus and Divided Opinion

Typically, public opinion is distributed among several different positions, and the distribution of opinion can tell us how divided the public is on an issue and whether compromise is possible. When polls show that a large proportion of the respondents (those who respond to a poll) appears to express the same view on an issue, we say that a **consensus** exists, at least at the moment the poll was taken. Figure 6.1 shows a pattern of opinion that might be called consensual. Issues on which the public holds widely differing attitudes result in **divided opinion** (see Figure 6.2).

Consensus
General agreement among the citizenry on an issue.

Divided Opinion
Public opinion that is polarized between two different positions.

  An interesting question arises as to when private opinion becomes public opinion. Everyone probably has a private opinion about the competence of the president, as well as about more personal concerns, such as the state of a neighbor's lawn. We say that private opinion becomes public opinion when the opinion is publicly expressed and concerns public issues. When someone's private opinion becomes so strong that the individual is willing to express it, then the opinion becomes a public opinion.

Forming Public Opinion: Political Socialization

Most Americans are willing to express opinions on political issues when asked. How do people acquire these opinions and attitudes? Typically, views that are expressed as political opinions are acquired through the process of **political socialization**. By this we mean that people acquire their political beliefs and values, often including their political party identification, through relationships with their families, friends, and coworkers.

Political Socialization
The process by which people acquire political beliefs and values.

  The most important early sources of political socialization are the family and the schools. Individuals' basic political orientations are formed in the family if other family members hold strong views. When the adults in a family view politics as relatively unimportant and are disaffected from the political system, however, children may receive very little political socialization.

  In the past few decades, more and more sources of information about politics have become available to all Americans, especially to young people through the internet, and in particular through social media. Thus, although their basic

| Figure 6.1 | **Consensus Opinion** |

Question: Do you think employers should be allowed to fire someone based on their sexual orientation or gender identity, or don't you think so? ► **How do you think Americans might have answered this question fifty years ago?**

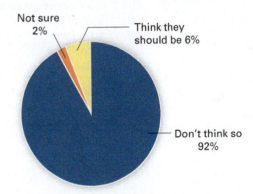

Source: Quinnipiac University Poll. April 26-29, 2019.

Figure 6.2 Divided Opinion

Question: Are new civil rights laws needed for LGBTQ+ people? ► Why might those who want new laws hold that opinion?

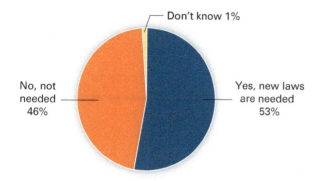

Source: Gallup News Service, May 2019.

outlook on the political system still may be formed by early family influences, young people are now exposed to many other sources of information about issues and values. Young people are exposed to many issues on TikTok, Twitter, Instagram, and Facebook, for example. This greater access to information may explain why young Americans are often more liberal than their parents on certain social issues such as LGBTQ+ rights.

The Family. How do primary caregivers transmit their political values to children? Studies suggest that the influence of family is due to two factors: communication and receptivity. Caregivers communicate their feelings and preferences to children constantly. Because children have such a strong need for approval, they are very receptive to these views.

Children are less likely to influence the adult caregivers in their family, because adults generally expect deference from children.[1] Nevertheless, other studies show that if children are exposed to political ideas at school and in the media, they will share these ideas with their families, giving the adults what some scholars call a "second chance" at political socialization.

Education as a Source of Political Socialization. From the early days of the republic, schools were perceived to be important transmitters of political information and attitudes. Children in the primary grades learn about their country mostly in patriotic ways. They learn about the Pilgrims, the flag, and some of the nation's presidents. By high school, students have a more complex understanding of the political system. Generally, the more education a person receives, the more likely it is that the person will be interested in politics, be confident in their ability to understand political issues, and be an active participant in the political process.

Peers and Peer Group Influence. Once a child enters school, the child's friends become an important influence on behavior and attitudes. For children and for adults, friendships and associations in **peer groups** affect political attitudes. We must, however, separate the effects of peer group pressure on attitudes in general from the effects of peer group pressure on political opinions. For the most part, associations among peers are nonpolitical. Political attitudes are more likely to be shaped by peer groups when those groups are involved directly in political activities. For example, individuals who share an ethnic identity may find a common political bond through working for the group's civil liberties and rights.

Opinion Leaders' Influence. We are all influenced by those with whom we are closely associated or whom we hold in high regard—friends at school, family members, other relatives, and teachers. In a sense, these people are **opinion leaders**, but on an informal level. That is, their influence on our political views is not necessarily intentional or deliberate. We are also influenced by formal opinion leaders, such as presidents, lobbyists,

Peer Groups
Groups consisting of members who share common social characteristics. Such groups play an important part in the socialization process, helping to shape attitudes and beliefs.

Opinion Leaders
One who is able to influence the opinions of others because of position, expertise, or personality.

---

1. Barbara A. Bardes and Robert W. Oldendick, *Public Opinion: Measuring the American Mind*, 5th ed. (Lanham, Md.: Rowman & Littlefield Publishers, 2016).

congresspersons, news commentators, and religious leaders, who have as part of their jobs the task of swaying people's views.

The Media and Public Opinion

The **media**—newspapers, television, radio, and internet sources—strongly influence public opinion. This is because the media inform the public about the issues and events of our times and thus have an **agenda-setting** effect. Consider Bernard Cohen's classic statement about the media and public opinion: The media may not be successful in telling people what to think, but they are "stunningly successful in telling their audience what to think about."[2]

The Popularity of the Media. Today, many contend that the media's influence on public opinion has grown to equal that of the family. For example, in her analysis of the role played by the media in American politics, media scholar Doris A. Graber points out that high school students, when asked where they obtain the information on which they base their views, mention the mass media far more than they mention their families, friends, and teachers.[3]

The Impact of the Newer Media. The extent to which newer forms of media have supplanted older ones—such as newspapers and the major broadcast networks—has been a major topic of discussion for quite a few years. Newer forms include not only the internet but also talk radio and cable television.

Talk radio would seem to be a very dated medium, given that radio first became important early in the twentieth century. Between 1949 and 1987, however, the Federal Communications Commission (FCC) enforced the Fairness Doctrine, which required radio and television to present controversial issues in a manner that was (in the FCC's view) honest, equitable, and balanced. Modern conservative talk radio took off only after the Fairness Doctrine was abolished. We examine further the Fairness Doctrine in the *Which Side Are You On?* feature in this chapter.

New Methods for Spreading Opinion. The impact of the various forms of newer media appears to vary considerably. Talk radio and cable networks such as Fox News have given conservatives new methods for promoting their views and socializing their audiences. It is possible, however, that such media mostly strengthen the beliefs of those who are already conservative, rather than recruiting new members to the political right. Indeed, cable news and talk radio are widely blamed for the increased polarization that has characterized American politics in recent years. Blogs have certainly aided in this polarization, too.

Social Media. The impact of social networking sites is more ambiguous. Facebook, for example, does have strongly political pages that, in effect, are political blogs. Many interactions on Facebook, however, are between members of peer groups, such as students who attend a particular school or individuals who work in the same profession. Members of such groups are more likely to hold a variety of views than are members of groups explicitly organized around a political viewpoint. Facebook, in other words, may enhance peer group influence.

Media
The channels of mass communication.

Agenda-Setting
Determining which public-policy questions will be debated or considered.

---

2. Bernard C. Cohen, *The Press and Foreign Policy* (Princeton, N.J.: Princeton University Press, 1963; repr. 2016), p. 81.
3. Doris A. Graber, *On Media: Making Sense of Politics* (New York: Oxford University Press, 2011).

Should the Federal Communications Commission Reinstate the Fairness Doctrine?

Way back in 1949 when there were few television stations and not that many radio stations, the Federal Communications Commission (FCC) created the Fairness Doctrine. It was an attempt to ensure that broadcast stations' coverage of controversial issues was fair and balanced. One of the reasons behind this rule, according to the FCC, was to assure that networks met their obligation to the public and showed views other than their own and those they agreed with. In essence, it only applied to ABC, NBC, and CBS because there were no other licensed networks available then. Civil libertarians fought the Fairness Doctrine for years, arguing that it was a violation of the First Amendment's free speech clause. The FCC had released a report called In the Matter of Editorializing by Broadcast Licensees that interpreted the public interest provisions of the Radio Act and the Communications Act as a mandate with a goal of promoting "a basic standard of fairness."

Is it time to bring back the Fairness Doctrine so that all reporting on controversial issues must present at least two sides to each issue?

It Is Only Fair That Consumers of Mass Media Information Hear at Least Two Sides to Every Story

Consider the facts. If a particular network presents only the liberal side of an issue, viewers will never know what the other side's arguments are all about. If a network presents only the conservative side, the same will be true. Given that broadcasters must obtain a license from the federal government, the federal government should be able to force them to be more objective when they present the news.

If the Fairness Doctrine could last for almost 40 years, there must have been something good that came out of it. That good was an increase in objective reporting compared to what that reporting would have been without it. Given the hyperpartisan way the media present news these days, a dose of objectivity would be welcomed.

Given the Number and Variety of Newer Media Sources of Information, We Do Not Need the Fairness Doctrine

When there were few licensed radio and television broadcast stations, perhaps the Fairness Doctrine was appropriate. But today it would be completely inappropriate. After all, if you do not like the particular conservative slant on Fox News, you have numerous other television stations to watch. If you do not like progressive talk radio, you have what seems to be an unlimited set of alternatives. Just consider SiriusXM. There are numerous progressive talk radio channels and at least one conservative channel.

Let's not forget the thousands of blogs that are out there. There are both right-wing and left-wing commentators and many in between. You can access political discussions on so many streaming platforms that you could never complain that there is not enough variety in the viewpoints presented. Today, the Fairness Doctrine would make no sense at all.

For Critical Analysis

Are there too many sources of political analysis and commentary today?

Political Events and Public Opinion

Generally, older Americans tend to be somewhat more conservative than younger Americans—particularly on social issues but also, to some extent, on economic issues. This effect probably occurs because older adults are likely to retain the social values that they learned years ago when various kinds of inequality were more widely accepted. Nevertheless, a more important factor than a person's age may be the impact of momentous political events that shape the political attitudes of an entire generation. When events produce such a long-lasting result, we refer to it as a **generational effect** (also called the cohort effect).

Working-class voters who grew up in the 1930s during the Great Depression were likely to form lifelong attachments to the Democratic Party, the party of Franklin D. Roosevelt. In the 1960s and 1970s, the war in Vietnam, the Watergate break-in, and the subsequent presidential cover-up fostered widespread cynicism toward government. (The Watergate break-in was the 1972 illegal entry into Democratic National Committee

Generational Effect
A long-lasting effect of the events of a particular time on the political opinions of those who came of political age at that time.

offices by members of President Richard Nixon's reelection organization.) There is evidence that the years of economic prosperity under President Ronald Reagan during the 1980s led many young people at that time to identify with the Republican Party. The high level of support that younger voters gave to Barack Obama may be good news for the Democratic Party in future years, although it was insufficient to propel the Democrats to victory in many recent elections.

Generational effects can be complicated by the widely recognized phenomenon of nostalgia. Throughout recorded history, older individuals have tended to view the world of their youth more positively than the world in which they currently live. As a presidential candidate, Donald Trump appealed to this tendency with the slogan "Make America Great Again."

a katz/Shutterstock.com

Image 6.1 His Holiness Pope Francis at the Cathedral Basilica of Saints Peter and Paul in Philadelphia. ▶ Why might this pope be an opinion leader for many people who are not Catholic?

The Influence of Demographic Factors

≫ **LO 6-2:** Identify the effects of various influences on opinion, including education, income, religion, race, ethnicity, gender, and geography.

Demographic characteristics, such as education, income, religion, race, ethnicity, gender, and geographic location, are strongly correlated with political party preferences and political ideologies. Table 6.1 illustrates the impact of some of these variables on voting behavior.

Educational Achievement

In the past, having a college education tended to be associated with voting for Republicans. In recent years, however, this correlation has vanished. Indeed, beginning with the 2016 elections, it has gone into reverse. In the 2018 midterm elections, among white Americans, 53 percent of those with a college education voted for Democrats. Among white Americans without a degree, only 37 percent did so. For some time now, individuals with a postgraduate education—more than a bachelor's degree—have become predominantly Democratic. Many people with postgraduate degrees are professionals, such as physicians, attorneys, and college instructors. In the 2016 primary and general elections, many observers remarked on the tendency of less-well-educated white voters to support Donald Trump. Some saw him as representing the white working class as a whole. There are plenty of less-well-educated white Democrats, however. In the 2016 Democratic primaries, such voters were more likely to pick Bernie Sanders than any other candidate. (Joe Biden was able to match or exceed Sanders' appeal in 2020.) Championing the working class has always been an essential part of Sanders' socialist ideology.

Table 6.1 **Voters by Groups in Presidential Elections, 2004–2020 (in Percentages)**

Why do African Americans and Latinos tend to support Democrats?

	2004		2008		2012		2016		2020	
	Kerry (Dem.)	Bush (Rep.)	Obama (Dem.)	McCain (Rep.)	Obama (Dem.)	Romney (Rep.)	Clinton (Dem.)	Trump (Rep.)	Biden (Dem.)	Trump (Rep.)
Gender										
Men	44	55	49	48	45	52	41	53	48	49
Women	51	48	56	43	55	44	54	42	56	43
Race and Ethnicity										
White	41	58	43	55	39	59	37	58	42	57
Black	88	11	95	4	93	6	88	8	87	12
Hispanic	58	40[a]	67	31	71	27	65	29	66	32
Educational Attainment										
Not a high school graduate[b]	50	50	63	35	54	35	45	51	48	51
High school only[c]	47	52	52	46	51	48	43	52	47	50
College graduate	46	52	50	48	47	51	49	45	51	46
Postgraduate education	54	45	58	40	55	42	58	37	62	32
Religion										
White Protestant[d]	32	68	34	65	30	69	37	60	NA	NA
Catholic	47	52	54	45	50	48	45	52	NA	NA
Jewish	75	24	78	21	69	30	71	24	NA	NA
White evangelical	21	79	24	74	21	78	16	81	23	76
Union Status										
Union household	59	40	59	39	58	40	51	43	57	40
Family Income										
Under $15,000	63	37	73	25	NA	NA	NA	NA	NA	NA
$15,000–29,000[e]	57	41	60	37	63	35	53	41	57	42
$30,000–49,000	50	49	55	43	57	42	51	42	58	41
Over $50,000[f]	43	56	49	49	45	53	47	49	56	43
Size of Place of Residence										
Population over 500,000[g]	60	40	70	28	69	29	59	35	60	37
Population 50,000 to 500,000[h]	50	50	59	39	58	40	45	50	51	48
Population 10,000 to 50,000	48	51	45	53	42	56	NA	NA	NA	NA
Rural	39	60	45	53	37	61	34	62	45	54

Note: Figures do not necessarily sum to 100 because of "other" or "no response" answers. NA = Not asked.

a. The official figure reported by the National Election Pool was 44. Studies later proved that this figure was impossibly high. NBC News lowered it to 40, but even that figure may have been too high. The 2016 figure for Trump had similar problems.
b. In 2016 and 2020, "high school or less."
c. In 2016 and 2020, "some college."
d. In 2012 and 2016, Protestant or "other Christian."
e. In 2012, 2016, and 2020, below $30,000.
f. In 2020, $50,000–$99,999. Also in 2020, $100,000–$199,999: Biden 41 and Trump 57; $200,000 or more: Biden 47 and Trump 43.
g. In 2016 and 2020, "urban."
h. In 2016 and 2020, "suburban."

Sources: The National Election Pool, as reported by CBS, the *New York Times*, CNN, Fox News, and Politico.

Economic Status

Family income is a strong predictor of economic liberalism or conservatism. Those with low incomes tend to favor government action to benefit people with low incomes or to promote economic equality. Those with high incomes tend to oppose government intervention in the economy or to support it only when it benefits business. The rich often tend toward the right and low-income voters often lean toward the left (at least in the past).

If we examine cultural as well as economic issues, however, the four-cornered ideological grid discussed at the beginning of this book becomes important. It happens that upper-income voters are more likely to endorse cultural liberalism, and lower-income individuals are more likely to favor cultural conservatism. Support for the right to have an abortion, for example, rises with income. It follows that libertarians—those who oppose government action on both economic and social issues—are concentrated among the wealthier members of the population. (Libertarians constitute the upper-right-hand corner of the four-cornered grid.) Those who favor government action both to promote traditional moral values and to promote economic equality—economic liberals, cultural conservatives—are concentrated among groups that are less well off. (This group fills up the lower-left-hand corner of the grid.) That said, it remains generally true that the higher a person's income, the more likely that person will be to vote Republican.

This creates an interesting paradox. Income and education are highly correlated. Yet income and education appear to pull in different directions politically. It follows that among white Americans at least, a highly educated, low-income voter is probably a Democrat, while someone with a high income but relatively little education is quite likely to be a Republican. Someone who works in the arts or literature will typically have much education, little income, and a tendency to vote Democratic. A construction contractor might have little formal education, strong earnings, and be attracted to the Republicans.

Religious Denomination

Traditionally, scholars have examined the impact of religion on political attitudes by dividing the population into such categories as Protestant, Catholic, and Jewish. In recent decades, however, such a breakdown has become less valuable as a means of predicting someone's political preferences. It is true that Jewish voters, as they were in the past, are notably more liberal than members of other groups on both economic and cultural issues. Persons reporting no religion are very liberal on social issues but have mixed economic views.

White Protestants and non-Latino Catholics, however, have grown closer to each other politically in recent years. This represents something of a change—in the late 1800s and early 1900s, northern Protestants were distinctly more likely to vote Republican, and northern Catholics were more likely to vote Democratic. Even now, in a few parts of the country, Protestants and Catholics tend to line up against each other when choosing a political party.

Religious Commitment and Beliefs

Today, two factors turn out to be major predictors of political attitudes among members of the various Christian denominations. One factor is the degree of religious commitment, as measured by such actions as regular churchgoing. The other is the degree to which the voter adheres to religious beliefs that (depending on the denomination) can be called conservative, evangelical, or fundamentalist. High scores on either factor are associated with cultural conservatism on political issues—that is, with beliefs that place a high value on social order.

In 2016, for example, 55 percent of those who attended services weekly voted for Republican candidate Donald Trump, compared with 46 percent of those who attended services a few times a year. Exit polls following the 2018 congressional elections showed the same pattern. Even though Trump's background revealed little evidence of religious commitment, many of the faithful expressed confidence that he would defend their interests. There is an exception to this trend—African Americans of all religious tendencies have been strongly supportive of Democrats.

The politics of white Americans who can be identified as holding evangelical Protestant or fundamentalist beliefs deserve special attention. According to Pew Research, 60 percent of American Protestants can be characterized as evangelical. The rest are conventionally described as mainline Protestants. As of 2021, evangelicals of all races were 24 percent of U.S. adults.[4]

Beliefs common to evangelicals include the full authority of the Bible, the importance of a conversion experience (being "born again"), and that God's gift of salvation is limited to those who accept Christ. Traditionally, not all evangelicals have been politically conservative. Some have been politically liberal, such as former Democratic presidents Jimmy Carter and Bill Clinton. In recent years, however, white evangelicals have swung sharply to the right. This phenomenon is limited to white evangelicals. Black churches are even more likely to be evangelical than white ones, but most of their members vote for Democrats.

Race and Ethnicity

Black Americans, on average, are somewhat conservative on certain cultural issues, such as LGBTQ+ rights and abortion. Yet they tend to be more liberal than white Americans on social-welfare matters, civil liberties, and even foreign policy. Black Americans voted principally for Republicans until Democrat Franklin D. Roosevelt's New Deal in the 1930s. Since then, they have largely identified with the Democratic Party. Indeed, in recent years, Democratic presidential candidates have received, on average, about 90 percent of the Black American vote.

Most Asian American groups lean toward the Democrats, although Vietnamese Americans tend to be Republican. Most Vietnamese Americans left Vietnam because of the Communist victory in the Vietnam War, and their strong anticommunism translates into conservative politics.

Muslim American immigrants and their descendants make up an interesting category.[5] In 2000, a majority of Muslim Americans of Middle Eastern ancestry voted for Republican George W. Bush because they shared his cultural conservatism. By 2016, the issues of Muslim civil liberties and discrimination against Muslims had turned Islamic voters into one of the nation's most Democratic blocs.

The Latino Vote

The diversity among Latino Americans has resulted in differing political behavior. The majority of Latino Americans vote Democratic. Cuban Americans, however, are often Republican. Most Cuban Americans left Cuba because of Fidel Castro's Communist

---

4. Pew Research Center, "About Three-in-Ten U.S. Adults Are Now Religiously Unaffiliated," December 14, 2021.

5. About one-third of U.S. Muslims are actually African Americans whose ancestors have been in this country for a long time. In terms of political preferences, African American Muslims are more likely to resemble other African Americans than Muslim immigrants from the Middle East.

regime. As with the Vietnamese, anticommunism leads to political conservatism. By 2016 and 2020, however, increasing numbers of young Cuban Americans were supporting the Democrats.

In 2004, Republican presidential candidate George W. Bush received almost 40 percent of the Latino vote. In 2008, however, Barack Obama won more than two-thirds of the Latino vote. Why did Latino support for the Republicans fall so sharply? In a word: immigration. Bush favored a comprehensive immigration reform that would have granted unauthorized immigrants a path to citizenship. Most Republicans in Congress, however, refused to support Bush on this issue. The harsh rhetoric of some Republicans convinced many Latinos that the Republicans were hostile to Latino interests.

Following the 2012 elections, some Republicans advocated a more welcoming line toward unauthorized immigrants in hopes of winning Latino support. Most Republicans rejected this proposal, however. In 2016, Republican Donald Trump won the presidency, and Trump's hostility toward undocumented immigrants may have alienated Latinos from the Republicans. In the 2018 midterm elections, Latinos supported Democrats over Republicans by a margin of 69 to 29 percent. During the 2020–2022 elections, Latinos generally favored Democrats, though by shrinking margins. One notable exception was in Florida, where, in 2022, Republican Governor Ron DeSantis benefitted from heavy Latino support.

The Gender Gap

Women won the right to vote in all states in 1920, and through the 1960 elections they gave somewhat more support to Republicans than men did. From 1964 through 1976, women did not demonstrate a clear partisan preference. Beginning in 1980, however, with the election of Ronald Reagan, scholars began to detect a **gender gap**. Women were now favoring the Democrats. In 2016, 54 percent of women voted for Democrat Hillary Clinton, compared with 41 percent of men, a gap of 13 percentage points. Clinton, of course, was the first female major-party candidate for president in U.S. history, and Republican Donald Trump was famous for his rude remarks about women.

Gender Gap
The difference between the percentage of women who vote for a particular candidate and the percentage of men who vote for the candidate.

Women's attitudes also appear to differ from those of their male counterparts on a range of issues other than presidential preferences. They are much more likely than men to oppose capital punishment and the use of force abroad. Studies also have shown that women are more concerned about risks to the environment, more supportive of social welfare, and more in agreement with extending civil rights to LGBTQ+ people than are men.

Geographic Region

Finally, where you live can influence your political attitudes.

City Versus Country. One of the most significant political developments of the last few years has been a growing gap in political allegiance between the Democratic city and the Republican countryside. Will Wilkinson, a former libertarian and current moderate, argues that this divide is largely due to a process of "self-sorting" among white voters. Urban areas continue to grow in population relative to the countryside, and those white Americans whose personal characteristics tend to draw them to liberalism are far more likely to move to a big city. Wilkinson's conclusion: "There is now *no such thing as a Republican city*." [Emphasis in original.] Even in the most conservative parts of the country, highly urban districts vote for Democrats.[6]

---

6. Will Wilkinson, *The Density Divide: Urbanization, Polarization, and Populist Backlash* (Niskanen Center Research Paper, June 2019).

REUTERS/Alamy Stock Photo

Image 6.2 Demonstrators call for comprehensive immigration reform outside the Capitol building in Washington, D.C. ▶ What kinds of changes to immigration policy have been recommended in recent years by members of Congress?

Our modern, high-tech economy has concentrated ever-greater numbers of people in our largest cities, while those left behind in rural areas and in smaller cities with declining industries lose out. These differing fortunes help explain the populist anger that has animated Trump voters in rural areas. Consider that urban areas with more than one million people, which account for 56 percent of the nation's population, enjoyed 93 percent of U.S. population growth between 2010 and 2016. In 2016, the 2,584 counties voting for Trump produced 36 percent of the nation's total output, or GDP. The 472 Clinton counties generated 64 percent.[7] The presidential contest between Donald Trump and Joe Biden in 2020 demonstrated a similar pattern. Trump was victorious throughout the majority of counties in the nation. But the most voters were obviously concentrated in highly populated urban areas. There is where Biden obtained most of his over 80 million votes.

North Versus South. The Civil War between the northern and southern states (1861–65) was the greatest trauma in American history, and its effects have reverberated down through the years. A major share of the Southern white population sees itself as the heirs and descendants of those who fought for the Confederacy. To this day, Southern whites retain a strong sense of cultural and political identity. Such an identity goes a long way in explaining the politics of the South—with Republicans as the party of white voters, while Democrats are heavily supported by Black voters.

In recent years, some parts of Confederate history have come under public scrutiny. Many statues of Confederate army officers have been removed, and the display of the Confederate flag is less acceptable than before.

Measuring Public Opinion

≫ LO 6-3: Describe the characteristics of a scientific opinion poll, and list some of the problems pollsters face in obtaining accurate results.

In a democracy, people express their opinions in a variety of ways, as mentioned in this chapter's introduction. One of the most common means of gathering and measuring public opinion on specific issues is through the use of **opinion polls**.

The History of Opinion Polls

Opinion Polls
A method of systematically questioning a small, selected sample of respondents who are deemed representative of the total population.

During the 1800s, certain American newspapers and magazines spiced up their political coverage by conducting face-to-face polls or mail surveys of their readers' opinions. In the early twentieth century, the magazine *Literary Digest* mailed large numbers of questionnaires to

---

7. Mark Muro and Sifan Liu, "Another Clinton-Trump Divide: High-Output America vs Low-Output America" (Brookings Institution, November 29, 2016).

individuals, many of whom were its own subscribers, to determine their political opinions. From 1916 to 1932, more than 70 percent of the magazine's election predictions were accurate.

In 1936, however, the magazine predicted that Republican Alfred Landon would defeat Democrat Franklin D. Roosevelt in the presidential race. Landon won in only two states. A major problem was that in 1936, several years into the Great Depression, the *Digest's* subscribers were considerably wealthier than the average American. In other words, they did not accurately represent all the voters in the U.S. population.

Several newcomers to the public opinion poll industry accurately predicted Roosevelt's landslide victory. These newcomers are still active in the poll-taking industry today: the Gallup poll of George Gallup and the Roper poll, founded by Elmo Roper. Gallup and Roper, along with Archibald Crossley, developed the modern polling techniques of market research. Using personal interviews with small samples of selected voters (fewer than two thousand), they showed that they could predict with relative accuracy the behavior of the total voting population.

Sampling Techniques

How can interviewing fewer than two thousand voters tell us what tens of millions of voters will do? Clearly, it is necessary that the sample of individuals be representative of all voters in the population.

The most important principle in sampling is randomness. Every person should have a known chance, and in particular an equal chance, of being sampled. If sampling follows this principle, then a small sample should be representative of the whole group, both in demographic characteristics (age, religion, race, region, and the like) and in opinions. The ideal way to sample the voting population of the United States would be to put all voter names into a jar—or a computer file—and randomly sample, say, two thousand of them. Because this is too costly and inefficient, pollsters have developed other ways to obtain good samples. One technique is simply to randomly select telephone numbers and interview the respective households. This technique used to produce a relatively accurate sample at a low cost. Today, most people will not answer telephone polls.

The Statistical Nature of Polling. Universally, when the results of an opinion poll are announced, the findings are reported as specific numbers. A poll might find, for example, that 10 percent of those surveyed approve of the job performance of Congress. Such precise figures can mislead you as to the essential nature of polling.

In reality, it makes more sense to consider the results of a particular survey question as a range of numbers, not a single integer. That could mean that the question about Congress's job performance yielded an answer that fell somewhere between 7 percent and 13 percent. The figure of 10 percent is only the midpoint of the possible spread—the most probable result. If we had been able to question all members of the public, the chances that they would give Congress exactly a 10 percent rating are not high. Even if the pollster in this case employed the best possible practices, the odds are better than 50-50 that the true answer is not 10 percent, but some other number in the 7 to 13 percent range.

Sampling Error. Reputable polling firms report the margin of error associated with their results. The results of a carefully conducted poll

Krista Kennell/Patrick McMullan/Getty Images

Image 6.3 Polling expert Nate Silver's FiveThirtyEight blog is now sponsored by ABC.
▶ Why might some people refuse to pay attention to the polls?

that surveys a large number of respondents—say, two thousand people—might have a 95 percent chance of falling within a 3-point margin of error. The 95 percent figure is an industry standard. What this means, however, is that the pollster believes that any given poll result has a 5 percent chance of landing four or more percentage points away from the true answer, which we would get if we really could interview everyone. In the example of the question about Congress, there is a 5 percent chance—one chance in twenty—that the approval rating is actually below 7 percent or above 13 percent.

Sampling Error
The difference between a sample result and the true result if the entire population had been interviewed.

These variations are called **sampling error**. They follow from the fact that the poll taker is examining a sample and not the entire population. Sampling error is one reason that knowledgeable poll watchers disregard small variations in poll results. Gallup, for example, polls the public on its approval of the president's job performance every day. Such continuous polls are known as tracking polls. Suppose that on Monday, the tracking poll shows that President Biden had a 40 percent approval rating. On Tuesday it was 42 percent, on Wednesday 41 percent, and on Thursday 39 percent. Was the president really more popular on Tuesday and Wednesday? Almost certainly not. These variations are simply so much "statistical noise."

The Difficulty of Obtaining Accurate Results

Reputable polling organizations devote substantial effort to ensuring that their samples are truly random. If they succeed, then the accuracy of their results should be limited only by sampling error. Unfortunately, obtaining a completely random sample of the population is difficult. Women are more likely to answer the telephone than men. Some kinds of people, such as students and individuals with low incomes, are relatively hard to contact.

Many poll takers now rely on automated scripts—"robocalls"—rather than live interviewers. Under the law, however, robocallers are not allowed to dial cell phones. As a result, automated surveys are less accurate than traditional ones. Pollsters currently have no way at all to reach people who rely on Skype, Facetime, WhatsApp, or similar systems for telephone service. Finally, more than 90 percent of households contacted by typical polls refuse to be interviewed.

Weighting the Sample. Polling firms address this problem of obtaining a true random sample by weighting their samples. That is, they correct for differences between the sample and the public by adding extra "weight" to the responses of underrepresented groups. For example, 20 percent of the respondents in a survey might state that they are evangelical Christians. Based on other sources of information, the poll taker believes that the true share of evangelicals in the target population is 25 percent. Therefore, the responses of the evangelical respondents receive extra weight so that they make up 25 percent of the reported result.

It is relatively easy to correct a sample for well-known demographic characteristics such as education, gender, race/ethnicity, religion, and geography. It is much harder—and riskier—to adjust for political ideology, partisan preference, or likelihood of voting. The formulas that firms use to weight their responses are typically trade secrets and are not disclosed to the public or the press.

House Effects. One consequence of the use of secret in-house weighting schemes is that the results reported by one polling firm may differ systematically from those reported by another. Pollster A might consistently rate the chances of Republican candidates as 2 percentage points higher than does pollster B. A consistent difference in polling results between firms is known as a **house effect**. (House here means the organization or firm, as when referring to casinos.) House effects are measured by comparing a firm's results with the average results of all other poll takers. A house effect does not necessarily mean that a firm's results are in error. It could be noticing something important that its rivals have missed.

House Effect
In public opinion polling, an effect in which one polling organization's results consistently differ from those reported by other poll takers.

How Accurate Are the Results? Despite all of the practical difficulties involved in poll taking, the major polling organizations have usually enjoyed a good record in predicting the outcome of presidential contests. (Predicting primary elections and state-level races is harder.) Some major poll takers, however, reported presidential results that were embarrassingly inaccurate. In 2016, almost all poll takers predicted that Hillary Clinton would win the presidency. She did not. Of course, polls attempt to predict the national popular vote, which Clinton won by 2 percentage points. Most polls still overstated her support at the national level. In addition, polls in the states essential to Trump's victory—Michigan, Pennsylvania, and Wisconsin—should have signaled trouble for Clinton. They didn't.

Figure 6.3 shows the 2020 presidential predictions of several prominent pollsters. In the 2020 elections, polling firms performed badly—the presidential polls were off by the largest margins in 72 years. On average, state-level presidential polls were about 6 percentage points more favorable to Biden than what was shown in the election results. (The state-level polls were more accurate in several states that Biden needed to carry.)

The number-one reason for the error appears to be that pollsters dramatically underestimated Republican voter turnout. Of course, Democratic turnout was way up as well, with the result that the 2020 elections posted the largest percentage voter turnout in more than a century. One problem that could have led to polling error may have been a tendency by Trump supporters to refuse to participate in polls. These voters may have seen polltakers as part of the despised "mainstream media."

Additional Problems With Polls

Public opinion polls are snapshots of the opinions and preferences of the people at a specific moment in time and as expressed in response to a specific question. Given that definition, it is fairly easy to understand situations in which the polls are wrong. For example, opinion polls leading up to the 1980 presidential elections showed President Jimmy Carter defeating challenger Ronald Reagan. Only a few analysts noted the large number of "undecided" respondents a week before the election. Those voters shifted massively to Reagan at the last minute, and Reagan won the election.

A similar development helped elect Donald Trump in 2016. At the last minute, the share of the electorate swinging from "undecided" to Trump was about 2 percentage points larger than the share that swung to Clinton. The result was that most poll takers predicted that Clinton would do about 2 percentage points better in the popular vote than she actually did.

Poll Questions. It makes sense to expect that the results of a poll will reflect the questions that are asked. Depending on what question is asked, voters could be said either to support a particular proposal or to oppose it. One of the problems with many polls is the yes/no answer format. For example, suppose that a poll question asks, "Do you support President Biden's policies toward China?" A respondent who has a complicated view of these events, as many people do, has no way of indicating this view because "yes" and "no" are the only possible answers.

How a question is phrased can change the polling outcome dramatically. The Roper polling organization once asked a double-negative question that many people found hard

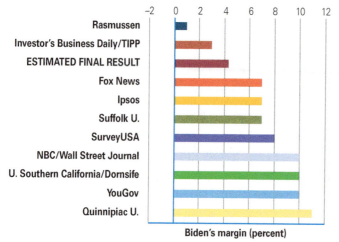

Figure 6.3 Joe Biden's Predicted Margin Over Donald Trump

These percentage points are predictions of the final popular vote margin. They are not the margin in the electoral college. The estimate of the actual popular vote margin comes from Nate Silver of the FiveThirtyEight blog. ▶ **Why is it so hard for polltakers to predict election results?**

Biden's margin (percent)

Source: FiveThirtyEight blog.

to understand: "Does it seem possible or does it seem impossible to you that the Nazi extermination of the Jews never happened?" The survey results showed that 20 percent of Americans seemed to doubt that the Holocaust ever occurred. When the Roper organization rephrased the question more clearly, the percentage of doubters dropped to less than 1 percent.

Respondents' answers are also influenced by the order in which questions are asked and, in some cases, by their interactions with the interviewer. To a certain extent, people try to please the interviewer.

Unscientific and Fraudulent Polls. A perennial issue is the promotion of surveys that are unscientific or even fraudulent. All too often, a magazine or website asks its readers to respond to a question—and then publishes the answers as if they were based on a scientifically chosen random sample. Other news media may then publicize the survey as if it were a poll taken by such reliable teams as Gallup, CBS and the *New York Times*, or the *Wall Street Journal* and NBC. Critical consumers should watch out for surveys with self-selected respondents and other types of skewed samples. These so-called polls may be used to deliberately mislead the public. In addition, some campaigns have used push polls, in which the respondents are given misleading information in the questions, in an effort to persuade them to vote against a particular candidate.

Public Opinion and the Political Process

≫ **LO 6-4:** Analyze the effect that public opinion may have on the political process.

Public opinion affects the political process in many ways. Politicians see public opinion as important to their careers. The president, members of Congress, governors, and other elected officials realize that strong support by the public as expressed in opinion polls is a source of power in dealing with other politicians. It is more difficult for a senator to say no to the president if the president is immensely popular and if polls show approval of the president's policies. Public opinion also helps political candidates identify voters' most important concerns and may help them shape their campaigns successfully.

Political Culture and Public Opinion

Americans are divided into a multitude of ethnic, religious, regional, and political subgroups. Given the diversity of American society and the wide range of opinions contained within it, how is it that the political process continues to function without falling into chaos?

One explanation is rooted in the concept of the American political culture, which can be described as a set of attitudes and ideas about the nation and the government. As discussed earlier, our political culture is widely shared by Americans of many different backgrounds. To some extent, it consists of symbols, such as the American flag, the Liberty Bell, and the Statue of Liberty. The elements of our political culture also include certain shared beliefs about the most important values in the American political system, including liberty, equality, and property.

The political culture provides a general environment of support for the political system. If the people share certain beliefs about the system and a reservoir of good feeling exists toward the institutions of government, the nation will be better able to weather periods of crisis. The political culture also helps Americans evaluate their government's performance.

Policymaking and Public Opinion

Policymakers cannot always be guided by opinion polls. In the end, politicians must make their own choices, and those choices necessarily involve trade-offs. If politicians vote for increased spending to improve education, for example, by necessity fewer resources are available for other worthy projects. Individuals who are polled do not have to make such trade-offs when they respond to questions. Indeed, survey respondents usually are not even given a choice of trade-offs in their policy opinions. Moreover, to make an informed policy choice requires an understanding not only of the policy area but also of the consequences of any given choice. Public opinion polls rarely ensure that those polled have such information.

Finally, government decisions cannot be made simply by adding up individual desires. Politicians regularly engage in "horse trading" (shrewd bargaining) with each other. Politicians also know that they cannot satisfy every desire of every constituent. Therefore, politicians attempt to maximize the net benefits to their constituents, while keeping within the limits of whatever the politicians believe the government can afford.

The Media in the United States

>> **LO 6-5:** Describe the different types of media and the changing roles they play in American society.

The study of people and politics must take into account the role played by the media. Historically, the print media played the most important role in informing public debate. The print media developed, for the most part, our understanding of how news is to be reported. Today, however, 50 percent of Americans use television news as their primary source of information. (Note that most young people don't watch TV.)

In addition, the internet has become a major source for news, political communication, and fundraising. The internet is now the second most widely used source of information—25 percent of all persons consider it their primary source of news. Only 7.5 percent of the public now relies on print publications as a primary news source.

The Roles of the Media

The mass media perform a number of different functions in any country. In the United States, we can list at least six media functions. Almost all of them can have political implications, and some are essential to the democratic process. These functions are as follows: (1) entertaining the public, (2) reporting the news, (3) identifying public problems, (4) socializing new generations, (5) providing a political forum, and (6) making profits.

Entertaining the Public. By far the greatest number of radio and television hours are dedicated to entertaining the public. The battle for prime-time ratings indicates how important successful entertainment is to the survival of networks and individual stations. A number of network shows have a highly political content. Many people have reported that they get much of their political information from programs such as *The Daily Show*, formerly hosted by Jon Stewart and now by Trevor Noah. Another important personality is John Oliver, who hosts *Last Week Tonight* on HBO.

For many Americans, especially younger ones, the internet is replacing television as a source of entertainment. While much time on the internet may be spent chatting with friends on services such as Skype and WhatsApp, or watching television programs online, politics is often a topic. YouTube, in particular, offers a large number of politically oriented videos, many of which are satirical. Talk radio and television shows that feature personalities are another form of politically oriented entertainment—one that is dominated by the political right.

Reporting the News. A primary function of the mass media in all their forms is the reporting of news. The media provide words and pictures about events, facts, personalities, and ideas. The protections of the First Amendment are intended to keep the flow of news as free as possible, because it is an essential part of the democratic process. If citizens cannot obtain unbiased information about the state of their communities and their leaders' actions, how can they make voting decisions? One of the more incisive comments about the importance of the media was made by James Madison, who said, "A popular government without popular information or the means of acquiring it, is but a prologue to a farce or a tragedy or perhaps both."[8]

Identifying Public Problems. The power of the media is important not only in revealing what the government is doing but also in determining what the government ought to do—in other words, in setting the **public agenda**. As we noted earlier in this chapter, the mass media identify public issues. American journalists have a long tradition of uncovering public wrongdoing, corruption, and bribery, and of bringing such wrongdoing to the public's attention. For its part, the internet offers an enormous collection of political sites, with policy proposals representing every point of view.

Public Agenda
Issues that are perceived by the political community as meriting public attention and governmental action.

Agenda setting by the media is enhanced by the various ways in which they can present the news. One technique, called **priming**, involves reporting certain facts, but not others. Priming can shape the public's response to an issue. A similar concept is **framing**, that is, embedding the issue in a particular story line. Attitudes toward government spending on people with incomes below the federal poverty threshold, for example, can be altered by stories that present such people as victims of bad luck—or who are suffering mostly due to their own behavioral problems.

Priming
In a media report, using only certain facts to shape the public's response to an issue.

Framing
In a media report, the technique of embedding an issue in particular examples or story lines to alter public perceptions of the issue.

Socializing New Generations. As mentioned earlier in this chapter, the media strongly influence the beliefs and opinions of Americans. Because of this influence, the media play a significant role in the political socialization of the younger generation and of immigrants

---

8. James Madison, "Letter to W. T. Barry," August 4, 1822, in Gaillard P. Hunt, ed., *The Writings of James Madison*, Vol. 9 (1910), p. 103.

to this country. Through the transmission of historical information (sometimes fictionalized), the presentation of American culture, and the portrayal of the diverse regions and groups in the United States, the media teach young people and immigrants about what it means to be an American. Many children's television shows are designed not only to entertain young viewers but also to instruct them in the moral values of American society. On the internet, young Americans participate in political forums, obtain information for writing assignments, and, in general, acquire much of their political socialization.

Providing a Political Forum. As part of their news function, the media also provide a political forum for leaders and the public. Candidates for office use news reporting to sustain interest in their campaigns, while officeholders use the media to gain support for their policies or to present an image of leadership. Presidential trips abroad are one way for the chief executive to get colorful, positive, and exciting news coverage that makes the president look "presidential." The media also offer ways for citizens to participate in public debate through letters to the editor, blog posts, Facebook and Twitter posts, and other channels.

Making Profits. Most of the news media in the United States are private, for-profit corporate enterprises. One of their goals is to make profits for expansion and for dividends to the stockholders who own the companies. In general, profits are made as a result of charging for advertising. Advertising revenues usually are related directly to circulation or to listener/viewer ratings.

Several well-known media outlets, in contrast, are publicly owned—public television stations in many communities and National Public Radio. These outlets operate without extensive commercials, are locally supported, and are often subsidized by the government and corporations.

For the most part, however, the media depend on advertisers for their revenues. Consequently, reporters may feel pressure from media owners and from advertisers. Media owners may take their cues from what advertisers want. If an important advertiser does not like the political bent of a particular newspaper reporter, for example, the reporter could be asked to alter their "style" of writing.

The Financial Crisis of the Press. Lately, newspapers have found it increasingly difficult to make a profit. Newspaper revenues have fallen because online services have taken over a greater share of classified advertising. The 2008 economic crisis, which depressed all forms of advertising spending, pushed many large daily newspapers over the edge. Newspapers in Chicago, Denver, and Seattle went out of business. Even some of the most famous papers, such as the *New York Times*, the *Chicago Tribune*, and the *Boston Globe*, were in serious financial trouble. The 2020 coronavirus recession reduced advertising even more.

Although all major newspapers are now online, they have found it difficult to turn a profit on their online editions. News sites typically cannot sell enough advertising to meet their costs. In response to this problem, major newspapers have begun charging for online access, a process dubbed as retreating behind a paywall. Access charges, however, reduce the number of users who are willing to view a site.

D Dipasupil/Getty Images

Image 6.4 MSNBC personality Rachel Maddow speaks at the Times Center Stage about the elections. Maddow is one of the most popular liberals on television. ▶ How might a network gain viewers by adopting a particular political line?

On the internet, news organizations that employ reporters and create articles are known as content providers, because they provide original content. Unfortunately for the content providers, they collect only a small share of the total revenue from online advertising. Most ad revenue goes to aggregators, such as Google, that provide search and aggregation services, but generate little or no original content. Google alone collects more than half of all U.S. online ad revenue. Google's ad revenue is substantially greater than the total ad revenue, print and online, of every newspaper in the nation put together. In other words, there is no absolute shortage of ad revenue—the problem is that it does not go to the content providers. Of course, without content providers, there is nothing to aggregate.

Television Versus the Newer Media

As we explained earlier, newer forms of media are displacing older ones as sources of information on politics and society in general. Although it is only recently that newspapers have experienced severe economic difficulties, they were losing ground to television as early as the 1950s. Today, the internet has begun to displace television.

Newer Patterns of Media Consumption. Not everyone, however, migrates to newer media at the same rate. Among Americans older than sixty-five years of age, only 6 percent obtained the greatest amount of information about political campaigns in 2016 by going online. In this older generation, 11 percent still relied on a printed daily newspaper, although that is down from 58 percent in 2000.[9]

The media consumption patterns are simply different from the past. Indeed, many younger people have abandoned e-mail, relying on Facebook, texting, and newer, more innovative social-networking platforms for messages. Television becomes something to watch only if you cannot find the program you want to see online.

Young people may find much of the offline media irrelevant to their lives. Yet television news, cable networks, talk radio, and other forms of media are not irrelevant to American politics. Older voters still do get their news from television, and they outnumber younger voters by a wide margin. It follows that television remains essential to American politics.

The Continuing Influence of Television. Television's continuing influence on the political process is recognized by all who engage in that process. Television news is often criticized for being superficial, particularly compared with the detailed coverage available in newspapers, magazines, and online articles. In fact, television news is constrained by its technical characteristics, the most important being the limitations of time—stories must be reported in only a few minutes.

The most interesting aspect of television—and of online videos—is the fact that it relies on images rather than words to attract the viewer's attention. Therefore, video that is chosen for a particular political story has exaggerated importance. Viewers do not know what other videos may have been taken or what other events may have been recorded—they see only those appearing on their screens. Video clips, whether they appear on network news or YouTube, can also use well-constructed stories to exploit the potential for drama. Some critics suggest that there is pressure to produce television news that has a story line, like a novel or movie. The story should be short, with exciting pictures and a clear plot. In extreme cases, the news media are satisfied with a **sound bite**, a several-second comment selected or crafted for its immediate impact on the viewer.

Sound Bite
A brief, memorable comment that can easily be fit into news broadcasts.

---

9. Pew Research Center for the People & the Press, "The 2016 Presidential Campaign—a News Event That's Hard to Miss," February 4, 2016.

It has been suggested that the format characteristics of video increase its influence on political events. As you are aware, real life is usually not dramatic, nor do all events have a plot that is neat or easily understood. Political campaigns are continuing events, lasting perhaps as long as two years. The significance of their daily turns and twists is only apparent later. The "drama" of Congress, with its 535 players and dozens of important committees and meetings, is also difficult for the media to present. Television requires, instead, dozens of daily three-minute stories.

Challenges Facing the Media

Media corporations can be large, and size usually translates into power. Have major media corporations used their power wisely? Two relevant issues are media consolidation and the net neutrality debate. A third issue is the possible impact of foreign governments on the administration of the internet.

Media Consolidation. Many media outlets are now owned by corporate conglomerates. A single entity may own a television network. It may also own studios that produce shows, news, and movies. Finally, it may own the means to deliver that content to the home through cable, satellite, or the internet. One concern advanced by observers of concentrated ownership is that media owners might use their power to steer the national agenda in a direction that they prefer. Indeed, several news organizations appear to have conservative or liberal viewpoints. Rupert Murdoch's Fox News clearly offers a conservative perspective. Both CNN and MSNBC have demonstrated their liberal perspectives for years. Some, however, believe that the great variety of internet news sources provides an ample counterweight to the advocacy of media moguls.

Kobby Dagan/Shutterstock.com

Image 6.5 Facebook founder Mark Zuckerberg supports his employees during San Francisco's LGBTQ+ pride parade. ▶ How are leaders of the newer media different from leaders of the old media?

The Unregulated Internet. The internet is widely regarded as a triumph of unregulated enterprise, even though it is directly descended from ARPANET, a project of the Advanced Research Projects Agency within the Department of Defense. The federal government may have created the internet, but internet pioneers were remarkably successful in preventing the government from imposing regulations that might limit the freedom of users. Almost all internet funding comes from the individuals and organizations that connect to it. An individual or organization can purchase connectivity from an **internet service provider (ISP)**.

Net Neutrality. The principle of **net neutrality** is that an ISP should treat all traffic equally. It should not block or degrade access to websites—for example, sites that compete with the ISP's own telephone or TV services. Nor should it create special "fast lanes" that allow favored content to load more quickly than the rest.

In the past, the structure of the internet tended to enforce the network neutrality principle. If an ISP attempted to block access to a site, for example, angry users would switch to a different ISP. Today, however, for many customers, high-speed broadband service is available only from a cable TV company such as Comcast that has a local monopoly, and cell phone providers such as Verizon Wireless. Secure in the knowledge that it would be difficult for their customers to switch to a different provider, large ISPs have explored the

Internet Service Provider (ISP)
A corporation or service that sells access to the internet.

Net Neutrality
The principle that an ISP should treat all traffic equally.

possibility of charging services such as Netflix for expedited transit. Such costs could be passed on to consumers.

As a result, net neutrality became a public issue. Advocates of the principle contended that net neutrality eased the creation of new services such as Facebook, YouTube, and Dropbox. Opponents argued that enforcing net neutrality would discourage investment in internet infrastructure. Attempts by the FCC to issue regulations on this issue were frustrated by a court ruling that the commission would have to classify the internet as a public utility before regulating it.[10] In February 2015, the FCC issued a proposal to do exactly that, proclaiming the internet a public utility. In March, the commission issued specific rules. ISPs could not block content, slow transmissions, or create special fast lanes. In 2016, a U.S. appeals court upheld the FCC rules. Republicans have been supportive of cable and cell phone companies, however. In December 2017, the FCC started dismantling the net neutrality rules.

Potential Problems With Foreign Governments. Could the actions of foreign governments impair internet freedom? After all, every country with an authoritarian regime tries to control its citizens' internet access. Witness China, home of the "Great Firewall of China." Many foreign websites are blocked. Bloggers and tweeters can be certain that government censors are analyzing their political statements.

The U.S. government, which sponsored the internet, has kept some control of it. For example, the Internet Corporation for Assigned Names and Numbers (ICANN) has been responsible to the U.S. Commerce Department. ICANN oversees the system of assigning internet domain names and addresses worldwide. In 2014, however, the Obama administration announced that it would end its control of ICANN. A controversy erupted. Some feared that if the U.S. government did not control ICANN, a United Nations (UN) body such as the International Telecommunication Union (ITU) might assume responsibility instead. The ITU, however, is run by governments, including authoritarian regimes such as China and Russia. These two nations have called for banning anonymity on the internet and for taxing access to sites such as Google and Facebook.

In response to criticisms, the Obama administration postponed action. In 2016, however, ICANN finally adopted new governance rules. It is now controlled by a nongovernmental panel of technical experts located in Los Angeles. Governments will have little input into ICANN decisions. In particular, the ITU is frozen out.

The Media and Political Campaigns

≫ LO 6-6: Indicate the ways in which political bias manifests itself in the mass media.

All forms of the media—television, newspapers, radio, magazines, and online services—have a significant political impact on American society. Although younger voters get a relatively small share of their news from television, it remains a significant news source for older voters. Therefore, candidates and their consultants spend much of their time devising strategies that use television to their benefit. Three types of TV coverage are generally employed in campaigns for the presidency and other offices: advertising, including negative ads; management of news coverage; and campaign debates.

---

10. *Verizon v. FCC*, 740 F.3d 623 (D.C. Cir. 2014).

Political Advertising

Political advertising has become increasingly important for the profitability of television station owners. Hearst Television, for example, obtains well over 10 percent of its revenues from political ads during an election year. During the 2012 presidential elections, total spending exceeded $7 billion. Among other expenses, candidates purchased more than 3 million campaign advertisements. At the presidential level, ad spending was down in 2016, but candidates in other races continued to increase their expenditures. All spending during the 2020 campaign increased dramatically. It is estimated that over $13 billion was spent then during the 2019-20 election cycle.

In recent elections, an ever-increasing share of political ads have been negative in nature. The public claims not to like negative advertising, but as one consultant put it, "Negative advertising works." Negative ads can backfire, though, when there are three or more candidates in the race, a typical state of affairs in the early presidential primaries. If one candidate attacks another, the attacker as well as the candidate who is attacked may come to be viewed negatively by the public. A candidate who "goes negative" may thus unintentionally boost the chances of a third candidate who is not part of the exchange.

Image 6.6 Republican presidential candidate Donald Trump at a press conference in New York City in July 2020. ▶ How did Trump's experience as host of a television reality show help him in his first campaign?

Management of News Coverage

Using political advertising to get a message across to the public is a very expensive tactic. Coverage by the news media, however, is free. The campaign simply needs to ensure that coverage takes place. In recent years, campaign managers have shown increasing sophistication in creating newsworthy events for journalists to cover. Uniquely, in 2015 and 2016 Donald Trump had no need of a campaign manager to help him attract free media coverage. Trump's personal talent for winning media attention was unprecedented. Trump's abilities meant that he was able to succeed even though his advertising budget was far smaller than that of any major-party candidate in many years.

The campaign staff uses several methods to try to influence the quantity and type of coverage the campaign receives. First, with an understanding of the technical aspects of media coverage—camera angles, necessary equipment, timing, and deadlines—the staff plans political events to accommodate the press. Second, the campaign organization is aware that political reporters and their sponsors—networks, newspapers, or blogs—are in competition for the best stories and can be manipulated through the granting of favors, such as a personal interview with the candidate. Third, the scheduler in the campaign has the important task of planning events that will be photogenic and interesting enough for the evening news.

A related goal, although one that is more difficult to attain, is to convince reporters that a particular interpretation of an event is true. Today, the art of putting the appropriate **spin** on a story or event is highly developed. Press advisers, often referred to as **spin doctors**, try to convince journalists that the advisers' interpetations of political events are correct.

Spin
An interpretation of political events that is favorable to a candidate or officeholder.

Spin Doctors
Political advisers who try to convince journalists of the truth of a particular interpretation of events.

For example, the Obama administration and Republicans in Congress engaged in a major spinning duel over Obama's 2014 executive order on unauthorized immigrants. The order allowed certain classes of unauthorized immigrants to remain in the country. Republicans sought to portray the order as overreach by an imperial presidency. Republicans in the House tried—unsuccessfully—to overturn the order by refusing to fund the Department of Homeland Security. Democrats then argued that Republicans were acting irresponsibly and threatening our national security. (The order was blocked by the Supreme Court in 2016.)

Going for the Knockout Punch—Presidential Debates

In presidential elections, perhaps just as important as political advertisements and general news coverage is the performance of the candidates in televised presidential debates. In the first such debate in 1960, John Kennedy, the young senator from Massachusetts, took on the vice president of the United States, Richard Nixon. Many observers concluded that Kennedy's performance in these debates provided the edge he needed to win a very close contest. Thereafter, candidates became aware of the great potential of television for changing the momentum of a campaign.

In general, challengers have much more to gain from debating than do incumbents. Challengers hope that the incumbent will make a mistake in the debate and undermine the "presidential" image. Incumbent presidents are loath to debate their challengers, because it puts their opponents on an equal footing with them, but the debates have become so widely anticipated that it is difficult for an incumbent to refuse to participate.

Clinton Versus Trump. In 2016, the first debate between Hillary Clinton and Donald Trump was seen by an unprecedented 80 million viewers. Going into the debates, Hillary Clinton's margin in the polls was narrow. After her successful performance, her margin approached 7 percentage points. By Election Day, however, most of her advantage had worn off. Some analysts suggested that the temporary bump in Clinton's support was an illusion. Good or bad news for a particular candidate may affect the willingness of the candidate's supporters to participate in polling. Clinton's 7-point advantage, in other words, may have been caused by discouraged Trump supporters who refused to talk to pollsters and by upbeat Clinton supporters who were more than happy to talk.

The Trump–Biden Debates. The first 2020 debate between Donald Trump and Joe Biden was notable for Trump's habit of interrupting and talking over Biden. Some commentators described it as the worst debate they had ever seen. Post-debate polls found that a majority of viewers disliked Trump's interruptions. Still, with 73 million viewers, it had the third-largest audience of any presidential debate ever. On October 2, the White House announced that the president had come down with COVID-19. Trump required hospitalization but recovered quickly.

Still, the second debate, planned for October 15, was replaced by two town halls, held simultaneously by ABC and NBC. The third debate proceeded on schedule. This time, the debate commission had the power to turn off a candidate's microphone. Both were therefore able to speak without undue interruption. Polls suggested that Trump's followers believed that he had won and that Biden's supporters thought he had done best.

Political Campaigns and the Internet

Today, the campaign staff of almost every candidate running for a significant political office includes an internet campaign strategist—a professional hired to create and maintain the campaign website, social media accounts, blogs, and podcasts. The work of this strategist includes designing a user-friendly and attractive website for the candidate and tracking campaign contributions made through the site. The strategist also manages the candidate's e-mail, Twitter, and Facebook communications. Finally, this staffer hires bloggers to promote the candidate's agenda on the web and monitors websites for favorable or unfavorable comments or video clips about the candidate.

Blogosphere Politics

Within the past few years, politicians have also felt obligated to post regular blogs on their websites. The word **blog** comes from web log, a regular updating of one's ideas at a specific website. Of course, many people besides politicians are also posting blogs. Most of the millions of blogs posted daily are not political. The ones that are can have a dramatic influence on events, giving rise to the term blogosphere politics.

Blog
A regular updating of one's ideas on a specific website. The word comes from web log.

Collective Blogs and Online Magazines. One development that has increasingly taken hold is the collective blog, in which writers—some of whom formerly had their own personal blogs—work together to produce the content. One example is Vox.com, a left-of-center news site. Another is RealClearPolitics, a right-of-center site that mostly aggregates articles from elsewhere (including from liberal sources). It is often hard to tell the difference between a collective blog and an online magazine. Among the sites we list in Table 6.2, only The Conscience of a Liberal is an old-fashioned, one-person blog.

Trump's Use of Twitter. One characteristic of the 2016 elections was the enhanced role of Twitter. With 310 million active users in 2016, Twitter was not the largest social media service. Famously, "tweets" were limited to 140 characters (now 280). Still, Twitter proved to be an ideal platform for Donald Trump, who reveled in his ability to issue short, colorful statements. Trump's Twitter presence was backed up by a veritable army of supporters who retweeted each of his observations to thousands of additional people. These supporters were also quite willing to pile onto anyone who criticized their candidate. Trump's tweets often provoked controversy. His campaign devoted little time to screening sources that Trump quoted, some of which turned out to be highly questionable.

Table 6.2	Selected Political Blog Sites and Online Magazines
Progressive	
The Conscience of a Liberal	https://twitter.com/paulkrugman
Mother Jones	www.motherjones.com
Talking Points Memo	talkingpointsmemo.com
ThinkProgress	thinkprogress.org
Conservative	
Daily Caller	dailycaller.com
Breitbart	www.breitbart.com
National Review Online	www.nationalreview.com
PJ Media	pjmedia.com

▶ Interact

Many blogs—and also online newspapers and magazines—allow readers to comment on posts or articles. Comments can be a way to build a community around a small blog. Sites with a huge readership, however, experience problems with comments. They can quickly deteriorate into "flame wars," in which readers insult each other instead of entering useful observations. One solution is to publish only those comments approved by a moderator. For most sites, however, this procedure involves an unacceptable amount of effort. Visit at least one progressive and one conservative site listed in Table 6.2. Take the time to look at posted comments. What topics are most important to these sites? How much of what they report is news, and how much is opinion? What kinds of readers does the site appear to have?

Bias
An inclination or a preference that interferes with impartial judgment.

Bias in the Media

Traditionally, newspapers and other media have tried to separate opinion pieces from "straight news." In recent years, many media observers have worried that opinion is "taking over" and displacing news sources that try to be objective. Many blogs, for example, are almost pure opinion, even if they also provide some facts. Another media format in which opinion is dominant is talk radio.

Talk Radio. The most conspicuous characteristic of talk radio is that it is almost completely controlled by conservatives, some of whom are quite radical. None of the top talk show hosts are liberal. Talk show hosts do not pretend to be journalists. Rather, they are personalities who entertain their audiences with red-meat politics. Exaggeration for effect is typical, and language that would be unacceptable in other contexts is common. As you will learn shortly, many conservatives believe that liberals dominate the "mainstream media." Conservative control of talk radio, however, makes it harder to argue that the media as a whole have a liberal bias.

The Mainstream Media. For decades, the contention that the mainstream media have a liberal **bias** has been repeated time and again. A number of studies appear to back up this claim. For example, research at the University of Connecticut has shown that journalists consider themselves Democrats three times as often as they identify with the Republicans. A recent Gallup poll reports that 47 percent of the public think that the news media are too liberal, while 13 percent see the media as too conservative. These views are strongly associated with the politics of the respondent: 75 percent of Republicans believe the media are too liberal, while only 20 percent of Democrats think that is true.

Bias and Professionalism. While many journalists may be Democrats at heart, many operate under a code of professional ethics that dictates "objectivity" and a commitment to the truth. Journalists may not always succeed in living up to such a code, but it helps that it exists.

To be sure, many media outlets have an explicit political point of view. This is especially common in the blogosphere, but it is true of some cable news channels as well. Fox News, for example, takes pride in avoiding what it sees as the liberal bias of the mainstream media. As stated earlier, both MSNBC and CNN do not hide their anti-conservative points of view.

The Media in 2016: Trump and Clinton. The media devoted ample resources to Trump's often questionable business dealings and his failure to release his income tax returns. Few voters could have remained ignorant of a tape in which Trump boasted that he had the ability to physically molest women. Still, the media found it difficult to respond to Trump's constant disregard for whether his statements were actually true. Indeed, Trump's objective was never

UPI/Alamy Stock Photo

Image 6.7 Rush Limbaugh was one of the most listened-to talk radio hosts in America. At times, he was considered the spokesperson for American conservatives. ▶ Should the Federal Communications Commission be able to have regulated what he said?

to report facts to assure his followers that he was on their side. Many of his supporters understood this and did not mind.

Clinton loathed the media, and many of its members hated her right back. Clinton's hostility was in part generated by a decades-long series of investigations into alleged scandals. None of these investigations revealed any wrongdoing, but they had a lethal impact on Clinton's relations with the media—and eventually, the public. An example was the controversy over Clinton's use of a private e-mail server while she was secretary of state. An investigation cleared her, though the FBI criticized her. According to the Tyndall Report, the three major networks devoted one hundred minutes to the e-mails—and thirty-two minutes to covering all policy issues taken together. As a result of this coverage, much of the media effectively supported Trump's contention that Clinton was a criminal who belonged in prison, not in the White House.

The Media in 2020: Trump and Biden. On Trump, there was always a large gap between reporting by the Fox News network and publications such as the *New York Times* or the *Washington Post*. Fox commentators argued that Trump could do little wrong. The *Times* and the *Post*, in contrast, were so hostile to Trump that some began to conclude that they were every bit as biased as Fox. One way in which journalists could reconcile professionalism with hostility to Trump was simply to report, again, and again, Trump's own tweets and statements, together with criticisms such as "without evidence" or "untrue." While many of Trump's strongest supporters were thrilled by his aggressiveness, his attitudes also tended to repel many of the middle-class moderates that he needed for his reelection bid.

Joe Biden, in contrast, was a more elusive target. Claims that Biden would be a puppet of the left contradicted the fact that Biden had run against the most progressive candidates in the Democratic primaries. Accusations that he was senile failed when people could see him for themselves. Press coverage of Biden, in short, tended to be neutral—to his advantage.

Being a Critical Consumer of the News

Television, print media, and the internet provide a wide range of choices for Americans who want to stay informed. Still, critics of the media argue that a substantial amount of what you read and see is colored either by the subjectivity of editors and bloggers or by the demands of profit making. Few Americans take the time to become critical consumers of the news. Many people, in fact, get almost all of their information from partisan sources, from within their own political "bubble." Some of these sources are famous for running stories that are flatly not true.

Why Should You Care? Even if you do not plan to engage in political activism, you have a stake in ensuring that your beliefs are truly your own and that they represent your values and interests. To guarantee this result, you need to obtain accurate information from the media. If you do not take care, you could find yourself voting for a candidate who is opposed to what you believe in or voting against measures that are in your interest. After all, even when journalists themselves are successful at remaining objective, they will of necessity give publicity to politicians and interest group representatives who are far from impartial.

What Can You Do? To become a critical news consumer, you must develop a critical eye and ear. Sources such as blogs often have strong political preferences, and you should try to determine what these are. Does a blog merely give opinions, or does it back up its arguments with data? It is possible to select anecdotes to support almost any argument—does an anecdote represent typical circumstances, or is it a rare occurrence highlighted to make a point?

Watching the evening news can be far more rewarding if you look at how much the news depends on video effects. You will note that stories on the evening news tend to be no more than three minutes long, that stories with excellent video footage get more attention, and that considerable time is taken up with "happy talk" or human-interest stories.

Another way to critically evaluate news coverage is to compare how the news is covered by different outlets. Table 6.2 in this chapter provides online sources that you can compare. You might want to compare a conservative site such as the *National Review* with one such as *Mother Jones*.

A variety of organizations try to monitor news sources for accuracy and bias. Consider visiting the following sites:

- Fairness & Accuracy in Reporting is a media watchdog with a strong liberal viewpoint.
- Accuracy in Media takes a combative conservative position on media issues.

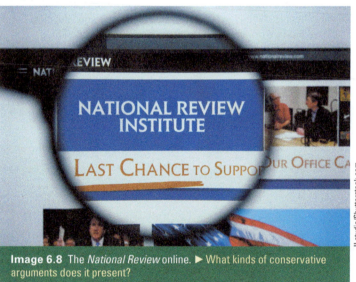

Image 6.8 The *National Review* online. ▶ What kinds of conservative arguments does it present?

Il.studio/Shutterstock.com

Key Terms

agenda-setting 125
bias 146
blog 145
consensus 123
divided opinion 123
framing 138
gender gap 131

generational effect 126
house effect 135
internet service
   provider (ISP) 141
media 125
net neutrality 141
opinion leaders 124

opinion polls 132
peer group 124
political
   socialization 123
priming 138
public agenda 138
public opinion 123

sampling error 134
sound bite 140
spin 143
spin doctor 143

Chapter Summary

» **LO 6-1** Public opinion is the aggregate of individual attitudes or beliefs shared by some portion of the adult population. A consensus exists when a large proportion of the public appears to express the same view on an issue. Divided opinion exists when the public holds widely differing attitudes on an issue.

People's opinions are formed through the political socialization process. Important factors in this process are the family, educational experiences, peer groups, opinion leaders, the media, and political events.

» **LO 6-2** Opinions are also influenced by demographic factors such as education, economic status, religion, race, ethnicity, gender, and geographic region.

» **LO 6-3** Most descriptions of public opinion are based on the results of opinion polls. An accurate poll includes a representative sample of the population being surveyed and ensures randomness in the selection of respondents.

Problems with polls include sampling error, the difficulty of persuading people to participate, badly weighted samples, and questions that are poorly worded. "Polls" that rely on self-selected respondents are inherently inaccurate and should be discounted.

» **LO 6-4** The political culture provides a general environment of support for the political system, allowing the nation to weather periods of crisis. The political culture also helps Americans to evaluate their government's performance.

Public opinion also plays an important role in policymaking. Politicians cannot always be guided by opinion polls, however. This is because respondents often do not understand the costs and consequences of policy decisions or the trade-offs involved in making such decisions.

» **LO 6-5** The media are enormously important in American politics today. They perform a number of functions, including (a) entertaining the public, (b) news reporting, (c) identifying public problems, (d) socializing new generations, (e) providing a political forum, and (f) making profits. Television remains the most important medium, in particular among older voters, who are the most likely to vote. More Americans are turning to the internet as a significant source of information.

» **LO 6-6** The political influence of the media is most obvious during political campaigns. Negative advertisements continue to be a major feature of campaigns. Today's campaigns use expert management of news coverage. For presidential candidates, how they appear in campaign debates is of major importance. Internet resources are transforming today's political campaigns.

Frequently, the mainstream media have been accused of liberal bias, although some observers contend that these accusations result from true stories that offend conservatives. Talk radio, which is overwhelmingly conservative, makes it harder to claim that the media as a whole tilt liberal.

Test Yourself

1. We can best define public opinion as:
   a. beliefs held by moderate voters.
   b. beliefs shared by both Democrats and Republicans.
   c. the aggregate of individual beliefs shared by some portion of adults.

2. Friends and coworkers who may influence your political attitudes are called:
   a. opinion leaders.
   b. agents of socialization.
   c. a peer group.

3. The gender gap refers to:
   a. the difference in college attendance rates for males and females.
   b. the tendency for women to be more likely to vote for a particular candidate than men.
   c. the tendency for men to dominate the political process.

4. One way to compensate for underrepresented groups in a polling sample is to:
   a. eliminate all answers from those who are part of the underrepresented group.
   b. reduce the weight given to the underrepresented group so that it does not count excessively.
   c. add extra weight to the responses of the underrepresented group to correct for the underrepresentation.

5. When one polling organization's results consistently differ from those of other poll takers, we call this:
   a. sampling error.
   b. a house effect.
   c. statistical noise.

6. The same polling question can result in different responses depending on how that question is:
   a. phrased.
   b. weighted.
   c. averaged.

7. Television remains a key medium in American politics because:
   a. it is the number-one source of information for older voters, who dominate the electorate.
   b. young people are avoiding the internet as a source of information.
   c. television advertisements are not that expensive to buy.

8. A major problem facing newspapers today is that they cannot collect enough online:
   a. clicks.
   b. advertising revenue.
   c. content.

9. A campaign press adviser who tries to convince reporters of a particular interpretation of an event is called a:
   a. campaign manager.
   b. media spokesperson.
   c. spin doctor.

10. The first televised major-party presidential debates were held between:
    a. Democrat Lyndon Johnson and Republican Barry Goldwater in 1964.
    b. Democrat Jimmy Carter and Republican Ronald Reagan in 1980.
    c. Democrat John F. Kennedy and Republican Richard Nixon in 1960.

11. The principle that all traffic on the internet should be treated equally is called:
    a. net neutrality.
    b. the Fairness Doctrine.
    c. professionalism.

Essay Questions

1. Years ago, people with postgraduate degrees were more likely to vote for Republican than Democratic candidates, but today, highly educated voters trend Democratic. Why might physicians and lawyers have become more likely to vote Democratic? For what reasons might college professors lean Democratic?

2. Individuals who respond to blog posts sometimes enter comments that are deliberately designed to foster disruption. (Such persons are commonly called trolls.) Consider also the prevalence of hostile and even threatening responses to posts by women on controversial topics. Why might people engage in such behaviors?

Answers to multiple-choice questions: 1. c, 2. c, 3. b, 4. c, 5. b, 6. a, 7. a, 8. b, 9. c, 10. c, 11. a.

7 Interest Groups and Political Parties

Students in Chicago march against climate change. They want government to do more. ▶ Why might other interest groups oppose efforts to reduce global warming?

MedSci/Alamy Stock Photo

The six **Learning Outcomes (LOs)** below are designed to help improve your understanding of this chapter. After reading this chapter, you should be able to:

≫ **LO 7-1** Describe the basic characteristics of interest groups, and explain why Americans join them.

≫ **LO 7-2** List the major types of interest groups, especially those with economic motivations.

≫ **LO 7-3** Discuss direct and indirect interest group techniques, and describe the main ways in which lobbyists are regulated.

≫ **LO 7-4** Cite some of the major activities of U.S. political parties, and discuss how they are organized.

≫ **LO 7-5** Explain how the history of U.S. political parties has led to the two major parties that exist today.

≫ **LO 7-6** Explain why a third-party presidential candidate has almost no chance of winning.

Check your understanding of the material with the Test Yourself section at the end of the chapter.

The structure of American government invites the participation of **interest groups** at various stages of the policymaking process. Americans can form groups in their neighborhoods or cities and lobby the city council or their state government. They can join statewide groups or national groups and try to influence government policy through Congress or through one of the executive agencies or cabinet departments. Representatives of large corporations may seek to influence members of Congress or the president

interest groups
Organized groups of individuals sharing common objectives who actively attempt to influence policymakers.

Political Party
A group of political activists who organize to win elections, operate the government, and determine public policy.

Lobbyists
Organizations or individuals who attempt to influence the passage, defeat, or content of legislation and the government's administrative decisions.

personally at social events or fundraisers. When attempts to influence government through the executive and legislative branches fail, interest groups can turn to the courts, filing suits in state or federal courts to achieve their political objectives.

Another way to influence policymaking is to become an active member of a political party and participate in the selection of political candidates, who, if elected, will hold government positions. A **political party** is formally defined as a group of political activists who organize to win elections, operate the government, and determine public policy. This definition explains the difference between an interest group and a political party. Interest groups do not want to operate the government, and they do not put forth political candidates—even though they support candidates who will promote their interests if elected or reelected.

In this chapter, we define interest groups, describe how they try to affect the government, and summarize the legal restrictions on **lobbyists**, groups or individuals hired to affect legislation and government administrative decisions. We also describe the major political parties, their history, and their organization. Finally, we explain why the two-party system has prevailed in the United States.

A Nation of Joiners

>> **LO 7-1:** Describe the basic characteristics of interest groups, and explain why Americans join them.

Alexis de Tocqueville observed in the early 1830s that "in no country of the world has the principle of association been more successfully used or applied to a greater multitude of objectives than in America."[1] The French traveler was amazed at the degree to which Americans formed groups to solve civic problems, establish social relationships, and speak for their economic or political interests. Perhaps James Madison, when he wrote *Federalist Paper* No. 10 (see Appendix C), had already judged the character of his country's citizens similarly. He supported the creation of a large republic with many states to encourage the formation of multiple interests. The multitude of interests, in Madison's view, would work to discourage the formation of an oppressive majority interest.

Thousands of Groups

The large number of pressure points in American government helps to explain why there are so many—more than one hundred thousand—interest groups at work in our society. Another reason for the multitude of interest groups is that the right to join a group is protected by the First Amendment to the U.S. Constitution. Not only are all people guaranteed the right "peaceably to assemble," but they are also guaranteed the right "to petition the Government for a redress of grievances." This constitutional provision encourages Americans to form groups and to express their opinions to the government or to their elected representatives as group members.

More than two-thirds of all Americans belong to at least one group or association. Although the majority of these affiliations could not be classified as interest groups in the political sense, Americans certainly understand the principles of working in groups.

Today, interest groups range from the elementary school parent-teacher association to the statewide association of insurance agents. They include small groups such as local environmental organizations and national groups such as the American Civil Liberties Union, the

---

1. Alexis de Tocqueville, *Democracy in America*, Vol. 1 [1835], ed. Phillips Bradley (New York: Knopf, 1980), p. 191.

National Education Association, and even the Association of Government Relations Professionals, formerly the American League of Lobbyists.

Interest Groups and Social Movements

Interest groups may be spawned by mass **social movements**. Such movements represent demands by a large segment of the population for change in the political, economic, or social system. A social movement is often the first expression of latent discontent with the existing system. It may be the authentic voice of weaker or oppressed groups in society that do not have the means or standing to organize as interest groups.

The civil rights movement of the 1950s and 1960s was clearly a social movement. To be sure, several formal organizations worked to support the movement—including the Southern Christian Leadership Conference, the National Association for the Advancement of Colored People, and the Urban League—but only a social movement could generate the kinds of civil disobedience that took place in hundreds of towns and cities across the country.

Social movements may generate interest groups with specific goals. In the example of the women's movement of the 1960s, the National Organization for Women was formed in part out of a demand to end gender-segregated job advertising in newspapers.

Reasons to Join—or Not Join

Individuals may join interest groups for a variety of reasons. We can identify three types of incentives for joining:

- People may join an interest group for companionship and the pleasure of associating with others who share their interests. We can call these benefits of association solidarity incentives.
- Some interest groups offer material incentives. For example, older Americans may join AARP because they can obtain low-cost supplemental health insurance. Those who join for this benefit may not care that AARP is also an interest group seeking to shape laws that affect senior citizens.
- Finally, members may join interest groups precisely because they want to pursue political or economic goals through joint action. Such purposive incentives are important when individuals feel strongly about issues.

It can be rational for someone not to join an interest group even when that person stands to benefit from the group's activities. Dairy farmers, for example, will benefit from the lobbying by the American Dairy Association whether they join the organization or not. The difficulty that interest groups face in recruiting members when benefits can be obtained without joining is referred to as the **free-rider problem**. This problem is especially acute for labor unions.

Image 7.1 Campaigners for woman suffrage in San Francisco, 1915. ▶ Did they have many supporters at that time?

Everett Historical/Shutterstock.com

Social Movements
Movements that represent the demands of a large segment of the public for political, economic, or social change.

Free-rider Problem
The difficulty that interest groups face in recruiting members when the benefits they achieve can be gained without joining the group.

Types of Interest Groups

» **LO 7-2:** List the major types of interest groups, especially those with economic motivations.

Thousands of groups exist to influence government. Among the major types of interest groups are those that represent the main sectors of the economy. In addition, a number of environmental groups and public-interest organizations have been formed to protect the environment and represent the needs of the general citizenry. Other types of groups include single-issue groups, ideological groups, and groups based on race, gender, or sexual orientation. The interests of foreign governments and foreign businesses are represented in the American political arena as well.

Economic Interest Groups

More interest groups are formed to represent economic interests than any other set of interests. The variety of economic interest groups mirrors the complexity of the American economy.

Business Interest Groups.   Thousands of business groups and trade associations work to influence government policies that affect their respective industries. Umbrella groups represent collections of businesses or other entities. For example, the National Association of Manufacturers is an umbrella group that represents manufacturing concerns. Some business groups are decidedly more powerful than others. Consider the U.S. Chamber of Commerce, which represents about 3 million member companies and organizations. It can bring constituent influence to bear on every member of Congress. Studies have shown that business groups—especially those representing specific industries such as banking or filmmaking—are often successful in winning beneficial legislation.

For example, pharmaceutical companies and Hollywood have been enormously successful in obtaining protection for intellectual property. The Walt Disney Company has long fought to ensure that its rights to Mickey Mouse never expire. U.S. law now protects Disney's control of Mickey Mouse until at least 2036. (Some economists have argued that lengthy copyright and patent protections discourage innovation and hurt the overall economy.)

Business interests scored a hard-fought victory in December 2017, when Congress passed and President Donald Trump signed the Tax Cuts and Jobs Act. The most important element of this very complicated legislation was a cut in the federal corporate income tax rate from 35 percent to 21 percent.

Beginning in 2018, Trump launched a campaign of imposing tariffs (taxes) on a wide variety of imported goods. Trump believed that he was helping businesses by injuring their overseas competitors. Some businesses, such as manufacturers of steel, benefited from the tariffs. For a greater number of businesses, however, the tariffs were a problem. The number of companies that buy steel—and which had to pay higher prices—is much larger than the number that make steel. Also, many businesses now rely on international supply chains, in which various items may be traded between nations multiple times before final sale. Tariffs could disrupt these supply chains. Business lobbyists opposed the tariffs, but their ability to combat them was undercut by their support for other Trump policies.

The business interests of the oil and natural gas industry suffered a blow when Joe Biden became president. On his first day in office, Biden cancelled the permit for the Keystone XL crude oil pipeline coming from Canada into the U.S. His administration cancelled some oil and gas leases already in effect on federal lands. He froze any further oil and gas leases in the Arctic National Wildlife Refuge (ANWR) of Alaska. He changed regulations with respect to liquifying natural gas and exporting it, thereby increasing the cost of LNG and delaying its growth. He signed an executive order declaring that the U.S. would become carbon neutral by 2050. If this goal is truly attained, the oil and gas industry would be negatively affected.

Agricultural Interest Groups.   American farmers and their employees represent less than 1 percent of the U.S. population. In spite of this, farmers' influence on legislation beneficial to their interests has been significant. Farmers have very strong interest groups. For example, the American Farm Bureau Federation, or Farm Bureau, established in 1919, represents nearly 6 million families (a majority of whom are not actually farm families).

Agricultural interest groups are among the most successful in obtaining subsidies from American taxpayers. The most recent farm bill was passed in 2018. This legislation provides $21 billion per year to the nation's farmers. Recent farm bills have eliminated direct payments—sums that formerly went to growers of corn, cotton, rice, soybeans, and wheat regardless of whether they actually planted the crops. Almost all of the funds saved were added back as crop insurance subsidies, however.

Labor Interest Groups. Interest groups representing the **labor movement** date back to at least 1886, when the American Federation of Labor (AFL) was formed. In 1955, the AFL joined forces with the Congress of Industrial Organizations (CIO). In 2005, however, four key unions left the federation and formed the Change to Win Coalition. Today, Change to Win has a membership of about 4.5 million workers, while the AFL-CIO's membership is about 12.5 million.

The role of unions in American society has been waning, as witnessed by a decline in union membership (see Figure 7.1). Unions traditionally have been strongest in the manufacturing and construction sectors. In the age of automation and with the rise of the **service sector**, blue-collar workers in basic industries (auto, steel, and the like) represent a smaller and smaller percentage of the total working population. As a result, unions are looking to other areas for their membership, including migrant farmworkers, service workers, and public employees. Part of such campaigns has been a call to raise the minimum wage established by the various states. We examine that controversy in this chapter's *Which Side Are You On?* feature.

Labor Movement
The economic and political expression of working-class interests.

Service Sector
The sector of the economy that provides services—such as health care, banking, and education—in contrast to the sector that produces goods.

| Figure 7.1 | Decline in Union Membership, 1948 to Present |

The percentage of the total workforce that consists of labor union members has declined greatly over the past forty years. The percentage of government workers who are union members, however, increased significantly in the 1960s and 1970s and has remained stable since then. ▶ **Why might it be easier to organize a union among public-sector workers than workers in the private sector?**

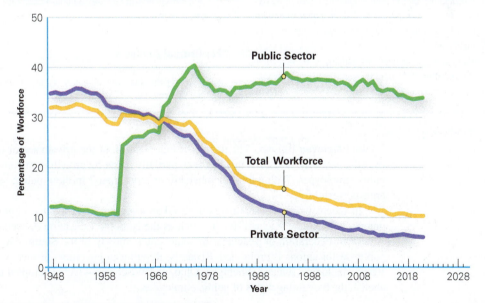

Source: Bureau of Labor Statistics [www.bls.gov/cps/cpsaat42.pdf].

Which Side Are You On?

Should States Raise the Minimum Wage?

A minimum wage is the lowest wage rate that an employer can legally pay. The national minimum wage is set by Congress. Currently, it is $7.25 per hour. Australia has the world's highest national minimum wage—$14.84 in U.S. dollars.

Twenty-nine states now have a minimum wage higher than the national rate. The New Mexico rate is only one dollar more than the national minimum. As of January 2022, Washington state had the highest state minimum wage at $14.49 per hour (though the minimum wage in the District of Columbia is $15.20). Forty-four localities have adopted minimum wages higher than their state minimum. A national movement has grown up around raising the minimum wage to $15.00 per hour, and a number of state and local governments have backed this effort.

Minimum wage laws are generally popular with voters. In a recent poll, 67 percent of Americans favored a $15 minimum wage. That included 86 percent of Democrats and 43 percent of Republicans. Traditionally, however, economists have been much less likely to favor such laws than are average voters.

Higher Minimum Wages Kill Jobs

Most conservative politicians—and some economists who aren't necessarily that conservative—oppose minimum wage laws. Obviously, hiking the minimum wage raises the pay of the lowest-paid workers. These workers become more expensive to hire. It is basic economics that in normal circumstances, if something costs more, people will buy less of it. A higher minimum wage should therefore reduce the number of low-skilled workers demanded by employers.

Many minimum-wage workers are employed by fast-food restaurants and retail stores that cater to people with low incomes. If minimum wages continue to rise, these businesses may need to raise their prices to recoup lost profits. The result: more expensive food and clothing for other workers with low incomes. Ultimately, no businessperson will consistently pay a worker a wage rate that exceeds the value of that worker's output. Teenagers—especially those from racial and ethnic minority groups—who cannot find a higher minimum-wage job would lose out on the opportunity to learn basic work skills that could help them find better jobs later.

Higher Minimum Wages Are Good Policy

Advocates of raising minimum wages accept that they would reduce employment if they were set too high. Advocates also argue, however, that the modest increases in the minimum wage seen in many states do not in fact have such a result. The forces of supply and demand for low-skilled labor are most effective when there are many employers who compete with each other in demanding such labor. In much of the country, there may not be enough employers demanding low-skilled workers to create an effective free market in labor.

We can predict that with a higher minimum wage, there would be less turnover—workers would stay longer in low-wage jobs. Also, minimum-wage workers are not all teenagers. The average age of minimum-wage workers is thirty-five. Paying workers a living wage is only fair. It can even save lives. A recent study finds that a one-dollar increase in the minimum wage leads to a 3.4 to 5.9 percent decline in suicides among adults with a high school education or less.

For Critical Analysis

If a San Francisco bookstore closes because it can't afford to pay its clerks the California minimum wage, would you blame the minimum-wage law—or Amazon?

Public Employee Unions. The degree of unionization in the private sector has declined over the past fifty years, but this has been partially offset by growth in the unionization of public employees. With a total membership of more than 7 million, public-sector unions are a powerful force.

In recent years, conservatives have taken a strong stand against public employee unions, particularly teachers' unions such as the National Education Association and the American Federation of Teachers. In some states, mostly in the South, bargaining with public-sector unions is prohibited. Recently, Republican governors in several midwestern states—including Indiana, Michigan, Ohio, and Wisconsin—have attempted to restrict or abolish the bargaining rights of public employees.

The Political Environment Faced by Labor. The success or failure of attempts to form unions depends greatly on popular attitudes. Many business-oriented conservatives have never accepted unions as legitimate institutions. In states where this view is widely held, local laws and practices can make it hard for labor to organize. For example, only 3.4 percent of workers in North Carolina are union members. In New York, where voters are more sympathetic to labor, the unionization rate is 22.7 percent. One way a state can make it more difficult to form unions is by adopting right-to-work laws. Such legislation bans contracts that require all employees to pay union dues or fees. The result is a free-rider problem for the unions. Twenty-eight states have such laws. Indiana, Kentucky, Michigan, West Virginia, and Wisconsin are the most recent states to adopt them.

With the election of Joe Biden, the political environment for unions did change. In 2022, the Biden administration mandated a union workforce at large federal construction projects. Any federal project costing more than $35 million must use project labor agreements. These are collective bargaining contracts between contractors and unions that set wages and the terms for workers' services before the start of the project. The result is estimated to be a guarantee of union jobs for over $260 billion in federal government construction contracts.

Image 7.2 Fast-food, home health care, and other workers with low wages rally in Chicago on behalf of the Fight for $15, a campaign that calls for better wages and working conditions. ▶ Why would organized labor favor a higher minimum wage for all workers, not just union members?

Marie Kanger Born/Shutterstock.com

Interest Groups of Professionals. Many professional organizations exist, including the American Bar Association, the Associated General Contractors of America, the Institute of Electrical and Electronics Engineers, and others. Some professional groups, such as those representing lawyers and physicians, are more influential than others because of their ability to restrict entry into their professions. Lawyers have a unique advantage—a large number of members of Congress share their profession.

Individuals With Low Incomes. Some have argued that the system of interest group politics leaves out Americans with incomes below the federal poverty threshold. Many of these individuals hold two or more jobs just to survive, leaving them no time to participate in interest groups. Consequently, some scholars suggest that interest groups and lobbyists are the privilege of Americans of the upper middle class and those who belong to unions or other special groups.

Others, however, observe that the low-income population does obtain benefits from government. Without federal tax and spending programs aimed at persons with low incomes, over 20 percent of U.S. families would have incomes below the official poverty line. If you consider all benefits that families with low incomes obtain, that number drops to about 10 percent. Programs with a major effect on reducing poverty include the Supplemental Nutrition Assistance Program (SNAP), formerly known as food stamps, and the Earned

Income Tax Credit (EITC). Social Security, unemployment insurance, and the Child Tax Credit also have a significant effect in reducing poverty, though these programs are not limited to people with low incomes.[2]

True, individuals with low incomes cannot easily represent themselves. But for decades, liberal groups and religious groups have campaigned on behalf of those experiencing poverty. These interest groups can bring the issues associated with poverty to the attention of policymakers in a way that an individual would not be able to achieve.

Environmental Interest Groups

The National Audubon Society was founded in 1905. The patron of the Sierra Club, John Muir, worked for the creation of national parks more than a century ago. But the blossoming of environmental groups with mass memberships did not occur until the 1970s.

Today's Environmental Groups. Since the first Earth Day, organized in 1972, many interest groups have sprung up in an attempt to protect the environment in general or unique ecological niches. The groups range from the National Wildlife Federation, with over 6 million members and supporters, to the Environmental Defense Fund, with a membership of 2.5 million.

Climate Change. The topic of climate change has become a major focus for environmental groups in recent years. This issue has pitted environmentalists against other interest groups—for example, interests representing industries that may be adding to global warming by releasing greenhouse gases into the atmosphere. Indeed, the reaction against environmentalism has been strong enough in such coal-producing states as West Virginia to transform them politically. Once a Democratic bastion, West Virginia now usually supports Republicans in national contests.

Public-Interest Groups

Public Interest
The best interests of the overall community. Also, the national good, rather than the narrow interests of a particular group.

Public interest is a difficult term to define because, as we noted earlier in the book, there are many publics in our nation of about 335 million. It is almost impossible for one particular public policy to benefit everybody, which in turn makes it practically impossible to define the public interest. Nonetheless, over the past few decades, a variety of lobbying organizations have been formed in the public interest.

The Consumer Movement. As an organized movement, consumerism began in 1936 with the founding of the Consumers Union, which continues to publish the popular magazine *Consumer Reports*. Consumerism took off during the 1960s. Ralph Nader, who gained notice by exposing allegedly unsafe automobiles, was a key figure in the new movement and a major sponsor of new organizations. These included Public Interest Research Groups (PIRGs)—campus organizations that emerged in the early 1970s and continue to provide students with platforms for civic engagement. Partly in response to a variety of consumer groups, several conservative public-interest legal foundations have sprung up that are often pitted against liberal groups in court.

Other Public-Interest Groups. One of the largest public-interest groups is Common Cause, founded in 1968. Its goal is to reorder national priorities toward "the public" and to make

---

2. Danilo Trisi and Matt Saenz, "Economic Security Programs Cut Poverty Nearly in Half Over Last 50 Years" (Center on Budget and Policy Priorities, November 26, 2019).

governmental institutions more responsive to the needs of the public. Another public-interest group is the League of Women Voters, founded in 1920. Although officially nonpartisan, it has supported a variety of progressive public policy positions, including abortion rights, universal healthcare, gun control, and climate change actions.

Additional Types of Interest Groups

A number of interest groups focus on just one issue. Single-interest groups, being narrowly focused, may be able to call attention to their causes because they have simple and straightforward goals and because their members tend to care intensely about the issues. Thus, such groups can easily motivate their members to contact legislators or to organize demonstrations in support of their policy goals.

The abortion debate has created groups opposed to abortion (such as the National Right to Life Committee) and groups in favor of abortion rights (such as NARAL Pro-Choice America). Further examples of single-issue groups are the National Rifle Association and the Great Lakes Commission.

Foreign Interest Groups. Homegrown interest groups are not the only players in the game. Washington, D.C., is also the center for lobbying by foreign governments, as well as private foreign interests. The governments of the largest U.S. trading partners, such as Japan, South Korea, Canada, and the European Union (EU) countries, maintain substantial research and lobbying staffs. Even smaller nations, such as those in the Caribbean, engage lobbyists when vital legislation affecting their trade interests is considered.

Ideological Groups. Among the most important interest groups are those that unite citizens around a common ideological viewpoint. Americans for Democratic Action, for example, was founded in 1947 to represent liberals who were explicitly anti-Communist. On the political right, Americans for Tax Reform, organized by Grover Norquist, has been successful in persuading almost all leading Republicans to sign a pledge promising never to vote to raise taxes.

Identity Groups. Still other groups represent Americans who share a common identity, such as membership in a particular race or ethnic group. The NAACP, founded in 1909 as the National Association for the Advancement of Colored People, represents Black Americans. The National Organization for Women (NOW) has championed women's rights since 1966.

Elderly Americans can be considered to have a common identity. AARP (formerly the American Association of Retired Persons) is one of the most powerful interest groups in Washington, D.C. It is the nation's largest interest group, with a membership of about 38 million. AARP played a significant role in the creation of Medicare and Medicaid, as well as in obtaining annual cost-of-living increases in Social Security payments. (Medicare pays for medical expenses incurred by those who are at least sixty-five years of age. Medicaid provides health care support for individuals with low incomes.)

There are competitors to AARP. One of them is the Association of Mature American Citizens (AMAC). Similar to AARP, AMAC members receive low-cost travel insurance, hotel discounts, life insurance products, and a prescription discount card. While AARP tends to support progressive government policies, the Association of Mature American Citizens tends to be more conservative in its political aims.

Interest Group Strategies

≫ **LO 7-3:** Discuss direct and indirect interest group techniques, and describe the main ways in which lobbyists are regulated.

Interest groups employ a wide range of techniques and strategies to promote their policy goals. Although few groups are successful at persuading Congress and the president to endorse their programs completely, many are able to block—or at least weaken—legislation injurious to their members. The key to success for interest groups is access to legislators and executive branch officials. To gain such access, interest groups and their representatives try to cultivate long-term relationships with these officials. The best of these relationships are based on mutual respect and cooperation. The interest group provides the official with sources of information and assistance, and the official in turn gives the group opportunities to express its views.

The techniques used by interest groups can be divided into direct and indirect techniques. With **direct techniques**, the interest group and its lobbyists approach officials personally to present their case. With **indirect techniques**, in contrast, the interest group uses the general public or individual constituents to influence the government on behalf of the interest group.

Direct Techniques
An interest group technique that uses direct interaction with government officials to further the group's goals.

Indirect Techniques
An interest group technique that uses third parties to influence government officials.

Direct Techniques

Lobbying, publicizing ratings of legislative behavior, and providing campaign assistance are three main direct techniques used by interest groups.

Lobbying Techniques. As you might have guessed, the term lobbying comes from the activities of private citizens regularly congregating in the lobbies of legislative chambers to petition legislators. In the latter part of the 1800s, railroad and industrial groups openly bribed state legislators to pass legislation beneficial to their interests, giving lobbying a well-deserved bad name. Today, in contrast, most lobbyists are professionals. They are either consultants to a company or interest group or members of one of the Washington, D.C., law firms that specialize in providing lobbying services. Such firms employ hundreds of former members of Congress and former government officials. Lobbyists are valued for their network of contacts in Washington.

Lobbyists engage in an array of activities to influence legislation and government policy. These include the following:

- Meeting privately with public officials. Although they are acting on behalf of their clients, lobbyists often furnish needed information to senators and representatives (and government agency appointees). It is to the lobbyists' advantage to provide useful information so that policymakers will rely on them in the future.
- Testifying before congressional committees for or against proposed legislation.
- Testifying before executive rulemaking agencies—such as the Federal Trade Commission or the Consumer Product Safety Commission—for or against proposed rules.
- Assisting legislators or bureaucrats in drafting legislation or regulations.
- Inviting legislators to social occasions, such as cocktail parties, boating expeditions, and other events, including conferences at exotic locations.
- Providing political information to legislators and other government officials. Sometimes, lobbyists have better information than the party leadership about how other legislators are going to vote.
- Suggesting nominations for federal appointments to the executive branch.

The Ratings Game. Many interest groups attempt to influence the overall behavior of legislators through their rating systems. Each year, these interest groups identify the legislation that they consider most important to their goals and then monitor how legislators vote on it. Legislators receive scores based on their votes. The usual ratings scheme ranges from 0 to 100 percent. In the scheme of the liberal Americans for Democratic Action, for example, a rating of 100 means that a member of Congress voted with the group on every issue and is, by that measure, very liberal.

Campaign Assistance. Groups recognize that the greatest concern of legislators is to be reelected, so they focus on the legislators' campaign needs. Associations with large memberships, such as labor unions, are able to provide workers for political campaigns, including precinct workers to get out the vote, volunteers to put up posters and pass out literature, and people to staff telephone banks at campaign headquarters.

Candidates vie for the groups' endorsements in a campaign. Gaining those endorsements may be automatic, or it may require that the candidates participate in debates or interviews with the interest groups. An interest group usually publicizes its choices in its membership publication, and the candidate can use the endorsement in campaign literature.

AP Images/John Hanna

Image 7.3 A Republican state senator in Kansas (left) meets with a lobbyist from Kansans for Life (right) at the statehouse in Topeka. They are discussing an amendment to the state constitution that would make it harder to obtain an abortion. ▶ Why would a legislator willingly be photographed with lobbyists?

Indirect Techniques

Interest groups can also try to influence government policy by working through others, who may be constituents or members of the general public. Indirect techniques mask an interest group's own activities and make the effort appear to be spontaneous. Furthermore, legislators and government officials are often more impressed by contacts from constituents than from an interest group's lobbyist.

Generating Public Pressure. In some instances, interest groups try to produce a groundswell of public pressure to influence the government. Such efforts may include advertisements online and in newspapers, mass e-mailings, texting members of Congress, contacting them on their social media accounts, television publicity, and demonstrations. To be sure, internet and social media make communication efforts even more effective. Interest groups may commission polls to find out what the public's sentiments are and then publicize the results. The intent of this activity is to convince policymakers that public opinion supports the group's position.

Using Constituents as Lobbyists. An interest group may also use constituents of elected officials to lobby for the group's goals. In the "shotgun" approach, the interest group tries to mobilize large numbers of constituents to write, phone, send e-mails, text messages, posts, and tweets to their legislators or to the president. Often, the group provides language that constituents can use in the communication, thus sparing people from the need of composing a message of their own. These efforts are effective on Capitol Hill only

ClassicStock/Alamy Stock Photo

Image 7.4 A cartoon from 1889 contends that the United States Senate is dominated by corporate interests. The term *trust* refers to a type of monopoly. Prior to the 1914 elections, members of the Senate were elected by state legislatures. ▶ Was such a body more likely to be corrupt than one elected directly by the people? Why or why not?

when the number of responses is very large, however. Legislators know that the voters did not initiate the communications on their own when many communications use exactly the same wording. Artificially manufactured grassroots activity has been aptly labeled Astroturf lobbying.

A variation on this technique uses only important constituents. With this approach, known as the "rifle" technique or the "Utah plant manager theory," the interest group might, for example, ask the manager of a local plant in Utah to contact the senator from Utah. Because the constituent is seen as influential and responsible for many jobs, the legislator is more likely to listen carefully to the constituent's concerns about legislation than to a paid lobbyist.

Regulating Lobbyists

Congress made its first attempt to control lobbyists and lobbying activities through Federal Regulation of the Lobbying Act of 1946. The act proved to be ineffective, however.

The Lobbying Disclosure Act. The reform-minded Congress of 1995–96 overhauled the lobbying legislation, fundamentally changing the ground rules for those who seek to influence the federal government. The Lobbying Disclosure Act passed in 1995 included the following provisions:

- A lobbyist is defined as anyone who spends at least 20 percent of their time lobbying members of Congress, their staffs, or executive-branch officials.
- Lobbyists must register with the clerk of the House and the secretary of the Senate.
- Semiannual reports must disclose the general nature of the lobbying effort.

Also in 1995, both the House and the Senate adopted new rules on gifts and travel expenses provided by lobbyists. The House adopted a flat ban on gifts, while the Senate established limits: Senators were prohibited from accepting any gift with a value of more than $50 and from accepting gifts worth more than $100 from a single source in a given year. These gift rules stopped the broad practice of taking members of Congress to lunch or dinner at high-priced restaurants, but the various exemptions and exceptions have allowed much gift giving to continue.

Since 2007, under the Honest Leadership and Open Government Act, lobbyists must report quarterly, and the registration threshold is $10,000 in spending per quarter. Organizations must report coalition activities if they contribute more than $5,000 to a coalition. The House and the Senate must now post lobbying information in a searchable file on the internet.

The Impact of Lobbying. No matter how professional their conduct, lobbyists continue to have a poor reputation. It is widely believed that by benefiting special interests, their activities injure everyone else. One argument for this proposition is known as **concentrated benefits and dispersed costs**. If a special law, such as a tax break, helps a relatively small number of people, those who receive the benefit will fight hard to keep or enlarge it. Other citizens, who pay for the benefit, may have little motivation to oppose it. For the general public, after all, the cost to each individual is usually a matter of pennies. Still, when many interest groups are able to obtain benefits, the total impact can be very large.

Concentrated Benefits and Dispersed Costs
The theory that a minority benefiting from a government program will make a stronger effort to keep it than the majority will ever make to abolish it.

Political Parties in the United States

» **LO 7-4:** Cite some of the major activities of U.S. political parties, and discuss how they are organized.

Every two years, the media concentrate on the state of the political parties. Prior to an election, a typical poll usually asks the following question: "Do you consider yourself to be a Republican, a Democrat, or an independent?" For many years, Americans were divided fairly evenly among these three choices. Today, about 44 percent of all voters call themselves **independents**, although in fact three-quarters or more of all independents lean toward either the Republicans or the Democrats.

Independents
A voter or candidate who does not identify with a political party.

In the United States, being a member of a political party does not require paying dues, passing an examination, or swearing an oath of allegiance. If nothing is really required to be a member of a political party, what, then, is a political party? As discussed earlier in this chapter, a political party is a group that seeks to win elections, operate the government, and determine public policy. Political parties are thus quite different from interest groups, which, as mentioned, seek to influence, not run, the government.

Functions of Political Parties in the United States

Political parties in the United States engage in a wide variety of activities, many of which are discussed in this chapter. Through these activities, parties perform a number of functions for the political system. These functions include the following:

1. **Recruiting candidates for public office.** Because it is the goal of parties to gain control of government, they must work to recruit candidates for elective offices.
2. **Organizing and running elections.** Although elections are a government activity, political parties actually organize voter registration drives, recruit volunteers to work at the polls, provide much of the campaign activity to stimulate interest in the election, and work to increase voter participation.

3. **Presenting alternative policies to the electorate.** Parties focus on a political program, which is typically detailed in the party platform. Party members, when elected, usually try to implement that program.

4. **Accepting responsibility for operating the government.** When a party elects the president or governor—or a majority of the members of a legislative body—it accepts responsibility for running the government. This includes developing linkages among elected officials in the various branches of government to gain support for policies and their implementation.

5. **Acting as the organized opposition to the party in power.** The "out" party, or the one that does not control the government, is expected to articulate its own policies and oppose the winning party when appropriate.

The major functions of American political parties are carried out by a small, relatively loose-knit nucleus of party activists. This arrangement is quite different from the more highly structured, mass-membership organization typical of many European parties. American parties concentrate on winning elections rather than on signing up large numbers of deeply committed, dues-paying members who believe passionately in the party's program.

The Party Organization

Party Organization
The formal structure and leadership of a political party, including election committees; local, state, and national executives; and paid professional staff.

American political parties are sometimes seen as hierarchical, but this perception is not accurate. In reality, the formal structure of each party—the **party organization**—reflects a high degree of decentralization. The parties have a confederal structure, and each unit has substantial independence from the rest of the party.

National Convention
The meeting held every four years by each major party to select presidential and vice-presidential candidates, write a platform, choose a national committee, and conduct party business.

The National Party Organization. Each party has a national organization, the most conspicuous part of which is the **national convention**, held every four years. The convention is used to officially nominate the presidential and vice-presidential candidates. In addition, the **party platform** is developed at the national convention. The platform sets forth the party's position on the issues and makes promises to initiate certain policies if the party wins control of the government.

Party Platform
A document drawn up at each national convention, outlining the policies, positions, and principles of the party.

After the convention, the platform sometimes is neglected or ignored when party candidates disagree with it. Still, once elected, the parties often do try to carry out platform promises, and many of the promises eventually become law. Of course, some general goals, such as economic prosperity, are included in the platforms of both major parties. Consider for example the 2020 Democratic Party platform that was approved by the Democratic National Convention on August 18, 2020. This platform outlined numerous progressive goals. They included leveling the economic playing field, achieving universal health care, achieving racial justice and equity, protecting LGBTQ+ rights, making Washington D.C., the fifty-first state, and mobilizing the world to address transnational challenges such as climate change. It is fair to say that the Biden administration made policy changes, especially during its first year, that corresponded quite well to the 2020 Democratic Party platform.

Convention Delegates. The party convention provides a striking illustration of the differences between the ordinary members of a party, or party identifiers, and party activists. Delegates to the Democratic National Convention are usually far more liberal than ordinary Democratic voters. Typically, delegates to the Republican National Convention are far more conservative than ordinary Republicans. Why does this happen? In part, it is because a person who wishes to become a delegate must be appointed by party leaders, or gather votes in a primary election from party members who care enough to vote in a primary. Voter turnout in primary elections is often quite low and those who do vote are likely to be among the most committed and ideological members of the party.

The National Committee. At the national convention, each of the parties formally chooses a national committee, elected by the individual state parties. This **national committee** directs and coordinates party activities during the following four years. One of the jobs of the national committee is to ratify the presidential nominee's choice of a national chairperson, who in principle acts as the spokesperson for the party. (If the presidential candidate loses, however, the national committee will often elect a new chair.) The national chairperson and the national committee plan the next campaign and the next convention, obtain financial contributions, and publicize the national party.

The State Party Organization. Every state party is unique. Nonetheless, state parties have several organizational features in common. Each state party has a chairperson, a committee, and a number of local organizations. In theory, the role of the **state central committee**—the principal organized structure of each political party within each state—is similar in the various states. The committee has responsibility for carrying out the policy decisions of the party's state convention. The committee also has control over the use of party campaign funds during political campaigns. Usually, the state central committee has little, if any, influence on party candidates once they are elected.

Local Party Machinery: The Grassroots. The lowest layer of party machinery is the local organization, supported by district leaders, precinct or ward captains, and party workers. In the 1800s, the institution of **patronage**—rewarding the party faithful with government jobs or contracts—held the local organization together. For immigrants and those with low incomes, the political machine often furnished important services and protections.

The last big-city local political machine to exercise substantial power was run by Chicago mayor Richard J. Daley (1955–76), who was also an important figure in national Democratic politics. City machines are now dead, mostly because their function of providing social services (and reaping the reward of votes) has been taken over by state and national agencies.

Local political organizations still provide the foot soldiers of politics—individuals who pass out literature and get out the vote on Election Day, which can be crucial in local elections. In many regions, local Democratic and Republican organizations still exercise some patronage, such as awarding courthouse jobs, contracts for street repair, and other construction contracts. The Supreme Court has ruled, however, that failing to hire or firing individuals because of their political affiliation is an infringement of these individuals' First Amendment rights to free expression.[3] Local party organizations are also the most important vehicles for recruiting young adults into political work.

The Party-in-the-Electorate

The party-in-the-electorate consists of everyone who identifies with the party in question who is not an elected official or part of the formal party organization. The party-in-the-electorate does not just consist of ordinary Americans, however, but of elites—media

Tom Williams/CQ-Roll Call, Inc./Getty Images

Image 7.5 Jaime Harrison is the chairperson of the Democratic National Committee. ▶ What does his job involve?

National Committee
A standing committee of a national political party established to direct and coordinate party activities between national party conventions.

State Central Committee
The principal organized structure of each political party within each state. This committee is responsible for carrying out policy decisions of the party's state convention.

Patronage
The practice of rewarding faithful party workers and followers with government employment and contracts.

---

3. *Rutan v. Republican Party of Illinois*, 497 U.S. 62 (1990).

personalities, fundraisers, and prominent figures of all types. These are people who identify with a party but who are not part of its formal organization and are not elected officials.

In *The Party Decides*, a modern classic work, a team of political scientists has argued that **policy demanders** are a key part of any major party. Policy demanders are interest group members or other ideologically motivated individuals who participate in parties with the intent to see that certain policies are adopted, or at least specific groups favored.[4] In the Democratic Party, for example, teachers' unions are policy demanders who favor increased spending on education and policies that benefit teachers. Among Republicans, a variety of policy demanders oppose legislation that would grant legal status to unauthorized immigrants.

Another elite group is opinion leaders. The late radio talk show host Rush Limbaugh, for example, held no office in the government or the Republican Party, but his influence was substantial. Large-scale contributors such as the brothers Charles and the late David Koch certainly qualify as elites. Entertainment celebrities are an elite group that is heavily Democratic.

The Party-in-Government

After the election is over and the winners are announced, the focus of party activity shifts from getting out the vote to organizing and controlling the government—to the activities of the party-in-government. Party membership plays an important role in the day-to-day operations of Congress, with partisanship determining everything from office space to committee assignments and power on Capitol Hill. For the president, the political party furnishes a pool of qualified applicants for political appointments to run the government. Presidents can, and occasionally do, appoint executive personnel, such as cabinet members, from the opposition party, but it is uncommon to do so. Judicial appointments also offer a great opportunity to the winning party. For the most part, presidents are likely to nominate federal judges and justices from their own party.

Divided Government. All of these party appointments suggest that the winning political party, whether at the national, state, or local level, has a great deal of control in the American system. Because of the checks and balances and the relative lack of cohesion in American parties, however, such control is the exception rather than the rule. One reason is that Americans have often seemed to prefer a **divided government**, with the executive and legislative branches controlled by different parties.

Party Polarization. In recent years, it has become increasingly difficult for legislators in either party to obtain support for legislation from members of the other party. More and more, voting takes place strictly along party lines. One reason for party-line voting is that political overlap between the two parties has vanished. Political scientists calculated that by 2009, the most conservative Democrat in the House was still more liberal than the most moderate Republican.

One effect of the new polarization is that interpersonal relationships between members of the two parties have deteriorated. A second effect is the growing tactic of blocking bills to

Jeff Kowalsky/Bloomberg/Getty Images

Image 7.6 Ronna Romney McDaniel is the chairperson of the Republican National Committee. ▶ Do all registered Republicans vote for this position?

Policy Demanders
Individuals or interest group members who participate in political parties with the intent to see that certain policies are adopted or specific groups favored.

Divided Government
A situation in which one major political party controls the presidency and the other controls one or more chambers of Congress, or in which one party controls a state governorship and the other controls the state legislature.

---

4. Marty Cohen et al., *The Party Decides: Presidential Nominations Before and After Reform* (Chicago: University of Chicago Press, 2008).

make the other party appear ineffective, without any attempt to reach a compromise. Today, major changes to the legislative landscape may depend on one party obtaining control of both the presidency and Congress. This can happen—the Democrats had such control in 2009–10. The Republicans gained it in 2017–18, following the 2016 elections. The Democrats regained one-party control from 2021 through January 2023.

A History of Political Parties in the United States

>> **LO 7-5:** Explain how the history of U.S. political parties has led to the two major parties that exist today.

The United States has a **two-party system**, and that system has been around since before 1800. The function and character of the political parties, as well as the emergence of the two-party system itself, have much to do with the unique historical forces operating from this country's beginning as an independent nation.

Two-party System
A political system in which only two parties have a reasonable chance of winning.

Generally, we can divide the evolution of our nation's political parties into seven periods:

1. The formation of parties, from 1789 to 1816.
2. The era of one-party rule, from 1816 to 1828.
3. The period from Andrew Jackson's presidency to the eve of the Civil War, from 1828 to 1856.
4. The Civil War and post–Civil War period, from 1856 to 1896.
5. The Republican ascendancy and the progressive period, from 1896 to 1932.
6. The New Deal period, from 1932 to about 1968.
7. The modern period, from approximately 1968 to the present.

The Formative Years: Federalists and Anti-Federalists

The first political division in the United States occurred before the adoption of the Constitution. The Federalists pushed for the adoption of the Constitution, whereas the Anti-Federalists were against ratification.

In September 1796, George Washington, who had served as president for two terms, decided not to run again. In his farewell address, he made a somber assessment of the nation's future. Washington felt that the country might be destroyed by the "baneful [harmful] effects of the spirit of party." He viewed parties as a threat to both national unity and the concept of popular government. Nevertheless, in the years after the ratification of the Constitution, Americans came to realize that some permanent mechanism would be necessary to identify candidates for office and represent political differences among the people. The result was two political parties.

Federalists and Republicans. One party was the Federalists, which included John Adams, the second president (1797–1801). The Federalists represented commercial interests such as merchants and large planters. They supported a strong national government.

Thomas Jefferson led the other party, which came to be called the Republicans. These Republicans should not be confused with the later Republican Party

PRISMA ARCHIVO/Alamy Stock Photo

Image 7.7 Thomas Jefferson, founder of the first Republican Party. His election to the presidency in 1800 was one of the world's first peaceful transfers of power from one party to another through a free election. ▶ What did Jefferson's party stand for?

Image 7.8 Andrew Jackson earned the name "Old Hickory" for exploits during the War of 1812. In 1828, Jackson was elected president as the candidate of the new Democratic Party. ▶ Whom did this party seek to represent?

Photo Researchers/Science History Images/Alamy Stock Photo

Democratic Party
One of the two major American political parties evolving out of the Republican Party of Thomas Jefferson. It was formed in 1828.

Whig Party
A major party in the United States during the first half of the nineteenth century, formally established in 1836. The Whig Party was anti-Jackson and advocated spending on infrastructure.

Republican Party
One of the two major American political parties. It emerged in the 1850s as an antislavery party and consisted of former northern Whigs, members of the Free Soil party, and antislavery Democrats.

of Abraham Lincoln. (To avoid confusion, some refer to Jefferson's party as the Democratic Republicans, but this name was never used during the time that the party existed.) Jefferson's Republicans represented artisans and farmers. They strongly supported states' rights. In 1800, when Jefferson defeated Adams in the presidential contest, one of the world's first peaceful transfers of power from one party to another was achieved.

The One-Party Interlude. From 1800 to 1820, a majority of U.S. voters regularly elected Jeffersonian Republicans to the presidency and to Congress. By 1816, the Federalist Party had nearly collapsed, and two-party competition did not really exist at the national level. Because there was no real political opposition to the Jeffersonian Republicans and thus little political debate, the administration of James Monroe (1817–25) came to be known as the era of good feelings.

Democrats and Whigs

Organized two-party politics returned after 1824. Following the election of John Quincy Adams as president, the Republican Party split in two. The supporters of Adams called themselves National Republicans. The supporters of Andrew Jackson, who defeated Adams in 1828, formed the **Democratic Party**. Later, the National Republicans took the name **Whig Party**, which had been a traditional name for British liberals. The Whigs stood for, among other things, federal spending on "internal improvements," such as roads. The Democrats opposed this policy. The Democrats, who were the stronger of the two parties, favored personal liberty and opportunity for the "common man." It was understood that the "common man" was a white man—hostility toward African Americans was an important force holding the disparate Democratic groups together.[5]

The Civil War Crisis

In the 1850s, hostility between the North and the South over the issue of slavery divided both parties. The Whigs were the first to split in two. The Whigs had been the party of an active federal government, but white Southerners had come to believe that "a government strong enough to build roads is a government strong enough to free your [enslaved people]." The southern Whigs therefore ceased to exist as an organized party. In 1854, the northern Whigs united with antislavery Democrats and members of the radical antislavery Free Soil Party to found the modern **Republican Party**. President Lincoln was a member of the Republic Party and obviously staunchly antislavery.

The Post–Civil War Period

After the Civil War, the Democratic Party was able to heal its divisions. Southern resentment of the Republicans' role in defeating the South and fears that the federal government would intervene on behalf of African Americans ensured that the Democrats would dominate the

---

5. Edward Pessen, *Jacksonian America: Society, Personality, and Politics* (Homewood, Ill.: Dorsey Press, 1969). See especially pages 246–247. The small number of free Black people who could vote were overwhelmingly Whig.

white South for the next century. It was in this period that the Republicans adopted the nickname **GOP**, which stands for "grand old party."

Cultural Politics. Northern Democrats feared a strong government for other reasons. The Republicans thought that the government should promote business and economic growth, but many Republicans also wanted to use the power of government to impose evangelical Protestant moral values on society. Democrats opposed what they saw as culturally coercive measures. Many Republicans wanted to limit or even prohibit the sale of alcoholic beverages. They favored the establishment of public schools—with a Protestant curriculum. As a result, Catholics were strongly Democratic. In this period, the parties were very evenly matched in strength.

The Triumph of the Republicans. In the 1890s, however, the Republicans gained a decisive edge. In that decade, the populist movement emerged in the West and South to champion the interests of small farmers, who were often greatly in debt. Populists supported inflation, which benefited debtors by reducing the real value of outstanding debts. In 1896, when William Jennings Bryan became the Democratic candidate for president, the Democrats embraced populism.

As it turned out, the few western farmers who were drawn to the Democrats by this step were greatly outnumbered by urban working-class voters who believed that inflation would reduce the purchasing power of their paychecks and who therefore became Republicans. Political scientists use the term **realignment** to refer to this kind of large-scale change in support for the two major parties. From 1896 until 1932, the GOP was successful in presenting itself as the party that knew how to manage the economy.

The Progressive Interlude

In the early 1900s, a spirit of political reform arose in both major parties. Called progressivism, this spirit was compounded by a fear of the growing power of large corporations and a belief that honest, impartial government could regulate the economy effectively. In 1912, the Republican Party temporarily split as former Republican president Theodore Roosevelt campaigned for the presidency on a third-party Progressive ticket. This Republican split permitted the election of Woodrow Wilson, the Democratic candidate, along with a Democratic Congress.

Like Roosevelt, Wilson considered himself a progressive, although he and Roosevelt did not agree on how progressivism ought to be implemented. Wilson's progressivism marked the beginning of a radical change in Democratic policies. Dating back to its very foundation, the Democratic Party had been the party of limited government. Under Wilson, the Democrats became for the first time at least as receptive as the Republicans to government action in the economy. (Wilson's progressivism did not extend to race relations—African Americans found the Wilson administration to be unremittingly hostile to their interests. Wilson resegregated federal government employment in 1913.)

GOP
A nickname for the Republican Party, which stands for "grand old party."

Realignment
A large-scale, lasting change in the types of voters who support each of the major political parties.

dpa picture alliance/Alamy Stock Photo

Image 7.9 Senator Marsha Blackburn (R-TN) listens to testimony before a Senate committee on Russian interference in the 2016 elections.
▶ Why are political parties more likely to pick senators than representatives as presidential candidates?

The New Deal Era

The Republican ascendancy resumed after Wilson left office. It ended with the election of 1932, in the depths of the Great Depression. Republican Herbert Hoover was president when the Great Depression began in 1929. While Hoover took some measures in an attempt to fight the Great Depression, they fell far short of what the public demanded. Significantly, Hoover opposed federal relief for the unemployed and the destitute. In 1932, Democrat Franklin D. Roosevelt was elected president by an overwhelming margin. As with the election of 1896, the vote in 1932 constituted a major political realignment.

The Great Depression shattered the working-class belief in Republican economic competence. Under Roosevelt, the Democrats began to make major interventions in the economy in an attempt to combat the Depression and to relieve the suffering of the unemployed. Roosevelt's New Deal relief programs were open to all citizens, both Black and white. As a result, African Americans began to support the Democratic Party in large numbers—a development that would have stunned any American politician of the 1800s.

Roosevelt's political coalition was broad enough to establish the Democrats as the new majority party, in place of the GOP. In the 1950s, Republican Dwight D. Eisenhower, the leading U.S. general during World War II, won two terms as president. Otherwise, with minor interruptions, the Democratic ascendancy lasted until about 1968.

An Era of Divided Government

The New Deal coalition managed the unlikely feat of including both African Americans and white people who were hostile to African American advancement. This balancing act came to an end in the 1960s, a decade that was marked by the civil rights movement, by several years of race riots in major cities, and by increasingly heated protests against the Vietnam War (1965–75). For many economically moderate, socially conservative voters, especially in the South, social issues had become more important than economic ones, and these individuals left the Democratic Party. These voters outnumbered the new voters who joined the Democrats—newly enfranchised African Americans and former liberal Republicans in New England and the upper Midwest.

The Parties in Balance. In 1964 and 1965, legislation was introduced to improve the civil rights of African Americans, among other underrepresented groups. In 1965, legislation was introduced to protect and strengthen the voting rights of African Americans. In both instances, Democratic Senators and Representatives from the South voted against this legislation. After 1968, there was a slow-motion realignment that left the nation almost evenly divided in politics. In presidential elections, the Republicans had more success than the Democrats. Until the 1990s, Congress remained Democratic, but official party labels can be misleading. Some of the Democrats were southern conservatives who normally voted with the Republicans on issues. As these conservative Democrats retired, they were largely replaced by Republicans. In 1994, Republicans were able to take control of both the House and the Senate for the first time in many years.

Red State, Blue State. Nothing demonstrated the nation's close political divisions more clearly than the 2000 presidential elections. Democratic presidential candidate Al Gore won the popular vote, but lost the electoral college by a narrow margin to Republican George W. Bush. The closeness of the vote in the electoral college led the press to repeatedly publish maps showing state-by-state results. Commentators discussed at length the supposed differences between the Republican "red states" and the Democratic "blue states."[6]

An interesting characteristic of the red state–blue state division is that it is an almost exact reversal of the results of the presidential elections of 1896, which established the Republican ascendancy that lasted until the Great Depression. Except for the state of Washington, every state that supported Democrat William Jennings Bryan in 1896 supported Republican George W. Bush in 2000 and 2004. This reversal parallels the transformation of the Democrats from an anti–civil rights to a pro–civil rights party and from a party that supported limited government to a party that favors extensive positive government action.

The Parties Today

Not only was the presidential election of 2000 very close, but the partisan balance in the U.S. Congress was also very close in the opening years of the twenty-first century. Until 2006, the Republicans generally controlled Congress. Their margins of control, however, were very narrow.

From time to time, voters demonstrate that they are relatively dissatisfied with the performance of one or another of the major parties. This dissatisfaction can produce a wave of support for the other party. Unlike a realignment, the effects of a **wave election** are temporary. The first decade of the twenty-first century was marked by a series of wave elections, in which the voters punished first one party and then the other.

Wave Elections Sweep out the Republicans. By 2006, an ever larger number of voters came to believe that U.S. intervention in Iraq had been a mistake, and in the midterm elections, the Democrats took control of the U.S. House and Senate. In September 2008, a worldwide financial panic developed into the greatest economic downturn since the Great Depression of the 1930s. That November, Democratic presidential candidate Barack Obama was elected with one of the largest margins in recent years.

Republicans on the Upswing. By 2010, many voters were convinced that Democrats were expanding government to an unacceptable degree, and a wave election returned control of the House to the Republicans. While President Obama won reelection in 2012, the Republicans retained control of the House, even though Democratic House candidates won more votes nationwide than Republican candidates. The 2014 midterm elections appeared to be another Republican wave, though some commentators attributed the strong Republican performance chiefly to very low turnout by Democrats, rather than any enthusiasm for the Republicans.

In 2016, Donald Trump won the electoral college while losing the popular vote. His unpopularity rose thereafter—two months after he was inaugurated, Trump's disapproval ratings in the polls rose above 50 percent and stayed there. In the 2018 midterms, Democratic turnout rose to unprecedented levels, though Republican turnout was up as well. Some of the 2018 Democratic

Genaro Molina/Los Angeles Times/Getty Images

Image 7.10 While a U.S. senator from California, Kamala Harris made a bid to become the Democratic presidential nominee in 2019. She pulled out before the primaries. In August 2020 she was named Joe Biden's vice-presidential running mate. ▶ What characteristics did she have that might have led Biden to pick her?

Wave Election
An election in which voters display dissatisfaction with one of the major parties through a "wave" of support for the other. In contrast to a realigning election, the results of a wave election are not permanent.

---

6. The use of red for Republicans and blue for Democrats is a twenty-first century development. It originated in the colors used by TV networks to display the results of presidential elections. This color scheme reverses the typical international pattern, which assigns red to the political left and blue to the right. Red is the traditional color of socialist and communist parties, and the U.S. color reversal was a deliberate attempt to avoid implying that Democrats were socialists.

2022 Elections:

Partisan Trends in the 2022 Elections

Over the past three decades, four sitting presidents have had approval ratings as low as Democrat Joseph Biden's on the eve of the 2022 midterm elections. Each time (Democrats Bill Clinton in 1994 and Barak Obama in 2014, Republicans George W. Bush in 2006 and Donald Trump in 2018), the president's party suffered heavy losses. Yet, in 2022, Democrats did fairly well, keeping control of the U.S. Senate and ceding the U.S. House of Representatives to the Republicans by a relatively small margin. For once, it seemed, a midterm election was *not* a referendum on an unpopular president.

This atypical result did not reflect any change in the partisan trends of American politics. Indeed, the population's unwillingness to cross the aisle was as strong as ever in 2022, with more than 90 percent of Republican voters supporting Republican candidates and more than 90 percent of Democratic voters supporting Democratic candidates. Both sides also voted predictably when it came to issues such as abortion, crime, and the economy. The most unpredictable voting group in 2022 was, as it turned out, independents, who split their vote between the two parties. In the four previous midterm elections, independent voters favored the opposition party (Republicans, in 2022) by double-digit margins.

Given how well "traditional" Republican candidates did when compared to the poor showing of their more extreme party-mates, the voting choices made by independents in 2022 probably represent a deviation rather than a trend. Democrats are hopeful that another recent pattern does become a long-term trend—youthful voters (aged 18-29), who generally back their party, turned out in record numbers for the second midterm election in a row.

---

voters were working-class white people returning home to the Democrats. Others were suburban moderates, often women, who were repelled by Trump's policies and behavior. As a result, Democrats had high hopes leading up to the 2020 elections. If they could defeat Trump and take the Senate, they might be able to pass much of their party platform. As it happened, Republican voter turnout was every bit as massive as the turnout by Democrats. The voters may have repudiated Trump, but not the Republican Party as a whole. The Democrats gained the majority in the House. The two parties were equally divided in the Senate, but with a tie-breaking Democratic vice president, some major legislation was able to be passed and signed into law by Biden.

Why Has the Two-Party System Endured?

» LO 7-6: Explain why a third-party presidential candidate has almost no chance of winning.

There are several reasons why two major parties have dominated the political landscape in the United States for almost two centuries. These reasons have to do with (1) the historical foundations of the system, (2) political socialization and practical considerations, (3) the winner-take-all electoral system, and (4) state and federal laws favoring the two-party system.

The Historical Foundations of the Two-Party System

As we have seen, at many times in American history one preeminent issue or dispute has divided the nation politically. In the beginning, Americans were at odds over ratifying the Constitution. After the Constitution went into effect, the power of the federal government became the major national issue. Thereafter, the dispute over slavery divided the nation, North versus South. At times—for example, in the North after the Civil War—cultural differences have been important. In that period, advocates of government-sponsored morality (such as banning alcoholic beverages) were pitted against advocates of personal liberty. During much of the twentieth century, economic differences were preeminent. In the New Deal period, the Democrats became known as the party of the working class, while the Republicans became known as the party of the middle and upper classes and commercial interests.

In situations like these, when politics is based on an argument between two opposing points of view, advocates of each viewpoint can mobilize most effectively by forming a single, unified party. The result is a two-party system. When such a system has been in existence for almost two centuries, it becomes difficult to imagine an alternative.

Political Socialization and Practical Considerations

Given that the majority of Americans identify with one of the two major political parties, it is not surprising that many children learn at a fairly young age to think of themselves as either Democrats or Republicans. This generates a built-in mechanism to perpetuate a two-party system. Also, most politically oriented people who aspire to work for change consider that the only realistic way to capture political power in this country is to be either a Republican or a Democrat.

The Winner-Take-All Electoral System

At almost every level of government in the United States, the outcome of elections is based on the **plurality**, winner-take-all principle. In a plurality system, the winner is the person who obtains the most votes, even if that person does not receive a majority (more than 50 percent) of the votes. Whoever gets the most votes gets everything. Most legislators in the United States are elected from single-member districts in which only one person represents the constituency, and the candidate who finishes second in such an election receives nothing for the effort.

Presidential Voting. The winner-take-all system also operates in the election of the U.S. president. Recall that the voters in each state do not vote for a president directly but vote for Electoral College delegates who are committed to the various presidential candidates. These delegates are called electors. (See Figure 7.2 for the 2020 results.)

In all but two states (Maine and Nebraska), if a presidential candidate wins a plurality in the state, then all the state's electoral votes go to that candidate. This is known as the **unit rule**. For example, suppose that the electors pledged to a particular presidential candidate receive a plurality of 40 percent of the votes in a state. That presidential candidate will receive all of the state's votes in the electoral college. Minor parties have a difficult time competing under such a system. Because voters know that minor parties rarely win any electoral votes, they often will not vote for minor-party candidates, even if the candidates are in tune with them ideologically.

Popular Election of the Governors and the President. In most of Europe, the chief executive (usually called the prime minister) is elected by the legislature, or parliament. If the parliament contains three or more parties, as is usually the situation, two or more of the parties can join together in a coalition to choose the prime minister and the other leaders of the government. In the United States, however, the people elect the president and the governors of all fifty states. There is no opportunity for two or more parties to negotiate a coalition. Here, too, the winner-take-all principle discriminates powerfully against any third party.

Proportional Representation. Many other nations use a system of proportional representation. If, during the national election, party X obtains 12 percent of the vote, party Y gets 43 percent of the vote, and party Z gets the remaining 45 percent of the vote, then party X gets 12 percent of the seats in the legislature, party Y

Plurality
A number of votes cast for a candidate that is greater than the number of votes for any other candidate but not necessarily a majority.

Unit Rule
A rule by which all of a state's electoral votes are cast for the presidential candidate who receives a plurality of the votes in that state.

 Interact

One of the most dangerous assumptions students can make is that something is true because they read it on the internet. To be sure, some internet sites are relatively reliable. Wikipedia, for example, receives much criticism. Yet studies have shown that its accuracy typically surpasses that of the *Encyclopedia Britannica* online. (Wikipedia does have the problem that its pages are occasionally subject to vandalism.) In contrast, statements made on the websites of political parties are utterly suspect. True facts that you can learn by visiting these sites may be limited to "What is the party trying to say?" and "Whom is it trying to say it to?" Anything that a party reports about another party is likely to be exaggerated, unfair, or flatly untrue. Try visiting the websites of the Republican and Democratic parties. Can you identify any statements that strike you as troublesome?

| Figure 7.2 | The 2020 Presidential Election Results |

▶ Joe Biden won the election by carrying Arizona, Georgia, Michigan, Pennsylvania, and Wisconsin, all of which went for Trump in 2016. Maine and Nebraska choose some of their electors by congressional district, and the red and blue dots indicate that each candidate won one of them.

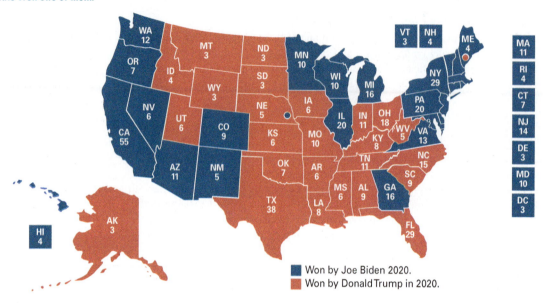

■ Won by Joe Biden 2020.
■ Won by Donald Trump in 2020.

gets 43 percent of the seats, and party Z gets 45 percent of the seats. Some nations implement proportional representation by creating districts that elect multiple representatives. An alternative system is to let voters choose both a local representative and a preferred party. Because even a minor party may still obtain at least a few seats in the legislature, smaller parties have a greater incentive to organize under such electoral systems than they do in the United States.

State and Federal Laws Favoring the Two Parties

Many state and federal election laws offer a clear advantage to the two major parties. In some states, the established major parties need to gather fewer signatures to place their candidates on the ballot than minor parties or independent candidates do. The criterion for determining how many signatures will be required is often based on the total party vote in the last general election, thus penalizing a new political party that did not compete in that election.

At the national level, minor parties face different obstacles. All of the rules and procedures of both chambers of Congress divide committee seats, staff members, and other privileges on the basis of party membership. A legislator who is elected on a minor-party ticket, such as the Conservative Party of New York, must choose to be counted with one of the major parties to obtain a committee assignment.

The Role of Minor Parties in U.S. Politics

For the reasons just discussed, minor parties have a difficult, if not impossible, time competing within the American two-party political system. Still, minor parties have played an important role in our political life. Parties other than the Republicans or Democrats are usually called a **third party**. (Technically, of course, there could be fourth, fifth, or sixth

Third Party
A political party other than the two major political parties (Republican and Democratic).

parties as well, but we use the term third party to describe any party that is not affiliated with the two major parties.) Third parties can come into existence in a number of ways. They may be founded from scratch by individuals or groups who are committed to a particular interest, issue, or ideology. They can split off from one of the major parties when a group becomes dissatisfied with the major party's policies. Finally, they can be organized around a particular charismatic leader and serve as that person's vehicle for contesting elections.

Frequently, third parties have acted as barometers of change in the political mood, forcing the major parties to recognize new issues or trends in the thinking of Americans. Political scientists also believe that third parties have acted as safety valves for dissident groups, preventing major confrontations and political unrest.

Ideological Third Parties. The longest-lived third parties have been those with strong ideological foundations that are typically at odds with the majority mindset. The Socialist Party is an example. The party was founded in 1901 and lasted until 1972, when it was finally dissolved. (It was replaced by nonparty advocacy organizations such as the Democratic Socialists of America.) The Socialists were never very popular in the United States. Conservatives revived the term socialist as an insult directed at President Obama. Given that, it is somewhat surprising that Bernie Sanders has done so well as a presidential candidate running as a democratic socialist.[7]

Library of Congress, Prints & Photographs Division, Reproduction number LC-DIG-hec-01584 (digital file from original negative)

Image 7.11 Eugene V. Debs was the nation's most popular socialist ever—at least until Senator Bernie Sanders (D-VT). Debs ran for president five times from 1900 to 1920, the last time from a prison cell. He had been convicted of speaking out against World War I. ▶ Why would such a conviction be impossible today?

Ideology has at least two functions in such parties. First, the members of the party regard themselves as outsiders and look to one another for support—ideology provides great psychological cohesiveness. Second, because the rewards of ideological commitment are partly psychological, these parties do not think in terms of immediate electoral success. A poor showing at the polls therefore does not dissuade either the leadership or the grassroots participants from continuing their quest for change in American government (and, ultimately, American society).

Today's active ideological parties include the Libertarian Party and the Green Party. The Libertarian Party supports a laissez-faire ("let it be") capitalist economic program, together with a hands-off policy on regulating matters of moral conduct. The Green Party began as a grassroots environmentalist organization with affiliated political parties across North America and Western Europe. It was established in the United States as a national party in 1996 and nominated Ralph Nader to run for president in 2000. Nader campaigned against what he called "corporate greed," advocated universal health insurance, and promoted environmental concerns. (He ran again for president as an independent in 2004 and 2008.)

Splinter Parties. Some of the more successful minor parties have been those that split from major parties. The impetus for these **splinter parties**, or factions, has usually been a situation in which a particular personality was at odds with the major party. The most successful of

Splinter Parties
A new party formed by a dissident faction within a major political party. Often, splinter parties have emerged when a particular personality was at odds with the major party.

---

7. Sanders has found many supporters among young people, particularly those in college. In surveys of his college supporters, though, a majority of them could not actually define what socialism meant.

these splinter parties was the "Bull Moose" Progressive Party, formed in 1912 to support Theodore Roosevelt for president. The Republican national convention of that year denied Roosevelt the nomination, despite the fact that he had won most of the primaries. He therefore left the GOP and ran against Republican William Howard Taft in the general elections. Although Roosevelt did not win the elections, he did split the Republican vote so that Democrat Woodrow Wilson became president.

Third parties have also been formed to back individual candidates who were not rebelling against a particular party. H. Ross Perot, for example, who challenged Republican George H. W. Bush and Democrat Bill Clinton for the presidency in 1992, had not previously been active in a major party. Perot's supporters probably would have split their votes between Bush and Clinton had Perot not been in the race. In theory, Perot ran in 1992 as a nonparty independent. In practice, he had to create a campaign organization. By 1996, Perot's organization was formalized as the Reform Party.

The Impact of Minor Parties. Third parties have rarely been able to affect American politics by actually winning elections. (One exception is that third-party and independent candidates have occasionally won races for state governorships—for example, Jesse Ventura was elected governor of Minnesota on the Reform Party ticket in 1998.) Instead, the impact of third parties has taken two forms. First, third parties can influence one of the major parties to take up one or more issues. Second, third parties can determine the outcome of a particular election by pulling votes from one of the major-party candidates in what is called the spoiler effect.

The presidential elections of 2000 were one instance in which a minor party may have altered the outcome. Green candidate Ralph Nader received almost one hundred thousand votes in Florida, a majority of which would probably have gone to Democrat Al Gore if Nader had not been in the race. The real question, however, is not whether the Nader vote had an effect—clearly, it did—but whether the effect was important. The problem is that in elections as close as the presidential elections of 2000, any factor with an impact on the outcome can be said to have determined the results.

The Rise of the Independents

Party Identification
Linking oneself to a particular political party

Straight-ticket Voting
Voting exclusively for the candidates of one party.

Polls that track **party identification** show increasing numbers of voters who identify themselves as independents. (See Figure 7.3.) Not only has the number of independents grown over the last half century, but voters also have been less willing to vote a straight ticket—that is, to vote for all the candidates of one party. In the early twentieth century, **straight-ticket voting** was nearly universal. By midcentury, 12 percent of voters engaged in split-ticket voting. By the 1970s and 1980s, 25 to 30 percent of all ballots cast in presidential election years were split-ticket. A major reason was that many voters, especially in the South, were pairing a Republican for president with a conservative Democrat for Congress. In recent years, however, conservative Democrats have become scarce, and the incidence of split-ticket voting has ranged only from 17 to 19 percent.

While the number of voters who identify as independents has never been greater, many voters who call themselves independents actually lean toward one or the other of the two major parties. When it comes to voting, these political leaners are every bit as loyal to their preferred party as those who accept a party label. As you can see in Figure 7.3, in a recent Gallup poll, 44 percent of those polled described themselves as independents. Yet 19 percent of all respondents admitted that they were independents who leaned Republican, and another 17 percent were independents who leaned Democratic. This left only 8 percent of the total who were true swing voters who could swing between the parties.

Figure 7.3	Party Identification from 1945 to the Present

▶ **Why would people who usually support one of the two major parties still call themselves independents?**

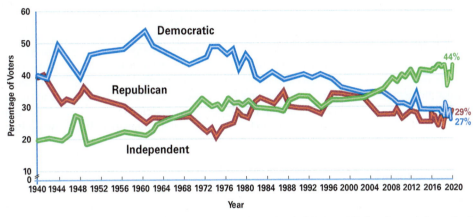

Sources: *Gallup Report*, August 1995; *New York Times*/CBS poll, June 1996; *Gallup Report*, February 1998; Pew Research Center for the People and the Press, November 2003; Gallup polls, 2004 through 2020, Pew Center, 2022. Percentages are quarterly averages. (Numbers do not add up to 100 due to undecided responses.)

Making A Difference

You Can Be a Convention Delegate

The most exciting political party event, staged every four years, is the national convention. State conventions also take place on a regular basis. Surprising as it might seem, there are opportunities for the individual voter to become a delegate.

Why Should You Care? How would you like to exercise a small amount of real political power yourself—power that goes beyond simply voting in an election? You might be able to become a delegate to a county, district, or even state party convention. Many of these conventions nominate candidates for various offices. For example, in Michigan, the state party conventions nominate the candidates for the Board of Regents of the state's top three public universities.

In much of the country, there are more openings for party precinct delegates than there are people willing to serve. In such circumstances, almost anyone can become a delegate by collecting a handful of signatures on a nominating petition or by mounting a small-scale write-in campaign.

What Can You Do? When the parties choose delegates for the national convention, the process begins at the local level—either the congressional district or the state legislative district. District delegates may be elected in party primary elections or chosen in neighborhood or precinct caucuses. If the delegates are elected in a primary, persons who want to run for these positions may need to file petitions with the board of elections.

It is even easier to get involved in the grassroots politics of presidential caucuses. In some states—Iowa being the earliest and most famous one—delegates are first nominated at the local precinct caucus. These caucuses select delegates to the county conventions who are pledged to specific presidential candidates. This is the first step toward the national convention. At both the county caucus and the convention levels, the parties often try to find younger members to fill some of the seats.

For further information about these opportunities, contact the state party office or your local state legislator.

Key Terms

concentrated benefits and dispersed costs 163	indirect techniques 160	patronage 165	splinter parties 175
	interest groups 151	plurality 173	state central committee 165
	labor movement 155	policy demanders 166	
Democratic Party 168	lobbyists 152	political party 152	straight-ticket voting 176
direct techniques 160	national committee 165	public interest 158	third party 174
divided government 166	national convention 164	realignment 169	two-party system 167
free-rider problem 153	party identification 176	Republican Party 168	unit rule 173
GOP 168	party organization 164	service sector 155	wave election 171
independents 163	party platform 164	social movements 153	Whig Party 168

Chapter Summary

» **LO 7-1** An interest group is an organization whose members share common objectives and actively attempt to influence government policy. Interest groups proliferate in the United States because they can influence government at many points in the political structure.

» **LO 7-2** Major types of economic interest groups include business, agricultural, labor, and professional groups. Other important groups include environmental, public-interest, ideological, and identity groups.

» **LO 7-3** Interest groups use direct and indirect techniques to influence government. Direct techniques include testifying before committees and rulemaking agencies, providing information to legislators, rating legislators' voting records, and aiding in political campaigns. Indirect techniques include conducting campaigns to rally public sentiment and using constituents to lobby for a group's interests.

In 1995, the Lobbying Disclosure Act defined lobbyists and their reporting requirements. In 2007, the Honest Leadership and Open Government Act increased the frequency of lobbyists' reports, required reports on coalition activity, and created a searchable internet file on lobbying activity.

» **LO 7-4** A political party is a group of political activists who organize to win elections, operate the government, and determine public policy. Functions of political parties include recruiting candidates for public office, organizing and running elections, presenting alternative policies to voters, assuming responsibility for operating the government, and acting as the opposition to the party in power.

A political party consists of those who identify with the party—the voters-in-the electorate, the party

organization, and the party-in-government. Each level of the party organization—local, state, and national—has considerable autonomy.

» **LO 7-5** The evolution of our nation's political parties can be divided into seven periods: (a) the creation and formation of political parties, from 1789 to 1816; (b) the era of one-party rule from 1816 to 1828; (c) the period from Andrew Jackson's presidency to the eve of the Civil War, from 1828 to 1856; (d) the Civil War and post–Civil War period, from 1856 to 1896; (e) the Republican ascendancy and the progressive period, from 1896 to 1932; (f) the New Deal period, from 1932 to about 1968; and (g) the modern period, from approximately 1968 to the present. Throughout most of the modern period, the Republican and Democratic parties have been closely matched in strength.

» **LO 7-6** Two major parties have dominated the political landscape in the United States for almost two centuries. The reasons for this include (a) the historical foundations of the system, (b) political socialization and practical considerations, (c) the winner-take-all electoral system, and (d) state and federal laws favoring the two-party system.

For these reasons, minor parties have found it extremely difficult to win elections. Still, third parties can affect the political process (even if they do not win) if major parties adopt their issues or if they help determine which major party wins an election.

From the 1940s to the present, independent voters have formed an increasing proportion of the electorate, with a consequent decline in Democratic and Republican party identification. Nevertheless, many independent voters lean toward one major party or the other.

Test Yourself

1. **When individuals benefit from the actions of an interest group but do not support that group, they are:**
   a. free riders.
   b. freeloaders.
   c. usually just waiting to join the group.

2. **Union membership in the United States has:**
   a. been growing, especially since 2000.
   b. stayed about the same since the Great Depression.
   c. been declining in recent years, except in the public sector.

3. **There are many direct techniques that interest groups can use to affect legislation. They include:**
   a. sending out large numbers of e-mail advertising pieces.
   b. attempts at weakening other interest groups.
   c. hiring lobbyists to argue their positions with members of Congress.

4. **Most lobbying is done by the following kind of people, who often work for Washington, D.C., law firms:**
   a. constituents.
   b. professionals.
   c. activists.

5. **Some interest groups try to organize campaigns that make it seem as if ordinary citizens are behind the effort. Such campaigns are called:**
   a. Astroturf lobbying.
   b. climate control.
   c. the rifle technique.

6. **A difficulty in limiting the effect of lobbying is:**
   a. opposition to new legislation by Democratic members of Congress.
   b. opposition to new legislation by Republican presidents.
   c. many legislators are proud of federal funds spent locally and are happy to tell their constituents all about it.

7. **An American political party includes:**
   a. the party-in-the-electorate, the party organization, and the members of the party.
   b. the party organization, the party-in-government, and the party-in-the-electorate.
   c. the party-in-government, the party-in-the-electorate, and the lobbyists for that party.

8. **In the years following the adoption of the Constitution, the first two organized political parties in the United States were the:**
   a. Democrats and Republicans.
   b. Whigs and Democrats.
   c. Federalists and Republicans.

9. **The elections of 1896, in which the Republicans gained a lasting advantage, were an example of:**
   a. political dealignment.
   b. a realigning election.
   c. the establishment of divided government.

10. **The New Deal era under Democratic president Franklin D. Roosevelt began:**
    a. at the beginning of the twentieth century.
    b. during the 1960s.
    c. during the Great Depression of the 1930s.

11. **At almost every level of government in this country, the outcome of elections is based on the plurality voting system, which means that:**
    a. the candidate with the largest number of votes wins, even if the winner does not receive 50 percent or more of the votes.
    b. when no one receives 50 percent of the vote, a runoff election is held.
    c. there is no need for everyone to vote in each election.

Essay Questions

1. About half of the paid lobbyists in Washington, D.C., are former government staff members or former members of Congress. Why would interest groups employ such people? Why might some reformers want to limit the ability of interest groups to employ them? On what basis might an interest group argue that such limits are unconstitutional?

2. Do you support (or lean toward) one of the major political parties today? If so, would you have supported the same party in the mid-to-late 1800s—or would you have supported a different party? Explain your reasoning.

Answers to multiple-choice questions: 1. a, 2. c, 3. c, 4. b, 5. a, 6. c, 7. b, 8. c, 9. b, 10. c, 11. a.

8 | Campaigns and Elections

During the 2020 election cycle, the call for voting by mail was heard around the country. Because the U.S. Constitution gives the states the task of setting the rules and regulations about voting, the federal government cannot impose mail-in voting on any state. ▶ What is the difference between mail-in voting and absentee voting?

The five **Learning Outcomes (LOs)** below are designed to help improve your understanding of this chapter. After reading this chapter, you should be able to:

≫ **LO 8-1** Discuss who runs for office and how campaigns are managed.

≫ **LO 8-2** Describe the current system of campaign finance.

≫ **LO 8-3** Summarize the process of choosing a president of the United States.

≫ **LO 8-4** Discuss why it matters (or does not matter) whether Americans vote on election day.

≫ **LO 8-5** Provide some of the reasons why people vote in particular ways.

Check your understanding of the material with the Test Yourself section at the end of the chapter.

Free elections are the cornerstone of the American political system. By casting ballots in local, state, and federal elections, voters choose one candidate over another to hold political office. There are thousands of elective offices in the United States and, consequently, thousands of elections. Although the major political parties strive to provide a slate of candidates for every election, recruiting candidates is easier for some offices than for others. Political parties may have difficulty finding candidates for the

180

board of the local water control district, for example, but they generally find a sufficient number of candidates for county commissioner or sheriff. The higher the office and the more prestige attached to it, the more candidates are likely to want to run. In many areas of the country, however, one major party may be considerably stronger than the other. In those situations, the minority party may have difficulty finding nominees for elections in which victory is unlikely.

The Twenty-First-Century Campaign

» **LO 8-1:** Discuss who runs for office and how campaigns are managed.

The presidential campaign provides the most colorful and exciting look at candidates and how they prepare to compete for office—in this instance, the highest office in the land. The individuals who wanted to be the Democratic Party's candidate in the 2020 presidential campaign faced a long and obstacle-filled path. First, they needed to tour the nation—particularly the states with an early **presidential primary**—to see if they had enough local supporters. They needed to create an organization and to win primary votes. Finally, when nominated as the party's candidate, the winner required funds to finance a successful campaign for president. Always, at every turn, there was the question of whether there were enough funds to effectively compete against primary opponents, and eventually against the Republican candidate in the general election.

Presidential Primary
A statewide primary election of delegates to a political party's national convention, held to determine a party's presidential nominee

Who Is Eligible?

There are few constitutional restrictions on who can be elected to national office in the United States. As detailed in the Constitution, the formal requirements are as follows:

1. **President.** Must be a natural-born citizen, have attained the age of thirty-five years, and be a resident of the country for fourteen years by the time of inauguration.
2. **Vice president.** Must meet the same requirements as the president and also not be a resident of the same state as the president.[1]
3. **Senator.** Must be a citizen for at least nine years, have attained the age of thirty by the time of taking office, and be a resident of the state from which elected.
4. **Representative.** Must be a citizen for at least seven years, have attained the age of 25 by the time of taking office, and be a resident of the state from which elected.

The qualifications for state legislators are set by state constitutions and likewise include age, place of residence, and citizenship. (Usually, the requirements for the state senate are somewhat higher than those for the lower chamber of the state legislature.) The legal qualifications for serving as governor or in other state offices are similar.

Who Runs?

In spite of these minimal legal qualifications for office at both the national and the state levels, a quick look at the slate of candidates in any election—or at the current members of Congress—will reveal that not all segments of the population enjoy these opportunities equally. Holders of political office in the United States have been predominantly white

---

1. Technically, a presidential and a vice-presidential candidate can be from the same state, but if they are, one of the two must forfeit the electoral votes of their home state.

and male. Until the twentieth century, presidential candidates were exclusively of northern European origin and of Protestant heritage.[2]

Laws that effectively denied voting rights made it impossible to elect African American public officials in many areas in which African Americans constituted a significant portion of the population. As a result of the passage of major civil rights legislation in the 1960s, however, the number of African American public officials has increased throughout the United States, and in a groundbreaking vote, the nation elected Barack Obama, an African American, president in 2008 and reelected him in 2012.

Women as Candidates. During much of the twentieth century, women generally were considered to be candidates only for lower-level offices, such as state legislator or school board member. The past thirty years have seen a tremendous increase in the number of women who run for office, not only at the state level but for the U.S. Congress as well. In 2022, about 250 women ran for Congress on major-party tickets, and at least 120 were elected. Today, a majority of Americans say they would vote for a qualified woman for president of the United States. Indeed, Hillary Clinton came close to winning the Democratic presidential nomination in 2008, a year in which the eventual Democratic nominee was favored to win the general election. Clinton did win the nomination in 2016, although she did not win the general election.

Professional Status. Political campaigning and officeholding are simply easier for some occupational groups than for others, and political involvement can make a valuable contribution to certain careers. Lawyers, for example, have more flexible schedules than do many other professionals, can take time off for campaigning, and can leave their jobs to hold public office full time. Furthermore, holding political office is good publicity for their professional practice. Perhaps most important, many jobs that lawyers aspire to—federal or state judgeships, state's attorney offices, or work in a federal agency—can be attained by political appointment.

Managing the Campaign

Primary Election
An election in which political parties choose their candidates for the general election.

General Election
An election, normally held on the first Tuesday in November, that determines who will fill various elected positions.

After the candidates have been nominated, typically through a **primary election**, the most exhausting and expensive part of the election process begins—the **general election** campaign, which actually fills the offices at stake. Political campaigns are becoming more complex and more sophisticated with every election. Even with the most appealing of candidates, today's campaigns require a strong organization with (1) expertise in political polling and marketing, (2) professional assistance in fundraising and accounting, (3) financial management, and (4) technological capabilities in every aspect of the campaign.

Campaign Goals. The goal is the same for all campaigns—to convince voters to choose a candidate or a slate of candidates for office. In recent decades, the typical campaign for high office has no longer been centered on the party but on the candidate. The candidate-centered campaign emerged in response to changes in the electoral system, the increased importance of television in campaigns, technological innovations such as the internet, and the increased cost of campaigning.

To run a successful and persuasive campaign, the candidate's organization must be able to raise funds for the effort, produce and pay for political commercials and advertising,

---

2. A number of early presidents were Unitarian. The Unitarian Church is not Protestant, but it is historically rooted in the Protestant tradition.

Sipa USA/Alamy Stock Photo

Image 8.1 The 2020 Democratic presidential candidates at the South Carolina primary debate in February. From left to right: former New York mayor Michael Bloomberg; South Bend, Indiana, mayor Pete Buttigieg; Massachusetts senator Elizabeth Warren; Vermont senator Bernie Sanders; former vice president Joe Biden; Minnesota senator Amy Klobuchar; and entrepreneur Tom Steyer. ▶ Did the COVID-19 pandemic change the debates?

and obtain coverage from the media. In addition, the organization needs to schedule the candidate's time effectively, convey the candidate's position on the issues to the voters, and conduct research on the opposing candidate. Finally, the campaign must get their voters to go to the polls.

The Role of the Parties. When party identification was more widespread among voters and before the advent of television campaigning, a strong party organization at the local, state, or national level could furnish most of the services and expertise that the candidate needed. Parties used their precinct organizations to distribute literature, register voters, and get out the vote on Election Day. Less effort was spent on advertising each candidate's positions and character, because the party label presumably communicated that information to many voters.

Modern parties cannot provide the level of services that they did many years ago, but parties remain central to the elections system. The high levels of political polarization seen in recent years mean that each major party is a strong ideological rallying point. The party organization as such may be less significant, but for politicians, party identification is more important than ever. Also, the candidate-centered campaign does not change the fact that candidates for top national and state positions must normally win the support of their party in a primary election.

The Professional Campaign. Whether the candidate is running for the state legislature, for the governor's office, for the U.S. Congress, or for the presidency, every campaign has some fundamental tasks to accomplish. Today, in national elections, most of these tasks are handled by paid professionals rather than volunteers or amateur politicians.

Hoo-Me/Storms Media Group/Alamy Stock Photo

Image 8.2 Brad Parscale was Donald Trump's advisor for data operations in 2016 and manager for much of 2020. ▶ What does a campaign manager do?

Political Consultant
A paid professional hired to devise a campaign strategy and manage a campaign.

The most sought-after and possibly the most criticized campaign expert is the **political consultant**, who, for a large fee, takes charge of the candidate's campaign. Paid political consultants began to displace volunteer campaign managers in the 1960s, about the same time that television became a force in campaigns. The paid consultant devises a campaign strategy and theme, oversees campaign advertising, and plans media appearances. Consultants and the firms they represent are not politically neutral. Most will work only for candidates from one party.

Opinion Polls. One of the major sources of information for both the media and the candidates is opinion polls. Poll taking is widespread during the primaries. Presidential hopefuls have private polls taken to make sure that there is at least some chance they could be nominated and, if nominated, elected. During the presidential campaign itself, polling is even more frequent. Polls are taken not only by the regular pollsters—Gallup, Mason-Dixon, and others—but also privately by each candidate's campaign organization. These private polls are for the exclusive and confidential use of the candidate and their campaign organization.

As the election approaches, many candidates use tracking polls, which are polls taken almost every day, to find out how well they are competing for votes. Tracking polls enable consultants to fine-tune advertising and the candidate's speeches in the last days of the campaign.

Focus Group
A small group of individuals who are led in discussion by a professional consultant to gather opinions on, and responses to, candidates and issues.

Focus Groups. Another tactic used by campaign organizations to gain insights into public perceptions of the candidate is the **focus group**. The ten to fifteen ordinary citizens who comprise the group discuss the candidate or certain political issues. Professional consultants, who conduct the discussion, select focus group members from specific target groups in the population—for example, working women, blue-collar men, senior citizens, or young voters. Recent campaigns have tried to reach groups such as "soccer moms," "Walmart shoppers," or "NASCAR dads."[3]

The group may discuss personality traits of the candidate, political advertising, and other candidate-related issues. Focus groups can reveal more emotional responses to candidates or the deeper anxieties of voters—feelings that consultants believe often are not tapped by more impersonal telephone surveys. The campaign then can shape its messages to respond to those feelings and perceptions.

Financing the Campaign

>> **LO 8-2:** Describe the current system of campaign finance.

The connection between money and elections is a sensitive issue in American politics. The belief is widespread that large campaign contributions by special interests corrupt the political system. Indeed, spending on all campaigns taken together reached new heights during the 2019–20 election cycle. In 2020, total spending on all candidates at all levels was $14.4 billion. These funds had to be provided by the candidates and their families, borrowed, or raised by contributions from individuals, organizations, or political action committees (PACs), which are set up under federal or state law for the express purpose of making political donations.

---

3. NASCAR stands for the National Association for Stock Car Auto Racing.

The way campaigns are financed has changed dramatically in the past several years. For decades, candidates and political parties had to operate within the constraints imposed by complicated laws regulating campaign financing. Some of these constraints still exist, but recent developments have opened up the process to a striking degree. Today, there are no limits on how much any person or institution can invest in the political process, and only modest limits on how this spending can take place.

The Evolution of the Campaign Finance System

Throughout much of early American history, campaign financing was unregulated. No limits existed on contributions, and no data were collected on campaign funding. During the twentieth century, however, a variety of federal corrupt practices acts were adopted to regulate campaign financing. The first of these acts, initially passed in 1910, contained many loopholes and proved to be ineffective. The **Hatch Act** (Political Activities Act) of 1939 is best known for restricting the political activities of civil servants. The act also made it unlawful for a political group to spend more than $3 million in any campaign and limited individual contributions to a campaign committee to $5,000. Of course, such restrictions were easily circumvented by creating additional political organizations.

Hatch Act
An act passed in 1939 that restricted the political activities of government employees. It also prohibited a political group from spending more than $3 million in any campaign and limited individual contributions to a campaign committee to $5,000.

The Federal Election Campaign Act. The Federal Election Campaign Act (FECA) of 1971, which became effective in 1972, replaced all previous laws. The act restricted the amount that could be spent on campaign advertising. It also limited the amount that candidates could contribute to their own campaigns and required disclosure of all contributions and expenditures over $100. In principle, the FECA limited the role of labor unions and corporations in political campaigns.

Amendments to the FECA passed in 1974 created the **Federal Election Commission (FEC)**. This commission consists of six bipartisan administrators whose duty is to enforce compliance with the requirements of the act. The 1974 amendments also placed limits on the sums that individuals and committees could contribute to candidates.

Federal Election Commission (FEC)
The federal regulatory agency with the task of enforcing federal campaign laws. As a practical matter, the FEC's role is largely limited to collecting data on campaign contributions.

The principal role of the FEC today is to collect data on campaign contributions. Candidate committees must file periodic reports with the FEC listing who contributed, how much was spent, and for what it was spent. As an enforcement body, however, the FEC is conspicuously ineffective and typically does not determine that a campaign has violated the rules until an election is over, if then.

The original FECA of 1971 limited the amount that each individual could spend on their own behalf. The Supreme Court overturned the provision in 1976, in *Buckley v. Valeo*, stating that it was unconstitutional to restrict in any way the amount congressional candidates could spend on their own behalf.[4] The Court later extended this principle to state elections as well.

Political Action Committees. Changes to the FECA in 1974 and 1976 allowed corporations, labor unions, and other interest groups to set up **political action committees (PACs)** to raise funds for candidates. PACs can contribute up to $5,000 to each candidate in each election. Each corporation or each union is limited to one PAC. The number of PACs grew significantly after 1976, as did the amounts that they spent on elections. Since the 1990s, however, the number of traditional PACs has leveled off because interest groups and activists have found alternative mechanisms for funneling resources into campaigns.

Political Action Committees (PACs)
Committees set up by and representing a corporation, labor union, or interest group. PACs raise campaign donations.

---

4. 424 U.S. 1 (1976).

Issue Advocacy Advertising
Advertising paid for by interest groups that support or oppose a candidate's position on an issue without mentioning the candidate, voting, or elections.

Soft Money
Campaign contributions unregulated by federal or state law, usually given to parties and party committees to help fund general party activities.

Independent Expenditures
Unregulated political expenditures by PACs, organizations, and individuals that are not coordinated with candidate campaigns or political parties.

Interact

It has been said that if you want to understand what is happening in politics, you need to "follow the money." A number of online resources can help you do that. One is the OpenSecrets site maintained by the Center for Responsive Politics. If you don't know the name of your U.S. representative, OpenSecrets can search for that (or you can simply enter "find your representative" into a search engine). Now that you have the name, find this representative in OpenSecrets. Take note of the industries that contribute to this politician. Then, use OpenSecrets or Wikipedia to identify the House committees—and especially subcommittees—on which this member sits. Does the representative receive contributions from the industries that they oversee?

Issue Advocacy Advertising. Business corporations, labor unions, and other interest groups have also developed ways of making independent expenditures that are not coordinated with those of a candidate or political party. A common tactic is **issue advocacy advertising**, which promotes positions on issues rather than candidates. Although promoting issue positions aligns very closely with promoting candidates who support those positions, the courts repeatedly have held that interest groups have a First Amendment right to advocate their positions.

Soft Money. Interest groups and PACs hit upon the additional strategy of generating **soft money**—that is, campaign contributions to political parties that escaped the limits of federal or state election law. No limits existed on contributions to political parties or party committees for activities such as voter education and voter-registration drives. This loophole enabled the parties to raise millions of dollars from corporations and individuals.

The Rise and Fall of the McCain-Feingold Act. The Bipartisan Campaign Reform Act of 2002, also known as the McCain-Feingold Act after its Republican and Democratic sponsors in the Senate, took effect on the day after the midterm elections of 2002. The law sought to regulate the new campaign-finance practices developed since the passage of the FECA. It banned soft money at the federal level, but it did not ban such contributions to state and local parties. It attempted to curb issue advocacy advertising, but also increased the sums that individuals could contribute directly to candidates.

The constitutionality of the 2002 act was immediately challenged. In December 2003, the Supreme Court upheld almost all of the clauses of the act.[5] In 2007, however, the Court eased the act's restrictions on issue advocacy ads when it ruled that only those ads "susceptible of no reasonable interpretation other than as an appeal to vote for or against a specific candidate" could be restricted prior to an election.[6] Finally, in 2010, *Citizens United v. FEC* swept away almost all remaining restrictions on independent expenditures, leading to the system we have today.[7]

The Current Campaign Finance Environment

As of 2022, political campaigns were financed in two distinct ways. One of these is spending by the candidate's own committee. Contributions made directly to the candidate's committee are subject to limitations: An individual can donate no more than $2,900 to a candidate in a single election, and contributions by committees are limited as well. In exchange for these limits, candidates have almost complete control over how their own campaign money is spent.

Another way in which campaigns are financed is through **independent expenditures**. These funds may be spent on advertising and other political activities, but in theory the expenditures cannot be coordinated with those of a candidate. No limits exist on how much can be spent in this fashion. This two-part system is the direct result of the 2010 *Citizens United v. FEC* ruling by the Supreme Court.

Citizens United v. FEC. In January 2010, the Supreme Court ruled that corporations, unions, and nonprofits may spend funds to support or oppose

---

5. *McConnell v. FEC*, 540 U.S. 93 (2003).

6. *FEC v. Wisconsin Right to Life*, 551 U.S. 449 (2007).

7. 558 U.S. 310 (2010).

candidates, so long as the expenditures are made independently and are not coordinated with candidate campaigns. Political parties may also make independent expenditures on behalf of candidates. These rulings overturned campaign-finance laws dating back decades.

Democrats, plus many journalists and bloggers, accused the Court of granting corporations rights that ought to be exercised only by flesh-and-blood human beings. Republicans and others defended the ruling as protecting freedom of speech. Two months later, a federal court of appeals held that it was not possible to limit contributions to independent-expenditure groups based on the size of the contribution.[8] These rulings effectively abolished all limits on independent expenditures.

Super PACs. These rulings led directly to a new type of political organization: the **super PAC**. Traditional PACs, which continue to exist, are set up to represent a corporation, labor union, or interest group. The super PAC, in contrast, is established to aggregate unlimited contributions by individuals and organizations and then funnel these sums into independent expenditures. By 2011, every major presidential candidate had a super PAC. It soon became clear that the supposed independence of these organizations is a fiction. Presidential super PACs are usually chaired by individuals who are closely associated with the candidate. Frequently, the chair is a former top member of the candidate's campaign. A variety of other super PACs have been established as well. These groups are often oriented toward a party, rather than a candidate.

One interesting development has been the tendency for super PACs to be supported primarily by very wealthy individuals, rather than by corporations or other organizations. The Koch brothers provide a striking example of this phenomenon.[9] For years, Charles and the late David Koch had been famous for their large contributions to Republican campaigns. A political network overseen by the brothers spent almost $400 million during the 2012 election cycle. For 2016, the network established an even more ambitious spending goal.

This plan, however, ran into trouble when Donald Trump became the Republican candidate. Trump was not acceptable to the libertarian-minded Koch brothers, who decided to devote whatever funds they could raise to other campaigns.

David Koch died in 2019. Charles Koch remains active but is not quite the titan that he was. Rather, in 2020, the most dramatic campaign finance story was the Democratic presidential campaign of Michael Bloomberg, one of the nation's richest individuals. Bloomberg had served two terms as mayor of New York City as a Republican and one term as an independent. Naturally, many long-time Democrats saw him as an interloper. Prior to the first major bloc of presidential primaries on March 3, 2020 (known as Super Tuesday), Bloomberg dropped about $500 million on television ads and on hiring 2,500 staff members.

This meant Bloomberg had a larger advertising budget and more paid staff than the rest of the candidates put together, with one exception. Tom Steyer, another Democratic billionaire, spent more than $250 million on his presidential campaign before dropping out of the race just prior to Super Tuesday. Clearly, in the world of politics, spending more money on campaigns does not necessarily lead to success.

The 527 Organization. Well before *Citizens United*, interest groups realized that they could set up new organizations outside the parties to encourage voter registration and to run issue ads aimed at energizing supporters. So long as these committees did not endorse candidates, they faced no limits on fundraising. These tax-exempt groups, called 527 organizations after the section of the tax code that provides for them, first had a major impact during the

Super PAC
A political organization that aggregates unlimited contributions by individuals and organizations to be spent independently of candidate committees.

Image 8.3 Charles Koch is head of Koch Industries. With his late brother David, he ran one of the largest fundraising operations in American politics. The brothers considered themselves libertarians and contributed to Republicans. ▶ Are super PACs a problem with American politics? Why or why not?

8. *SpeechNow.org v. FEC*, 599 F.3d 686 (D.C.Cir. 2010).

9. The name is pronounced *coke*.

2003–2004 election cycle. Since then, they have largely been replaced by super PACs, but a number continue to be active to the present day.

The 501(c)(4) Organization. In the 2007–2008 election cycle, campaign-finance lawyers began recommending a new type of independent group—the 501(c)(4) organization, which, like the 527 organization, is named after the relevant provision of the tax code. A 501(c)(4) is ostensibly a "social welfare" group and, unlike a 527, is not required to disclose the identity of its donors or to report spending to the FEC.

Lawyers then began suggesting that 501(c)(4) organizations claim a special exemption that would allow the organization to ask people to vote for or against specific candidates as long as a majority of the group's effort was devoted to issues. Only those funds spent directly to support candidates had to be reported to the FEC, and the 501(c)(4) could continue to conceal its donors. One result, beginning with the 2008 elections, was to make it all but impossible to determine exactly how much was spent by independent groups. Critics claimed that 501(c)(4)s were being used illegally. The FEC has never ruled on their validity, however.

Image 8.4 *"Most of all, I want to thank the people of my district for their unflagging support and disturbingly short-term memories."*

Christopher Weyant/The New Yorker Collection/The Cartoon Bank.com

Candidate Committees. Despite the limits on contributions to candidate committees, these organizations continue to collect large sums. In 2016, Hillary Clinton's committee raised about $1.2 billion, though Donald Trump brought in only $650 million. In 2020, Democrat Joe Biden amassed more than $1.0 billion, while Trump pulled in more than $1.5 billion.

Candidate committees at all levels received a boost in April 2014 as a result of the Supreme Court's latest ruling on campaign finance. The Court continued to hold that limits on the amount that any one individual could contribute to any one candidate were permissible. An overall cap on the total amount that an individual could contribute, however, was unconstitutional. In other words, there can be no limit on the number of different candidates a wealthy individual can support. A billionaire could, for example, give the $2,900 maximum contribution to every single candidate of a particular party running for the U.S. Congress. The ruling also freed up the amounts that individuals could give to the political parties.[10] The likely consequence will be to divert some funds away from super PACs and to candidate and party committees.

The Decline and Fall of Public Financing. From 1976 through 2004, most presidential candidates relied on a system of public funding financed by a checkoff on federal income tax forms. This system provided funds to match what a candidate could raise during the primary season. During the general election campaign, the system would pay for a candidate's entire campaign. Publicly funded candidates, however, could not raise funds independently for the general election or exceed the program's overall spending limits.

The system began to break down after 2000, when many candidates rejected public support during the primaries in the belief that they could raise larger sums privately. In 2008, Barack Obama became the first candidate since the program was founded to opt out of federal funding for the general elections as well. By 2012, the public financing system was essentially out of business. None of the major candidates in either party was willing to use it.

---

10. *McCutcheon v. FEC*, 134 S.Ct. 1434 (2014).

2022 Elections:

Financing the Congressional Races

For all the surprises that unfolded over the course of the 2022 midterm elections, the amount spent on congressional races was not one of them. Since the United States Supreme Court's 2010 ruling allowing political committees to raise unlimited funds, such spending has increased each election cycle. For the 2022 elections, federal candidates and political committees were expected to disburse roughly $9 billion, easily beating the previous midterm record of $7.1 billion set in 2018.

Of the ten most expensive congressional races in the 2022 election cycle, five involved contests considered "toss ups" between Republican and Democratic candidates for the U.S. Senate. Two of these races—in Georgia and Pennsylvania—saw spending top $100 million. A good chunk of these funds come from outside sources, particularly super PACs. According to data gathered by the nonpartisan organization OpenSecrets, a super PAC aligned with Senator Mitch McConnell (R-KY) called the Senate Leadership Fund spent about $150 million, more than any other outside group during the 2022 cycle. In a single October day, the Senate Majority PAC—aligned with Senator Chuck Schumer (D-NY)—spent $4.6 million in advertising to discredit Pennsylvania's Republican Senate candidate Mehmet Oz.

Freed from the $2,900 cap limiting the amount one can donate to a candidate in a single election, individuals can contribute large sums to super PACs. They do so not only to impact the course of elections, but also to gain influence with candidates once they take office. Indeed, for all the billions of dollars, including approximately $7.5 billion in political advertising, spent on these elections, such influence may be the best value for large donors. Nobody knows, for sure though, exactly to what extent spending leads to victory in electoral politics.

Running for President: The Longest Campaign

» LO 8-3: Summarize the process of choosing a president of the United States.

The American presidential election is the culmination of two different campaigns: the presidential primary campaign and the general election campaign following the party's national convention. Traditionally, both the primary campaigns and the final campaigns take place during the first ten months of an election year. Increasingly, though, the states are holding their primaries earlier in the year, which has motivated the candidates to begin their campaigns earlier as well. Indeed, candidates in the 2020 presidential races began campaigning in early 2019, thus launching one of the longest presidential campaigns to date. Almost immediately after the 2022 midterm elections, campaigning for the presidential election of 2024 started. This primary campaigning timing has become a pattern.

Primary elections were first organized for choosing state officials in 1904 in Wisconsin. The purpose of the primary was to open the nomination process to ordinary party members and to weaken the influence of party bosses. Until 1968, however, there were fewer than twenty primary elections for the presidency. They were often "beauty contests," in which the candidates competed for popular votes but the results did not control the selection of delegates to the national convention. National conventions were meetings of the party elite—legislators, mayors, county chairpersons, and loyal party workers—who were mostly appointed to their delegations. The leaders of large blocs of delegates could direct their delegates to support a favorite candidate.

Reforming the Presidential Primaries

In recent decades, the character of the presidential primary process and the makeup of the national convention have changed dramatically. The public, rather than party elites, now generally controls the nomination process. After the disruptive riots outside the doors of the 1968 Democratic convention in Chicago, many party leaders pushed for serious reforms of the convention system.

The Power of Elected Delegates. The Democratic National Committee appointed a special commission to study the problems of the presidential primary system. During the next several years, the group—called the McGovern-Fraser Commission—formulated new rules for delegate selection that had to be followed by state Democratic parties beginning in 1972.

The reforms instituted by the Democratic Party, which were mostly imitated by the Republicans, revolutionized the nomination process for the presidency. The most important changes require that a majority of the convention delegates be elected by the voters in primary elections, in caucuses held by local parties, or at state conventions. Delegates are normally pledged to a particular candidate, although the pledge is not always formally binding at the convention. The delegation from each state must also include a proportion of women, younger party members, and representatives of the racial and ethnic minority groups within the party. At first, almost no special privileges were given to party leaders and elected party officials, such as senators and governors. In 1984, however, many of these individuals returned to the Democratic convention as **superdelegates**. Republicans had an equivalent category of delegates, although the Republicans were fewer in number and pledged to support the nominee who carried their state in the primaries.

The Role of the Superdelegates. The Democratic superdelegates became an issue in 2016, when most superdelegates with a preferred candidate lined up behind Hillary Clinton. Bernie Sanders claimed that the convention was therefore rigged against him. Of course, Clinton also outperformed Sanders in electing regular delegates, so Sanders's charge was somewhat beside the point. Still, the rules were altered for the 2020 convention. As with the Republicans, superdelegates were now pledged to support the candidate who carried their state, at least on the first ballot.

The Invisible Primary

Before the primary season even begins, presidential candidates must begin lining up as much support within their party as is possible. This process has been called the **invisible primary** because much of the action occurs behind closed doors. Potential candidates try to win support among elected officials, fundraisers, interest groups, and opinion leaders. If a candidate can "win" the invisible primary, their chances in the actual primaries go way up. Historically, Republicans have been even more ready than Democrats to rally around the presumptive candidate. This process was described in *The Party Decides*, a widely acclaimed work of political science.[11]

As it happens, the 2015–16 election cycle featured the primary election victories of Donald Trump, a candidate with almost no support among the party leaders who typically participate in the invisible primary. The resulting joke: "The party decides—except when it doesn't." Trump was not the first candidate ever to win a party's nomination after decisively losing the invisible primary, though such a result had not been seen in decades. Democratic candidates George McGovern and Jimmy Carter managed that feat in 1972 and 1976, respectively. These were, however, the first two Democratic contests after the party reforms of 1972, and it may have taken that long for Democratic elders to adjust to the new system. Trump, an unconventional candidate, won because the large field of "regular Republican" candidates divided the rest of the vote.

Superdelegates
A party leader or elected official who is given the right to vote at the party's national convention. Superdelegates are not elected at the state level.

Invisible Primary
The preprimary campaign to win supporters among elected officials, fundraisers, interest groups, and opinion leaders.

---

11. Marty Cohen et al., *The Party Decides: Presidential Nominations Before and After Reform* (Chicago: University of Chicago Press, 2008).

The Party Decides

In 2020, it seemed possible that Vermont senator Bernie Sanders, a democratic socialist, might also win because his opponents could not unite. Regular Democrats, who were very conscious of what had happened to the Republicans in 2016, proceeded to organize one of the most astonishing displays of political unity seen in many years. Between the South Carolina primary on February 29 and March 5, two days after Super Tuesday, the Democratic candidates who were in third, fourth, fifth, sixth, and seventh place in the polls all withdrew, with four of the five endorsing Biden.

It seems that Barack Obama had some words with Pete Buttigieg, after which he withdrew and endorsed Biden. Former Senate majority leader Harry Reid talked with Amy Klobuchar, who did the same. A majority of Klobuchar's supporters in Minnesota then turned in formation and voted for Biden. The ultimate result was a two-person race between Biden and Sanders. The Democrats may not have held an effective invisible primary in 2020, but "the party decides" process was definitely back in business.

Primaries and Caucuses

Various types of primaries are used by the states. One notable difference is between proportional and winner-take-all primaries. Another important consideration is whether independent voters can take part in a primary. Some states also use caucuses and conventions to choose candidates for various offices.

Direct and Indirect Primaries. A **direct primary** is one in which voters decide party nominations by voting directly for candidates. In an **indirect primary**, voters instead choose convention delegates, and the delegates determine the party's candidate in the general election. Delegates may be pledged to a particular candidate. Indirect primaries are rare except when choosing a presidential candidate. Most candidates in state and local elections are chosen by direct primaries.

Direct Primary
A primary election in which voters decide party nominations by voting directly for candidates.

Indirect Primary
A primary election in which voters choose convention delegates, and the delegates determine the party's candidate in the general election.

Proportional and Winner-Take-All Primaries. Most primaries are winner-take-all. Proportional primaries are used mostly to elect delegates to the national conventions of the two major parties—delegates who are pledged to one or another candidate for president. Under the proportional system, if one candidate for president wins 40 percent of the vote in a primary, that candidate receives about 40 percent of the pledged delegates.

In recent years, the Democrats have used the proportional system for all of their presidential primaries and caucuses. For the most part, the Republicans have relied on the winner-take-all principle. In 2012, however, the Republican National Committee began requiring that early primaries be proportional. Republicans made even greater use of proportional primaries in 2016 and in 2020.

Closed and Open Primaries. A closed primary is one of several types of primaries distinguished by how independent voters are handled. In a **closed primary**, only declared members of a party can vote in that party's primary. In other words, voters must declare their party affiliation, either when they register to vote or at the primary election. In a closed-primary system, voters cannot cross over into the other party's primary in order to nominate the weakest candidate of the opposing party or to affect the ideological direction of that party.

In an **open primary**, any voter can vote in either party's primary without declaring a party affiliation. Basically, the voter makes the choice in the privacy of the voting booth. The voter must, however, choose one party's list from which to select candidates.

Closed Primary
A type of primary in which the voter is limited to choosing candidates of the party of which they are a member.

Open Primary
A primary in which any voter can vote in either party primary (but must vote for candidates of only one party).

Image 8.5 Vermont senator Bernie Sanders and former vice president Joe Biden were the last remaining Democratic presidential candidates in 2020 after the other major candidates dropped out. All, including Sanders, eventually endorsed Biden. ▶ Was Biden wise when he adopted some of Sanders's policies, in part to unify the party?

UPI/Alamy Stock Photo

Blanket Primary. A blanket primary is one in which the voter can vote for candidates of more than one party. Until 2000, a few states, including Alaska, California, and Washington, had blanket primaries. In 2000, however, the Supreme Court abolished the blanket primary. The Court ruled that the blanket primary violated political parties' First Amendment right of association. Because the nominees represent the party, party members—not the general electorate—should have the right to choose the party's nominee.[12]

Run-Off Primary. Some states have a two-primary system. If no candidate receives a majority of the votes in the first primary, the top two candidates must compete in another primary, called a run-off primary.

The "Top-Two" Primary. Louisiana has long used a special type of primary for filling some offices. Under the system, all candidates appear on a single ballot. A party cannot prevent a candidate from appearing on the primary ballot—an insurgent Republican, for example, could appear on the ballot alongside the party-supported Republican. The two candidates receiving the most votes, regardless of party, then move on to the general election. Following the abolition of the blanket primary, the state of Washington adopted this system. In 2008, the Supreme Court upheld the new plan.[13] In 2010, Californians voted to use this system beginning in 2012.

Caucus System
A meeting of party members to select candidates and propose policies.

Conventions and Caucuses. The number of states using the **caucus system** has declined considerably in recent years. In 2020, only four states picked their delegates to the Democratic national convention in this way. These four, however, included two of the earliest states to vote—Iowa and Nevada.

Strictly speaking, the caucus system is a convention system. In North Dakota, for example, local citizens gather in party meetings, called caucuses, at the precinct level. They choose delegates to district conventions. The district conventions elect delegates to the state convention, and the state convention actually chooses the delegates to the national convention. The national delegates, however, are pledged to reflect the presidential preferences that voters expressed at the caucus level.

In 2020, in a number of states, Republicans used a state convention instead of a presidential primary to pick national convention delegates. The thinking was that because Trump was the inevitable victor, conventions could save expense—and prevent Trump from being embarrassed by a handful of rebellious delegates.

Front-Loading the Primaries

As soon as potential presidential candidates realized that winning as many primary elections as possible guaranteed them the party's nomination for president, their tactics changed dramatically. Candidates concentrated on building organizations in states that

12. *California Democratic Party v. Jones*, 530 U.S. 567 (2000).
13. *Washington State Grange v. Washington State Republican Party*, 552 U.S. 442 (2008).

held early, important primary elections. By the 1970s, candidates recognized that the winner of an early contest, such as the Iowa caucuses or the New Hampshire primary election (both now held in January), would instantly become seen as the **front-runner**, increasing the candidate's media exposure, and escalating the pace of contributions to their campaign.

The Rush to Be First. The state political parties began to see that early primaries had a much greater effect on the outcome of the presidential contest than did later ones. Accordingly, in every successive presidential election, more and more states moved their primaries into the first months of the year, a process known as **front-loading** the primaries. One result was a series of "Super Tuesdays," when multiple states held simultaneous primaries. In 2008, twenty-four states held their primaries or caucuses on February 5, making it the largest Super Tuesday ever. So many states were in play on February 5 that it was impossible for the candidates to campaign strongly in all of them. Rather than winning more attention, many Super Tuesday states found that they were ignored. Because the Democratic race was not decided until the very end of the process in June 2008, the later Democratic primaries, such as those in Indiana, North Carolina, Ohio, Pennsylvania, and Texas, were hotly contested.

Front-loading, in short, had become counterproductive. As a result, in 2012 Super Tuesday was held on March 6, a month later than in 2008. Only ten states participated. In 2016, twelve states participated. Super Tuesday 2020 was held on March 3, with participation back up to fourteen states. These included California and Texas, the two largest states by population. As a result, about one third of all Democratic convention delegates were chosen on that one day.

The National Parties Seek to Regain Control. The process of front-loading the primaries alarmed many observers, who feared that a front-runner might wrap up the nomination before voters were able to make a thorough assessment of the candidates. In response, the national Democratic and Republican parties took steps to regain control of the primary schedule. Such steps included a requirement that states could not hold primaries or caucuses before a specified date. States would need special permission to choose delegates before that date. Traditional lead-off states such as Iowa and New Hampshire were allowed to go first, and a limited number of other states also received such permission. Initially, a few states were unwilling to follow the official schedule, and as a result they were penalized by the national parties. By 2016, however, all states were obeying the rules.

On to the National Convention

Presidential candidates have been nominated by the convention method in every election since 1832. Extra delegates are allowed from states won by the party in the preceding elections. Parties also accept delegates from the District of Columbia, the territories, and U.S. citizens living abroad.

Ron Adar/Shutterstock.com

Image 8.6 President Trump at a campaign rally in Hershey, Pennsylvania, in December 2019. Giant rallies attended by adoring fans were Trump's favorite method of campaigning.
► How likely would it be for you or any of your friends to swing your support to a candidate based on a rally?

Front-runner
The presidential candidate who appears to be ahead at a given time in the primary season.

Front-loading
The practice of moving presidential primary elections to the early part of the campaign to maximize the impact of these primaries on the nomination.

Credentials Committee
A committee used by political parties at their national conventions to determine which delegates may participate.

Seating the Delegates. At the convention, each political party uses a **credentials committee** to determine which delegates may participate. Controversy may arise when rival groups claim to be the official party organization. The Mississippi Democratic Party split along racial lines in 1964 at the height of the civil rights movement. Two sets of delegates were selected at the state level—one made up of white delegates and the other including both white and African American delegates—and both factions showed up at the national convention. The committee decided to seat the pro–civil rights delegates and exclude those who represented the traditional "white" party.

Convention Activities. Most delegates arrive at the convention committed to a presidential candidate. No convention since 1952 has required more than one ballot to choose a nominee. Conventions normally last four days, but in both 2008 and 2012 the Republican convention was shortened to three days due to hurricanes. On each night, featured speakers seek to rally the party faithful and draw in uncommitted voters who are watching on television.

A major goal of the conventions is to unite each party around the winning candidate. Party members who supported losing candidates must be encouraged to switch their support to the winner.

What occurred in 2020 was quite different from any other conventions in U.S. history. The COVID-19 pandemic forced both parties to completely alter their convention plans. The Democrats chose to have only a "virtual" set of speeches while they nominated Joe Biden for president and Kamala Harris for vice president. The Republicans chose to have a mixed convention during which the final day included President Trump's appearance outside the White House in front of over a thousand supporters. All other speeches were virtual.

The Electoral College

Some people who vote for the president and vice president think that they are voting directly for a candidate. In actuality, they are voting for **electors** who will cast their ballots in the Electoral College. Article II, Section 1, of the Constitution outlines in detail the method of choosing electors for president and vice president.

Electors
Members of the Electoral College, which selects the president and vice president. Each state's electors are chosen in each presidential election year according to state laws.

The Choice of Electors. Electors are selected during each presidential election year. The selection is governed by state laws. After the national party convention, the electors are pledged to the candidates chosen. Each state's number of electors equals that state's number of senators (two) plus its number of representatives. The total number of electors today is 538, equal to 100 senators, 435 members of the House, and 3 electors for the District of Columbia. (The Twenty-third Amendment, ratified in 1961, added electors for the District of Columbia.)

The Electors' Commitment. In all but two states, a plurality of voters in the state chooses a slate of electors. (A plurality is the largest number, but not necessarily a majority.) Those electors are pledged to cast their ballots on the first Monday after the second Wednesday in December in the state capital for the presidential and vice-presidential candidates of their party.[14] The Constitution does not, however, require the electors to cast their ballots for the candidates of their party, and on rare occasions so-called faithless electors have voted for a candidate to whom they were not pledged. The 2016 presidential elections were marked by

---

14. In Maine and Nebraska, electoral votes are based in part on congressional districts. Each district chooses one elector. The remaining two electors are chosen by a plurality of all votes cast statewide.

an unusual number of faithless electors. Five Clinton electors refused to vote for her, and two Trump electors jumped ship as well. Apparently, most of the faithless Clinton electors were promoting a scheme under which electors from both parties would vote for a moderate Republican such as Ohio governor John Kasich. Such votes are illegal in twenty-nine states, but no faithless elector has ever been prosecuted.

The ballots are counted and certified before a joint session of Congress early in January. The candidates who receive a majority (270) of the electoral votes are certified as president-elect and vice president–elect. According to the Constitution, if no candidate receives a majority of the electoral votes, the election of the president is decided in the House of Representatives from among the candidates with the three highest numbers of votes, with each state having one vote (decided by a plurality of each state delegation). The selection of the vice president is determined by the Senate in a choice between the two candidates with the most votes, each senator having one vote. The House was required to choose the president in 1801 (Thomas Jefferson), and again in 1825 (John Quincy Adams).

Problems With the Electoral College System. It is possible for a candidate to become president without obtaining a majority of the popular vote. There have been many presidents in our history who did not win such a majority. Such an event becomes more likely when there are important third-party candidates. Perhaps more distressing is the possibility of a candidate's being elected when an opposing candidate receives a plurality of the popular vote. Through 2019, this had occurred on five occasions—in the elections of John Quincy Adams in 1824, Rutherford B. Hayes in 1876, Benjamin Harrison in 1888, George W. Bush in 2000, and Donald Trump in 2016. All of these candidates won elections in which an opponent received more popular votes than they did.

The 2016 elections were particularly troublesome because the gap between the popular vote and the electoral vote was so large. Hillary Clinton's popular vote margin over Donald Trump exceeded 2.8 million votes, or about 2.1 percent. In previous cases when the winner lost the popular vote, the margin was very close. This was not so in 2016.

Clinton's loss was the second time in sixteen years that the Democratic presidential candidate won the popular vote but lost in the Electoral College. Inevitably, many Democrats have become hostile to this system. Replacing it through a constitutional amendment seems almost impossible, however.

The 2020 Election and the January 6, 2021 Demonstrations at the Capitol

There is no question about who won the popular vote in 2020—Joe Biden received over 81 million votes versus Trump's 74 million votes. There was no question who won in the Electoral College either—306 for Biden versus 232 for Trump. When the Joint Session of Congress convened on January 6, 2021 to formally count the electoral votes, about 30,000 of those who did not think that the election had been fairly run showed up for a speech by President Trump. What ensued after he gave his speech is now referred to as the January 6th attack on the Capitol. Note, though, that there was no way that the rioters who entered the building could have changed the election outcome. That is because at that moment in time, the actions by Congress within the Capitol were just a formality. Nonetheless, many continue to refer to that demonstration as an insurrection, which is a violent uprising against an authority or government. To this date, none of those arrested (or tried) have been charged for an act of insurrection. (Some individuals have, however, been charged with sedition, which is defined as overt conduct that tends toward rebellion against the established order.)

How Are Elections Conducted?

>> **LO 8-4:** Discuss why it matters (or does not matter) whether Americans vote on election day.

Australian Ballot
A secret ballot prepared, distributed, and tabulated by government officials at public expense. Since 1888, all states have used the Australian ballot rather than an open, public ballot.

The United States uses the **Australian ballot**—a secret ballot that is prepared, distributed, and counted by government officials at public expense. Since 1888, all states have used the Australian ballot. Before that, many states used oral voting or differently colored ballots prepared by the parties. Obviously, knowing which way a person was voting made it easy to apply pressure on the person to change their vote, and vote buying was common.

Voting by Mail

Voting by mail has been accepted for absentee ballots for many decades (for example, for individuals who are doing business away from home or for members of the armed forces). Recently, several states have offered mail ballots to all of their voters. The rationale for using the mail-in ballot is to make voting easier and increase turnout.

Oregon has gone one step further: Since 1998, that state has employed postal ballots exclusively, and there are no polling places. (Voters who do not prepare their ballots in time for the U.S. Postal Service to deliver them can drop off their ballots at drop boxes on Election Day.) In addition, Colorado, Hawaii, Utah, and Washington now use mail-in ballots exclusively. By national standards, voter turnout in those three states has been high, especially in midterm elections when turnout in most states is substantially reduced.

Voting by mail became much more widespread in 2020, in part because of the COVID-19 pandemic. In some states, ballots were mailed to everyone, whether requested or not. In other states, mail-in ballots were accepted without signature verification or address verification. Indeed, many of the complaints about the 2020 election process concerned the inability of state and local officials to make sure that only eligible voters could vote.

Voting Fraud and Voter ID Laws

Voting fraud is something regularly suspected and increasingly proved. Voting in the 1800s, when secret ballots were rare and people had a cavalier attitude toward the open buying of votes, was probably much more conducive to fraud than modern elections are. Still, some observers claim that the potential for voting fraud is high in many states, particularly through the use of phony voter registration, absentee ballots, and mail-in ballots. Other observers claim, however, that errors due to fraud are small in number and that a few mistakes are inevitable in a system involving millions of voters. These people argue that an excessive concern with voting fraud makes it harder for underrepresented groups and people with low incomes to vote.

Voter ID Requirements. In recent years, many states have adopted laws requiring enhanced proof of identity before voters can cast their ballots. Indiana imposed what was then the nation's toughest voter identification (ID) law in 2005. Indiana legislators claimed that they were motivated by a desire to prevent voting fraud, but critics argued that they were really trying to suppress voter turnout among racial and ethnic minority group members and people with low incomes—the individuals least likely to possess adequate identification. In 2008, the Supreme Court upheld the Indiana voter ID law.[15]

Voting Restrictions. Since 2008, dozens of states have moved to tighten voter ID requirements. Republicans provided almost all of the support for the new ID laws. By 2020,

---

15. *Crawford v. Marion County Election Board*, 553 U.S. 181 (2008).

Image 8.7 Senator Charles Schumer (D-NY) points to a blowup of a flyer with misleading voting information. Schumer cosponsored a bill to make the distribution of fraudulent election material a federal offense. ▶ How likely is it that a voter would be misled by such a flyer?

twenty-five states had enacted new laws that made it harder to vote. Cumbersome voter ID rules were the most common, but other laws limited early voting or absentee ballots. In some states, however, state or federal courts overturned the new laws. In a few states, they were repealed by the voters. Also, twenty states passed laws making it easier to vote.

Until 2013, most southern states with a history of racial discrimination had to obtain preclearance from the federal government for any significant change to their voting laws and procedures under the 1965 Voting Rights Act. The Department of Justice refused to preclear voter ID laws in South Carolina and Texas on the ground that the laws impose a greater burden on racial and ethnic minority voters than on white voters. In 2013, however, the Supreme Court effectively suspended the preclearance procedure. As a result, many southern states were able to implement strict voter ID laws in time for the 2014 elections.

The Impact of Restrictive Voting Laws on Voter Turnout. In any election, the number of Americans who fail to vote is very large. Any factor that affects voter turnout, therefore, can have a major impact on election results. In 2012, a belief by racial and ethnic minority group members that their voting rights were at risk seems to have increased voter turnout measurably. If the new voting laws really were meant to reduce the Democratic vote in 2012, those new laws apparently backfired. In the 2020 elections, voter turnout was perhaps the highest in modern history. Moreover, racial and ethnic minority voter participation was almost as high as white voter participation.

In 2021, the Biden Administration supported two sweeping voter rights bills. One argument in favor of those bills was to ensure that no underrepresented individuals were discriminated against in our elections. The proposed federal legislation received much criticism from Republican lawmakers. Among other things, Republicans argued that the Constitution in Article I, Section 4, gives almost all the power to run elections to the state legislatures. Ultimately, no voting rights legislation passed in the Senate.

Turning Out to Vote

In 2018, the number of Americans eligible to vote was about 237.1 million people. Of that number, about 118.6 million, or 50.0 percent of the eligible population, actually cast a ballot. This was the best turnout in the midterm elections since 1966, far exceeding the 36.7 percent who voted in 2014. Still, when voter turnout is this low, it means, among other things, that the winner of a close election may be voted in by a very small share of those eligible to vote.

Figure 8.1 shows **voter turnout** for presidential and **midterm elections** from 1920 to 2022. Each of the peaks in the figure represents voter turnout in a presidential election. Thus, we can also see that turnout for congressional elections is influenced greatly by whether there is a presidential election in the same year. Whereas voter turnout during the presidential elections of 2016 was 60.0 percent, it was 50.0 percent in the midterm elections of 2018. Voter turnout in the 2020 election was 66.2 percent. In the 2022 midterm elections it was about 46 percent. In the 2020 elections, nearly 158.4 million ballots were counted. If one looks only at the voting-age population, then voter turnout was 61.7 percent. But looking at only estimated eligible voters, voter turnout, as just mentioned, was 66.2 percent.

The same is true at the state level. When there is a race for governor, more voters participate in the elections than when only state legislators are on the ballot. Voter participation rates in gubernatorial elections are also greater in presidential election years. The average turnout in state elections is about 14 percentage points higher when a presidential election is held.

Now consider local elections. In races for mayor, city council, county auditor, and the like, it is fairly common for only 25 percent or less of the electorate to vote. Is something amiss here? It would seem that people should be more likely to vote in elections that directly

Voter Turnout
The percentage of citizens taking part in the election process. Also, the number of eligible voters who actually "turn out" to cast their ballots.

Midterm Elections
National elections in which candidates for president are not on the ballot. In midterm elections, voters choose all members of the U.S. House of Representatives and one-third of the members of the U.S. Senate.

Figure 8.1 **Voter Turnout for Presidential and Midterm Elections, 1920–2022**

The peaks represent voter turnout in presidential election years. The troughs represent voter turnout in midterm years with no presidential elections. ▶ **Why might turnout have been higher in 2016 than in 2012?**

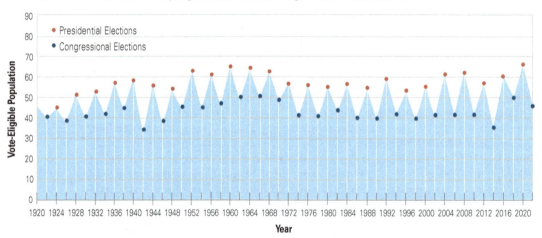

Sources: Historical Data Archive, Inter-university Consortium for Political and Social Research; Michael P. McDonald and Samuel L. Popkin, "The Myth of the Vanishing Voter," *American Political Science Review*, Vol. 95, No. 4 (December 2001), p. 966; and the United States Elections Project.

Note: Prior to 1948, the voting-age population is used as a proxy for the population eligible to vote.

affect them. At the local level, each person's vote counts more because there are fewer voters. Furthermore, the issues—crime control, school bonds, sewer bonds, and the like—touch the immediate interests of the voters. In reality, however, potential voters are most interested in national elections, when a presidential choice is involved. Otherwise, voter participation in our representative government is low and, as we have seen, it is not overwhelmingly high even in presidential elections.

The Voting-Age Population and the Vote-Eligible Population. In the past, the press and even many political scientists calculated voter turnout by taking the number of people who vote as a percentage of the nation's **voting-age population**. Until about 1972, this was a reasonable way to obtain an approximate figure for turnout. In recent decades, however, turnout figures based on the voting-age population have become less and less reliable. The problem is that the voting-age population is not the same as the population of eligible voters, the **vote-eligible population**. The figure for the voting-age population includes felons and ex-felons who have lost the right to vote. Above all, it includes a large number of new immigrants who are not yet citizens. Finally, it does not include Americans living abroad, who can cast absentee ballots.

Voting-age Population
The number of people of voting age living in the country at a given time, regardless of whether they have the right to vote.

Vote-eligible Population
The number of people who, at a given time, enjoy the right to vote in national elections.

Legal Restrictions on Voting

Legal restrictions on voter registration have existed since the founding of our nation. Most groups in the United States have been concerned with the suffrage (voting) issue at one time or another. The writers of the Constitution allowed the states to decide who could vote. Thus, women were allowed to vote in Wyoming in 1870 but not in the entire nation until the Nineteenth Amendment was ratified in 1920.

Property Requirements. Many government functions concern property rights and the distribution of income and wealth, and some of the founders believed it was appropriate that only people who had an interest in property should vote. In colonial times, therefore, only white males who owned property with a certain minimum value were eligible to vote, leaving more Americans ineligible to take part in elections than were eligible. By about 1850, however, most white adult males in almost all the states could vote without any property qualification.

Further Extensions of the Franchise. Extension of the franchise (the right to vote) to Black males occurred with the passage of the Fifteenth Amendment in 1870. This enfranchisement was short lived, however, as the "redemption" of the South by white supremacists had rolled back those gains by the end of the century. It was not until the 1960s that African Americans, both male and female, were able to participate in the electoral process in all states. The most recent extension of the franchise occurred when the voting age was reduced from 21 to 18 by the Twenty-Sixth Amendment in 1971. One result of lowering the voting age was to depress voter turnout for several decades beginning in 1972, as you can see in Figure 8.1. Young people are less likely to vote than older citizens.

Is the Franchise Still Too Restrictive?

There continue to be certain classes of people who do not have the right to vote. These include noncitizens and, in many states, convicted felons who have been released from prison. Also, no one under the age of 18 can vote. A number of political activists have argued that some of these groups should be allowed to vote. Should noncitizens be allowed to vote? We examine this issue in this chapter's *Which Side Are You On?* feature.

Most other democracies do not prevent convicts from voting after they have completed their sentences. According to the American Civil Liberties Union, eleven states currently

Which Side Are You On?

Should Noncitizens Be Able to Vote in the United States?

As of 2022, fourteen local jurisdictions allow noncitizen voting. Of course, if this were to occur during federal elections, it would be illegal since the enactment of the Illegal Immigration Reform and Immigrant Responsibility Act of 1996. This act prohibits noncitizens from voting in federal elections. If caught, noncitizens can be fined, imprisoned, and even deported. No federal law, in contrast, prohibits noncitizens from voting in state and municipal elections.

Different municipalities have different rules when it comes to noncitizen voting. For example, in November 2016 voters in San Francisco approved a proposal that allows all parents of children in the San Francisco school district to vote in school board elections regardless of their immigration or citizenship status. In 2021, New York City gave legal immigrants the right to vote in city and borough elections (struck down in 2022). Montpelier, Vermont, passed a city charter change that affords full voting rights in municipal elections to any legal noncitizens who reside in the city.

Does all of this make sense?

This Is Crazy—Citizenship Has to Mean Something

Those opposed to noncitizen voting argue that only citizens should vote in any elections throughout the United States. After all, isn't that one of the privileges of citizenship? It is against the law for any noncitizen to vote in federal elections, so why would it not

follow that noncitizens are also ineligible to vote in any elections? People who come from other countries to live legally in the United States must spend years to obtain citizenship. Why should other immigrants—legal or unauthorized—be able immediately to have the same rights as foreign-born citizens? Allowing noncitizens to vote makes a mockery of our Constitution.

If You Are a Resident Somewhere, You Should Have the Right to Vote

According to former law professor and politician, Jamie Raskin, the blanket exclusion of noncitizens from the ballot is neither constitutionally required nor historically normal.[16] Consider the fact that 12 to 20 million unauthorized immigrants live in the United States. They contribute as much as any natural-born American to this country's cultural and economic life. But they do not have a say in matters of politics or policy. That is just not right. Noncitizens who vote strengthen communities and give more residents an investment in politics that affect their daily lives. If we want true representation, we should encourage noncitizen voting. The more voters show up, the more accurately elections reflect residents' desires.

For Critical Analysis
Which groups are most in favor of noncitizen voting? Why?

prevent at least some felons from voting after they have completed their sentences. Those disenfranchised in most of these states are typically guilty of violent crimes such as murder. In Iowa, Kentucky, and Virginia, reenfranchisement requires a petition to the governor or a state court. In all three of these states, however, governors have restored the voting rights of a substantial number of felons. Barring felons from the polls injures racial and ethnic minority groups because they make up a disproportionate share of former prison inmates.

Maine and Vermont allow those currently imprisoned to vote. In contrast, Florida has disenfranchised more felons than any other state—more than 10 percent of those who would otherwise be eligible to vote. In 2018, Florida voters approved an amendment to the state constitution that automatically restored voting rights to most felons who had served their sentences. The Republican-controlled state legislature then restricted reenfranchisement to those without financial obligations to the state. Because Florida imposes many fines and restitution requirements on convicts, a majority of those who had been reenfranchised by the voters once again lost their voting rights. In May 2020, a Federal district court overturned the new restrictive law, but in September a Federal appeals court reinstated it.[17] In Iowa, a 2005 executive order by a Democratic governor restored voting rights to all felons. In 2011, however, a new Republican governor revoked the order, disenfranchising thousands.

16. Raskin, Jamie B., "Legal Aliens, Local Citizens: The Historical, Constitutional and Theoretical Meanings of Alien Suffrage," *University of Pennsylvania Law Review*, Volume 141, pp. 391–470, April 1993.
17. *Jones v. Governor of Florida*, 950 F.3d 795 (11th Cir. 2020).

Current Eligibility and Registration Requirements. Voting generally requires **registration**, and to register, a person must meet the following legal requirements: (1) citizenship, (2) age (18 or older), and (3) residency. Since 1972, states cannot impose residency requirements of more than thirty days.

Each state has different laws for voting and registration. In 1993, Congress passed the "motor voter" bill, which requires that states provide voter-registration materials when people receive or renew driver's licenses, that all states allow voters to register by mail, and that voter-registration forms be made available at a wider variety of public places and agencies.

In 2015, Oregon passed a law under which any citizen who obtains an Oregon driver's license is automatically registered to vote. Anyone who does not want to be registered can opt out, but doing so requires an explicit act by the nonvoter. Automatic voter registration quickly took off around the country. By 2022, eighteen states and the District of Columbia had adopted similar legislation.

In general, a person must register well in advance of an election, although voters in twenty states are allowed to register up to, or even on, Election Day. North Dakota has no voter registration at all. Some argue that registration requirements are responsible for much of the nonparticipation in our political process. There also is a partisan dimension to the debate over registration and nonvoting. Republicans generally fear that an expanded electorate would help to elect more Democrats—because more Democrats than Republicans are the kinds of persons who have trouble registering.

The Voting Rights Act. The Voting Rights Act was enacted in 1965 to ensure that African Americans had equal access to the polls. Section 5 of the act requires that new voting practices or procedures in jurisdictions with a history of discrimination in voting be approved by the national government before being implemented.

In June 2013, in *Shelby County v. Holder*, the Supreme Court effectively invalidated the requirement that changes to voting procedures in covered states and districts receive preclearance.[18] The Court did not throw out Section 5. Rather, it overturned Section 4, which determined those states and localities that should be covered by Section 5. The Court contended that Section 4, which dated back to the 1960s, was obsolete. In principle, Congress could adopt a new set of Section 4 formulas based on more current conditions. The chances of such legislation making its way through recent sessions of Congress, however, have been zero.

How Do Voters Decide?

>> **LO 8-5:** Provide some of the reasons why people vote in particular ways.

A variety of factors appear to influence political preferences. Party identification is among the most important. Other factors include the perception of the candidates and issue preferences. Various demographic factors influence political preferences as well.

Party Identification

With the possible exception of race, party identification is the most important determinant of voting behavior in national elections. Party affiliation is influenced by family and peer groups, by generational effects, by the media, and by the voter's assessment of candidates and issues.

Registration
The entry of a person's name onto the list of registered voters for elections. To register, a person must meet certain legal requirements of age, citizenship, and residency.

---

18. 133 S.Ct. 2612 (2013).

As we have observed on more than one occasion, the number of independent voters has grown over the years. While party identification may have little effect on the voting behavior of true independents, it remains a crucial determinant for the majority of the voters, who have established party preferences.

Other Political Factors

Factors such as perception of the candidates and issue preferences also affect how people vote. While most people do not change their party identification from year to year, candidates and issues can change greatly, and voting behavior can therefore change as well.

Perception of the Candidates. The image of the candidate seems to be important in a voter's choice, especially of a president. To some extent, voter attitudes toward candidates are based on emotions (such as trust) rather than on any judgment about experience or policy. In some years, voters have been attracted to a candidate who appeared to share their concerns and worries. In other years, voters have sought a candidate who appeared to have high integrity and honesty.

Perceptions of candidates were especially important in 2016. In that year, Hillary Clinton suffered from a strong perception that she was untrustworthy. For his part, Donald Trump's negative ratings in polls set new records. It appeared that many voters would have to decide which candidate they disliked the least.

In the 2020 election, there was a strong dichotomy in voters' minds. There were ardent supporters of Trump despite what many considered his non-presidential persona. Indeed, some political scientists argued that many of those who voted for Joe Biden did so simply as a vote against Donald Trump.

Issue Preferences. Issues can make a difference in presidential and congressional elections. Although personality or image factors may be very persuasive, most voters have some notion of how the candidates differ on basic issues or at least know which candidates want a change in the direction of government policy.

Historically, economic concerns have been among the most powerful influences on public opinion. When the economy is doing well, it is very difficult for a challenger, especially at the presidential level, to defeat the incumbent. In contrast, inflation, unemployment, or high interest rates are likely to work to the disadvantage of the incumbent.

While true swing voters may be influenced by the issues when picking a candidate, issue preferences may have little influence on strong party loyalists. In fact, much evidence suggests that such persons often change their issue preferences to match those of their party. One example occurred when President Obama, after a long delay, finally endorsed same-sex marriage. Some conservatives hoped that this stand would alienate conservative African Americans who opposed such unions. Nothing of the sort happened. Instead, opinion polls reported a marked increase in Black people's support for same-sex marriage.

Demographic Characteristics

Demographic characteristics that influence political preferences include race, religion, education, income and **socioeconomic status**, and similar traits. People who share the same religion or any other demographic trait are likely to influence one another and may also have common political concerns that follow from the common characteristic. We examined these

Image 8.8 These young voters—all Haitian immigrants—sport t-shirts from Citizen Change, a get-out-the-vote group backed by musician P. Diddy along with Mary J. Blige, Mariah Carey, and 50 Cent. ▶ Why are young people often less likely to vote?

RosalreneBetancourt 11/Alamy Stock Photo

factors, such as race and religion, earlier in this book as part of the discussion of political socialization.

Demographic influences reflect an individual's personal background and place in society. Some factors have to do with the family into which a person was born: race and (for most people) religion. Others may be the result in large part of choices made throughout an individual's life. They include place of residence, educational achievement, and profession.

Most of these factors are interrelated. People who have more education are likely to have higher incomes and to hold professional jobs. Similarly, children born into wealthier families are far more likely to complete college than children from families with low incomes. A number of other interrelationships are not so immediately obvious. For example, many people might not realize that 75 percent of African Americans report that religion is very important in their lives, compared with only 49 percent of white people.[19]

Making A Difference

Registering and Voting

Very close elections demonstrate that your vote can make a difference. In local races, elections have sometimes been decided by one or two votes. In nearly every state, before you are allowed to cast a vote in an election, you must first register. Registration laws vary considerably from state to state.

Residency and Age Requirements What do you have to do to register and cast a vote? In general, you must be a citizen of the United States, at least 18 years old on or before Election Day, and a resident of the state in which you intend to register. A number of states require that you meet a minimum-residency requirement. The minimum-residency requirement is very short in some states—for example, ten days in Wisconsin. No state requires more than thirty days. Thirty states do not have any minimum-residency requirement.

Time Limits Nearly every state also specifies a closing date by which you must be registered before an election. You may not be able to vote if you register too close to the day of the election. The closing date for registration varies from Election Day itself to thirty days before the election. In North Dakota, no registration is necessary.

In most states, your registration can be revoked if you do not vote within a certain number of years or do not report a change of address. Federal regulations place limits on how purges are conducted, but Democrats have frequently accused Republican state officials of violating the rules. The belief is that those who move frequently or who often fail to vote—and who are therefore purged—tend to be Democrats. For their part, Republicans contend that aggressive purges limit voter fraud.

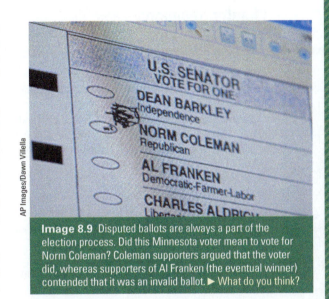

AP Images/Dawn Villella

Image 8.9 Disputed ballots are always a part of the election process. Did this Minnesota voter mean to vote for Norm Coleman? Coleman supporters argued that the voter did, whereas supporters of Al Franken (the eventual winner) contended that it was an invalid ballot. ▶ What do you think?

An Example Let us look at voter registration in Texas as an example. If you live in Texas, you may have registered to vote when you obtained your Texas driver's license. If not, you can find a voter registration form online by searching on "texas vrapp." You must mail the application to the voter registrar in your county. (The registrar's address appears on the form after you finish filling it out.) Applications are also available at post offices, libraries, Texas Department of Public Safety offices, and Texas Department of Human Services offices. Your application must be postmarked thirty days before Election Day.

---

19. The Pew Forum on Religion and Public Life, "U.S. Public Becoming Less Religious," November 3, 2015, p. 46.

Key Terms

Australian ballot 196

caucus system 192

closed primary 191

credentials
 committee 194

direct primary 191

electors 194

Federal Election
 Commission
 (FEC) 185

focus group 184

front-loading 193

front-runner 193

general election 182

Hatch Act 185

independent
 expenditures 186

indirect primary 191

invisible primary 190

issue advocacy
 advertising 186

midterm elections 198

open primary 191

political action
 committees
 (PACs) 185

political consultant 184

presidential
 primary 181

primary election 182

registration 201

socioeconomic
 status 202

soft money 186

superdelegates 190

super PAC 187

vote-eligible
 population 199

voter turnout 198

voting-age
 population 199

Chapter Summary

» LO 8-1 The legal qualifications for holding political office are minimal at the national, state, and local levels, but holders of political office still are predominantly white and male and are likely to have professional status.

American political campaigns are lengthy and extremely expensive. In recent decades, they have become more candidate centered rather than party centered in response to a relative decline in party resources.

» LO 8-2 Interest groups are major sources of campaign funds. The contributions are often made through political action committees, or PACs. Other methods of contributing include issue advocacy advertising. The McCain-Feingold Act of 2002 imposed significant restrictions on campaign finance, but in 2010 these restrictions were largely swept away by the Supreme Court in its ruling *Citizens United v. FEC.*

Campaign finance today is largely based on two types of committees. Super PACs can raise unlimited funds from any source, but supposedly are not allowed to coordinate with candidate campaigns. Candidate committees face restrictions on contributions but are not limited in how they may spend their funds to support a campaign.

» LO 8-3 After the Democratic convention of 1968, the McGovern-Fraser Commission formulated new rules for primaries, most of which were also adopted by Republicans. These reforms opened up the nomination process for the presidency to all voters. A presidential primary is a statewide election to help a political party determine its presidential nominee at the national convention. Some states use the caucus system of choosing convention delegates.

In the general elections, a voter technically does not vote directly for president but chooses between slates of presidential electors. In most states, the slate that wins the most popular votes throughout the state gets to cast all the electoral votes for the state. The candidate receiving a majority (270) of the electoral votes wins the election.

» LO 8-4 The United States uses the Australian ballot, a secret ballot that is prepared, distributed, and counted by government officials. Voter participation in the United States is often considered to be low, especially in elections that do not feature a presidential contest. Turnout is lower when measured as a percentage of the voting-age population than it is when measured as a percentage of the population actually eligible to vote.

In colonial times, only white males who owned property were eligible to vote. The suffrage issue has concerned, at one time or another, most groups in the United States. Today, to be eligible to vote, a person must satisfy registration, citizenship, age, and residency requirements. Each state has different qualifications.

» **LO 8-5** The two most important determinants of voting behavior are party identification and race. Perceptions of candidates' characters and their stand on the issues are also important, as are the demographic characteristics described earlier in this book.

Test Yourself

1. **The most sought-after (and most criticized) campaign expert, who for a large fee takes over the candidate's campaign, is the:**
   a. spin doctor.
   b. political consultant.
   c. campaign organizer.

2. **The Supreme Court ruling that was most important in creating our current campaign finance system was:**
   a. *McConnell v. FEC.*
   b. *Citizens United v. FEC.*
   c. *California Democratic Party v. Jones.*

3. **Today, presidential candidates do not accept matching public funds because:**
   a. candidates can raise far more outside of the public system than they would receive if they participated in it.
   b. once candidates accept public funds for the primaries, they must match public funds in a ratio of two to one for the general elections.
   c. public funds are no longer available.

4. **In an indirect primary:**
   a. voters decide party nominations by voting directly for candidates.
   b. voters make no decisions directly about convention delegates.
   c. voters choose convention delegates, and those delegates determine the party's candidate in the general elections.

5. **Any voter can vote in either party primary without declaring a party affiliation in:**
   a. an open primary.
   b. a closed primary.
   c. a "top-two" primary.

6. **The practice of moving presidential primary elections to the early part of the campaign is called:**
   a. the strategy of winning.
   b. front-running.
   c. front-loading.

7. **The Electoral College has become controversial because:**
   a. it can award the presidency to a candidate who did not receive a plurality of the popular vote.
   b. "faithless electors" have changed the outcome of presidential elections.
   c. it discriminates against residents of small states.

8. **In the United States today, all states use secret ballots that are prepared, distributed, and counted by government officials at public expense. This system is called:**
   a. the Australian ballot.
   b. the Massachusetts ballot.
   c. the open ballot.

9. **In statistics on voter participation, the voting-age population is typically larger than the:**
   a. total population.
   b. vote-eligible population.
   c. adult population.

10. **In colonial times, the right to vote was typically limited to persons who were:**
    a. of English ancestry.
    b. adult white males.
    c. adult white males who owned some property.

11. Perhaps the two most important factors in determining how voters cast their ballots are:
   a. perception of the candidates and issue preferences.
   b. party identification and race.
   c. level of education and gender.

Essay Questions

1. Some have argued that limits on campaign spending violate First Amendment guarantees of freedom of speech. How strong is this argument? Can such spending be seen as a form of protected expression? Under what circumstances can contributions be seen instead as a method of bribing elected officials?

2. Some people are more likely to vote than others. Older persons vote more frequently than younger people. Wealthy voters make it to the polls more often than voters with low incomes. What might cause older and wealthier individuals to exhibit greater turnout?

Answers to multiple-choice questions: 1. b, 2. b, 3. a, 4. c, 5. a, 6. c, 7. a, 8. a, 9. b, 10. c, 11. b.

Congress

From left to right, U.S. representatives Liz Cheney (R-WY), Tom Cole (R-OK), Kay Granger (R-TX), and House Republican leader Kevin McCarthy (CA). Granger helped work out a compromise with Democrats on border security to avert a government shutdown. ▶ **Why are bipartisan compromises so hard?**

AP Images/J. Scott Apple white

The five **Learning Outcomes (LOs)** below are designed to help improve your understanding of this chapter. After reading this chapter, you should be able to:

≫ LO 9-1 Describe the various roles played by Congress and the constitutional basis of its powers.

≫ LO 9-2 Explain some of the differences between the House and the Senate, and some of the privileges enjoyed by members of Congress.

≫ LO 9-3 Examine the implications of apportioning House seats.

≫ LO 9-4 Outline the arguments for and against using seniority to choose leadership positions in the House and the Senate.

≫ LO 9-5 Discuss the process by which a bill becomes law and how the federal government establishes its budget.

Check your understanding of the material with the Test Yourself section at the end of the chapter.

Most Americans view Congress in a less-than-flattering light. In recent years, Congress has appeared to be deeply split, highly partisan in its conduct, and not very responsive to public needs. Polls show that the share of the public with a favorable opinion of Congress as a whole has at times fallen as low as 7 percent. In one poll, respondents rated traffic jams, root canal operations, and cockroaches more favorably than Congress. (Congress did beat North Korea and meth labs.) Yet individual members of Congress often receive much higher approval ratings from the voters in their districts. This is one of the paradoxes of the relationship between the people and Congress. Members of the public hold the institution in relatively low regard compared with the satisfaction they express with their individual representatives.

Part of the explanation for these seemingly contradictory appraisals is that members of Congress spend considerable time and effort serving their **constituents**. If the federal bureaucracy makes a mistake that affects a legislator's constituent, the office of that senator or representative tries to resolve the issue. On a personal level, what most Americans see, therefore, is the work of these local representatives in their home states. Congress, however, was created to work not just for local constituents but also for the nation as a whole. Understanding the nature of the institution and the process of lawmaking is an important part of understanding how the policies that shape our lives are made.

Constituents
Persons represented by a legislator or other elected or appointed official.

The Nature and Functions of Congress

> **LO 9-1:** Describe the various roles played by Congress and the constitutional basis of its powers.

The founders of the American republic believed that the bulk of the power that would be exercised by a national government should be in the hands of the legislature. The leading role envisioned for Congress in the new government is apparent from its primacy in the Constitution. Article I deals with the structure, the powers, and the operation of Congress.

Bicameralism

Bicameralism
The division of a legislature into two separate assemblies.

The **bicameralism** of Congress—its division into two legislative houses—was in part the result of the Connecticut Compromise, which tried to balance the large-state population advantage, reflected in the House, and the small-state demand for equality in policy making, which was satisfied in the Senate. Beyond that, the two chambers of Congress also reflected the social class biases of the founders. They wished to balance the interests and the numerical superiority of the common citizens with the property interests of the less numerous landowners, bankers, and merchants.

They achieved this goal by providing that members of the House of Representatives should be elected directly by "the People," whereas members of the Senate were to be chosen by the elected representatives sitting in state legislatures, who were more likely to be members of the elite. (The latter provision was changed in 1913 by the passage of the Seventeenth Amendment, which provides that senators are also to be elected directly by the people.)

The logic of the bicameral Congress was reinforced by differences in length of tenure. Members of the House are required to face the electorate every two years, whereas senators can serve for a much more secure term of six years—even longer than the four-year term provided for the president. Furthermore, the senators' terms are staggered so that only one-third of the senators face the electorate every two years, along with all of the House members.

The bicameral Congress was designed to perform certain functions for the political system. These functions include lawmaking, representation, service to constituents, oversight (regulatory supervision), public education, and conflict resolution. Of these, the two most important and the ones that most often interfere with each other are lawmaking and representation.

The Lawmaking Function

The principal and most obvious function of any legislature is **lawmaking**. Congress is the highest elected body in the country, charged with making binding rules for all Americans. This does not mean, however, that Congress initiates most of the ideas for legislation that it eventually considers. A majority of the bills that Congress acts on originate in the executive branch. Many other bills are traceable to interest groups and political party organizations. In dealing with legislation, members engage in compromise and logrolling (offering to support a fellow member's bill in exchange for that member's promise to support your bill in the future). Through such tactics, as well as debate and discussion, backers of legislation attempt to fashion a winning majority coalition.

Traditionally, logrolling often involved agreements to support another member's legislative **earmarks**, also known as pork. Earmarks are special provisions in legislation to set aside funds for projects that have not passed an impartial evaluation by agencies of the executive branch. (Normal spending projects pass through such evaluations.) Recent attempts to curtail pork did not eliminate the process altogether but substantially reduced its frequency for a while. Both parties in Congress voted to reinstate earmarks at the beginning of the Biden administration. In the March 2022 $1.5 trillion omnibus spending bill, members of Congress added more than 4,000 earmarks.

The Representation Function

Representation includes both representing the desires and demands of the constituents in the member's home district or state and representing larger national interests, such as the nation's security. Because the interests of constituents in a specific district may be at odds with the demands of national policy, the representation function is often a source of conflict for lawmakers. For example, although it may be in the interest of the nation to reduce defense spending by closing certain military bases, such closures are not in the interest of the states and districts that will lose jobs and local spending. Every legislator faces votes that set local representational issues against lawmaking realities.

How should the legislators fulfill the representation function? There are several views on how this task should be accomplished.

The Trustee View of Representation. One approach to the question of how representation should be achieved is that legislators should act as **trustees** of the broad interests of the entire society. They should vote against the narrow interests of their constituents if their conscience and their perception of national needs so dictate. For example, in 2011 Congress approved trade agreements with Colombia, Panama, and South Korea, despite the widely held belief that such agreements cost specific Americans their jobs.

The Instructed-Delegate View of Representation. Directly opposed to the trustee view of representation is the notion that members of Congress should behave as **instructed delegates**—that is, they should mirror the views of the majority of the constituents who elected them.

Generally, most legislators hold neither a pure trustee view nor a pure instructed-delegate view. Typically, they combine both perspectives in a pragmatic mix.

Interact

We have observed that Congress is not popular. For more background, locate the page "Confidence in Institutions" on the Gallup website. You'll find how the public rates fourteen institutions. The military almost always ranks first and Congress last. As of 2019, only 11 percent of poll respondents had a "great deal" or "quite a lot" of confidence in Congress. Those answering "very little" or "none" made up 52 percent of the total. If you scroll down, you can find how people responded to this poll dating back to 1973. Congress wasn't always so unpopular. As recently as 2001, people who rated Congress favorably outnumbered those who rated it unfavorably. Like most American institutions, Congress enjoyed greater confidence for several years following the 9/11 terrorist attacks. Why might this be so? In general, why might Congress be so unpopular—and the military so well regarded?

Lawmaking
The process of establishing the legal rules that govern society.

Earmarks
Special provisions in legislation to set aside funds for projects that have not passed an impartial evaluation by agencies of the executive branch. Also known as pork.

Representation
The function of members of Congress as elected officials representing the views of their constituents as well as larger national interests.

Trustees
In a legislature, members who act according to their conscience and the broad interests of the entire society.

Instructed Delegates
Legislators or convention delegates who are agents of the voters who elected them and who vote according to the views of constituents, regardless of personal beliefs.

Service to Constituents

Constituents expect individual members of Congress to act as brokers between private citizens and the federal government. This function of providing service to constituents usually takes the form of **casework**. Legislators and their staffs spend a considerable portion of their time in casework activities, such as explaining the meaning of particular bills to people who may be affected by them, promoting a local business interest, or interceding with a regulatory agency on behalf of constituents who disagree with proposed agency regulations.

Casework
In the example of Congress, personal work for constituents.

The Oversight Function

Oversight of the bureaucracy is essential if the decisions made by Congress are to have any force. **Oversight** is the process by which Congress follows up on the laws it has enacted to ensure that they are being enforced and administered in the way Congress intended. This is done by holding committee hearings and investigations, changing the size of an agency's budget, or cross-examining high-level presidential nominees to head major agencies.

Oversight
In a legislature, the process by which it follows up on laws it has enacted to ensure that they are being enforced and administered as Congress intended.

Oversight and Partisan Politics. A problem with oversight is that it has become entangled in partisan politics. Oversight can become intense, and even excessive, when the president faces a chamber of Congress that is controlled by the other party. For example, in 2015 and 2016 the Republicans launched a series of investigations of former secretary of state Hillary Clinton. Some say the reason was that she was expected to be the Democratic candidate for president in 2016. A committee unsuccessfully tried to find improper conduct by Clinton during and after an attack on the U.S. consulate in Benghazi, Libya. In contrast, members of Congress have tended to ease up on oversight whenever the president is of their political party.

Image 9.1 Representative Steve Scalise (R-LA) in December 2019. Scalise, House Republican whip, was shot and seriously injured by a left-wing terrorist while playing baseball in 2017. ▶ Why might Republicans be popular in Louisiana?

ZUMA Press, Inc./Alamy Stock Photo

Oversight of the Trump Administration. The question of whether congressional investigations were excessively partisan was raised after the Democrats took control of the House in January 2019. By the middle of that year, fourteen House committees had launched at least 50 investigations into Trump's businesses, his campaigns, and his presidency. Republicans contended that these investigations amounted to an improper witch hunt. Democrats argued that they were merely responding to a "target-rich environment."

The First Impeachment Investigation. The investigations reached their peak after September 2019, when a complaint about Trump's interaction with the president of Ukraine became public. The accusation was that Trump refused to release military aid to Ukraine that it desperately needed to counteract Russian aggression. Purportedly, the aid would be released if Ukraine announced an investigation of Hunter Biden, son of Joe Biden, Trump's most likely opponent in the 2020 elections. The younger Biden had been appointed to the board of a Ukraine energy company, allegedly because his father was the vice president of the United States.

Given that Trump was presumably soliciting interference in the 2020 elections by a foreign power, House Speaker Nancy Pelosi switched from opposing an impeachment investigation to supporting it. Trump was impeached by the House, but he was acquitted by the Senate in February 2020. The Democratic leadership knew perfectly well that they would not find the twenty Republican votes in the Senate that would be needed to convict. As it turned out, they found exactly one. Still, the Democrats wanted to "go on the record" against Trump.

Trump refused to allow any of his staff to respond to congressional **subpoenas** (orders to appear), both in the impeachment investigation and in most other investigations as well. Some testified anyway. Several House committees sued to enforce the subpoenas, but it soon became clear that the courts were unlikely to decide these issues in time for them to be relevant to the impeachment. Rather than waiting for the courts to act, the House simply added an obstruction of Congress charge to the initial one covering the Ukraine issue.

Subpoenas
An order by a court or legislative committee requiring that an individual appear and testify.

The Second Impeachment Investigation

During the several weeks after the January 6th violence by demonstrators at the Capitol building, the House yet again investigated President Trump. This time he was impeached on a single count—incitement of an insurrection. As with the first impeachment, the House voted in favor of the impeachment, but the Senate did not convict Trump.

Oversight of the Biden Administration

When the Republicans became the House majority party after the 2022 midterm elections, there was certainty that at least some of the actions of Biden during his first two years in office would be investigated. Potential topics of investigation included, but would not be limited to, the way in which the Biden administration handled the withdrawal of American troops from Afghanistan in August and September of 2021 and the relative openness of the southern border and the consequent unauthorized immigration crisis.

The Public-Education Function

Educating the public is a function that Congress performs whenever it holds public hearings, exercises oversight of the bureaucracy, or engages in committee and floor debate on such major issues and topics as immigration, oil pipelines, and the concerns of small businesses. In so doing, Congress presents a range of viewpoints on pressing national questions. Congress also decides what issues will come up for discussion and decision. This **agenda setting** is a major facet of its public-education function.

Agenda Setting
Determining which public-policy questions will be debated or considered.

The Conflict-Resolution Function

Congress is commonly seen as an institution for resolving conflicts within American society. Organized interest groups and spokespersons for different racial, religious, economic, and ideological interests look to Congress as an access point for airing their grievances and seeking help. This view of Congress puts it in the position of trying to resolve the differences among competing points of view by passing laws to accommodate as many interested parties as possible. To the extent that Congress meets pluralist expectations in accommodating competing interests, it tends to build support for the entire political process. Its failure to do so, however, tends to bring the political process into disrepute.

The Powers of Congress

The Constitution is both highly specific and extremely vague about the powers that Congress may exercise. The first seventeen clauses of Article I, Section 8, specify most of the **enumerated powers** of Congress—that is, powers expressly given to that body.

Enumerated Powers
Powers specifically granted to the national government by the Constitution. The first seventeen clauses of Article I, Section 8, specify most of the enumerated powers of Congress.

Enumerated Powers. The enumerated, or expressed, powers of Congress include the right to:

- Impose a variety of taxes, including tariffs on imports
- Borrow funds
- Regulate interstate commerce and international trade
- Establish procedures for naturalizing citizens
- Make laws regulating bankruptcies
- Coin (and print) currency and regulate its value
- Establish standards of weights and measures
- Punish counterfeiters
- Establish post offices and post roads
- Regulate copyrights and patents
- Establish the federal court system
- Punish illegal acts on the high seas
- Declare war
- Raise and regulate an army and a navy
- Call up and regulate the state militias to enforce laws, to suppress insurrections, and to repel invasions
- Govern the District of Columbia

The most important of the domestic powers of Congress, listed in Article I, Section 8, are the rights to impose taxes, to spend, and to regulate commerce. The most important foreign policy power is the power to declare war. Other sections of the Constitution allow Congress to establish rules for its own members, to regulate congressional elections, and to override a presidential veto. Congress may also regulate the extent of the Supreme Court's authority to review cases decided by the lower courts, regulate relations among states, and propose amendments to the Constitution.

Powers of the Senate. Some functions are restricted to one chamber. The Senate must advise on, and consent to, the ratification of treaties and must accept or reject presidential nominations of ambassadors, Supreme Court justices, other federal judges, and "all other Officers of the United States." But the Senate may delegate to the president or lesser officials the power to make lower-level appointments.

Constitutional Amendments. Amendments to the Constitution provide for other congressional powers. Congress must certify the election of a president and a vice president or choose those officers itself if no candidate has a majority of the electoral vote (Twelfth Amendment). It may levy an income tax (Sixteenth Amendment) and determine who will act as president in case of the death or incapacity of the president or vice president (Twentieth Amendment and Twenty-fifth Amendment).

The Necessary and Proper Clause. Beyond these numerous specific powers, Congress enjoys the right under clause 18 of Article I, Section 8 (the elastic, or "necessary and proper," clause),

Image 9.2 Senator Elizabeth Warren (D-MA) campaigns for president in New Hampshire in 2019. Warren was a strong advocate of bank regulation.
▶ Why might a stand against bankers be popular with many voters?

Maverick Pictures/Shutterstock.com

"to make all Laws which shall be necessary and proper for carrying into Execution the foregoing Powers [of Article I], and all other Powers vested by this Constitution in the Government of the United States, or in any Department or Officer thereof." This vague statement of congressional responsibilities has provided, over time, the basis for a greatly expanded national government. It has also constituted, at least in theory, a check on the expansion of presidential powers.

House–Senate Differences and Congressional Perks

>> **LO 9-2:** Explain some of the differences between the House and the Senate, and some of the privileges enjoyed by members of Congress.

Congress is composed of two markedly different—but co-equal—chambers. Although the Senate and the House of Representatives exist within the same legislative institution, each has developed certain distinctive features that distinguish one from the other.

Size and Rules

The central difference between the House and the Senate is simply that the House is much larger than the Senate. The House has 435 voting representatives, plus delegates from the District of Columbia, Puerto Rico, Guam, American Samoa, and the Virgin Islands, compared with just 100 senators. This size difference means that a greater number of formal rules are needed to govern activity in the House, whereas correspondingly looser procedures can be followed in the less-crowded Senate. This difference is most obvious in the rules governing debate on the floors of the two chambers.

The Senate usually permits extended debate on all issues that arise before it. In contrast, the House generally operates with an elaborate system in which its **Rules Committee** proposes time limitations on debate for any bill, and a majority of the entire body accepts or modifies those suggested time limits. As a consequence of its stricter time limits on debate, the House, despite its greater size, often is able to act on legislation more quickly than the Senate.

Debate and Filibustering

The Senate tradition of the **filibuster**, or the use of unlimited debate as a blocking tactic, dates back to 1790.[1] In that year, a proposal to move the U.S. capital from New York to Philadelphia was stalled by such time-wasting maneuvers. This unlimited-debate tradition—which also existed in the House until 1811—is not absolute, however.

Cloture. Under Senate Rule 22, debate may be ended by invoking cloture. Cloture shuts off discussion on a bill. Amended in 1975 and 1979, Rule 22 states that debate may be closed off on a bill if sixteen senators sign a petition requesting it and if, after two days have elapsed,

Rules Committee
A standing committee of the House of Representatives that provides special rules under which specific bills can be debated, amended, and considered by the House.

Filibuster
The use of the Senate's tradition of unlimited debate as a delaying tactic to block bills or nominations.

Image 9.3 Charles "Chuck" Grassley of Iowa is the most senior Republican in the Senate and holds the honorary post of president pro tem.
▶ How can long service make a senator more influential?

Drew Angerer/Getty Images News/Getty Images

---

1. Filibuster comes from a Spanish word for pirate, which in turn came from the Dutch term *vrijbuiter*, or freebooter. The word was first used in 1851 to accuse senators of pirating or hijacking debate.

Which Side Are You On?

Is It Time to Get Rid of the Filibuster?

It is not in the Constitution, but it is an important institution. It is the filibuster, and it follows from Senate Rule 22, which allows for unlimited debate. Throughout American history, senators could tie up the Senate's business by talking indefinitely. In 1975, Rule 22 was revised. Since that year, a vote by sixty senators is required to stop floor debate (instead of the previous sixty-seven). A second significant change in Senate practice developed, however—today, senators don't actually have to talk to hold a filibuster. All they have to do to maintain a filibuster is to announce that a filibuster exists. Some want the filibuster abolished. Others do not agree.

The Filibuster Is Not Even Constitutional

Critics of the filibuster argue that it has no constitutional basis and implicitly violates many actual provisions of the Constitution. After all, the Constitution requires a supermajority—more than a simple majority—only for special situations such as ratifying treaties, proposing constitutional amendments, overriding presidential vetoes, and convicting impeached officials.

Consider this statement by Alexander Hamilton in *Federalist Paper* No. 75: "All provisions which require more than a majority of any [legislative] body to its resolutions have a direct tendency to embarrass the operations of the government and an indirect one to subject the sense of the majority to that of the minority." Hamilton was writing about a proposal to require that more than half of a chamber's members be present to convene a session, but his argument certainly applies to whether a body should need more than a majority of its members to take a vote.

The Filibuster as Damage Control

True, filibusters today are not as colorful as they were before 1975, when senators were forced to read out of a telephone book or even wear diapers to keep a filibuster going. Yet supporters of the current filibuster system argue that it continues to provide an important protection for minority rights. Why shouldn't Congress be forced to obtain broad support for important legislation? It would be dangerous to allow major taxation and spending measures to be decided by a bare majority. Polling has shown that the filibuster is quite popular among the public at large. Clearly, Americans see the importance of slowing down legislation created by only a single party in Congress. The filibuster still serves a useful purpose, so let's keep it.

■ For Critical Analysis

What would be likely to happen if the filibuster were abolished?

---

three-fifths of the entire membership (sixty votes, assuming no vacancies) vote for cloture. After cloture is invoked, each senator may speak on a bill for a maximum of one hour before a vote is taken.

Increased Use of the Filibuster. Traditionally, filibusters were rare, and the tactic was employed only on issues of principle. Filibustering senators spoke for many hours, sometimes reading names from a telephone book. By the twenty-first century, however, filibusters could be invoked without such speeches, and senators were threatening to filibuster almost every significant piece of legislation to come before the body. The threats were sufficient to create a new, ad hoc rule that important legislation needed the support of sixty senators, not fifty. As a result of the increased use of the filibuster, some have called for its abolition. We discuss that topic in this chapter's *Which Side Are You On?* feature.

Reconciliation
In Congress, a special rule that can be applied to budget bills sent from the House to the Senate. Reconciliation measures cannot be filibustered.

Reconciliation. An additional way of bypassing the filibuster is known as **reconciliation**. Budget bills sent from the House of Representatives to the Senate can be handled under special reconciliation rules that do not permit filibusters. Under the rules, reconciliation can be used only to handle budgetary matters. Also, in principle, the procedure is to be invoked only for measures that would have the net effect of reducing the federal deficit. This last restriction, however, has frequently been avoided by the use of misleading bookkeeping.

One of the most striking examples of reconciliation took place in March 2010, when the Democrats used the procedure to make a series of amendments to the just-passed Affordable Care Act, also known as Obamacare. Reconciliation was necessary because at the end of January, the Republicans won a special U.S. Senate election, thus reducing the number of Democratic senators to fifty-nine.

The Nuclear Option. It takes sixty senators to invoke cloture. Senate rules, however, can be changed by a simple majority vote. It is possible, therefore, to limit or abolish the filibuster by a majority vote. Such an act has been dubbed the nuclear option, in comparison to the most extreme option in warfare. In the past, such a procedure would have been considered an unthinkable violation of Senate tradition. In the polarized Congress of the twenty-first century, however, very few tricks are still unthinkable.

In 2005, after Democratic senators blocked a vote on a series of Republican judicial candidates, the Republican leadership threatened to employ the nuclear option. A bipartisan group arranged a compromise. Filibusters of nominees were to be reserved for "extraordinary circumstances." In 2013, Democrats contended that Republicans had violated this understanding. No compromise was reached, and so Democrats voted to abolish filibusters against all executive branch nominees and judicial nominees other than to the Supreme Court. (Court nominations were added in 2017.) The rules change did not affect use of the filibuster against proposed legislation. It is quite possible, however, that future changes to the rules may put additional limits on the filibuster—or even abolish it altogether.

The so-called nuclear option resurfaced during the end of Biden's first year in office. The Democrats wanted to pass a multi-trillion-dollar spending bill, plus bills related to the federal takeover of voting procedures. The only way these bills would pass appeared to be by eliminating the filibuster rule for important legislation in the Senate. The attempt to eliminate the filibuster failed and so too did the proposed legislation.

The Hastert Rule. Speakers of the House from the Republican Party have used another procedure that can prevent action on a bill. Under the Hastert Rule, a Republican Speaker will only allow a bill to reach the floor of the House for a vote if it has the support of a majority of the Republican members. In other words, no bill is allowed to pass with the support of a minority of the Republicans plus some Democrats. Of course, Democratic Speakers have also employed this tactic, but they have never formalized it as a rule. Further, even Republican Speakers will violate the rule when it is absolutely necessary. Then-Speaker John Boehner, for example, abandoned the Hastert rule to end a government shutdown in 2013.

Congresspersons and the Citizenry: A Comparison

Members of the Senate and the House of Representatives are not typical American citizens. Members of Congress are older than most Americans, partly because of constitutional age requirements and partly because a good deal of political experience normally is an advantage in running for national office. Members of Congress are also disproportionately white, male, and trained in high-status occupations.

While women are about half the nation's population, they make up only about a fifth of the members of Congress. Years ago, of course, this share was lower still. Racial and ethnic minority group members have also increased their representation over time. Still, they constitute only about 20 percent of the House and 10 percent of the Senate, compared to 35 percent of the nation as a whole.

Members of Congress are much more likely than ordinary citizens to report a religious affiliation. The percentage of Protestants in Congress matches their share in the general population. Catholics are slightly overrepresented in the House. Latter-day Saints (Mormons) and Jewish Americans are overrepresented in Congress, but for both groups the numbers are still small. Lawyers are by far the largest occupational group among congresspersons, although the proportion of lawyers in the House is lower now than it was in the past.

Compared with the average American citizen, members of Congress are well paid. Annual congressional salaries are now $174,000. Increasingly, members of Congress are also much wealthier than the average citizen. Currently, the average member is worth $4.5 million, not counting the value of a primary residence.

Perks and Privileges

Legislators have many benefits that are not available to most people. These range from subsidized meals in the congressional dining rooms to free parking at Washington, D.C., airports.

Among the most important perks is a team of staff members. More than thirty thousand people are employed on Capitol Hill. About half of them are personal and committee staff members. The personal staff includes office clerks and assistants; professionals who deal with media relations, draft legislation, and satisfy constituency requests for service; and staffers who maintain local offices in the member's home district or state.

The average Senate office on Capitol Hill employs about thirty staff members, and twice that number work on the personal staffs of senators from the most populous states. House office staffs typically are about half as large as those of the Senate.

Members of Congress also benefit from a number of special constitutional protections. Under Article I, Section 6, of the Constitution, for example, "for any Speech or Debate in either House, they shall not be questioned in any other Place." The "speech or debate" clause means that members may make any allegations or other statements they wish in connection with official duties and normally not be sued for defamation (libel or slander) or otherwise be subject to legal action.

Congressional Elections and Apportionment

» **LO 9-3:** Examine the implications of apportioning House seats.

The process of electing members of Congress is decentralized. Congressional elections are conducted by the individual state governments. The states, however, must conform to the rules established by the U.S. Constitution and federal statutes. The Constitution states that representatives are to be elected every second year by popular ballot, and the number of seats awarded to each state is to be determined every ten years by the results of the census. Each state has at least one representative, with most congressional districts having almost 770,000 residents. Senators are elected by popular vote every six years. Approximately one-third of the seats are chosen every two years. Each state has two senators. Under Article I, Section 4, of the Constitution, state legislatures are given control over "[t]he Times, Places and Manner of holding Elections for Senators and Representatives," although "the Congress may at any time by Law make or alter such Regulations."

Candidates for Congressional Elections

Congressional campaigns have changed considerably in the past two decades. Like all other campaigns, they are much more expensive. In 2022, candidate and independent committees spent about $9 billion on congressional elections. Once in office, legislators spend time almost every day raising funds for their next campaign.

Presidential Effects. Congressional candidates are always hopeful that a strong presidential candidate will sweep in other members of their party. (In fact, in some presidential elections such "coattail effects" have not materialized at all.) One way to measure the coattail effect is to look at the subsequent midterm elections, held in the even-numbered years following the presidential contests. In these years, voter turnout usually falls sharply. The party controlling the White House frequently loses seats in Congress in the midterm elections, in part because the coattail effect ceases to apply. Table 9.1 shows the pattern for midterm elections since 1946.

The Power of Incumbency. The power of incumbency in the outcome of congressional elections cannot be overemphasized. Figure 9.1 shows that a sizable majority of representatives and senators who decide to run for reelection are successful. This conclusion holds for both presidential-year and midterm elections. Even in elections when one party makes significant gains, most incumbents remain safe.

Apportionment of the House

Two of the more complicated aspects of congressional elections are apportionment issues—**reapportionment** (the allocation of seats in the House to each state after a census) and **redistricting** (the redrawing of the boundaries of the districts within each state). In a landmark vote in 1962, the Supreme Court made the redistricting of state legislative seats a justiciable (that is, a reviewable) question.[2] The Court did so by invoking the Fourteenth Amendment principle that no state can deny to any person "the equal protection of the laws." In 1964, the Court held that both chambers of a state legislature must be designed so that all districts are equal in population.[3] Later that year, the Court applied this "one person, one vote" principle to U.S. congressional districts on the basis of Article I, Section 2, of the

Table 9.1	Midterm Gains and Losses by the Party of the President, 1946–2022

▶ What effect might voter turnout have had on these numbers?

Seats Gained or Lost by the Party of the President in the House of Representatives		
Year	President's Party	Outcome
1946	D.	−55
1950	D.	−29
1954	R.	−18
1958	R.	−47
1962	D.	−4
1966	D.	−47
1970	R.	−12
1974	R.	−48
1978	D.	−15
1982	R.	−26
1986	R.	−5
1990	R.	−8
1994	D.	−52
1998	D.	+5
2002	R.	+5
2006	R.	−30
2010	D.	−64
2014	D.	−15
2018	R.	−41
2022	D.	−10 (est.)

Sources: Norman Ornstein, Thomas E. Mann, and Michael J. Malbin, *Vital Statistics on Congress, 2001–2002* (Washington, D.C.: The AEI Press, 2002); and authors' updates.

Reapportionment
The allocation of seats in the House of Representatives to each state after a census.

Redistricting
The redrawing of the boundaries of the congressional districts within each state.

---

2. *Baker v. Carr*, 369 U.S. 186 (1962). The term justiciable is pronounced juhs-*tish*-a-buhl.
3. *Reynolds v. Sims*, 377 U.S. 533 (1964).

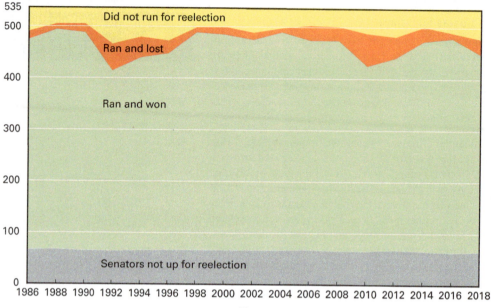

| Figure 9.1 | The Power of Incumbency |

Senators and members of the House taken together. ▶ **Why did so many incumbents lose in 2010?**

Sources: Norman Ornstein, Thomas E. Mann, and Michael J. Malbin, *Vital Statistics on Congress,* 2001–2002 (Washington, D.C.: The AEI Press, 2002); and authors' updates.

Constitution, which requires that members of the House be chosen "by the People of the several States."[4]

As a result of severe malapportionment of congressional districts before 1964, some districts contained two or three times the population of other districts in the same state, thereby diluting the effect of a vote cast in the more populous districts. This system generally benefited the conservative residents of rural areas and small towns and harmed the interests of the more heavily populated and liberal cities.

Gerrymandering

Gerrymandering
The drawing of legislative district boundary lines for the purpose of obtaining partisan advantage. A district is said to be gerrymandered when its shape is altered substantially to determine which party will win it.

Although the general issue of apportionment has been dealt with fairly successfully by the one person, one vote principle, the **gerrymandering** issue has not yet been resolved. This term refers to the tactics that were used under Elbridge Gerry, the governor of Massachusetts, in the 1812 elections to draw legislative boundaries (see Figure 9.2). A district is said to have been gerrymandered when its shape is altered substantially to determine which party will win it.

In 1986, the Supreme Court heard a case that challenged gerrymandered congressional districts in Indiana. The Court ruled for the first time that redistricting for the political

---

4. *Wesberry v. Sanders,* 376 U.S. 1 (1964).

benefit of one group could be challenged on constitutional grounds.[5] In this specific case, however, the Court did not agree that the districts had been drawn unfairly.

In Pennsylvania, the state Supreme Court ruled in 2018 that the state's Republican gerrymander of congressional districts violated the Pennsylvania Constitution. The state court eventually issued its own district map, which was more balanced. In June 2019, however, the United States Supreme Court finally closed the door on any claims that gerrymandering violated the U.S. Constitution. The 5–4 vote split Court conservatives and liberals. Chief Justice John Roberts wrote: "We conclude that partisan gerrymandering claims present political questions beyond the reach of the federal courts."[6]

Independent Redistricting Commissions. A number of states have attempted to resolve the problem of gerrymandering by taking the power to set district lines away from the state legislature. Instead, an independent or bipartisan commission draws the lines. The Arizona legislature challenged the constitutionality of such commissions, but in 2015 the Supreme Court ruled that they were constitutional.[7]

How Gerrymandering Works. Congressional and state legislative redistricting decisions are often made by a small group of political leaders within a state legislature. Typically, their goal is to shape voting districts in such a way as to maximize their party's chances of winning state legislative seats, as well as seats in Congress. Two of the techniques in use are called **packing** and **cracking**. By employing powerful computers and software, voters supporting the opposing party are "packed" into as few districts as possible or the opposing party's supporters are "cracked" into different districts.

Figure 9.3 illustrates the redistricting process. In these three examples, sixty-four individuals must be distributed among four districts, each of which has a population of sixteen. Two political parties are involved: the O Party and the X Party.

In Example 1, supporters of the two parties are sorted so that each district contains only one kind of voter. Such a pattern sometimes appears when the members of a state legislature are most interested in preserving the seats of incumbents, regardless of party. In this example, it would be almost impossible to dislodge a sitting member in a general election. Example 2 is the reverse case. Every district is divided evenly between the parties, and even a very slight swing toward one of the parties could give that party all four seats.

Figure 9.2	The Original Gerrymander

In 1812, the Massachusetts legislature carved out of Essex County a district that had a dragon-like contour. An illustrator penciled in a head, wings, and claws and exclaimed, "That will do for a salamander!" Editor Benjamin Russell replied, "Better say a Gerrymander." (Here, salamander is an old name for a monster, not an amphibian.)

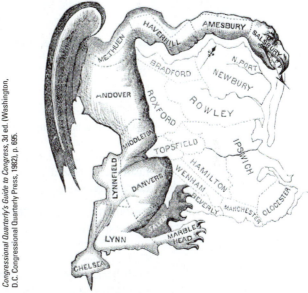

Congressional Quarterly's Guide to Congress, 3d ed. (Washington, D.C. Congressional Quarterly Press, 1982), p. 695.

Source: Boston's *Columbian Centinel*, 1812.

Packing
In gerrymandering, packing as many voters as possible of the opposing party into a single district.

Cracking
In gerrymandering, splitting the opposing party's voters into many different districts.

---

5. *Davis v. Bandemer*, 478 U.S. 109 (1986).

6. *Rucho v. Common Cause*, 139 S.Ct. 2484 (2019).

7. *Arizona State Legislature v. Arizona Independent Redistricting Commission*, 135 S.Ct. 2652 (2015).

| Figure 9.3 | Examples of Districting |

▶ Why might a nonpartisan redistricting board tend to favor solutions such as Example 2?

Example 1. A "bipartisan gerrymander" aimed at protecting incumbents in both the O Party and the X Party.

Example 2. An unstable system. All districts have the same number of supporters in each party.

Example 3. A classic partisan gerrymander. The X Party is almost guaranteed to carry three districts.

Example 3 is a classic partisan gerrymander benefiting the X Party. The district in the lower right is an example of packing—the maximum possible number of supporters of the O Party are packed into that district. The other three districts are examples of cracking. The O Party supporters are cracked so that they do not have a majority in any of the three districts. In these districts, the X Party has majorities of eleven to five, ten to six, and eleven to five.

Redistricting After the 2020 Census. The 2020 census created an opportunity for both parties to redistrict many states. As always, redistricting kicks off a fight over who will control Congress. Some states lost congressional representatives (and therefore Electoral College votes) and other states gained. After every redistricting action, there are lawsuits to challenge the outcomes. Most were not going to change the voting districts for the 2022 mid-term elections. Many observers predicted that the Republicans would benefit from the 2020 census results. In reality, the number of Democratic-leaning seats increased by six, while the number of truly competitive seats was reduced by six. There are still more Republican-leaning seats than Democratic-leaning seats.

"Minority-Majority" Districts

Under the mandate of the Voting Rights Act of 1965, the Justice Department issued directives to states after the 1990 census instructing them to create congressional districts that would maximize the voting power of underrepresented groups—that is, create districts in which racial and ethnic minority group voters were the majority. The result was a number of creatively drawn congressional districts—see, for example, the depiction of Illinois's Fourth Congressional District in Figure 9.4, which is commonly described as "a pair of earmuffs."

These districts were challenged in a number of lawsuits. Plaintiffs claimed that district boundaries based on race alone violate the equal protection clause of the Constitution. For example, the Supreme Court has issued five rulings on cases involving North Carolina's Twelfth District. The most recent decision, in 2017, found that the district's radically elongated boundaries were in fact unconstitutional.[8]

---

8. *Cooper v. Harris*, 137 S.Ct. 1455 (2017), 581 U.S. __.

Figure 9.4   The Fourth Congressional District of Illinois

This district, which is mostly within Chicago's city limits, was drawn to connect two Hispanic neighborhoods separated by an African American majority district. ▶ **Given that Democrats are in the majority in every central Chicago district, why might Illinois's Democratic legislature have bothered to shape this district as they did?**

Source: *National Atlas of the United States*, U.S. Department of the Interior.

How Congress Is Organized

> **» LO 9-4:** Outline the arguments for and against using seniority to choose leadership positions in the House and the Senate.

Congress is organized by party. The limited amount of centralized power that exists in Congress is exercised through party-based mechanisms. When the Republican Party, for example, wins a majority of seats in either the House or the Senate, Republicans control the official positions of power in that chamber, and every important committee has a Republican chairperson and a majority of Republican members. The same process holds when Democrats are in the majority.

In each chamber of Congress, members of the two major political parties meet separately in caucuses. In these meetings, members elect leaders who coordinate party action and negotiate with the other chamber and with the president. Still, much of the actual work of legislating is normally performed by the committees and subcommittees within Congress.

Thousands of bills are introduced in every session of Congress, and no single member can possibly be adequately informed on all the issues that arise. The committee system is a way to provide for specialization, or a division of the legislative labor. Members of a committee can concentrate on just one area or topic—such as taxation or energy—and develop sufficient expertise to draft appropriate legislation when needed. The flow of legislation through both the House and the Senate is determined largely by the speed with which the members of these committees act on bills and resolutions.

Party Control After the 2022 Midterm Elections

Following the 2022 midterm elections, Representative Kevin McCarthy (R-CA) was undoubtably pleased to assume the mantle of Speaker of the House, a post he had sought for a number of years. Still, he had to be disappointed by his party's small majority. For leaders like McCarthy and Nancy Pelosi (CA), his Democratic predecessor as Speaker, small majorities often mean big headaches.

Under these circumstances, if a group of like-minded House members decide to band together, they can pressure party leadership by threatening to withhold their support for crucial legislation. Presently, one such group is the pro-Donald Trump Freedom Caucus. With about forty staunchly conservative members, the Freedom Caucus will potentially be able to block McCarthy's efforts on immigration reform, government funding, and other important legislative areas if their concerns aren't allayed. The group is also in a position to make controversial demands, such as starting impeachment proceedings against Joe Biden and other high-ranking Democrats, as a bargaining chip for their cooperation.

On the Senate side, even the narrowest of majorities is enough to ensure success confirming federal judges nominated by the president—one of the upper chamber's most impactful responsibilities. From 2021 to 2023, when Senate party control was split 50-50, majority leader Charles Schumer (D-NY) was able to get almost all of Biden's judicial nominees confirmed, thanks to Vice President Kamala Harris's tie-breaking votes. Given the Democrats' Senate victory in the 2022 midterm elections, this trend is almost certain to continue through 2025. Thus, even if House Speaker McCarthy is able to block large portions of Biden's and the Senate Democrat's agenda, he will be powerless when it comes to thwarting judicial nominees.

The Power of Committees

Sometimes called "little legislatures," committees usually have the final say on pieces of legislation.[9] Committee actions may be overturned on the floor by the House or Senate, but this rarely happens. Legislators normally defer to the expertise of the chairperson and other members of the committee who speak on the floor in defense of a committee decision. Chairpersons of committees exercise control over the scheduling of hearings and formal actions on bills. They also decide which subcommittee will act on legislation falling within their committee's jurisdiction. Committees normally have the power to kill proposed legislation by refusing to act on it—that is, by never sending it to the entire chamber for a vote.

In the past, committees very rarely were deprived of control over bills—although this kind of action is provided for in the rules of each chamber. In the House, if a bill has been considered by a standing committee for thirty days, the signatures of a majority (218) of the House membership on a **discharge petition** can pry a bill out of an uncooperative committee's hands. From 1909 to 2023, more than nine hundred and thirty such petitions were initiated. About two dozen resulted in successful discharge efforts.[10]

Discharge Petition
A procedure by which a bill in the House of Representatives may be forced (discharged) out of a committee that has refused to report it for consideration by the House.

Committees Versus the Leadership

While ordinary members of Congress are poorly placed to challenge the committee system, party leaders are in a much more powerful position. Traditionally, if a measure was important to the majority caucus, party leaders would take over once the bill was reported out of committee. Once the bill was on the floor of the House or Senate, the leadership would try to control the amendment process and to steer the legislation toward passage.

In 2017, however, the Republican leadership in both chambers employed a much more centralized process for their two major legislative efforts. These two were the failed attempt

---

9. The term *little legislatures* is from Woodrow Wilson, *Congressional Government* (New York: Meridian Books, 1956 [first published in 1885]).

10. *Congressional Quarterly's Guide to Congress*, 6th ed. (Washington, D.C.: Congressional Quarterly Press, 2007); and authors' updates.

to repeal (and possibly replace) Obamacare, and the successful writing of a major new tax bill. The role of committees was essentially nominal. Neither legislative effort was discussed in open hearings. There were no committee **markup** (revision) sessions. Rather, the Republican leadership kept tight control from the very beginning.

In short, the **regular order**, which consists of committee hearings, solicitation of interest-group opinion, and multiple votes, had broken down. A major reason was that the leadership feared that open hearings would generate enough opposition to doom legislative projects. The Democrats regained control of the House in the 2018 midterm elections. When the COVID-19 pandemic hit the U.S. in March of 2020, the Speaker of the House, Nancy Pelosi, basically closed the U.S. Capitol for in-person voting and discussion. As a result, regular order for legislation disappeared and did not return for many months.

Types of Congressional Committees

Over the past two centuries, Congress has created several types of committees, each of which serves particular needs of the institution.

Standing Committees. By far, the most important committees in Congress are the **standing committees**—permanent bodies that are established by the rules of each chamber and that continue from session to session. We present a list of the standing committees of the 118th Congress in Table 9.2. In addition, most of the standing committees have created subcommittees to carry out their work. For example, the 118th Congress had 70 subcommittees in the Senate and 104 in the House. Each standing committee is given a specific area of legislative policy jurisdiction, and almost all legislative measures are considered by the appropriate standing committees.

Because of the importance of their work and the traditional influence of their members in Congress, certain committees are considered to be more prestigious than others. Seats on standing committees that handle spending issues are especially sought after because members can use these positions to benefit their constituents. Committees that control spending include the Appropriations Committee in either chamber and the Ways and Means Committee in the House. Members also normally seek seats on committees that handle matters of special interest to their constituents. A member of the House from an agricultural district, for example, will have an interest in joining the House Agriculture Committee.

Select Committees. In principle, a **select committee** is created for a limited time and for a specific legislative purpose. For example, a select committee may be formed to investigate a public problem, such as child nutrition or aging. In practice, a select committee, such as the Select Committee on Intelligence in each chamber, may continue indefinitely. Select committees rarely create original legislation.

Joint Committees. A **joint committee** is formed by the concurrent action of both chambers of Congress and consists of members from each chamber. Joint committees, which may be permanent or temporary, have dealt with the economy, taxation, and the Library of Congress.

Conference Committees. Special joint committees—**conference committees**—are formed for the purpose of achieving agreement between the House and the Senate on the exact

Alex Edelman/Bloomberg/Getty Images

Image 9.4 Representative Alexandria Ocasio-Cortez (D-NY), a democratic socialist, is a rising star on the left of the Democratic Party. She is co-author of the Green New Deal, a proposal to counter climate change. ▶ Why might younger voters be concerned about the environment?

Markup
In the U.S. Congress, the process by which committees and subcommittees amend or rewrite proposed legislation.

Regular Order
In Congress, channeling proposed legislation through committee and subcommittee hearings, with solicited testimony and votes on revised language.

Standing Committees
Permanent committees in the House or Senate that consider bills within a certain subject area.

Select Committee
A temporary legislative committee established for a limited time period and for a special purpose.

Joint Committee
A legislative committee composed of members from both chambers of Congress.

Conference Committees
Special joint committees appointed to reconcile differences when bills pass the two chambers of Congress in different forms.

Table 9.2	Standing Committees of the 118th Congress, 2022–2024

In 2011, House Republicans changed the name of the Committee on Education and Labor to the Committee on Education and the Workforce. In 2019, Democrats changed it back. ▶ **"Labor" often refers to unions. Why might Republicans have a problem with labor unions?**

House Committees	Senate Committees
Agriculture	Agriculture, Nutrition, and Forestry
Appropriations	Appropriations
Armed Services	Armed Services
Budget	Banking, Housing, and Urban Affairs
Education and Labor	Budget
Energy and Commerce	Commerce, Science, and Transportation
Ethics	Energy and Natural Resources
Financial Services	Environment and Public Works
Foreign Affairs	Finance
Homeland Security	Foreign Relations
House Administration	Health, Education, Labor, and Pensions
Judiciary	Homeland Security and Governmental Affairs
Natural Resources	Judiciary
Oversight and Government Reform	Rules and Administration
Rules	Small Business and Entrepreneurship
Science, Space, and Technology	Veterans' Affairs
Small Business	
Transportation and Infrastructure	
Veterans' Affairs	
Ways and Means	

wording of legislative acts when the two chambers pass legislative proposals in different forms. No bill can be sent to the White House to be signed into law unless it first passes both chambers in identical form. Conference committees are in a position to make significant alterations to legislation and frequently become the focal point of policy debates.

The House Rules Committee. Due to its special gatekeeping power over the terms on which legislation will reach the floor of the House of Representatives, the House Rules Committee holds a uniquely powerful position. For each bill, the committee passes a special rule that sets the time limit on debate and determines whether and how a bill may be amended. The Rules Committee has the unusual power to convene while the House is meeting as a whole, to have its resolutions considered immediately on the floor, and to initiate legislation on its own.

The Selection of Committee Members

In both chambers, members are appointed to standing committees by the steering committee of their party. The majority-party member with the longest term of continuous service on a standing committee is given preference when the committee selects its chairperson. The most senior member of the minority party is called the ranking committee member for that party. This **seniority system** is not required by law but is an informal, traditional process, and it applies to other significant posts in Congress as well. The system provides a predictable means of assigning positions of power within Congress.

The general pattern until the 1970s was that members of the House or Senate who represented safe seats would be reelected repeatedly and eventually could accumulate enough years of continuous committee service to enable them to become the chairpersons of their committees. In the 1970s, reforms to the chairperson selection process somewhat modified the seniority system in the House. The reforms introduced the use of a secret ballot in electing House committee chairpersons and allowed for the possibility of choosing a chairperson on a basis other than seniority. The Democrats immediately replaced three senior chairpersons who were out of step with the rest of their party. In 1995, the Republicans chose relatively junior House members as chairpersons of several key committees, thus ensuring conservative control of the committees. The Republicans also passed a rule limiting the term of a chairperson to six years.

Image 9.5 Senator Lindsey Graham (R-SC) in March 2020. Graham sought to limit unemployment benefits in the $2 trillion bipartisan pandemic relief package passed that month. ▶ Why do you think Graham eventually voted for the package, generous benefits included?

Leadership in the House

The House leadership is made up of the Speaker, the majority and minority leaders, and the party whips.

The Speaker. The foremost power holder in the House of Representatives is the **Speaker of the House**. The Speaker's position is technically a nonpartisan one, but in reality, the Speaker is the official leader of the majority party in the House.[11] When a new Congress convenes in January of odd-numbered years, each party nominates a candidate for Speaker. All Republican members of the House are expected to vote for their party's nominee, and all Democrats are expected to support their candidate. The vote to organize the House is the one vote in which representatives are strongly expected to vote with their party. In a sense, this vote defines a member's partisan status.

The major formal powers of the Speaker include the following:

- Presiding over meetings of the House
- Appointing members of joint committees and conference committees
- Scheduling legislation for floor action
- Deciding points of order and interpreting the rules with the advice of the House parliamentarian
- Referring bills and resolutions to the appropriate standing committees of the House

A Speaker may take part in floor debate and vote, as can any other member of Congress, but recent Speakers usually have voted only to break a tie.

Seniority System
A custom followed in both chambers of Congress specifying that the member of the majority party with the longest term of continuous service will be given preference when a committee chairperson (or a holder of some other significant post) is selected.

Speaker of the House
The presiding officer in the House of Representatives. The Speaker is chosen by the majority party and is the most powerful and influential member of the House.

Media Punch/MediaPunch Inc/Alamy Stock Photo

---

11. The Constitution does not require that the Speaker of the House be a member of the House of Representatives.

Image 9.6 California Democrat Nancy Pelosi was Speaker of the House from 2007 to 2011 and again from 2019 through January 2023. Maryland Democrat Steny Hoyer was first elected in 1981. He was majority leader from 2019 through January 2023. California Republican Kevin McCarthy was House majority leader from 2014 to 2019 and then became minority leader from 2019 to 2023. In 2023, he became the Speaker of the House. ▶ Who chooses congressional leaders?

Majority Leader of the House
A leader elected by the majority party in the House to assist the Speaker and foster party cohesion.

The Majority Leader. The **majority leader of the House** is elected by the caucus of the majority party to foster cohesion among party members and to act as a spokesperson for the party. The majority leader influences the scheduling of debate and acts as the chief deputy of the Speaker. The majority leader cooperates with the Speaker and other party leaders, both inside and outside Congress, to formulate the party's legislative program and to guide that program through the legislative process in the House. The parties have often recruited future Speakers from those who hold the position of majority leader.

Minority Leader of the House
The party leader elected by members of the minority party in the House.

The Minority Leader. The **minority leader of the House** is the candidate nominated for Speaker by the caucus of the minority party. Like the majority leader, the leader of the minority party has as their primary responsibility the maintaining of cohesion within the party's ranks. The minority leader speaks on behalf of the president if the minority party controls the White House. In relations with the majority party, the minority leader consults with both the Speaker and the majority leader on recognizing members who wish to speak on the floor, on House rules and procedures, and on the scheduling of legislation. Minority leaders have no actual power in these areas, however.

Whips
A member of Congress who aids the majority or minority leader of the House or the Senate.

Whips. The leadership of each party includes assistants to the majority and minority leaders known as **whips**.[12] The whips are members of Congress who assist the party leaders by passing information down from the leadership to party members and by ensuring that members show up for floor debate and cast their votes on important issues. Whips conduct polls among party members about the members' views on legislation, inform the leaders about whose vote is doubtful and whose is certain, and may exert pressure on members to support the leaders' positions.

---

12. Whip comes from "whipper-in," a fox-hunting term for someone who keeps the hunting dogs from straying.

Photo courtesy of Senator McConnell

Ron Sachs/CNP/Polaris/Newscom

Image 9.7 After Republicans took control of the U.S. Senate in the 2014 elections, Republican senator Mitch McConnell of Kentucky, left, was elected Senate majority leader. Democratic senator Chuck Schumer of New York, right, was elected minority leader in November 2016. The roles were reversed in 2020 and remained so in 2022. It is rare for a congressional leader to become president. ▶ How might a congressional leadership position interfere with presidential aspirations?

Leadership in the Senate

The Senate is less than one-fourth the size of the House. This fact alone probably explains why a formal, complex, and centralized leadership structure is not as necessary in the Senate as it is in the House.

The two highest-ranking formal leadership positions in the Senate are essentially ceremonial in nature. Under the Constitution, the vice president of the United States is the president (that is, the presiding officer) of the Senate and may vote to break a tie. The vice president, however, is only rarely present for a meeting of the Senate. The Senate elects instead a **president pro tempore** ("pro tem") to preside over the Senate in the vice president's absence. Ordinarily, the president pro tem is the member of the majority party with the longest continuous term of service in the Senate. As mentioned, the president pro tem is mostly a ceremonial position. More junior senators take turns actually presiding over the sessions of the Senate.

The real leadership power in the Senate rests in the hands of the **Senate majority leader**, the **Senate minority leader**, and their respective whips. The Senate majority and minority leaders have the right to be recognized first in debate on the floor and generally exercise the same powers available to the House majority and minority leaders. They control the scheduling of debate on the floor in conjunction with the majority party's policy committee, influence the allocation of committee assignments for new members or for senators attempting to transfer to a new committee, influence the selection of other party officials, and participate in selecting members of conference committees.

The leaders are expected to mobilize support for partisan legislative or presidential initiatives. They act as liaisons with the White House when the president is of their party, try to obtain the cooperation of committee chairpersons, and seek to facilitate the smooth functioning of the Senate through the senators' unanimous consent to various procedural motions. The majority and minority leaders are elected by their respective party caucuses.

President Pro Tempore
The temporary presiding officer of the Senate in the absence of the vice president.

Senate Majority Leader
The chief spokesperson of the majority party in the Senate, who directs the legislative program and party strategy.

Senate Minority Leader
The party officer in the Senate who commands the minority party's opposition to the policies of the majority party and directs the legislative program and strategy of the minority party.

Senate party whips, like their House counterparts, maintain communication within the party on platform positions and try to ensure that party colleagues are present for floor debate and important votes. The Senate whip system is far less elaborate than its counterpart in the House, because there are fewer members to track and senators have a greater tradition of independence.

Lawmaking and Budgeting

» **LO 9-5:** Discuss the process by which a bill becomes law and how the federal government establishes its budget.

Each year, Congress and the president propose and approve many laws. Some are "money bills" that require extensive bargaining but must be passed for the government to continue to function. Other laws are relatively free of controversy and are passed with little dissension. Still other proposed legislation is extremely controversial and reaches to the roots of differences between Republicans and Democrats.

Figure 9.5 shows that each law begins as a bill, which must be introduced in either the House or the Senate. Often, similar bills are introduced in both chambers. A budget bill, however, must start in the House. In each chamber, the bill follows similar steps. It is referred to a committee and its subcommittees for study, discussion, hearings, and markup (rewriting). When the bill is reported out to the full chamber, it must be scheduled for debate (by the Rules Committee in the House and by the leadership in the Senate). After the bill has been passed in each chamber, if the two versions of the bill contain different provisions, a conference committee is formed to write a compromise bill, which must be approved by both chambers before it is sent to the president to sign or veto.

The procedure summarized in Figure 9.5 is the regular order, mentioned earlier. If the congressional leadership abandons the regular process, a different series of steps applies. During the period when the Speaker of the House did not allow most members to enter the Capitol for legislative discussions and votes, the Democratic leadership essentially substituted itself for the committee actions shown in the yellow and dark blue boxes in Figure 9.5.

A second departure from normal procedure was the use of reconciliation, also described earlier, for both measures. Obamacare repeal was attached to the fiscal year 2017 budget resolution, and the tax-cutting bill was part of the budget resolution for 2018. By using reconciliation, Republicans hoped to avoid Democratic filibusters. The traditional way to pass such bills would be to alter them to win support from at least a few Democrats. The Republican leadership, however, was set on passing legislation with no Democratic input. Given that the Republicans had only a two-vote majority in the Senate, doing so required complete Republican unity to overcome united Democratic opposition. The Republicans achieved such unity on taxation, but not on the issue of health care.

In the spring of 2021, the Senate Parliamentarian ruled that the Senate could pass two budget reconciliation bills in that year—one concerning fiscal year 2021 and one focused on fiscal year 2022. The American Rescue Plan Act of 2021 was enacted into law using reconciliation.

How Much Will the Government Spend?

The Constitution is very clear about where the power of the purse lies in the national government: All taxing or spending bills must originate in the House of Representatives. Much of the business of Congress is concerned with approving government expenditures through the budget process and with raising the revenues to pay for government programs.

| Figure 9.5 | How a Bill Becomes Law |

This illustration shows the most typical way in which proposed legislation is enacted into law. Most legislation begins as similar bills introduced into the House and the Senate. The process is illustrated here with two hypothetical bills, House Bill No. 100 (HR 100) and Senate Bill No. 200 (S 200). The path of HR 100 is shown on the left and that of S 200 on the right.

▶ **Where does the filibuster fit into this process?**

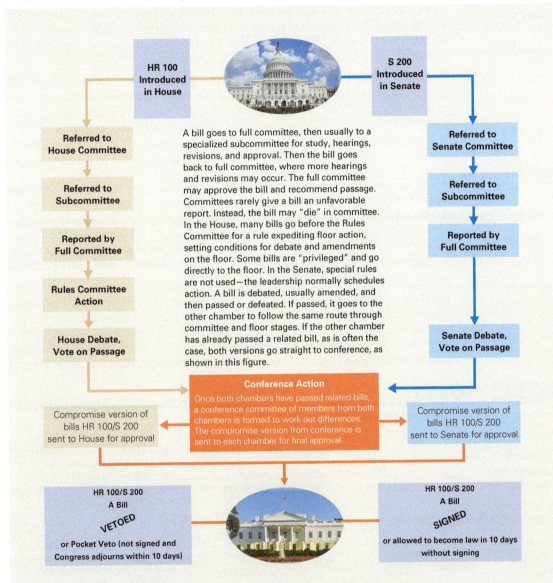

HR 100 Introduced in House

S 200 Introduced in Senate

Referred to House Committee

Referred to Senate Committee

Referred to Subcommittee

Referred to Subcommittee

Reported by Full Committee

Reported by Full Committee

Rules Committee Action

House Debate, Vote on Passage

Senate Debate, Vote on Passage

A bill goes to full committee, then usually to a specialized subcommittee for study, hearings, revisions, and approval. Then the bill goes back to full committee, where more hearings and revisions may occur. The full committee may approve the bill and recommend passage. Committees rarely give a bill an unfavorable report. Instead, the bill may "die" in committee. In the House, many bills go before the Rules Committee for a rule expediting floor action, setting conditions for debate and amendments on the floor. Some bills are "privileged" and go directly to the floor. In the Senate, special rules are not used—the leadership normally schedules action. A bill is debated, usually amended, and then passed or defeated. If passed, it goes to the other chamber to follow the same route through committee and floor stages. If the other chamber has already passed a related bill, as is often the case, both versions go straight to conference, as shown in this figure.

Conference Action
Once both chambers have passed related bills, a conference committee of members from both chambers is formed to work out differences. The compromise version from conference is sent to each chamber for final approval.

Compromise version of bills HR 100/S 200 sent to House for approval

Compromise version of bills HR 100/S 200 sent to Senate for approval

HR 100/S 200 A Bill VETOED or Pocket Veto (not signed and Congress adjourns within 10 days)

HR 100/S 200 A Bill SIGNED or allowed to become law in 10 days without signing

A compromise bill approved by both chambers is sent to the president, who can sign it into law or veto it and return it to Congress. Congress may override a veto by a two-thirds majority vote in both chambers. The bill then becomes law without the president's approval.

Orhan Cam/Shutterstock.com

Preparing the Budget

The federal government operates on a **fiscal year (FY)** cycle. (See Figure 9.6 for a graphic illustration of the budget cycle.) The fiscal year runs from October through September, so fiscal 2024, or FY24, runs from October 1, 2023, through September 30, 2024. Eighteen months before a fiscal year starts, the executive branch begins preparing the **executive budget**. The Office of Management and Budget (OMB) outlines the budget and then sends it to the various departments and agencies. Bargaining follows, in which—to use only two of many examples—the Department of Health and Human Services may argue for more antipoverty spending, and the armed forces for more defense spending.

The OMB Reviews the Budget. Even though the OMB has fewer than 550 employees, it is one of the most powerful agencies in Washington. It assembles the budget documents and monitors federal agencies throughout each year. Every year, it begins the budget process with a spring review, in which it requires all the agencies to review their programs, activities, and goals. At the beginning of each summer, the OMB sends out a letter instructing agencies to submit their requests for funding for the next fiscal year. By the end of the summer, each agency must submit a formal request to the OMB.

In actuality, the "budget season" begins with the fall review. At this time, the OMB looks at budget requests and, in almost all cases, routinely cuts them back. Although the OMB works within guidelines established by the president, specific decisions often are left to the OMB director and the director's associates. By the beginning of November, the director's review begins. The director meets with cabinet secretaries and budget officers. Time becomes crucial. The budget must be completed by January so that it can be included in the *Economic Report of the President*.

The Election-Year Budget. The schedule just described cannot apply to a year in which the voters elect a new president or to a year in which a new president is inaugurated. For obvious reasons, an out-going president cannot engage in the fall review of the following year's budget because that president would no longer be in office. Just as obvious, a first-term presidential candidate can hardly undertake a fall review either, given that campaigning is

---

| **Figure 9.6** | **The Budget Cycle** |

▶ Why does Congress have so much trouble meeting its deadlines?

Executive Budgeting Process

Executive agency requests: about twelve to eighteen months before the start of the fiscal year, or in March to September

Office of Management and Budget (OMB) review and presidential approval: nine to twelve months before the start of the fiscal year, or in September to December

Legislative Budgeting Process

Second budget resolution: by October 1

First budget resolution: by May 15

Executive branch submits a budget to Congress: eight to nine months before the start of the fiscal year, at the end of January

Execution

Start of fiscal year: October 1

Outlays and obligations: October 1 to September 30

Audit of fiscal year outlays: on a selective basis by the Government Accountability Office (GAO)

still going on. Following the selection of a new president, the budget is compressed into the first months of the new administration. Biden presented his first budget in late May 2021. That budget projected total federal spending of a little over $6 trillion—a record.

Congress Faces the Budget

In January, nine months before the fiscal year starts, the president takes the OMB's proposed budget, approves it, and submits it to Congress. Then the congressional budgeting process takes over. The budgeting process involves two steps: authorization and appropriation.

The Authorization Process. First, Congress must authorize funds to be spent. The **authorization** is a formal declaration by the appropriate congressional committee that a certain amount of funding may be available to an agency. Congressional committees and subcommittees look at the proposals from the executive branch and the Congressional Budget Office in making the decision to authorize funds.

The Appropriation Process. After the funds have been authorized, they must be appropriated by Congress. The appropriations committees of both the House and the Senate forward spending bills to their respective bodies. The **appropriation** of funds occurs when the final bill is passed. In this process, large sums are in play. Representatives and senators, especially those who chair key committees, have traditionally found it easy to slip earmarks, or pork, into a variety of bills. These proposals may have nothing to do with the explicitly stated purpose of the bill.

Budget Resolutions and Crises

The first budget resolution by Congress is due in May. It sets overall revenue goals and spending targets. Spending and tax laws that are drawn up over the summer are supposed to be guided by the first budget resolution. By September, Congress is scheduled to pass its second budget resolution, one that will set binding limits on taxes and spending for the fiscal year beginning October 1.

The Continuing Resolution. In actuality, Congress has finished the budget on time in only three years since 1977. The budget is usually broken into a series of appropriations bills. If Congress has not passed one of these bills by October 1, it normally passes a **continuing resolution** that allows the affected agencies to keep on doing whatever they were doing the previous year with the same amount of funding.

The Federal Debt Ceiling. If the federal government runs a budget deficit—if it spends more than it takes in—it must issue new debt. The government has, in fact, run a deficit in most years. Current law limits the amount of debt the government can issue. If the federal debt approaches the debt ceiling, Congress must raise the ceiling to allow additional debt. Many people mistakenly believe that raising the ceiling is a prerequisite for new, future spending, but that is not the case. If the debt ceiling is not raised as needed, the government might be forced to default on its existing obligations.

Traditionally, members of Congress often "grandstanded" by voting against the debt ceiling hike, even though passage was never in doubt. Occasionally, both parties engage in brinkmanship before voting on an increase in the federal debt ceiling. At the end of 2021, an increase in the debt ceiling by $2.5 trillion was finally agreed upon by Congress on December 14. Most of the arguments surrounding increasing the debt ceiling do not matter, however. The U.S. government will never default on its debt.

Authorization
A formal declaration by a legislative committee that a certain amount of funding may be available to an agency. Some authorizations terminate in a year. Others are renewable automatically without further congressional action.

Appropriation
The passage, by Congress, of a spending bill specifying the amount of authorized funds that actually will be allocated for an agency's use.

Continuing Resolution
A temporary funding law that Congress passes when an appropriations bill has not been passed by the beginning of the new fiscal year on October 1.

Chip Somodevilla/Getty Images News/Getty Images

Image 9.8 U.S. Representative Hakeem Jeffries (D-NY) at a hearing on the impeachment of President Trump in December 2019. ▶ Why do you think that Republican senators were almost unanimous in refusing to convict Trump?

Failure to Pass a Continuing Resolution. It was assumed at the time that the debt ceiling tactic would not be revived any time soon. Still, there is another way to suspend normal government activity—Congress can fail to approve a continuing resolution in a timely fashion. With no appropriation bill or continuing resolution, the administration is required to temporarily shut down part or all of the federal government. (Generally, the most vital services are exempt from such a shutdown.)

Historically, Congress has often forced such shutdowns, and it did so at least twice in 2018. One such instance was trivial—a Republican senator held up debate long enough to trigger a several-hour shutdown in the middle of the night. In January, however, Senate Democrats forced a three-day shutdown by refusing to vote for a continuing resolution. The goal was to pressure Republicans to insert protection for the "DREAMers" into the bill. DREAMers are unauthorized immigrants who were brought into the country as children by their parents. While these immigrants enjoy much popular support, the public also opposed shutting down the government on their behalf, and the Democratic effort failed.

In the winter of 2018–2019, a dispute between President Trump and Congress led to the longest government shutdown in history—35 days. The shutdown stemmed from Trump's demand for billions in federal funds for a proposed wall on the U.S.–Mexico border. Funding for the wall was rejected by almost all Democrats and was not universally popular among Republicans. In January 2019, in the face of growing popular opposition, Trump relented and the Senate Republican leadership allowed a continuing resolution to pass, ending the shutdown. Trump then declared a national emergency in a further attempt to fund the wall by diverting military funds from other projects. Legal challenges to the declaration were ultimately rejected by the Supreme Court.[13]

Realize that government shutdowns certainly make the news, but they are never truly complete shutdowns of the U.S. government. All essential services keep functioning. The military continues to protect us. Most of the federal bureaucracies continue to operate. At best, some small parts of the federal government temporarily stop functioning.

---

13. *Trump v. Sierra Club*, 140 S.Ct. 1 (2019).

Making A Difference

Learning About Your Representatives

Do you know the names of your senators and your representative in Congress? A surprising number of Americans do not. Even if you know the names and parties of your elected delegates, there is still much more you could learn about them that would be useful.

Why Should You Care? The legislation that Congress passes can directly affect your life. For instance, federally guaranteed student loans are a major issue. By 2023, outstanding student loans amounted to $1.84 trillion, substantially larger than U.S. credit-card debt. Student loans issued by the private sector cannot be discharged through bankruptcy. Congress has recently made a number of adjustments beneficial to students, yet more could be done. No such reforms are possible without congressional action—so it matters a great deal who is elected to Congress.

You can make a difference on major legislation simply by voting for the candidates you prefer. In between elections, you can lobby your senators or your representative and ask that they support legislation that meets your approval. To do so effectively, however, you need to know what positions these officials are currently advocating.

What Can You Do? To contact a member of Congress, start by going to the websites of the U.S. House of Representatives and the U.S. Senate.

Although you can communicate easily with your representatives by e-mail, using it has some drawbacks. Representatives and senators now receive large volumes of e-mail from constituents, which they rarely read themselves. They have staff members who read and respond to e-mail instead. Many interest groups argue that U.S. mail, or even express mail or a phone call, is more likely to capture the attention of a representative than e-mail. You can easily obtain information on your representative by going to the website house.gov. Then put in your zip code. You will be taken to your House of Representatives member's webpage.

Key Terms

agenda setting 211
appropriation 231
authorization 231
bicameralism 208
casework 210
conference
    committees 223
constituents 208
continuing
    resolution 231
cracking 219
discharge petition 222
earmarks 209

enumerated powers 211
executive budget 230
filibuster 213
fiscal year (FY) 230
gerrymandering 218
instructed delegates 209
joint committee 223
lawmaking 209
majority leader of the
    House 226
minority leader of the
    House 226
markup 223

oversight 210
packing 219
president pro
    tempore 227
reapportionment 217
reconciliation 214
redistricting 217
regular order 223
representation 209
Rules Committee 213
select committee 223
Senate majority
    leader 227

Senate minority
    leader 227
seniority system 225
Speaker of the
    House 225
standing
    committees 223
subpoenas 211
trustees 209
whips 226

Chapter Summary

» **LO 9-1** The authors of the U.S. Constitution believed that the bulk of national power should be in the legislature. The Connecticut Compromise established the House of Representatives with a membership based on population, and the Senate based on the equality of states.

The functions of Congress include (a) lawmaking, (b) representation, (c) service to constituents, (d) oversight, (e) public education, and (f) conflict resolution.

The Constitution specifies the enumerated, or expressed, powers of Congress, including the rights to impose taxes, to borrow funds, to regulate commerce, and to declare war. In addition, Congress enjoys the right, under the elastic, or "necessary and proper," clause, to make all laws necessary and proper for executing the various powers of the national government.

» **LO 9-2** There are 435 members of the House of Representatives and 100 members of the Senate. Owing to its larger size, the House has a greater number of formal rules. The Senate tradition of unlimited debate, expressed in the filibuster, has been used over the years to frustrate the passage of bills. Budget bills can be exempt from a filibuster, and by 2017 most presidential nominations were exempt as well.

Members of Congress are older and wealthier than most Americans, disproportionately white and male, and more likely to be lawyers.

» **LO 9-3** Most incumbent representatives and senators who run for reelection are successful. The Supreme Court's "one person, one vote" rule means that the populations of congressional and state legislative districts must be effectively equal. Still, district boundaries are frequently drawn to benefit one of the parties by gerrymandering.

» **LO 9-4** Most of the work of legislating is performed by committees and subcommittees within Congress. Legislation introduced into the House or Senate is assigned to standing committees. Joint committees are formed by the action of both chambers and consist of members from each. Conference committees are joint committees set up to achieve agreement between the House and the Senate on the wording of legislative acts that were passed by the chambers in different forms. The seniority rule, which is usually followed, specifies that the longest-serving member of the majority party will be the chair of a committee.

The foremost power in the House is the Speaker of the House. Other leaders are the House majority leader, the House minority leader, and the majority and minority whips. Formally, the vice president is the presiding officer of the Senate. Actual Senate leadership rests with the majority leader, the minority leader, and their whips.

» **LO 9-5** A bill becomes law by progressing through both chambers of Congress and—presuming that the regular order is followed—their appropriate committees before submission to the president.

The budget process for a fiscal year begins with the preparation of an executive budget by the president. This is reviewed by the Office of Management and Budget and then sent to Congress, which is supposed to pass a final budget by the end of September. Since 1977, Congress generally has not followed its own time rules.

Test Yourself

1. The bicameralism of Congress means that
   a. every district has two members.
   b. every state has two senators.
   c. Congress is divided into two legislative bodies.

2. The process of compromise in which members of Congress support each other's bills is called
   a. agenda setting.
   b. logrolling.
   c. reconciliation.

3. The central difference between the House and the Senate is that
   a. the House is much larger than the Senate.
   b. the Senate is much larger than the House.
   c. the Senate meets only occasionally, but the House meets all of the time.

4. In contrast to the House, only the Senate has the power to accept or reject
   a. treaties with foreign nations.
   b. executive agreements with foreign governments.
   c. the recognition of foreign governments.

5. A high percentage of senators and representatives are reelected, and we describe this as due to
   a. coattail effects.
   b. presidential effects.
   c. the power of incumbency.

6. Congressional redistricting often involves gerrymandering, which means that the redistricting
   a. results in an equal number of Democratic and Republican districts.
   b. results in strange-shaped districts designed to favor one party.
   c. results in districts that have almost no representation.

7. Gerrymandering can be accomplished by
   a. cracking and packing.
   b. varying the population of districts.
   c. more frequent redistricting.

8. The typical method of appointing committee chairpersons in Congress is based on
   a. rotation.
   b. presidential appointment.
   c. the seniority system.

9. The leader of the majority party in the House of Representatives is the
   a. House majority leader.
   b. Speaker of the House.
   c. president pro tempore.

10. When an appropriations bill has not been passed by the beginning of the new fiscal year, Congress may pass a temporary funding law called
    a. a continuing resolution.
    b. a second budget resolution.
    c. a temporary authorization.

Essay Questions

1. The District of Columbia is not represented in the Senate and has a single, nonvoting delegate to the House. Should the District of Columbia be represented in Congress by voting legislators? Why or why not?

2. Identify some advantages to the nation that might follow when one party controls the House, the Senate, and the presidency. Identify some of the disadvantages that might follow from such a situation.

Answers to multiple-choice questions: 1. c, 2. b, 3. a, 4. a, 5. c, 6. b, 7. a, 8. c, 9. b, 10. a.

10 The President

Joe Biden won the 2020 election to become the 46th president of the United States. During his almost half-decade of public service, he previously tried to become president on two separate occasions. ▶ **Why do you think that he won?**

Geopix/Alamy Stock Photo

The five **Learning Outcomes (LOs)** below are designed to help improve your understanding of this chapter. After reading this chapter, you should be able to:

» **LO 10-1** Identify the types of people who typically undertake serious campaigns for the presidency.

» **LO 10-2** Distinguish among the major roles of the president.

» **LO 10-3** Describe some of the special powers of the president, and tell how a president can be removed from office.

» **LO 10-4** Explain the organization of the executive branch and, in particular, the executive office of the president.

» **LO 10-5** Explain why most vice presidents have little to do with running the federal government.

Check your understanding of the material with the Test Yourself section at the end of the chapter.

The writers of the Constitution had no models to follow when they created the presidency of the United States. Nowhere else in the world was there an elected head of state. What the founders did not want was a king. The two initial plans considered by the founders—the Virginia and New Jersey plans—both called for a relatively weak executive elected by Congress. Other delegates, especially those who had witnessed the need for a strong leader in the Revolutionary Army, believed a powerful executive would be necessary for the new republic. The delegates, after much debate, created a chief executive who had enough powers granted in the Constitution to balance those of Congress.

235

Who Can Become President?

» **LO 10-1:** Identify the types of people who typically undertake serious campaigns for the presidency.

The requirements for becoming president, as outlined in Article II, Section 1, of the Constitution, are not overwhelmingly strict:

> *No person except a natural born Citizen, or a Citizen of the United States, at the time of the Adoption of this Constitution, shall be eligible to the Office of President; neither shall any Person be eligible to that Office who shall not have attained to the Age of thirty-five Years, and been fourteen Years a Resident within the United States.*

The president receives a salary of $400,000, plus $169,000 for expenses and a vast array of free services, beginning with residence in the White House.

Birthplace and Age

The only question that arises about these constitutional requirements relates to the term "natural born Citizen." Does that mean only citizens born in the United States and its territories? What about a child born to U.S. citizens visiting or living in another country? Although the question has not been dealt with directly by the United States Supreme Court, it is reasonable to expect that someone would be eligible if their parents were Americans.

Birth Controversies. These questions were debated when opponents of President Barack Obama (2009–16) claimed that Obama was not a natural born citizen. In fact, Obama was born in Honolulu, Hawaii, in 1961. Those who disputed Obama's birth claimed that his birth certificate was a forgery, even though Obama's birth was also recorded by two Honolulu newspapers.

The Age and Background of the President. Although the Constitution states that the minimum-age requirement for the presidency is 35 years, most presidents have been much older than that when they assumed office. Theodore Roosevelt (1901-09) at the age of 42, was the youngest elected president, and the oldest is Joe Biden, at age 78. The average age at initial inauguration has been 55. There has clearly been a demographic bias in the selection of presidents. All have been male, white, and from the Protestant tradition, except for John F. Kennedy and Joe Biden, both Roman Catholics, and Barack Obama, an African American.

Image 10.1 At the age of 69, President Ronald Reagan (1981–89) was the oldest person to be elected until Donald Trump (age 70) and then Joe Biden (age 78). ▶ What problems might result if presidents serve while in their seventies or eighties?

AP Images

The Process of Becoming President

Major and minor political parties nominate candidates for president and vice president at national conventions every four years. The nation's voters do not elect a president and vice president directly but rather cast ballots for presidential electors, who then vote for president and vice president in the Electoral College.

The Electoral College. Because victory goes to the candidate with a majority in the Electoral College, someone can be elected to the office of the presidency without having a plurality of the popular vote cast. This occurred several times in U.S. history. In elections in which more than two candidates were running for office, many presidential candidates have won with less than 50 percent of the total popular votes cast for all candidates—including Abraham Lincoln (1861–65), Woodrow Wilson (1913–21), Harry Truman (1945–53), John F. Kennedy (1961–63), Richard Nixon (1969–74), and Bill Clinton (1993–2001). It is possible for a presidential candidate to win when another candidate has received more popular votes. This occurred in the 2016 election when Hillary Clinton received 48.2 percent of the popular vote. Donald Trump received 46.1 percent. Does this fact mean that the Electoral College should be bypassed or abolished? We examine that question in the *Which Side Are You On?* feature in this chapter.

When the Electoral College Fails to Choose a President. Thus far, on two occasions the Electoral College has failed to give any candidate a majority. At that point, the House of Representatives takes over, and the president is then chosen from among the three candidates having the most Electoral College votes. In 1800, Thomas Jefferson and Aaron Burr tied in the Electoral College. This happened because the Constitution had not been explicit in indicating which of the two electoral votes was for president and which was for vice president.

In 1804, the **Twelfth Amendment** clarified the matter by requiring that the president and the vice president be chosen separately. In 1824, the House again had to make a choice, this time among John Quincy Adams, William H. Crawford, and Andrew Jackson. It chose Adams, even though Jackson had more electoral and popular votes.

Pictorial Press/Pictorial Press Ltd/Alamy Stock Photo

Image 10.2 In 1960, John F. Kennedy became the second youngest person elected president of the United States. Despite his youth, Kennedy had serious health problems that he kept secret. ▶ Could a presidential candidate easily do such a thing today?

The Many Roles of the President

≫ LO 10-2: Distinguish among the major roles of the president.

The Constitution speaks briefly about the duties and obligations of the president. Based on this brief list of powers and on the precedents of history, the presidency has grown into a very complicated job that requires fulfilling at least five constitutional roles. These are (1) head of state, (2) chief executive, (3) commander in chief of the armed forces, (4) chief diplomat, and (5) chief legislator of the United States. In addition to these constitutional roles, presidents serve as the leaders of their political parties—the president is also the nation's most prominent and successful politician. Here we examine each of these significant presidential functions, or roles. It is worth noting that one person plays all these roles simultaneously and that the needs of the roles may at times come into conflict.

Twelfth Amendment
An amendment to the Constitution, adopted in 1804, that specifies the separate election of the president and the vice president by the Electoral College.

Head of State

Every nation has at least one person who is the ceremonial head of state. In most democratic nations, the role of **head of state** is given to someone other than the chief executive, who leads the executive branch of government. In Britain, for example, the head of state is the

Head of State
The role of the president as ceremonial head of the government.

Which Side Are You On?

Should We Elect the President by Popular Vote?

It is possible for a presidential candidate to be elected when an opposing candidate receives a plurality of the popular vote. This has occurred on five occasions. Most recently, it happened in the elections of George W. Bush in 2000 and Donald Trump in 2016. These candidates won elections in which an opponent received more popular votes than they did. In 2000, Democrat Al Gore received 547,000 more votes than George W. Bush, the Republican. Still, Bush won enough Electoral College votes to become president. In 2016, Hillary Clinton won 2,865,000 more votes than Donald Trump. This was by far the largest popular vote margin ever won by a candidate who lost in the Electoral College. Such results have led to calls for replacing the Electoral College with a popular-vote system.

Abolishing the College would require a constitutional amendment, however, and the likelihood that such an amendment would be ratified is remote. As an alternative, the National Popular Vote Interstate Compact advocates a compact to bypass the existing system. This proposal would require each participating state to cast all of its electoral votes for the candidate who receives the most popular votes nationwide. The plan would be triggered if the number of participating states grows to the point at which these states can elect a majority of the Electoral College. As of 2022, fifteen states and the District of Columbia had joined. For the compact to go into effect, however, it would need the approval of Congress and the United States Supreme Court. Is bypassing the Electoral College a good idea?

We Should Keep the Existing System

Supporters of the Electoral College argue that without it, small states would be ignored. Candidates would concentrate on large states with plenty of voters. Also, the current system typically encourages certainty in elections by exaggerating the winner's margin of victory. Under the existing system, if the election is close and votes must be recounted, the recounts will take place in only a few jurisdictions. If the popular vote determined the winner, votes might have to be recounted in every corner of the country. Finally, we have a federal system in this country, and the Electoral College reflects that. If you leave aside Clinton's huge margin in California, Trump won the popular vote in the rest of the country in 2016. Why should we let California choose the president?

Let's Bypass the Electoral College

In contrast, supporters of the interstate compact say that it is unfair and undemocratic for a president to be elected without winning the popular vote. Further, the existing system tends to disenfranchise voters in much of the nation. Presidential candidates have little reason to campaign in states where they are certain either to win or to lose by a large margin. During recent presidential elections, major campaigns took place in only a few swing states. If presidential candidates had to win the popular vote, they would be forced to campaign everywhere that they could find persuadable voters, regardless of state lines. And as to the California argument just made, you can change the outcome of any election if you don't count the votes of one or more states. Exactly when did California cease to be part of the Union?

■ For Critical Analysis

All of the states that have recently joined the interstate compact are solidly Democratic. Why might that be?

queen or king. In much of Europe, the head of state is a relatively powerless president, and the prime minister is the chief executive. But in the United States, the president is both chief executive and head of state.

Some observers of the American political system believe that having the president serve as both the chief executive and the head of state limits the time available to do "real" work. Most presidents have not agreed with this conclusion, however—particularly those presidents who have skillfully blended these two roles with their role as politician. Being head of state gives the president much public exposure. When that exposure is positive, it helps the president deal with Congress over proposed legislation and increases the chances of being reelected—or getting the candidates of the president's party elected.

Chief Executive

According to the Constitution, "The executive Power shall be vested in a President of the United States of America. … [H]e may require the Opinion, in writing, of the principal Officer in each of the executive Departments, upon any Subject relating to the Duties of their respective Offices … and he shall nominate, and by and with the Advice and Consent of the Senate, shall appoint … Officers of the United States. … [H]e shall take Care that the Laws be faithfully executed." As **chief executive**, the president is constitutionally bound to enforce the acts of Congress, the judgments of federal courts, and treaties signed by the United States.

The Powers of Appointment and Removal. To assist in the various tasks of the chief executive, the president has a federal bureaucracy, which currently consists of 2.1 million federal civilian employees, not counting the U.S. Postal Service (516,600 career employees). You might think that the president, as head of the largest bureaucracy in the United States, wields enormous power.

The president, however, only nominally runs the executive branch. Most government positions are filled by **civil service** employees, who generally gain government employment through a merit system rather than presidential appointment. Therefore, even though the president has important **appointment power**, that power is limited to cabinet and subcabinet jobs, federal judgeships, agency heads, and several thousand lesser jobs—about nine thousand positions in total. This means that most of the 2.9 million civilian employees of the executive branch (USPS included) owe no political allegiance to the president. They are more likely to owe loyalty to congressional committees or to interest groups representing the sector of society that they serve.

The president's power to remove from office those officials who are not doing a good job or who do not agree with the president is not explicitly granted by the Constitution and has been limited. In 1926, however, a Supreme Court decision prevented Congress from interfering with the president's ability to fire those executive-branch officials whom the president had appointed with Senate approval.[1]

Harry Truman spoke candidly of the difficulties a president faces in trying to control the executive bureaucracy. On leaving office, he referred to the problems that Dwight Eisenhower (1953–61), as a former general of the army, was going to have: "He'll sit here and he'll say do this! do that! and nothing will happen. Poor Ike—it won't be a bit like the Army. He'll find it very frustrating."[2]

The Power to Grant Reprieves and Pardons. Section 2 of Article II of the Constitution gives the president the power to grant **reprieves**, **pardons**, and **commutations** of sentence for offenses against the United States except in cases of impeachment. All pardons are administered by the Office of the Pardon Attorney in the Department of Justice. Note that the pardon power extends only to offenses against the United States, and not individual states. The president cannot pardon someone convicted in a state court.

The Supreme Court upheld the president's power to grant pardons, reprieves, and commutations in a 1925 case concerning a pardon granted by the president to an individual convicted of contempt of court. A federal circuit court had contended that only judges had

Chief Executive
The role of the president as head of the executive branch of the government.

Civil Service
A collective term for employees of the government. Generally, civil service is understood to apply to all those who gain government employment through a merit system.

Appointment Power
The president's authority to fill a government office or position.

Reprieves
Formal postponements of the execution of a sentence imposed by a court of law.

Pardons
A release from the punishment for, or legal consequences of, a crime. A pardon can be granted by the president before or after a conviction.

Commutations
A reduction in the length of the sentence of someone convicted of a crime. Commutation does not overturn the conviction itself.

---

1. *Meyers v. United States*, 272 U.S. 52 (1926).
2. Quoted in Richard E. Neustadt, *Presidential Power: The Politics of Leadership* (New York: Wiley, 1960), p. 9. Note that Truman may not have considered the amount of politics involved in decision making in the upper ranks of the army.

the authority to convict individuals for contempt of court when court orders were violated and that the courts should be free from interference by the executive branch. The Supreme Court simply stated that the president could grant reprieves or pardons for all offenses "either before trial, during trial, or after trial, by individuals, or by classes, conditionally or absolutely, and this without modification or regulation by Congress."[3]

Commander in Chief

The president, according to the Constitution, "shall be Commander in Chief of the Army and Navy of the United States, and of the Militia of the several States, when called into the actual Service of the United States." In other words, the armed forces are under civilian, rather than military, control.

Wartime Powers. Those who wrote the Constitution had George Washington (1789–97) in mind when they made the president the **commander in chief**. Presidents as commanders in chief have wielded dramatic power.

Commander in Chief
The role of the president as supreme commander of the military forces of the United States and of the state National Guard units when they are called into federal service.

- Harry Truman made the fateful decision to drop atomic bombs on Hiroshima and Nagasaki in 1945 with the goal of forcing Japan to surrender and thus bring World War II to an end.
  - Lyndon Johnson (1963–69) ordered bombing missions against North Vietnam in the 1960s, and he personally selected some of the targets.
  - Richard Nixon decided to invade Cambodia in 1970.
  - Ronald Reagan sent troops to Lebanon and Grenada in 1983 and ordered U.S. fighter planes to attack Libya in 1986.
  - George H.W. Bush (1989–93) sent troops to Panama in 1989 and to the Middle East in 1990.
  - Bill Clinton sent troops to Haiti in 1994 and to Bosnia in 1995, ordered missile attacks on alleged terrorist bases in 1998, and sent American planes to bomb Serbia in 1999.
  - George W. Bush (2001–2009) ordered the invasion of Afghanistan in 2002 and of Iraq in 2003.
  - Barack Obama ordered more troops into Afghanistan in 2009, authorized air strikes in Libya in 2011, and increased U.S. troop strength in Iraq in an attempt to combat ISIS in 2014–2016.
  - Donald Trump authorized a variety of military actions in Iraq and Syria in 2019 and 2020.
  - Joe Biden authorized an increase in U.S. troops in NATO nations during the Russian invasion of Ukraine in 2022.

    The president is the ultimate decision maker in military matters. Everywhere the president goes, so too goes the "football"—a briefcase filled with all of the codes necessary to order a nuclear attack. Only the president has the power to order the use of nuclear force.

    As commander in chief, the president exercises more authority than in any other role. Constitutionally, Congress has the sole power to declare war, but the president can send the armed forces into situations that are certainly the equivalent of war. Harry Truman

George Skadding/The LIFE Picture Collection/Getty Images

Image 10.3 President Harry Truman (at left), stands with General Dwight Eisenhower in 1951. A year later, Eisenhower successfully ran for president. ▶ Why might a general make a good president?

---

3. Ex parte *Grossman*, 267 U.S. 87 (1925).

dispatched troops to Korea in 1950. Johnson and Nixon waged an undeclared war in South-east Asia, where more than 58,000 Americans were killed and 300,000 were wounded. In neither of these situations had Congress declared war.

The War Powers Resolution. In an attempt to gain more control over such military activities, in 1973 Congress passed the **War Powers Resolution** over President Nixon's veto. The act requires that the president consult with Congress when sending American forces into action. Once they are sent, the president must report to Congress within forty-eight hours. Unless Congress approves the use of troops within sixty days or extends the sixty-day time limit, the forces must be withdrawn. In spite of the War Powers Resolution, the effective powers of the president as commander in chief are more extensive today than they were in the past.

Chief Diplomat

The Constitution gives the president the power to recognize foreign governments and to make treaties with the **advice and consent** of the Senate. The president also nominates U.S. ambassadors to other countries. As **chief diplomat**, the president dominates American foreign policy, a role that has been supported many times by the Supreme Court.

Diplomatic Recognition. An important power of the president as chief diplomat is that of **diplomatic recognition**, or the power to recognize—or refuse to recognize—foreign governments as legitimate. In the role of ceremonial head of state, the president has always received foreign diplomats. In modern times, the simple act of receiving a foreign diplomat has been equivalent to accrediting the diplomat and officially recognizing their governments. Such recognition of the legitimacy of another country's government is a prerequisite to diplomatic relations or treaties between that country and the United States.

Deciding when to recognize a foreign power is not always simple. The United States, for example, did not recognize the Soviet Union until 1933—sixteen years after the Russian Revolution of 1917. All attempts to reverse the effects of that revolution—including military invasion of Russia and diplomatic isolation—proved futile. Only then did Franklin D. Roosevelt (1933–45) extend recognition to the Soviet government. In December 1978, long after the Communist victory in China in 1949, President Jimmy Carter (1977–81) granted official recognition to the People's Republic of China.[4]

Proposal and Ratification of Treaties. The president has the sole power to negotiate treaties with other nations. These treaties must be presented to the Senate. A two-thirds vote in the Senate is required for approval, or ratification. After ratification, the president can approve the treaty as adopted by the Senate. Approval poses a problem when the Senate has added substantive amendments or reservations to a treaty, particularly when such changes may require reopening negotiations with the other signatory governments. Sometimes, a president may decide to withdraw a treaty if the senatorial changes are too extensive—as Woodrow Wilson (1913–21) did with the Versailles Treaty in 1919 that concluded World War I. Wilson believed that the senatorial reservations would weaken the treaty so much that it would be ineffective.

AP Images/Barry Thumma

Image 10.4 President George H.W. Bush meets with the foreign minister of Saudi Arabia in 1990. George H.W. Bush was the father of George W. Bush, making the Bush family a true political dynasty. ▶ Is it common for the children of elected officials to go into politics?

---

4. The Nixon administration first encouraged new relations with the People's Republic of China by allowing a cultural exchange of table tennis teams. Nixon subsequently traveled to China.

Ratifying a treaty may be a difficult process, but revoking a treaty appears to be easier. The Constitution says nothing about how a treaty can be terminated, and on at least two occasions presidents have revoked treaties unilaterally, without the approval of Congress. One of these terminations was challenged by a lawsuit. Ultimately, the Supreme Court refused to overrule the president's decision.[5]

Executive Agreements. Presidential power in foreign affairs is enhanced greatly by the use of **executive agreements** made between the president and other heads of state. Such agreements do not require Senate approval, although the House and Senate may refuse to appropriate the funds necessary to implement them. Whereas treaties are normally binding on succeeding administrations, executive agreements require each new president's consent to remain in effect.

Among the advantages of executive agreements are speed and secrecy. The former is essential during a crisis. The latter is important when the administration fears that open senatorial debate may be detrimental to the best interests of the United States or to the interests of the president.[6] There have been far more executive agreements (about nine thousand) than treaties (about thirteen hundred). Many executive agreements contain secret provisions calling for American military assistance or other support.

The Constitution makes no mention—explicit or implicit—of executive agreements. The Supreme Court, however, has given executive agreements the same legal weight as formal treaties.[7] This conclusion follows from earlier cases in which the Court found the president's powers in the international realm to be "plenary and exclusive." Executive agreements are clearly an attractive way for a president to bypass Congress when making foreign policy.

President Obama used an executive agreement when endorsing the nuclear arms deal with Iran and five other world powers in 2015. The problem with using executive agreements in this way was exposed when President Trump pulled the United States out of the deal in 2018. President Biden did not submit a modified nuclear arms deal with Iran to the Senate in 2022. Indeed, as of that summer, no agreement had been reached. Even if it does become reality, the next Republican president can easily pull the United States out of that deal, unless of course the deal is approved as a treaty by the Senate.

Chief Legislator

Constitutionally, presidents must recommend to Congress legislation that they judge necessary and expedient. Not all presidents have wielded their power as **chief legislator** in the same manner. Some presidents have been almost completely unsuccessful in getting their legislative programs implemented by Congress. Presidents Franklin D. Roosevelt and Lyndon Johnson, however, saw much of their proposed legislation put into effect.

Creating the Congressional Agenda. In modern times, the president has played a dominant role in creating the congressional agenda. In the president's annual **State of the Union message,** which is required by the Constitution (Article II, Section 3) and is usually given in late January shortly after Congress reconvenes, the president presents a legislative program. The message gives a broad, comprehensive view of what the president wishes the

Executive Agreements
International agreements made by the president, without senatorial ratification, with the head of a foreign state.

Chief Legislator
The role of the president in influencing the making of laws.

State of the Union Message
An annual message to Congress in which the president proposes a legislative program. The message is addressed not only to Congress but also to the American people and to the world.

---

5. *Goldwater v. Carter*, 444 U.S. 996 (1979).
6. The Case Act of 1972 requires that all executive agreements be transmitted to Congress within sixty days after taking effect. Secret agreements are transmitted to the foreign relations committees as classified information.
7. *United States v. Belmont*, 301 U.S. 324 (1937); and *United States v. Pink*, 315 U.S. 203 (1942).

legislature to accomplish during its session. It is as much a message to the American people and to the world as it is to Congress.

Since 1913, the president has delivered the State of the Union message in a formal address to Congress. Today, this address is one of the great ceremonies of American governance, and many customs have grown up around it. For example, one cabinet member, the "designated survivor," stays away to ensure that the country will always have a president even if someone manages to blow up the Capitol building. Everyone gives the president an initial standing ovation out of respect for the office, but this applause does not necessarily represent support for the individual who holds the office. During the speech, senators and House members either applaud or remain silent to indicate their opinion of the policies that the president announces.

Getting Legislation Passed. The president can propose legislation, but Congress is not required to pass—or even introduce—any of the administration's bills. How, then, does the president get those proposals made into law? One way is by exercising the power of persuasion. The president writes to, telephones, and meets with various congressional leaders. The president makes public announcements to influence public opinion. Finally, as head of a party, the president exercises leadership over the party's members in Congress. A president whose party holds a majority in both chambers of Congress usually has an easier time getting legislation passed than does a president who faces a hostile Congress.

Saying No to Legislation—the Veto. The president has the power to say no to legislation through use of the veto, by which the White House returns a bill unsigned to Congress with a **veto message** attached.[8] Because the Constitution requires that every bill passed by the House and the Senate be sent to the president before it becomes law, the president must act on each bill:

1. If the bill is signed, it becomes law.
2. If the bill is not sent back to Congress after ten congressional working days, it becomes law without the president's signature.
3. The president can reject the bill and send it back to Congress with a veto message setting forth objections. Congress then can change the bill, hoping to secure presidential approval, and repass it. Or Congress can simply reject the president's objections by overriding the veto with a two-thirds roll-call vote of the members present in both the House and the Senate.
4. If the president refuses to sign the bill and Congress adjourns within ten working days after the bill has been submitted to the president, the bill is killed for that session of Congress. This is called a **pocket veto**. If Congress wishes the bill to be reconsidered, the bill must be reintroduced during the following session.

Presidents employed the veto power infrequently until after the Civil War, but it has been used with increasing vigor since then. Presidents George W. Bush, Barack Obama, Donald Trump, and Joe Biden, however, made little or no use of the veto during the periods when their parties controlled Congress.

Congress's Power to Override Presidential Vetoes. A veto is a clear-cut indication of the president's dissatisfaction with congressional legislation. Congress, however, can override a presidential veto, although it rarely exercises this power. Consider that two-thirds of the

Veto Message
The president's formal explanation of a veto, which accompanies the vetoed legislation when it is returned to Congress.

Pocket Veto
A special veto exercised by the chief executive after a legislative body has adjourned. Bills not signed by the chief executive die after a specified period of time.

8. Veto in Latin means "I forbid."

members of each chamber who are present must vote to override the president's veto in a roll-call vote. This means that if only one-third plus one of the members voting in one of the chambers of Congress do not agree to override the veto, the veto holds. In American history, only about 4 percent of all vetoes have been overridden.

Party Chief and Politician

Presidents are by no means above political partisanship, and one of their many roles is that of chief of party. Although the Constitution says nothing about the function of the president within a political party (the mere concept of political parties was abhorrent to most of the authors of the Constitution), today presidents are the actual leaders of their parties.

The President as Chief of Party. As party leader, the president chooses the national committee chairperson and can try to discipline party members who fail to support presidential policies. One way of exerting political power within the party is through **patronage**—rewarding the faithful by appointing them to government, or public, jobs. This power was more extensive in the past, before the establishment of the civil service in 1883, but the president still retains important patronage power. As we noted earlier, the president can appoint several thousand individuals to jobs in the cabinet, the White House, and the federal regulatory agencies.

Patronage
The practice of rewarding faithful party workers and followers with government employment and contracts.

Perhaps the most important partisan role that the president has played in the late 1900s and early 2000s has been that of fundraiser. The president is able to raise large sums for the party through appearances at dinners, speaking engagements, and other social occasions. President Clinton may have raised more than half a billion dollars for the Democratic Party during his two terms. President Bush was even more successful than Clinton. Barack Obama and Donald Trump carried on this fundraising tradition. Joe Biden initially appeared to be a less successful fundraiser while president.

Presidents have a number of other ways of exerting influence as party chief. The president may make it known that a particular congressperson's choice for federal judge will not be appointed unless that member of Congress is more supportive of the president's legislative program. The president may agree to campaign for a particular program or for a particular candidate. Presidents also reward loyal members of Congress with support for the funding of local projects, tax breaks for regional industries, and other forms of "pork."

Presidential Constituencies. Presidents have many constituencies. In principle, they are beholden to the entire electorate—the public of the United States—even those who did not vote. Presidents are certainly beholden to their party, because its members helped to put them in office. The president's constituencies also include members of the opposing party whose cooperation the president needs. Finally, the president must take into consideration a constituency that has come to be called the Washington community, also known as those "inside the beltway."[9] This community consists of individuals who—whether in or out of political office—are intimately familiar with the workings of government, thrive on gossip, and measure daily the political power of the president.

Public Approval. All of these constituencies are impressed by presidents who maintain a high level of public approval, partly because doing so is very difficult to accomplish. Presidential popularity, as measured by national polls, gives the president an extra political

---

9. Here, the beltway refers to I-495, the interstate highway that completely encircles the District of Columbia as well as many close-in Washington suburbs.

resource to use in persuading legislators to pass legislation. A president who suffers a dramatic loss of popularity will have trouble getting legislation through Congress. In such circumstances, a president can even fail to be reelected. That was the fate of President Jimmy Carter, who lost to Ronald Reagan after a disastrous collapse in popular support.

Recent Presidents and the Public Opinion Polls. Immediately after 9/11, President George W. Bush had the highest job-approval ratings ever recorded. By the time he left office, however, only 25 percent of the public approved of his performance as president.

Obama's popularity figures were also very high when he took office. Some of that initial popularity came from Republicans, however, and could not survive the partisan battles that began in 2009. President Trump's approval ratings, which fell as low as 37 percent in his first year of office, were around 42 percent in 2018 and 2019. Such low numbers were a problem for the Republicans in the run-up to the 2020 elections. Joe Biden's popularity after his first year in office was only around 38 percent. Some commentators argued at that time that his low approval rating was because he had embraced too many progressive policies. Others pointed out that high gas prices and rising inflation reduced Biden's popularity.

Samuel Corum/Anadolu Agency/Getty Images

Image 10.5 President Barack Obama at one of his last news conferences. Obama was more popular at the end of his presidency than he had been for much of his time in office. ▶ Why might he have left office on a high note?

"Going Public." Since the early 1900s, presidents have spoken more to the public and less to Congress. In the 1800s, only 7 percent of presidential speeches were addressed to the public. Since 1900, 50 percent have been addressed to the public. Presidents frequently go over the heads of Congress and the political elites, taking their cases directly to the people.

This strategy, dubbed "going public," gives the president additional power through the ability to persuade and manipulate public opinion. By identifying their own positions so clearly, presidents can weaken the legislators' positions. In times when the major political parties are highly polarized, however, the possibility of compromise with the opposition party may actually be reduced if the president openly takes a strong position. Legislation that might have won bipartisan support can fail if it comes to be seen as a partisan issue. As a result, going public is not as effective as it once was.

Presidential Powers

≫ LO 10-3: Describe some of the special powers of the president, and tell how a president can be removed from office.

Presidents have at their disposal a variety of special powers and privileges not available in the other branches of the U.S. government. Most of the powers of the president discussed earlier in this chapter in the section on the roles of the president are called **constitutional powers**, because their basis lies in the Constitution. In addition, Congress has established by law, or statute, numerous other presidential powers—such as the ability to declare national emergencies. These are called **statutory powers**. Both constitutional and statutory powers have been labeled the **expressed powers** of the president, because they are expressly written into the Constitution or into law.

Constitutional Powers
Powers vested in the president by Article II of the Constitution.

Statutory Powers
Powers created for the president through laws enacted by Congress.

Expressed Powers
Powers of the president that are expressly written into the Constitution or into statutory law.

National Archives

Image 10.6 Secretary of State Colin Powell, President George W. Bush, and Vice President Dick Cheney at a National Security Council meeting held the day after the 9/11 terrorist attacks. ▶ What effect did that crisis have on the powers of the president?

Inherent Powers
Powers of the president derived from the statements in the Constitution that "the executive Power shall be vested in a President" and that the president should "take Care that the Laws be faithfully executed."

Emergency Powers
An inherent power exercised by the president during a period of national crisis.

Presidents also have what have come to be known as **inherent powers**. These depend on the statements in the Constitution that "the executive Power shall be vested in a President" and that the president should "take Care that the Laws be faithfully executed." The most common example of inherent powers is those emergency powers invoked by the president during wartime. Franklin D. Roosevelt, for example, used his inherent powers to move Japanese Americans living on the West Coast into internment camps for the duration of World War II. President George W. Bush often justified expanding the powers of the presidency by saying that such powers were necessary to fight the war on terrorism.

Emergency Powers

If you read the Constitution, you will find no mention of the additional powers that the executive office may exercise during national emergencies. Indeed, the Supreme Court has stated that an "emergency does not create power."[10] But it is clear that presidents have made strong use of their inherent powers during times of emergency, particularly in the realm of foreign affairs.

The **emergency powers** of the president were first enunciated in the Supreme Court's decision in *United States v. Curtiss-Wright Export Corp.*[11] In that case, President Franklin Roosevelt, without authorization by Congress, ordered an embargo on the shipment of weapons to two warring South American countries. The Court recognized that the president may exercise inherent powers in foreign affairs and that the national government has primacy in these affairs.

Examples of emergency powers are abundant, coinciding with crises in domestic and foreign affairs. Abraham Lincoln suspended certain civil liberties at the beginning of the Civil War (1861–65) and called the state militias into national service. These actions and his subsequent governance of conquered areas—and even of areas of northern states—were justified by claims that they were essential to preserve the Union. Franklin Roosevelt declared an "unlimited national emergency" following the fall of France in World War II (1939–45) and took steps to ready the federal budget and the economy for war.

President Harry Truman authorized the federal seizure of steel plants and their operation by the national government in 1952 during the Korean War. Truman claimed that he was using his inherent emergency power as chief executive and commander in chief to safeguard the nation's security, as an ongoing steel mill strike threatened the supply of weapons to the armed forces. The Supreme Court did not agree, holding that the president had no authority under the Constitution to seize private property or to legislate such action.[12] According to legal scholars, this was the first time a limit had been placed on the exercise of the president's emergency powers.

---

10. *Home Building and Loan Association v. Blaisdell*, 290 U.S. 398 (1934).
11. 299 U.S. 304 (1936).
12. *Youngstown Sheet and Tube Co. v. Sawyer*, 343 U.S. 579 (1952).

Executive Orders

Congress allows the president (as well as administrative agencies) to issue **executive orders** that have the force of law. These executive orders can do the following: (1) enforce legislative statutes, (2) enforce the Constitution or treaties with foreign nations, and (3) establish or modify rules and practices of executive administrative agencies.

An executive order, then, represents the president's legislative power. The only apparent requirement is that under the Administrative Procedure Act of 1946, all executive orders must be published in the *Federal Register*, a daily publication of the U.S. government. Executive orders have been used to implement national affirmative action regulations, to restructure the White House bureaucracy, and to establish military tribunals for suspected terrorists. In recent years, presidents have also accomplished such goals with presidential memoranda. In practice, these are identical to executive orders except for a politically motivated change in name. They do not have to be numbered nor do they have to be published.

Executive orders can be controversial. President Obama, recognizing that he could expect little from the Republicans in Congress, repeatedly used executive orders in an attempt to implement his policies. By the time Obama left office, however, some of his most controversial orders were tied up in the courts. One was an order deferring the deportation of several million unauthorized immigrants, most of whom had children who are citizens. Regardless of whether the courts agreed that Obama had a right to issue this order, President Trump planned to revoke it. Trump's action revealed a problem with executive orders—they can be reversed by the next president. Reversing legislation passed by Congress and signed by the president is much harder.

As stated previously, President Biden started issuing executive orders and presidential memoranda on his first day in office. As of March 2, 2022, he had signed 81 executive orders, 60 presidential memoranda, 2,007 proclamations, and 40 notices. Here some examples of Biden's executive orders and memoranda:

- Halted construction of the southern border wall
- Canceled the Keystone XL pipeline
- Extended the pause on student loan payments
- Required mask wearing in airports, on trains, and airplanes due to the COVID-19 pandemic
- Revoked a Trump order creating an industry-led apprenticeship program
- Raised the minimum wage of federal contract workers to $15 per hour

Executive Privilege

Another inherent executive power that has been claimed by presidents concerns the right of the president and the president's executive officials to withhold information from, or refuse to appear before, Congress or the courts. This is called **executive privilege**, and it relies on the constitutional separation of powers for its basis.

Invoking Executive Privilege. Presidents have frequently invoked executive privilege to avoid having to disclose information to Congress about actions of the executive branch. Executive privilege rests on the assumption that a certain degree of secrecy is essential to national security. Critics of executive privilege believe that it can be used to shield from public scrutiny actions of the executive branch that should be open to Congress and to the American citizenry.

Executive Orders
Rules or regulations issued by the president that have the effect of law.

Federal Register
A daily publication of the U.S. government that prints executive orders, rules, and regulations.

Executive Privilege
The right of executive officials to withhold information from, or to refuse to appear before, a legislative committee or a court.

Limiting Executive Privilege. Limits to executive privilege went untested until the Watergate affair in the early 1970s. Five men had broken into the headquarters of the Democratic National Committee and were caught searching for documents that might damage the candidacy of the Democratic nominee, George McGovern. Later investigation showed that the break-in had been planned by members of Richard Nixon's campaign committee and that Nixon and his closest advisers had devised a strategy for impeding the investigation of the crime. After it became known that all conversations held in the Oval Office had been recorded on a secret system, Nixon was ordered to turn over the tapes to the special prosecutor in charge of the investigation.

Nixon refused to do so, claiming executive privilege. He argued that "no president could function if the private papers of his office, prepared by his personal staff, were open to public scrutiny." In 1974, in one of the Supreme Court's most famous cases, *United States v. Nixon*, the justices unanimously ruled that Nixon had to hand over the tapes.[13] The Court held that executive privilege could not be used to prevent evidence from being heard in criminal proceedings.

Trump's Claim of "Absolute Immunity." During its many investigations of the Trump administration in 2019, the Democratic House attempted to subpoena—require the appearance—of a number of Trump staff members. Some of the staff did in fact appear, but others refused. The White House itself claimed that advisers who work with the president have "absolute immunity" from congressional subpoena on matters related to their official duties. Such a doctrine would be broader than the existing principle of executive privilege. Earlier presidents had made such claims, but the issue was never settled in court.

Signing Statements

Are presidents allowed to refuse to enforce certain parts of legislation if they believe that they are unconstitutional? This question came to the forefront in recent years because of President George W. Bush's extensive use of signing statements. A **signing statement** is a written declaration that a president may make when signing a bill into law regarding the law's enforcement.

Signing Statement
A written declaration that the president may make when signing a bill into law. It may contain instructions to the bureaucracy on how to administer the law or point to sections of the law that the president considers unconstitutional or contrary to national security interests.

Presidents have been using such statements for decades, but President Bush used 161 statements to invalidate more than one thousand provisions of federal law. No previous president used signing statements to make such sweeping claims on behalf of presidential power. Earlier presidents often employed statements to serve notice that parts of bills might be unconstitutional, but they were just as likely to issue statements that were purely rhetorical. That is, statements might praise Congress and the measure just passed—or denounce the opposition party.

During his first presidential campaign, Barack Obama criticized Bush's use of signing statements. As president, Obama's statements were more in line with tradition. The same was true of President Trump. At least during the first two years of the Biden administration, the number of signing statements issued were in line with the historical average. In Biden's first year in office, he issued three signing statements.

Abuses of Executive Power and Impeachment

Presidents normally leave office in one of two ways. It may be that their first term has expired and they have not sought (or won) reelection. They may leave because, having served two full terms, they are not allowed to be elected for a third term (owing to the

---

13. 318 U.S. 683 (1974).

Twenty-second Amendment, passed in 1951). Eight presidents have died in office. But there is still another way for a president to leave office—by **impeachment** and conviction. Articles I and II of the Constitution authorize the House and Senate to remove the president, the vice president, or other civil officers of the United States for committing "Treason, Bribery, or other high Crimes and Misdemeanors." According to the Constitution, the impeachment process begins in the House, which impeaches (accuses) the federal officer involved. If the House votes to impeach the officer, it draws up articles of impeachment and submits them to the Senate, which conducts the actual trial.

Presidents Andrew Johnson and Richard Nixon. In the history of the United States, no president has ever actually been impeached and also convicted—and thus removed from office—by means of this process. President Andrew Johnson (1865–69), who succeeded to the office after the assassination of Abraham Lincoln, was impeached by the House but acquitted by the Senate. More than a century later, the House Judiciary Committee approved articles of impeachment against President Richard Nixon for his involvement in the cover-up of the Watergate break-in of 1972. Informed by members of his own party that he had no hope of surviving the trial in the Senate, Nixon resigned on August 9, 1974, before the full House voted on the articles. Nixon is the only president to have resigned from office.

President Bill Clinton. The second president to be impeached by the House but not convicted by the Senate was President Bill Clinton. In 1998, the Republican House approved two charges against Clinton: lying to a grand jury about his affair with White House intern Monica Lewinsky and obstruction of justice. The articles of impeachment were then sent to the Senate, which acquitted Clinton. The attempt to remove Clinton was very unpopular, although the allegations against him did damage his popularity as well. Part of the problem for Clinton's Republican opponents was that the charges against the president essentially boiled down to his lying about sex. As one observer put it, "Everyone lies about sex." Of course, not everyone lies about sex when under oath.

President Trump and the Mueller Investigation. The FBI, under director James Comey, sought to investigate communications between the Russians and former Trump national security adviser Michael Flynn. In May 2017, Trump fired Comey. In the resulting storm of publicity, Deputy Attorney General Rod Rosenstein appointed former FBI director Robert Mueller as special counsel to oversee the Russia investigation.[14] (Attorney General Jeff Sessions had already recused, or removed, himself from participation in the investigation because of his own contacts with the Russians.)

Impeachment
An action by the House of Representatives to accuse the president, vice president, or other civil officers of the United States of committing "Treason, Bribery, or other high Crimes and Misdemeanors."

Richard Ellis / Alamy Stock Photo

Image 10.7 President Bill Clinton announces the first federal budget surplus in twenty-nine years at the White House in 1998. The economy boomed while Clinton was president. ▶ What effect does the state of the economy have on a president's popularity?

---

14. Note that Republicans in general were suspicious of the Russian investigation against Trump while he was a candidate and while he was president. A special counsel, John Durham, was appointed to investigate charges that Hillary Clinton's campaign might have paid for some of the information used in pursuing Trump's campaign associates. Durham issued indictments against several Democrats who worked for the Clinton campaign. Clinton campaign lawyer Michael Sussmann was charged with lying to the FBI but was acquitted in a jury trial.

After a two-year investigation, the Mueller Report was presented to the American and indeed the world public. Its conclusion was that no credible evidence existed for the accusations against Donald Trump with respect to his involvement with Russian President Vladimir Putin or his associates. Thus, Trump's election was most likely unrelated to any of Putin's purported influence.

The First Impeachment of President Trump. Later, there were allegations that Trump had tried to pressure the president of Ukraine into announcing an investigation that could be used against former vice president Joe Biden, Trump's likely opponent in the 2020 elections. Trump was impeached in December 2019 by a near-party-line vote in the House. The two charges were abuse of power and obstruction of Congress. The Senate acquitted Trump, again on a near-party-line vote, in February 2020.

The Second Impeachment of President Trump. After a fiery speech by Donald Trump to thousands of supporters gathered in Washington, D.C., on January 6, many of those supporters marched to the Capitol building. During a violent altercation with Capitol police, some protesters broke in through windows, others were let in by some members of the Capitol police force. Business at the Capitol was disrupted for three hours, and most of that business had to do with confirming the electoral votes for Joe Biden.

One week before Trump left office, the House voted to impeach him on one count—incitement to insurrection. A month later, when Trump was already a private citizen, the Senate acquitted him.

The Executive Organization

> **LO 10-4:** Explain the organization of the executive branch and, in particular, the executive office of the president.

Gone are the days when presidents answered their own mail, as George Washington did. It was not until 1857 that Congress authorized a private secretary for the president, to be paid by the federal government. Woodrow Wilson typed most of his correspondence, even though he did have several secretaries. At the beginning of Franklin Roosevelt's long tenure in the White House, the entire staff consisted of thirty-seven employees. With the New Deal and World War II, however, the presidential staff became a sizable organization.

The Cabinet

Although the Constitution does not include the word cabinet, it does state that the president "may require the Opinion, in writing, of the principal Officer in each of the executive Departments." Since the time of George Washington, these officers have formed an advisory group, or **cabinet**, to which the president may turn for counsel.

Cabinet
An advisory group selected by the president to aid in making decisions. The cabinet includes the heads of fifteen executive departments and others named by the president.

Members of the Cabinet. Originally, the cabinet consisted of only four officials—the secretaries of state, treasury, and war and the attorney general. Today, the cabinet numbers fourteen department secretaries and the attorney general. The cabinet may include others as well. Presidents at their discretion can, for example, ascribe cabinet rank to the vice president, the head of the Office of Management and Budget, the national security adviser, or additional officials. Under President Joe Biden, the additional members of the cabinet are the following:

- The administrator of the Environmental Protection Agency
- The administrator of the Small Business Administration
- The chair of the Council of Economic Advisors
- The director of National Intelligence
- The U.S. ambassador to the United Nations
- The U.S. trade representative
- The vice president
- The White House chief of staff

When Biden took over the presidency, he decided not to include the director of the Central Intelligence Agency in his cabinet.

Often, a president will use a **kitchen cabinet** to replace the formal cabinet as a major source of advice. The term kitchen cabinet originated during the presidency of Andrew Jackson (1829–37), who relied on the counsel of close friends who allegedly met with him in the kitchen of the White House. A kitchen cabinet is a very informal group of advisers. Usually, they are friends with whom the president worked before being elected.

Kitchen Cabinet
The informal advisers to the president.

Presidential Use of Cabinets. Because neither the Constitution nor statutory law requires the president to consult with the cabinet, its use is purely discretionary. Some presidents have relied on the counsel of their cabinets more than others. Dwight Eisenhower was used to the team approach to solving problems from his experience as supreme allied commander during World War II, and therefore he frequently turned to his cabinet for advice on a wide range of issues. More often, presidents have solicited the opinions of their cabinets and then have done what they wanted to do. Lincoln supposedly said—after a cabinet meeting in which a vote was seven nays against his one aye—"Seven nays and one aye; the ayes have it."

It is not surprising that presidents tend to disregard their cabinet members' advice. Often, the departmental heads are more responsive to the wishes of their own staffs or to their own political ambitions than they are to the president. They may be more concerned with obtaining resources for their departments than with achieving the president's goals. So, there is often a conflict of interest between presidents and their cabinet members.

The Executive Office of the President

When President Franklin Roosevelt appointed a special committee on administrative management, he knew that the committee would conclude that the president needed help. Indeed, the committee proposed a major reorganization of the executive branch. Congress did not approve the entire reorganization, but it did create the **Executive Office of the President (EOP)** to provide staff assistance for the chief executive and to help coordinate the executive bureaucracy. Since that time, a number of agencies have been created within the EOP to supply the president with advice and staff members. Presidents reorganize the EOP and the White House Office constantly, and any table of organization is therefore temporary. As of 2023, the EOP agencies under Joe Biden were the following:

Executive Office of the President (EOP)
An organization established by President Franklin Roosevelt to assist the president in carrying out major duties.

- Council of Economic Advisers
- Council on Environmental Quality
- Executive Residence
- National Security Council (NSC)

- Office of Administration
- Office of Management and Budget
- Office of National Drug Control Policy
- Office of Science and Technology Policy
- Office of the United States Trade Representative
- Office of the Vice President
- White House Office

White House Office
The personal office of the president, which tends to presidential political needs and manages the media.

The White House Office. The **White House Office** includes most of the key personal and political advisers to the president. Among the jobs held by these aides are those of secretary, press secretary, appointments secretary, and legal counsel to the president. Often, the individuals who hold these positions are recruited from the president's campaign staff. Their duties—mainly protecting the president's political interests—are similar to campaign functions. In 2023, the White House Office was made up of the following units:

- Domestic Policy Council
- National Security Adviser
- National Economic Council
- Office of Cabinet Affairs
- Office of the Chief of Staff
- Office of Communications
- Office of Digital Strategy
- Office of the First Lady
- Office of Public Engagement and Intergovernmental Affairs
- Office of Legislative Affairs
- Office of Management and Administration
- Office of Presidential Personnel
- Office of Scheduling and Advance
- Office of the Staff Secretary
- Office of the United States Trade Representative
- Office of the White House Counsel
- Oval Office Operations

Chief of Staff
The person who is named to direct the White House Office and advise the president.

Key White House Staff. In all recent administrations, one member of the White House Office has been named **chief of staff**. This person, who is responsible for coordinating the office, is also one of the president's chief advisers. In addition to civilian advisers, the president is supported by a large number of military personnel, who are organized under the White House Military Office. These members of the military provide communications, transportation, medical care, and food services to the president and the White House staff.

Office of Management and Budget (OMB)
A division of the Executive Office of the President. The OMB assists the president in preparing the annual budget, clearing and coordinating departmental agency budgets, and supervising the administration of the federal budget.

The Office of Management and Budget. The **Office of Management and Budget (OMB)** was originally the Bureau of the Budget, which was created in 1921 within the Department of the Treasury. Recognizing the importance of this agency, Franklin Roosevelt moved it into the White House Office in 1939. Richard Nixon reorganized the Bureau of the Budget in 1970 and changed its name to reflect its new managerial function. It is headed by a director, who drafts the annual federal budget that the president presents to Congress each January for approval.

In principle, the director of the OMB has broad fiscal powers in planning and estimating various parts of the federal budget, because all agencies must submit their proposed budget to the OMB for approval. In reality, it is not so clear that the OMB truly can affect the greater scope of the federal budget. The OMB may be more important as a clearinghouse for legislative proposals initiated in the executive agencies.

The National Security Council. The **National Security Council (NSC)** is a link between the president's key foreign and military advisers and the president. Its members consist of the president, the vice president, and the secretaries of state and defense, plus other informal members. The NSC is managed by the president's assistant for national security affairs, also known as the national security adviser.

National Security Council (NSC)
An agency in the Executive Office of the President that advises the president on national security.

The Vice President

> **LO 10-5:** Explain why most vice presidents have little to do with running the federal government.

The Constitution does not give much power to the vice president. The only formal duty is to preside over the Senate—which is rarely necessary. This obligation is fulfilled when the Senate organizes and adopts its rules and also when the vice president is needed to decide a tie vote. In all other cases, the president pro tem manages parliamentary procedures in the Senate. The vice president is expected to participate only informally in senatorial deliberations, if at all.

The Vice President's Job

Vice presidents have traditionally been chosen by presidential nominees to balance the ticket by attracting groups of voters or appeasing party factions. If a presidential nominee is from the North, it is not a bad idea to have a vice-presidential nominee who is from the South. If the presidential nominee is from a rural state, perhaps someone with an urban background would be most suitable as a running mate. Presidential nominees who are strongly conservative or strongly liberal would do well to have vice-presidential nominees whose views lie more in the middle of the political road.

Strengthening the Ticket. In recent presidential elections, however, vice-presidential candidates have often been selected for other reasons. Barack Obama picked Joe Biden to be his running mate in 2008 to add gravitas (seriousness) and foreign policy experience to the ticket. In 2012, Republican presidential candidate Mitt Romney chose Representative Paul Ryan of Wisconsin as his running mate. Ryan, the author of conservative House budget proposals, was greeted with enthusiasm by Republicans who were skeptical of Romney's conservative credentials.

In 2016, Republican candidate Donald Trump picked Indiana governor Mike Pence to be his running mate. Pence was a fairly conventional conservative Republican. By choosing him, Trump sought to rally Republicans who were uncomfortable with Trump's insurgent politics. Democratic presidential candidate Joe Biden chose Senator Kamala Harris (D-CA) as his running mate in 2020. She was the first woman of color to be named to this position for a major political party in the United States. She balanced the ticket in terms of age (55 versus Biden's 77) and diversity (she is half Jamaican and half Indian).

Supporting the President. Traditionally, the job of the vice president has not been very demanding. In recent years, however, presidents have granted their running mates increased responsibilities and power. President Jimmy Carter was the first modern president to rely on his vice president—Walter Mondale—as a major adviser. Under President George W. Bush, Dick Cheney became the most powerful vice president in history. Cheney was able to place his supporters throughout the bureaucracy and exert influence on a wide range of issues. He could exercise this degree of power, however, only because he had the support of the president. In contrast, Vice President Biden's relationship to President Obama was more conventional, and the same was true of Vice President Pence and Vice President Harris.

Archive Image / Alamy Stock Photo

Image 10.8 Members of the national security team receive an update on the mission against Osama bin Laden in the Situation Room of the White House on May 1, 2011. Those present included Vice President Joe Biden (left), President Barack Obama (second left), Secretary of State Hillary Clinton (second right), and Secretary of Defense Robert Gates (right).
▶ What power does the president have to deal with known terrorists?

Presidential Succession

Eight vice presidents have become president because of the death of the president. John Tyler, the first to do so, took over William Henry Harrison's position in 1841 after Harrison had served for only one month. No one knew whether Tyler should simply be a caretaker until a new president could be elected three and a half years later or whether he actually should be president. Tyler assumed that he was supposed to be the chief executive, and he acted as such—although his political opponents referred to him as "His Accidency." Since then, vice presidents taking over the position of the presidency because of the incumbent's death have assumed all presidential powers.

But what should a vice president do if a president becomes incapable of carrying out necessary duties while in office? This question was not addressed in the original Constitution. Article II, Section 1, says only that "[i]n Case of the Removal of the President from Office, or of his Death, Resignation, or Inability to discharge the Powers and Duties of the said Office, the same shall devolve on [the same powers shall be exercised by] the Vice President." In October 1919, President Woodrow Wilson was incapacitated by a stroke. He had seventeen months left in his term of office. No one was willing to take responsibility for certifying that Wilson was unable "to discharge the powers and duties" of the presidency. In fact, most of his duties were assumed by cabinet members and by the First Lady.

When Dwight Eisenhower became ill for a second time in 1958, he entered into a pact with Richard Nixon specifying that the vice president could determine whether the president was incapable of carrying out his duties if the president could not communicate. John F. Kennedy and Lyndon Johnson entered into similar agreements with their vice presidents.

Finally, in 1967, the **Twenty-Fifth Amendment** was passed, establishing procedures in the event of presidential incapacity, death, or resignation.

When the President Becomes Incapacitated. According to the Twenty-Fifth Amendment, when a president believes that they are incapable of performing the duties of office, the president must inform Congress in writing. Then the vice president serves as acting president until the president can resume normal duties. When the president is unable to communicate, a majority of the cabinet, including the vice president, can declare that fact to Congress. Then the vice president serves as acting president until the president resumes normal duties. If a dispute arises over the return of the president's ability, a two-thirds vote of both chambers of Congress is required to allow the vice president to remain acting president. Otherwise, the president resumes normal duties.

When the Vice Presidency Becomes Vacant. The Twenty-Fifth Amendment also addresses the issue of how the president should fill a vacant vice presidency. Section 2 of the amendment states, "Whenever there is a vacancy in the office of the Vice President, the President shall nominate a Vice President who shall take office upon confirmation by a majority vote of both Houses of Congress."

The question of who shall be president if both the president and the vice president die is answered by the Presidential Succession Act of 1947. If the president and vice president die, resign, or are disabled, the Speaker of the House will become president, after resigning from Congress. Next in line is the president pro tem of the Senate, followed by the cabinet officers in the order of the initial creation of their departments (see Table 10.1).

Twenty-fifth Amendment
A 1967 amendment to the Constitution that establishes procedures for filling presidential and vice-presidential vacancies and makes provisions for presidential incapacity.

ZUMA Press, Inc./Alamy Stock Photo

Image 10.9 Vice President Kamala Harris. Harris had been a U.S. senator and before that the attorney general of California. ▶ What are the official duties of the vice president?

Table 10.1	Line of Succession to the Presidency of the United States

▶ How might the public react if the Speaker of the House became president—and was of a different political party than the deceased president?

1. Vice president	10. Secretary of Commerce
2. Speaker of the House of Representatives	11. Secretary of Labor
3. Senate president pro tempore	12. Secretary of Health and Human Services
4. Secretary of State	13. Secretary of Housing and Urban Development
5. Secretary of the Treasury	14. Secretary of Transportation
6. Secretary of Defense	15. Secretary of Energy
7. Attorney general (head of the Justice Department)	16. Secretary of Education
8. Secretary of Interior	17. Secretary of Veterans Affairs
9. Secretary of Agriculture	18. Secretary of Homeland Security

Communicating With the White House

When it comes to caring about the presidency, most people do not need much encouragement. Many people, however, believe the president is such a remote figure that nothing they can do will affect what the president does. That is not always true. On many issues, your voice—combined, of course, with the voices of many others—can have an impact. Writing to the president is a traditional way for citizens to express their opinions.

Why Should You Care? The president makes many decisions that directly influence your life. For example, in 2020, our response to the COVID-19 coronavirus pandemic depended in part on presidential leadership. Many Americans with opinions about how the president should have addressed this crisis "cast their vote" by adding their e-mail to the many others that the president received on the issue. You can do likewise on an issue that is important to you.

What Can You Do? The most traditional way to communicate with the White House is by letter. Letters to the president should be addressed to:

> The President of the United States
> The White House
> 1600 Pennsylvania Avenue NW
> Washington, DC 20500

Will you get an answer? Almost certainly. The White House mail room is staffed by volunteers and paid employees who sort the mail for the president and tally the public's concerns. You may receive a standard response to your comments or a more personal, detailed response.

You can also send your comments and ideas to the White House using e-mail: comments@whitehouse.gov. E-mail may be the fastest way to communicate with the president.

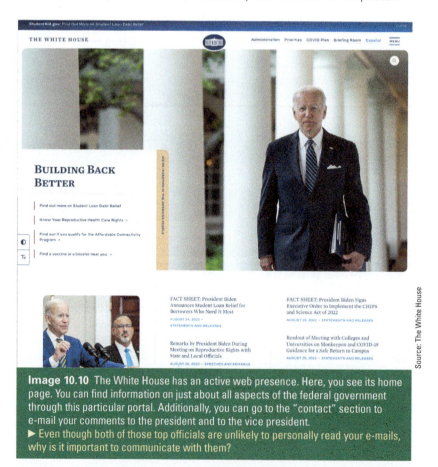

Source: The White House

Image 10.10 The White House has an active web presence. Here, you see its home page. You can find information on just about all aspects of the federal government through this particular portal. Additionally, you can go to the "contact" section to e-mail your comments to the president and to the vice president.

▶ Even though both of those top officials are unlikely to personally read your e-mails, why is it important to communicate with them?

Key Terms

advice and consent 245
appointment power 243
cabinet 254
chief diplomat 245
chief executive 243
chief legislator 246
chief of staff 256
civil service 243
commander in chief 244
commutations 243
constitutional
    powers 249

diplomatic
    recognition 245
emergency powers 250
executive agreements 246
Executive Office of the
    President (EOP) 255
executive orders 251
executive privilege 251
expressed powers 249
Federal Register 251
head of state 241
impeachment 253

inherent powers 250
kitchen cabinet 255
National Security
    Council (NSC) 257
Office of Management
    and Budget
    (OMB) 256
pardons 243
patronage 248
pocket veto 247
reprieves 243
signing statement 252

state of the union
    message 246
statutory powers 249
twelfth amendment 241
twenty-fifth
    amendment 259
veto message 247
war powers
    resolution 245
white house office 256

Chapter Summary

» LO 10-1 The office of the president of the United States, combining as it does the functions of chief of state and chief executive, was unique at the time of its creation. The framers of the Constitution were divided over whether the president should be a weak or a strong executive. The requirements for the office of the presidency are outlined in Article II, Section 1, of the Constitution.

» LO 10-2 The president's roles include both formal and informal duties. These roles include head of state, chief executive, commander in chief, chief diplomat, chief legislator, party chief, and politician.

As head of state, the president is ceremonial leader of the government. As chief executive, the president is bound to enforce the acts of Congress, the judgments of the federal courts, and treaties. The chief executive has the power of appointment and the power to grant reprieves and pardons.

As commander in chief, the president is the ultimate decision maker in military matters. As chief diplomat, the president recognizes foreign governments, negotiates treaties, signs agreements, and nominates and receives ambassadors.

The role of chief legislator includes recommending legislation to Congress, lobbying for the legislation, approving laws, and exercising the veto power. Presidents are also politicians and

leaders of their political parties. Presidents rely on their personal popularity to help them fulfill these functions.

» LO 10-3 In addition to constitutional and inherent powers, the president has statutory powers written into law by Congress. Presidents also have a variety of special powers not available to other branches of the government. These include emergency powers and the power to issue executive orders, to invoke executive privilege, and to issue signing statements.

Abuses of executive power are dealt with by Articles I and II of the Constitution, which authorize the House and Senate to impeach and remove the president, vice president, or other officers of the federal government for committing "Treason, Bribery, or other high Crimes and Misdemeanors."

» LO 10-4 The president receives assistance from the cabinet and from the Executive Office of the President (including the White House Office).

» LO 10-5 The vice president is the constitutional officer assigned to preside over the Senate and to assume the presidency in case of the death, resignation, removal, or disability of the president. The Twenty-Fifth Amendment, passed in 1967, established procedures to be followed in case of presidential incapacity, death, or resignation, and when filling a vacant vice presidency.

Test Yourself

1. Anyone can become president of the United States, as long as that individual:
   a. is at least 35 years old.
   b. is at least 35 years old and a natural born citizen.
   c. is at least 40 years old and a natural born citizen.

2. To date, only two presidents have been Roman Catholic, and they are:
   a. George W. Bush and Joe Biden.
   b. Ronald Reagan and Joe Biden.
   c. John F. Kennedy and Joe Biden.

3. If no presidential candidate has a majority in the Electoral College, the question of who should become president is decided by the:
   a. U.S. House.
   b. U.S. Senate.
   c. U.S. Supreme Court.

4. Our president is both head of state and chief executive, which means that the president:
   a. engages in ceremonial activities both at home and abroad, and faithfully ensures that the acts of Congress are enforced.
   b. designates the vice president to represent the United States in public ceremonies abroad.
   c. makes sure that treaties are upheld but delegates other actions to the cabinet.

5. The president may grant pardons, reprieves, and commutations:
   a. with the advice and consent of the Senate.
   b. with the approval of the attorney general.
   c. without modification or regulation by Congress.

6. When the president issues an executive order, such action represents the president's:
   a. constitutional powers.
   b. legislative powers.
   c. emergency powers.

7. A president who disagrees with a part of legislation that they have signed into law can make a written declaration regarding the law's enforcement. This declaration is called:
   a. a signing statement.
   b. a veto message.
   c. executive privilege.

8. Upon impeachment by the House of Representatives, the president:
   a. must leave office immediately.
   b. cannot run for reelection.
   c. is tried by the Senate.

9. The White House chief of staff, the ambassador to the United Nations, and the head of the Environmental Protection Agency:
   a. have at different times been named members of the president's cabinet.
   b. are all part of the Executive Office of the President (EOP).
   c. are not subject to presidential appointment.

10. The only formal duty imposed on the vice president by the Constitution is to preside over the:
    a. U.S. House.
    b. U.S. Senate.
    c. cabinet.

Essay Questions

1. What characteristics do you think voters look for when choosing a president? Might these characteristics change as a result of changes in the political environment and the specific problems facing the nation? If you believe voters almost always look for the same characteristics, why do they do so? If voters seek somewhat different people as president, which circumstances favor which kinds of leaders?

2. Many presidents have been lawyers, though George W. Bush was a businessman, Ronald Reagan was an actor, and Jimmy Carter was a naval officer and owned a peanut warehouse. What advantages might these three presidents have gained from their career backgrounds? In particular, what benefits might Ronald Reagan have derived from his experience as an actor?

Answers to multiple-choice questions: 1. b, 2. c, 3. a, 4. a, 5. c, 6. b, 7. a, 8. c, 9. a, 10. b.

11 The Executive Branch

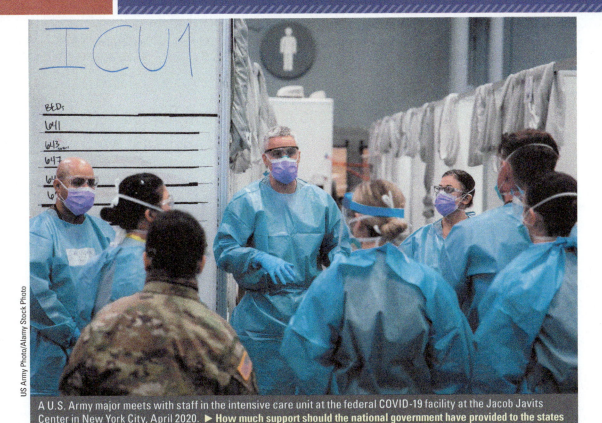

A U.S. Army major meets with staff in the intensive care unit at the federal COVID-19 facility at the Jacob Javits Center in New York City, April 2020. ▶ **How much support should the national government have provided to the states to combat the pandemic?**

US Army Photo/Alamy Stock Photo

The five **Learning Outcomes (LOs)** below are designed to help improve your understanding of this chapter. After reading this chapter, you should be able to:

» **LO 11-1** Discuss the nature of the federal bureaucracy, and identify the largest federal spending programs.

» **LO 11-2** Describe the various types of agencies and organizations that make up the federal executive branch.

» **LO 11-3** Explain how government employees are hired and how the civil service is administered.

» **LO 11-4** Discuss why it has been so difficult to reform federal bureaucracies.

» **LO 11-5** Discuss how federal agencies make rules and what the role of Congress is in this process.

Check your understanding of the material with the Test Yourself section at the end of the chapter.

aceless bureaucrats—this is how many Americans visualize the civil servants and political appointees who make up the executive branch of the federal government. Polls consistently report that the majority of Americans support "less government." The same polls, however, report that the majority of Americans support almost every specific program that the government undertakes. The conflict between the desire for small government and the desire for the benefits that only a large government can provide has been a constant feature of American politics. For example, the goal of preserving endangered species has widespread support. At the same time, many people believe that restrictions imposed under the Endangered Species Act violate the rights of landowners. Helping the elderly pay their medical bills is a popular objective, but hardly anyone enjoys paying the Medicare tax that supports this effort.

The Nature and Scope of the Federal Bureaucracy

>> **LO 11-1:** Discuss the nature of the federal bureaucracy, and identify the largest federal spending programs.

Bureaucracy
A large organization that is structured hierarchically to carry out specific functions.

A **bureaucracy** is an organization that is structured hierarchically to carry out specific functions. Generally, bureaucracies are characterized by an organization chart. Different units of the organization have different functions and expertise.

Public and Private Bureaucracies

We should not think of bureaucracy as unique to government. Any large corporation or university can be considered a bureaucratic organization, even though the term bureaucracy is most often applied to government agencies. The fact is that the handling of complex problems requires a division of labor. Individuals must concentrate their skills on specific, well-defined aspects of a problem and depend on others to solve the rest of it.

Public, or government, bureaucracies differ from private organizations in some important ways, however. A private corporation has a single leader—its chief executive officer (CEO). Public bureaucracies do not have a single leader. Although the president is the chief administrator of the federal system, all agencies are subject to the dictates of Congress for their funding, staffing, and, indeed, their continued existence. Public bureaucracies supposedly serve all citizens, while private ones serve private interests.

One other important difference between private corporations and government bureaucracies is that government bureaucracies are not organized to make a profit. Rather, they are supposed to perform their functions as efficiently as possible to conserve taxpayers' dollars.

The Size of the Bureaucracy

In 1789, the new government's executive branch was tiny. There were three departments—State (with nine employees), War (with two employees), and Treasury (with thirty-nine employees)—and the Office of the Attorney General (which later became the Department of Justice). The bureaucracy was still small in 1798. At that time, the secretary of state had seven clerks and spent a total of $500 (about $3,000 in 2023 dollars) on stationery and printing. In that same year, an appropriations act allocated $1.4 million (about $36 million in 2023 dollars), to the War Department.

Government Employment Today. Times have changed. Excluding 1.4 million military service members, but including employees of Congress, the courts, and the U.S. Postal Service, the federal bureaucracy includes approximately 2.9 million employees. That number has remained relatively stable for the past several decades. It is somewhat deceiving, however, because many other individuals work directly or indirectly for the federal government as subcontractors or consultants and in other capacities.

Figure 11.1 shows the combined growth in government employment at the federal, state, and local levels. Since 1960, this growth has been mainly at the state and local levels. If all government employees are included, about 15 percent of civilian employment is accounted for by government.

The Impact of Ronald Reagan. Notice in Figure 11.1 that government employment as a share of the total U.S. population grew rapidly until 1980. In that year, Republican Ronald Reagan was elected president. Under Reagan, government employment actually fell, in large part because of the elimination of revenue sharing, a program through which the federal government transferred large sums to state and local governments. While government employment picked up later in Reagan's administration, it never resumed the constant upward course characteristic of the 1960s and 1970s. In short, Reagan's "conservative revolution" had a genuine impact on the trajectory of government.

Impact of the COVID-19 Pandemic. When the pandemic first hit in 2020, employment in the government sector fell, as it did in the private sector. During the years after the shutdowns in both the private and public sector, some states and localities lagged in rehiring laid-off workers. By 2023, however, all government employment combined was approximately where it was prior to the pandemic.

Figure 11.1   Government Employees: Local, State, and Federal, as a Percentage of the U.S. Population (1960–2021)

▶ Why might a majority of government workers be employed by local government?

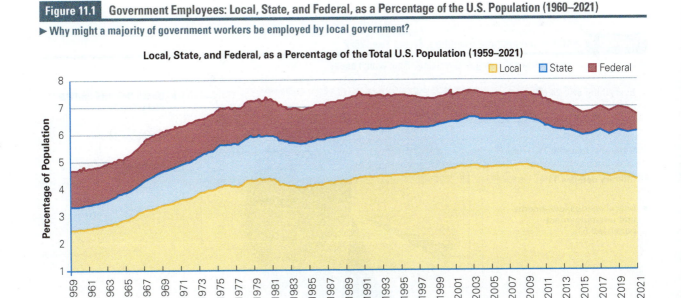

Local, State, and Federal, as a Percentage of the Total U.S. Population (1959–2021)

Source: The Federal Reserve Economic Data (FRED) service of the St. Louis Federal Reserve, U.S. Census Bureau, Bureau of Labor Statistics, and authors' calculations.

The Federal Budget

In 1929, spending by all levels of government was equivalent to only about 11 percent of the nation's gross domestic product (GDP). For fiscal year 2023, it was about 46 percent.

Social Spending. Studies repeatedly show that most Americans have a very inaccurate idea of how the federal budget is spent. Figure 11.2 can help. This pie chart demonstrates that almost 40 percent of all federal spending goes to two programs that benefit older Americans—Social Security and Medicare. Additional social programs, many aimed at individuals and families with low incomes, push the total amount of social spending to the 60 percent mark.

Because of these additional social programs, the federal government spends much more on the poor than many people realize. Medicaid, a joint federal-state program that provides health care services, is the largest of these programs. (CHIP, which is combined with Medicaid in the figure, is the Children's Health Insurance Program.) In contrast, traditional welfare—Temporary Assistance for Needy Families (TANF)—accounts for only 0.34 percent of the budget ($16.9 billion) and is buried in the "Miscellaneous low-income support" slice. Out of TANF funds, only $3.5 billion goes to actual cash payments to the poor.

Defense and All the Rest. Military defense and veterans' benefits are almost a fifth of the whole. Interest payments on the national debt are about 5 percent. "Everything else," which includes education and transportation, amounts to 24.9 percent of the budget. Foreign aid, which is included in the "Everything else" slice, is about $38 billion. This is a substantial sum, but it is much smaller than many people imagine.

Figure 11.2 | **Federal Government Spending, Fiscal Year 2022**

▶ Do you find some of these percentages surprising? If so, which ones?

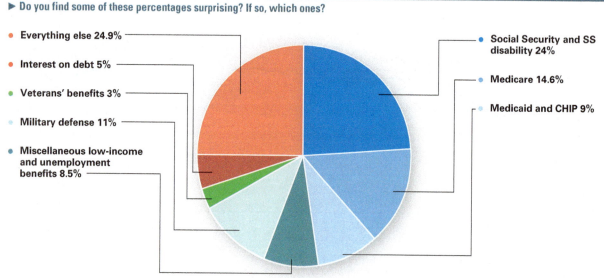

- Everything else 24.9%
- Interest on debt 5%
- Veterans' benefits 3%
- Military defense 11%
- Miscellaneous low-income and unemployment benefits 8.5%

- Social Security and SS disability 24%
- Medicare 14.6%
- Medicaid and CHIP 9%

Source: usgovernmentspending.com.

Revenue Sources. Where does the federal government get the funds that support its spending? Figure 11.3 can help answer this question. As you might expect, the personal income tax provides the largest share of federal revenues, about 51 percent. More than 12 percent is borrowed. How much of a problem is the borrowing? We look at that issue in this chapter's *Which Side Are You On?* feature.

The Organization of the Executive Branch

> **LO 11-2:** Describe the various types of agencies and organizations that make up the federal executive branch.

Within the federal bureaucracy are a number of different types of government agencies and organizations. Figure 11.4 outlines the several bodies within the executive branch, as well as the separate organizations that provide services to Congress, to the courts, and directly to the president.

The executive branch, which employs most of the government's staff, has four major types of structures. They are (1) cabinet departments, (2) independent executive agencies, (3) independent regulatory agencies, and (4) government corporations. Each has a distinctive relationship to the president, and some have unusual internal structures, overall goals, and grants of power.

Figure 11.3	Federal Revenue Sources 2022

▶ Why are corporate income taxes so small relative to individual income taxes?

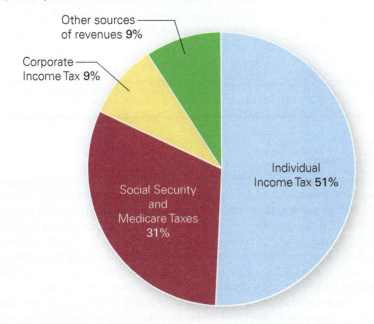

Other sources of revenues 9%

Corporate Income Tax 9%

Individual Income Tax 51%

Social Security and Medicare Taxes 31%

Source: Economic Indicators, various issues.

Which Side Are You On?

We Have to Stop Overspending by the Federal Government

"A billion here, a billion there. Pretty soon you're talking about real money." Today that statement must be changed to—"a trillion dollars here and a trillion dollars there, pretty soon you're talking about real money." The fact is that the federal government has spent more than it receives almost every year. The difference between federal government revenues and federal government spending is called the federal deficit. It used to be measured in the billions, but now it can be measured in the trillions. Obviously, an individual or family could not do the same thing year after year. But can the federal government? And even if it can, is it right? Another question is, can America survive all of this overspending?

We Cannot Borrow Forever

Those who believe that the federal budget deficit has been dangerously high are often called "deficit hawks." (Their opponents are "deficit doves.") When deficit hawks project our current rates of borrowing into the future, they see disaster unfolding. Just a few years ago in 2019, the deficit was 4 percent of the total economy. Today it is estimated at 13 percent in 2023. Every year that we run a deficit, we add to the national debt. Currently, the net national debt is 140.1 of total economic activity. That is a lot of dollars that our grandchildren will have to repay. Why should we load such a burden on their backs?

Deficit hawks have always said that too much government spending would eventually lead to inflation. That is exactly what started to happen in the later part of 2021. While government officials and some economists predicted that the inflation would only be temporary, they were sadly proven wrong by early 2022. Inflation hit a 40-year high by March of that year. By June 2022, it

is estimated to be 9.1 percent. Inflation is defined as the continuing loss in the purchasing power of dollars.

The Government Still Has Plenty of Room to Borrow

Deficit doves have a number of arguments. We will limit ourselves to two. The first concerns the burden on our grandchildren. Must they repay the national debt? That is doubtful. We never did pay off the sums we borrowed to finance World War II (1939–45). The economy just grew so much that these debts became irrelevant. Also, we are not, as some put it, "borrowing from our grandchildren." Most goods and services produced in 2022 were consumed in 2022. Most production in 2050 will be consumed in 2050. To take anything of value from our grandchildren would require a time machine. Let the people of 2050 make their own decisions about how to distribute the nation's yearly income.

Second, if large deficits create high interest rates, where are these sky-high interest rates? Deficit hawks have been predicting this result since early in the Obama administration (2009–17), and they have almost always been wrong. If a theory regularly fails to make accurate predictions, it is time to abandon it. We had to borrow to fight the COVID-19 pandemic, and we did so at low interest rates. Perhaps if we borrow too much, we will see higher interest rates, or some other problem. That will be the sign that we need to stop. But we are not there yet. (In all fairness, interest rates started to rise in the latter half of 2022.)

■ For Critical Analysis

Should we worry about how much the federal government must pay in interest on its debt?

Cabinet Departments

Cabinet Departments
One of the fifteen major departments of the executive branch.

Line Organizations
In the federal government, an administrative unit that is directly accountable to the president.

The fifteen **cabinet departments** are the major service organizations of the federal government. They can also be described in management terms as **line organizations**. This means that they are directly accountable to the president and are responsible for performing government functions, such as printing money and training troops. These cabinet departments were created by Congress when the need for each department arose. The first department to be created was State, and the most recent one was Homeland Security, established in 2003. A president might ask that a new department be created or an old one abolished, but the president has no power to do so without legislative approval from Congress.

Each department is headed by a secretary (except for the Justice Department, which is headed by the attorney general). Each department also has several levels of undersecretaries, assistant secretaries, and other personnel.

Figure 11.4   **Organization Chart of the Federal Government, 2022**

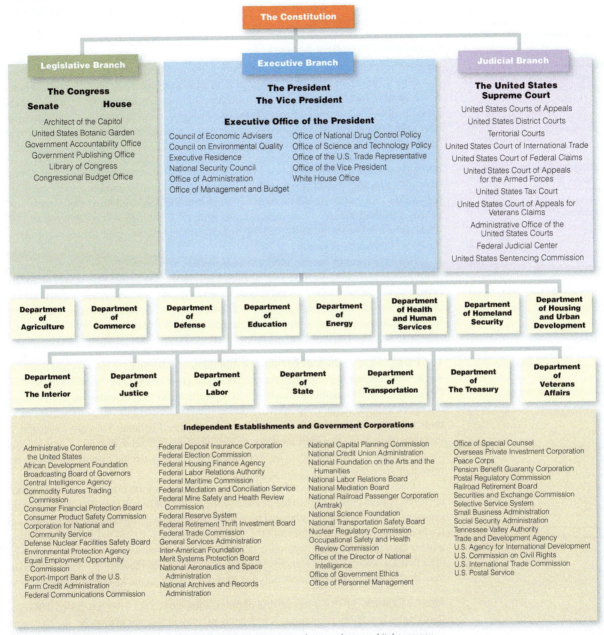

Sources: *United States Government Manual* at www.usgovernmentmanual.gov. and www.whitehouse.gov.

Presidents theoretically have considerable control over the cabinet departments, because presidents are able to appoint or fire all of the top officials. Even cabinet departments do not always respond to the president's wishes, though. One reason why presidents are frequently unhappy with their departments is that the entire bureaucratic structure below the top political levels is staffed by permanent employees. Many of these employees are committed to established programs or procedures and resist change. Table 11.1 shows each cabinet department. The table also describes some of the functions of each of the departments.

Independent Executive Agencies

Independent executive agencies are bureaucratic organizations that are not located within a department but report directly to the president, who appoints their chief officials. When a new federal agency is created—the Environmental Protection Agency, for example—Congress decides where it will be located in the bureaucracy. In recent decades, presidents often have asked that a new organization be kept separate or independent rather than added to an existing department, particularly if a department may be hostile to the agency's creation.

Independent Regulatory Agencies Typically, an **independent regulatory agency** is responsible for a specific type of public policy. Its function is to make and implement rules and regulations in a particular sphere of action to protect the public interest. The earliest such agency was the Interstate Commerce Commission (ICC), which was established in 1887 when Americans began to seek some form of government control over the rapidly growing business and industrial sector.

This new form of organization, the independent regulatory agency, was supposed to make technical, nonpolitical decisions about rates, profits, and rules that would be for the benefit of all and that did not require congressional legislation. In the years that followed the creation of the ICC, other agencies were formed to regulate communication (the Federal Communications Commission) and nuclear power (the Nuclear Regulatory Commission). (The ICC was abolished in 1995.)

The Purpose and Nature of Regulatory Agencies. In practice, regulatory agencies are administered independently of all three branches of government. They were set up because Congress felt it was unable to handle the complexities and technicalities required to carry out specific laws. Regulatory agencies and commissions combine some functions of all three branches of government—legislative, executive, and judicial. They are legislative in that they make rules that have the force of law. They are executive in that they provide for the enforcement of those rules. They are judicial in that they decide disputes involving the rules they have made.

Heads of regulatory agencies and members of agency boards or commissions are appointed by the president with the consent of the Senate, although they do not report to the president. When an agency is headed by a board rather than an individual, the members of the board cannot, by law, all be from the same political party. Presidents can influence regulatory agency behavior by appointing people of their own parties or individuals who share their political views when vacancies occur, in particular when the chair is vacant. Members may be removed by the president only for causes specified in the law creating the agency.

Agency Capture. Over the last several decades, some observers have concluded that regulatory agencies, although nominally independent, may in fact not always be so. They contend that many agencies have been captured by the very industries and firms that they were supposed to regulate and therefore make decisions based on the interests of the industry, not the general public. The results of **agency capture** have been less competition rather than more competition, higher prices rather than lower prices, and fewer choices rather than more choices for consumers.

Independent Executive Agencies
A federal agency that is not part of a cabinet department but reports directly to the president.

Independent Regulatory Agency
An agency outside the major executive departments charged with making and implementing rules and regulations within a specific area.

Agency Capture
The act by which an industry being regulated by a government agency gains direct or indirect control over agency personnel and decision makers.

Table 11.1 Cabinet Departments

Department and Year Established	Principal Functions	Selected Subagencies
State (1789) (11,507 employees)	Negotiates treaties, develops foreign policy, protects citizens abroad	Passport Services Office, Foreign Service
Treasury (1789) (92,115 employees)	Pays all federal bills, borrows money, collects federal taxes, mints coins and prints paper currency, supervises national banks	Internal Revenue Service, U.S. Mint
Interior (1849) (68,121 employees)	Supervises federally owned lands and parks, supervises Native American affairs	National Park Service, Bureau of Indian Affairs
Justice (1870)[a] (113,311 employees)	Furnishes legal advice to the president, enforces federal criminal laws, supervises federal prisons	Federal Bureau of Investigation, Drug Enforcement Administration, Bureau of Prisons
Agriculture (1889) (92,187 employees)	Provides assistance to farmers and ranchers, conducts agricultural research, works to protect forests	Food Safety and Inspection Service, Federal Crop Insurance Corporation, Forest Service
Commerce (1913)[b] (48,934 employees)	Grants patents and trademarks, conducts a national census, monitors the weather, protects the interests of businesses	Bureau of the Census, Patent and Trademark Office, National Oceanic and Atmospheric Administration
Labor (1913)[b] (13,910 employees)	Administers federal labor laws, promotes the interests of workers	Occupational Safety and Health Administration, Bureau of Labor Statistics
Defense (1947)[c] (748,780 employees)	Manages the armed forces (army, navy, air force, and marines), operates military bases, is responsible for civil defense	National Security Agency; Departments of the Air Force, Navy, Army
Housing and Urban Development (1965) (7,358 employees)	Deals with the nation's housing needs, develops and rehabilitates urban communities, oversees resale of mortgages	Government National Mortgage Association, Office of Community Planning and Development
Transportation (1967) (53,408 employees)	Finances improvements in mass transit; develops and administers programs for highways, railroads, and aviation	Federal Aviation Administration, National Highway Traffic Safety Administration
Energy (1977) (14,289 employees)	Promotes the conservation of energy and resources, analyzes energy data, conducts research and development	Federal Energy Regulatory Commission, National Nuclear Security Administration
Health and Human Services (1979)[d] (80,319 employees)	Promotes public health, enforces pure food and drug laws, conducts and sponsors health-related research	Food and Drug Administration, Centers for Disease Control and Prevention, Centers for Medicare and Medicaid Services
Education (1979)[d] (3,653 employees)	Coordinates federal programs and policies for education, administers aid to education, promotes educational research	Office of Elementary and Secondary Education, Office of Federal Student Aid
Veterans Affairs (1988) (400,773 employees)	Promotes the welfare of veterans of the U.S. armed forces	Veterans Health Administration, Veterans Benefits Administration
Homeland Security (2003) (208,254 employees)	Attempts to prevent terrorist attacks within the United States, control America's borders, and minimize the damage from natural disasters	U.S. Coast Guard, Secret Service, Federal Emergency Management Agency, U.S. Immigration and Customs Enforcement

[a]Formed from the Office of the Attorney General (created in 1789).
[b]Formed from the Department of Commerce and Labor (created in 1903).
[c]Formed from the Department of War (created in 1789) and the Department of the Navy (created in 1798).
[d]Formed from the Department of Health, Education, and Welfare (created in 1953).

Interact

In this modern age, many government agencies have developed attractive and entertaining websites. The NASA site is enormously popular, especially for its striking photos of celestial objects. The page you can find by searching on "nasa benefits to you" shows the practical benefits of space exploration. An all-time favorite, however, has to be the zombie apocalypse comic written by the Centers for Disease Control (CDC). When you've finished reading it, consider whether it does a good job of providing useful information on disaster preparedness. You can find it by searching for "cdc zombie comic."

Deregulation and Reregulation. During the presidency of Jimmy Carter (1977–81), significant deregulation (the removal of regulatory restraints—the opposite of regulation) was initiated. For example, Carter appointed a chairperson of the Civil Aeronautics Board (CAB) who gradually eliminated regulation of airline fares and routes. Deregulation continued under President Ronald Reagan (1981–89).

Under President Bill Clinton (1993–2001), the Interstate Commerce Commission was eliminated, and the banking and telecommunications industries, along with many other sectors of the economy, were deregulated. At the same time, there was extensive regulation to protect the environment, a trend somewhat attenuated by the George W. Bush administration.

Regulation Under Obama and Trump. After the financial crisis of September 2008, many people saw inadequate regulation of the financial industry as a major cause of the nation's economic difficulties. During President Barack Obama's administration, therefore, reregulation of that industry became a major objective. After intense debate, Congress passed a comprehensive financial industry regulation plan in 2010.

Donald Trump became president with a powerful desire to cut back on government regulation. Initially, he found that difficult to do. Many of his staff had little experience in government and did not understand the processes that are necessary to change regulations. An agency cannot pull a new regulation out of thin air—the change must be justified by a detailed analysis. Many proposed regulatory changes, especially in Trump's first year in office, lacked the needed justification. Therefore, they could not stand up to challenges in the courts. By 2019, however, the administration had a better understanding of how to undertake deregulation in a lawful fashion. The result was a series of major cutbacks in regulation by the Environmental Protection Agency, the Consumer Financial Protection Agency, and other agencies.

Reregulation Yet Again Under the Biden Administration. From the very beginning of the Biden administration, there began a trend toward reregulation of the economy. For example, in 2021 and 2022, there were new rules and regulations concerning the energy sector. Many of those were fought in court, but some survived. After the invasion of Ukraine by Russia in 2022, many Republicans and some Democrats called for a loosening of regulations in the energy sector in order to ween America from importing oil from Russia. (Almost none were rescinded.) Additionally, from a strategic point of view, some called for aggressive increases in natural gas exploration and natural gas exporting (via liquified natural gas) to Europe so that European nations would not rely on Russia for this energy source.

Government and Government-Controlled Corporations

Government Corporation
An agency of government that administers a quasi-business enterprise. These corporations are used when government activities are primarily commercial.

Another form of bureaucratic organization in the United States is the **government corporation**. Although the concept is borrowed from the world of business, there are important differences between public and private corporations.

A private corporation has shareholders (stockholders) who in principle elect a board of directors, who in turn choose the corporate officers, such as the chief executive officer (CEO). When a private corporation makes a profit, it must pay taxes (unless it avoids them through various legal loopholes). It distributes the after-tax profits to shareholders as dividends or plows the profits back into the corporation to make new investments, or both.

A government corporation has a board of directors and managers, but it does not usually have any stockholders. The public cannot buy shares of stock in a typical government corporation, and if the entity makes a profit, it does not distribute the profit as dividends. Nor does it have to pay taxes on profits—the profits remain in the corporation. The largest and most famous government corporation is the U.S. Postal Service, with 520,000 career employees. Another well-known example is Amtrak, the passenger railway service, with a staff of about 20,000.

Bankruptcy. The federal government can also take effective control of a private corporation in a number of different circumstances. One is bankruptcy. When a company files for bankruptcy, it asks a federal judge for relief from its creditors. The judge, operating under bankruptcy laws established by Congress (as specified in the Constitution), is ultimately responsible for the fate of the enterprise. When a bank fails, the government has a special interest in protecting customers who have deposited funds with the bank. For that reason, the failing institution is taken over by the Federal Deposit Insurance Corporation (FDIC), which ensures continuity of service to bank customers.

Image 11.1 Even at $0.60 for the one-ounce first-class rate, postage in the United States is a bargain by international standards. First-class rates are $0.82 in Japan, $1.12 in Britain, and $1.43 in France. ▶ What are some of the reasons the U.S. Postal Service has experienced financial difficulties?

Government Ownership of Private Enterprises. The federal government can also obtain partial or complete ownership of a private corporation by purchasing its stock. Before 2008, such takeovers were rare, although they occasionally happened. When Continental Illinois, then the nation's seventh-largest bank, failed in 1984, the FDIC wound up in control of the institution for ten years before it could find a buyer.

The Continental Illinois rescue provided a blueprint for the massive bank bailout initiated under President George W. Bush in October 2008. The government made investments in more than eight hundred businesses, including banks, automobile companies, and the giant insurance company AIG. The bailout program was tremendously unpopular. Still, in time, the government recovered its investments.

Government-Sponsored Enterprises. An additional type of corporation is the government-sponsored enterprise, a business created by the federal government itself, which then sells part or all of the corporation's stock to private investors.

Until 2008, the leading examples of this kind of company were the Federal Home Loan Mortgage Corporation, known as Freddie Mac, and the Federal National Mortgage Association, commonly known as Fannie Mae. Both of these firms buy mortgages from banks and bundle them into securities that can be sold to investors. When the housing market collapsed, so—eventually—did Freddie Mac and Fannie Mae. Investors had always assumed that the federal government backed the obligations of the two enterprises, even though the government had never issued an explicit guarantee. In September 2008, the implicit guarantee became real when the government seized the two companies in what was effectively a bankruptcy. Freddie Mac and Fannie Mae became government-owned corporations. Eventually, they returned to profitability, and today all profits go to the U.S. Treasury.

Staffing the Bureaucracy

» **LO 11-3:** Explain how government employees are hired and how the civil service is administered.

There are two categories of executive branch employees: political appointees and civil servants. As noted earlier, the president can make political appointments to most of the top jobs in the federal bureaucracy. The president also can appoint ambassadors to foreign posts. All of the jobs that are considered "political plums" and that usually go to the politically well connected are listed in *Policy and Supporting Positions*, a book published by the Government Printing Office after each presidential election. Informally (and appropriately), this has been called the "Plum Book." The rest of the national government's employees belong to the civil service and obtain their jobs through a much more formal process.

Political Appointees

To fill the positions listed in the Plum Book, the president and the president's advisers solicit suggestions from politicians, businesspersons, and other prominent individuals. Appointments to these positions offer the president a way to pay off outstanding political debts. Presidents often use ambassadorships to reward individuals for their campaign contributions. But the president must also take into consideration such things as the candidate's ability to actually do the job.

The Aristocracy of the Federal Government. Political appointees are in some sense the aristocracy of the federal government. But their powers, although they appear formidable on paper, are often exaggerated. Like the president, political appointees will occupy their position for a comparatively brief time. Political appointees often leave office before the president's term ends. In fact, the average term of service for political appointees is less than two years. As a result, most appointees have little background for their positions and may be mere figureheads. Often, they only respond to the paperwork that flows up from below. Additionally, the professional civil servants who make up the permanent executive branch workforce may not feel compelled to carry out their current chief's directives quickly, because they know that the chief will not be around for very long.

The Difficulty in Firing Civil Servants. This inertia is compounded by the fact that it is very difficult to discharge civil servants. In recent years, fewer than 0.1 percent of federal employees have been fired for incompetence. Because discharged employees may appeal their dismissals, many months or even years can pass before the issue is resolved conclusively. This occupational rigidity helps to ensure that most political appointees, no matter how competent or driven, may not be able to exert much meaningful influence over their subordinates, let alone implement dramatic changes in the bureaucracy itself.

History of the Federal Civil Service

When the federal government was formed in 1789, it had no career public servants but rather consisted of amateurs who were almost all Federalists. When Thomas Jefferson took over as president, few federal administrative jobs were held by members of his party, so he fired more than one hundred officials and replaced them with his own supporters. Then, for the next twenty-five years, a growing body of federal administrators gained experience and expertise, becoming in the process professional public servants. These administrators stayed in office regardless of who was elected president. The bureaucracy had become a self-maintaining, long-term element within government.

To the Victors Belong the Spoils. When Andrew Jackson took over the White House in 1828, he could not believe how many appointed officials (appointed before he became president, that is) were overtly hostile toward him and his Democratic Party. Because the bureaucracy was reluctant to carry out his programs, Jackson did the obvious: He fired federal officials—more than all his predecessors combined. The **spoils system**—an application of the principle that to the victors belong the spoils—became the standard method of filling federal positions. Whenever a new president was elected from a party different from the party of the previous president, there would be an almost complete turnover in the staffing of the federal government.

The Civil Service Reform Act of 1883. Jackson's spoils system survived for a number of years, but it became increasingly corrupt. In addition, the size of the bureaucracy increased by 300 percent between 1851 and 1881. As the bureaucracy grew larger, the cry for civil service reform became louder. Reformers began to look to the example of several European countries—in particular, Germany. That country had established a professional civil service that operated under a **merit system**, in which job appointments were based on competitive examinations.

In 1883, the **Pendleton Act**—or **Civil Service Reform Act**—was passed, placing the first limits on the spoils system. The act established the principle of employment on the basis of open, competitive examinations and created the **Civil Service Commission** to administer the personnel service. Only 10 percent of federal employees were covered by the merit system initially. Later laws and executive orders, however, increased the coverage to more than 90 percent of federal employees. The effects of these reforms were felt at all levels of government.

The Supreme Court strengthened the civil service system in 1976 and in 1980.[1] In those two cases, the Court used the First Amendment to forbid government officials from discharging or threatening to discharge public employees solely for not being supporters of the political party in power unless party affiliation is an appropriate requirement for the position. A 1990 ruling added further enhancements to the civil service system.[2] The Court's ruling in that year effectively prevented the use of

Spoils System
The awarding of government jobs to political supporters and friends.

Merit System
The selection, retention, and promotion of government employees on the basis of competitive examinations.

Pendleton Act (Civil Service Reform Act)
An act that established the principle of federal government employment based on merit and created the Civil Service Commission to administer the personnel service.

Civil Service Commission
The initial central personnel agency of the national government, created in 1883.

Library of Congress, Prints & Photographs Division, Reproduction number [LC-US262-7622]

Image 11.2 President James A. Garfield was assassinated in 1881 by a disappointed office seeker. The long-term effect of this crime was to replace the spoils system with a permanent career civil service. ▶ What kinds of problems would result today if we relied, even in part, on the spoils system?

---

1. *Elrod v. Burns*, 427 U.S. 347 (1976); and *Branti v. Finkel*, 445 U.S. 507 (1980).
2. *Rutan v. Republican Party of Illinois*, 497 U.S. 62 (1990).

partisan political considerations as the basis for hiring, promoting, or transferring most public employees. An exception was permitted, however, for senior policymaking positions, which usually go to officials who will support the programs of the elected leaders.

The Civil Service Reform Act of 1978. In 1978, the Civil Service Reform Act abolished the Civil Service Commission and created two new federal agencies to perform its duties. To administer the civil service laws, rules, and regulations, the act created the Office of Personnel Management (OPM). The OPM is empowered to recruit, interview, and test potential government workers and determine who should be hired. The OPM makes recommendations to the individual agencies as to which persons meet the standards (typically, the top three applicants for a position), and the agencies then decide whom to hire. To oversee promotions, employees' rights, and other employment matters, the act created the Merit Systems Protection Board (MSPB). The MSPB evaluates charges of wrongdoing, hears employee appeals of agency decisions, and can order corrective action against agencies and employees.

Federal Employees and Political Campaigns. In 1933, when President Franklin D. Roosevelt set up his New Deal, a veritable army of civil servants was hired to staff the many new agencies that were created. Because the individuals who worked in these agencies owed their jobs to the Democratic Party, it seemed natural for them to campaign for Democratic candidates. The Democrats who controlled Congress in the mid-1930s did not object.

In 1938, a coalition of conservative Democrats and Republicans took control of Congress and forced through the Hatch Act—or Political Activities Act—of 1939. The act prohibited federal employees from actively participating in the political management of campaigns. It also forbade the use of federal authority to influence nominations and elections, and it outlawed the use of bureaucratic rank to pressure federal employees to make political contributions.

Hatch Act Controversies. The Hatch Act created controversies that lasted for decades. Many contended that the act deprived federal employees of their First Amendment freedoms of speech and association. In 1972, a federal district court declared the act unconstitutional. The United States Supreme Court, however, reaffirmed the challenged portion of the act in 1973, stating that the government's interest in preserving a nonpartisan civil service was so great that the prohibitions should remain.[3]

Twenty years later, Congress addressed the criticisms of the Hatch Act by passing the Federal Employees Political Activities Act of 1993. This act, which amended the Hatch Act, lessened the harshness of the 1939 act in several ways. Among other things, the 1993 act allowed federal employees to run for office in nonpartisan elections, participate in voter-registration drives, make campaign contributions to political organizations, and campaign for candidates in partisan elections.

Modern Attempts at Bureaucratic Reform

≫ LO 11-4: Discuss why it has been so difficult to reform federal bureaucracies.

As long as the federal bureaucracy exists, attempts to make it more open, efficient, and responsive to the needs of U.S. citizens will continue. The most important reforms in the last several decades include sunshine laws, privatization, and attempts to protect so-called whistleblowers.

---

3. *United States Civil Service Commission v. National Association of Letter Carriers*, 413 U.S. 548 (1973).

Sunshine Laws Before and After 9/11

In 1976, Congress enacted the **Government in the Sunshine Act**. It required for the first time that all multiheaded federal agencies—agencies headed by a committee instead of an individual—hold their meetings regularly in public session. The bill defined meeting as almost any gathering, formal or informal, of agency members, including a conference telephone call. The only exceptions to this rule of openness are discussions of matters such as court proceedings or personnel problems, and these exceptions are specifically listed in the bill. Sunshine laws now exist at all levels of government.

Government in the Sunshine Act
A law that requires all committee-directed federal agencies to conduct their business regularly in public sessions.

Information Disclosure. In 1966, the federal government passed the Freedom of Information Act (FOIA), which required federal government agencies, with certain exceptions, to disclose to individuals information contained in government files. FOIA requests are helpful not just to individuals. Indeed, the major beneficiaries of the act have been news organizations, which have used it to uncover government waste, scandals, and incompetence.

There are many examples of FOIA disclosures of varying levels of importance starting in 1919 through the 1960s. We discovered that the U.S. narrowly escaped detonating a nuclear bomb over North Carolina in 1961 when the plane carrying it crashed. We also discovered, through a four-year-old request, that a major American supplier of Parmesan cheese was using wood pulp in its products.

In recent years, news organizations have found it more difficult to use the FOIA. The Obama administration set new records for censoring government files, denying access to information, and failing to address FOIA requests in a timely fashion. These problems became even worse under President Trump. According to the Associated Press (AP), those requesting records from the Trump administration under the FOIA received censored files or nothing in 78 percent of cases, a record number.

At least at the beginning of the Biden administration, Freedom of Information Act experts saw little improvement in the response of government agencies to journalists' request for information. In the first two years, the Biden administration did not announce any new or revised Freedom of Information Act directives.

Curbs on Information Disclosure. Since the terrorist attacks of September 11, 2001, the trend toward open government has been reversed at both the federal and the state levels. Within weeks after September 11, 2001, federal agencies removed hundreds, if not thousands, of documents from internet sites, public libraries, and the reading rooms found in various federal government departments. Information contained in some of the documents included diagrams of power plants and pipelines, structural details on dams, and safety plans for chemical plants. The military also immediately began restricting information about its current and planned activities, as did the Federal Bureau of Investigation. These agencies were concerned that terrorists could make use of this information to plan attacks.

Privatization, or Contracting Out

Another approach to bureaucratic reform is **privatization**, which occurs when government services are replaced by services from the private sector. For example, state governments have contracted with private firms to operate prisons. Supporters of privatization argue that some services can be provided more efficiently by the private sector. A similar scheme involves furnishing vouchers to government "clients" in lieu of services. Instead of supplying housing, the government could offer vouchers that recipients could use to "pay" for housing in privately owned buildings.

Privatization
The replacement of government services with services provided by private firms.

National Park Service

Image 11.3 A park ranger at the Upper Delaware Scenic and Recreational River, a national park on the New York–Pennsylvania border. ▶ Why might the national parks be popular with most citizens?

The privatization, or contracting-out, strategy has been most successful on the local level. Some municipalities have contracted with private companies for such services as trash collection. This approach is not a cure-all, however, because many functions, particularly on the national level, cannot be contracted out in any meaningful way.

The increase in the amount of government work being contracted out to the private sector has led to significant controversy in recent years. Some have criticized the lack of competitive bidding for many contracts that the government has awarded. Another concern is the perceived lack of federal government oversight over the work done by private contractors.

The Issue of Whistleblowers

A **whistleblower** is someone who "blows the whistle," or publicly discloses information on gross governmental inefficiency or illegal action. Whistleblowers may be clerical workers, managers, or specialists, such as scientists.

Whistleblower
In the context of government, someone who brings gross governmental inefficiency or an illegal action to the public's attention.

Laws Protecting Whistleblowers. The 1978 Civil Service Reform Act prohibits reprisals against whistleblowers by their superiors, and it set up the Merit Systems Protection Board as part of this protection. Many federal agencies also have toll-free hotlines that employees can use anonymously to report bureaucratic waste and inappropriate behavior. About 35 percent of all calls result in agency action or follow-up.

Further protection for whistleblowers was provided in 1989, when Congress passed the Whistleblower Protection Act. That act established an independent agency, the Office of Special Counsel (OSC), to investigate complaints brought by government employees who have been demoted, fired, or otherwise punished for reporting government fraud or waste.

Some state and federal laws encourage employees to blow the whistle on their employers' wrongful actions by providing monetary incentives to the whistleblowers. At the federal level, the False Claims Act of 1986 allows a whistleblower who has disclosed information about a fraud against the U.S. government to receive a monetary award. If the government chooses to prosecute the case and wins, the whistleblower receives between 15 and 25 percent of the proceeds. If the government declines to intervene, the whistleblower can bring a suit on behalf of the government and, if the suit is successful, will receive between 25 and 30 percent of the proceeds.

The Problem Continues. Despite these efforts to help whistleblowers, there is little evidence that they truly receive much protection. According to a survey, more than 41 percent of the employees who turned to the OSC for assistance stated that they were no longer employees of the government agencies on which they had blown the whistle. The government's difficulty in dismissing employees seems to magically disappear when the employee is a whistleblower.

Whistleblowers Under President Obama. During his 2008 campaign, Obama promised to protect whistleblowers. Many observers believe, however, that in fact the Obama administration's record on whistleblowers was one of the worst ever. This conclusion is based, in large part, on the administration's use of the Espionage Act of 1917 to prosecute persons who leaked national security information to the press. By 2013, the administration had launched seven such prosecutions. The Espionage Act has been used regularly against persons spying for foreign governments. Not since 1984, however, had the government initiated such a case based on leaks to the press.

One dramatic case involved Edward Snowden, a National Security Agency (NSA) contractor. Snowden delivered a vast collection of information on NSA surveillance to journalists. Snowden was aware of how the government had treated Private First Class Chelsea (formerly Bradley) Manning, an earlier leaker. Manning had been held in solitary confinement in ways that some critics saw as abusive. Snowden therefore relocated to Hong Kong, hoping that the Chinese government would grant him asylum. On learning that asylum would not be granted, Snowden fled to Russia where he received permanent residence in 2020.

Whistleblowers and Private Data. While many applaud whistleblowers when they reveal government waste, government scandals, and fraud, what about whistleblowers who reveal and publish private data? For example, is it appropriate for whistleblowers to reveal information about people's income taxes? This is not hypothetical because someone in the Internal Revenue Service (IRS) provided the website ProPublica with the tax returns of many of the nation's billionaires, including Jeff Bezos, Elon Musk, George Soros, and Michael Bloomberg. The Biden administration, including Attorney General Merrick Garland and IRS Commissioner Charles Rettig, promised that they would find the leaker and prosecute them.

As another example, an employee of the U.S. Treasury's Financial Crimes Division, Natalie Edwards, revealed that officials there had collected and stored data on American citizens. When nothing was done, she leaked suspicious activity reports (SARs) to BuzzFeed News and to the International Consortium of Investigative Journalists. She claimed that the information leaked showed that there was a global failure to police money laundering. The Treasury Department responded—she was sentenced to six months in prison for "violating her oath." Biden refused to pardon her.

@xychelsea/twitter/ZUMA Press/Newscom

Image 11.4 Chelsea Manning was sentenced to thirty-five years in prison for giving classified U.S. government information to the website WikiLeaks. Her sentence was later commuted by President Obama, and she was released from prison in May 2017 after serving seven years. ▶ Is Manning a criminal, a hero—or both?

Bureaucrats as Politicians and Policymakers

≫ **LO 11-5:** Discuss how federal agencies make rules and what the role of Congress is in this process.

Because Congress is unable to oversee the day-to-day administration of its programs, it must delegate certain powers to administrative agencies. Congress delegates power to agencies through **enabling legislation**. For example, the Federal Trade Commission was created by the Federal Trade Commission Act of 1914, the Equal Employment Opportunity Commission was created by the Civil Rights Act of 1964, and the Occupational Safety and Health Administration was created by the Occupational Safety and Health Act of 1970.

Enabling Legislation
A statute enacted by Congress that authorizes the creation of an administrative agency and specifies the name, purpose, composition, functions, and powers of the agency being created.

The enabling legislation generally specifies the name, purpose, composition, functions, and powers of the agency.

In theory, the agencies should put into effect laws passed by Congress. Laws are often drafted in such vague and general terms, however, that they provide limited guidance to agency administrators as to how they should be implemented. This means that the agencies themselves must decide how best to carry out the wishes of Congress.

The discretion given to administrative agencies is not accidental. Congress has long realized that it lacks the technical expertise and the resources to monitor the implementation of its laws. Hence, administrative agencies are created to fill the gaps. This gap-filling role requires an agency to formulate administrative rules (regulations) to put flesh on the bones of the law. But it also forces the agency itself to become an unelected policymaker.

The Rulemaking Environment

Rulemaking does not occur in a vacuum. Suppose that Congress passes a new air pollution law. The Environmental Protection Agency (EPA) might decide to implement the new law through a technical regulation on power plant emissions. This proposed regulation would be published in the *Federal Register*, a daily government publication, so that interested parties would have an opportunity to comment on it. Individuals and companies that oppose all or parts of the rule might then try to convince the EPA to revise or redraft the regulation. Some parties might try to persuade the agency to withdraw the proposed regulation altogether. In any event, the EPA would consider these comments in drafting the final version of the regulation.

Waiting Periods and Court Challenges. Once the final regulation has been published in the *Federal Register*, there is a sixty-day waiting period before the rule can be enforced. During that period, businesses, individuals, and state and local governments can ask Congress to overturn the regulation. After the sixty-day period has lapsed, the regulation can still be challenged in court by a party having a direct interest in the rule, such as a company that expects to incur significant costs in complying with it. The company could argue that the rule misinterprets the applicable law or goes beyond the agency's legal authority. An allegation by the company that the EPA made a mistake in judgment probably would not be enough to convince the court to throw out the rule. The company instead would have to demonstrate that the rule itself was "arbitrary and capricious."

Controversies. How agencies implement, administer, and enforce legislation has resulted in controversy. For example, decisions made by agencies charged with administering the Endangered Species Act have led to protests from farmers, ranchers, and others whose economic interests have been harmed.

At times, a controversy may arise when an agency refuses to issue regulations to implement a particular law. During the George W. Bush administration, the EPA refused to issue regulations designed to curb the emission of carbon dioxide and other greenhouse gases. State and local governments, as well as a number of environmental groups, then sued the agency. Those bringing the suit claimed that the EPA was not fulfilling its obligation to implement the provisions of the Clean Air Act. Ultimately, the Supreme Court held that the EPA had the authority to—and should—regulate such gases.[4] The Supreme Court changed its view of this issue in 2022. Speaking for the Court, Chief Justice John Roberts argued that

---

4. *Massachusetts v. EPA*, 549 U.S. 497 (2007).

the EPA does not have the power to regulate carbon dioxide emissions "at a level that will force a nationwide transition away from the use of coal to generate electricity."[5]

Revoking an Existing Rule. As noted earlier, one goal of the Trump administration was to cut back regulation. In particular, the administration wanted to reverse a number of specific rules long opposed by Republicans. One was the Clean Power Plan (CPP) advanced by the EPA that would have made it much harder to use coal to generate electrical power. True, the CPP was in substantial danger of being struck down by the Supreme Court. But the president could also simply direct the EPA to withdraw the CPP.

That step is not as easy as it sounds, however. The rulemaking process just described applies not only to creating new rules, but to revoking existing ones as well. The agency responsible for the rule must prepare a justification for the revocation. Comments and waiting periods are required. Lawsuits are possible. The process of making a rule can take years, and unmaking one can take just as long.

The Biden Administration's Push for More Regulations. While much of the proposed social change legislation did not occur as planned for the Biden administration, many new regulations were proposed prior to the 2022 midterm elections. Some of the areas where regulations were proposed included:

- Financial regulations, particularly with respect to cryptocurrency
- Pro-competition rules, particularly with respect to the beer, wine, and spirits industry
- Changes to promote competition in the agricultural sector
- Lower prescription drug prices
- New rules about the use of certain suspected carcinogens, such as ethylene oxide
- Regulations promoting a faster transition toward alternative energy sources

Negotiated Rulemaking

Since the end of World War II in 1945, companies, environmentalists, and other special interest groups have challenged government regulations in court. In the 1980s, however, the sheer wastefulness of attempting to regulate through litigation became increasingly apparent. Today, a growing number of federal agencies encourage businesses and public interest groups to become directly involved in drafting regulations. Agencies hope that such participation may help to prevent later courtroom battles over the regulations.

Congress formally approved such a process, which is called negotiated rulemaking, in the Negotiated Rulemaking Act of 1990. The act authorizes agencies to allow those who will be affected by a new rule to participate in the rule drafting process. If an agency chooses to engage in negotiated rulemaking, it must publish in the *Federal Register* the subject and scope of the rule to be developed, the names of the parties that will be affected significantly by the rule, and other information.

Representatives of the affected groups and other interested parties then may apply to be members of the negotiating committee. The agency is represented on the committee, but a trained public policy mediator from the private sector presides over the proceedings. Once the committee members have reached agreement on the terms of the proposed rule, a notice is published in the *Federal Register*, followed by a period for comments by any person or organization interested in the proposed rule. Negotiated rulemaking often is conducted under the condition that the participants promise not to challenge in court the outcome of any agreement to which they were a party.

---

5. *West Virginia v. Environmental Protection Agency*, 597 U.S. __ (2022).

Bureaucrats as Policymakers

Theories of public administration once assumed that bureaucrats do not make policy decisions but only implement the laws and policies developed by the president and legislative bodies. A more realistic view is that the agencies and departments of government play important roles in policymaking. The bureaucracy often initiates regulations and programs based on its expertise and on scientific studies. The views and beliefs of the bureaucrats themselves may also influence the results. How a law passed by Congress eventually is translated into action—from the forms to be filled out to decisions about who gets what benefits—usually is determined within each agency or department. Even the evaluation of whether a policy has achieved its purpose usually is based on studies that are commissioned and interpreted by the agency administering the program.

The bureaucracy's policymaking role often has been depicted as an *iron triangle*. Recently, many political scientists have come to see the concept of an *issue network* as a more accurate description of the typical policymaking process.

Iron Triangles. In the past, scholars often described the bureaucracy's role in the policy-making process by using the concept of an **iron triangle**—a three-way alliance among legislators in Congress, bureaucrats, and interest groups. Consider as an example the development of agricultural policy. Congress, as one component of the triangle, includes two major committees concerned with agricultural policy, the House Committee on Agriculture and the Senate Committee on Agriculture, Nutrition, and Forestry. The Department of Agriculture, the second component of the triangle, has more than 100,000 employees, plus thousands of contractors and consultants. Agricultural interest groups, the third component of the triangle, include many large and powerful associations, such as the American Farm Bureau Federation, the National Cattlemen's Beef Association, and the National Corn Growers Association. These three components of the iron triangle work together, formally or informally, to create policy.

For example, the various agricultural interest groups lobby Congress to develop policies that benefit their groups' economic welfare. Members of Congress cannot afford to ignore the wishes of interest groups because those groups are potential sources of voter support and campaign contributions. The legislators in Congress also work closely with the Department of Agriculture, which, in implementing a policy, can develop rules that benefit—or at least do not hurt—various industries or groups. The Department of Agriculture, in turn, supports policies that enhance the department's budget and powers. In this way, according to theory, agricultural policy is created that benefits all three components of the iron triangle.

Issue Networks. With the growth in the complexity of government, policymaking also has become more complicated. The bureaucracy is larger, Congress has more committees and subcommittees, and interest groups are more powerful than ever. Although iron triangles still exist, often they are inadequate as descriptions of how policy is made today. Frequently, different interest groups concerned about a certain area of policy have conflicting demands, which makes agency decision making difficult. Additionally, during periods of divided government, departments are pressured by the president to take one approach and by Congress to take another.

Many scholars now use the term issue network to describe the policymaking process. An **issue network** consists of individuals or organizations that support a particular policy position on the environment, taxation, consumer safety, or some other issue. Typically, an issue network includes legislators and/or their staff members, interest group leaders, bureaucrats, scholars and other experts, and representatives from the media. Members of a particular issue network work together to influence the president, members of Congress,

Iron Triangle
A three-way alliance among legislators in Congress, bureaucrats, and interest groups to make or preserve policies that benefit their respective interests.

Issue Network
A group of individuals or organizations—which may consist of legislators and legislative staff members, interest group leaders, bureaucrats, scholars and other experts, and media representatives—that supports a particular policy position on a given issue.

administrative agencies, and the courts to affect public policy on a specific issue. Each policy issue may involve conflicting positions taken by two or more issue networks.

Congressional Control of the Bureaucracy

Many political pundits doubt whether Congress can meaningfully control the federal bureaucracy. These commentators forget that Congress specifies in an agency's enabling legislation the powers of the agency and the parameters within which it can operate. Additionally, Congress has "the power of the purse" and theoretically could refuse to authorize or appropriate funds for a particular agency. Whether Congress would actually take such a drastic measure would depend on the circumstances. It is clear, however, that Congress does have the legal authority to decide whether or not to fund administrative agencies.

Congress also can exercise oversight over agencies. Congressional committees conduct investigations and hold hearings to oversee an agency's actions, reviewing them to ensure compliance with congressional intentions. The agency's officers and employees can be ordered to testify before a committee about the details of various actions. Through the questions and comments of members of the House or Senate during the hearings, Congress indicates its positions on specific programs and issues. The views expressed in any investigations and hearings are taken seriously by agency officials, who often act on them.

Gary Fandel/Bloomberg/Getty Images

Image 11.5 Two farmers walking together near their cattle.
▶ What part do farmers play in agricultural policymaking at the federal level?

Making A Difference

What the Government Knows About You

The federal government collects billions of pieces of information on tens of millions of Americans each year. You are probably the subject of several federal records (for example, in the Social Security Administration, the Internal Revenue Service, and, if you are male, the Selective Service).

Why Should You Care? Verifying the information that the government has about you can be important. On several occasions, the records of two people with similar names have become confused. Sometimes innocent persons have had the criminal records of other persons erroneously inserted into their files. Such disasters are not always caused by bureaucratic error. One of the most common crimes in today's world is "identity theft," in which one person makes use of another individual's personal identifiers (such as a Social Security number) to commit fraud.

What Can You Do? The 1966 Freedom of Information Act (FOIA) requires that the federal government release, at your request, any identifiable information it has about you or about any other subject.

(Some categories of material are exempted, however.) To request material, write directly to the Freedom of Information Act officer at the agency in question. You must have a relatively specific idea about the document or information you want to obtain.

A second law, the Privacy Act of 1974, gives you access specifically to information the government may have collected about you. This law allows you to review records on file with federal agencies and to check those records for possible inaccuracies.

If you want to look at any records or find out if an agency has a record on you, write to the agency head or Privacy Act officer, and address your letter to the specific agency. State that "under the provisions of the Privacy Act of 1974, 5 U.S.C. 522a, I hereby request a copy of (or access to)." Then describe the record that you wish to investigate.

The General Services Administration (GSA) has published a citizen's guide, *Your Right to Federal Records*. You can locate this manual by entering its name into your favorite search engine.

Key Terms

agency capture 270	government corporation 272	independent regulatory agencies 270	Pendleton Act (Civil Service Reform Act) 275
bureaucracy 264		iron triangle 282	
cabinet departments 268	Government in the Sunshine Act 277	issue network 282	privatization 277
civil Service Commission 275	independent executive agencies 270	line organizations 268	spoils system 275
enabling legislation 279		merit system 275	whistleblower 278

Chapter Summary

>> **LO 11-1** Bureaucracies are hierarchical organizations characterized by division of labor and extensive procedural rules. Bureaucracy is the primary form of organization of most major corporations and universities, as well as governments.

Since the founding of the United States, the federal bureaucracy has grown from a few to about 2.9 million employees (including the U.S. Postal Service, Congress, and the judiciary, but excluding the military). Federal, state, and local employees together make up about 10 percent of the nation's civilian labor force. Social Security, Medicare, Medicaid, and military defense are the largest components of federal spending. Major sources of federal revenue include the individual and corporate income taxes, Social Security and Medicare payroll taxes, and borrowing.

>> **LO 11-2** The executive branch consists of fifteen cabinet departments, as well as a large number of independent executive agencies, independent regulatory agencies, and government corporations. These entities enjoy varying degrees of autonomy, visibility, and political support.

>> **LO 11-3** A federal bureaucracy of career civil servants was formed during Thomas Jefferson's presidency. Andrew Jackson implemented a spoils system through which he appointed his own political supporters. A civil service based on professionalism and merit was the goal of the Civil Service Reform Act of 1883. Concerns that the civil service be freed from the pressures of politics prompted the passage of the Hatch Act in 1939. The Civil Service Reform Act of 1978 made significant changes in the administration of the civil service by creating the Office of Personnel Management and the Merit Systems Protection Board.

>> **LO 11-4** There have been many attempts to make the federal bureaucracy more open, efficient, and responsive to the needs of U.S. citizens. The most important reforms have included sunshine laws, privatization, and protection for whistleblowers, who are often subject to reprisals.

>> **LO 11-5** Congress delegates much of its authority to federal agencies when it creates new laws. The bureaucrats who run these agencies may become important policymakers, because Congress has neither the time nor the technical expertise to oversee the administration of its laws. The agency rulemaking process begins when a proposed regulation is published. A comment period follows, during which interested parties may offer suggestions for changes. The process is lengthy, and so is the process for repealing or changing a rule.

Congress exerts ultimate control over all federal agencies, because it controls the federal government's purse strings. The appropriations process provides a way to send messages of approval or disapproval to particular agencies, as do congressional hearings and investigations of agency actions.

Test Yourself

1. **In terms of federal dollars spent, the most important programs are:**
   a. social programs, including Social Security and Medicare.
   b. the military and subsidies for corporations.
   c. foreign aid.

2. **After the individual income tax, the next two largest sources of funds to support the federal government are:**
   a. the Social Security payroll tax and the Medicare payroll tax.
   b. the corporate income tax and the Social Security payroll tax.
   c. the Social Security payroll tax and borrowing.

3. **When a federal agency's function is to make and implement rules and regulations to protect the public interest, it is called:**
   a. an independent executive agency.
   b. an independent regulatory agency.
   c. a government corporation.

4. **The heads of federal regulatory agencies and members of agency boards and commissions are appointed by:**
   a. the president acting alone.
   b. the president with the consent of the Senate.
   c. the Supreme Court.

5. **When an agency serves the industry it is meant to regulate rather than serving the public, we call this:**
   a. agency capture.
   b. deregulation.
   c. an iron triangle.

6. **In the early days of this country, when a new president was of a different party than the outgoing president, government employees were often fired and replaced with supporters of the incoming president's party. This was called the:**
   a. civil service system.
   b. spoils system.
   c. patronage system.

7. **The first significant legislation aimed at making the federal civil service nonpartisan and independent was:**
   a. the Civil Service Act of 1978.
   b. the Hatch Act.
   c. the Pendleton Act of 1883.

8. **Privatization means that:**
   a. the government must provide individuals with the information it has on them.
   b. private companies replace members of the civil service in providing a government service.
   c. bonuses are awarded for efficient work.

9. **Under the Obama administration, whistleblowers:**
   a. received increased protection from reprisals.
   b. became less active.
   c. faced criminal charges with unprecedented frequency.

10. **Because Congress cannot oversee the daily administration of its many programs, it delegates power to agencies through:**
    a. enabling legislation.
    b. negotiated rulemaking.
    c. congressional oversight.

11. **An issue network consists of individuals or organizations that support a particular policy position. A typical issue network includes:**
    a. Congress, the president's cabinet, and the Supreme Court.
    b. federal judges, congressional staff, and the heads of certain private corporations.
    c. legislators (or their staff), interest group leaders, bureaucrats, scholars and other experts, and the media.

Essay Questions

1. The U.S. attorney general, head of the Justice Department, is appointed by the president and is frequently the president's close political ally. Should the attorney general and other U.S. attorneys be appointed on a partisan basis? Why or why not?

2. If Congress tried to make civil servants easier to fire, what political forces might stand in the way?

Answers to multiple-choice questions: 1. a, 2. c, 3. b, 4. b, 5. a, 6. b, 7. c, 8. b, 9. c, 10. a, 11. c.

Demonstrators outside the Supreme Court building in 2019. The court was hearing arguments about whether the 2020 Census should include a question on U.S. citizenship proposed by the Trump administration. Opponents of the question believed it would damage response rates in immigrant communities. The Court eventually held that the process used to add the question was improper. ► **Why are so many of the cases brought before the Court political in nature?**

Win McNamee/Getty Images News/Getty Images

The five **Learning Outcomes (LOs)** below are designed to help improve your understanding of this chapter. After reading this chapter, you should be able to:

» **LO 12-1** Explain the main sources of American law, including constitutions, statutes and regulations, and the common law tradition.

» **LO 12-2** Describe the structure of the federal court system and basic judicial requirements such as jurisdiction and standing to sue.

» **LO 12-3** Discuss the procedures used by the United States Supreme Court and the various types of opinions it hands down.

» **LO 12-4** Evaluate the manner in which federal judges are selected.

» **LO 12-5** Describe your views on whether the Supreme Court should make policy.

Check your understanding of the material with the Test Yourself section at the end of the chapter.

A s Alexis de Tocqueville, a French commentator on American society in the 1800s, noted, "scarcely any political question arises in the United States that is not resolved, sooner or later, into a judicial question."[1] Our judiciary forms part of our political process. The instant that judges interpret the law, they become actors in the political arena—policymakers working within a political institution. The most important political force within our judiciary is the United States Supreme Court. The justices of the Supreme Court are not elected but are appointed by the president and confirmed by the Senate, as are all other federal court judges.

How do courts make policy? Why do the federal courts play such an important role in American government? The answers to these questions lie, in part, in our colonial heritage. Most of American law is based on the English system, particularly the English common law tradition. In that tradition, the decisions made by judges constitute an important source of law. We open this chapter with an examination of this tradition and of the various other sources of American law. We then look at the federal court system—how it is organized, how its judges are selected, how these judges affect policy, and how they are restrained by our system of checks and balances.

Sources of American Law

> **LO 12-1:** Explain the main sources of American law, including constitutions, statutes and regulations, and the common law tradition.

The body of American law includes the federal and state constitutions, statutes passed by legislative bodies, administrative law, and case law—the legal principles expressed in court decisions. Case law is based in part on the common law tradition, which dates to the earliest English settlements in North America.

The Common Law Tradition

In 1066, the Normans conquered England, and William the Conqueror and his successors began the process of unifying the country. For years after the conquest, most disputes were settled according to local courts and customs. Under Henry II Plantagenet (1114–89), however, the king's courts sought to establish a common, or uniform, set of rules for the whole country. As the number of courts and cases increased, portions of the most important decisions of each year were gathered together and recorded in *Year Books*. Judges who were settling disputes similar to ones that had been decided before used the *Year Books* as the basis for their decisions. If a case was unique, judges had to create new rules, but they based their decisions on the general principles suggested by earlier cases. The body of judge-made law that developed under this system is still used today and is known as the **common law**.

Common Law
The body of law developed from judicial decisions in English and U.S. courts, not attributable to a legislature.

Stare Decisis. The practice of deciding new cases with reference to former decisions—that is, according to **precedent**—became a cornerstone of the English and American judicial systems. It is embodied in the doctrine of *stare decisis* (pronounced *ster*-ay dih-*si*-ses), a Latin phrase that means "to stand on decided cases." The doctrine of *stare decisis* obligates judges to follow the precedents set previously by their own courts or by higher courts that have authority over them.

Precedent
A court ruling bearing on subsequent legal decisions in similar cases. Judges rely on precedents in deciding cases.

Stare Decisis
To stand on decided cases—the judicial policy of following precedents established by past decisions.

---

1. Alexis de Tocqueville, *Democracy in America*, trans. George Lawrence (New York: Harper & Row, 1966), p. 248.

Image 12.1 A law student looks up cases in a law library.
▶ Would it be easier to find cases online? Why or why not?

VStock LLC/Tanya Constantine/Getty Images

Examples of Precedents. *Stare decisis* means that a lower state court in California would be obligated to follow a precedent set by the California Supreme Court. That lower court, however, would not be obligated to follow a precedent set by the supreme court of another state, because each state court system is independent. Of course, when the United States Supreme Court decides an issue, all of the nation's other courts are obligated to abide by the Court's decision, because the Supreme Court is the highest court in the land.

The doctrine of *stare decisis* provides a basis for judicial decision making in all countries that have common law systems. Today, the United States, Britain, and several dozen other countries have common law systems. Generally, those countries that were once colonies of Britain, including Australia, Canada, India, New Zealand, and others, have retained their English common law heritage.

Constitutions

The constitutions of the federal government and the states set forth the general organization, powers, and limits of government. The U.S. Constitution is the supreme law of the land. A law in violation of the Constitution, no matter what its source, may be declared unconstitutional and thereafter cannot be enforced. Similarly, the state constitutions are supreme within their respective borders (unless they conflict with the U.S. Constitution or federal laws and treaties made in accordance with it). The Constitution thus defines the political playing field on which state and federal powers are reconciled.

Statutes and Administrative Regulations

Although the English common law provides the basis for both our civil and our criminal legal systems, statutes (laws enacted by legislatures) have become increasingly important in defining the rights and obligations of individuals. Federal statutes may relate to any subject that is a concern of the federal government and may apply to areas ranging from hazardous waste to federal taxation. State statutes include criminal codes, commercial laws, and laws covering a variety of other matters. Cities, counties, and other local political bodies also pass statutes, which are called ordinances. These ordinances may deal with such issues as real estate zoning and public safety.

Rules and regulations issued by administrative agencies are another source of law. Today, much of the work of the courts consists of interpreting these laws and regulations and applying them to the specific circumstances of the cases that come before the courts.

Case Law

Because we have a common law tradition, in which the doctrine of *stare decisis* plays an important role, the decisions rendered by the courts also form an important body of law, collectively referred to as **case law**. Case law includes judicial interpretations of common law principles and doctrines, as well as interpretations of constitutional provisions, statutes, and administrative agency regulations. As you learned in previous chapters, it is up to the courts—and ultimately, if necessary, the Supreme Court—to decide what a

Case Law
Judicial interpretations of common law principles and doctrines, as well as interpretations of constitutional law, statutory law, and administrative law.

constitutional provision or a statutory phrase means. In doing so, the courts, in effect, establish law.

The Federal Court System

The United States has a dual court system, with state courts and federal courts. Each of the fifty states, as well as the District of Columbia, has its own independent system of courts. This means that there are fifty-two court systems in total. Here we focus on the federal courts.

Basic Judicial Requirements

In any court system, state or federal, certain requirements must be met before a case can be brought. Two important requirements are jurisdiction and standing to sue.

Jurisdiction. A state court can exercise **jurisdiction** (the authority of the court to hear and decide a case) over the residents of a particular geographic area, such as a county or district. A state's highest court, or supreme court, has jurisdictional authority over all residents within the state.

Because the Constitution established a federal government with limited powers, federal jurisdiction is also limited. Article III, Section 1, of the U.S. Constitution limits the jurisdiction of the federal courts to cases that involve either a federal question or diversity of citizenship. A **federal question** arises when a case is based, at least in part, on the U.S. Constitution, a treaty, or a federal law. Persons who claim that their rights under the Constitution, such as the right to free speech, have been violated could bring a case in a federal court. **Diversity of citizenship** exists when the parties to a lawsuit are from different states or (more rarely) when the suit involves a U.S. citizen and a government or citizen of a foreign country. The amount in controversy must be at least $75,000 before a federal court can take jurisdiction in a diversity case, however.

Given the significant limits on federal jurisdiction, most lawsuits and criminal cases are heard in state, rather than federal, courts. A defendant or a party to a dispute handled by a state court may file an appeal with a state appeals court, or even the state's supreme court. Appeals cannot be taken to a federal court, however, unless a federal question is involved.

Standing to Sue. Another basic judicial requirement is standing to sue, or a sufficient "stake" in a matter to justify bringing suit. The party bringing a lawsuit must have suffered a harm, or have been threatened by a harm, as a result of the action that led to the dispute in question. Standing to sue also requires that the controversy at issue be a justiciable (pronounced just-*tish*-a-bul) controversy. A **justiciable controversy** is a controversy that is real and substantial, as opposed to hypothetical or academic. In other words, a court will not give advisory opinions on hypothetical questions.

Parties to Lawsuits

In most lawsuits, the parties are the plaintiff (the person or organization that initiates the lawsuit) and the defendant (the person or organization against whom the lawsuit is brought). There may be a number of plaintiffs and defendants in a single lawsuit. Many lawsuits are

Jurisdiction
The authority of a court to decide certain cases. Not all courts have the authority to decide all cases. When a case arises and what is its subject matter are two separate jurisdictional issues.

Federal Question
A question that has to do with the U.S. Constitution, acts of Congress, or treaties. A federal question provides a basis for federal jurisdiction.

Diversity of Citizenship
The condition that exists when the parties to a lawsuit are from different states or when the suit involves a U.S. citizen and a government or citizen of a foreign country. Diversity of citizenship can provide a basis for federal jurisdiction.

Justiciable Controversy
A controversy that is real and substantial, as opposed to hypothetical or academic.

Litigate
To engage in a legal proceeding or seek relief in a court of law. To carry on a lawsuit.

Amicus Curiae Briefs
A written legal argument filed by a third party, or *amicus curiae* (Latin for "friend of the court"), who is not directly involved in the litigation but who has an interest in the outcome of the case.

Class-Action suit
A lawsuit filed by an individual seeking damages for "all persons similarly situated."

brought by interest groups. Interest groups play an important role in our judicial system, because they **litigate**—bring to trial—or assist in litigating most cases of racial or gender-based discrimination, almost all civil liberties cases, and more than one-third of the cases involving business matters. Interest groups also file *amicus curiae* (pronounced ah-*mee*-kous *kur*-ee-eye) **briefs**, or "friend of the court" briefs, in more than 50 percent of these kinds of cases.

Sometimes, interest groups or other plaintiffs will bring a **class-action suit**, in which whatever the court decides will affect all members of a class similarly situated (such as users of a particular product manufactured by the defendant in the lawsuit). The strategy of class-action lawsuits was pioneered by such groups as the National Association for the Advancement of Colored People (NAACP), the Legal Defense Fund, and the Sierra Club.

Procedural Rules

Both the federal and the state courts have established procedural rules that shape the litigation process. These rules are designed to protect the rights and interests of the parties and to ensure that the litigation proceeds in a fair and orderly manner. The rules also serve to identify the issues that must be decided by the court—thus saving court time and expense. Court decisions may also apply to trial procedures. For example, the Supreme Court has held that the parties' attorneys cannot discriminate against prospective jurors on the basis of race or gender. Some lower courts have also held that people cannot be excluded from juries because of their sexual orientation or religion.

The parties must comply with procedural rules and with any orders given by the judge during the course of the litigation. When a party does not follow a court's order, the court can cite that person for contempt. A party who commits civil contempt (failing to comply with a court's order for the benefit of another party to the proceeding) can be taken into custody, fined, or both, until that person complies with the court's order. A party who commits criminal contempt (obstructing the administration of justice or disrespecting the rules of the court) also can be taken into custody and fined but cannot avoid punishment by complying with a previous order.

Types of Federal Courts

As you can see in Figure 12.1, the federal court system is basically a three-tiered model consisting of (1) U.S. district courts and various specialized courts of limited jurisdiction (not all of the latter are shown in the figure), (2) intermediate U.S. courts of appeals, and (3) the United States Supreme Court.

Trial Court
The court in which most cases begin.

General Jurisdiction
A court's authority to hear cases that is not significantly restricted. A court of general jurisdiction normally can hear a broad range of cases.

Limited Jurisdiction
A court's authority to hear cases that is restricted to certain types of claims, such as tax claims or bankruptcy petitions.

U.S. District Courts. The U.S. district courts are trial courts. A **trial court** is what the name implies—a court in which trials are held and testimony is taken. The U.S. district courts are courts of **general jurisdiction**, meaning that they can hear cases involving a broad array of issues. Federal cases involving most matters typically are heard in district courts. The other courts on the lower tier of the model shown in Figure 12.1 are courts of **limited jurisdiction**, meaning that they can try cases involving only certain types of claims, such as tax claims or bankruptcy petitions.

There is at least one federal district court in every state. The number of judicial districts has varied historically owing to population changes and corresponding caseloads, but no entirely new district has been created since California was redivided in 1966. Today, there are ninety-four federal judicial districts and 677 authorized district court judgeships. The Southern District of New York has the largest number of judges—28.

Figure 12.1	The Organization of the Federal Court System

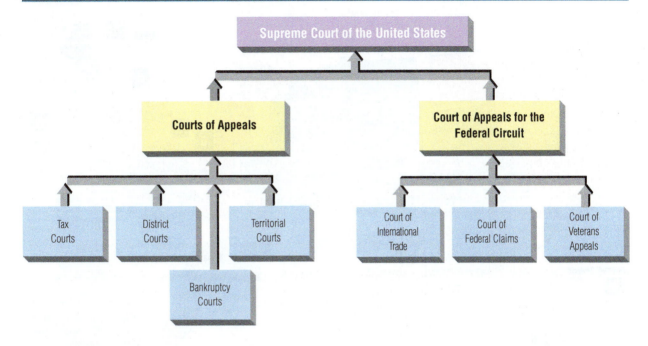

A party who is dissatisfied with the decision of a district court can appeal the case to the appropriate U.S. court of appeals, or federal **appellate court**. Figure 12.2 shows the jurisdictional boundaries of the district courts (which are state boundaries, unless otherwise indicated by dotted lines within a state) and of the U.S. courts of appeals.

Appellate Court
A court having jurisdiction to review cases and issues that were originally tried in lower courts.

U.S. Courts of Appeals. There are thirteen U.S. courts of appeals—also referred to as U.S. circuit courts of appeals. Twelve of these courts, including the U.S. Court of Appeals for the District of Columbia, hear appeals from the federal district courts located within their respective judicial circuits (geographic areas over which they exercise jurisdiction). The Court of Appeals for the Thirteenth Circuit, called the Federal Circuit, has national appellate jurisdiction over certain types of cases, such as cases involving patent law and those in which the U.S. government is a defendant.

Note that when an appellate court reviews a case decided in a district court, the appellate court does not conduct another trial. Rather, a panel of three or more judges reviews the record of the case on appeal, which includes a transcript of the trial proceedings. The panel determines whether the trial court committed an error. Usually, appellate courts do not look at questions of fact (such as whether a party did commit a certain action, such as burning a flag). Instead, they look at questions of law (such as whether the act of flag burning is a form of speech protected by the First Amendment to the Constitution). An appellate court will challenge a trial court's finding of fact only when the finding is clearly contrary to the evidence presented at trial or when there is no evidence to support the finding.

A party can petition the United States Supreme Court to review an appellate court's decision. The likelihood that the Supreme Court will grant the petition is slim, however,

Figure 12.2 | **The Federal Court System—Courts of Appeal and District Courts**

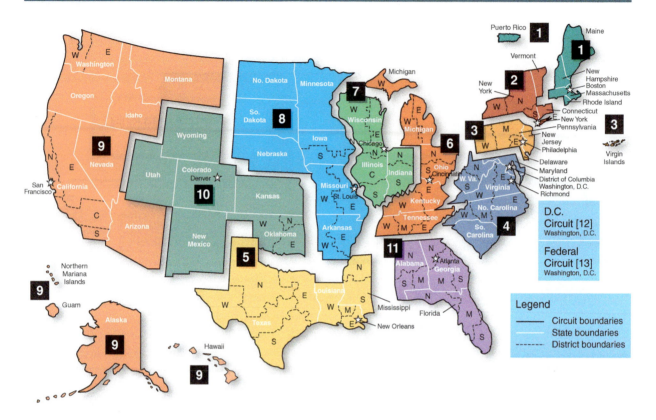

because the Court reviews only a small percentage of the cases decided by the appellate courts. This means that decisions made by appellate courts usually are final.

The United States Supreme Court. The highest level of the three-tiered model of the federal court system is the United States Supreme Court. Although the Supreme Court can exercise original jurisdiction (that is, act as a trial court) in certain cases, such as those affecting foreign diplomats and those in which a state is a party, most of its work is as an appellate court. The Court hears appeals not only from the federal appellate courts, but also from the highest state courts. Note, though, that the United States Supreme Court can review a state supreme court decision only if a federal question is involved. Because of its importance in the federal court system, we look more closely at the Supreme Court later in this chapter.

Administrative Law Tribunals. In addition to the federal court system, federal administrative agencies and executive departments often employ administrative law judges, who resolve disputes arising under the rules governing their agencies. For example, the Social Security Administration might hold a hearing to determine whether an individual is entitled to collect a particular benefit. If all internal agency appeals processes have been exhausted, a party may have a right to take the case into the federal court system.

Federal Courts and the War on Terrorism

As noted, the federal court system includes a variety of trial courts of limited jurisdiction, dealing with matters such as tax claims or international trade. The government's attempts to combat terrorism have drawn attention to certain specialized courts that meet in secret. We look next at these courts, as well as at the role of the federal courts with respect to the detainees accused of terrorism.

The FISA Court. The federal government created the first secret court in 1978. In that year, Congress passed the Foreign Intelligence Surveillance Act (FISA), which established a court to hear requests for warrants for the surveillance of suspected spies. Officials can request a warrant without having to reveal to the suspect or to the public the information used to justify the warrant or even that the warrant exists. The FISA court has approved almost all of the thousands of requests for warrants that federal officials have submitted. There is no public access to the court's proceedings or records. All FISA court judges are appointed by the chief justice of the Supreme Court without review by any other authority.

In the aftermath of the terrorist attacks on September 11, 2001, the George W. Bush administration expanded the powers of the FISA court. Previously, the FISA had allowed secret domestic surveillance only if the purpose was to combat intelligence gathering by foreign powers. Amendments to the FISA enacted after 9/11 changed this wording to "a significant purpose"—meaning that warrants may now be requested to obtain evidence that can be used in criminal trials.

Image 12.2 Ketanji Brown Jackson is the 116th justice of the Supreme Court. ▶ Who nominated her?

Anna Moneymaker/Getty Images News/Getty Images

The FISA Court and the National Security Agency. Some of the National Security Agency (NSA) material that Edward Snowden leaked to the press in 2013 dealt with the FISA court. One of the first stories described a FISA court order that required Verizon to provide a daily, ongoing feed of all domestic landline metadata (data about data) to the NSA. Metadata, in this case, includes information about calls, such as time and duration of the call, the phone number that originated the call, and the phone number that received the call. Metadata does not include the content of actual conversations. It soon came out that the FISA court had effectively granted the NSA the right to collect metadata on all phone calls, regardless of carrier.

The FISA court apparently justified the massive data collection through a "special needs" exception to the Fourth Amendment's requirement of a warrant for searches and seizures. It would seem that under this exception the Fourth Amendment does not apply to national security surveillance. These revelations touched off a massive debate between advocates of civil liberties and those concerned about national security.

Many of the actions authorized by the FISA court were based on the USA Patriot Act, which was passed in 2001 in the wake of the 9/11 terrorist attacks. In 2015, Congress passed the USA Freedom Act. This law reauthorized some of the actions permitted under the Patriot Act, but curbed others. The new law placed several new limits on surveillance authorized by the FISA court. In addition, the court was now required to release any new precedents that it might set, as well as any new guidance the court might issue on surveillance activities.

Alien "Removal Courts." In 1996, Congress passed the Anti-Terrorism and Effective Death Penalty Act. The new law was a response to the bombing of a federal building in 1995 in

AP Images/Jim Lo Scalzo

Image 12.3 Amy Coney Barrett became an associate justice of the U.S. Supreme Court on October 27, 2020.

Oklahoma City, which killed 168 people. Even though the perpetrators of this crime were U.S. citizens whose motives were entirely domestic, the new law focused on noncitizens. For example, the act created an alien "removal court" to hear evidence against suspected "alien terrorists." The judges in this court rule on whether there is probable cause for deportation. If so, a public deportation proceeding is held in a U.S. district court. The prosecution does not need to follow procedures that normally apply in criminal cases. In addition, the defendant cannot see the evidence that the prosecution used to secure the hearing.

The Federal Courts and Suspected Terrorists. After the 9/11 attacks, the U.S. military took custody of hundreds of suspected terrorists seized in Afghanistan and elsewhere and held them at Guantánamo Bay, Cuba. According to the George W. Bush administration, they could be held indefinitely. The handling of the prisoners at Guantánamo has been a source of ongoing controversy. The Supreme Court held, first in 2004 and then in 2006, that the Bush administration's treatment of these detainees violated the U.S. Constitution.[2]

In response to the Court's 2006 decision, Congress passed an act that eliminated federal court jurisdiction over challenges by these detainees based on *habeas corpus.* (This term refers to the right of detained persons to challenge the legality of their detention before a judge.) In 2008, in *Boumediene v. Bush,* the Court ruled that the provisions restricting the federal courts' jurisdictional authority over detainees' *habeas corpus* challenges were illegal.[3] The decision gave Guantánamo detainees the right to challenge their detention in federal civil courts. In 2010, however, a federal appeals court ruled that the administration had the right to detain prisoners indefinitely at Bagram Air Force Base in Afghanistan because the prison was located on foreign soil and within a war zone.[4] (The Biden administration pulled out all U.S. forces from Afghanistan in 2021.) As of 2022, thirty-nine prisoners remained indefinitely detained in the Guantánamo prison. Twenty-seven of them have never been charged with any crime. Guantánamo Bay remains the longest standing war prison in United States history. In January 2022, the Biden administration approved the release of almost half of those retained. The problem was to find countries that would take them.

The Supreme Court at Work

» **LO 12-3:** Discuss the procedures used by the United States Supreme Court and the various types of opinions it hands down.

The Supreme Court begins its regular annual term on the first Monday in October and usually adjourns in late June or early July of the next year. Special sessions may be held after the regular term ends, but only a few cases are decided in this way. More commonly, cases are carried over until the next regular session.

---

2. *Hamdi v. Rumsfeld*, 542 U.S. 507 (2004); *Hamdan v. Rumsfeld*, 548 U.S. 557 (2006).
3. 553 U.S. 723 (2008).
4. *Maqaleh v. Gates*, 605 F.3d 84 (D.C.Cir. 2010).

Of the total number of cases that are decided each year in U.S. courts, those reviewed by the Supreme Court represent less than one in four thousand. Included in these, however, are decisions that profoundly affect our lives. In recent years, the United States Supreme Court has decided issues involving the right to bear arms, health care reform, and campaign finance. Other cases have involved affirmative action programs, religious freedom, abortion, and many other matters with significant consequences for the nation.

Because the Supreme Court exercises a great deal of discretion over the types of cases it hears, it can influence the nation's policies by issuing decisions in some types of cases and refusing to hear appeals in others, thereby allowing lower court decisions to stand. Indeed, the fact that George W. Bush assumed the presidency in 2001 instead of Al Gore, his Democratic opponent, was largely due to a Supreme Court decision to review a Florida court's ruling. In *Bush v. Gore,* the Supreme Court reversed the Florida court's order to recount manually the votes in selected Florida counties—a decision that effectively handed the presidency to Bush.[5]

Which Cases Reach the Supreme Court?

Many people are surprised to learn that in a typical case, there is no absolute right of appeal to the Supreme Court. The Court's appellate jurisdiction is almost entirely discretionary—the Court chooses which cases it will decide. The justices never explain their reasons for hearing certain cases and not others, so it is difficult to predict which case or type of case the Court might select.

Factors That Bear on the Decision. A number of factors bear on the decision to accept a case. If a legal question has been decided differently by various lower courts, it may need resolution by the highest court. A ruling may be necessary if a lower court's decision conflicts with an existing Supreme Court ruling. In general, the Court considers whether the issue could have significance beyond the parties to the dispute.

Another factor is whether the solicitor general is asking the Court to take a case. The solicitor general, a high-ranking presidential appointee within the Justice Department, represents the national government before the Supreme Court and promotes presidential policies in the federal courts. The solicitor general decides what cases the government should request the Supreme Court to review and what position the government should take in cases before the Court.

Granting Petitions for Review. If the Court decides to grant a petition for review, it issues a **writ of *certiorari*** (pronounced sur-shee-uh-*rah*-ree). The writ orders a lower court to send the Supreme Court a record of the case for review. The vast majority of the petitions for review are denied. A denial is not a decision on the merits of a case, nor does it indicate agreement with the lower court's opinion. (The judgment of the lower court remains in force, however.) Therefore, denial of the writ has no value as a precedent. The Court will not issue a writ unless at least four justices approve of it. This is called the **rule of four**.[6]

Writ of *Certiorari*
An order issued by a higher court to a lower court to send up the record of a case for review.

Rule of Four
A United States Supreme Court procedure by which four justices must vote to grant a petition for review if a case is to come before the full court.

---

5. 531 U.S. 98 (2000).
6. The "rule of four" is modified when seven or fewer justices participate, which occurs from time to time. When that happens, as few as three justices can grant *certiorari*.

Court Procedures

Once the Supreme Court grants *certiorari* in a particular case, the justices do extensive research on the legal issues and facts involved in the case. (Of course, some preliminary research is necessary before deciding to grant the petition for review.) Each justice is entitled to four law clerks, who undertake much of the research and preliminary drafting necessary for the justice to form an opinion.

The Court normally does not hear any evidence, as is true with all appeals courts. The Court's consideration of a case is based on the abstracts, the record, and the briefs. The attorneys are permitted to present **oral arguments**. Unlike the practice in most courts, lawyers addressing the Supreme Court can be (and often are) questioned by the justices at any time during oral arguments. All statements and the justices' questions during oral arguments are recorded.

The justices meet to discuss and vote on cases in conferences held throughout the term. In these conferences, in addition to deciding cases already before the Court, the justices determine which new petitions for *certiorari* to grant. These conferences are strictly private—no stenographers, audio recorders, or video cameras are allowed.

Decisions and Opinions

When the Court has reached a decision, its opinion is written. The **opinion** contains the Court's ruling on the issue or issues presented, the reasons for its decision, the rules of law that apply, and other information. In many cases, the decision of the lower court is **affirmed**, resulting in the enforcement of that court's judgment or decree. If the Supreme Court believes that the lower court made the wrong decision, however, the decision will be **reversed**. Sometimes, the case will be **remanded** (sent back to the court that originally heard the case) for a new trial or other proceeding. For example, a lower court might have held that a party was not entitled to bring a lawsuit under a particular law. If the Supreme Court holds to the contrary, it will remand (send back) the case to the trial court with instructions that the trial go forward.

The Court's written opinion sometimes is unsigned. This is called an opinion *per curiam* ("by the court"). Typically, the Court's opinion is signed by all the justices who agree with it. When in the majority, the chief justice decides who writes the opinion and may write it personally. When the chief justice is in the minority, the senior justice on the majority side assigns the opinion.

Types of Opinions. When all justices unanimously agree on an opinion, the opinion is written for the entire Court (all the justices) and can be deemed a **unanimous opinion**. When there is not a unanimous opinion, a **majority opinion** is written, outlining the views of the majority of the justices involved in the case. Often, one or more justices who feel strongly about making or emphasizing a particular point that is not made or emphasized in the majority written opinion will write a **concurring opinion**. That means the justice writing the concurring opinion agrees (concurs) with the conclusion given in the majority written opinion but wants to make or clarify a particular point or to voice disapproval of the grounds on which the decision was made.

Note that it is also possible for a group of justices to issue a **plurality opinion**. Such an opinion does not represent a majority of the Court, but it will still decide the case because one or more concurring opinions agrees with its verdict.

Finally, in other than unanimous opinions, one or more dissenting opinions are usually written by those justices who do not agree with the majority. The **dissenting opinion** is important because it often forms the basis of the arguments used years later if the Court reverses the previous decision and establishes a new precedent.

Oral Arguments
The arguments presented in person by attorneys to an appellate court.

Opinion
A statement by a judge or a court of the decision reached in a case. An opinion sets forth the applicable law and details the reasoning on which the ruling was based.

Affirmed
To declare that a court ruling is valid and must stand.

Reversed
To annul or make void a court ruling on account of some error or irregularity.

Remanded
To send a case back to the court that originally heard it.

Unanimous Opinion
A court opinion or determination on which all judges agree.

Majority Opinion
A court opinion reflecting the views of the majority of the judges.

Concurring Opinion
A separate opinion prepared by a judge who supports the decision of the majority of the court but for different reasons.

Plurality Opinion
An opinion by a minority of the Court that decides a case because it is supported by one or more concurring opinions.

Dissenting Opinion
A separate opinion in which a judge dissents from (disagrees with) the conclusion reached by the majority of the court and expounds their own views about the case.

Publishing Opinions. Shortly after an opinion is written, the Supreme Court announces its decision from the bench. The clerk of the Court also releases the opinion for online publication. Ultimately, the opinion is published in the *United States Reports,* which is the official printed record of the Court's decisions. Because it takes some years for a case to be printed in the official record, citations of recent cases often refer to the *Supreme Court Reporter,* a compilation published by a private company. Citations containing the abbreviation "U.S." refer to the official reporter, and the abbreviation "S.Ct." refers to the commercial reporter.

Image 12.4 Justice Clarence Thomas with his clerks. ▶ Why is a Supreme Court clerkship a desirable position for a young attorney?

The Court's Dwindling Caseload. Some have complained that the Court reviews too few cases each term, thus giving the lower courts insufficient guidance on important issues. Indeed, the number of signed opinions issued by the Court has dwindled notably since the 1980s. For example, in its 1982–83 term, the Court issued signed opinions in 151 cases. By the early 2000s, this number had dropped to between 70 and 80 per term. In the term ending in June 2022, the number was 66.

The Selection of Federal Judges

≫ **LO 12-4:** Evaluate the manner in which federal judges are selected.

All federal judges are appointed. The Constitution, in Article II, Section 2, states that the president is to appoint the justices of the Supreme Court with the advice and consent of the Senate. Congress has established the same procedure for staffing other federal courts. This means that the Senate and the president jointly decide who shall fill every vacant judicial position, no matter what the level.

There are currently 870 federal judicial posts at all levels, although at any given time many of these positions are vacant. Once appointed to a federal judgeship, a person holds that job for life. Judges serve until they resign, retire voluntarily, or die. Federal judges who engage in blatantly illegal conduct may be removed through impeachment and conviction, although such action is rare.

In contrast to federal judges, many state judges—including the judges who sit on state supreme courts—are chosen by the voters in elections. What arguments favor the election of judges? What problems can such a system create? We examine such questions in this chapter's *Which Side Are You On?* feature.

Judicial Appointments

Candidates for federal judgeships are suggested to the president by the Department of Justice, senators, other judges, the candidates themselves, and lawyers' associations and other interest groups. In selecting a candidate to nominate for a judgeship, the president

Which Side Are You On?

Should State Judges Be Elected?

The nation's founders sought to insulate the courts from popular passions, and as a result, all of the judges and justices in the federal court system are appointed by the president and confirmed by the Senate. Federal judges and justices are appointed for life. In thirty-nine states, in contrast, some or all state judges must face election and reelection.

The question of whether state judges should be elected or whether they should be appointed has proved to be very divisive. Many in the legal community agreed with a former Oregon Supreme Court justice, Hans A. Linde, when he pointed out that "to the rest of the world, American adherence to judicial elections is as incomprehensible as our rejection of the metric system." Public opinion polls, however, regularly show strong public support for electing judges.

The People's Will Should Prevail

Those who advocate the election of state judges see the issue as a simple matter of democracy. Judges cannot be insulated from politics. Governors who appoint judges are highly political creatures and are likely to appoint members of their own party. If politics is going to play a role, the people ought to have their say directly. In addition, researchers at the University of Chicago School of Law found that elected judges write more opinions than do appointed judges.

We let ordinary people participate in the legal process through the jury system, and they ought to be able to choose judges as well.

That way, the people can be confident that judges will respond to popular concerns, such as the fear of crime. Without elections, judges living in safe, upscale neighborhoods may fail to appreciate what it is like to fear for your safety on an everyday basis.

Electing Judges Leads to Corruption

Former United States Supreme Court justice Sandra Day O'Connor condemned the practice of electing judges: "No other nation in the world does that because they realize you are not going to get fair and impartial judges that way." Opponents of judicial elections observe that most voters do not have enough information to make sensible choices when they vote for judicial candidates.

Judicial candidates raise considerable funds from the lawyers who will appear before them if they win. Additional campaign funds are raised by special interest groups. People in favor of electing judges think that the candidates they vote for will, for example, be "tough on crime." Often, they are. But those who oppose judicial elections contend that elected judges will also tilt toward the wealthy groups that put them in office, and away from the interests of ordinary people.

■ For Critical Analysis

In some states, judicial candidates are nominated by political parties. What consequences can follow from such explicit partisan identification?

---

considers not only the person's competence but also other factors, including the person's political philosophy (as will be discussed shortly), ethnicity, and gender.

The nomination process—no matter how the nominees are obtained—always works the same way. The president makes the actual nomination, submitting the name to the Senate. To reach a conclusion, the Senate Judiciary Committee (operating through subcommittees) invites testimony, both written and oral, at its various hearings. The Senate then either confirms or rejects the nomination.

Federal District Court Judgeship Nominations. Although the president officially nominates federal judges, in the past the nomination of federal district court judges actually originated with a senator or senators of the president's party from the state in which there was a vacancy (if such a senator existed). In effect, judicial appointments were a form of political patronage. President Jimmy Carter (1977–81) ended this tradition by establishing independent commissions to oversee the initial nomination process. President Ronald Reagan (1981–89) abolished Carter's nominating commissions and established complete presidential control of nominations.

For many years after President Reagan took control of nominations, a practice called senatorial courtesy continued to constrain the president's freedom to appoint federal district judges. Senatorial courtesy allowed senators of the president's political party to veto judicial appointments in their state. Senators from the "opposition" party (the party to which the president does not belong) also enjoyed the right of senatorial courtesy, although their veto power varied over time. Home-state senators expressed their opinion of judicial candidates on blue slips that were returned to the chair of the Senate Judiciary Committee. Under the Trump administration, however, the Senate abandoned the tradition altogether.

When Joe Biden was seeking the Democratic nomination to be the presidential candidate, he proclaimed that he would nominate a Black female for the next vacancy on the Supreme Court. When that vacancy was going to occur, he did indeed choose a Black female—Ketanji Brown Jackson.

Federal Courts of Appeals Appointments. There are many fewer federal courts of appeals appointments than federal district court appointments, but they are more influential. Federal appellate judges handle more important matters, and therefore presidents take a keener interest in the nomination process for such judgeships. Also, the U.S. courts of appeals have become "stepping-stones" to the Supreme Court.

Supreme Court Appointments. Table 12.1 summarizes the background of all Supreme Court justices to 2023. As you can see, the most common occupational background of the justices at the time of their appointment has been private legal practice or state or federal judgeship. Those nine justices who were in federal executive posts at the time of their appointment held the high offices of secretary of state, comptroller of the treasury, secretary of the navy, postmaster general, secretary of the interior, chairman of the Securities and Exchange Commission, and secretary of labor. In the "Other" category under "Occupational Position Before Appointment" in Table 12.1 are two justices who were professors of law (including William H. Taft, a former president) and one justice who was a North Carolina state employee with responsibility for organizing and revising the state's statutes.

Partisanship and Judicial Appointments

In most circumstances, the president appoints judges or justices who belong to the president's own political party. Presidents see their federal judiciary appointments as one sure way to institutionalize their political views long after they have left office. George W. Bush appointed 322 federal district and appeals court judges, ensuring a majority of Republican-appointed judges in the federal courts. Barack Obama then appointed a total of 329 judges, and the balance shifted again. Under President Trump, the Senate confirmed new judges at a rapid pace. Under President Biden, the confirmation of new judges also continued at a fast pace principally because there was a possibility that the Democratic-controlled Senate might become Republican controlled after the November 2022 elections.

Supreme Court Appointments by Bush. President George W. Bush was also able to fill two Supreme Court vacancies—those left by the death of Chief Justice William Rehnquist and by the retirement of Justice Sandra Day O'Connor. Bush appointed two conservatives to these positions—John G. Roberts, Jr., who became chief justice, and Samuel Alito, Jr., who replaced O'Connor. The appointment of Alito, in particular, strengthened the rightward movement of the Court that had begun years before with the appointment of Rehnquist as chief justice. This was because Alito was a reliable member of the Court's conservative wing, whereas O'Connor had been a "swing voter."

| Table 12.1 | Background of Supreme Court Justices to 2023 |

Number of Justices (116 = Total)		Number of Justices (116 = Total)	
Occupational Position Before Appointment		**Political Party Affiliation**	
Federal judgeship	35	Federalist (to 1835)	13
Private legal practice	25	Jeffersonian Republican (to 1828)	7
State judgeship	21	Whig (to 1861)	1
U.S. attorney general	7	Democrat	47
Deputy or assistant U.S. attorney general	2	Republican	46
U.S. solicitor general	3	Independent	1
U.S. senator	6	**Age on Appointment**	
U.S. representative	2	Under 40	5
State governor	3	41–50	36
Federal executive post	9	51–60	61
Other	3	61–70	14
Religious Background		**Gender**	
Protestant	85	Male	110
Roman Catholic	16	Female	6
Jewish	7	**Race**	
Unitarian	7	White (non-Latino)	112
No religious affiliation	1	African American	3
Educational Background		Latino	1
College graduate	100		
Not a college graduate	16		

Sources: Congressional Quarterly, *Congressional Quarterly's Guide to the U.S. Supreme Court* (Washington, D.C.: Congressional Quarterly Press, 1996); and authors' updates.

Supreme Court Appointments by Obama. President Barack Obama had two opportunities to fill Supreme Court vacancies in the first two years of his term. The vacancies resulted from the retirement of justices David Souter and John Paul Stevens. Both had been members of the Court's so-called liberal wing, so Obama's appointments did not change the ideological balance of the Court. Obama chose two women: Sonia Sotomayor, who had been an appeals court judge and is the Court's first Latino member, and Elena Kagan, who had been Obama's solicitor general.

The Senate's Role

Ideology also plays a large role in the Senate's confirmation hearings, and presidential nominees to the Supreme Court have not always been confirmed. In fact, almost 20 percent of presidential nominations to the Supreme Court have either been rejected or not been acted on by the Senate.

Controversial Supreme Court Appointments. One of the most memorable of these rejections was the Senate's refusal to confirm Robert Bork—a conservative nominee—in 1987.

Many observers saw the Bork confirmation battle as a turning point after which confirmations became more partisan. Another controversial appointment was that of Clarence Thomas, who underwent a volatile and acrimonious confirmation hearing in 1991, replete with charges against him of sexual harassment. Still, he was ultimately confirmed by the Senate.

President Clinton had little trouble gaining approval for both of his nominees to the Supreme Court: Ruth Bader Ginsburg (who died in September 2020) and Stephen G. Breyer. President George W. Bush's nominees faced hostile grilling in their confirmation hearings, however, and Bush was forced to withdraw the nomination of White House counsel Harriet Miers when it became clear she would not be confirmed.

The Controversy Following the Death of Justice Scalia. In February 2016, Justice Antonin Scalia died unexpectedly. Scalia had been the lion of the Court's conservative wing. (It is a sign of the Court's collegiality that Scalia was also a close personal friend of liberal Justice Ruth Ginsburg.) President Obama then nominated as Scalia's replacement Merrick Garland, an appeals court judge. Garland was as moderate a judge as Obama could be expected to name. By replacing Scalia, however, Garland would inevitably swing the Court to the left.

The nomination was issued in the middle of the 2016 presidential primaries. Republicans in the Senate recognized that if they could postpone action on Scalia's replacement until 2017, there was a chance that a new Republican president might make the nomination. Senate Republicans therefore announced that they would not hold hearings on Garland's nomination. While this step was not unprecedented, it was unusual.

Republican Donald Trump was in fact elected president. As one of his first acts following his inauguration, he nominated Neil Gorsuch to the Court. An appeals court judge, Gorsuch was widely respected and also quite conservative. Democrats, angered over the treatment of Garland, filibustered the appointment. Republicans then abolished the filibuster as it applies to Supreme Court appointments. Gorsuch was confirmed and took office in April 2017.

The Kavanaugh Appointment. In June 2018, Justice Anthony Kennedy announced his retirement. In July, President Trump nominated Brett Kavanaugh, a federal appeals court judge, to replace Kennedy. Kavanaugh was far more conservative than Kennedy, and Democrats objected to the nomination. In September, a California professor accused Kavanaugh of sexually assaulting her when they were both in high school. Two other women made similar claims. The result was a major national controversy. Still, Republicans were able to confirm Kavanaugh in October by a narrow margin.

The Death of Justice Ginsburg and the Barrett Appointment. In September 2020, Justice Ruth Bader Ginsburg died at the age of 87 following a long battle with cancer. Ginsburg had been a leader of the Court's liberal wing. She was also widely revered across the country as a feminist leader. Her death took place less than seven weeks before the November 2020 elections. Senate majority leader Mitch McConnell announced that Senate Republicans would approve a nomination by President Trump either before the elections or at least before the next president took office on January 20, 2021. Trump nominated Amy Coney Barrett, an appeals court judge known to be both talented and extremely conservative. Given that McConnell had earlier argued that Justice Scalia's seat should not be filled in an election year (Scalia died in February 2016), Democrats were outraged. Replacing Ginsburg with Barrett would move the Court sharply to the right. As with most recent nominees, Barrett would not comment on any case that might come before her. She did, however, distinguish between precedents that were liable to be overturned and "super-precedents" that were not.

According to Barrett, *Brown v. Board of Education* was a super-precedent. Barrett was approved on a near-party-line vote.

Justice Stephen Breyer formally announced his retirement from the Supreme Court in late January 2022, to take effect at the end of the 2021-22 session. As stated before, Joe Biden had previously announced that he would replace any vacancy with a Black woman. After a short selection process, Biden announced his choice—U.S. Court of Appeals for the District of Columbia judge Ketanji Brown Jackson. The vetting process in the Senate was also relatively short. There was never any question that Brown Jackson would be approved. She was sworn in on June 30, 2022.

Policymaking and the Courts

>> **LO 12-5:** Describe your views on whether the Supreme Court should make policy.

The partisan battles over judicial appointments reflect an important reality in today's American government: the importance of the judiciary in national politics. Because appointments to the federal bench are for life, the ideology of judicial appointees can affect national policy for years to come. Although the primary function of judges in our system of government is to interpret and apply the laws, inevitably judges make policy when carrying out this task. One of the major policymaking tools of the federal courts is their power of judicial review.

Image 12.5 Chief Justice John Roberts.
▶ Which president nominated Roberts to be chief justice?

BRENDAN SMIALOWSKI/Getty Images

Judicial Review

Remember from earlier in this text that the power of the courts to determine whether a law or action by the other branches of government is constitutional is known as the power of judicial review. This power enables the judicial branch to act as a check on the other two branches of government, in line with the system of checks and balances established by the U.S. Constitution.

The power of judicial review is not mentioned in the Constitution, however. Rather, it was established by the Supreme Court's decision in *Marbury v. Madison*.[7] In that case, in which the Court declared that a law passed by Congress violated the Constitution, the Court claimed such a power for the judiciary:

It is emphatically the province and duty of the Judicial Department to say what the law is. Those who apply the rule to a particular case must of necessity expound and interpret that rule. If two laws conflict with each other, the courts must decide on the operation of each.

If a federal court declares that a federal or state law or policy is unconstitutional, the court's decision affects the application of the law or policy only within that court's jurisdiction. For this reason, the higher the level of the court, the greater the impact of the decision on society. Because of the Supreme Court's national jurisdiction, its decisions have the greatest impact. For example,

---

7. 5 U.S. 137 (1803).

when the Supreme Court held that an Arkansas state constitutional amendment limiting the terms of congresspersons was unconstitutional, laws establishing term limits in twenty-three other states also were invalidated.[8]

Judicial Activism and Judicial Restraint

Judicial scholars like to characterize judges and justices as being either "activist" or "restraintist."

Judicial Activism. The doctrine of **judicial activism** rests on the conviction that the federal judiciary should take an active role by using its powers to check the activities of Congress, state legislatures, and administrative agencies when those governmental bodies exceed their authority. One of the Supreme Court's most activist eras was the period from 1953 to 1969, when the Court was headed by Chief Justice Earl Warren. The Warren Court propelled the civil rights movement forward by holding, among other things, that laws permitting racial segregation violated the equal protection clause of the Fourteenth Amendment.

Judicial Restraint. In contrast, the doctrine of **judicial restraint** rests on the assumption that the courts should defer to the decisions made by the legislative and executive branches, because members of Congress and the president are elected by the people, whereas members of the federal judiciary are not. Because administrative agency personnel normally have more expertise than the courts do in the areas regulated by the agencies, the courts likewise should defer to agency rules and decisions. In other words, under the doctrine of judicial restraint, the courts should not thwart the implementation of legislative acts and agency rules unless they are clearly unconstitutional.

Political Implications. In the past, judicial activism was often linked with liberalism, and judicial restraint with conservatism. In fact, though, a conservative judge can be activist, just as a liberal judge can be restraintist. In the 1950s and 1960s, the Supreme Court was activist and liberal. Many observers believe that the Roberts Court, with its conservative majority, has become increasingly activist over time.

Some believed that the Court was stepping back from conservative judicial activism when it upheld most of Obama's health care reform legislation in June 2012. In fact, however, the Court's decision was mostly based on precedent. In one major departure from precedent, the Court set new limits on the commerce clause, a conservative goal. These limits did not change the outcome of the case, however.

Other terms that are often used to describe a justice's philosophy are strict construction and broad construction. Justices who believe in strict construction look to the "letter of the law" when they attempt to interpret the Constitution or a particular statute. Those who favor broad construction try to determine the context and purpose of the law.

The Roberts Court

John Roberts became chief justice in 2005, following the death of Chief Justice William H. Rehnquist. Replacing one conservative chief justice with another did not immediately change the Court's ideological balance. The real change came in January 2006, when Samuel Alito replaced Sandra Day O'Connor. Unlike O'Connor, Alito was firmly in the conservative camp. This fact had consequences. In a 2007 case, for example, the Court upheld a

Judicial Activism
A doctrine holding that the federal judiciary should take an active role by using its powers to check the activities of governmental bodies when those bodies exceed their authority.

Judicial Restraint
A doctrine holding that courts should defer to the decisions made by the elected representatives of the people in the legislative and executive branches when possible.

8. *U.S. Term Limits, Inc. v. Thornton*, 514 U.S. 779 (1995).

2003 federal law banning partial birth abortion, by a close (five-to-four) vote.[9] This ruling reversed an earlier decision. The Supreme Court's conservative drift continued in the following years. In 2008, for example, the Court established the right of individuals to own guns for private use.[10] It also upheld lethal injection as an execution method.[11]

The Nature of the Court's Conservatism. Although the Roberts Court is widely characterized as conservative, its philosophy is not identical to the conservatism of the Republicans in Congress or the broader conservative movement. True, justices such as Thomas could rightly be characterized as in full agreement with the conservative movement. Former Justice Kennedy and even Chief Justice Roberts, however, clearly "marched to their own drummer." As one example, the Court has shown a degree of sympathy for the rights of LGBTQ+ people that cannot be found in the Republican Party platform. It was Justice Kennedy, after all, who in 2003 wrote the opinion in *Lawrence v. Texas* striking down laws

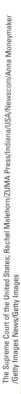

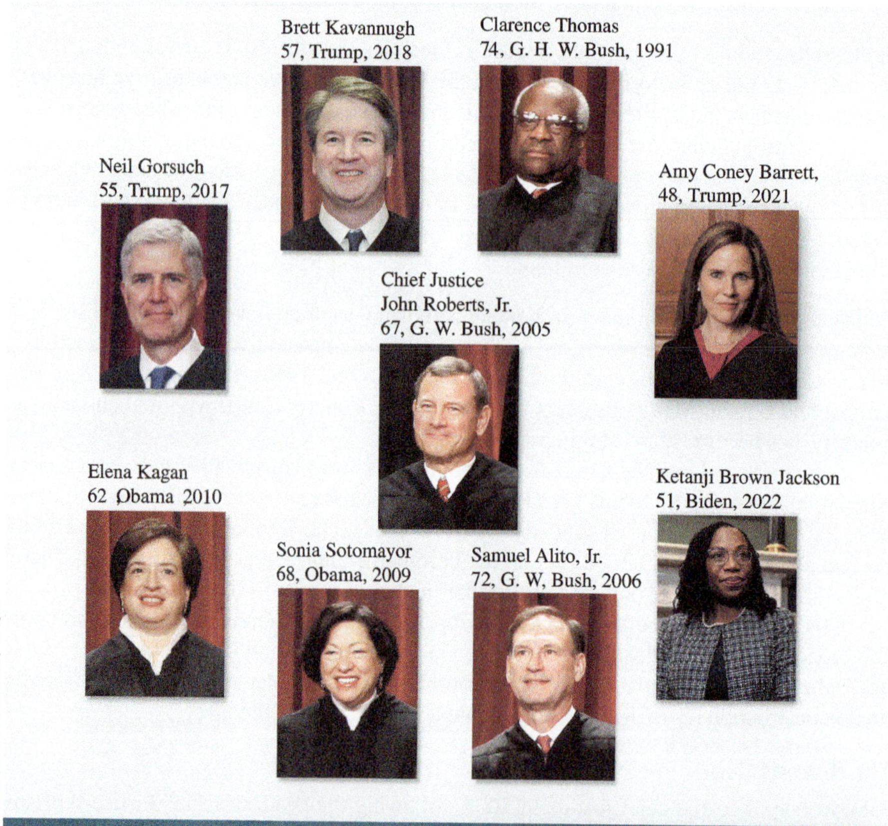

Brett Kavannugh
57, Trump, 2018
Clarence Thomas
74, G. H. W. Bush, 1991
Neil Gorsuch
55, Trump, 2017
Amy Coney Barrett,
48, Trump, 2021
Chief Justice
John Roberts, Jr.
67, G. W. Bush, 2005
Elena Kagan
62, Obama, 2010
Ketanji Brown Jackson
51, Biden, 2022
Sonia Sotomayor
68, Obama, 2009
Samuel Alito, Jr.
72, G. W, Bush, 2006

The Supreme Court of the United States; Rachel Malehorn/ZUMA Press/Indiana/USA/Newscom/Anna Moneymaker/Getty Images News/Getty Images

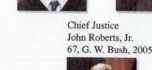

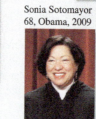

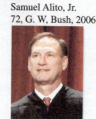

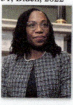

Image 12.6 Supreme Court justices along with their ages as of 2023, the president who appointed them, and the year they assumed office. ▶ What has to occur for one of these nine justices to be replaced by someone else?

9. *Gonzales v. Carhart*, 550 U.S. 124 (2007).
10. *District of Columbia v. Heller*, 554 U.S. 570 (2008).
11. *Baze v. Rees*, 553 U.S. 35 (2008).

that had banned same-sex sexual activity nationwide.[12] Chief Justice Roberts demonstrated his independence in 2012 by authoring the opinion that affirmed the constitutionality of the Affordable Care Act (also known as Obamacare).[13]

The Court provided more examples of its brand of conservatism in 2013. The Court continued to take a favorable approach to LGBTQ+ people's rights. In *United States v. Windsor,* it ruled that the federal government could not refuse to recognize same-sex marriages authorized by the states.[14] In contrast, to the satisfaction of conservatives, the Court struck down part of the Voting Rights Act of 1965.[15]

Many of the most important rulings in 2014 also gave heart to conservatives. For example, the Court decided that closely held corporations had the right to deny their employees certain birth control benefits in insurance plans that conformed to the Affordable Care Act.[16] This ruling, *Burwell v. Hobby Lobby,* was applauded by religious conservatives and denounced by feminist groups.

In the term ending in 2015, however, several important rulings confirmed the limits of the Court's conservatism. *Obergefell v. Hodges,* for example, established a nationwide constitutional right to same-sex marriage.[17]

A Divided Court. The death of Justice Scalia in February 2016 left the Court with a four-to-four split between conservative and liberal justices. For the next fourteen months, the Court was at least somewhat more liberal than before. The four-to-four split also raised the possibility of tie votes. When that happens, the decision of the lower court is sustained. The Court's action does not, however, serve as a precedent. Chief Justice Roberts sought consensus on the Court, but a few four-to-four deadlocks did occur. In several cases, the Court was able to stop attempts by President Obama to use his executive powers to set policy. For example, in a four-to-four decision, the Court blocked Obama's attempt to prevent the deportation of up to 5 million unauthorized immigrants.[18]

Conservative Justice Neil Gorsuch joined the Court in April 2017, too late to have an effect on most cases. As a result, the term ending in June 2017 was marked by an unusual degree of consensus and an absence of groundbreaking decisions.

Conservatism Restored. With the Court's conservative majority back in place, the term ending in 2018 was marked by a variety of conservative victories. The Court backed a Colorado baker who refused to create a wedding cake for a gay couple.[19] The Court supported Trump's third attempt to restrict travel from several mostly Muslim countries.[20] Finally, the court ruled that state governments may not require government workers who do not join a labor union to pay fees to support collective bargaining, a major blow to labor.[21]

The replacement of Justice Kennedy by Justice Kavanaugh in late 2018 guaranteed that the terms ending in 2019 and 2020 would be even more successful for conservatives. In June 2019, for example, the Court, after equivocating in earlier years, ruled that the issue

---

12. 539 U.S. 558 (2003).
13. *National Federation of Independent Business v. Sebelius*, 132 S.Ct. 2566 (2012).
14. 570 U.S. 744 (2013).
15. *Shelby County v. Holder*, 570 U.S. 529 (2013).
16. 573 U.S. 682 (2014).
17. 135 S.Ct. 2584 (2015).
18. *United States v. Texas*, 136 S.Ct. 2271 (2016).
19. *Masterpiece Cakeshop v. Colorado Civil Rights Commission*, 138 S.Ct. 1719 (2018).
20. *Trump v. Hawaii*, 138 S.Ct. 2392 (2018).
21. *Janus v. AFSCME*, 138 S.Ct. 2448 (2018).

of partisan gerrymanders could not be addressed by the federal courts.[22] Given the recent heavy use of the gerrymander by Republicans, this ruling was a victory for that party.

The Swing Vote on Occasion—Chief Justice John Roberts. In June and July 2020, the Court issued a number of headline rulings that some members of the conservative movement viewed almost as a betrayal. These included a pro-LGBTQ+ rights opinion, *Bostock v. Clayton County, Georgia.*[23] Some conservatives wondered whether it was really correct to call the Court conservative.

Consider *June Medical Services v. Russo,* a Louisiana abortion case that overturned a verdict by the Fifth Circuit Court.[24] Chief Justice Roberts wrote the concurring opinion that decided the case, and by doing so helped confirm his status as the new swing vote on the Court. Conservatives denounced this ruling as a betrayal of the right-to-life cause. In that case, Louisiana had adopted a series of restrictions on abortion clinics severe enough to force most or even all of them to close. The Louisiana law was almost identical to one that Texas had adopted earlier. But the Court had overturned the Texas law in 2016 in *Whole Woman's Health v. Hellerstedt,* which reversed a finding by the Fifth Circuit Court.[25] So the latest ruling was consistent.

John Roberts—The Swing Vote No More. Once Amy Coney Barrett joined the Court, Chief Justice John Roberts could no longer be considered a swing vote. Conservatives had a six-three majority. If Roberts voted with liberals all the time, he would still not be a swing vote. Even though Brown Jackson is considered more progressive than the justice who she replaced (Stephen Breyer), her left-leaning tendencies would have little impact on future decisions taken by the Court.

The conservatism of the current Court is no longer in doubt. For example, in the June 2022 *Hobbes* decision, the court overruled *Roe v. Wade*, thereby sending all issues related to abortion regulation back to the fifty state legislatures.[26] At around the same time, the Court issued several other decisions that most observers labeled conservative.

What Checks Our Courts?

Our judicial system is one of the most independent in the world. But the courts do not have absolute independence, for they are part of the political process. Political checks limit the extent to which courts can exercise judicial review and engage in an activist policy. These checks are exercised by the executive branch, the legislature, the public, and, finally, the judiciary itself.

Executive Checks. President Andrew Jackson was once supposed to have said, after Chief Justice John Marshall made an unpopular decision, "John Marshall has made his decision; now let him enforce it."[27]

Image 12.7 Justice Neil Gorsuch became a member of the Supreme Court in 2017, replacing the late Justice Antonin Scalia.
▶ Why was the nomination of Gorsuch controversial?

Mario Tama/Getty Images News/Getty Images

22. *Rucho v. Common Cause*, 139 S.Ct. 2484 (2019) and *Lamone v. Benisek*, 139 S.Ct. 1316 (2019).
23. 590 U.S. __ (2020).
24. 591 U.S. __ (2020).
25. 579 U.S. __ (2016).
26. *Dobbs v. Jackson Women's Health Organization, et al.*, 597 U.S. __ (2022).
27. The decision that Jackson was referring to was *Cherokee Nation v. Georgia*, 30 U.S. 1 (1831).

This purported remark goes to the heart of **judicial implementation**—the enforcement of judicial decisions in such a way that those decisions are translated into policy. The Supreme Court simply does not have any enforcement powers, and whether a decision will be implemented depends on the cooperation of the other two branches of government. Rarely, though, will a president refuse to enforce a Supreme Court decision, as President Jackson did.

Executives at the state level may also refuse to implement court decisions with which they disagree. A notable example of such a refusal occurred in Arkansas after the Supreme Court ordered schools to desegregate "with all deliberate speed" in 1955.[28] Arkansas governor Orval Faubus refused to cooperate with the decision and used the state's National Guard to block the integration of Central High School in Little Rock. Ultimately, President Dwight Eisenhower had to federalize the Arkansas National Guard to force it to stand down and also send federal troops to Little Rock to quell the violence that had erupted.

Legislative Checks. Courts may make rulings, but often the legislatures at local, state, and federal levels are required to appropriate funds to carry out the courts' rulings. A court, for example, may decide that prison conditions must be improved, but it is up to the legislature to authorize the funds necessary to carry out the ruling. When such funds are not appropriated, the court that made the ruling, in effect, has been checked.

Court rulings can be overturned by constitutional amendments at both the federal and the state levels. For example, the Sixteenth Amendment to the U.S. Constitution, ratified in 1913, overturned a Supreme Court ruling that found the income tax to be unconstitutional.

Finally, Congress or a state legislature can rewrite (amend) old laws or enact new ones to overturn a court's rulings if the legislature concludes that the court is interpreting laws or legislative intentions erroneously. For example, in 2009 Congress passed (and President Obama signed) the Lilly Ledbetter Fair Pay Act, which resets the statute of limitations for filing an equal-pay lawsuit each time an employer issues a discriminatory paycheck. The law was a direct answer to *Ledbetter v. Goodyear,* in which the Supreme Court held that the statute of limitations begins at the date the pay was agreed upon, not at the date of the most recent paycheck.[29] The new legislation made it much easier for employees to win pay discrimination lawsuits.

Public Opinion. Public opinion plays a significant role in shaping government policy, and certainly the judiciary is not free from this rule. One problem is that persons affected by a Supreme Court decision that is contrary to their views may simply ignore it. Officially sponsored prayers were banned in public schools in 1962, yet it was widely known that the ban was (and still is) ignored in many southern and rural districts. What can the courts do in this situation? Unless someone complains about the prayers and initiates a lawsuit, the courts can do nothing.

Judicial Implementation
The way in which court decisions are translated into action.

dpa picture alliance/Alamy Stock Photo

Image 12.8 The confirmation of Justice Brett Kavanaugh was controversial in part because of accusations that he had committed sexual assault when in high school. ▶ How much weight should senators give to such issues when they vote on judicial confirmations?

28. *Brown v. Board of Education*, 349 U.S. 294 (1955)—referred to as the second *Brown* decision.
29. 550 U.S. 618 (2007).

Naturally, liberal and conservative justices may look to different strands of public opinion. With conservative majorities, the Court tended to reflect conservative opinion. Two cases on states' rights illustrate this tendency. In 1995, the Court held, for the first time in sixty years, that Congress had overreached its powers under the commerce clause when it attempted to regulate the possession of guns in school zones. According to the Court, the possession of guns in school zones had nothing to do with the commerce clause.[30] Yet in a 2005 case, the Court ruled that Congress's power to regulate commerce allowed it to ban marijuana use even when a state law permitted such use, and the growing and use of the drug were strictly local in nature.[31] What these two rulings had in common was that they supported policies generally considered to be conservative—the right to possess firearms on the one hand, and strict laws against marijuana on the other.

Judicial Traditions and Doctrines. Supreme Court justices (and other federal judges) typically exercise self-restraint in fashioning their decisions. To a large degree, this restraint is mandated by various judicially established traditions and doctrines. For example, in exercising its discretion to hear appeals, the Supreme Court will not hear a meritless appeal just so it can rule on the issue.

Also, when reviewing a case, the Supreme Court frequently narrows its focus to just one issue involved in the case. In the past, the court has rarely made broad, sweeping decisions on issues. Furthermore, the doctrine of *stare decisis* acts as a restraint because it obligates the courts, including the Supreme Court, to follow established precedents when deciding cases. Only rarely will courts overrule a precedent.

Hypothetical and Political Questions. As already mentioned, the courts will hear only what are called justiciable disputes—disputes that arise out of actual cases. In other words, a court will not hear a case that involves a merely hypothetical issue.

Additionally, if a political question is involved, the Supreme Court often will exercise judicial restraint and refuse to rule on the matter. A **political question** is one that the Supreme Court declares should be decided by the elected branches of government—the executive branch, the legislative branch, or those two branches acting together. For example, the Supreme Court has refused to rule on whether women in the military should be allowed to serve in combat units, preferring instead to defer to the executive branch's decisions on the matter. (In January 2013, the Department of Defense lifted the ban on women serving in combat units.) Generally, though, fewer questions are deemed political questions by the Supreme Court today than in the past.

The Impact of the Lower Courts. Higher courts can reverse the decisions of lower courts. Lower courts can act as a check on higher courts, too. Lower courts can ignore—and have ignored—Supreme Court decisions. Usually, they do so indirectly. A lower court might conclude, for example, that the precedent set by the Supreme Court does not apply to the exact circumstances in the case before the court. Alternatively, the lower court may decide that the Supreme Court's decision was ambiguous with respect to the issue before the lower court. The fact that the Supreme Court rarely makes broad and clear-cut statements makes it easier for lower courts to interpret the Supreme Court's decisions in different ways.

Political Question
An issue that a court believes should be decided by the executive or legislative branch, or both.

---

30. *United States v. Lopez,* 514 U.S. 549 (1995).
31. *Gonzales v. Raich,* 545 U.S. 1 (2005).

Making a Difference

Changing the Legal System

The U.S. legal system may seem too complex to be influenced by one individual, but its power nonetheless depends on the support of individuals. The public has many ways of resisting, modifying, or overturning statutes and rulings of the courts.

Why Should You Care? You may find it worthwhile to attend one or more court sessions to see how the law works. Legislation is given its practical form by court rulings. Therefore, if you care about the effects of a particular law, pay attention to how the courts are interpreting it. For example, do you believe that sentences handed down for certain crimes are too lenient—or too strict?

What Can You Do? Public opinion can have an effect on judicial policies. There is probably an organization that pursues lawsuits to benefit whichever causes that you support. A prime example is the modern women's movement, which undertook long series of lawsuits to change the way women are treated in American life. The courts only rule on cases that are brought before them, and the women's movement changed American law by filing—and winning—case after case.

- In 1965, a federal circuit court opened a wide range of jobs for women by overturning laws that kept women out of work that was "too hard" for them.
- In 1974, the Court ruled that employers could not use the "going market rate" to justify lower wages for women.
- In 1978, an Oregon court became the first of many to find that a man could be prosecuted for raping his wife.

Today, groups such as the National Organization for Women continue to support lawsuits to advance women's rights.

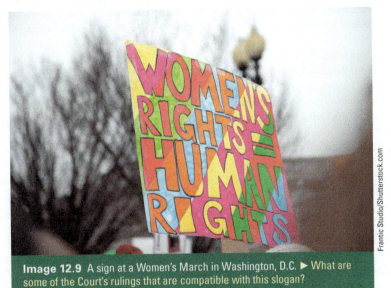

Image 12.9 A sign at a Women's March in Washington, D.C. ▶ What are some of the Court's rulings that are compatible with this slogan?

Frantic Studio/Shutterstock.com

Key Terms

affirmed 292
amicus curiae brief 286
appellate court 287
case law 284
class-action suit 286

common law 283
concurring opinion 292
dissenting opinion 292
diversity of citizenship 285

federal question 285
general jurisdiction 286
judicial activism 299
judicial implementation 303

judicial restraint 299
jurisdiction 285
justiciable controversy 285
limited jurisdiction 286

litigate 286
majority opinion 292
opinion 292
oral arguments 292

plurality opinion 292
political question 304
precedent 283
remanded 292

reversed 292
rule of four 291
stare decisis 283
trial court 286

unanimous opinion 292
writ of *certiorari* 291

Chapter Summary

» LO 12-1 American law is rooted in the common law tradition. The common law doctrine of *stare decisis* (which means "to stand on decided cases") obligates judges to follow precedents established previously by their own courts or by higher courts that have authority over them. Precedents established by the United States Supreme Court, the highest court in the land, are binding on all lower courts. Fundamental sources of American law include the U.S. Constitution and state constitutions, statutes enacted by legislative bodies, regulations issued by administrative agencies, and case law.

» LO 12-2 Article III, Section 1, of the U.S. Constitution limits the jurisdiction of the federal courts to cases involving (a) a federal question, which is a question based, at least in part, on the U.S. Constitution, a treaty, or a federal law, or (b) diversity of citizenship, which arises when parties to a lawsuit are from different states or when the lawsuit involves a foreign citizen or government.

The federal court system is a three-tiered model consisting of (a) U.S. district (trial) courts and various lower courts of limited jurisdiction, (b) intermediate U.S. courts of appeals, and (c) the United States Supreme Court. Cases may be appealed from the district courts to the appellate courts. In most cases, the decisions of the federal appellate courts are final because the Supreme Court hears relatively few cases.

» LO 12-3 The Supreme Court's decision to review a case is influenced by many factors, including the significance of the issues involved and whether lower courts have issued conflicting opinions. After a case is accepted, the justices undertake research (with the help of their law clerks) on the issues involved in the case, hear oral arguments from the parties, meet in conference to discuss and vote on the issues, and announce one or more opinions, which are then released for publication. Types of opinions include unanimous, majority, plurality, concurring, and dissenting opinions.

» LO 12-4 Federal judges are nominated by the president and confirmed by the Senate. Once appointed, they hold office for life, barring gross misconduct. The nomination and confirmation process, particularly for Supreme Court justices, is often extremely politicized. Democrats and Republicans alike realize that justices may occupy seats on the Court for decades and want to have persons appointed who share their views. Nearly 20 percent of all presidential nominations to the Supreme Court have either been rejected or not acted on by the Senate.

» LO 12-5 In interpreting and applying the law, judges inevitably become policymakers. The most important policymaking tool of the federal courts is the power of judicial review. This power was not mentioned specifically in the Constitution, but the Supreme Court claimed this power for the federal courts in its 1803 decision in *Marbury v. Madison.*

Judges who take an active role in checking the activities of the other branches of government sometimes are characterized as "activist" judges, and judges who defer to the decisions of the other branches sometimes are regarded as "restraintist" judges. The Warren Court of the 1950s and 1960s was activist in a liberal direction, whereas the Roberts Court has become increasingly activist in a conservative direction.

Checks on the powers of the federal courts include executive checks, legislative checks, public opinion, and judicial traditions and doctrines.

Test Yourself

1. **One important source of American law is:**
   a. the rights and duties of workers as expressed in employment agreements.
   b. case law based in part on the common law tradition.
   c. case law based in part on the federal tradition.

2. **The supreme law of the land in the United States is:**
   a. the Bible.
   b. the Declaration of Independence.
   c. the United States Constitution.

3. **To bring a lawsuit, parties must show that they suffered an actual harm or are threatened by an actual harm as a result of the action that led to the dispute. If so, then those parties have:**
   a. a federal question.
   b. standing to sue.
   c. jurisdiction.

4. **The distinction between federal district courts and federal appellate courts can be summarized by the following statement:**
   a. federal district courts are trial courts that hear evidence, but federal appellate courts do not hear evidence.
   b. federal district courts only hear appeals from federal appellate courts.
   c. federal appellate courts only accept cases involving state constitutions.

5. **The secret court set up to issue warrants in national security cases is called:**
   a. the FISA court.
   b. the Court of Federal Claims.
   c. an administrative law tribunal.

6. **"I'll take it all the way to the Supreme Court." A lawyer cannot truthfully promise this because:**
   a. the Supreme Court may be too far away from the state in which the controversy occurred.
   b. the Supreme Court hears only a limited number of cases in which a federal question is involved.
   c. the Supreme Court is not in session for a full twelve months each year.

7. **Supreme Court justices who do not agree with the majority opinion of the Court often write a:**
   a. concurring opinion.
   b. dissenting opinion.
   c. plurality opinion.

8. **In an attempt to keep the minority party from holding up judicial appointments, the Senate has restricted the scope of:**
   a. the filibuster.
   b. seniority.
   c. presidential appointment authority.

9. **The most common occupational position held by a Supreme Court justice before appointment has been:**
   a. U.S. senator.
   b. state governor.
   c. federal judgeship.

10. **When a federal court declares that a federal or state law or policy is unconstitutional, that court is engaging in:**
    a. judicial review.
    b. congressional condemnation.
    c. administrative oversight.

11. **The belief that the federal judiciary should actively use its powers to check the laws passed by Congress and state legislatures is called:**
    a. broad construction.
    b. judicial restraint.
    c. judicial activism.

Essay Questions

1. What are the benefits of having lifetime appointments to the United States Supreme Court? What problems might such appointments cause? What would be the likely result if Supreme Court justices faced term limits?

2. In "Public Opinion" in the section "What Checks Our Courts," we described how the Supreme Court ruled in favor of states' rights in a gun-control case and against states' rights in a marijuana case. Why do you think the justices might have come to different conclusions in these two cases?

Answers to multiple-choice questions: 1. b, 2. c, 3. b, 4. a, 5. a, 6. b, 7. b, 8. a, 9. c, 10. a, 11. c.

13 Domestic and Economic Policy

ZUMA Press/ZUMA Press, Inc./Alamy Stock Photo

Asylum seekers from Central America walk atop the fence at the U.S./Mexico border in Tijuana. ► **Why do you think unauthorized immigration is still an important political issue?**

The five **Learning Outcomes (LOs)** below are designed to help improve your understanding of this chapter. After reading this chapter, you should be able to:

» **LO 13-1** Describe the five steps of the policy-making process, using the CARES Act as an example.

» **LO 13-2** Outline the effects of health care entitlement programs such as Medicare and Medicaid, as well as the Affordable Care Act.

» **LO 13-3** Evaluate how the federal government has responded to the issue of energy security and to the controversy over climate change.

» **LO 13-4** Define unemployment, inflation, fiscal policy, public debt, and monetary policy.

» **LO 13-5** Explain how taxpayers can alter their behavior in response to changes in tax rates.

Check your understanding of the material with the Test Yourself section at the end of the chapter.

Part of the public policy debate in our nation involves domestic problems. **Domestic policy** can be defined as all laws, government planning, and government actions that concern internal issues of national importance. Consequently, the span of such policies is enormous. Domestic policies range from relatively simple issues, such as what the speed limit should be on interstate highways, to more complex ones, such as how best to protect our environment. Many of our domestic policies are formulated and implemented by the federal government, but a number of others are the result of the combined efforts of federal, state, and local governments.

We can define several types of domestic policy. Regulatory policy seeks to define what is and is not legal. Setting speed limits is obviously regulatory policy. Redistributive policy transfers income from certain individuals or groups to others, often based on the belief that these transfers enhance fairness. Social Security is an example. Promotional policy seeks to foster or discourage various economic or social activities, typically through subsidies and tax breaks. A tax credit for buying an electric car would qualify as promotional. Except under unusual circumstances, whenever a policy decision is made, some groups will be better off, and some groups will be hurt. All policy making generally involves such a dilemma.

In this chapter, we look at domestic policy issues involving health care and also energy and the environment. This chapter's *Which Side Are You On?* feature looks at whether we should be worried about increasing government transfers to help certain groups. We also examine national economic policies undertaken by the federal government—for example, the issue of the federal budget deficit.

Domestic Policy
All government laws, planning, and actions that concern internal issues of national importance, such as health care, the environment, and the economy.

Which Side Are You On?

Does Entitlement Spending Corrupt Us?

Certain federal benefits are called entitlements because you are entitled to receive them if you meet specific requirements. If you meet certain age and previous earnings requirements, you can receive a monthly Social Security check. If you lose your job, you may be entitled to unemployment benefits for a certain number of weeks. If your family income is below a certain level, you are typically entitled to benefits from the Supplemental Nutrition Assistance Program (SNAP, formerly called food stamps).

In recent years, federal entitlement spending has ballooned. Indeed, big government has gotten bigger in large part because Americans are receiving more entitlement payments every year. At all levels combined, government spending now has a value equivalent to about 38 percent of GDP. Some have argued that large-scale entitlement spending is corrupting us.

The More You Give People, the Less They'll Work

Conservatives point out that entitlement transfers—adjusted for rising prices and population growth—are now more than seven times what they were in 1960. (In part, this is because major programs such as Medicare and Medicaid were created in the 1960s.)

Currently, almost half of Americans live in a household that receives at least one government benefit. If you count tax deductions, almost every household receives benefits.

Consider SNAP benefits. In 2007, 26 million Americans received them. By 2023, about 46 million Americans received them. The same story applies to Social Security disability payments. Four million people received disability checks in 1988. Today, disability checks are distributed to about 12 million people. Fewer people are now in the labor force, and those who are work fewer hours per year. Since 2000, the labor force participation rate has fallen continuously, even during boom times. Many believe that increased entitlement benefits have reduced people's desire to join the labor force. Also consider that in 2020 and 2021 during the COVID-19 pandemic, the federal government provided additional payments to those who were already receiving state unemployment benefits. As a result, millions of Americans were receiving more from the government than they could earn if they reentered the labor market. They reacted rationally, stayed unemployed, and kept receiving the government payments instead. In other words, entitlements corrupt.

(Continued)

Entitlements Are a Needed Part of the Social Contract

While the statistics just presented are accurate, political progressives do not accept the conclusions drawn. With an aging society, we should expect to pay more for Social Security. The same is true for government-financed health care. Health care expenses are driven up not only by larger numbers of the elderly, but also by increasingly expensive (and effective) medical procedures and medicines.

Contrary to what some have argued, Americans are not divided between "makers" and "takers." At various times in our lives, we are all takers, and almost all of us are makers. As President Obama said in his second inaugural address, "The commitments we make to each other—through Medicare, and Medicaid, and Social Security—these things do not sap our initiative; they strengthen us … they free us to take the risks that make this country great."

Americans believe in hard work as much as they always have. The Pew Economic Mobility Project sampled Americans on what is essential for getting ahead. More than 90 percent responded, "hard work," and almost 90 percent answered "ambition." That doesn't sound like corruption.

■ For Critical Analysis

Who ultimately pays for entitlement programs?

The Policy-Making Process: The CARES Act

» **LO 13-1:** Describe the five steps of the policy-making process, using the CARES Act as an example.

How does any issue get resolved? First, of course, the issue must be identified as a problem. Often, policy makers have only to open their local newspapers or e-mails, texts, and posts from their constituents to discover that a problem is brewing. On rare occasions, a crisis—such as that brought about by the terrorist attacks of September 11, 2001—creates the need to formulate policy. Like most Americans, however, policy makers receive much of their information from the national media. Finally, various lobbying groups provide information to members of Congress.

No matter how simple or how complex the problem, those who make policy follow a number of steps. We can divide the process of policy making into five steps: (1) agenda building, (2) policy formulation, (3) policy adoption, (4) policy implementation, and (5) policy evaluation. The CARES Act (Coronavirus Aid, Relief, and Economic Security Act) passed in 2020 can be used to illustrate this process.

The CARES Act: Agenda Building

First of all, an issue must get on the agenda. In other words, Congress must become aware that a problem requires congressional action. Agenda building may occur as the result of a crisis, a technological change, or a mass media campaign, as well as through the efforts of strong political personalities and effective lobbying groups. To understand how the COVID-19 pandemic became an important issue, and how action in response to it became part of the national agenda, we need to examine the background of the issue.

In March 2020, the nation experienced the most rapid economic contraction in its history. The practice of "social distancing" to slow the spread of the COVID-19 virus meant the universal cancellation of festivals, concerts, and sporting events. Those who could work from home began doing so. Restaurants either closed or offered take-out only. Colleges and universities either canceled classes or moved to online learning. International air travel was almost completely banned, and the domestic flights that remained were largely empty. Some of the collapse of economic activity was voluntary, but state governors across the country also issued stay-at-home orders that made social distancing a legal requirement.

Business observers predicted that the shutdowns would force the entire world airline industry into bankruptcy. A major share of the nation's restaurants would never reopen. In the week ending March 21, almost 3.3 million people filed for unemployment benefits, nearly five times the previous record. Unemployment claims were in the millions the next week as well, and the week after. Clearly, the national government would have to take action.

The CARES Act: Policy Formulation

During the next step in the policy-making process, various policy proposals are discussed among government officials and the public. Such discussions may take place in the printed media, on television, and in the halls of Congress. Congress holds hearings, the president voices the administration's views, and the topic may even become a campaign issue.

In response to the COVID-19 crisis, senators and members of the House from both parties demanded direct payments to people with low and middle incomes. Senate majority leader Mitch McConnell proposed a $1 trillion plan to provide loans and grants to businesses, and also tax rebates to Americans with incomes below $75,000. This plan was put together entirely by Republican senators. Upon passage it was sent to the House. Democrats criticized the package as biased toward business. Democrats also contended that relief for individuals should pass through the unemployment insurance system, not only the tax system. The House did not accept McConnell's plan.

The CARES Act: Policy Adoption

The third step in the policy-making process involves choosing a specific policy from among the proposals that have been discussed.

Despite its enormous cost, the CARES Act was passed as emergency legislation. Therefore, all the policy formation steps were accelerated. Normally, major legislation might spend more than a year working its way through the legislative process. The CARES Act was put together in a matter of days.

Negotiations between Republicans and Democrats in the Senate determined the final shape of the bill. Treasury secretary Steven Mnuchin played a major role in the discussions. President Trump was not directly involved, but fortunately for the bill's prospects, he had called for a large package. The final $2 trillion package included:

- Tax deferrals and reductions
- Loans to large corporations
- Loans and grants to small businesses and to the airlines
- Grants to the health care industry
- Enhanced unemployment insurance, and
- Direct payments to households, including $1,200 to most individuals

The final bill passed the Senate and the House unanimously on March 27 and was immediately signed into law by President Trump.

The CARES Act: Policy Implementation

The fourth step in the policy-making process involves the implementation of the policy alternative chosen by Congress. Government action must be implemented by bureaucrats, the courts, police, and individual citizens.

To move the money out quickly, the government would have to make use of existing institutions such as the tax system and the unemployment insurance system. Neither of these were prepared for the task ahead. Unemployment insurance is administered by the states, and many of them used obsolete software that could not be reprogrammed on short notice. It was not easy to locate individuals with very low incomes, who often did not have bank accounts with direct deposit.

Loans and grants to businesses were largely disbursed through commercial banks, which in many cases gave special consideration to their existing customers. The initial $349 billion allocated to the Paycheck Protection Program, a major source of funds for small businesses, was exhausted by April 16. On April 24, President Trump signed a new bill with an additional allocation of $320 billion.

The CARES Act: Policy Evaluation

After a policy has been implemented, it is evaluated. When a policy has been in place for a given period of time, groups inside and outside the government conduct studies to determine how the program has actually worked. Based on this feedback and the perceived success or failure of the policy, a new round of policy-making initiatives may be undertaken to improve on the effort.

The CARES Act passed so quickly that few people—in Congress or the media—had time to examine it thoroughly. Potential problems soon surfaced. One was that the small business funding allowed franchises and subsidiaries of large corporations to file as small businesses, even though they had access to the financial markets through their parent company. Public pressure persuaded some, but not all, of these corporations to give the money back. Likewise, some universities with huge endowments, such as Harvard and Stanford, agreed not to participate. Some wealthy schools kept the funds, however.

As is typical of such a vast package, some of the benefits had nothing to do with the stated goals of the legislation. A 2017 tax reform, described later in this chapter, contained caps on some of its business tax breaks, so that the very largest firms would not benefit excessively. The CARES Act repealed many of these caps.

Some Republicans objected to the unemployment provisions because many unemployed persons could receive benefits in excess of their previous pay. Among Democrats, a major objection was that the package contained very little to benefit state and local governments, which were bearing much of the financial burden of the crisis. The House began work on an additional bill largely aimed at funding the states.

Health Care in the Twenty-first Century

> » **LO 13-2:** Outline the effects of health care entitlement programs such as Medicare and Medicaid, as well as the Affordable Care Act.

Dealing with the COVID-19 pandemic is only one of the most recent examples of how the federal government has sought to intervene in the nation's health care system. Before the CARES Act, before Obamacare, the federal government had already established massive programs to fund health care spending, notably Medicaid and Medicare.

Health Care's Role in the American Economy

In 1965, about 6 percent of our national income was spent on health care, but that percentage has risen since, as you can see in Figure 13.1. As of 2022, health care was estimated to account for 19.6 percent of the total U.S. economy. Per capita spending on health care is greater in the United States than almost anywhere else in the world. Measured by the percentage of the **gross domestic product (GDP)** devoted to health care, America spends about 70 percent more than Britain or Canada. (The GDP is the dollar value of all final goods and services produced in a one-year period.)

Gross Domestic Product (GDP)
The dollar value of all final goods and services produced in a one-year period.

| Figure 13.1 | Percentage of Total National Income Spent on Health Care in the United States |

▶ What happened to this type of spending in the last twenty years?

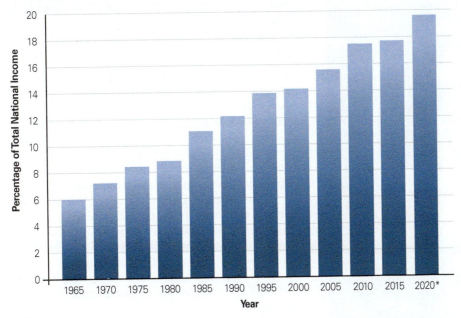

* estimate

Sources: U.S. Department of Commerce; U.S. Department of Health and Human Services; Deloitte and Touche LLP; VHA, Inc.; and Centers for Medicare and Medicaid Services.

Before the COVID-19 pandemic, government spending on health care constituted about 45 percent of total health care spending. Private insurance accounted for about 34 percent of payments for health care. The remainder was paid directly by individuals or by charities. The government programs **Medicare** and **Medicaid** are the main sources of hospital and other medical benefits for about 137 million Americans—more than two-fifths of the nation's population. Many of these people are elderly. Like Social Security, Medicare and Medicaid are **entitlement programs**. Anyone who meets specific requirements is entitled to benefits under such programs.

Medicare. The Medicare program, which was created in 1965 under President Lyndon Johnson, pays hospital and physician bills (for eligible services, after deductibles and copays) for U.S. residents over the age of sixty-five. Since 2006, Medicare has also paid for at least part of the prescription drug expenses of the elderly. In return for paying a tax on their lifetime earnings (for most people currently set at 2.9 percent of wages and salaries), retirees are assured that the majority of their hospital and physician bills will be paid for with public funds.

Medicaid. In recent decades, the joint federal-state, taxpayer-funded Medicaid program for individuals with no or low income has generated a major expansion of government entitlements. In 1990, total Medicaid spending was about $40 billion. By fiscal year 2023, the total cost of Medicaid and the Children's Health Insurance Program was about $800 billion. In 2000, 34 million people were enrolled in the programs. As of 2023, about 90 million were enrolled.

Medicare
A federal health insurance program that covers U.S. residents over the age of sixty-five. The costs are met, in part, by a tax on wages and salaries.

Medicaid
A joint state-federal program that provides medical care to the poor (including indigent elderly persons in nursing homes). The program is funded out of general government revenues.

Entitlement Programs
A government program that entitles a defined class of people to obtain benefits. Entitlements operate under open-ended budget authorizations that do not limit how much can be spent.

Image 13.1 A booth to promote Medicaid in the "Little Pakistan" neighborhood of Brooklyn, New York. Legal immigrants who are not citizens are barred from collecting Medicaid for the first five years that they are in the United States. In some states the rules are even more restrictive. *Are such rules fair? Why or why not?*

Ethel Wolvovitz/Alamy Stock Photo

Currently, the federal government pays more than 85 percent of Medicaid's total cost. The states pay the rest. Wealthy states must pick up a greater share of the tab than poor states. As you will learn later in this section, the Affordable Care Act (also known as Obamacare) expanded considerably the share of the population that is eligible for Medicaid, as well as the costs to the federal government.

The Problem of the Uninsured. In 2013, before Obamacare was fully implemented, about 42 million Americans—more than 18 percent of the population—did not have health insurance. The uninsured population has been relatively young, in part due to Medicare, which covers almost everyone over the age of sixty-five. Also, younger workers are more likely to be employed in entry-level jobs without health insurance benefits.

The traditional system of health care in the United States was based on the assumption that employers would provide health insurance to working-age persons. Many small businesses, however, simply have not been able to afford to offer their workers health insurance. In 2021, employer-provided health insurance cost an average of $22,000 for family coverage, according to the Kaiser Family Foundation.

The Problem of High Costs. High medical costs are a problem not only for individuals with inadequate or non-existent insurance coverage. They are also a problem for the system as a whole. Over the last four decades, per capita spending on health care in the United States grew at an average rate of 4.9 percent per year (when corrected for inflation). A main driver of the growth in health care spending is new medical technologies and services.

In addition, people over the age of sixty-five run up health care bills that are far larger than those incurred by the rest of the population. As a federal problem, therefore, health care spending growth remains chiefly a Medicare issue, even after the implementation of Obamacare.

The Affordable Care Act—Obamacare

Affordable Care Act (ACA)
A law passed in 2010 that seeks, among other things, to ensure the right to health care insurance for American citizens. The act is nicknamed "Obamacare."

In March 2010, President Barack Obama signed into law the **Affordable Care Act (ACA)**, a massive overhaul of the nation's health care funding system. A few days later, Obama signed the Health Care and Education Reconciliation Act, a series of adjustments to the main legislative package. They have become known by the nickname "Obamacare".

For more than half a century, liberals have sought to establish a universal health insurance system in this country. All attempts went nowhere. After the 2008 elections, however, the Democrats were in complete control of Congress and the presidency. Universal health insurance now appeared to be politically possible. The Affordable Care Act was a major step toward universal coverage. For a variety of reasons, however, not everyone was covered by the legislation.

Democratic Plans for Reform. Under the Democratic plans, all citizens were expected to obtain health insurance from some source—an employer, Medicare or Medicaid, or a new plan sponsored by the federal government or a state government. Individuals with low income would receive a subsidy to help them pay their insurance premiums. Funding the legislation required heavier taxes on the rich and taxes on drug and insurance companies.

One key element of the proposed legislation was the individual mandate, a requirement to buy insurance. Unfortunately for the Democrats, the individual mandate allowed the Republicans to accuse the Democrats of "forcing" people to do something, never a popular position in America. The individual mandate, passed as part of the ACA, was abolished in 2017.

Passage. The House and Senate passed different versions of the legislation in late 2009. In January 2010, a special election cost Senate Democrats their sixtieth vote which was necessary to end filibusters. If the House and Senate versions of the bill were reconciled in a conference committee—the normal procedure—Senate Democrats would not be able to pass the resulting compromise. Democrats, however, assembled enough support in the House to pass the Senate bill unaltered in March 2010, thus eliminating the need for a conference committee.

Details of the Legislation. Some provisions took effect quickly. Young adults were allowed to stay on their parents' health plans until they turned twenty-six, and insurance companies could not drop people when they became sick.

In 2014, most of the program kicked in, including the following:

- A ban on excluding people with preexisting conditions from insurance plans.
- Creation of state health insurance exchanges where individuals and small businesses can buy policies from commercial insurance companies.
- Subsidies to help persons with incomes up to four times the federal poverty level purchase coverage on the exchanges.
- Medicaid coverage for individuals with incomes up to 133 percent of the poverty level (but only in participating states).

Implementing the ACA. Implementation would not occur, of course, if Obamacare could be repealed. Complete repeal of the legislation, however, was hard. Repeal would have to pass both chambers of Congress and survive a presidential veto.

Many conservative state officials challenged the constitutionality of the ACA in court. In 2012, however, the Supreme Court ruled that most of the act was constitutional. The one exception: The Court threw out the mechanism by which the federal government could force states to expand their Medicaid programs.

Medicaid expansion was fully funded by the federal government for the first six years and funded at 90 percent thereafter. Still, a large number of conservative state governments exercised their option to refuse expansion. As a result, several million persons with low income were not eligible for coverage.

In October 2013, the state and federal exchanges were scheduled to open. The federal exchanges had many technical difficulties for several months. By January 2014, however, they were functioning adequately.

By 2017, those who purchased insurance policies through the online exchanges were generally pleased that they could obtain coverage. Still, many believed that their policies were too stingy. Many people faced large out-of-pocket expenses for co-pays (the patient's share of an expense) and deductibles (the sums charged before insurance kicks in). The minority of persons with incomes too high for them to receive subsidies often found

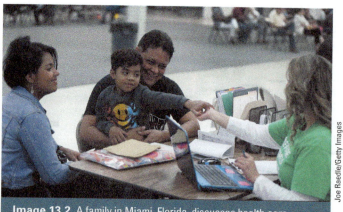

Joe Raedle/Getty Images

Image 13.2 A family in Miami, Florida, discusses health care insurance options with an insurance agent. The family is eligible for coverage under the Affordable Care Act. ▶ Why does Obamacare remain unpopular with many people?

their premiums (monthly bills) to be uncomfortably large. Still, in 2017, for the first time ever, a majority of respondents supported the ACA in opinion polls.

Attempts to Repeal Obamacare. The criticisms just mentioned were picked up by Republican leaders. Some critics of Republican legislation to replace the ACA argued that the true conservative problem with the program was the taxes necessary to fund it. Replacements for the ACA uniformly reduced taxes on upper-income individuals by cutting the funds available for coverage—the opposite of what many people wanted. Still, in May 2017, the Republican House passed the American Health Care Act.

When the Congressional Budget Office finally evaluated this bill, it estimated that millions of people would eventually lose coverage. In addition, some people with low income in their early sixties could be charged premiums that exceeded half of their income.

The bill then went to the Senate, where it failed. A final vote sought to repeal parts of the ACA. This proposal was defeated by a single vote in July 2017.

Energy and the Environment

>> **LO 13-3:** Evaluate how the federal government has responded to the issue of energy security and to the controversy over climate change.

Energy policy addresses two major problems: (1) America's energy security, which often involved reliance on foreign oil, and (2) climate change (global warming), purportedly caused by increased emissions of carbon dioxide (CO_2) and other greenhouse gases.

Energy Independence—A Strategic Issue

Petroleum was the lifeblood of the twentieth century economy. In the first part of the century, America was a major oil exporter. As of 1945, at the end of World War II, the nation still produced more oil than it could consume. By 1950, however, we were a net importer. Imports grew year by year, much of the supply coming from unfriendly regimes. By 1973, 30 percent of U.S. petroleum consumption was imported. In that year, Arab nations suspended oil exports to the United States in response to our support of Israel in the Yom Kippur War. Because of price controls, hours-long lines formed at U.S. gasoline stations. The Arab oil embargo lasted five months. In 1977, when fully half of our oil was imported, the Islamic revolution in Iran sparked a second panic. Ensuring the nation's energy security was now a major foreign policy objective.

By 2006, almost 60 percent of our oil came from abroad. Fortunately, much of it came from friendly neighbors—Canada and Mexico. Still, the world's largest oil exporters included nations that are not our friends. Russia was the world's second-largest oil exporter, after Saudi Arabia. Other major exporters included Venezuela and Iran, both openly hostile to the United States.

Supply shortages pushed the price of oil up to $147 a barrel in 2008, leading to gasoline prices above $4 per gallon at the pump. By 2014, however, U.S. oil imports hit a two-decade low. In 2017, imports were down to 19 percent of consumption. In September 2019, for the first time in seventy years, the United States became a net oil exporter. What happened?

High Prices and New Production. If the price of a commodity goes up, producers of that commodity have an incentive to produce more of it. Clearly, U.S. petroleum producers had an incentive to extract more crude oil, if possible. The question was, could they? For many years, they could not.

To increase domestic supplies, the U.S. oil industry developed new technologies for hydraulic fracturing, or **fracking**. This process involves injecting water, sand, and chemicals under high pressure into hydrocarbon-bearing rocks, releasing oil or natural gas. Expensive oil made fracking profitable.

Fracking has had an even greater impact on the supply of natural gas. Years ago, it seemed likely that the United States would need to import natural gas. By 2012, however, so much natural gas was available domestically that the nation had run out of storage space. Low natural gas prices plus new air pollution regulations made coal uncompetitive as a source of electricity. As a result, by 2020, 752 coal-based power plant units had retired, and only 310 were still in business. Despite concerns that fracking might harm drinking water supplies or otherwise damage the environment, use of the process grew rapidly.

The Politics of Energy. Oil at $40 to $50 per barrel in 2015 forced a pause in the fracking boom, because marginal wells were no longer profitable at such prices. As prices moved back above $60, however, fracking was able to gear up again rapidly. The United States, not Saudi Arabia, was now the world's number one oil producing nation. In early 2020, Russia sought to flood the markets with oil to drive down prices and destroy the U.S. fracking industry. Saudi Arabia then launched a price war with Russia to force the Russians to stop. These plans were implemented mere weeks before the arrival of the coronavirus pandemic, which slashed demand for petroleum everywhere.

Russia and Saudi Arabia tried to backtrack. Unusually, they had support from the United States—President Trump was on very good terms with the leaders of both nations. But it was too late. Prices fell so fast that in April 2020, the price of West Texas Intermediate, a benchmark, was briefly negative. In other words, Texas producers had to pay distributors to take oil off their hands—the industry had run out of storage space. Many small fracking firms went out of business. The oil was still there, though, waiting for higher prices.

The government has also taken steps to curb the consumption—and hence the price—of gasoline. President Obama issued higher fuel efficiency standards for vehicles in 2009 and 2012. By 2016, the requirement was 39 miles per gallon (MPG) for cars and 30 MPG for light trucks. By 2025, the nation's combined fleet of new cars and light trucks were to have an average fuel efficiency of 54.5 miles per gallon.

The federal government also subsidizes the development of alternative fuels. Subsidies to encourage the production of ethanol from corn are controversial. Critics charge that ethanol production is an inefficient method of producing energy and makes food more expensive. Subsidies for renewable energy sources, such as windmills and solar power panels, have also attracted criticism. A past problem with wind and especially solar power had been high costs. Prices have fallen rapidly, however. Both wind and solar are now cheaper than coal and often competitive with natural gas. While these renewable energy sources are still a small fraction of the nation's power supply, they represent more than half of all new energy supplies currently being put into production.

Fracking
Short for hydraulic fracturing, the injection of a high-pressure solution of water, sand, and chemicals into hydrocarbon-bearing rocks, releasing oil or natural gas.

Some environmentalists have championed nuclear power as a carbon-free source of energy. The major problem has been that nuclear power could not compete on cost with natural gas. A second problem is safety. In March 2011, a giant tsunami struck northeast Japan and severely damaged four nuclear reactors located on the coast. The resulting radiation leaks convinced many people that new nuclear power plants would be dangerous.

Energy Prices and Russia's Invasion of Ukraine. Starting in 2021, Russia began amassing troops and equipment on the border between Ukraine and Russia. These hostile actions were occurring at a time when the Biden administration was curtailing some production of oil and gas in the United States. Actually, Biden issued an executive order on the first day of his presidency that shut down the Keystone XL pipeline from Canada. His administration continued to put restraints on the energy industry through increased regulation and the freezing of oil leases on federal lands. Many of these actions were undertaken as part of a so-called green new deal that would gradually ween Americans away from petroleum-based energy sources.

When Putin finally invaded Ukraine in early 2022, the U.S. was importing 600,000 barrels of oil a day from Russia. The world price of a barrel of petroleum rose to $124. What was to be a short "war" in Ukraine turned out to be a long slog. Months later, fighting continued. Western nations attempted to punish Russia by no longer buying energy sources from that country. But China and India made up the difference in demand. The price per barrel initially went down but rose again during the summer of 2022. Gas prices at the pump spiked in the U.S., reaching over $7 per gallon in some parts of California. Then a world recession became a real possibility and world demand for oil fell. By September it had dropped to $90 per barrel and gas prices fell accordingly.

Climate Change

In the 1990s, many scientists working on climate issues began to conclude that average world temperatures would rise significantly in the twenty-first century. Gases released by human activity, principally carbon dioxide (CO_2), may be producing a greenhouse effect, trapping the sun's heat and slowing its release into outer space.

The Climate Change Debate. Many scientists who perform research on the world's climate believe that climate change will be significant, but there is disagreement as to how much warming will actually occur. It is generally accepted that world temperatures have already increased by about 1 degree Celsius over the last century. The United Nations' Intergovernmental Panel on Climate Change predicts further increases ranging from 1.0 to 4.8 degrees Celsius by 2100. This range of estimates is rather wide in part because it is not clear how much will be done to limit greenhouse gas emissions.

Climate change has become a major political football to be kicked back and forth by conservatives and liberals. Environmental groups and others have been pressing the federal government to take action now to avert a planet-threatening crisis. Their efforts are complicated by the fact that a portion of the American electorate does not believe that global warming is happening or, if it is happening, that it is caused by human activities.

Disbelief in climate change has become a partisan phenomenon. Skepticism about climate change among Republicans is substantial. The opinions of Democrats have not changed—about four-fifths of them accept that climate change is a problem. If there is no global warming, of course, there would be no reason to limit emissions of CO_2 and other greenhouse gases. Since 2014, in the wake of superstorms and droughts, skepticism about climate change among Republicans had eased somewhat—but opposition to CO_2 restrictions remained strong.

Addressing the Issue. In 2009, Democrats made an initial attempt to legislate on CO_2 emissions. The bill sank without a trace in the Senate. With Republicans in control of the House beginning in 2011, no further legislation was possible. Despite the lack of government action, by 2011 CO_2 emissions in the United States were down from 2008 levels. The most important cause was new power plants that used natural gas instead of coal. (Natural gas does release some CO_2, but less than half as much as coal.) More fuel-efficient cars also contributed to the reduction.

It was also possible that the Environmental Protection Agency (EPA) might act without new legislation. In 2007, the Supreme Court found that the EPA had the authority to regulate the emission of CO_2 and other greenhouse gases

Image 13.3 A Tesla Roadster plugged into a recharging station in Santa Cruz, California. The Roadster can travel 244 miles on a single charge of its battery pack. ▶ What are some of the problems that prevent more U.S. drivers from switching to electric cars?

under the Clean Air Act.[1] (The Court overruled this decision in 2022, as we discuss below.) In 2009, the EPA issued a finding that greenhouse gases did in fact threaten the public health and welfare. In 2013, it issued rules covering new power plants. Coal-based power plants were already suffering serious price competition from natural gas, and the EPA's rules made the construction of new coal-based plants almost impossible.

In 2014, the EPA proposed rules covering existing power plants. The rules sought to cut emissions from such plants by 30 percent by 2030. In 2014, several states sued the EPA in an attempt to overturn the rules. As a result, federal courts stayed (suspended) the new rules pending a decision by the Supreme Court. In 2016, the Court split four-to-four over the case, which meant the stays remained in place. In 2017, however, President Trump ordered the EPA to revoke the rules covering new power plants

The question about the power of the EPA reached the Supreme Court again in 2022. In *West Virginia v. Environmental Protection Agency*,[2] the Court examined the question of whether the EPA has the authority to regulate greenhouse gas emissions in all industries. The Court held that EPA did not have such power because Congress did not grant it such power. The Court was unpersuaded by the EPA's argument that Congress implicitly tasked that agency with regulation of how Americans obtain their energy.

An additional controversy centered on the proposed Keystone XL pipeline. This project would carry petroleum from the Alberta oil sands (and also from North Dakota) to refineries on the Gulf Coast. Opponents of the pipeline claimed that the oil sands were one of the world's most pollution-intense sources of oil. Proponents argued for the economic benefits of greater supply. Republicans in Congress tried to force President Obama to approve the project. In 2015, he canceled the pipeline instead. Upon taking office, however, President Trump announced plans to revive the project. As mentioned before, upon taking office, President Joe Biden canceled the project again.

---

1. *Massachusetts v. EPA*, 549 U.S. 497 (2007).
2. *West Virginia v. Environmental Protection Agency*, 597 U.S. __ (2020).

The Politics of Economic Decision Making

» **LO 13-4:** Define unemployment, inflation, fiscal policy, public debt, and monetary policy.

Nowhere are the principles of public policy making more obvious than in the economic decisions made by the federal government. The president and Congress are constantly faced with questions of economic policy. Economic policy becomes especially important when the nation enters a recession.

Good Times, Bad Times

Like any economy that is fundamentally capitalist, the U.S. economy experiences ups and downs. Good times—booms—are followed by lean years. If a slowdown is severe enough, it is called a **recession**. Recessions are characterized by increased **unemployment**, the inability of those who are in the workforce to find a job. The government tries to moderate the effects of such downturns. In contrast, booms are historically associated with another economic problem that the government must address—rising prices, or **inflation**.

Recession
An economic downturn, usually characterized by a fall in the GDP and rising unemployment.

Unemployment
The inability of those who are in the labor force to find a job.

Inflation
A sustained rise in the general price level of goods and services.

Unemployment. Some psychologists say that unemployment is one of the most traumatizing events in a person's life. Certainly, unemployment imposes costs on the entire economy, not just on the unemployed individuals. Since the Great Depression of the 1930s, fighting unemployment has been a major goal of the federal government. The federal government also provides unemployment insurance. Not all unemployed workers are eligible, however. In fact, in recent years, only about one-third of the unemployed have received benefits. Benefits are not available to employees who quit their jobs voluntarily or are fired for cause. They are also not paid to individuals who are self-employed or workers who are entering the labor force for the first time but cannot find a job.

Measuring Unemployment. Estimates of the number of unemployed are prepared by the U.S. Department of Labor. The Bureau of the Census also generates estimates using survey research data. Critics of the published unemployment rate calculated by the federal government believe that it fails to reflect the true numbers of discouraged workers and "hidden unemployed." There is no exact way to measure discouraged workers, however. The Department of Labor defines them as people who have dropped out of the labor force and are no longer looking for a job because they believe that the job market has little to offer them. As a result, some economists believe that a better way to look at the unemployment issue is to calculate the share of the population that is actually working.

Inflation. Rising prices, or inflation, can also be a serious economic and political problem. Inflation is a sustained upward movement in the average level of prices. Another way of defining inflation is as a decline in the purchasing power of money over time. The government measures inflation using the consumer price index, or CPI. The Bureau of Labor Statistics identifies a market basket of goods and services purchased by the typical consumer and regularly checks the price of that basket. Over a period of many years, inflation can add up. For example, today's dollar is worth (very roughly) about a twentieth of what it was worth a century ago. In effect, today's dollar is a pre–World War I nickel.

Certain prices started to rise in 2021. Inflation—a general rise in all prices—became a major concern by the end of 2021 and the beginning of 2022. Indeed, by June 2022, the annual rate of inflation had hit 9.1 percent, the highest in 40 years. Inflation became a major policy topic during the 2022 midterm elections. Critics of Congress claim that it had spent too much money on too many programs, thereby increasing overall national demand so much that inflation was inevitable.

The Business Cycle. Economists refer to the regular succession of economic expansions and contractions as the business cycle. An extremely severe recession is called a depression, as in the example of the Great Depression of the 1930s. By 1933, actual output was 35 percent below the nation's productive capacity. Unemployment reached 25 percent. Compared with this catastrophe, recessions since 1945 have usually been mild. Nevertheless, the United States has experienced recessions with some regularity. Recession years since 1960 have included 1970, 1974, 1980, 1982, 1990, 2001, 2008–2009, 2020, and 2022.

To try to control the ups and downs of the national economy, the government has several policy options. One is to change the level of taxes or government spending. The other possibility involves influencing interest rates and the money side of the economy. We will examine taxing and spending, or fiscal policy, first.

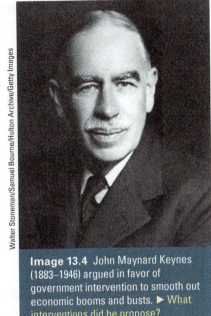

Image 13.4 John Maynard Keynes (1883–1946) argued in favor of government intervention to smooth out economic booms and busts. ▶ What interventions did he propose?

Fiscal Policy

Fiscal policy is the domain of Congress. A fiscal policy approach to stabilizing the economy is often associated with the twentieth-century British economist John Maynard Keynes (1883–1946). Keynes originated the school of thought that today is called **Keynesian economics**, which supports the use of government spending and taxing to help stabilize the economy. (Keynesian is pronounced *kayn-zee-un*.) Keynes believed that there was a need for government intervention in the economy, in part because after falling into a recession or depression, a modern economy may become trapped in an ongoing state of less-than-full employment.

Government Spending and Borrowing. Keynes developed his fiscal policy theories during the Great Depression of the 1930s. He believed that the forces of supply and demand operated too slowly on their own in such a serious recession. Unemployment meant people had less to spend, and because they could not buy things, more businesses failed, creating additional unemployment. It was a vicious cycle. Keynes's idea was simple: In such circumstances, the government should step in and engineer the spending that is needed to return the economy to a more normal state.[3]

The spending promoted by the government could take either of two forms. The government could increase its own spending, or it could cut taxes, allowing the taxpayer to undertake the spending instead. To have the effect Keynes wanted, however, it was essential that the spending be financed by a **budget deficit**—the government should spend more than it takes in.

Discretionary Fiscal Policy. Keynes originally developed his fiscal theories as a way of lifting an economy out of a major disaster such as the Great Depression. Beginning with the presidency of John F. Kennedy (1961–63), however, policy makers have attempted to use Keynesian methods to fine-tune the economy. This is discretionary fiscal policy— discretionary meaning left to the judgment, or discretion, of a policy maker.

Fiscal Policy
The federal government's use of taxation and spending policies to affect overall business activity.

Keynesian Economics
A school of economic thought that favors active federal government policy making to stabilize economy-wide fluctuations, including the use of discretionary fiscal policy.

Budget Deficit
Government expenditures that exceed receipts.

---

3. Robert Skidelsky, *Keynes: The Return of the Master* (New York: Public Affairs, 2010).

The Timing Problem. Attempts to fine-tune the economy encounter a timing problem. There will be an action time lag between the recognition of a problem and the implementation of policy to solve it. Fiscal policy time lags are long and variable, so a policy designed to combat a recession may not produce results until the economy is already out of the recession.

Because of the timing problem, attempts by the government to employ fiscal policy in the last sixty years have typically taken the form of tax cuts or increases. Tax changes can take effect more quickly than government spending. In 2009, therefore, the Obama administration was employing an exceptional approach when it secured from Congress a roughly $900 billion package consisting largely of hoped-for economic stimulus spending. Supported congressional spending packages also provided economic stimulus subsequent to the COVID-19 economic slowdown.

Criticisms of Keynes. Following World War II (1939–45), Keynes's theories were integrated into the mainstream of economic thinking. There have always been economic schools of thought, however, that consider Keynesian economics to be fatally flawed. These schools argue either that fiscal policy has no effect or that it has negative side effects that outweigh any benefits. Some opponents of fiscal policy believe that the federal government should limit itself to monetary policy, which we will discuss shortly. Others believe that it is best for the government to do nothing at all.

The Eclipse of Fiscal Policy. It is worth noting that most voters have neither understood nor accepted Keynesian economics. Despite popular attitudes, politicians of both parties accepted Keynesian ideas for many years. Democratic president John F. Kennedy was perhaps the first Keynesian in the White House. Republican president Richard Nixon (1969–74) is alleged to have said, "We are all Keynesians now." During the first years of Obama's presidency, however, Keynesian thinking among Republicans in Congress vanished almost completely. Instead, Republicans rejected "countercyclical" policies, reflecting the popular belief that during a recession the government should "tighten its belt."

It did not help the Keynesian cause that Obama's stimulus package failed to end high rates of unemployment—Keynesian economists argued that the stimulus was less than half of what was needed to accomplish such a goal. When Obama, in his 2010 State of the Union address, employed the belt-tightening metaphor, Keynesians realized that they had lost control of the political discourse.

By the time of the 2016 elections, the size of the federal budget deficit was no longer a top political issue, in part because economic recovery had reduced the size of the deficit substantially. As a result, legislators from both major parties were more receptive to proposals that might have the side effect of increasing the deficit. These included the massive tax cut bill passed by the Republicans in December 2017. The huge increases in federal spending touched off by the coronavirus pandemic in 2020 and 2021 revived concerns about deficits, however.

The Public Debt and Deficit Spending

Treasuries
U.S. Treasury securities—bills, notes, and bonds. Debt issued by the federal government.

Public, or National, Debt
The total amount of debt carried by the federal government.

The government typically borrows by selling U.S. Treasury bills, notes, and bonds, known collectively as Treasury securities and informally as **treasuries**. The sale of these federal obligations to corporations, private individuals, pension plans, foreign governments, foreign businesses, and foreign individuals adds to this nation's **public debt**, or **national debt**. In the last few years, foreign governments, especially those of China and Japan, have come to own about half of the U.S. public debt. Thirty years ago, the share of the U.S. public debt held by foreigners was only 15 percent.

The Public Debt. There are two types of public debt—gross and net. The gross public debt includes all federal government interagency borrowings, which really do not matter. This is similar to your taking an IOU ("I owe you") out of your left pocket and putting it into your right pocket. What is important is the net public debt—the public debt that does not include interagency borrowing. The best way to examine the relative importance of the public debt is to compare it with the gross domestic product (GDP), as is done in Figure 13.2. (Remember from earlier in this chapter that the gross domestic product is the dollar value of all final goods and services produced in a one-year period.) In the figure, you see that the public debt reached its peak during World War II and fell until 1975. From about 1960 to 2008, the net public debt as a percentage of GDP ranged between 25 and 50 percent. Thereafter, deficits incurred during the Great Recession drove the debt up rapidly.

Note that the net public debt as a percentage of GDP can fall even when the federal government is still running a budget deficit. If the economy is growing faster than the debt, then the debt as a share of the economy will fall even if it is still rising slowly. For example, the government never actually paid off the sums it borrowed to finance World War II. Rather, the economy grew fast enough that, over time, the wartime debt ceased to be important.

The Public Debt in Perspective. From 1960 until 1998, the federal government spent more than it received in all but two years. Some observers considered those ongoing budget

Figure 13.2	Net Public Debt as a Percentage of the Gross Domestic Product

The net public debt as a percentage of GDP fell after World War II. It rose dramatically in 2009 in response to the Great Recession, but then leveled off. ▶ **Why has it risen recently?**

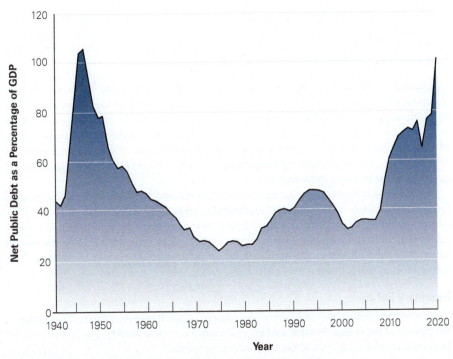

Source: Office of Management and Budget and the Congressional Budget Office.

deficits to be the negative result of Keynesian policies. Others argued that the deficits actually resulted from the abuse of Keynesianism. Politicians have been more than happy to run budget deficits in recessions. They have sometimes refused to implement the other side of Keynes's recommendations—to run a budget surplus during boom times, or at least to keep the percentage growth of the debt well below the growth of GDP.

In 1993, however, President Bill Clinton (1993–2001) obtained a tax increase as the nation emerged from a mild recession. Between the tax increase and the "dot-com boom," the United States had a budget surplus each year from 1998 to 2002. Some commentators predicted that we would be running federal government surpluses for years to come.

Back to Deficit Spending.   All of those projections went by the wayside because of several events. One event was the "dot-com bust," followed by the 2001–2002 recession, which lowered the rate of growth of not only the economy but also federal government tax receipts. A third event was the spending resulting from the terrorist attacks of 9/11 and the war in Iraq. These events ended the reduction in the debt seen under Clinton. Under George W. Bush, the debt rose, but moderately.

The Great Recession (2007–2008) dramatically increased the budget deficit and the level of public debt. Tax revenues collapsed, and spending on such items as unemployment compensation rose automatically. In addition, immediately upon taking office, President Obama obtained legislation from Congress that helped push the public debt to levels not seen since World War II. By 2013, however, due to spending curbs and increased tax collections, the annual federal deficit was falling. From a peak of 9.8 percent of GDP in 2009, the deficit was down to 2.6 percent in 2017. With the tax cut act of 2017, the deficit began to grow again. Spending in response to the coronavirus, plus a collapse in tax receipts, then caused the deficit to take off like a rocket, pushing the debt to new heights.

Both Presidents Trump and Biden did not seem overly concerned about deficit spending. Whereas talk in the past was always about hundreds of billions of dollars of that type of spending, now trillions of dollars of deficit spending do not seem to raise eyebrows, at least among those who make economic policy.

The Future of Deficit Spending.   Can high levels of deficit spending go on forever? Before the onset of the Great Recession, many economists feared that if high levels of deficit spending went on long enough, the rest of the world—which owns about 50 percent of all treasuries—might lose faith in our government. So far, however, there has been little sign of such a problem. On the contrary, following the financial crisis that struck on September 15, 2008, panicked investors bought large amounts of treasuries in the belief that they were the safest instruments in existence.

These developments have convinced some economists that as long as the dollar remains the world's dominant currency, "runs" on the dollar are not actually possible. Still, the larger the national debt, the more interest the federal government must pay to sustain it. If interest rates, which were very low until the summer of 2022, go back up substantially, the burden becomes greater. This poses the question of whether paying interest to the holders of U.S. treasuries is a desirable use of our tax dollars.

Monetary Policy

Controlling the rate of growth of the money supply is called **monetary policy**. This policy is the domain of the **Federal Reserve System**, also known simply as **the Fed**. The Fed is the most important regulatory agency in the U.S. monetary system.

Monetary Policy
The use of changes in the amount of money in circulation to alter credit markets, employment, and the rate of inflation.

Federal Reserve System (the Fed)
The system created by Congress in 1913 to serve as the nation's central banking organization.

The Fed performs a number of important functions. Perhaps the Fed's most important task is regulating the amount of money in circulation, which can be defined loosely as checking account balances and currency. The Fed also provides a system for transferring checks from one bank to another. In addition, it holds reserves deposited by most of the nation's banks, savings and loan associations, savings banks, and credit unions. Finally, it plays a role in supervising the banking industry.

Organization of the Federal Reserve System. A board of governors manages the Fed. This board consists of seven full-time members appointed by the president with the approval of the Senate. There are twelve Federal Reserve district banks. The most important unit within the Fed is the **Federal Open Market Committee**. This is the body that actually determines the future growth of the money supply and other important economy-wide financial variables. This committee is composed of the members of the Board of Governors, the president of the New York Federal Reserve Bank, and presidents of four other Federal Reserve banks, rotated periodically.

The Board of Governors of the Federal Reserve System is independent. The president can attempt to influence the board, and Congress can threaten to merge the Fed into the Treasury Department, but as long as the Fed retains its independence, its chairperson and governors can do what they please. Hence, any talk about "the president's monetary policy" or "Congress's monetary policy" is inaccurate. The Fed remains an independent entity.

Loose and Tight Monetary Policies. The Federal Reserve System seeks to stabilize nation-wide economic activity by controlling the amount of money in circulation. Credit, like any good or service, has a cost. The cost of borrowing—the interest rate—is similar to any other

Federal Open Market Committee
The most important body within the Federal Reserve System. The Federal Open Market Committee decides how monetary policy should be carried out.

Media Punch/MediaPunch Inc/Alamy Stock Photo

Image 13.5 Jerome Powell became chair of the Federal Reserve in 2018. Here, he testifies before a committee of the U.S. House. ▶ Why do some people argue that he is the single most important player in the world economy?

cost of doing business. When the cost of borrowing falls, businesspersons can undertake more investment projects. When it rises, businesspersons undertake fewer projects. Consumers also react to interest rates when deciding whether to borrow funds to buy houses, cars, or other big-ticket (high-priced) items.

If the Fed implements a loose monetary policy (often called an expansionary policy), the supply of credit increases and its cost falls. If the Fed implements a tight monetary policy (often called a contractionary policy), the supply of credit falls (or fails to grow) and its cost increases. A loose monetary policy is often implemented as an attempt to encourage economic growth. You may be wondering why any nation would want a tight monetary policy. The answer is to control inflation.

Monetary Policy During Recessions. A tight monetary policy is a powerful tool for taming inflation. (Some would argue that it is the only way that inflation can be stopped.) If interest rates go high enough, people will stop borrowing. How effective, though, is a loose monetary policy at ending a recession? Under normal conditions, it is very effective. A loose monetary policy will spur an expansion in economic activity.

To combat the Great Recession, however, the Fed reduced its interest rate almost to zero. The rate could hardly go any lower. Yet when consumers had credit, they were still reluctant to make major purchases. Many businesses found that they had little need to borrow to invest in new activities—and no need to hire new staff. Overall demand for goods and services was so low that companies could produce all they needed with their existing capacity and workforce.

Monetary policy had run out of steam—using it was like "pushing on a string." Even if the Fed created large amounts of new money, banks would not loan out these funds. Instead, they would pile up as unused reserves that banks leave on deposit with the Fed. After all, the government has little power to force banks to lend, and it certainly has no power to make people borrow and spend. As a result, the Obama administration placed its bets on fiscal policy.

Innovative Policies. During 2008 and 2009, the Fed developed a new way to respond to the failure of banks to lend. Relying on its ability to create money, it began to make loans itself, without turning to Congress for appropriations. The Fed bought debt issued by corporations. It bought securities that were based on student loans and credit card debt. By 2009, the Fed had loaned out close to $2 trillion in fresh credit. In 2010 and 2011, the Fed implemented yet another new policy, called quantitative easing, in an attempt to make monetary policy more effective. Quantitative easing essentially means buying quantities of long-term treasuries and mortgage-backed securities to hold down long-term interest rates.

In 2013, the Fed began a policy of tapering. Under this plan, the Fed slowly reduced the size of its quantitative easing purchases. (The purchases were ended altogether in October 2014.) The Fed also developed a program of forward guidance. Under this policy, the Fed made it clear that interest rates would remain low for a long time to come. In 2015, however, for the first time since the onset of the Great Recession, the Fed began to consider raising interest rates. The Fed in fact raised the federal funds rate incrementally in 2015 and 2016, and then several times in 2017 and 2018. In short, the special measures that the Fed had used in an attempt to fight the Great Recession were coming to an end.

The federal funds rate peaked at 2.5 percent in December 2018. Thereafter, the Fed reduced rates slightly out of concern for economic growth. The rate was 1.75 percent beginning in November 2019. In March 2020, in response to the pandemic, the Fed dropped the rate to a range from 0.25 percent to zero. It also announced that it would buy up to $2.3 trillion in commercial debt, thus making it easier to borrow during the pandemic.

In late 2021, because of increasing inflation, the Federal Reserve announced that it planned to increase interest rates in stages over the next several years. Then the Russian–Ukrainian war entered the discussion. Fed policy makers did not want to precipitate a recession, so they backed off a bit in their attempts to control inflation through increasing interest rates. Starting in June, though, the Fed increased its benchmark interest rate by more than it had done in decades. The Fed felt that fighting inflation was worth the risk of creating another recession. The Fed continued to raise interest rates through the fall of 2022.

The Politics of Taxation

» **LO 13-5:** Explain how taxpayers can alter their behavior in response to changes in tax rates.

Federal taxes are enacted by Congress. The Internal Revenue Code, which is the federal tax code, encompasses thousands of pages, thousands of sections, and thousands of subsections—our tax system is not very simple.

Americans pay a variety of taxes. At the federal level, the income tax is levied on most sources of income. Social Security and Medicare taxes are assessed on wages and salaries. There is an income tax for corporations, which has an indirect effect on many individuals. The estate tax is collected from property left behind by wealthy persons who have died. State and local governments also assess taxes on income, sales, and land. Altogether, the value of all taxes collected by the federal government and by state and local governments was 38 percent of GDP in 2022. This is a substantial sum, but it is less than what many other countries collect.

Federal Income Tax Rates

Individuals and businesses pay income taxes based on tax rates. Not all of your income is taxed at the same rate. The first few dollars of income that you earn are not taxed at all. The highest rate is imposed on the "last" dollar you make. This highest rate is the marginal tax rate. Table 13.1 shows the 2021 marginal tax rates for individuals and married couples (which applied to income earned in the previous year, 2020). The higher the tax rate, the greater the public's reaction to that tax rate. If the highest tax rate you pay on the income you make is 12 percent, then any method you can use to reduce your taxable income by one dollar saves you twelve cents in tax liabilities that you owe the federal government.

Table 13.1	Marginal Tax Rates for Single Persons and Married Couples (Filed in 2022 for Income Earned in 2021)	
Marginal Tax Bracket	**Single Persons**	**Married Filing Jointly**
10%	Up to $9,875	Up to $19,750
12%	$9,876 to $40,125	$19,751 to $80,250
22%	$40,126 to $85,525	$80,251 to $171,050
24%	$85,526 to $163,300	$171,051 to $326,600
32%	$163,301 to $207,350	$326,601 to $414,700
35%	$207,351 to $518,400	$414,701 to $622,050
37%	$518,401 or more	$622,051 or more

Source: Tax-Brackets.org (www.tax-brackets.org/federaltaxtable/2022).

Individuals paying a 12 percent rate have a relatively small incentive to avoid paying taxes but consider individuals who were faced with a tax rate of 94 percent in the 1940s during and after World War II. They had a tremendous incentive to find legal ways to reduce their taxable incomes. For every dollar of income that was somehow deemed nontaxable, the tax liabilities of these taxpayers would be reduced by ninety-four cents.

Income Tax Loopholes and Other Types of Taxes

Individuals and corporations facing high tax rates will adjust their earning and spending behavior to reduce their taxes. They will also make concerted attempts to get Congress to add **loopholes** to the tax law that allow them to reduce their taxable incomes. When Congress imposed very high tax rates on high incomes, it also provided more loopholes than it does today. For example, special provisions enabled investors in oil and gas wells to reduce their taxable incomes.

Progressive and Regressive Taxation. As Table 13.1 shows, the greater your taxable income, the higher the marginal tax rate. Persons with large incomes pay a larger share of their income in income tax. A tax system in which rates go up with income is called a **progressive tax** system. The federal income tax is clearly progressive.

The income tax is not the only tax you must pay. For example, the federal Social Security tax is levied on all wage and salary income at a flat rate of 6.2 percent. (Employers pay another 6.2 percent, making the total effective rate 12.4 percent.) In 2021, however, there was no Social Security tax on wages and salaries in excess of $147,000. (This "cap" changes from year to year.) Persons with very high salaries, therefore, pay no Social Security tax on much of their wages.

In addition, the tax is not levied on investment income (including capital gains, rents, royalties, interest, dividends, and profits from a business). The wealthy receive a much greater share of their income from these sources than others do. As a result, the wealthy pay a much smaller portion of their income in Social Security taxes than do the working poor. The Social Security tax is therefore a **regressive tax**.

To fund Medicare, a combined employer/employee 2.9 percent tax is also assessed on all wage income. The income of individuals that exceeds $200,000, however, is subject to a rate of 3.8 percent. For married couples filing jointly, the threshold is $250,000. Note that three-quarters of all taxpayers owe more in payroll taxes, such as Social Security and Medicare taxes, than they do in income taxes.

Capital Gains. Finally, as part of the income tax system, the federal government also taxes capital gains, that is, increases in the value of property over time. If you own stocks, for example, and sell them for a higher price than you bought them, the difference is a capital gain. The tax rate on long-term capital gains is lower than the rate for wage or salary income, on the theory that this lower rate encourages investment. Individuals with taxable incomes that do not exceed $40,000 and married couples whose income does not exceed $80,000 pay no tax on long-term capital gains. Individuals with a taxable income from $40,000 to $441,450 pay a 15 percent rate. Couples are taxed at 15 percent if their taxable income is from $80,000 to $496,050. For anyone above these income levels the rate is 20 percent. A special capital gains tax of 3.8 percent is also levied on certain high earners to help fund the Affordable Care Act. Because long-term capital gains are taxed at a lower rate than ordinary income, taxpayers have an interest in defining as much of their income as possible as capital gains.

Loopholes
A legal method by which individuals and businesses are allowed to reduce the tax liabilities they owe to the government.

Progressive Tax
A tax that rises in percentage terms as incomes rise.

Regressive Tax
A tax that falls in percentage terms as incomes rise.

What Kind of Tax System Do We Have? The various taxes Americans pay pull in different directions. The federal estate tax is extremely progressive, because it is not imposed at all on smaller estates. Sales taxes are regressive, because the wealthy spend a relatively smaller portion of their income on items subject to the sales tax. Add everything up, and the tax system as a whole is neither progressive nor regressive.

Making a Difference

Learning About Entitlement Reform

As discussed earlier in the chapter, programs such as Medicare, Medicaid, Social Security, unemployment compensation, and several others are known as entitlement programs. They are called entitlements because if you meet certain qualifications—of age or income, for example—you are entitled to specified benefits. The federal government can estimate how much it will have to pay out in entitlements but cannot set an exact figure in advance. In this way, entitlement spending differs from other government spending. When Congress decides what it will give to the national park system, for example, it allocates an exact sum, and the park system cannot exceed that budget. Along with national defense, entitlements make up by far the greatest share of the federal budget. This fact led a Bush administration staff member to joke, "It helps to think of the government as an insurance company with an army."

Why Should You Care? What happens to entitlement programs will affect your life in two major ways. Entitlement spending will largely determine how much you pay in taxes throughout your working lifetime. Entitlement policy will also determine how much support you receive from the federal government when you grow old. Because entitlements make up such a large share of the federal budget, it is not possible to address the issue of budget deficits without considering entitlement spending. Further, under current policies, spending on Medicare will rise in future years, placing ever greater pressure on the federal budget. Sooner or later, entitlement reform will be impossible to avoid. However these programs are changed, you will feel the effects in your wallet throughout your life.

What Can You Do? Should Medicare and Social Security benefits be high, with the understanding that taxes must therefore go up? Should these programs be cut back in the hope of avoiding deficits and tax

increases? Do entitlements mean that the old are fleecing the young—or is that argument irrelevant because we will all grow old someday? Progressives and conservatives disagree strongly about these questions. You can develop your own opinions by learning more about entitlement reform. The following organizations take a conservative position on entitlements:

- The Cato Institute, a conservative libertarian organization. Find its webpage on social security at www.cato.org/research/social-security.
- The Heritage Foundation. See what it has to say at www.heritage.org/issues/retirement-security.

The following organizations take a liberal stand on entitlements:

- National Committee to Preserve Social Security and Medicare presents its views at www.ncpssm.org.
- AARP (formerly the American Association of Retired Persons) defends retirement benefits at www.aarp.org/advocacy.

Image 13.6 ▶ Who is entitled to Medicare?

Key Terms

Affordable Care Act
(ACA) 318
budget deficit 325
domestic policy 313
entitlement programs
317
Federal Open Market
Committee 329

Federal Reserve System
(the Fed) 328
fiscal policy 325
fracking 321
gross domestic product
(GDP) 316
inflation 324

Keynesian economics
325
loopholes 332
Medicaid 317
Medicare 317
monetary policy 328
progressive tax 332

public, or national, debt
326
recession 324
regressive tax 332
treasuries 326
unemployment 324

Chapter Summary

» **LO 13-1** Domestic policy consists of laws, government planning, and government actions that concern internal issues of national importance. The policy-making process is initiated when policy makers become aware—through the media or from their constituents—of a problem that needs to be addressed. The process of policy making includes agenda building, policy formulation, policy adoption, policy implementation, and policy evaluation.

» **LO 13-2** Health care spending accounts for almost 18 percent of the U.S. economy. A major source of funding is Medicare, the federal program that pays health care expenses of U.S. residents over the age of sixty-five.

Much of the population has lacked health insurance—a major political issue. In the past, individual health insurance policies (not obtained through an employer) were expensive and often unobtainable at any price. In 2010, Congress passed a health care reform package—the Affordable Care Act, nicknamed "Obamacare"—that provides greatly expanded coverage in the United States. It initially required residents not already covered to purchase coverage, which is subsidized for individuals with low income.

» **LO 13-3** Issues concerning energy and the environment are on the nation's agenda. One problem has been our reliance on petroleum imports, given that many petroleum exporters are hostile to American interests. In recent years, however, production techniques such as fracking have greatly increased the domestic supply of crude oil (thereby lowering its cost) and especially of natural gas. Climate change, caused by the emission of CO_2 and other greenhouse gases, is a second major problem, although some dispute how serious it is.

» **LO 13-4** Fiscal policy is the use of taxes and spending to affect the overall economy. Lower taxes or higher spending can increase the budget deficit, which some believe can stimulate the economy.

The federal government has run a deficit in most years since 1960. The deficit is met by U.S. Treasury borrowing. This adds to the public debt of the U.S. government. Although the budget was temporarily in surplus from 1998 to 2002, large deficits now seem likely for many years to come.

Monetary policy is controlled by the Federal Reserve System, or the Fed. Monetary policy consists of changing the rate of growth of the money supply in an attempt to either stimulate or cool the economy. A loose monetary policy, in which more money is created, encourages economic growth. A tight monetary policy, in which less money is created, may be the only effective way of ending an inflationary spiral.

» **LO 13-5** U.S. taxes amount to about 26 percent of the gross domestic product. The federal individual income tax is progressive, that is, higher earners pay a larger share of their income. Individuals and corporations that pay taxes at the highest rates will try to pressure Congress into creating exemptions and tax loopholes. Loopholes allow earners with high incomes to reduce their taxable incomes.

Test Yourself

1. The policy-making process includes, but is not limited to:
   a. agenda building, policy formulation, and judicial approval.
   b. agenda building, policy formulation, and policy adoption.
   c. agenda building, policy formulation, and state referendums.

2. Entitlement programs include:
   a. Social Security and unemployment insurance.
   b. welfare and foreign aid.
   c. highway construction and veterans' benefits.

3. The last two phases of the policy-making process involve policy:
   a. formulation and adoption.
   b. adoption and implementation.
   c. implementation and evaluation.

4. The $2 trillion bill passed in March 2020 to address the COVID-19 pandemic was called:
   a. The Affordable Care Act (ACA).
   b. The American Health Care Act (AHCA).
   c. The Coronavirus Aid, Relief, and Economic Security Act (CARES Act).

5. The national minimum wage is:
   a. $15 per hour.
   b. $7.25 per hour.
   c. $10.00 per hour.

6. A major new source of increased energy supplies within the United States comes from:
   a. running existing wells at a faster pace.
   b. fracking (hydraulic fracturing).
   c. the new oil boom in Alaska.

7. Emissions of carbon dioxide (CO_2) have leveled off since 2008 in part because of the increased use in power plants of:
   a. natural gas.
   b. uranium.
   c. hydrogen.

8. When an economic slowdown is severe enough, it is officially called a:
   a. depression.
   b. recession.
   c. contraction.

9. Economic boom times are sometimes accompanied by:
   a. inflation.
   b. unemployment.
   c. lower taxes.

10. Fiscal policy involves:
    a. government spending and changes in the money supply in circulation.
    b. government taxation and the changes in the money supply in circulation.
    c. government taxing and spending policies.

11. The federal personal income tax system can be called:
    a. a progressive tax.
    b. a regressive tax.
    c. a degressive tax.

12. Americans who work for a salary typically pay federal income taxes, as well as payroll taxes that fund:
    a. Social Security and Medicaid.
    b. Medicare and Medicaid.
    c. Social Security and Medicare.

Essay Questions

1. Until recently, Congress always opposed the establishment of a universal health insurance system for the United States. What could the reasons for this stance have been? Are the reasons compelling? What political interests might oppose a universal system, and why?

2. Liberals have long favored progressive taxes, while conservatives prefer taxes that are either proportional or regressive. Which side has the stronger arguments? Explain your reasoning.

Answers to multiple-choice questions: 1. b, 2. a, 3. c, 4. c, 5. b, 6. b, 7. a, 8. b, 9. a, 10. c, 11. a, 12. c.

14 | Foreign Policy

U.S. Navy recruits wear face masks to prevent the spread of COVID-19 during basic seamanship training in April 2020. ▶ **What role does the military play in U.S. foreign policy?**

The five **Learning Outcomes (LOs)** below are designed to help improve your understanding of this chapter. After reading this chapter, you should be able to:

≫ LO 14-1 Define foreign policy and discuss moral idealism versus political realism in foreign policy.

≫ LO 14-2 Describe recent foreign policy challenges that involve the use of force.

≫ LO 14-3 Discuss the use of diplomacy in addressing such issues as nuclear proliferation, the rise of China, and the confrontation between Israel and the Palestinians.

≫ LO 14-4 Explain why U.S. foreign policy is mainly carried out by the president rather than Congress.

≫ LO 14-5 Cite the main themes in the history of U.S. foreign policy.

Check your understanding of the material with the Test Yourself section at the end of the chapter.

On September 11, 2001, Americans were forced to change their view of national security and of their relations with the rest of the world—literally overnight. No longer could citizens of the United States believe that national security issues involved only threats overseas or that the American homeland could not be attacked. Within a few days, it became known that the 9/11 attacks on the World Trade Center and on the Pentagon had been planned and carried out by a terrorist network named al Qaeda that was directed by the radical Islamist leader Osama bin Laden. The network was closely linked to the Taliban government of Afghanistan, which had ruled that nation since 1996.

Americans were shocked by the success of the attacks. They wondered how the airport security systems could have failed so drastically. Shouldn't the intelligence community have known about and defended against this terrorist network? How could U.S. foreign policy have been so blind to the anger of Islamist groups throughout the world?

In this chapter, we examine the tools of foreign policy and national security policy in the light of the many challenges facing the United States. One such challenge for U.S. foreign policy makers today is how best to respond to the threat of terrorism. We also review the history of American foreign policy.

Facing the World: Foreign and Defense Policies

>> **LO 14-1:** Define foreign policy and discuss moral idealism versus political realism in foreign policy.

The United States is only one nation in a world with almost two hundred independent countries, many located in regions where armed conflict is ongoing. What tools does the U.S. have to deal with the many challenges to its peace and prosperity? One tool is **foreign policy**. By this term, we mean both the goals the government wants to achieve in the world and the techniques and strategies used to achieve them. These techniques and strategies include **diplomacy**, **economic aid**, and military intervention.

As you will read later in this chapter, in the United States the foreign policy process usually originates with the president and those agencies that provide advice on foreign policy matters. Congressional action and national public debate often affect foreign policy formulation as well.

Aspects of Foreign Policy

As one aspect of overall foreign policy, **national security policy** is designed primarily to protect the independence and the political integrity of the United States. It concerns itself with the defense of the United States against actual or potential enemies.

U.S. national security policy is based on determinations made by the Department of Defense, the Department of State, and a number of other federal agencies, including the National Security Council (NSC). The NSC acts as an advisory body to the president, and it has often been a rival of the State Department in influencing the foreign policy process.

Defense policy is a subset of national security policy. Generally, defense policy refers to the set of policies that direct the nature and activities of the U.S. armed forces. Defense policies are proposed by the leaders of the nation's military forces and the secretary of Defense, and are influenced by congressional decision makers.

Diplomacy refers to the settling of disputes and conflicts among nations by peaceful methods. Diplomacy is also the set of negotiating techniques by which a nation attempts to carry out its foreign policy. Of course, diplomacy can be successful only if the parties involved are willing to negotiate.

Foreign Policy
A nation's external goals and the techniques and strategies used to achieve them.

Diplomacy
The process by which states carry on political relations with each other. Also, the process of settling conflicts among nations by peaceful means.

Economic Aid
Assistance to other nations in the form of grants, loans, or credits to buy the assisting nation's products.

National Security Policy
Foreign and domestic policy designed to protect the nation's independence and political integrity. Policy that is concerned with the safety and defense of the nation.

Defense Policy
A subset of national security policy concerning the U.S. armed forces.

Image 14.1 A U.S. paratrooper after a military exercise with allied forces. ▶ Under what circumstances is it appropriate for the United States to intervene abroad using ground forces?

Petras Malukas/Getty Images

Idealism Versus Realism in Foreign Policy

Since the earliest years of the republic, Americans have felt that the United States has a special destiny. The American experiment in political and economic liberty, it was thought, would provide the best possible life for its citizens and be a model for other nations. As the United States became a power in world politics, Americans came to believe that the nation's actions in the world should be guided by American political and moral principles.

Moral Idealism. This view of America's mission has led to the adoption of many foreign policy initiatives that are rooted in **moral idealism**. This philosophy views the world as fundamentally benign and assumes that most nations can be persuaded to take moral considerations into account when setting their policies.[1] In this perspective, nations should come together and agree to keep the peace, as President Woodrow Wilson (1913–21) proposed for the League of Nations. Many foreign policy initiatives taken by the United States have been based on this idealistic view of the world. These include humanitarian relief efforts following great natural disasters. For example, the United States provided aid to West Africa in response to an outbreak of the Ebola virus in 2014. After the gigantic volcanic eruption in Tonga on December 20, 2021, the United States sent millions of dollars of aid.

Political Realism. In opposition to the moral perspective is **political realism**. Realists see the world as a dangerous place in which each nation strives for its own survival and interests, regardless of moral considerations. The United States must therefore base its foreign policy decisions on cold calculations without regard to morality. Realists believe that other nations are, by definition, dangerous. A strong defense will show the world that the United States is willing to protect its interests.

Donald Trump was an advocate of political realism—his doctrine of "America first" was as far away from moral idealism as we have seen in an American president. Trump explicitly rejected the policy—endorsed by most recent U.S. presidents—of promoting human rights in his meetings with foreign leaders. He also exhibited a realistic attitude toward authoritarian rulers such as Russia's Vladimir Putin and Rodrigo Duterte of the Philippines. Trump's foreign policy was described as "transactional." That is, he emphasized exchanging favors with individual nations. Trump also showed some skepticism toward collective international

Moral Idealism
A philosophy that views nations as normally willing to cooperate and to agree on moral standards for conduct.

Political Realism
A philosophy that views each nation as acting principally in its own interest.

---

1. Quoted in James M. McCormick, *American Foreign Policy and Process*, 6th ed. (Independence, Ky.: Cengage Learning, 2013).

organizations such as the North Atlantic Treaty Organization (NATO), a military alliance that includes the United States, Canada, and most of the nations of Europe.

It is difficult to label the Biden administration's foreign policy. In the lead-up to Putin's February 2022 invasion of Ukraine (an independent nation), Biden's statements and actions seemed to be a blend of moral idealism and political realism.

American Foreign Policy—A Mixture of Both. It is important to note that the United States has rarely been guided by only one of these principles. Typically, both moral idealism and political realism affect foreign policy making. At times, idealism and realism can pull in different directions, making it difficult to establish a coherent policy. The so-called Arab Spring of 2011 serves as an example of such cross-currents in American foreign policy.

Acting on the basis of political realism, the United States built up long-standing relationships with various dictators in the Arab world, such as Hosni Mubarak of Egypt. Given such alliances, the United States had to determine whether to support existing governments when they came under attack by popular rebellions.

President Obama and then Secretary of State Hillary Clinton, however, did not believe that realism and idealism were necessarily in conflict. The United States could support democratic movements and remain true to its values. Initially, this course of action appeared to be workable, because in Egypt and Tunisia, at least, the democratic rebels were winning. In 2013, however, the military seized power in Egypt, ending its experiment with democracy. In 2014, speaking at the graduation ceremony for the U.S. Military Academy, Obama was blunt: American relations with Egypt were again based on political realism.

As it turned out, Tunisia was the only nation in which the Arab Spring rebellions were a success. In Libya, rebels were initially successful in taking power only in the eastern region. The United States and its European allies then intervened with air strikes to assist the rebels. The Libyan dictator, Muammar Gaddafi, was overthrown and killed. Libya was unable to establish a coherent national government in subsequent years, however, and the country wound up divided between rival regimes. Critics accused idealists of supporting an irresponsible intervention.

Terrorism and Warfare

> **» LO 14-2:** Describe recent foreign policy challenges that involve the use of force.

The foreign policy of the United States—whether idealist, realist, or both—must be formulated to deal with world conditions. In some instances, these policies have involved the use of force.

The Emergence of Terrorism

Terrorism is a systematic attempt to inspire fear to gain political ends. Typically, terrorism involves the indiscriminate use of violence against noncombatants. In the past, terrorism was a strategy generally employed by radicals who wanted to change the status of a particular nation or province. For example, over many years the Irish Republican Army undertook terrorist attacks in the British province of Northern Ireland with the aim of driving out the British and uniting the province with the Republic of Ireland. In the twenty-first century, however, the United States has confronted a new form of terrorism that is not associated with such clear-cut aims.

Terrorism
A systematic attempt to inspire fear to gain political ends, typically involving the indiscriminate use of violence against noncombatants.

Dha/ZUMA Press/Newscom

Image 14.2 Thousands of Syrian refugees walk back into Syria from Turkey to celebrate the Eid festival in June 2017. ▶ Why has the United States been reluctant to intervene in the Syrian civil war?

September 11. In 2001, nineteen terrorists hijacked four airplanes and crashed three of them into buildings—two into the World Trade Center towers in New York City and one into the Pentagon in Washington, D.C. The fourth airplane crashed in a field in Pennsylvania, after the passengers fought the hijackers.

Why did the al Qaeda network plan and launch attacks on the United States? In part, the attacks were intended to frighten and demoralize America so that it would withdraw its troops from the Middle East.

Al Qaeda's Ultimate Aims. Al Qaeda's ultimate goals, however, were not limited to forcing the United States to withdraw from the Middle East. Al Qaeda envisioned worldwide revolutionary change, with all nations brought under the theocratic rule of an Islamist empire. Governments have successfully negotiated with terrorists who profess limited aims—today, radicals associated with the Irish Republican Army are part of a coalition government in Northern Ireland. There is little way to negotiate with an organization such as al Qaeda.

Domestic Terrorism. Al Qaeda is not the only group ever to launch a terrorist attack on U.S. soil. Radicals opposed to the U.S. war in Vietnam set off bombs in the 1960s and 1970s (usually without fatalities). Right-wing terrorists were an issue in the 1990s—notably, a bomb set off at a federal office building in Oklahoma City killed 168 people.

In more recent years, however, attacks by domestic Islamists have been the major concern. Such individuals are typically "self-radicalized" through the internet and are not controlled by a foreign organization. A bombing at the Boston Marathon in 2013 killed three people and cost fourteen victims at least one of their legs. The alleged perpetrators were two self-radicalized Muslim brothers, one of them a U.S. citizen. A husband-and-wife team killed fourteen people in San Bernardino, California, in 2015. A lone gunman murdered forty-nine people at a nightclub in Orlando, Florida, in 2016. Other nations have experienced devastating incidents. In 2015, terrorists murdered 130 people in Paris, France. In a 2016 atrocity in the French city of Nice, eighty-six were killed, and an additional 434 were injured. Most of the casualties inflicted by terrorist attacks, however, have been in predominantly Muslim nations, notably war-torn Afghanistan, Iraq, and Syria.

The War on Terrorism. After 9/11, President George W. Bush implemented stronger security measures, including heightened airport security, new laws allowing greater domestic surveillance of potential terrorists, and increased funding for the military. In addition, Bush launched two military efforts abroad. The first was to attack al Qaeda's bases in Afghanistan, as well as the Taliban government of that country, which was allied with the terrorists. The second, which began in 2003, was a war against the dictatorial regime in Iraq.

Wars in Iraq

In 1990, the Persian Gulf became the setting for a major challenge to the international system set up after World War II (1939–45). President Saddam Hussein of Iraq sent troops into the neighboring oil sheikdom of Kuwait, occupying that country. This was the most clear-cut case of aggression against an independent nation in half a century. In January 1991, U.S.-led coalition forces retook Kuwait, and the First Gulf War ended.

As part of the cease-fire that ended the First Gulf War, Iraq agreed to allow United Nations (UN) weapons inspectors to oversee the destruction of its missiles and all chemical and nuclear weapons development. In 1999, though, Iraq placed so many obstacles in the path of the UN inspectors that they withdrew from the country.

The Second Gulf War—The Iraq War. In 2002 and early 2003, President George W. Bush began assembling an international coalition that might support further military action in Iraq. Bush was unable to convince the UN Security Council that military force was necessary in Iraq, so the United States took the initiative. In March 2003, U.S. and British forces invaded Iraq and within a month had toppled Hussein's dictatorship. The process of establishing order in Iraq turned out to be very difficult, however.

Occupied Iraq. The people of Iraq are divided into three principal ethnic groups. The Kurdish-speaking people of the north were overjoyed by the invasion. The Arabs adhering to the Shiite branch of Islam live principally in the south and constitute a majority of the population. They were deeply skeptical of U.S. intentions. The Arabs belonging to the Sunni branch of Islam live mainly to the west of Baghdad. Many Sunnis considered the occupation to be a disaster.

In short order, a Sunni guerrilla insurgency arose and launched attacks against the coalition forces. A newly organized al Qaeda in Iraq sponsored suicide bombings and other attacks against coalition troops and the forces of the new Iraqi government. Al Qaeda also attacked Iraqi Shiites. A major bloodletting in the country took place between Sunnis and Shiites. By late 2006, polls indicated that about two-thirds of Americans wanted to see an end to the Iraq War—a sentiment expressed in the 2006 midterm elections.

Iraqi Endgame? In January 2007, President Bush announced a major increase, or "surge," in U.S. troop strength. Skeptics doubted that the new troop levels would have much effect on the outcome. In April 2007, however, Sunni tribal leaders rose up against al Qaeda and called in U.S. troops to help them. Al Qaeda, it seems, had badly overplayed its hand by terrorizing the Sunni population.

During subsequent months, the Iraqi government gained substantial control over its own territory. Still, American attitudes toward the war remained negative. In 2008, President Bush and the Iraqi prime minister negotiated a deadline for withdrawing U.S. troops. U.S. combat forces left Iraq in August 2010. The rest of the American troops were out by the end of 2011.

Afghanistan

The Iraq War was not the only military effort launched by the Bush administration as part of the war on terrorism. The first military effort was directed against al Qaeda camps in Afghanistan and the Taliban regime, which had ruled most of Afghanistan since 1996. In late 2001, after building a coalition of international allies and anti-Taliban rebels within Afghanistan, the United States began an air campaign against the Taliban regime. The anti-Taliban rebels, known as the Northern Alliance, were able to take Kabul, the capital, and oust the Taliban from power.

The Return of the Taliban. The Taliban were defeated, but not destroyed. The Taliban and al Qaeda both retreated to the rugged mountains between Afghanistan and Pakistan, where they were able to establish bases on the Pakistani side of the border. In 2003, the Taliban began to launch attacks against Afghan soldiers, foreign aid workers, and American troops.

During 2009 and 2010, President Obama almost doubled the number of U.S. troops stationed in Afghanistan. At the same time, he announced that he would begin making troop withdrawals in 2011. By 2015, the number of troops was down to about 10,000. In 2017, President Trump raised U.S. troop levels back up to 14,000.

The Death of bin Laden. In 2011, intelligence agencies obtained evidence that bin Laden might be living in a residential compound in Abbottabad, Pakistan, possibly under the protection of members of Pakistan's military. On May 1, 2011, U.S. Navy SEALs launched a helicopter raid that killed bin Laden and four others.

Withdrawing From Afghanistan. While many have called our presence in Afghanistan America's longest war, it really was not a war after 2011. Indeed, almost no Americans were killed by the end of the 2010s. Nonetheless, the Trump administration wanted the U.S. to get out of that conflict. The Trump administration began negotiations with the Taliban. In February of 2020, an agreement was reached with the Taliban, and the Trump administration began to draw down forces.

When Joe Biden became president, he, too, wanted Americans to leave Afghanistan. His goal was to be completely out of that country by the anniversary of 9/11. The precipitous withdrawal of U.S. troops occurred on August 30, 2021. Many concerned individuals had been kept in the dark prior to that date. For example, personnel at the U.S. embassy had less than 24 hours to pack their bags and leave. What ensued was a foreign policy embarrassment. U.S. troops stopped providing air cover support for Afghan government troops. The U.S. left over $80 billion of sophisticated military equipment at the Bagram Air Force Base. Thousands of Afghans who held U.S. passports or green cards were left stranded without any support from the U.S. government. The Taliban was able to enter the capital of Afghanistan and took over Kabul and the rest of that country in less than three days.

The Civil War in Syria and the Rise of ISIS

In 2011, Syrians rebelled against their dictator, Bashar al-Assad. The rebellion soon turned into a stalemate. Assad's forces inflicted horrifying casualties on the civilian population. By 2017, the death toll was well over 400,000, and almost half the country's people had been driven from their homes. The rebels were also fighting among themselves and were increasingly dominated by radical Islamists who held beliefs similar to those of al Qaeda. With few forces that America could back, political realism left the Obama administration reluctant to intervene.

The Rise of ISIS. The most hard-line Islamist group in Syria was the Islamic State in Iraq and Greater Syria (ISIS), also known as the Islamic State in Iraq and the Levant (ISIL) and as Daesh, an Arabic acronym. This group was a reorganized version of al Qaeda in Iraq, but in 2014, the al Qaeda movement expelled ISIS due to its vicious tactics.

As its name implies, ISIS was active in both Syria and Iraq. In June 2014, ISIS launched a major offensive in Iraq that soon left it in control of Mosul, Iraq's second largest city. ISIS was aided in its advance by the acquiescence of various Sunni groups that had grievances against the Shiite-led government of Iraq. At the end of June, ISIS changed its name to simply the "Islamic State" (IS). It announced that it sought to rule not only the Middle East, but the entire world.

The Islamic State in Iraq. IS soon began expelling, killing, and even enslaving religious minority groups in the lands it controlled. These included Christians and members of the small Yazidi faith. IS also clashed with the Peshmerga, the militia of Iraq's autonomous Kurdish region. President Obama authorized air strikes to assist the Peshmerga and later began to provide air support to the Iraqi government as well. In 2017, Iraqi forces retook Mosul. By that point, U.S. forces in Iraq were back up to almost 5,000 soldiers.

The Ongoing Catastrophe in Syria. By 2015, the civil war in Syria had developed into a three-way conflict among the government, IS, and more moderate rebel factions. Syrian Kurds located along the Turkish border constituted a fourth element. IS conquests in Iraq resulted in U.S. intervention in Syria for the first time. This included the bombing of IS targets and

dpa picture alliance/Alamy Stock Photo

Image 14.3 Female soldiers of the Peshmerga, the militia of Iraq's autonomous Kurdish region. They were to join the fight against ISIS in Iraq. ▶ Why might most Arab armies be men-only?

also support for the small number of Syrian rebels who were not Islamist radicals. President Obama was opposed to any additional U.S. involvement, arguing that such a step would not have positive results. Many foreign policy experts disagreed with that calculation, however. President Trump's actions were not greatly different from those undertaken by Obama.

At the request of the Syrian government, in 2015 the Russian air force began air strikes against both IS and the more moderate rebels. Russia claimed to be attacking IS, but the majority of its strikes actually hit moderate targets. It appeared that the Syrian civil war was developing into an international war by proxy. Iran and Russia were in support of the Assad government, while the United States and Saudi Arabia supported various rebel factions. While Turkey was hostile to the Assad regime, its main interest was in suppressing Assad's Kurdish opponents, who were seen as allied with Kurdish rebels in Turkey itself.

In 2015, more than a million Syrian refugees poured into Europe through Turkey, precipitating a crisis in that continent. By 2017, the Russian-backed Assad government had clearly obtained the upper hand in the fighting. Non-IS rebels were confined to small pockets of territory and forced into a series of cease-fires. For the time being, Turkish forces in the area prevented a complete collapse of the rebel enclave and the massacre of its inhabitants. IS itself had lost essentially all of its territory, primarily to a combined U.S.–Kurdish operation. IS was therefore essentially reduced to a stateless terrorist group much like al Qaeda before it.

U.S. Diplomatic Efforts

>> **LO 14-3:** Discuss the use of diplomacy in addressing such issues as nuclear proliferation, the rise of China, and the confrontation between Israel and the Palestinians.

The United States has dealt with many international problems through diplomacy, rather than the use of armed force. Some of these issues include the proliferation of nuclear weapons, the confrontation between Israel and the Palestinians, the growing power of China, and ongoing economic problems in Europe.

Nuclear Weapons

In 1945, the United States was the only nation to possess nuclear weapons. Several nations quickly joined the "nuclear club," however, including the Soviet Union in 1949, Britain in 1952, France in 1960, and China in 1964. India and Pakistan detonated nuclear devices within a few weeks of each other in 1998. North Korea conducted an underground nuclear explosive test in October 2006. Several other nations, Israel in particular, are believed to possess nuclear weapons or the capability to produce them in a short time.

About 15,000 nuclear warheads are known to be stockpiled worldwide, though the exact number is uncertain. The United States and Russia dismantled some of their nuclear weapons systems after the end of the **Cold War** and the breakup of the Soviet Union in 1991 (discussed later in this chapter). Still, both retain sizable nuclear arsenals.

Nuclear Proliferation: Iran. For years, the United States, the European Union (EU), and the United Nations have tried to prevent Iran from becoming a nuclear power. In spite of these efforts, many observers believed that Iran was in the process of developing nuclear weapons. The group of nations trying to negotiate with Iran included Britain, China, France, Germany, Russia, and the United States.

By 2009, the UN Security Council had voted three rounds of penalties, called sanctions, against Iran in reaction to its nuclear program. By 2012, the sanctions were beginning to damage Iran's economy. In 2012, it was disclosed that the United States had successfully destroyed many of Iran's nuclear enrichment centrifuges by deploying a specially designed computer virus. Threats that Israel or the United States might bomb Iran's nuclear sites added to the pressure.

Before 2013, talks between Iran and the six nations just mentioned went nowhere. In 2013, however, Iran elected a new president, Hassan Rouhani, who initiated a charm offensive directed at the West. It appeared that for the first time, Iran was prepared to negotiate seriously.

Reaching a Deal. In July 2015, Iran reached a deal with the six world powers and the European Union. The agreement lifted most sanctions in exchange for substantial restrictions on Iran's nuclear program. Until 2030, Iran could produce only limited amounts of low-enriched uranium. The International Atomic Energy Agency would be able to inspect all Iranian nuclear facilities.

Advocates of the deal contended that even if Iran were to drop out of it, the country would still be at least a year away from building a usable nuclear bomb. In that time, other nations would be able to impose pressure on Iran to change course. Opponents of the deal included most Republicans and some Democrats in Congress plus the government of Israel. These opponents wanted Iran to stop its destabilizing military and financial support for rebel factions in neighboring countries. These demands had no connection to the nuclear issue. Indeed, some opponents would accept nothing less than the overthrow of Iran's theocratic government.

President Trump was also opposed to the deal. In April 2018 he withdrew from it and announced that all U.S. sanctions on Iran would be reimposed. The other participating nations tried to keep the deal alive. European businesses, however, would be banned from doing business with America if they invested in Iran. Most were forced to pull out. Attempts by European governments to find a way to bypass American financial institutions largely failed.

By 2019, Iran was again suffering severe economic pain from the sanctions. Iran announced deliberate steps to violate its nuclear commitments, but it was careful to choose violations that were reversible. Upon taking office in 2021, Joe Biden indicated that he

Cold War
The ideological, political, and economic confrontation between the United States and the Soviet Union following World War II.

wished to resurrect the old deal with Iran, with some changes. Negotiations were restarted. Ironically, a new deal was fashioned with the help of Russia. We say ironically because at the same time Putin was preparing to invade Ukraine, his diplomat was acting as a go-between for the U.S. Then Putin ordered the shelling of civilian targets in cities throughout Ukraine while the Iran negotiations proceeded. Iran fired ballistic missiles on the U.S. consulate in Iraq on March 23, 2022, and then launched a cyberattack on Israeli government websites.

Several European countries offered a "final" deal in August 2022. Iran thought the deal was constructive although the U.S. did not agree. During that time, the U.S. learned that Iran had plotted to assassinate former National Security Advisor John Bolton. Some experts believe that Iran is very close to creating a nuclear bomb.

Nuclear Proliferation: North Korea. North Korea tested a nuclear device in 2006. An agreement reached in February 2007 provided that North Korea would start disabling its nuclear facilities and allow UN inspectors into the country. In July 2007, North Korea dismantled one of its nuclear reactors and admitted UN inspectors.

By 2009, however, North Korea was pulling back from its treaty obligations. In April, the country tested a long-range missile capable of delivering a nuclear warhead. After the UN Security Council issued a statement condemning the test, North Korea ordered UN inspectors out of the country, broke off negotiations, and conducted a second nuclear test. Since that time, North Korea has tested rockets capable of reaching the U.S. mainland.

The United States and other parties have sought to persuade China to take the lead in bringing North Korea back to the negotiating table—China is the one nation that has significant economic leverage over North Korea. China, however, is concerned over the consequences that could follow if sanctions or other measures were to lead to a collapse of the North Korean regime.

President Trump responded to North Korea's steps with a series of insulting tweets, and the North Koreans responded in kind. Surprisingly, Trump then offered to meet North Korean leader Kim Jong-un personally. The meeting took place in June 2018. Both parties called it a success. Kim offered to give up his nuclear weapons, but his price for doing so appeared to be high. It might include the abandonment of the U.S. defense treaty with South Korea—or even Japan. Such a U.S. withdrawal was inconceivable, and no agreement was reached. During Biden's first few years in office, North Korea launched several missile tests to show that it was improving its offensive military capabilities. Its apparent goal has been for some time to both miniaturize its nuclear warheads and develop missiles that could reach the United States.

Chemical Weapons in Syria. Most nations have signed treaties banning the use of chemical weapons. In 2013, however, Bashar al-Assad's regime in Syria used nerve gas

Itar-Tass Photo Agency/Alamy

Image 14.4 Iranian president Hassan Rouhani. ▶ How successful has Rouhani been in nuclear negotiations with major world powers?

against districts under rebel control, with massive fatalities. President Obama proposed to respond to this act by launching air strikes and asked Congress for approval. Russia then announced that Syria would sign a treaty banning chemical weapons and yield up its weapons.

To the surprise of many, the Assad regime cooperated with international inspectors. In 2014, President Obama announced that the destruction of the weapons was complete. That same year, however, Assad allegedly used chlorine gas against rebels. Chlorine is not a controlled substance, but its use as a weapon is banned.

After President Trump took office, the Assad regime employed nerve gas against rebel-held communities on at least two occasions. Clearly, either Assad had failed to yield up all of his chemical weapon stocks, or he had managed to obtain a new supply. On both occasions, Trump ordered limited retaliatory bombings of regime targets. U.S. military leaders admitted that the bombings were unlikely to eliminate Assad's ability to gas his own people.

Israel and the Palestinians

As a longtime supporter of the state of Israel, the United States has undertaken to persuade the Israelis to negotiate with the Palestinian Arabs who live in the territories occupied by Israel. The conflict between Israel and the Palestinians, which began in 1948, has been extremely hard to resolve. The internationally recognized solution is for Israel to yield the West Bank and the Gaza Strip to the Palestinians in return for effective security commitments and abandonment by the Palestinians of any right of return to Israel proper.

The Palestinians, however, have been unwilling to stop terrorist attacks on Israel, and Israel has been unwilling to dismantle its settlements in the occupied territories. Further, the two parties have been unable to come to an agreement on how much of the West Bank should go to the Palestinians and what compensation (if any) the Palestinians should receive for abandoning all claims to settlement in Israel proper. Although it is clear that any peace deal would require that Palestinians give up the right of return to Israel, the Palestinians have not yet abandoned that claim.

Talks With the PLO. In 1991, under pressure from the United States, the Israelis opened talks with the Palestine Liberation Organization (PLO). In 1993, the PLO and Israel agreed to set up Palestinian self-government—the Palestinian Authority—in the West Bank and the Gaza Strip.

Further agreements were rejected by Palestinian radicals, who began a campaign of suicide bombings in Israeli cities. In 2002, the Israeli government moved tanks and troops into Palestinian towns to kill or capture the terrorists. One result of the Israeli reoccupation was an almost complete—if temporary—collapse of the Palestinian Authority. In February 2004, Israeli prime minister Ariel Sharon announced a plan under which Israel would withdraw from the Gaza Strip, regardless of whether a deal could be reached with the Palestinians.

The Rise of Hamas. In January 2006, the militant group Hamas won a majority of the seats in the Palestinian legislature. American and European politicians refused to talk to Hamas until it agreed to rescind its avowed desire to destroy Israel. In 2007, after fighting between Hamas and the PLO, Hamas wound up in complete control of the Gaza Strip, and the PLO retained exclusive power in the West Bank.

Israel sought to pressure the Hamas regime in the Gaza Strip to relinquish power through an economic blockade. Hamas retaliated by firing a series of rockets into Israel. In January 2009, Israel temporarily reoccupied the Gaza Strip. In June 2014, fighting again broke out between Israel and the Hamas regime in the Gaza Strip. A cease-fire was finally established in August. By that time, Gaza had suffered massive destruction and loss of life.

Talks Fail Again. In 2013, the United States attempted to restart negotiations between Israel and the Palestinians. By 2014, however, the talks had collapsed again. One obstacle to peace was the tough positions taken by Prime Minister Benjamin Netanyahu, who was elected in 2009. Despite opposition from the Obama administration, Netanyahu accelerated the growth of Israeli settlements in the West Bank.

In May 2017, President Trump visited the region and announced his desire to restart the peace talks. Such a step, however, would require an investment of time and energy that the Trump administration was not able to

Xinhua/Alamy Stock Photo

Image 14.5 President Trump meets with Israeli prime minister Benjamin Netanyahu in May 2017. ▶ Why has the Israeli–Palestinian dispute been so hard to resolve?

maintain. In December 2017, Trump formally recognized Jerusalem as the capital of Israel. Given the previous understanding that such recognition would only be granted as part of a final peace deal, Trump's action was strongly criticized by many in the international community. In September 2020, President Trump successfully brokered a peace accord between Israel and the United Arab Emirates and also one between Israel and Bahrain. In effect, these other countries decided to ignore Palestine.

These agreements are now known as the Abraham Accords. Even though the Biden administration has not shown much support for Israel, Israel is attempting to add other Middle East countries to the Abraham Accords.

The New Power: China

The growth of the Chinese economy during the last forty years is one of the most important developments in world history. For much of that time, the Chinese economy grew at a rate of about 10 percent annually, a long-term growth rate previously unknown in human history. Never have so many escaped poverty so quickly.

China now produces 45 percent of the world's output of steel and 60 percent of the world's cement. China's electrical generating capacity continues to grow rapidly. The new plants, which are often coal fired, may promote global warming and also generate some of the world's worst air pollution. Skyscrapers fill the skyline of every major Chinese city.

In 2007, for the first time, China manufactured more passenger automobiles than did the United States. China is building a limited-access highway system that, when complete, will be longer than the U.S. interstate highway system. Depending on how it is measured, the economy of China may already be larger than that of the United States. China, in short, is becoming the world's second superpower.

Trade Relationships Between China and the United States. An important factor in U.S.–Chinese relations has been the large and growing trade ties between the two countries. While officially Communist, China today permits much free enterprise. China has become substantially integrated into the world economic system, and it exports considerably more goods and services to the United States than it imports. The resulting economic imbalances are good for Chinese exporters, but create financial problems in both countries.

Recently, Chinese authorities have sought to rebalance their economy toward greater domestic consumption. China's own people are to consume more of the goods and services it produces. As a result, China's current account surplus (the most comprehensive measurement of excess exports) has fallen since 2011.

Political observers point out that China may appear to be tending towards a free enterprise economy, but it still remains a communist country. The Communist Party now, more than in the last ten years, controls an ever-increasing part of the economy. China's President Xi Jinping has moved China toward isolationism. He is no longer encouraging Chinese citizens to learn English. He has throttled successful Chinese entrepreneurs who seem to have too much popularity and success. He has made it clear that he will remain leader of China as long as he wants to.

In the process of "re-communizing" his country, Xi Jinping has been responsible for a reduction in the amount of innovation by China's younger, vibrant population. After all, what is the future benefit of being innovative if one's innovations can simply be taken over by the Communist Party? The world saw the Chinese economy start to sputter in 2021 and 2022 when its growth rate dropped. Needless to say, Chinese–American relations have not improved as of late, particularly when China would not condemn Putin's invasion of Ukraine in 2022.

The Issue of Taiwan. Inevitably, economic power translates into military potential. Is this a problem? It could be if China had territorial ambitions. At this time, China does not appear to have a blatant appetite for non-Chinese territory. China's leaders, however, seem to have a rather expansive concept of what is meant by "Chinese territory." For example, China has always considered the island of Taiwan to be Chinese. In principle, Taiwan agrees. Taiwan calls itself the "Republic of China" and officially considers its government to be the legitimate ruler of the entire country—both Taiwan and mainland China. This diplomatic fiction has remained in effect since 1949, when the Chinese Communist Party won a civil war and drove the anti-Communist forces off the mainland.

China's position is that sooner or later, Taiwan must rejoin the rest of China. The position of the United States is that this reunification must not come about by force. Is peaceful reunification possible? China holds up Hong

Elizabeth Ruiz/Getty Images

Image 14.6 Chinese president Xi Jinping and his wife, Peng Liyuan, visit Mexico. Peng Liyuan, a People's Liberation Army folksinger, was nationally famous years before her husband became China's leader.
▶ What has happened with China's economy in recent years?

Kong as an example. Hong Kong came under Chinese sovereignty peacefully in 1997. The people of Taiwan, however, are far from considering Hong Kong to be an acceptable precedent. Indeed, in 2019 and 2020 millions of Hong Kong citizens took to the streets to demonstrate against China's imposition of greater control over their country. Certainly, Taiwan does not want to suffer the recent fate of Hong Kong. In 2020, the Hong Kong people lost any independence they had previously enjoyed. China's Communist Party simply indicated that it would take over political control of Hong Kong's people—and it did.

Chinese Nationalism. Growing expressions of Chinese nationalism have raised concern in some of China's neighbors. China has recently engaged in disputes with Japan, the Philippines, Vietnam, and other Asian nations over the ownership of uninhabited islands in the East China and South China seas. In one arena—cyberspace—Chinese–American relations were already quite heated. In 2014 and 2015, the United States accused the Chinese military of sponsoring cyberattacks on U.S. computer networks.

Within China, much of the most damaging nationalism takes the form of discrimination against ethnic groups. These include the Muslim Uyghurs and the people of Tibet. In 2019, the world learned that up to 1 million Uyghurs and members of other Muslim minority groups were being held in "re-education" camps. Inmates were pressured to abandon Islamic traditions and forced to work under conditions approaching enslaved persons' labor. As of the end of 2022, there has been no improvement in the condition of Muslim Uyghurs enslaved by China.

If silence can indicate anything, it did when China did not condemn Putin's invasion of Ukraine.

Economic Troubles in Europe

Many Europeans consider the European Union (EU) to be one of their most important achievements. The EU, which grew out of the earlier European Economic Community, has been seen as guaranteeing a permanent peace in Europe. Given that Europe was home to World Wars I and II—arguably the two greatest disasters in human history—such a peace is of the utmost importance to the United States and the world. In 2000, a majority of EU members sought to deepen their union through a common currency, the euro.

The Debt Crisis. The nineteen nations that share the euro were hit hard by the worldwide financial panic of 2008. In Greece and, to a lesser extent, Portugal, governments had borrowed irresponsibly. In Ireland and Spain, many real estate loans went sour, and these countries found themselves in danger when their governments assumed the debts of the threatened banks.

These nations began running out of funds to service their debts, and they faced ruinous interest rates if they attempted to borrow in the financial markets. If a nation such as Britain, Japan, or the United States faced such a crisis, it could rely on its central bank—in America, the Fed—to serve as lender of last resort and simply "print" the necessary money. But the "Eurozone" nations did not control their own money supplies, and the European Central Bank (ECB) was barred from acting as lender of last resort. Investors began pulling funds out of the troubled nations, reducing their money supplies further. The panic threatened to spread to Italy. Eventually, Eurozone nations did come up with bailout plans for Greece, Ireland, Portugal, and Spain. Perhaps of even more importance, the ECB developed indirect methods of functioning as a lender of last resort.

Interact

One way to learn more about foreign affairs is to consult news sources from countries that are either not allied with the United States or actively hostile toward it. You can find English-language news reports from China by searching online for "cctv news." Find news from Russia simply by entering "rt." Both websites are controlled by their governments. As you scan these sites, ask yourself these questions:

- How does the site report on its own national leaders?
- According to the site, what appear to be the most important issues?
- What attitudes does the site project toward the United States?
- Do the reports from either nation suggest that it might pose a threat to world peace?

The German Question. An additional problem has been Germany's large trade surplus. In 2011, Germany's current account surplus passed that of China to become the largest in the world. According to most economists, the size of a nation's current account balance has little to do with trade agreements. For any country, the current account balance is actually a function of the nation's own economic policy. If America as a whole consumes more than it produces, it will have to make up the difference through imports from abroad. In other words, it will run a current account deficit. Attempts to reduce imports from one nation will simply result in more imports from somewhere else.

The same principle applies—in reverse—to Germany. If Germany as a whole consumes less than it produces, it will run a surplus. Many economists, therefore, argued that the German government should encourage the nation to consume more, through lower taxes or more spending on infrastructure. The result would be a more balanced German economy and greater economic growth throughout Europe and the world. The Germans, however, rejected this argument.

Brexit. In 2013, for domestic political reasons, British prime minister David Cameron promised a referendum on U.K. membership in the EU if his Conservative Party won the 2015 elections. The Conservatives won, and the referendum was duly held in June 2016. The United States, almost every other world power, and all major U.K. institutions backed "remain." (Donald Trump was a major exception in endorsing "leave.") Still, the "leave" campaign won by a narrow margin. Cameron was forced to resign.

The number-one issue for those endorsing "Brexit"—Britain's exit from the EU—was immigration. The vote was held in the wake of massive refugee flows into continental Europe from Syria and other troubled nations. Britain faced little pressure to accept Syrian refugees. Under EU law, however, all members are required to accept the free movement of labor. By 2016, thousands of Eastern Europeans had entered Britain seeking work.

Victory by the Brexit forces plunged the United Kingdom into an unprecedented political crisis. "Brexiteers" and "Remainers" were at daggers drawn. After years of controversy, in 2019 a provisional exit plan was devised by British prime minister Teresa May and EU negotiators. Parliament repeatedly refused to approve the plan. May was forced to resign. Boris Johnson became prime minister and called a new election. Victory by his conservatives guaranteed that Brexit would go forward. The U.K. left the EU on January 31, 2020.

Who Makes Foreign Policy?

» **LO 14-4:** Explain why U.S. foreign policy is mainly carried out by the president rather than Congress.

Developing a comprehensive U.S. foreign policy is a demanding task. Does this responsibility fall to the president, to Congress, or to both acting jointly? There is no easy answer to this question because, as constitutional authority Edwin S. Corwin once observed, the U.S. Constitution created an "invitation to struggle" between the president and Congress for control over the foreign policy process. Let us look first at the powers given to the president by the Constitution.

Constitutional Powers of the President

The Constitution confers broad powers on the president. Article II vests the executive power of the government in the president. The presidential oath of office, given in Article II, Section 1, requires that the president "solemnly swear" to "preserve, protect and defend the Constitution of the United States."

War Powers. In addition, and perhaps more important, Article II, Section 2, designates the president as "Commander in Chief of the Army and Navy of the United States." Starting with Abraham Lincoln, all presidents have interpreted this authority broadly. Indeed, since George Washington's administration, the United States has been involved in at least 125 undeclared wars that were conducted under presidential authority. For example, in 1950 Harry Truman ordered U.S. armed forces in the Pacific to counter North Korea's invasion of South Korea. Bill Clinton sent troops to Haiti and Bosnia. George W. Bush initiated wars in Afghanistan and Iraq, and Barack Obama undertook air strikes to support rebels in Libya.

Treaties and Executive Agreements. Article II, Section 2, of the Constitution also gives the president the power to make treaties, provided that the Senate concurs. In addition to this formal treaty-making power, the president makes use of executive agreements. Since World War II (1939–45), executive agreements have accounted for almost 95 percent of the understandings reached between the United States and other nations.

Doug Mills/AP Images

Image 14.7 President George W. Bush, fourth from the right, with his National Security Council (NSC) the day after the terrorist attacks on September 11, 2001. Secretary of State Colin Powell is to the left of the president. Vice President Dick Cheney is to the right. National Security Adviser Condoleezza Rice is at the far end of the table. ▶ What is the NSC's role in determining U.S. foreign policy?

Other Constitutional Powers. An additional power conferred on the president in Article II, Section 2, is the right to appoint ambassadors, other public ministers, and consuls. In Section 3 of that article, the president is given the power to recognize foreign governments by receiving their ambassadors.

The Executive Branch and Foreign Policy Making

There are at least four foreign policy-making sources within the executive branch, in addition to the president. These are the (1) Department of State, (2) National Security Council, (3) intelligence community, and (4) Department of Defense.

The Department of State. In principle, the State Department is the executive agency that has primary authority over foreign affairs. It supervises U.S. relations with the nearly two hundred independent nations around the world and with the United Nations and other multinational groups. It staffs embassies and consulates throughout the world. It does this with one of the smallest budgets of the cabinet departments.

The National Security Council. The National Security Council (NSC) is managed by the national security adviser. Other members are the president, the vice president, the secretaries of State and Defense, and often the chairperson of the Joint Chiefs of Staff and the director of the Central Intelligence Agency (CIA). The role of national security adviser has changed from president to president. National Security Adviser Henry Kissinger was President Nixon's most important confidant. Under President Obama, however, the adviser was relatively unimportant. The role of national security adviser regained some of its former importance under President Trump and President Biden.

Intelligence Community
The government agencies that gather information about the capabilities and intentions of foreign governments or that engage in covert actions.

The Intelligence Community. The **intelligence community** consists of the forty or more government agencies and bureaus that are involved in intelligence activities. The CIA, created as part of the National Security Act of 1947, is the key official member of the intelligence community.

Intelligence activities consist mostly of overt information gathering, but they include covert actions as well. Covert actions, as the name implies, are carried out in secret, and the American public rarely finds out about them. The CIA covertly aided in the overthrow of the Mossadegh regime in Iran in 1953 and was instrumental in destabilizing the Allende government in Chile from 1970 to 1973.

The Intelligence Community and the War on Terrorism. With the rise of terrorism as a threat, the intelligence agencies have received more funding and enhanced surveillance powers, but these moves have also provoked fears of civil liberties violations. Legislation enacted in 2004 established the Office of the Director of National Intelligence to oversee the intelligence community.

A simmering controversy that came to a boil in 2009 concerned the CIA's use of a technique called waterboarding while interrogating prisoners in the years after 9/11. Before 9/11, the government had defined waterboarding as a form of torture, but former vice president Dick Cheney, an advocate of the practice, denied that it was torture. In May 2009, President Obama, even as he denounced waterboarding, assured CIA employees that no member of the agency would be penalized for following Justice Department rulings that had legitimized harsh interrogation methods. As a candidate, Trump advocated methods that would be "worse than waterboarding." As president, he accepted advice from his secretary of defense not to restore such tactics.

President Joe Biden reaffirmed the United States' unequivocal ban on torture and its opposition to all forms of inhuman treatment. He did this on June 26, 2021, which was the anniversary of the United Nation's Convention Against Torture and Other Cruel, Inhuman, or Degrading Treatment or Punishment.

The Department of Defense. The Department of Defense (DoD) was created in 1947 to bring all of the various activities of the American military establishment under the jurisdiction of a single department headed by a civilian secretary of Defense. At the same time, the Joint Chiefs of Staff, consisting of the commanders of the various military branches and a chairperson, was created to formulate a unified military strategy.

Although the Department of Defense is larger than any other federal department, it declined in size after the fall of the Soviet Union in 1991. In the subsequent ten years, the total number of civilian employees was reduced by about 400,000, to approximately 665,000. Military personnel were also reduced in number. The wars in Afghanistan and Iraq drove the defense budget up again. After Russia invaded Ukraine in 2022, there were calls for increased military spending.

Congress Balances the Presidency

A new interest in the balance of power between Congress and the president on foreign policy questions developed during the Vietnam War (1965–75). Sensitive to public frustration over the long and costly war and angry at Richard Nixon for some of his other actions as president, Congress attempted to establish limits on the power of the president in setting foreign and defense policy.

The War Powers Resolution. In 1973, Congress passed the War Powers Resolution over President Nixon's veto. The act limited the president's use of troops in military action without congressional consultation and approval. Most presidents, however, have not interpreted the "consultation" provisions of the act as meaning that Congress should be involved before military action is taken. Instead, Presidents Ford, Carter, Reagan, George H. W. Bush, Clinton, and Obama undertook military actions and then informed congressional leaders.

The Power of the Purse. One of Congress's most significant constitutional powers is the so-called power of the purse. The president may order that a certain action be taken, but that order cannot be executed unless Congress funds it. When the Democrats took control of Congress in January 2007, many asked whether the new Congress would use its power of the purse to bring an end to the Iraq War, in view of strong public opposition to the war.

Hisham Ibrahim/Getty Images

Image 14.8 The Pentagon takes its name from its unusual shape. When the media refer to "the Pentagon," they are making reference to the Department of Defense. ▶ What does it say about American self-confidence that its military headquarters is so obvious from the air?

Congress's decision was to add conditions to an emergency war-funding request submitted by the president. The conditions required the president to establish a series of timelines for the removal of American troops from Iraq. President George W. Bush immediately threatened to veto any bill that imposed such conditions on the funding. His threat carried the day. The Democrats simply did not have a large enough majority to override a veto.

The Major Foreign Policy Themes

>> **LO 14-5:** Cite the main themes in the history of U.S. foreign policy.

In the early years of the nation, presidents and the people generally agreed that the United States should avoid foreign entanglements and concentrate instead on its own development. From the beginning of the twentieth century until the present, however, a major theme has been increasing global involvement. The theme of the post–World War II years was the containment of communism. A theme for at least the first part of the twenty-first century has been combating terrorism.

The Formative Years: Avoiding Entanglements

The founders of the United States had a basic mistrust of European governments. This was a logical position at a time when the United States was so weak militarily that it could not influence European developments directly. Moreover, being protected by oceans that took weeks to cross certainly allowed the nation to avoid foreign entanglements. During the 1800s, therefore, the United States generally stayed out of European conflicts and politics. In the Western Hemisphere, however, the United States pursued an active policy of expansion. The nation purchased Louisiana in 1803, annexed Texas in 1845, gained substantial territory from Mexico in 1848, purchased Alaska in 1867, and annexed Hawaii in 1898.

The Monroe Doctrine. President James Monroe, in his message to Congress in 1823, set out three principles: (1) European nations should not establish new colonies in the Western Hemisphere, (2) European nations should not intervene in the affairs of independent nations of the Western Hemisphere, and (3) the United States would not interfere in the affairs of European nations. The **Monroe Doctrine** was the underpinning of the U.S. **isolationist foreign policy** toward Europe, which continued throughout the 1800s.

Monroe Doctrine
A policy statement made by President James Monroe in 1823. The United States would not accept any new European intervention in the Western Hemisphere. In return, the United States would not meddle in European affairs.

Isolationist Foreign Policy
A policy of abstaining from an active role in international affairs or alliances, which characterized U.S. foreign policy toward Europe during most of the 1800s.

The Spanish–American War and World War I. The end of the isolationist policy started with the Spanish–American War in 1898. Winning the war gave the United States possession of Guam, Puerto Rico, and the Philippines (which gained independence in 1946). Then came World War I (1914–18). The United States declared war on Germany in 1917 because that country refused to give up its campaign of sinking all ships headed for Britain, including passenger ships from America.

In the 1920s, the United States went "back to normalcy," as President Warren G. Harding urged it to do. U.S. military forces were largely disbanded, and the nation returned to a period of isolationism.

The Era of Internationalism

Isolationism was permanently shattered by the bombing of the U.S. naval base at Pearl Harbor, Hawaii, on December 7, 1941. The surprise attack by the Japanese caused the deaths of 2,403 American servicemen. President Franklin Roosevelt asked Congress to declare war on Japan immediately, and the United States entered World War II. Germany then declared war on the United States.

At the conclusion of the war, the United States was the only major participating country to emerge with its economy intact, and even strengthened. The United States was also the only country to have control over operational nuclear weapons. President Harry Truman had made the decision to use two atomic bombs in August 1945 to end the war with Japan. (A few historians and certain commentators still argue over the necessity of this action, which ultimately killed more than 100,000 Japanese and left an equal number permanently injured.) The United States truly had become the world's superpower.

The Cold War. The United States had become an uncomfortable ally of the Soviet Union after Adolf Hitler's invasion of that country. Soon after World War II ended, relations between the Soviet Union and the West deteriorated. The Soviet Union wanted a weakened Germany, and to achieve this, it insisted that Germany be divided in two, with East Germany becoming a buffer against the West. Little by little, the Soviet Union helped to install Communist governments in Eastern European countries, which were soon referred to collectively as the **Soviet bloc**. In response, the United States encouraged the rearming of Western Europe. The Cold War had begun.

Containment Policy. In 1947, a remarkable article was published in *Foreign Affairs* magazine, signed by "X." The actual author was George F. Kennan, chief of the policy-planning staff for the State Department. The doctrine of **containment** set forth in the article became—according to many—the bible of Western foreign policy. "X" argued that whenever and wherever the Soviet Union could successfully challenge the West, it would do so. He recommended that our policy toward the Soviet Union be "firm and vigilant containment of Russian expansive tendencies."[2]

The containment theory was expressed clearly in the **Truman Doctrine**, which was enunciated by President Harry Truman in 1947. Truman held that the United States must help countries in which a Communist takeover seemed likely. Later that year, he backed the Marshall Plan, an economic assistance plan for Europe that was intended to prevent the expansion of Communist influence there. In 1949, the United States, along with several European nations, entered into a military alliance called the North Atlantic Treaty Organization, or NATO, to offer a credible response to any Soviet military attack.

Superpower Relations

During the Cold War, there was never any direct military conflict between the United States and the Soviet Union. Only on occasion did the United States enter a conflict with any Communist-led country. Two such occasions were in Korea and in Vietnam.

The Korean War. After the end of World War II, northern Korea was occupied by the Soviet Union, and southern Korea was occupied by the United States. The result was two rival Korean governments. In 1950, North Korea invaded South Korea. Under UN authority, the United States entered the war, which prevented an almost certain South Korean defeat. When U.S. forces were on the brink of conquering North Korea, however, China joined the war on the side of the North, resulting in a stalemate. An armistice signed in 1953 led to the

Image 14.9 President Truman ordered two atomic bomb attacks on Japan in 1945. ▶ Was his decision justified?

Soviet Bloc
The Soviet Union and the Eastern European countries that installed Communist regimes after World War II and that were dominated by the Soviet Union.

Containment
A U.S. diplomatic policy adopted by the Truman administration to contain Communist power within its existing boundaries.

Truman Doctrine
The policy adopted by President Harry Truman in 1947 to halt Communist expansion.

2. X, "The Sources of Soviet Conduct," *Foreign Affairs*, July 1947, p. 575.

Image 14.10 In a famous meeting in Yalta in February 1945, British prime minister Winston Churchill (left), U.S. president Franklin Roosevelt (center), and Soviet leader Joseph Stalin (right) decided the fate of several nations in Europe, including Germany. ▶ What happened to Germany immediately after World War II?

two Koreas that exist today. U.S. forces have remained in South Korea since that time.

The Vietnam War. The Vietnam War (1965–75) also involved the United States in a civil war between a Communist north and pro-Western south. When the French army in Indochina was defeated by the Communist forces of Ho Chi Minh in 1954, two Vietnams were created. The United States assumed the role of supporting the South Vietnamese government against North Vietnam. American forces in Vietnam at the height of the U.S. involvement totaled more than 500,000 troops. More than 58,000 Americans were killed in the conflict. A peace agreement in 1973 allowed U.S. troops to leave the country, and in 1975, North Vietnam easily occupied Saigon (the South Vietnamese capital) and unified the nation.

Over the course of the Vietnam War, the debate concerning U.S. involvement became extremely heated and, as mentioned previously, spurred congressional efforts to limit the ability of the president to commit forces to armed combat. The military draft was also a major source of contention during the Vietnam War.

The Cuban Missile Crisis. Perhaps the closest the two superpowers came to a nuclear confrontation was the Cuban missile crisis in 1962. The Soviets placed missiles in Cuba, ninety miles off the U.S. coast, in response to Cuban fears of an American invasion and to try to balance an American nuclear advantage. President John F. Kennedy and his advisers rejected the option of invading Cuba, setting up a naval blockade around the island instead. In October, the Soviet Union announced the withdrawal of its missile operations from Cuba. In exchange, the United States agreed not to invade Cuba in the future.

Still, the United States maintained a comprehensive economic embargo of Cuba following this crisis. The relationship between the United States and Cuba did not substantially improve until 2015, when President Obama announced plans to establish diplomatic relations with the Cuban government. The election of President Trump in 2016, however, put those plans on hold. Upon taking office in 2021, President Joe Biden expressed a desire to seek normalization of relations with Cuba. When Cubans protested the Communist regime there in July 2021, National Security Council Senior Director Juan Gonzalez indicated that Biden had "hit the pause button" on Cuba policy.

Détente
A French word meaning a relaxation of tensions. The term characterized U.S.–Soviet relations as they developed under President Richard Nixon and Secretary of State Henry Kissinger.

A Period of Détente. The French word **détente** means a relaxation of tensions. By the end of the 1960s, it was clear that some efforts had to be made to reduce the threat of nuclear war between the United States and the Soviet Union. The Soviet Union had gradually begun to catch up in the building of bombers and missiles, thus balancing the nuclear scales between the two countries. Each nation had acquired the military capacity to destroy the other.

As the result of lengthy negotiations under Secretary of State Henry Kissinger and President Richard Nixon, the United States and the Soviet Union signed the Strategic Arms Limitation Treaty (SALT I) in May 1972. That treaty limited the number of offensive missiles each country could deploy.

The policy of détente was not limited to the U.S. relationship with the Soviet Union. Seeing an opportunity to capitalize on increasing friction between the Soviet Union and the People's Republic of China, Kissinger secretly began negotiations to establish a new relationship with China. President Nixon eventually visited that nation in 1972. The visit set the stage for the formal diplomatic recognition of that country, which occurred during the Carter administration (1977–81).

Nuclear Arms Agreements With the Soviet Union and Russia. In subsequent years, several American presidents negotiated and signed arms control agreements with the Soviet Union (and later, with Russia). These presidents included Republicans Ronald Reagan (1981–89) and George H. W. Bush (1989–93). The most recent such treaty, New START, was signed in 2010 by President Obama and Dmitry Medvedev, who was then the president of Russia. New START reduced the number of permitted warheads to 1,550 for each side, a drop of about 30 percent from previous agreements. After some delays, the Senate ratified the treaty.

The Dissolution of the Soviet Union. In 1989, the fall of the Berlin Wall that had divided that city into eastern and western sectors marked the first step in the reunification of Germany. By then, it was clear that the Soviet Union had relinquished much of its political and military control over the nations of Eastern Europe that formerly had been part of the Soviet bloc. No one expected the Soviet Union to dissolve into separate states as quickly as it did, however. Demands for political, ethnic, and religious autonomy grew. On the day after Christmas in 1991, the Soviet Union was officially dissolved into fifteen independent nations.

Russia After the Soviet Union. Vladimir Putin became Russia's second president in 2000, following Boris Yeltsin. Putin chipped away at Russia's democratic institutions, slowly turning the country into what was, in essence, an elected autocracy.

In recent years, the United States has become concerned over Russia's aggressive attitude toward its neighbors. For example, in 2008, Russian troops entered Georgia to prevent that nation from retaking an autonomous region that was under Russian protection. On several occasions since 2005, Russia has cut off the transmission of natural gas to Europe as a result of disputes.

Crisis in Ukraine. In November 2013, Ukraine's pro-Russian president Viktor Yanukovych abruptly broke off economic talks with the European Union, apparently under pressure from Putin. The resulting tumult was so intense that Yanukovych fled the country in February 2014. Parliament assumed power and began steering the country back toward Europe.

Putin denounced the new government as "fascist." Claiming the right to protect

kpzfoto/Alamy

Image 14.11 A roadblock set up by pro-Russian militias in eastern Ukraine to control traffic between rebel-held areas and the rest of the country. ▶ Why is Russia so hostile to the Ukrainian government?

Russian-speaking populations in Ukraine, Putin annexed the Crimean Peninsula, which has an ethnic-Russian majority. Pro-Russian militias, with Russian support, forcibly took control of parts of two eastern provinces. Western nations responded with a series of sanctions. Attempts to obtain a cease-fire in eastern Ukraine had mixed results. The annexation of Crimea, however, appeared to be irreversible.

Putin started amassing troops and military equipment on Ukraine's border in 2021. He invaded that independent country in February 2022. Seeking quick control over that country, Russian troops instead met with stiff resistance from Ukraine's military and civilian population. By March, Putin had ordered the shelling of civilian targets and implicitly the killing of civilians, which many observers claimed were war crimes.

Putin showed his willingness to use any means necessary to gain an increased foothold in Ukraine. His forces continued to drop bombs and missiles near the Zaporishshia nuclear power plant—Europe's largest—in the late summer of 2022. Many nearby residents were asked to leave their homes. Millions of Ukrainians already had relocated within that country or moved to other countries, such as Poland. In the early fall, Ukraine launched major counteroffensives. The end of hostilities did not appear imminent.

How much of a lingering problem is Putin's belligerence? This chapter's *Which Side Are You On?* feature addresses that question.

Russia's Future. Even as Russia reasserts itself as a great power, its future is in doubt. Its population is dropping and may fall as low as 138 million by 2050, down from 150 million currently. Russia has not only a low birthrate but also a very high death rate—Russian life expectancy for men is below that of India, despite the widespread poverty in that latter country. If Russia's population continues to fall, its ability to project power may decline as well.

Which Side Are You On?

How Dangerous Is Putin's Russia for the World?

A little over twenty years ago, the former head of the Soviet Union's secret police, Vladimir Putin, took over as the leader of the Russian government. (He did not do so by winning any elections, though.) Many hoped he would support integration with the West and the rule of law. Today, no one believes that Putin ever agreed with these goals. Rather, they see an autocrat who rules his country with an iron fist. Putin has called the collapse of the Soviet Union "the greatest geopolitical catastrophe of the century." His actions indicate that he wants to reverse it and dominate all the nations that were once part of the Soviet Union. He has occupied several disputed districts in neighboring countries. He has also invaded and annexed Ukraine's Crimea province. In 2022, he invaded all of Ukraine and continued to aim missiles at civilian targets. Almost all journalists who have opposed him have either fled Russia or are dead. The free press in Russia is extinct.

Putin May Be the Most Dangerous Leader in the World Today

Many warned the Biden administration that Putin could not be trusted. They turned out to be correct. Putin's amassing of troops and equipment on Ukraine's border was not for any other purpose than

to invade that country. Secretly, he has been placing his pro-Russian people throughout that country for years. Ironically, Russia was head of the Security Council of the United Nations while Putin was invading Ukraine. When a resolution to condemn that invasion was put before the council, obviously Russia (and China) vetoed it.

Putin has sent sophisticated air defense systems to Iran. In essence, Putin has supported leaders throughout the world who are anti-American. He became close to China's dictator, Xi Jinping, prior to the Ukrainian invasion. He even agreed with Xi Jinping to not invade Ukraine until after the Winter Olympics in China. Putin has threatened all of the small Baltic countries—Estonia, Latvia, and Lithuania. Russia's air force flies nuclear-armed bombers around the world on an ongoing basis. Russian jets have constantly violated the airspace of the Scandinavian and Baltic nations. Some of Putin's government officials have casually mentioned in off-the-record discussions that Russia was prepared to use its nuclear weapons. That threat became explicit when Putin put his nuclear forces on high alert in February 2022.

Putin was able to hide his true intentions in Ukraine because of his control over virtually all Russian media. Russians

(Continued)

were told during the Ukraine invasion that he was rooting out Nazis in Eastern Ukraine (quite a laugh given that the president of that country is Jewish). Some of the real news did get out in Russia and there were demonstrations. Putin jailed thousands of protestors in response.

Let there be no doubt about Russia's ability to threaten the entire world order.

Russia Presents a Problem, But One We Can Eventually Handle

Others believe that providing Ukraine with arms would be a mistake. Unless NATO is prepared for all-out war in Ukraine, Putin can always provide his minions with more military support than we can offer the Ukrainian government. Besides, does the U.S. really want to start World War III over the fate of Ukraine—a country thousands of miles away which has little trade with our own country?

Unfortunately, the problem with Russia is not just Putin. Most Russians do not accept that their country should be one nation among many, playing by universal rules. They believe Russia is a great power that deserves special respect. In particular, Russia must have a "sphere of influence" over neighboring countries, which cannot be allowed to pursue policies that conflict with Russian interests. After all, aren't Western European nations mere puppets of the Americans? When the Soviet Union put missiles on the island of Cuba, how did the U.S. react? It brought both countries to the brink of nuclear war and annihilation. Shouldn't the current leader of Russia be able to express his desire to not be surrounded by well-armed NATO nations? Russia has been invaded by its neighbors every 33 years on average since 1800. It has a right be weary of its neighbors.

We need to resurrect the policy of containment once used against the Soviet Union. We must be firm, but not reckless. Containment can succeed. Russia is fundamentally weak. It has few real friends. Its economy and its military power are puny compared to ours. In time, Russians will realize that belligerence is self-defeating.

■ For Critical Analysis

How can a country with a small economy still be a threat to the United States?

Working for Human Rights

In many countries throughout the world, human rights are not protected. In some nations, people are imprisoned, tortured, or killed because they oppose the current regime. In other nations, certain ethnic or racial groups are oppressed by the majority population.

Why Should You Care? The defense of human rights is unlikely to put a single dollar in your pocket, so why get involved? The strongest reason for involving yourself with human rights issues in other countries is simple moral altruism—unselfish regard for the welfare of others.

What Can You Do? How can you work for the improvement of human rights in other nations? One way is to join an organization that attempts to keep watch over human rights violations. By publicizing human rights violations, such groups try to pressure nations into changing their practices. Sometimes, they are able to apply enough

Ann Little/Alamy

Image 14.12 Amnesty International members in front of the White House protest America's use of drone strikes in the war on terrorism. Activists claim that too many innocent civilians die in drone attacks against terrorists. ▶ Are such deaths something that Americans should worry about?

pressure and cause enough embarrassment that victims may be freed from prison or allowed to emigrate.

If you want to obtain general information about the position of the United States on human rights violations, enter "state human rights" into a search engine.

Amnesty International U.S.A. and the American Friends Service Committee (AFSC) are well known for their watchdog efforts in countries that violate human rights for political reasons. To find Amnesty International, go to www.amnestyusa.org. For the AFSC, type "afsc" into a search engine.

Key Terms

Cold War 344
containment 355
defense policy 337
détente 356
diplomacy 337
economic aid 337

foreign policy 337
intelligence community 352
isolationist foreign policy 354
Monroe Doctrine 354

moral idealism 338
national security policy 337
political realism 338
Soviet bloc 355
terrorism 339

Truman Doctrine 355

Chapter Summary

» **LO 14-1** Foreign policy includes the nation's external goals and the techniques and strategies used to achieve them. Diplomacy involves the nation's external relationships and is an attempt to resolve conflict without resort to arms. U.S. foreign policy is based both on moral idealism and on political realism.

» LO 14-2 Terrorism is the attempt to create fear to gain political ends by violence against noncombatants. It has become a major challenge facing the United States and other nations. The United States waged war on terrorism after the attacks of September 11, 2001.

In 1991 and again in 2003, the United States sent combat troops to Iraq. The second war in Iraq, begun in 2003, succeeded in toppling the dictatorship of Saddam Hussein, but led to a long, grinding conflict with insurgent forces. The United States also went to war in Afghanistan to track down al Qaeda, which was responsible for the 9/11 attacks, and to expel the Taliban government that had supported the terrorists. The growth of the terrorist group ISIS drew the United States back into Iraq and, to some extent, into Syria as well.

» **LO 14-3** Recent diplomatic efforts by the United States include containing the nuclear

ambitions of Iran and North Korea. The rise of China as a superpower raises a series of issues, including trade concerns. American efforts to promote the peace process between Israel and the Palestinians have had limited success.

» **LO 14-4** The U.S. Constitution designates the president as commander in chief of the army and navy. Presidents have interpreted this authority broadly. They also have the power to make treaties and executive agreements. The State Department is the executive agency with primary authority over foreign affairs. The National Security Council also plays a major role. The intelligence community engages in information gathering and covert operations. To establish some limits on the power of the president to intervene abroad, Congress passed the War Powers Resolution in 1973.

» LO 14-5 In the early years of the nation, isolationism was the foreign policy strategy. With the start of the twentieth century, isolationism gave way to global involvement. The end of the policy of isolationism toward Europe started with the Spanish–American War of 1898. U.S. involvement in Europe became more extensive when the United States entered World War I. The United States was the only major country to emerge from World War II with its economy intact and with operating nuclear weapons.

After World War II, the Cold War with the Soviet Union began. A policy of containment of the Soviet Union was enunciated in the Truman Doctrine.

The United States signed nuclear arms control agreements with the Soviet Union under several presidents. After the fall of the Soviet Union, Russia emerged as a less threatening state. Under President Vladimir Putin, however, Russia has moved away from democracy and begun threatening its neighbors, even invading all of Ukraine.

Test Yourself

1. **As part of foreign policy, national security policy is designed to:**
   a. provide economic assistance to other nations.
   b. ensure that all other countries respect each other's borders.
   c. protect the independence and political integrity of the United States.

2. **In foreign policy, U.S. support for disaster relief is sometimes an example of:**
   a. moral idealism.
   b. political realism.
   c. strategic balancing.

3. **Acts of terrorism are:**
   a. the result of governments' attempts to gain new territory.
   b. attempts to inspire fear to gain political ends.
   c. due to governments that failed in diplomacy.

4. **The three major groups in Iraq are:**
   a. the Arabs, the Kurds, and the Christians.
   b. the Sunni Arabs, the Shiite Arabs, and the Taliban.
   c. the Sunni Arabs, the Shiite Arabs, and the Kurds.

5. **The two countries that today represent the most serious problems with nuclear proliferation are:**
   a. Iran and North Korea.
   b. Japan and Germany.
   c. China and Brazil.

6. **China considers the following to be part of its territory:**
   a. Vietnam.
   b. Taiwan.
   c. Mongolia.

7. **The Palestinian territories are made up of:**
   a. Judea and Samaria.
   b. The West Bank and the Golan Heights.
   c. The West Bank and the Gaza Strip.

8. **The intelligence community is involved in foreign policy and consists of:**
   a. the CIA and the Department of Defense.
   b. more than forty government agencies and bureaus involved in intelligence activities.
   c. the CIA and the National Security Council.

9. **In the 1820s, the United States proclaimed that it would not accept any new European intervention in the Western Hemisphere, and in turn it would not intervene in European affairs. This was the:**
   a. Monroe Doctrine.
   b. Jackson Doctrine.
   c. policy of détente.

10. **After World War II, President Harry Truman vowed that the United States must help countries in which a Communist takeover seemed likely. This became known as the:**
    a. rollback policy.
    b. Marshall Plan.
    c. Truman Doctrine.

11. The Cold War refers to a period during which:
   a. the Soviet Union and the United States faced off throughout the world.
   b. the United States reverted back to isolationist policies.
   c. the United States engaged in economic conflict with many Asian countries.

12. Prior to the invasion of all of Ukraine, Russia had already annexed:
   a. Armenia.
   b. Kiev.
   c. Crimea.

Essay Questions

1. Some people believe that if no U.S. military personnel were stationed abroad, terrorists would have less desire to harm Americans or the United States. Do you agree? Why or why not?
2. Why do you think that North Korea and Iran might want to possess nuclear weapons, even though they can never hope to match the nuclear arsenals of the original nuclear powers?

Answers to multiple-choice questions: 1. c, 2. a, 3. b, 4. c, 5. a, 6. b, 7. c, 8. b, 9. a, 10. c, 11. a, 12. c.

The Declaration of Independence

In Congress, July 4, 1776

A Declaration by the Representatives of the United States of America, in General Congress assembled. When in the Course of human Events, it becomes necessary for one People to dissolve the Political Bands which have connected them with another, and to assume among the Powers of the Earth, the separate and equal Station to which the Laws of Nature and of Nature's God entitle them, a decent Respect to the Opinions of Mankind requires that they should declare the causes which impel them to the Separation.

We hold these Truths to be self-evident, that all Men are created equal, that they are endowed by their Creator with certain unalienable Rights, that among these are Life, Liberty, and the Pursuit of Happiness—That to secure these Rights, Governments are instituted among Men, deriving their just Powers from the Consent of the Governed, that whenever any Form of Government becomes destructive of these Ends, it is the Right of the People to alter or to abolish it, and to institute new Government, laying its Foundation on such Principles, and organizing its Powers in such Forms, as to them shall seem most likely to effect their Safety and Happiness. Prudence, indeed, will dictate that Governments long established should not be changed for light and transient Causes; and accordingly all Experience hath shewn, that Mankind are more disposed to suffer, while Evils are sufferable, than to right themselves by abolishing the Forms to which they are accustomed. But when a long Train of Abuses and Usurpations, pursuing invariably the same Object, evinces a Design to reduce them under absolute Despotism, it is their Right, it is their Duty, to throw off such Government, and to provide new Guards for their future Security. Such has been the patient Sufferance of these Colonies; and such is now the Necessity which constrains them to alter their former Systems of Government. The History of the present King of Great-Britain is a History of repeated Injuries and Usurpations, all having in direct Object the Establishment of an absolute Tyranny over these States. To prove this, let Facts be submitted to a candid World.

He has refused his Assent to Laws, the most wholesome and necessary for the public Good.

He has forbidden his Governors to pass Laws of immediate and pressing Importance, unless suspended in their Operation till his Assent should be obtained; and when so suspended, he has utterly neglected to attend to them.

He has refused to pass other Laws for the Accommodation of large Districts of People, unless those People would relinquish the Right of Representation in the Legislature, a Right inestimable to them, and formidable to Tyrants only.

He has called together Legislative Bodies at Places unusual, uncomfortable, and distant from the Depository of their Public Records, for the sole Purpose of fatiguing them into Compliance with his Measures.

He has dissolved Representative Houses repeatedly, for opposing with manly Firmness his Invasions on the Rights of the People.

He has refused for a long Time, after such Dissolutions, to cause others to be elected; whereby the Legislative Powers, incapable of Annihilation, have returned to the People at large for their exercise; the State remaining in the mean time exposed to all the Dangers of Invasion from without, and Convulsions within.

He has endeavoured to prevent the Population of these States; for that Purpose obstructing the Laws for Naturalization of Foreigners; refusing to pass others to encourage their Migrations hither, and raising the Conditions of new Appropriations of Lands.

He has obstructed the Administration of Justice, by refusing his Assent to Laws for establishing Judiciary Powers.

He has made Judges dependent on his Will alone, for the Tenure of their offices, and the Amount and payment of their Salaries.

He has erected a Multitude of new Offices, and sent hither Swarms of Officers to harass our People, and eat out their Substance.

He has kept among us, in Times of Peace, Standing Armies, without the consent of our Legislatures.

He has affected to render the Military independent of, and superior to the Civil Power.

He has combined with others to subject us to a Jurisdiction foreign to our Constitution, and unacknowledged by our Laws; giving his Assent to their Acts of pretended Legislation:

For quartering large Bodies of Armed Troops among us:

For protecting them, by a mock Trial, from Punishment for any Murders which they should commit on the Inhabitants of these States:

For cutting off our Trade with all Parts of the World:

For imposing Taxes on us without our Consent:

For depriving us, in many cases, of the Benefits of Trial by Jury:

For transporting us beyond Seas to be tried for pretended Offences:

For abolishing the free System of English Laws in a neighbouring Province, establishing therein an arbitrary Government, and enlarging its Boundaries, so as to render it at once an Example and fit Instrument for introducing the same absolute Rule into these Colonies:

For taking away our Charters, abolishing our most valuable Laws, and altering fundamentally the Forms of our Governments:

For suspending our own Legislatures, and declaring themselves invested with Power to legislate for us in all Cases whatsoever.

He has abdicated Government here, by declaring us out of his Protection and waging War against us.

He has plundered our Seas, ravaged our Coasts, burnt our towns, and destroyed the Lives of our People.

He is, at this Time, transporting large Armies of foreign Mercenaries to compleat the works of Death, Desolation, and Tyranny, already begun with circumstances of Cruelty and Perfidy, scarcely paralleled in the most barbarous Ages, and totally unworthy the Head of a civilized Nation.

He has constrained our fellow Citizens taken Captive on the high Seas to bear Arms against their Country, to become the Executioners of their Friends and Brethren, or to fall themselves by their Hands.

He has excited domestic Insurrections amongst us, and has endeavoured to bring on the Inhabitants of our Frontiers, the merciless Indian Savages, whose known Rule of Warfare, is an undistinguished Destruction, of all Ages, Sexes and Conditions.

In every state of these Oppressions we have Petitioned for Redress in the most humble Terms: Our repeated Petitions have been answered only by repeated Injury. A Prince, whose Character is thus marked by every act which may define a Tyrant, is unfit to be the Ruler of a free People.

Nor have we been wanting in Attentions to our British Brethren. We have warned them from Time to Time of Attempts by their Legislature to extend an unwarrantable Jurisdiction over us. We have reminded them of the Circumstances of our Emigration and Settlement here. We have appealed to their native Justice and Magnanimity, and we have conjured them by the Ties of our common Kindred to disavow these Usurpations, which, would inevitably interrupt our Connections and Correspondence. They too have been deaf to the Voice of Justice and of Consanguinity. We must, therefore, acquiesce in the Necessity, which denounces our Separation, and hold them, as we hold the rest of Mankind, Enemies in War, in Peace, Friends.

We, therefore, the Representatives of the UNITED STATES OF AMERICA, in General Congress Assembled, appealing to the Supreme Judge of the World for the Rectitude of our Intentions, do, in the Name, and by the Authority of the good People of these Colonies, solemnly Publish and Declare, That these United Colonies are, and of Right ought to be, Free and Independent States; that they are absolved from all Allegiance to the British Crown, and that all political Connection between them and the State of Great-Britain, is and ought to be totally dissolved; and that as Free and Independent States, they have full Power to levy War, conclude Peace, contract Alliances, establish Commerce, and to do all other Acts and Things which Independent States may of right do. And for the support of this declaration, with a firm Reliance on the Protection of divine Providence, we mutually pledge to each other our lives, our Fortunes, and our sacred Honor.

Appendix B

The Constitution of the United States*

The Preamble

We the People of the United States, in Order to form a more perfect Union, establish Justice, insure domestic Tranquility, provide for the common defence, promote the general Welfare, and secure the Blessings of Liberty to ourselves and our Posterity, do ordain and establish this Constitution for the United States of America.

The Preamble declares that "We the People" are the authority for the Constitution (unlike the Articles of Confederation, which derived their authority from the states). The Preamble also sets out the purposes of the Constitution.

Article I. (Legislative Branch)

The first part of the Constitution, Article 1, deals with the organization and powers of the lawmaking branch of the national government, the Congress.

Section 1. Legislative Powers

All legislative Powers herein granted shall be vested in a Congress of the United States, which shall consist of a Senate and House of Representatives.

Section 2. House of Representatives

Clause 1: Composition and Election of Members. The House of Representatives shall be composed of Members chosen every second Year by the People of the several States, and the Electors in each State shall have the Qualifications requisite for Electors of the most numerous Branch of the State Legislature.

Each state has the power to decide who may vote for members of Congress. Within each state, those who may vote for state legislators may also vote for members of the House of Representatives (and, under the Seventeenth Amendment, for U.S. senators). When the Constitution was written, nearly all states limited voting rights to white male property owners or taxpayers at least twenty-one years old. Subsequent amendments granted voting power to African American men, all women, and everyone at least eighteen-years-old.

Clause 2: Qualifications. No Person shall be a Representative who shall not have attained to the Age of twenty five Years, and been seven Years a Citizen of the United States, and who shall not, when elected, be an Inhabitant of that State in which he shall be chosen.

Each member of the House must be at least twenty-five years old, a citizen of the United States for at least seven years, and a resident of the state in which she or he is elected.

Clause 3: Apportionment of Representatives and Direct Taxes. Representatives [and direct Taxes][1] shall be apportioned among the several States which may be included within this Union, according to their respective Numbers [which shall be determined by adding to the whole Number of free Persons, including those bound to Service for a Term of Years, and excluding Indians not taxed, three fifths of all other Persons].[2] The actual Enumeration shall be made within three Years after the first Meeting of the Congress of the United States, and within every subsequent Term of ten Years, in such Manner as they shall by Law direct. The Number of Representatives shall not exceed one for every thirty Thousand, but each State shall have at Least one Representative; and until such enumeration shall be made, the State of New Hampshire shall be entitled to chuse three, Massachusetts eight, Rhode Island and Providence Plantations one, Connecticut five, New York six, New Jersey four, Pennsylvania eight, Delaware one, Maryland six, Virginia ten, North Carolina five, South Carolina five, and Georgia three.

A state's representation in the House is based on the size of its population. Population is counted in each decade's census, after which Congress reapportions House seats. Since early in the twentieth century, the number of seats has been limited to 435.

---

* The spelling, capitalization, and punctuation of the original have been retained here. Brackets indicate passages that have been altered by amendments to the Constitution. We have added article titles (in parentheses), section titles, and clause designations. We have also inserted annotations in blue italic type.

---

1. Modified by the Sixteenth Amendment.
2. Modified by the Fourteenth Amendment.

Clause 4: Vacancies. When vacancies happen in the Representation from any State, the Executive Authority thereof shall issue Writs of Election to fill such Vacancies.

The "Executive Authority" is the state's governor. When a vacancy occurs in the House, the governor calls a special election to fill it.

Clause 5: Officers and Impeachment. The House of Representatives shall chuse their Speaker and other Officers; and shall have the sole Power of Impeachment.

The power to impeach is the power to accuse. In this case, it is the power to accuse members of the executive or judicial branch of wrongdoing or abuse of power. Once a bill of impeachment is issued, the Senate holds the trial.

Section 3. The Senate

Clause 1: Term and Number of Members. The Senate of the United States shall be composed of two Senators from each State [chosen by the Legislature thereof],[3] for six Years; and each Senator shall have one Vote.

Every state has two senators, each of whom serves for six years and has one vote in the upper chamber. Since the Seventeenth Amendment was passed in 1913, all senators have been elected directly by voters of the state during the regular election.

Clause 2: Classification of Senators. Immediately after they shall be assembled in Consequence of the first Election, they shall be divided as equally as may be into three Classes. The Seats of the Senators of the first Class shall be vacated at the Expiration of the second Year, of the second Class at the Expiration of the fourth Year, and of the third Class at the Expiration of the sixth Year, so that one third may be chosen every second Year; [and if Vacancies happen by Resignation, or otherwise, during the Recess of the Legislature of any State, the Executive thereof may make temporary Appointments until the next Meeting of the Legislature, which shall then fill such Vacancies].[4]

One-third of the Senate's seats are open to election every two years (in contrast, all members of the House are elected simultaneously).

Clause 3: Qualifications. No Person shall be a Senator who shall not have attained to the Age of thirty Years, and been nine Years a Citizen of the United States, and who shall not, when elected, be an Inhabitant of that State for which he shall be chosen.

---

3. Repealed by the Seventeenth Amendment.
4. Modified by the Seventeenth Amendment.

Every senator must be at least thirty years old, a citizen of the United States for a minimum of nine years, and a resident of the state in which he or she is elected.

Clause 4: The Role of the Vice President. The Vice President of the United States shall be President of the Senate, but shall have no Vote, unless they be equally divided.

The vice president presides over meetings of the Senate but cannot vote unless there is a tie. The Constitution gives no other official duties to the vice president.

Clause 5: Other Officers. The Senate shall chuse their other Officers, and also a President pro tempore, in the Absence of the Vice President, or when he shall exercise the Office of President of the United States.

The Senate votes for one of its members to preside when the vice president is absent. This person is usually called the president pro tempore because of the temporary nature of the position.

Clause 6: Impeachment Trials. The Senate shall have the sole Power to try all Impeachments. When sitting for that Purpose, they shall be on Oath or Affirmation. When the President of the United States is tried, the Chief Justice shall preside: And no Person shall be convicted without the Concurrence of two thirds of the Members present.

The Senate conducts trials of officials that the House impeaches. The Senate sits as a jury, with the vice president presiding if the president is not on trial.

Clause 7: Penalties for Conviction. Judgment in Cases of Impeachment shall not extend further than to removal from Office, and disqualification to hold and enjoy any Office of honor, Trust, or Profit under the United States: but the Party convicted shall nevertheless be liable and subject to Indictment, Trial, Judgment, and Punishment, according to Law.

On conviction of impeachment charges, the Senate can only force an official to leave office and prevent him or her from holding another office in the federal government. The individual, however, can still be tried in a regular court.

Section 4. Congressional Elections: Times, Manner, and Places

Clause 1: Elections. The Times, Places and Manner of holding Elections for Senators and Representatives, shall be prescribed in each State by the Legislature thereof; but the Congress may at any time by Law make or alter such Regulations, except as to the Places of chusing Senators.

Congress set the Tuesday after the first Monday in November in even-numbered years as the date for congressional elections. In states with more than one seat in the House, Congress requires that representatives be elected from districts within each state. Under the Seventeenth Amendment, senators are elected at the same places as other officials.

Clause 2: Sessions of Congress. [The Congress shall assemble at least once in every Year, and such Meeting shall be on the first Monday in December, unless they shall by Law appoint a different Day.][5]

Congress has to meet every year at least once. The regular session now begins at noon on January 3 of each year, subsequent to the Twentieth Amendment, unless Congress passes a law to fix a different date. Congress stays in session until its members vote to adjourn. Additionally, the president may call a special session.

Section 5. Powers and Duties of the Houses

Clause 1: Admitting Members and Quorum. Each House shall be the Judge of the Elections, Returns, and Qualifications of its own Members, and a Majority of each shall constitute a Quorum to do Business; but a smaller Number may adjourn from day to day, and may be authorized to compel the Attendance of absent Members, in such Manner, and under such Penalties as each House may provide.

Each chamber may exclude or refuse to seat a member-elect.
The quorum rule requires that 218 members of the House and 51 members of the Senate be present to conduct business. This rule normally is not enforced in the handling of routine matters.

Clause 2: Rules and Discipline of Members. Each House may determine the Rules of its Proceedings, punish its Members for disorderly Behaviour, and, with the Concurrence of two thirds, expel a Member.

The House and the Senate may adopt their own rules to guide their proceedings. Each may also discipline its members for conduct that is deemed unacceptable. No member may be expelled without a two-thirds majority vote in favor of expulsion.

Clause 3: Keeping a Record. Each House shall keep a Journal of its Proceedings, and from time to time publish the same, excepting such Parts as may in their Judgment require Secrecy; and the Yeas and Nays of the Members of either House on any question shall, at the Desire of one fifth of those Present, be entered on the Journal.

The journals of the two chambers are published at the end of each session of Congress.

5. Changed by the Twentieth Amendment.

Clause 4: Adjournment. Neither House, during the Session of Congress, shall, without the Consent of the other, adjourn for more than three days, nor to any other Place than that in which the two Houses shall be sitting.

Congress has the power to determine when and where to meet, provided, however, that both chambers meet in the same city. Neither chamber may recess for more than three days without the consent of the other.

Section 6. Rights of Members

Clause 1: Compensation and Privileges. The Senators and Representatives shall receive a Compensation for their services, to be ascertained by Law, and paid out of the Treasury of the United States. They shall in all Cases, except Treason, Felony and Breach of the Peace, be privileged from Arrest during their Attendance at the Session of their respective Houses, and in going to and returning from the same; and for any Speech or Debate in either House, they shall not be questioned in any other Place.

Congressional salaries are to be paid by the U.S. Treasury rather than by the members' respective states. The original salaries were $6 per day; in 1857 they were $3,000 per year. Both representatives and senators were paid $165,200 in 2007.
Treason is defined in Article III, Section 3. A felony is any serious crime. A breach of the peace is any indictable offense less than treason or a felony. Members cannot be arrested for things they say during speeches and debates in Congress. This immunity applies to the Capitol Building itself and not to their private lives.

Clause 2: Restrictions. No Senator or Representative shall, during the Time for which he was elected, be appointed to any civil Office under the Authority of the United States, which shall have been created, or the Emoluments whereof shall have been encreased during such time; and no Person holding any Office under the United States, shall be a Member of either House during his Continuance in Office.

During the term for which a member was elected, he or she cannot concurrently accept another federal government position.

Section 7. Legislative Powers: Bills and Resolutions

Clause 1: Revenue Bills. All Bills for raising Revenue shall originate in the House of Representatives; but the Senate may propose or concur with Amendments as on other Bills.

All tax and appropriation bills for raising money have to originate in the House of Representatives. The Senate, though, often amends such bills and may even substitute an entirely different bill.

Clause 2: The Presidential Veto. Every Bill which shall have passed the House of Representatives and the Senate, shall, before it becomes a Law, be presented to the President of the United States; If he approve he shall sign it, but if not he shall return it, with his Objections to the House in which it shall have originated, who shall enter the Objections at large on their Journal, and proceed to reconsider it. If after such Reconsideration two thirds of that House shall agree to pass the Bill, it shall be sent together with the Objections, to the other House, by which it shall likewise be reconsidered, and if approved by two thirds of that House, it shall become a Law. But in all such Cases the Votes of both Houses shall be determined by Yeas and Nays, and the Names of the Persons voting for and against the Bill shall be entered on the Journal of each House respectively. If any Bill shall not be returned by the President within ten Days (Sundays excepted) after it shall have been presented to him, the Same shall be a Law, in like Manner as if he had signed it, unless the Congress by their Adjournment prevent its Return in which Case it shall not be a Law.

When Congress sends the president a bill, he or she can sign it (in which case it becomes law) or send it back to the chamber in which it originated. If it is sent back, a two-thirds majority of each chamber must pass it again for it to become law. If the president neither signs it nor sends it back within ten days, it becomes law anyway, unless Congress adjourns in the meantime.

Clause 3: Actions on Other Matters. Every Order, Resolution, or Vote to which the Concurrence of the Senate and House of Representatives may be necessary (except on a question of Adjournment) shall be presented to the President of the United States; and before the Same shall take Effect, shall be approved by him, or being disapproved by him, shall be repassed by two thirds of the Senate and House of Representatives, according to the Rules and Limitations prescribed in the Case of a Bill.

The president must have the opportunity to either sign or veto everything that Congress passes, except votes to adjourn and resolutions not having the force of law.

Section 8. The Powers of Congress
Clause 1: Taxing. The Congress shall have Power to lay and collect Taxes, Duties, Imposts and Excises, to pay the Debts and provide for the common Defence and general Welfare of the United States; but all Duties, Imposts and Excises shall be uniform throughout the United States;

Duties are taxes on imports and exports. Impost is a generic term for tax. Excises are taxes on the manufacture, sale, or use of goods.

Clause 2: Borrowing. To borrow Money on the credit of the United States;

Congress has the power to borrow money, which is normally carried out through the sale of U.S. treasury bonds on which interest is paid. Note that the Constitution places no limit on the amount of government borrowing.

Clause 3: Regulation of Commerce. To regulate Commerce with foreign Nations, and among the several States, and with the Indian Tribes;

This is the commerce clause, which gives to Congress the power to regulate interstate and foreign trade. Much of the activity of Congress is based on this clause.

Clause 4: Naturalization and Bankruptcy. To establish an uniform Rule of Naturalization, and uniform Laws on the subject of Bankruptcies throughout the United States;

Only Congress may determine how aliens can become citizens of the United States. Congress may make laws with respect to bankruptcy.

Clause 5: Money and Standards. To coin Money, regulate the Value thereof, and of foreign Coin, and fix the Standard of Weights and Measures;

Congress mints coins and prints and circulates paper money. Congress can establish uniform measures of time, distance, weight, and so on. In 1838, Congress adopted the English system of weights and measurements as our national standard.

Clause 6: Punishing Counterfeiters. To provide for the Punishment of counterfeiting the Securities and current Coin of the United States;

Congress has the power to punish those who copy American money and pass it off as real. Currently, the punishment is a fine up to $5,000 and/or imprisonment for up to fifteen years.

Clause 7: Roads and Post Offices. To establish Post Offices and post Roads;

Post roads include all routes over which mail is carried—highways, railways, waterways, and airways.

Clause 8: Patents and Copyrights. To promote the Progress of Science and useful Arts, by securing for limited Times to Authors and Inventors the exclusive Right to their respective Writings and Discoveries;

Authors' and composers' works are protected by copyrights established by copyright law, which currently is the Copyright Act of 1976, as amended. Copyrights are valid for the life of the author or composer plus seventy years. Inventors' works are protected by patents, which vary in length of protection from fourteen to twenty years. A patent gives a person the exclusive right to control the manufacture or sale of her or his invention.

Clause 9: Lower Courts. To constitute Tribunals inferior to the supreme Court;

Congress has the authority to set up all federal courts, except the Supreme Court, and to decide what cases those courts will hear.

Clause 10: Punishment for Piracy. To define and punish Piracies and Felonies committed on the high Seas, and Offences against the Law of Nations;

Congress has the authority to prohibit the commission of certain acts outside U.S. territory and to punish certain violations of international law.

Clause 11: Declaration of War. To declare War, grant Letters of Marque and Reprisal, and make Rules concerning Captures on Land and Water;

Only Congress can declare war, although the president, as commander in chief, can make war without Congress's formal declaration. Letters of marque and reprisal authorized private parties to capture and destroy enemy ships in wartime. Since the middle of the nineteenth century, international law has prohibited letters of marque and reprisal, and the United States has honored the ban.

Clause 12: The Army. To raise and support Armies, but no Appropriation of Money to that Use shall be for a longer Term than two Years;

Congress has the power to create an army; the funds used to pay for it must be appropriated for no more than two-year intervals. This latter restriction gives ultimate control of the army to civilians.

Clause 13: Creation of a Navy. To provide and maintain a Navy;

This clause allows for the maintenance of a navy. In 1947, Congress created the U.S. Air Force.

Clause 14: Regulation of the Armed Forces. To make Rules for the Government and Regulation of the land and naval Forces;

Congress sets the rules for the military mainly by way of the Uniform Code of Military Justice, which was enacted in 1950 by Congress.

Clause 15: The Militia. To provide for calling forth the Militia to execute the Laws of the Union, suppress Insurrections and repel Invasions;

The militia is known today as the National Guard. Both Congress and the president have the authority to call the National Guard into federal service.

Clause 16: How the Militia Is Organized. To provide for organizing, arming, and disciplining the Militia, and for governing such Part of them as may be employed in the Service of the United States, reserving to the States respectively, the Appointment of the Officers, and the Authority of training the Militia according to the discipline prescribed by Congress;

This clause gives Congress the power to "federalize" state militia (National Guard). When called into such service, the National Guard is subject to the same rules that Congress has set forth for the regular armed services.

Clause 17: Creation of the District of Columbia. To exercise exclusive Legislation in all Cases whatsoever, over such District (not exceeding ten Miles square) as may, by Cession of particular States, and the Acceptance of Congress, become the Seat of the Government of the United States, and to exercise like Authority over all Places purchased by the Consent of the Legislature of the State in which the Same shall be, for the Erection of Forts, Magazines, Arsenals, dock-Yards, and other needful Buildings;—And

Congress established the District of Columbia as the national capital in 1791. Virginia and Maryland had granted land for the District, but Virginia's grant was returned because it was believed it would not be needed. Today, the District covers sixty-nine square miles.

Clause 18: The Elastic Clause. To make all Laws which shall be necessary and proper for carrying into Execution the foregoing Powers, and all other Powers vested by this Constitution in the Government of the United States, or in any Department or Officer thereof.

This clause—the necessary and proper clause, or the elastic clause—grants no specific powers, and thus it can be stretched to fit different circumstances. It has allowed Congress to adapt the government to changing needs and times.

Section 9. The Powers Denied to Congress
Clause 1: Question of Slavery. The Migration or Importation of such Persons as any of the States now existing shall think proper to admit, shall not be prohibited by the Congress prior to the Year one thousand eight hundred and eight, but a Tax or duty may be imposed on such Importation, not exceeding ten dollars for each Person.

"Persons" referred to slaves. Congress outlawed the slave trade in 1808.

Clause 2: Habeas Corpus. The privilege of the Writ of Habeas Corpus shall not be suspended, unless when in Cases of Rebellion or Invasion the public Safety may require it.

A writ of habeas corpus is a court order directing a sheriff or other public officer who is detaining another person to "produce the body" of the detainee so the court can assess the legality of the detention.

Clause 3: Special Bills. No Bill of Attainder or ex post facto Law shall be passed.

A bill of attainder is a law that inflicts punishment without a trial. An ex post facto law is a law that inflicts punishment for an act that was not illegal when it was committed.

Clause 4: Direct Taxes. [No Capitation, or other direct, Tax shall be laid, unless in Proportion to the Census or Enumeration herein before directed to be taken.][6]

A capitation is a tax on a person. A direct tax is a tax paid directly to the government, such as a property tax. This clause was intended to prevent Congress from levying a tax on slaves per person and thereby taxing slavery out of existence.

Clause 5: Export Taxes. No Tax or Duty shall be laid on Articles exported from any State.

Congress may not tax any goods sold from one state to another or from one state to a foreign country. (Congress does have the power to tax goods that are bought from other countries, however.)

Clause 6: Interstate Commerce. No Preference shall be given by any Regulation of Commerce or Revenue to the Ports of one State over those of another: nor shall Vessels bound to, or from, one State, be obliged to enter, clear, or pay Duties in another.

Congress may not treat different ports within the United States differently in terms of taxing and commerce powers. Congress may not give one state's port a legal advantage over the ports of another state.

Clause 7: Treasury Withdrawals. No Money shall be drawn from the Treasury, but in Consequence of Appropriations made by Law; and a regular Statement and Account of the Receipts and Expenditures of all public Money shall be published from time to time.

Federal funds can be spent only as Congress authorizes. This is a significant check on the president's power.

Clause 8: Titles of Nobility. No Title of Nobility shall be granted by the United States: And no Person

holding any Office of Profit or Trust under them, shall, without the Consent of the Congress, accept of any present, Emolument, Office, or Title, of any kind whatever, from any King, Prince, or foreign State.

No person in the United States may hold a title of nobility, such as duke or duchess. This clause also discourages bribery of American officials by foreign governments.

Section 10. Those Powers Denied to the States
Clause 1: Treaties and Coinage. No State shall enter into any Treaty, Alliance, or Confederation; grant Letters of Marque and Reprisal; coin Money; emit Bills of Credit; make any Thing but gold and silver Coin a Tender in Payment of Debts; pass any Bill of Attainder, ex post facto Law, or Law impairing the Obligation of Contracts, or grant any Title of Nobility.

Prohibiting state laws "impairing the Obligation of Contracts" was intended to protect creditors. (Shays' Rebellion—an attempt to prevent courts from giving effect to creditors' legal actions against debtors—occurred only one year before the Constitution was written.)

Clause 2: Duties and Imposts. No State shall, without the Consent of the Congress, lay any Imposts or Duties on Imports or Exports, except what may be absolutely necessary for executing its inspection Laws; and the net Produce of all Duties and Imposts, laid by any State on Imports or Exports, shall be for the Use of the Treasury of the United States; and all such Laws shall be subject to the Revision and Controul of the Congress.

Only Congress can tax imports. Further, the states cannot tax exports.

Clause 3: War. No State shall, without the Consent of Congress, lay any Duty of Tonnage, keep Troops, or Ships of War in time of Peace, enter into any Agreement or Compact with another State, or with a foreign Power or engage in War, unless actually invaded, or in such imminent Danger as will not admit of delay.

A duty of tonnage is a tax on ships according to their cargo capacity. No states may tax ships according to their cargo unless Congress agrees. Additionally, this clause forbids any state to keep troops or warships during peacetime or to make a compact with another state or foreign nation unless Congress so agrees. A state, in contrast, can maintain a militia, but its use has to be limited to disorders that occur within the state—unless, of course, the militia is called into federal service.

---

6. Modified by the Sixteenth Amendment.

Article II. (Executive Branch)

Section 1. The Nature and Scope of Presidential Power

Clause 1: Four-Year Term. The executive Power shall be vested in a President of the United States of America. He shall hold his Office during the Term of four Years, and, together with the Vice President, chosen for the same Term, be elected, as follows.

The president has the power to carry out laws made by Congress, called the executive power. He or she serves in office for a four-year term after election. The Twenty-second Amendment limits the number of times a person may be elected president.

Clause 2: Choosing Electors from Each State. Each State shall appoint, in such Manner as the Legislature thereof may direct, a Number of Electors, equal to the whole Number of Senators and Representatives to which the State may be entitled in the Congress; but no Senator or Representative, or Person holding an Office of Trust or Profit under the United States, shall be appointed an Elector.

The "Electors" are known more commonly as the "electoral college." The president is elected by electors—that is, representatives chosen by the people—rather than by the people directly.

Clause 3: The Former System of Elections. [The Electors shall meet in their respective States, and vote by Ballot for two Persons, of whom one at least shall not be an Inhabitant of the same State with themselves. And they shall make a List of all the Persons voted for, and of the Number of Votes for each; which List they shall sign and certify, and transmit sealed to the Seat of the Government of the United States, directed to the President of the Senate. The President of the Senate shall, in the Presence of the Senate and House of Representatives, open all the Certificates, and the Votes shall then be counted. The Person having the greatest Number of Votes shall be the President, if such Number be a Majority of the whole Number of Electors appointed; and if there be more than one who have such Majority, and have an equal Number of Votes, then the House of Representatives shall immediately chuse by Ballot one of them for President; and if no Person have a Majority, then from the five highest on the List the said House shall in like Manner chuse the President. But in chusing the President, the Votes shall be taken by States, the Representation from each State having one Vote; A quorum for this Purpose shall consist of a Member or Members from two thirds of the States, and a Majority of all the States shall be necessary to a Choice. In every Case, after the Choice of the President, the Person having the greater Number of Votes of the Electors shall be the Vice President. But if there should remain two or more who have equal Votes, the Senate shall chuse from them by Ballot the Vice President.][7]

The original method of selecting the president and vice president was replaced by the Twelfth Amendment. Apparently, the framers did not anticipate the rise of political parties and the development of primaries and conventions.

Clause 4: The Time of Elections. The Congress may determine the Time of chusing the Electors, and the Day on which they shall give their Votes; which Day shall be the same throughout the United States.

Congress set the Tuesday after the first Monday in November every fourth year as the date for choosing electors. The electors cast their votes on the Monday after the second Wednesday in December of that year.

Clause 5: Qualifications for President. No person except a natural born Citizen, or a Citizen of the United States, at the time of the Adoption of this Constitution, shall be eligible to the Office of President; neither shall any Person be eligible to that Office who shall not have attained to the Age of thirty five Years, and been fourteen Years a Resident within the United States.

The president must be a natural-born citizen, be at least thirty-five years of age when taking office, and have been a resident within the United States for at least fourteen years.

Clause 6: Succession of the Vice President. [In Case of the Removal of the President from Office, or of his Death, Resignation or Inability to discharge the Powers and Duties of the said Office, the same shall devolve on the Vice President, and the Congress may by Law provide for the Case of Removal, Death, Resignation or Inability, both of the President and Vice President, declaring what Officer shall then act as President, and such Officer shall act accordingly, until the Disability be removed, or a President shall be elected.][8]

This section provided for the method by which the vice president was to succeed to the presidency, but its wording is ambiguous. It was replaced by the Twenty-fifth Amendment.

---

7. Changed by the Twelfth Amendment.
8. Modified by the Twenty-fifth Amendment.

Clause 7: The President's Salary. The President shall, at stated Times, receive for his Services, a Compensation, which shall neither be encreased nor diminished during the Period for which he shall have been elected, and he shall not receive within that Period any other Emolument from the United States, or any of them.

The president maintains the same salary during each four-year term. Moreover, she or he may not receive additional cash payments from the government. Originally set at $25,000 per year, the salary is currently $400,000 a year plus a $50,000 nontaxable expense account.

Clause 8: The Oath of Office. Before he enter on the Execution of his Office, he shall take the following Oath or Affirmation: "I do solemnly swear (or affirm) that I will faithfully execute the Office of President of the United States, and will to the best of my Ability, preserve, protect and defend the Constitution of the United States."

The president is "sworn in" prior to beginning the duties of the office. Currently, the taking of the oath of office occurs on January 20, following the November election. The ceremony is called the inauguration. The oath of office is administered by the chief justice of the United States Supreme Court.

Section 2. Powers of the President
Clause 1: Commander in Chief. The President shall be Commander in Chief of the Army and Navy of the United States, and of the Militia of the several States, when called into the actual Service of the United States; he may require the Opinion, in writing, of the principal Officer in each of the executive Departments, upon any Subject relating to the Duties of their respective Offices, and he shall have Power to grant Reprieves and Pardons for Offences against the United States, except in Cases of Impeachment.

The armed forces are placed under civilian control because the president is a civilian but still commander in chief of the military. The president may ask for the help of the head of each of the executive departments (thereby creating the cabinet). The cabinet members are chosen by the president with the consent of the Senate, but they can be removed without Senate approval.

The president's clemency powers extend only to federal cases. In those cases, he or she may grant a full or conditional pardon, or reduce a prison term or fine.

Clause 2: Treaties and Appointment. He shall have Power, by and with the Advice and Consent of the Senate, to make Treaties, provided two thirds of the Senators present concur; and he shall nominate, and by and with the Advice and Consent of the Senate, shall appoint Ambassadors, other public Ministers and Consuls, Judges of the supreme Court, and all other Officers of the United States, whose Appointments are not herein otherwise provided for, and which shall be established by Law; but the Congress may by Law vest the Appointment of such inferior Officers, as they think proper, in the President alone, in the Courts of Law, or in the Heads of Departments.

Many of the major powers of the president are identified in this clause, including the power to make treaties with foreign governments (with the approval of the Senate by a two-thirds vote) and the power to appoint ambassadors, Supreme Court justices, and other government officials. Most such appointments require Senate approval.

Clause 3: Vacancies. The President shall have Power to fill up all Vacancies that may happen during the Recess of the Senate, by granting Commissions which shall expire at the end of their next Session.

The president has the power to appoint temporary officials to fill vacant federal offices without Senate approval if the Congress is not in session. Such appointments expire automatically at the end of Congress's next term.

Section 3. Duties of the President
He shall from time to time give to the Congress Information of the State of the Union, and recommend to their Consideration such Measures as he shall judge necessary and expedient; he may, on extraordinary Occasions, convene both Houses, or either of them, and in Case of Disagreement between them, with Respect to the Time of Adjournment, he may adjourn them to such Time as he shall think proper; he shall receive Ambassadors and other public Ministers; he shall take Care that the Laws be faithfully executed, and shall Commission all the Officers of the United States.

Annually, the president reports on the state of the union to Congress, recommends legislative measures, and proposes a federal budget. The State of the Union speech is a statement not only to Congress but also to the American people. After it is given, the president proposes a federal budget and presents an economic report. At any time, the president may send special messages to Congress while it is in session. The president has the power to call special sessions, to adjourn Congress when its two chambers do not agree on when to adjourn, to receive diplomatic representatives of other governments, and to ensure the proper execution of all federal laws. The president further has the ability to empower federal officers to hold their positions and to perform their duties.

Section 4. Impeachment

The President, Vice President and all civil Officers of the United States, shall be removed from Office on Impeachment for, and Conviction of, Treason, Bribery, or other high Crimes and Misdemeanors.

Treason denotes giving aid to the nation's enemies. The definition of high crimes and misdemeanors is usually given as serious abuses of political power. In either case, the president or vice president may be accused by the House (called an impeachment) and then removed from office if convicted by the Senate. (Note that impeachment does not mean removal but rather refers to an accusation of treason or high crimes and misdemeanors.)

ARTICLE III. (Judicial Branch)

Section 1. Judicial Powers, Courts, and Judges

The judicial Power of the United States, shall be vested in one supreme Court, and in such inferior Courts as the Congress may from time to time ordain and establish. The Judges, both of the supreme and inferior Courts, shall hold their Offices during good Behaviour, and shall, at stated Times, receive for their Services a Compensation, which shall not be diminished during their Continuance in Office.

The Supreme Court is vested with judicial power, as are the lower federal courts that Congress creates. Federal judges serve in their offices for life unless they are impeached and convicted by Congress. The payment of federal judges may not be reduced during their time in office.

Section 2. Jurisdiction

Clause 1: Cases under Federal Jurisdiction. The judicial Power shall extend to all Cases, in Law and Equity, arising under this Constitution, the Laws of the United States, and Treaties made, or which shall be made, under their Authority;—to all Cases affecting Ambassadors, other public Ministers and Consuls;—to all Cases of admiralty and maritime Jurisdiction;—to Controversies to which the United States shall be a Party;—to Controversies between two or more States; [—between a State and Citizens of another State;—][9] between Citizens of different States;—between Citizens of the same State claiming Lands under Grants of different States, [and between a State, or the Citizens thereof, and foreign States, Citizens or Subjects.][10]

---

9. Modified by the Eleventh Amendment.
10. Modified by the Eleventh Amendment.

The federal courts take on cases that concern the meaning of the U.S. Constitution, all federal laws, and treaties. They also can take on cases involving citizens of different states and citizens of foreign nations.

Clause 2: Cases for the Supreme Court. In all Cases affecting Ambassadors, other public Ministers and Consuls, and those in which a State shall be a Party, the supreme Court shall have original Jurisdiction. In all the other Cases before mentioned, the supreme Court shall have appellate Jurisdiction, both as to Law and Fact, with such Exceptions, and under such Regulations as the Congress shall make.

In a limited number of situations, the Supreme Court acts as a trial court and has original jurisdiction. These cases involve a representative from another country or involve a state. In all other situations, the cases must first be tried in the lower courts and then can be appealed to the Supreme Court. Congress may, however, make exceptions. Today, the Supreme Court acts as a trial court of first instance on rare occasions.

Clause 3: The Conduct of Trials. The Trial of all Crimes, except in Cases of Impeachment, shall be by Jury; and such Trial shall be held in the State where the said Crimes shall have been committed; but when not committed within any State, the Trial shall be at such Place or Places as the Congress may by Law have directed.

Any person accused of a federal crime is granted the right to a trial by jury in a federal court in that state in which the crime was committed. Trials of impeachment are an exception.

Section 3. Treason

Clause 1: The Definition of Treason. Treason against the United States, shall consist only in levying War against them, or, in adhering to their Enemies, giving them Aid and Comfort. No Person shall be convicted of Treason unless on the Testimony of two Witnesses to the same overt Act, or on Confession in open Court.

Treason is the making of war against the United States or giving aid to its enemies.

Clause 2: Punishment. The Congress shall have Power to declare the Punishment of Treason, but no Attainder of Treason shall work Corruption of Blood, or Forfeiture except during the Life of the Person attainted.

Congress has provided that the punishment for treason ranges from a minimum of five years in prison and/or a $10,000 fine to a maximum of death. "No Attainder of Treason shall work Corruption of Blood" prohibits punishment of the traitor's heirs.

ARTICLE IV. (Relations among the States)

Section 1. Full Faith and Credit
Full Faith and Credit shall be given in each State to the public Acts, Records, and judicial Proceedings of every other State. And the Congress may by general Laws prescribe the Manner in which such Acts, Records and Proceedings shall be proved, and the Effect thereof.

All states are required to respect one another's laws, records, and lawful decisions. There are exceptions, however. A state does not have to enforce another state's criminal code. Nor does it have to recognize another state's grant of a divorce if the person obtaining the divorce did not establish legal residence in the state in which it was given.

Section 2. Treatment of Citizens
Clause 1: Privileges and Immunities. The Citizens of each State shall be entitled to all Privileges and Immunities of Citizens in the several States.

A citizen of a state has the same rights and privileges as the citizens of another state in which he or she happens to be.

Clause 2: Extradition. A Person charged in any State with Treason, Felony, or other Crime, who shall flee from Justice, and be found in another State, shall on Demand of the executive Authority of the State from which he fled, be delivered up, to be removed to the State having Jurisdiction of the Crime.

Any person accused of a crime who flees to another state must be returned to the state in which the crime occurred.

Clause 3: Fugitive Slaves. [No Person held to Service or Labour in one State, under the Laws thereof, escaping into another, shall, in Consequence of any Law or Regulation therein, be discharged from such Service or Labour, but shall be delivered up on Claim of the Party to whom such Service or Labour may be due.][11]

This clause was struck down by the Thirteenth Amendment, which abolished slavery in 1865.

Section 3. Admission of States
Clause 1: The Process. New States may be admitted by the Congress into this Union; but no new State shall be formed or erected within the Jurisdiction of any other State; nor any State be formed by the Junction of two or more States, or Parts of States, without the Consent of the Legislatures of the States concerned as well as of the Congress.

---

11. Repealed by the Thirteenth Amendment.

Only Congress has the power to admit new states to the Union. No state may be created by taking territory from an existing state unless the state's legislature so consents.

Clause 2: Public Land. The Congress shall have Power to dispose of and make all needful Rules and Regulations respecting the Territory or other Property belonging to the United States; and nothing in this Constitution shall be so construed as to Prejudice any Claims of the United States, or of any particular State.

The federal government has the exclusive right to administer federal government public lands.

Section 4. Republican Form of Government
The United States shall guarantee to every State in this Union a Republican Form of Government, and shall protect each of them against Invasion; and on Application of the Legislature, or of the Executive (when the Legislature cannot be convened) against domestic Violence.

Each state is promised a republican form of government—that is, one in which the people elect their representatives. The federal government is bound to protect states against any attack by foreigners or during times of trouble within a state.

ARTICLE V. (Methods of Amendment)

The Congress, whenever two thirds of both Houses shall deem it necessary, shall propose Amendments to this Constitution, or on the Application of the Legislatures of two thirds of the several States, shall call a Convention for proposing Amendments, which, in either Case, shall be valid to all Intents and Purposes, as Part of this Constitution, when ratified by the Legislatures of three fourths of the several States, or by Conventions in three fourths thereof, as the one or the other Mode of Ratification may be proposed by the Congress; Provided that no Amendment which may be made prior to the Year One thousand eight hundred and eight shall in any Manner affect the first and fourth Clauses in the Ninth Section of the First Article; and that no State, without its Consent, shall be deprived of its equal Suffrage in the Senate.

Amendments may be proposed in either of two ways: by a two-thirds vote of each chamber (Congress) or at the request of two-thirds of the states. Ratification of amendments may be carried out in two ways: by the legislatures of three-fourths of the states or by the voters in three-fourths of the states. No state may be denied equal representation in the Senate.

ARTICLE VI. (National Supremacy)

Clause 1: Existing Obligations. All Debts contracted and Engagements entered into, before the Adoption of this Constitution shall be as valid against the United States under this Constitution, as under the Confederation.

During the Revolutionary War and the years of the Confederation, Congress borrowed large sums. This clause pledged that the new federal government would assume those financial obligations.

Clause 2: Supreme Law of the Land. This Constitution, and the Laws of the United States which shall be made in Pursuance thereof; and all Treaties made, or which shall be made, under the Authority of the United States, shall be the supreme Law of the Land; and the Judges in every State shall be bound thereby, any Thing in the Constitution or Laws of any State to the Contrary notwithstanding.

This is typically called the supremacy clause; it declares that federal law takes precedence over all forms of state law. No government at the local or state level may make or enforce any law that conflicts with any provision of the Constitution, acts of Congress, treaties, or other rules and regulations issued by the president and his or her subordinates in the executive branch of the federal government.

Clause 3: Oath of Office. The Senators and Representatives before mentioned, and the Members of the several State Legislatures, and all executive and judicial Officers, both of the United States and of the several States, shall be bound by Oath or Affirmation, to support this Constitution; but no religious Test shall ever be required as a Qualification to any Office or public Trust under the United States.

Every federal and state official must take an oath of office promising to support the U.S. Constitution. Religion may not be used as a qualification to serve in any federal office.

ARTICLE VII. (Ratification)

The Ratification of the Conventions of nine States shall be sufficient for the Establishment of this Constitution between the States so ratifying the Same.

Nine states were required to ratify the Constitution. Delaware was the first and New Hampshire the ninth.

Done in Convention by the Unanimous Consent of the States present the Seventeenth Day of September in the Year of our Lord one thousand seven hundred and Eighty seven and of the Independence of the United States of America the Twelfth. In witness whereof we have hereunto subscribed our Names,

Attest William Jackson Secretary

Go. WASHINGTON
Presid't. and deputy from Virginia

DELAWARE
- Geo. Read
- Gunning Bedford jun
- John Dickinson
- Richard Bassett
- Jaco. Broom

MARYLAND
- James McHenry
- Dan of St. Thos. Jenifer
- Danl. Carroll

VIRGINIA
- John Blair
- James Madison Jr.

NORTH CAROLINA
- Wm. Blount
- Richd. Dobbs Spaight
- Hu. Williamson

SOUTH CAROLINA
- J. Rutledge
- Charles Cotesworth Pinckney
- Charles Pinckney
- Pierce Butler

GEORGIA
- William Few
- Abr. Baldwin

NEW HAMPSHIRE
- John Langdon
- Nicholas Gilman

MASSACHUSETTS
- Nathaniel Gorham
- Rufus King

CONNECTICUT
- Wm. Saml. Johnson
- Roger Sherman

NEW YORK
- Alexander Hamilton

NEW JERSEY
- Wh. Livingston
- David Brearley
- Wm. Paterson
- Jona. Dayton

PENNSYLVANIA
- B. Franklin
- Thomas Mifflin
- Robt. Morris
- Geo. Clymer
- Thos. FitzSimons
- Jared Ingersoll
- James Wilson
- Gouv. Morris

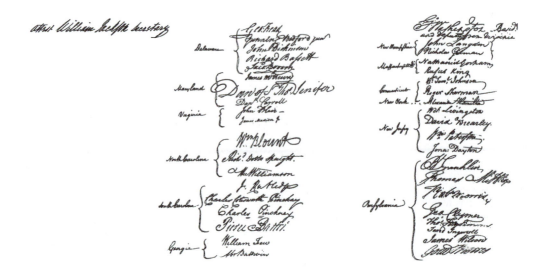

Articles in addition to, and amendment of, the Constitution of the United States of America, proposed by Congress and ratified by the Legislatures of the several states, pursuant to the Fifth Article of the original Constitution.

Amendments to the Constitution of the United States

(The Bill of Rights)[12]

AMENDMENT I.
(Religion, Speech, Assembly, and Petition)

Congress shall make no law respecting an establishment of religion, or prohibiting the free exercise thereof; or abridging the freedom of speech, or of the press; or the right of the people peaceably to assemble, and to petition the Government for a redress of grievances.

Congress may not create an official church or enact laws limiting the freedom of religion, speech, the press, assembly, and petition. These guarantees, like the others in the Bill of Rights (the first ten amendments), are not absolute—each may be exercised only with regard to the rights of other persons.

---

12. On September 25, 1789, Congress transmitted to the state legislatures twelve proposed amendments, two of which, having to do with congressional representation and congressional pay, were not adopted. The remaining ten amendments became the Bill of Rights. In 1992, the amendment concerning congressional pay was adopted as the Twenty-seventh Amendment.

AMENDMENT II. (Militia and the Right to Bear Arms)

A well regulated Militia, being necessary to the security of a free State, the right of the people to keep and bear Arms, shall not be infringed.

To protect itself, each state has the right to maintain a volunteer armed force. States and the federal government may regulate but not completely ban the possession and use of firearms by individuals.

AMENDMENT III.
(The Quartering of Soldiers)

No Soldier shall, in time of peace be quartered in any house, without the consent of the Owner, nor in time of war, but in a manner to be prescribed by law.

Before the Revolutionary War, it had been common British practice to quarter soldiers in colonists' homes. Military troops do not have the power to take over private houses during peacetime.

AMENDMENT IV.
(Searches and Seizures)

The right of the people to be secure in their persons, houses, papers, and effects, against unreasonable searches and seizures, shall not be violated, and no Warrants shall issue, but upon probable cause, supported by Oath or affirmation, and particularly describing the place to be searched, and the persons or things to be seized.

Here the word warrant means "justification" and refers to a document issued by a magistrate or judge indicating the name, address, and possible offense committed. Anyone asking for the warrant, such as a police officer, must be able to convince the magistrate or judge that an offense probably has been committed.

AMENDMENT V.
(Grand Juries, Self-Incrimination, Double Jeopardy, Due Process, and Eminent Domain)

No person shall be held to answer for a capital, or otherwise infamous crime, unless on a presentment or indictment of a Grand Jury, except in cases arising in the land or naval forces, or in the Militia, when in actual service in time of War or public danger; nor shall any person be subject for the same offence to be twice put in jeopardy of life or limb; nor shall be compelled in any criminal case to be a witness against himself, nor be deprived of life, liberty, or property, without due process of law; nor shall private property be taken for public use, without just compensation.

There are two types of juries. A grand jury considers physical evidence and the testimony of witnesses and decides whether there is sufficient reason to bring a case to trial. A petit jury hears the case at trial and decides it. "For the same offence to be twice put in jeopardy of life or limb" means to be tried twice for the same crime. A person may not be tried for the same crime twice or forced to give evidence against herself or himself. No person's right to life, liberty, or property may be taken away except by lawful means, called the due process of law. Private property taken in public purposes must be paid for by the government.

AMENDMENT VI.
(Criminal Court Procedures)

In all criminal prosecutions, the accused shall enjoy the right to a speedy and public trial, by an impartial jury of the State and district wherein the crime shall have been committed, which district shall have been previously ascertained by law, and to be informed of the nature and cause of the accusation; to be confronted with the witnesses against him; to have compulsory process for obtaining witnesses in his favor, and to have the Assistance of Counsel for his defence.

Any person accused of a crime has the right to a fair and public trial by a jury in the state in which the crime took place. The charges against that person must be indicated. Any accused person has the right to a lawyer to defend him or her and to question those who testify against him or her, as well as the right to call people to speak in his or her favor at trial.

AMENDMENT VII.
(Trial by Jury in Civil Cases)

In Suits at common law, where the value in controversy shall exceed twenty dollars, the right of trial by jury shall be preserved, and no fact tried by jury, shall be otherwise re-examined in any Court of the United States, than according to the rules of the common law.

A jury trial may be requested by either party in a dispute in any case involving more than $20. If both parties agree to a trial by a judge without a jury, the right to a jury trial may be put aside.

AMENDMENT VIII.
(Bail, Cruel and Unusual Punishment)

Excessive bail shall not be required, nor excessive fines imposed, nor cruel and unusual punishments inflicted.

Bail is an amount of money that a person accused of a crime may be required to deposit with the court as a guaranty that she or he will appear in court when requested. The amount of bail required or the fine imposed as punishment for a crime must be reasonable compared with the seriousness of the crime involved. Any punishment judged to be too harsh or too severe for a crime is prohibited.

AMENDMENT IX.
(The Rights Retained by the People)

The enumeration in the Constitution, of certain rights, shall not be construed to deny or disparage others retained by the people.

Many civil rights that are not explicitly enumerated in the Constitution are still held by the people.

AMENDMENT X.
(Reserved Powers of the States)

The powers not delegated to the United States by the Constitution, nor prohibited by it to the States, are reserved to the States respectively, or to the people.

Those powers not delegated by the Constitution to the federal government or expressly denied to the states belong to the states and to the people. This amendment in essence allows the states to pass laws under their "police powers."

AMENDMENT XI.
(Ratified on February 7, 1795—Suits against States)

The Judicial power of the United States shall not be construed to extend to any suit in law or equity, commenced or prosecuted against one of the United States by Citizens of another State, or by Citizens or Subjects of any Foreign State.

This amendment has been interpreted to mean that a state cannot be sued in federal court by one of its own citizens, by a citizen of another state, or by a foreign country.

AMENDMENT XII.
(Ratified on June 15, 1804—Election of the President)

The Electors shall meet in their respective states, and vote by ballot for President and Vice-President, one of whom, at least, shall not be an inhabitant of the same State with themselves; they shall name in their ballots the person voted for as President, and in distinct ballots the person voted for as Vice-President, and they shall make distinct lists of all persons voted for as President, and of all persons voted for as Vice-President, and of the number of votes for each, which lists they shall sign and certify, and transmit sealed to the seat of the government of the United States, directed to the President of the Senate;—The President of the Senate shall, in the presence of the Senate and House of Representatives, open all the certificates and the votes shall then be counted;—The person having the greatest number of votes for President, shall be the President, if such number be a majority of the whole number of Electors appointed; and if no person have such majority, then from the persons having the highest numbers not exceeding three on the list of those voted for as President, the House of Representatives shall choose immediately, by ballot, the President. But in choosing the President, the votes shall be taken by States, the representation from each State having one vote; a quorum for this purpose shall consist of a member or members from two-thirds of the States, and a majority of all States shall be necessary to a choice. [And if the House of Representatives shall not choose a President whenever the right of choice shall devolve upon them, before the fourth day of March next following, then the Vice-President shall act as President, as in the case of the death or other constitutional disability of the President.][13]—The person having the greatest number of votes as Vice-President, shall be the Vice-President, if such number be a majority of the whole number of Electors appointed, and if no person have

a majority, then from the two highest numbers on the list, the Senate shall choose the Vice-President; a quorum for the purpose shall consist of two-thirds of the whole number of Senators, and a majority of the whole number shall be necessary to a choice. But no person constitutionally ineligible to the office of President shall be eligible to that of Vice-President of the United States.

The original procedure set out for the election of president and vice president in Article II, Section 1, resulted in a tie in 1800 between Thomas Jefferson and Aaron Burr. It was not until the next year that the House of Representatives chose Jefferson to be president. This amendment changed the procedure by providing for separate ballots for president and vice president.

AMENDMENT XIII.
(Ratified on December 6, 1865—Prohibition of Slavery)

Section 1.

Neither slavery nor involuntary servitude, except as a punishment for crime whereof the party shall have been duly convicted, shall exist within the United States, or any place subject to their jurisdiction.

Some slaves had been freed during the Civil War. This amendment freed the others and abolished slavery.

Section 2.

Congress shall have power to enforce this article by appropriate legislation.

AMENDMENT XIV.
(Ratified on July 9, 1868—Citizenship, Due Process, and Equal Protection of the Laws)

Section 1.

All persons born or naturalized in the United States, and subject to the jurisdiction thereof, are citizens of the United States and of the State wherein they reside. No State shall make or enforce any law which shall abridge the privileges or immunities of citizens of the United States; nor shall any State deprive any person of life, liberty, or property, without due process of law; nor deny to any person within its jurisdiction the equal protection of the laws.

Under this provision, states cannot make or enforce laws that take away rights given to all citizens by the federal government. States cannot act unfairly or arbitrarily toward, or discriminate against, any person.

---

13. Changed by the Twentieth Amendment.

Section 2.

Representatives shall be apportioned among the several States according to their respective numbers, counting the whole number of persons in each State, excluding Indians not taxed. But when the right to vote at any election for the choice of electors for President and Vice President of the United States, Representatives in Congress, the Executive and Judicial officers of a State, or the members of the Legislature thereof, is denied to any of the male inhabitants of such State, being [twenty-one][14] years of age, and citizens of the United States, or in any way abridged, except for participation in rebellion, or other crime, the basis of representation therein shall be reduced in the proportion which the number of such male citizens shall bear to the whole number of male citizens twenty-one years of age in such State.

Section 3.

No person shall be a Senator or Representative in Congress, or elector of President and Vice President, or hold any office, civil or military, under the United States, or under any State, who having previously taken an oath, as a member of Congress, or as an officer of the United States, or as a member of any State legislature, or as an executive or judicial officer of any State, to support the Constitution of the United States, shall have engaged in insurrection or rebellion against the same, or given aid or comfort to the enemies thereof. But Congress may by a vote of two-thirds of each House, remove such disability.

This provision forbade former state or federal government officials who had acted in support of the Confederacy during the Civil War to hold office again. It limited the president's power to pardon those persons. Congress removed this "disability" in 1898.

Section 4.

The validity of the public debt of the United States, authorized by law, including debts incurred for payment of pensions and bounties for services in suppressing insurrection or rebellion, shall not be questioned. But neither the United States nor any State shall assume or pay any debt or obligation incurred in aid of insurrection or rebellion against the United States, or any claim for the loss or emancipation of any slave, but all such debts, obligations and claims shall be held illegal and void.

14. Changed by the Twenty-sixth Amendment.

Section 5.

The Congress shall have power to enforce, by appropriate legislation, the provisions of this article.

AMENDMENT XV.
(Ratified on February 3, 1870—The Right to Vote)

Section 1.

The right of citizens of the United States to vote shall not be denied or abridged by the United States or by any State on account of race, color, or previous condition of servitude.

No citizen can be refused the right to vote simply because of race or color or because that person was once a slave.

Section 2.

The Congress shall have power to enforce this article by appropriate legislation.

AMENDMENT XVI.
(Ratified on February 3, 1913—Income Taxes)

The Congress shall have power to lay and collect taxes on incomes, from whatever source derived, without apportionment among the several States, and without regard to any census or enumeration.

This amendment allows Congress to tax income without sharing the revenue so obtained with the states according to their population.

AMENDMENT XVII.
(Ratified on April 8, 1913—The Popular Election of Senators)

Section 1.

The Senate of the United States shall be composed of two Senators from each State, elected by the people thereof, for six years; and each Senator shall have one vote. The electors in each State shall have the qualifications requisite for electors of the most numerous branch of the State legislatures.

Section 2.

When vacancies happen in the representation of any State in the Senate, the executive authority of such State shall issue writs of election to fill such vacancies: Provided, That the legislature of any State may empower the executive thereof to make temporary appointments until the people fill the vacancies by election as the legislature may direct.

Section 3.

This amendment shall not be so construed as to affect the election or term of any Senator chosen before it becomes valid as part of the Constitution.

This amendment modified portions of Article I, Section 3, that related to election of senators. Senators are now elected by the voters in each state directly. When a vacancy occurs, either the state may fill the vacancy by a special election, or the governor of the state involved may appoint someone to fill the seat until the next election.

AMENDMENT XVIII.
(Ratified on January 16, 1919—Prohibition)

Section 1.

After one year from the ratification of this article the manufacture, sale, or transportation of intoxicating liquors within, the importation thereof into, or the exportation thereof from the United States and all territory subject to the jurisdiction thereof for beverage purposes is hereby prohibited.

Section 2.

The Congress and the several States shall have concurrent power to enforce this article by appropriate legislation.

Section 3.

This article shall be inoperative unless it shall have been ratified as an amendment to the Constitution by the legislatures of the several States, as provided in the Constitution, within seven years from the date of the submission hereof to the States by the Congress.[15]

This amendment made it illegal to manufacture, sell, and transport alcoholic beverages in the United States. It was repealed by the Twenty-first Amendment.

AMENDMENT XIX.
(Ratified on August 18, 1920—Women's Right to Vote)

Section 1.

The right of citizens of the United States to vote shall not be denied or abridged by the United States or by any State on account of sex.

---

15. The Eighteenth Amendment was repealed by the Twenty-first Amendment.

Section 2.

Congress shall have power to enforce this article by appropriate legislation.

Women were given the right to vote by this amendment, and Congress was given the power to enforce this right.

AMENDMENT XX.
(Ratified on January 23, 1933—The Lame Duck Amendment)

Section 1.

The terms of the President and Vice President shall end at noon on the 20th day of January, and the terms of Senators and Representatives at noon on the 3d day of January, of the years in which such terms would have ended if this article had not been ratified; and the terms of their successors shall then begin.

This amendment modified Article I, Section 4, Clause 2, and other provisions relating to the president in the Twelfth Amendment. The taking of the oath of office was moved from March 4 to January 20.

Section 2.

The Congress shall assemble at least once in every year, and such meeting shall begin at noon on the 3d day of January, unless they shall by law appoint a different day.

Congress changed the beginning of its term to January 3. The reason the Twentieth Amendment is called the Lame Duck Amendment because it shortens the time between when a member of Congress is defeated for reelection and when he or she leaves office.

Section 3.

If, at the time fixed for the beginning of the term of the President, the President elect shall have died, the Vice President elect shall become President. If a President shall not have been chosen before the time fixed for the beginning of his term, or if the President elect shall have failed to qualify, then the Vice President elect shall act as President until a President shall have qualified; and the Congress may by law provide for the case wherein neither a President elect nor a Vice President elect shall have qualified, declaring who shall then act as President, or the manner in which one who is to act shall be selected, and such person shall act accordingly until a President or Vice President shall have qualified.

This part of the amendment deals with problem areas left ambiguous by Article II and the Twelfth Amendment. If the president dies before January 20 or fails to qualify for office, the presidency is to be filled as described in this section.

Section 4.

The Congress may by law provide for the case of the death of any of the persons from whom the House of Representatives may choose a President whenever the right of choice shall have devolved upon them, and for the case of the death of any of the persons from whom the Senate may choose a Vice President whenever the right of choice shall have devolved upon them.

Congress has never created legislation pursuant to this section.

Section 5.

Sections 1 and 2 shall take effect on the 15th day of October following the ratification of this article.

Section 6.

This article shall be inoperative unless it shall have been ratified as an amendment to the Constitution by the legislatures of three-fourths of the several States within seven years from the date of its submission.

AMENDMENT XXI.
(Ratified on December 5, 1933—The Repeal of Prohibition)

Section 1.

The eighteenth article of amendment to the Constitution of the United States is hereby repealed.

Section 2.

The transportation or importation into any State, Territory, or possession of the United States for delivery or use therein of intoxicating liquors, in violation of the laws thereof, is hereby prohibited.

Section 3.

This article shall be inoperative unless it shall have been ratified as an amendment to the Constitution by conventions in the several States, as provided in the Constitution, within seven years from the date of the submission hereof to the States by Congress.

The amendment repealed the Eighteenth Amendment but did not make alcoholic beverages legal everywhere. Rather, they remained illegal in any state that so designated them. Many such "dry" states existed for a number of years after 1933. Today, there are still "dry" counties within the United States, in which the sale of alcoholic beverages is illegal.

AMENDMENT XXII.
(Ratified on February 27, 1951— Limitation of Presidential Terms)

Section 1.

No person shall be elected to the office of the President more than twice, and no person who has held the office of President, or acted as President, for more than two years of a term to which some other person was elected President shall be elected to the office of President more than once. But this Article shall not apply to any person holding the office of President when this Article was proposed by the Congress, and shall not prevent any person who may be holding the office of President, or acting as President, during the term within which this Article becomes operative from holding the office of President or acting as President during the remainder of such term.

Section 2.

This article shall be inoperative unless it shall have been ratified as an amendment to the Constitution by the legislatures of three-fourths of the several States within seven years from the date of its submission to the States by the Congress.

No president may serve more than two elected terms. If, however, a president has succeeded to the office after the half-way point of a term in which another president was originally elected, then that president may serve for more than eight years, but not to exceed ten years.

AMENDMENT XXIII.
(Ratified on March 29, 1961—Presidential Electors for the District of Columbia)

Section 1.

The District constituting the seat of Government of the United States shall appoint in such manner as the Congress may direct:

A number of electors of President and Vice President equal to the whole number of Senators and Representatives in Congress to which the District would be entitled if it were a State, but in no event more than the least populous State; they shall be in addition to those appointed by the States, but they shall be considered, for the purposes of the election of President and Vice President, to be electors appointed by a State; and they shall meet in the District and perform such duties as provided by the twelfth article of amendment.

Section 2.

The Congress shall have power to enforce this article by appropriate legislation.

Citizens living in the District of Columbia have the right to vote in elections for president and vice president. The District of Columbia has three presidential electors, whereas before this amendment it had none.

AMENDMENT XXIV.
(Ratified on January 23, 1964—The Anti–Poll Tax Amendment)

Section 1.

The right of citizens of the United States to vote in any primary or other election for President or Vice President, for electors for President or Vice President, or for Senator or Representative in Congress, shall not be denied or abridged by the United States, or any State by reason of failure to pay any poll tax or other tax.

Section 2.

The Congress shall have power to enforce this article by appropriate legislation.

No government shall require a person to pay a poll tax to vote in any federal election.

AMENDMENT XXV.
(Ratified on February 10, 1967— Presidential Disability and Vice Presidential Vacancies)

Section 1.

In case of the removal of the President from office or of his death or resignation, the Vice President shall become President.

Whenever a president dies or resigns from office, the vice president becomes president.

Section 2.

Whenever there is a vacancy in the office of the Vice President, the President shall nominate a Vice President who shall take office upon confirmation by a majority vote of both Houses of Congress.

Whenever the office of the vice presidency becomes vacant, the president may appoint someone to fill this office, provided Congress consents.

Section 3.

Whenever the President transmits to the President pro tempore of the Senate and the Speaker of the House of Representatives his written declaration that he is unable to discharge the powers and duties of his office, and until he transmits to them a written declaration to the contrary, such powers and duties shall be discharged by the Vice President as Acting President.

Whenever the president believes she or he is unable to carry out the duties of the office, she or he shall so indicate to Congress in writing. The vice president then acts as president until the president declares that she or he is again able to carry out the duties of the office.

Section 4.

Whenever the Vice President and a majority of either the principal officers of the executive departments or of such other body as Congress may by law provide, transmit to the President pro tempore of the Senate and the Speaker of the House of Representatives their written declaration that the President is unable to discharge the powers and duties of his office, the Vice President shall immediately assume the powers and duties of the office as Acting President.

Thereafter, when the President transmits to the President pro tempore of the Senate and the Speaker of the House of Representatives his written declaration that no inability exists, he shall resume the powers and duties of his office unless the Vice President and a majority of either the principal officers of the executive department or of such other body as Congress may by law provide, transmit within four days to the President pro tempore of the Senate and the Speaker of the House of Representatives their written declaration that the President is unable to discharge the powers and duties of his office. Thereupon Congress shall decide the issue, assembling within forty-eight hours for that purpose if not in session. If the Congress, within twenty-one days after receipt of the latter written declaration, or, if Congress is not in session, within twenty-one days after Congress is required to assemble, determines by two-thirds vote of both Houses that the President is unable to discharge the powers and duties of his office, the Vice President shall continue to discharge the same as Acting President; otherwise, the President shall resume the powers and duties of his office.

Whenever the vice president and a majority of the members of the cabinet believe that the president cannot carry out her or his duties, they shall so indicate in writing to Congress. The vice president shall then act as president. When the president believes that she or he is able to carry out her or his duties again, she or he shall so indicate to the Congress. However, if the vice president and a majority of the cabinet do not agree, Congress must decide by a two-thirds vote within three weeks who shall act as president.

AMENDMENT XXVI.
(Ratified on July 1, 1971—Voting Rights for Eighteen-Year-Olds)

Section 1.
The right of citizens of the United States, who are eighteen years of age or older, to vote shall not be denied or abridged by the United States or by any State on account of age.

No one eighteen years of age or older can be denied the right to vote in federal or state elections by virtue of age.

Section 2.
The Congress shall have power to enforce this article by appropriate legislation.

AMENDMENT XXVII.
(Ratified on May 7, 1992— Congressional Pay)

No law, varying the compensation for the services of the Senators and Representatives, shall take effect, until an election of representatives shall have intervened.

This amendment allows the voters to have some control over increases in salaries for congressional members. Originally submitted to the states for ratification in 1789, it was not ratified until 203 years later, in 1992.

Appendix C

Federalist Papers No. 10 and No. 51

In 1787, after the newly drafted U.S. Constitution was submitted to the thirteen states for ratification, a major political debate ensued between the Federalists (who favored ratification) and the Anti-Federalists (who opposed ratification). Anti-Federalists in New York were particularly critical of the Constitution, and in response to their objections, Federalists Alexander Hamilton, James Madison, and John Jay wrote a series of eighty-five essays in defense of the Constitution. The essays were published in New York newspapers and reprinted in other newspapers throughout the country.

For students of American government, the essays, collectively known as the Federalist Papers, are particularly important because they provide a glimpse of the founders' political philosophy and intentions in designing the Constitution—and, consequently, in shaping the American philosophy of government.

We have included in this appendix three of these essays: Federalist Papers Nos. 10, 51, and 78. Each essay has been annotated by the authors to indicate its importance in American political thought and to clarify the meaning of particular passages.

Federalist Paper No. 10

Federalist Paper No. 10, penned by James Madison, has often been singled out as a key document in American political thought. In this essay, Madison attacks the Anti-Federalists' fear that a republican form of government will inevitably give rise to "factions"—small political parties or groups united by a common interest—that will control the government. Factions will be harmful to the country because they will implement policies beneficial to their own interests but adverse to other people's rights and to the public good. In this essay, Madison attempts to lay to rest this fear by explaining how, in a large republic such as the United States, there will be so many different factions, held together by regional or local interests, that no single one of them will dominate national politics.

Madison opens his essay with a paragraph discussing how important it is to devise a plan of government that can control the "instability, injustice, and confusion" brought about by factions.

Among the numerous advantages promised by a well-constructed Union, none deserves to be more accurately developed than its tendency to break and control the violence of faction. The friend of popular governments never finds himself so much alarmed for their character and fate as when he contemplates their propensity to this dangerous vice. He will not fail, therefore, to set a due value on any plan which, without violating the principles to which he is attached, provides a proper cure for it. The instability, injustice, and confusion introduced into the public councils have, in truth, been the mortal diseases under which popular governments have everywhere perished, as they continue to be the favorite and fruitful topics from which the adversaries to liberty derive their most specious declamations. The valuable improvements made by the American constitutions on the popular models, both ancient and modern, cannot certainly be too much admired; but it would be an unwarrantable partiality to contend that they have as effectually obviated the danger on this side, as was wished and expected. Complaints are everywhere heard from our most considerate and virtuous citizens, equally the friends of public and private faith and of public and personal liberty, that our governments are too unstable, that the public good is disregarded in the conflicts of rival parties, and that measures are too often decided, not according to the rules of justice and the rights of the minor party, but by the superior force of an interested and overbearing majority. However anxiously we may wish that these complaints had no foundation, the evidence of known facts will not permit us to deny that they are in some degree true. It will be found, indeed, on a candid review of our situation, that some of the distresses under which we labor have been erroneously charged on the operation of our governments; but it will be found, at the same time, that other causes will not alone account for many of our heaviest misfortunes; and, particularly, for that prevailing and increasing distrust of public engagements and alarm for private rights which are echoed from one end of the continent to the other. These must be chiefly, if not wholly, effects of the unsteadiness and injustice with which a factious spirit has tainted our public administration.

Madison now defines what he means by the term faction.

By a faction I understand a number of citizens, whether amounting to a majority or minority of the whole, who are united and actuated by some common impulse of passion, or of interest, adverse to the rights of other citizens, or the permanent and aggregate interests of the community.

Madison next contends that there are two methods by which the "mischiefs of faction" can be cured: by removing the causes of faction or by controlling their effects. In the following paragraphs, Madison explains how liberty itself nourishes factions. Therefore, to abolish factions would involve abolishing liberty—a cure "worse than the disease."

There are two methods of curing the mischiefs of faction: the one, by removing its causes; the other, by controlling i ts effects.

There are again two methods of removing the causes of faction: the one, by destroying the liberty which is essential to its existence; the other, by giving to every citizen the same opinions, the same passions, and the same interests.

It could never be more truly said than of the first remedy that it was worse than the disease. Liberty is to faction what air is to fire, an aliment without which it instantly expires. But it could not be a less folly to abolish liberty, which is essential to political life, because it nourishes faction than it would be to wish the annihilation of air, which is essential to animal life, because it imparts to fire its destructive agency.

The second expedient is as impracticable as the first would be unwise. As long as the reason of man continues fallible, and he is at liberty to exercise it, different opinions will be formed. As long as the connection subsists between his reason and his self-love, his opinions and his passions will have a reciprocal influence on each other; and the former will be objects to which the latter will attach themselves. The diversity in the faculties of men, from which the rights of property originate, is not less an insuperable obstacle to a uniformity of interests. The protection of these faculties is the first object of government. From the protection of different and unequal faculties of acquiring property, the possession of different degrees and kinds of property immediately results; and from the influence of these on the sentiments and views of the respective proprietors ensues a division of the society into different interests and parties.

The latent causes of faction are thus sown in the nature of man; and we see them everywhere brought into different degrees of activity, according to the different circumstances of civil society. A zeal for different opinions concerning religion, concerning government, and many other points, as well of speculation as of practice; an attachment to different leaders ambitiously contending for pre-eminence and power; or to persons of other descriptions whose fortunes have been interesting to the human passions, have, in turn, divided mankind into parties, inflamed them with mutual animosity, and rendered them much more disposed to vex and oppress each other than to co-operate for their common good. So strong is this propensity of mankind to fall into mutual animosities that where no substantial occasion presents itself the most frivolous and fanciful distinctions have been sufficient to kindle their unfriendly passions and excite their most violent conflicts. But the most common and durable source of factions has been the various and unequal distribution of property. Those who hold and those who are without property have ever formed distinct interests in society. Those who are creditors, and those who are debtors, fall under a like discrimination. A landed interest, a manufacturing interest, a mercantile interest, a moneyed interest, with many lesser interests, grow up of necessity in civilized nations, and divide them into different classes, actuated by different sentiments and views. The regulation of these various and interfering interests forms the principal task of modern legislation and involves the spirit of party and faction in the necessary and ordinary operations of government.

No man is allowed to be a judge in his own cause, because his interest would certainly bias his judgment, and, not improbably, corrupt his integrity. With equal, nay with greater reason, a body of men are unfit to be both judges and parties at the same time; yet what are many of the most important acts of legislation but so many judicial determinations, not indeed concerning the rights of single persons, but concerning the rights of large bodies of citizens? And what are the different classes of legislators but advocates and parties to the causes which they determine? Is a law proposed concerning private debts? It is a question to which the creditors are parties on one side and the debtors on the other. Justice ought to hold the balance between them. Yet the parties are, and must be, themselves the judges; and the most numerous party, or in other words, the most powerful faction must be expected to prevail. Shall domestic manufacturers be encouraged, and in what degree, by restrictions on foreign manufacturers? [These] are questions which would be differently decided by the landed and the manufacturing classes, and probably by neither with a sole regard to justice and the public good. The apportionment of taxes on the various descriptions of property is an act which seems to require the most exact impartiality; yet there is, perhaps, no legislative act in which greater opportunity and temptation are given to a predominant party to trample on the rules of justice. Every shilling with which they overburden the inferior number is a shilling saved to their own pockets.

It is in vain to say that enlightened statesmen will be able to adjust these clashing interests and render them all subservient to the public good. Enlightened statesmen will not always be at the helm. Nor, in many cases, can such an adjustment be made at all without taking into view indirect and remote considerations, which will rarely prevail over the immediate interest which one party may find in disregarding the rights of another or the good of the whole.

The inference to which we are brought is that the causes of faction cannot be removed and that relief is only to be sought in the means of controlling its effects.

Having concluded that "the causes of faction cannot be removed," Madison now looks in some detail at the other method by which factions can be cured—by controlling their effects. This is the heart of his essay. He begins by positing a significant question: How can you have self-government without risking the possibility that a ruling faction, particularly a majority faction, might tyrannize over the rights of others?

If a faction consists of less than a majority, relief is supplied by the republican principle, which enables the majority to defeat its sinister views by regular vote. It may clog the administration, it may convulse the society; but it will be unable to execute and mask its violence under the forms of the Constitution. When a majority is included in a faction, the form of popular government, on the other hand, enables it to sacrifice to its ruling passion or interest both the public good and the rights of other citizens. To secure the public good and private rights against the danger of such a faction, and at the same time to preserve the spirit and the form of popular government, is then the great object to which our inquiries are directed. Let me add that it is the great desideratum by which alone this form of government can be rescued from the opprobrium under which it has so long labored and be recommended to the esteem and adoption of mankind.

Madison now sets forth the idea that one way to control the effects of factions is to ensure that the majority is rendered incapable of acting in concert in order to "carry into effect schemes of oppression." He goes on to state that in a democracy, in which all citizens participate personally in government decision making, there is no way to prevent the majority from communicating with each other and, as a result, acting in concert.

By what means is this object attainable? Evidently by one of two only. Either the existence of the same passion or interest in a majority at the same time must be prevented, or the majority, having such coexistent passion or interest, must be rendered, by their number and local situation, unable to concert and carry into effect schemes of oppression. If the impulse and the opportunity be suffered to coincide, we well know that neither moral nor religious motives can be relied on as an adequate control. They are not found to be such on the injustice and violence of individuals, and lose their efficacy in proportion to the number combined together, that is, in proportion as their efficacy becomes needful.

From this view of the subject it may be concluded that a pure democracy, by which I mean a society consisting of a small number of citizens, who assemble and administer the government in person, can admit of no cure for the mischiefs of faction. A common passion or interest will, in almost every case, be felt by a majority of the whole; a communication and concert results from the form of government itself; and there is nothing to check the inducements to sacrifice the weaker party or an obnoxious individual. Hence it is that such democracies have ever been spectacles of turbulence and contention; have ever been found incompatible with personal security or the rights of property; and have in general been as short in their lives as they have been violent in their deaths. Theoretic politicians, who have patronized this species of government, have erroneously supposed that by reducing mankind to a perfect equality in their political rights, they would at the same time be perfectly equalized and assimilated in their possessions, their opinions, and their passions.

Madison now moves on to discuss the benefits of a republic with respect to controlling the effects of factions. He begins by defining a republic and then pointing out the "two great points of difference" between a republic and a democracy: a republic is governed by a small body of elected representatives, not by the people directly; and a republic can extend over a much larger territory and embrace more citizens than a democracy can.

A republic, by which I mean a government in which the scheme of representation takes place, opens a different prospect and promises the cure for which we are seeking. Let us examine the points in which it varies from pure democracy, and we shall comprehend both the nature of the cure and the efficacy which it must derive from the Union.

The two great points of difference between a democracy and a republic are: first, the delegation of the government, in the latter, to a small number of citizens elected by the rest; secondly, the greater number of citizens and greater sphere of country over which the latter may be extended.

In the following four paragraphs, Madison explains how in a republic, particularly a large republic, the delegation of authority to elected representatives will increase the likelihood that those who govern will be "fit" for their positions and that a proper balance will be achieved between local (factional) interests and national interests. Note how he stresses that the new federal Constitution, by dividing powers between state governments and the national government, provides a "happy combination in this respect."

The effect of the first difference is, on the one hand, to refine and enlarge the public views by passing them through the medium of a chosen body of citizens, whose wisdom may best discern the true interest of their country and whose patriotism and love of justice will be least likely to sacrifice it to temporary or partial considerations. Under such a regulation it may well happen that the public voice, pronounced by the representatives of the people, will be more consonant to the public good than if pronounced by the people themselves, convened for the purpose. On the other hand, the effect may be inverted. Men of factious tempers, of local prejudices, or of sinister designs, may, by intrigue, by corruption, or by other means, first obtain the suffrages, and then betray the interests of the people. The question resulting is, whether small or extensive republics are most favorable to the election of proper guardians of the public weal; and it is clearly decided in favor of the latter by two obvious considerations.

In the first place, it is to be remarked that however small the republic may be the representatives must be raised to a certain number in order to guard against the cabals of a few; and that however large it may be, they must be limited to a certain number in order to guard against the confusion of a multitude. Hence, the number of representatives in the two cases not being

in proportion to that of the constituents, and being proportionally greater in the small republic, it follows that if the proportion of fit characters be not less in the large than in the small republic, the former will present a greater option, and consequently a greater probability of a fit choice.

In the next place, as each representative will be chosen by a greater number of citizens in the large than in the small republic, it will be more difficult for unworthy candidates to practice with success the vicious arts by which elections are too often carried; and the suffrages of the people being more free, will be more likely to center on men who possess the most attractive merit and the most diffusive and established characters.

It must be confessed that in this, as in most other cases, there is a mean, on both sides of which inconveniencies will be found to lie. By enlarging too much the number of electors, you render the representative too little acquainted with all their local circumstances and lesser interests; as by reducing it too much, you render him unduly attached to these, and too little fit to comprehend and pursue great and national objects. The federal Constitution forms a happy combination in this respect; the great and aggregate interests being referred to the national, the local and particular to the State legislatures.

Madison now looks more closely at the other difference between a republic and a democracy—namely, that a republic can encompass a larger territory and more citizens than a democracy can. In the remaining paragraphs of his essay, Madison concludes that in a large republic, it will be difficult for factions to act in concert. Although a factious group—religious, political, economic, or otherwise—may control a local or regional government, it will have little chance of gathering a national following. This is because in a large republic, there will be numerous factions whose work will offset the work of any one particular faction ("sect"). As Madison phrases it, these numerous factions will "secure the national councils against any danger from that source."

The other point of difference is the greater number of citizens and extent of territory which may be brought within the compass of republican than of democratic government; and it is this circumstance principally which renders factious combinations less to be dreaded in the former than in the latter. The smaller the society, the fewer probably will be the distinct parties and interests composing it; the fewer the distinct parties and interests, the more frequently will a majority be found of the same party; and the smaller the number of individuals composing a majority, and the smaller the compass within which they are placed, the more easily will they concert and execute their plans of oppression. Extend the sphere and you take in a greater variety of parties and interests; you make it less probable that a majority of the whole will have a common motive to invade the rights of other citizens; or if such a common motive exists, it will be more difficult for all who feel it to discover their own strength and to act in unison with each other. Besides other impediments, it may be remarked that, where there is a consciousness of unjust or dishonorable purposes, communication is always checked by distrust in proportion to the number whose concurrence is necessary.

Hence, it clearly appears that the same advantage which a republic has over a democracy in controlling the effects of faction is enjoyed by a large over a small republic—is enjoyed by the Union over the States composing it. Does this advantage consist in the substitution of representatives whose enlightened views and virtuous sentiments render them superior to local prejudices and to schemes of injustice? It will not be denied that the representation of the Union will be most likely to possess these requisite endowments. Does it consist in the greater security afforded by a greater variety of parties, against the event of any one party being able to outnumber and oppress the rest? In an equal degree does the increased variety of parties comprised within the Union increase this security. Does it, in fine, consist in the greater obstacles opposed to the concert and accomplishment of the secret wishes of an unjust and interested majority? Here again the extent of the Union gives it the most palpable advantage.

The influence of factious leaders may kindle a flame within their particular States but will be unable to spread a general conflagration through the other States. A religious sect may degenerate into a political faction in a part of the Confederacy; but the variety of sects dispersed over the entire face of it must secure the national councils against any danger from that source. A rage for paper money, for an abolition of debts, for an equal division of property, or for any other improper or wicked project, will be less apt to pervade the whole body of the Union than a particular member of it, in the same proportion as such a malady is more likely to taint a particular county or district than an entire State.

In the extent and proper structure of the Union, therefore, we behold a republican remedy for the diseases most incident to republican government. And according to the degree of pleasure and pride we feel in being republicans ought to be our zeal in cherishing the spirit and supporting the character of federalists.

Publius
(James Madison)

Federalist Paper No. 51

Federalist Paper No. 51, also authored by James Madison, is another classic in American political theory. Although the Federalists wanted a strong national government, they had not abandoned the traditional American view, particularly notable during the revolutionary era, that those holding powerful government positions could not be trusted to put national interests and the common good above their own personal interests. In this essay, Madison explains why the separation of the national government's powers into three branches—executive, legislative, and judicial—and a federal structure of government offer the best protection against tyranny.

To what expedient, then, shall we finally resort, for maintaining in practice the necessary partition of power among the several departments as laid down in the Constitution? The only answer that can be given is that as all these exterior provisions are found to be inadequate the defect must be supplied, by so contriving the interior structure of the government as that its several constituent parts may, by their mutual relations, be the means of keeping each other in their proper places. Without presuming to undertake a full development of this important idea I will hazard a few general observations which may perhaps place it in a clearer light, and enable us to form a more correct judgment of the principles and structure of the government planned by the convention.

In the next two paragraphs, Madison stresses that for the powers of the different branches (departments) of government to be truly separated, the personnel in one branch should not be dependent on another branch for their appointment or for the "emoluments" (compensation) attached to their offices.

In order to lay a due foundation for that separate and distinct exercise of the different powers of government, which to a certain extent is admitted on all hands to be essential to the preservation of liberty, it is evident that each department should have a will of its own; and consequently should be so constituted that the members of each should have as little agency as possible in the appointment of the members of the others. Were this principle rigorously adhered to, it would require that all the appointments for the supreme executive, legislative, and judiciary magistracies should be drawn from the same fountain of authority, the people, through channels having no communication whatever with one another. Perhaps such a plan of constructing the several departments would be less difficult in practice than it may in contemplation appear. Some difficulties, however, and some additional expense would attend the execution of it. Some deviations, therefore, from the principle must be admitted. In the constitution of the judiciary department in particular, it might be inexpedient to insist rigorously on the principle: first, because peculiar qualifications being essential in the members, the primary consideration ought to be to select that mode of choice which best secures these qualifications; second, because the permanent tenure by which the appointments are held in that department must soon destroy all sense of dependence on the authority conferring them.

It is equally evident that the members of each department should be as little dependent as possible on those of the others for the emoluments annexed to their offices. Were the executive magistrate, or the judges, not independent of the legislature in this particular, their independence in every other would be merely nominal.

In the following passages, which are among the most widely quoted of Madison's writings, he explains how the separation of the powers of government into three branches helps to counter the effects of personal ambition on government. The separation of powers allows personal motives to be linked to the constitutional rights of a branch of government. In effect, competing personal interests in each branch will help to keep the powers of the three government branches separate and, in so doing, will help to guard the public interest.

But the great security against a gradual concentration of the several powers in the same department consists in giving to those who administer each department the necessary constitutional means and personal motives to resist encroachments of the others. The provision for defense must in this, as in all other cases, be made commensurate to the danger of attack. Ambition must be made to counteract ambition. The interest of the man must be connected with the constitutional rights of the place. It may be a reflection on human nature that such devices should be necessary to control the abuses of government. But what is government itself but the greatest of all reflections on human nature? If men were angels, no government would be necessary. If angels were to govern men, neither external nor internal controls on government would be necessary. In framing a government which is to be administered by men over men, the great difficulty lies in this: you must first enable the government to control the governed; and in the next place oblige it to control itself. A dependence on the people is, no doubt, the primary control on the government; but experience has taught mankind the necessity of auxiliary precautions.

This policy of supplying, by opposite and rival interests, the defect of better motives, might be traced through the whole system of human affairs, private as well as public. We see it particularly displayed in all the subordinate distributions of power, where the constant aim is to divide and arrange the several offices in such a manner as that each may be a check on the other—that the private interest of every individual may be a sentinel over the public rights. These inventions of prudence cannot be less requisite in the distribution of the supreme powers of the State.

Madison now addresses the issue of equality among the branches of government. The legislature will necessarily predominate, but if the executive is given an "absolute negative" (absolute veto power) over legislative actions, this also could lead to an abuse of power. Madison concludes that the division of the legislature into two "branches" (parts, or chambers) will act as a check on the legislature's powers.

But it is not possible to give to each department an equal power of self-defense. In republican government, the legislative authority necessarily predominates. The remedy for this inconveniency is to divide the legislature into different branches; and to render them, by different modes of election and different principles of action, as little connected with each other as the nature of their common functions and their common dependence on the society will admit. It may even be necessary to guard against dangerous encroachments by still further precautions. As the weight of the legislative authority requires that it should be thus divided, the weakness of the executive may require, on the other hand, that it should be fortified. An absolute negative on the legislature appears, at first view, to be the natural defense with which the executive magistrate should be armed. But perhaps it would be neither altogether safe nor alone sufficient. On ordinary occasions it might not be exerted with the requisite firmness, and on extraordinary occasions it might be perfidiously abused. May not this defect of an absolute negative be supplied by some qualified connection between this weaker department and the weaker branch of the stronger department, by which the latter may be led to support the constitutional rights of the former, without being too much detached from the rights of its own department?

If the principles on which these observations are founded be just, as I persuade myself they are, and they be applied as a criterion to the several State constitutions, and to the federal Constitution, it will be found that if the latter does not perfectly correspond with them, the former are infinitely less able to bear such a test.

In the remainder of the essay, Madison discusses how a federal system of government, in which powers are divided between the states and the national government, offers "double security" against tyranny.

There are, moreover, two considerations particularly applicable to the federal system of America, which place that system in a very interesting point of view.

First. In a single republic, all the power surrendered by the people is submitted to the administration of a single government; and the usurpations are guarded against by a division of the government into distinct and separate departments. In the compound republic of America, the power surrendered by the people is first divided between two distinct governments, and then the portion allotted to each subdivided among distinct and separate departments. Hence a double security arises to the rights of the people. The different governments will control each other, at the same time that each will be controlled by itself.

Second. It is of great importance in a republic not only to guard the society against the oppression of its rulers, but to guard one part of the society against the injustice of the other part. Different interests necessarily exist in different classes of citizens. If a majority be united by a common interest, the rights of the minority will be insecure. There are but two methods of providing against this evil: the one by creating a will in the community independent of the majority—that is, of the society itself; the other, by comprehending in the society so many separate descriptions of citizens as will render an unjust combination of a majority of the whole very improbable, if not impracticable. The

first method prevails in all governments possessing an hereditary or self-appointed authority. This, at best, is but a precarious security; because a power independent of the society may as well espouse the unjust views of the major as the rightful interests of the minor party, and may possibly be turned against both parties. The second method will be exemplified in the federal republic of the United States. Whilst all authority in it will be derived from and dependent on the society, the society itself will be broken into so many parts, interests and classes of citizens, that the rights of individuals, or of the minority, will be in little danger from interested combinations of the majority.

In a free government the security for civil rights must be the same as that for religious rights. It consists in the one case in the multiplicity of interests, and in the other in the multiplicity of sects. The degree of security in both cases will depend on the number of interests and sects; and this may be presumed to depend on the extent of country and number of people comprehended under the same government. This view of the subject must particularly recommend a proper federal system to all the sincere and considerate friends of republican government, since it shows that in exact proportion as the territory of the Union may be formed into more circumscribed Confederacies, or States, oppressive combinations of a majority will be facilitated; the best security, under the republican forms, for the rights of every class of citizen, will be diminished; and consequently the stability and independence of some member of the government, the only other security, must be proportionally increased. Justice is the end of government. It is the end of civil society. It ever has been and ever will be pursued until it be obtained, or until liberty be lost in the pursuit. In a society under the forms of which the stronger faction can readily unite and oppress the weaker, anarchy may as truly be said to reign as in a state of nature, where the weaker individual is not secured against the violence of the stronger; and as, in the latter state, even the stronger individuals are prompted, by the uncertainty of their condition, to submit to a government which may protect the weak as well as themselves; so, in the former state, will the more powerful factions or parties be gradually induced, by a like motive, to wish for a government which will protect all parties, the weaker as well as the more powerful. It can be little doubted that if the State of Rhode Island was separated from the Confederacy and left to itself, the insecurity of rights under the popular form of government within such narrow limits would be displayed by such reiterated oppressions of factious majorities that some power altogether independent of the people would soon be called for by the voice of the very factions whose misrule had proved the necessity of it. In the extended republic of the United States, and among the great variety of interests, parties, and sects which it embraces, a coalition of a majority of the whole society could seldom take place on any other principles than those of justice and the general good; whilst there being thus less danger to a minor from the will of a major party, there must be less pretext, also, to provide for the security of the former, by introducing into the government a will not dependent on the latter, or, in other words, a will independent of the society itself. It is no less certain than it is important, notwithstanding the contrary opinions which have been entertained, that the larger the society, provided it lie within a practicable sphere, the more duly capable it will be of self-government. And happily for the republican cause, the practicable sphere may be carried to a very great extent by a judicious modification and mixture of the *federal principle*.

Publius
(James Madison)

Government Spending and Revenue Charts

Do you find some of these percentages surprising? If so, which ones?

Federal Government Spending

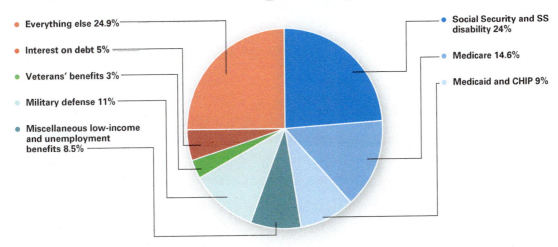

- Everything else 24.9%
- Interest on debt 5%
- Veterans' benefits 3%
- Military defense 11%
- Miscellaneous low-income and unemployment benefits 8.5%

- Social Security and SS disability 24%
- Medicare 14.6%
- Medicaid and CHIP 9%

Federal Government Revenues

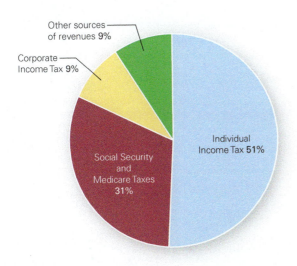

Other sources of revenues 9%

Corporate Income Tax 9%

Individual Income Tax 51%

Social Security and Medicare Taxes 31%

Source: Economic Indicators, various issues.

Glossary

A

Actual Malice Either knowledge of a defamatory statement's falsity or a reckless disregard for the truth.

Advice and Consent Terms in the Constitution describing the U.S. Senate's power to review and approve treaties and presidential appointments.

Affirmed To declare that a court ruling is valid and must stand.

Affirmative Action A policy in educational admissions or job hiring that gives special attention or compensatory treatment to traditionally disadvantaged groups in an effort to overcome present effects of past discrimination.

Affordable Care Act (ACA) A law passed in 2010 that seeks, among other things, to provide health care insurance to all American citizens. The act has been nicknamed "Obamacare."

Agency Capture The act by which an industry being regulated by a government agency gains direct or indirect control over agency personnel and decision makers.

Agenda Setting Determining which public-policy questions will be debated or considered.

***Amicus Curiae* Brief** A written legal argument filed by a third party, or *amicus curiae* (Latin for "friend of the court"), who is not directly involved in the litigation but who has an interest in the outcome of the case.

Anti-Federalist An individual who opposed the ratification of the new Constitution in 1787. The Anti-Federalists were opposed to a strong central government.

Appellate Court A court having jurisdiction to review cases and issues that were originally tried in lower courts.

Appointment Power The president's authority to fill a government office or position.

Appropriation The passage, by Congress, of a spending bill specifying the amount of authorized funds that actually will be allocated for an agency's use.

Arraignment The first act in a criminal proceeding, in which the defendant is brought before a court to hear the charges against them and enter a plea of guilty or not guilty.

Australian Ballot A secret ballot prepared, distributed, and tabulated by government officials at public expense. Since 1888, all states have used the Australian ballot rather than an open, public ballot.

Authoritarianism A type of regime in which only the government itself is fully controlled by the ruler. Social and economic institutions exist that are not under the government's control.

Authority The right and power of a government or other entity to enforce its decisions.

Authorization A formal declaration by a legislative committee that a certain amount of funding may be available to an agency. Some authorizations terminate in a year. Others are renewable automatically without further congressional action.

B

Bias An inclination or a preference that interferes with impartial judgment.

Bicameral Legislature A legislature made up of two parts, called chambers. The U.S. Congress, composed of the House of Representatives and the Senate, is a bicameral legislature.

Bicameralism The division of a legislature into two separate assemblies.

Bill of Attainder A law that inflicts punishment without a trial.

Bill of Rights The first ten amendments to the U.S. Constitution.

Block Grants Federal grants that provide funds to a state or local government for a general functional area, such as criminal justice or mental-health programs.

Blog A regular updating of one's ideas on a specific website. The word comes from web log.

Budget Deficit Government expenditures that exceed receipts.

Bureaucracy A large organization that is structured hierarchically to carry out specific functions.

C

Cabinet An advisory group selected by the president to aid in making decisions. The cabinet includes the heads of fifteen executive departments and others named by the president.

Cabinet Departments One of the fifteen major departments of the executive branch.

Capitalism An economic system characterized by the private ownership of wealth-creating assets, free markets, and freedom of contract.

Case Law Judicial interpretations of common law principles and doctrines, as well as interpretations of constitutional law, statutory law, and administrative law.

Casework In the example of Congress, personal work for constituents.

Categorical Grants Federal grants to a state or local government for a specific program or project.

Caucus System A meeting of party members to select candidates and propose policies.

Checks and Balances A major principle of the American system of government whereby each branch of the government can check the actions of the others.

Chief Diplomat The role of the president in recognizing foreign governments, making treaties, and effecting executive agreements.

Chief Executive The role of the president as head of the executive branch of the government.

Chief Legislator The role of the president in influencing the making of laws.

Chief of Staff The person who is named to direct the White House Office and advise the president.

Civil Disobedience A nonviolent, public refusal to obey allegedly unjust laws.

Civil Liberties Those personal freedoms, including freedom of religion and of speech, that are protected for all individuals in a society.

Civil Rights Generally, all rights rooted in the Fourteenth Amendment's guarantee of equal protection under the law.

Civil Service A collective term for employees of the government. Generally, civil service is understood to apply to all those who gain government employment through a merit system.

Civil Service Commission The initial central personnel agency of the national government, created in 1883.

Class-Action Suit A lawsuit filed by an individual seeking damages for "all persons similarly situated."

Closed Primary A type of primary in which the voter is limited to choosing candidates of the party of which they are a member.

Cold War The ideological, political, and economic confrontation between the United States and the Soviet Union following World War II.

Commander in Chief The role of the president as supreme commander of the military forces of the United States and of the state National Guard units when they are called into federal service.

Commerce Clause The section of the Constitution in which Congress is given the power to regulate trade among the states and with foreign countries.

Commercial Speech Advertising statements, which increasingly have been given First Amendment protection.

Common Law The body of law developed from judicial decisions in English and U.S. courts, not attributable to a legislature.

Commutations A reduction in the length of the sentence of someone convicted of a crime. Commutation does not overturn the conviction itself.

Concentrated Benefits and Dispersed Costs The theory that a minority benefiting from a government program will make a stronger effort to keep it than the majority will ever make to abolish it.

Concurrent Powers Powers held jointly by the national and state governments.

Concurring Opinion A separate opinion prepared by a judge who supports the decision of the majority of the court but for different reasons.

Confederal System A system consisting of a league of independent states, in which the central government created by the league has only limited powers over the states.

Confederation A political system in which states or regional governments retain ultimate authority except for those powers they expressly delegate to a central government.

Conference Committees Special joint committees appointed to reconcile differences when bills pass the two chambers of Congress in different forms.

Consensus General agreement among the citizenry on an issue.

Conservatism A set of beliefs that includes a limited role for the national government in helping individuals, support for traditional values and lifestyles, and a cautious response to change.

Conservative Movement An American movement founded in the 1950s that provides a comprehensive ideological framework for conservative politics.

Constituents Persons represented by a legislator or other elected or appointed official.

Constitutional Powers Powers vested in the president by Article II of the Constitution.

Containment A U.S. diplomatic policy adopted by the Truman administration to contain Communist power within its existing boundaries.

Continuing Resolution A temporary funding law that Congress passes when an appropriations bill has not been passed by the beginning of the new fiscal year on October 1.

Cooperative Federalism A model of federalism in which the states and the national government cooperate in solving problems.

Cracking In gerrymandering, splitting the opposing party's voters into many different districts.

Credentials Committee A committee used by political parties at their national conventions to determine which delegates may participate.

D

De Facto Segregation Racial segregation that occurs because of patterns of racial residence and similar social conditions.

De Jure Segregation Racial segregation that occurs because of laws or administrative decisions by public agencies.

Defamation of Character Wrongfully hurting a person's good reputation.

Defense Policy A subset of national security policy concerning the U.S. armed forces.

Democracy A system of government in which political authority is vested in the people.

Democratic Party One of the two major American political parties evolving out of the Republican Party of Thomas Jefferson. It was formed in 1828.

Democratic Republic A republic in which leaders elected by the people make and enforce laws and policies.

Détente A French word meaning a relaxation of tensions. The term characterized U.S.-Soviet relations as they developed under President Richard Nixon and Secretary of State Henry Kissinger.

Devolution The transfer of powers from a national or central government to a state or local government.

Diplomacy The process by which states carry on political relations with each other. Also, the process of settling conflicts among nations by peaceful means.

Diplomatic Recognition The formal acknowledgment of a foreign government as legitimate.

Direct Democracy A system of government in which political decisions are made by the people directly, rather than by their elected representatives.

Direct Primary A primary election in which voters decide party nominations by voting directly for candidates.

Direct Techniques An interest group technique that uses direct interaction with government officials to further the group's goals.

Discharge Petition A procedure by which a bill in the House of Representatives may be forced (discharged) out of a committee that has refused to report it for consideration by the House.

Dissenting Opinion A separate opinion in which a judge dissents from (disagrees with) the conclusion reached by the majority of the court and expounds their own views about the case.

Diversity of Citizenship The condition that exists when the parties to a lawsuit are from different states or when the suit involves a U.S. citizen and a government or citizen of a foreign country. Diversity of citizenship can provide a basis for federal jurisdiction.

Divided Government A situation in which one major political party controls the presidency and the other controls one or more chambers of Congress, or in which one party controls a state governorship and the other controls the state legislature.

Divided Opinion Public opinion that is polarized between two different positions.

Domestic Policy All government laws, planning, and actions that concern internal issues of national importance, such as health care, the environment, and the economy.

Dual Federalism A model of federalism that looks on national and state governments as co-equal sovereign powers. Neither the state government nor the national government should interfere in the other's sphere.

E

Earmarks Special provisions in legislation to set aside funds for projects that have not passed an impartial evaluation by agencies of the executive branch. Also known as pork.

Economic Aid Assistance to other nations in the form of grants, loans, or credits to buy the assisting nation's products.

Elastic Clause, or Necessary and Proper Clause The clause in Article I, Section 8, that grants Congress the power to do whatever is necessary to execute its specifically delegated powers.

Electors Members of the Electoral College, which selects the president and vice president. Each state's electors are chosen in each presidential election year according to state laws.

Electoral College A group of persons, called electors, that officially elects the president and the vice president of the United States. The electors are selected by each state and the District of Columbia.

Elite Theory The argument that society is ruled by a small number of people who exercise power to further their self-interest.

Emergency Powers An inherent power exercised by the president during a period of national crisis.

Enabling Legislation A statute enacted by Congress that authorizes the creation of an administrative agency and specifies the name, purpose, composition, functions, and powers of the agency being created.

Entitlement Programs A government program that entitles a defined class of people to obtain benefits. Entitlements operate under open-ended budget authorizations that do not limit how much can be spent.

Enumerated Powers Powers specifically granted to the national government by the Constitution. The first seventeen clauses of Article I, Section 8, specify most of the enumerated, or expressed, powers of the national government.

Equality As a political value, the idea that all people are of equal worth.

Establishment Clause The part of the First Amendment prohibiting the establishment of a church officially supported by the national government.

Ex Post Facto Law A law that inflicts punishment for an act that was not illegal at the time it was committed.

Exclusionary Rule A judicial policy prohibiting the admission at trial of illegally seized evidence.

Executive Agreements International agreements made by the president, without senatorial ratification, with the head of a foreign state.

Executive Budget The budget prepared and submitted by the president to Congress.

Executive Office of the President (EOP) An organization established by President Franklin Roosevelt to assist the president in carrying out major duties.

Executive Orders Rules or regulations issued by the president that has the effect of law.

Executive Privilege The right of executive officials to withhold information from, or to refuse to appear before, a legislative committee or a court.

Expressed Powers Powers of the president that is expressly written into the Constitution or into statutory law.

F

Federal Election Commission (FEC) The federal regulatory agency with the task of enforcing federal campaign laws. As a practical matter, the FEC's role is largely limited to collecting data on campaign contributions.

Federal Mandates Requirements in federal legislation that force states and municipalities to comply with certain rules.

Federal Open Market Committee The most important body within the Federal Reserve System. The Federal Open Market Committee decides how monetary policy should be carried out.

Federal Question A question that has to do with the U.S. Constitution, acts of Congress, or treaties. A federal question provides a basis for federal jurisdiction.

Federal Register A daily publication of the U.S. government that prints executive orders, rules, and regulations.

Federal Reserve System (the Fed) The system created by Congress in 1913 to serve as the nation's central banking organization.

Federalist An individual who was in favor of the adoption of the U.S. Constitution and the creation of a federal union with a strong central government.

Feminism The movement that supports political, economic, and social equality for women.

Filibuster The use of the Senate's tradition of unlimited debate as a delaying tactic to block bills or nominations.

Fiscal Having to do with government revenues and expenditures.

Fiscal Federalism A process by which funds raised through taxation or borrowing by one level of government (usually the national government) are spent by another level (typically, state or local governments).

Fiscal Policy The federal government's use of taxation and spending policies to affect overall business activity.

Fiscal Year (FY) A twelve-month period that is used for bookkeeping or accounting purposes. Usually, the fiscal year does not coincide with the calendar year. For example, the federal government's fiscal year runs from October 1 through September 30.

Focus Group A small group of individuals who are led in discussion by a professional consultant to gather opinions on, and responses to, candidates and issues.

Foreign Policy A nation's external goals and the techniques and strategies used to achieve them.

Fracking Short for hydraulic fracturing, the injection of a high-pressure solution of water, sand, and chemicals into hydrocarbon-bearing rocks, releasing oil or natural gas.

Framing In a media report, the technique of embedding an issue in particular examples or story lines to alter public perceptions of the issue.

Free Exercise Clause The provision of the First Amendment guaranteeing the free exercise of religion.

Free-Rider Problem The difficulty that interest groups face in recruiting members when the benefits they achieve can be gained without joining the group.

Front-Loading The practice of moving presidential primary elections to the early part of the campaign to maximize the impact of these primaries on the nomination.

Front-Runner The presidential candidate who appears to be ahead at a given time in the primary season.

G

Gender Discrimination Any practice, policy, or procedure that denies equality of treatment to an individual or to a group because of gender.

Gender Gap The difference between the percentage of women who vote for a particular candidate and the percentage of men who vote for the candidate.

General Election An election, normally held on the first Tuesday in November, that determines who will fill various elected positions.

General Jurisdiction A court's authority to hear cases that is not significantly restricted. A court of general jurisdiction normally can hear a broad range of cases.

Generational Effect A long-lasting effect of the events of a particular time on the political opinions of those who came of political age at that time.

Gerrymandering The drawing of legislative district boundary lines for the purpose of obtaining partisan advantage. A district is said to be gerrymandered when its shape is altered substantially to determine which party will win it.

GOP A nickname for the Republican Party, which stands for "grand old party."

Government The institution that has the ultimate authority for making decisions that resolve conflicts and allocate benefits and privileges within a society.

Government Corporation An agency of government that administers a quasi-business enterprise. These corporations are used when government activities are primarily commercial.

Government in the Sunshine Act A law that requires all committee-directed federal agencies to conduct their business regularly in public sessions.

Grandfather Clause A device used by southern states to disenfranchise African Americans. It restricted voting to those whose ancestors had voted before 1867.

Great Compromise The compromise between the New Jersey and Virginia plans that created one chamber of the Congress based on population and one chamber representing each state equally; also called the Connecticut Compromise.

Gross Domestic Product (GDP) The dollar value of all final goods and services produced in a one-year period.

H

Hatch Act An act passed in 1939 that restricted the political activities of government employees. It also prohibited a political group from spending more than $3 million in any campaign and limited individual contributions to a campaign committee to $5,000.

Head of State The role of the president as ceremonial head of the government.

Hispanic Someone who can claim a heritage from a Spanish-speaking country. Hispanics may be of any race.

House Effect In public opinion polling, an effect in which one polling organization's results consistently differ from those reported by other poll takers.

I

Ideology A comprehensive set of beliefs about the nature of people and about the role of an institution or government.

Imminent Lawless Action Test The current standard established by the Supreme Court for evaluating the legality of advocacy speech. Such speech can be forbidden only when it is "directed to inciting . . . imminent lawless actions."

Impeachment An action by the House of Representatives to accuse the president, vice president, or other civil officers of the United States of committing "Treason, Bribery, or other high Crimes and Misdemeanors."

Incorporation Theory The view that the protections of the Bill of Rights apply to state governments through the Fourteenth Amendment's due process clause.

Independents A voter or candidate who does not identify with a political party.

Independent Executive Agencies A federal agency that is not part of a cabinet department but reports directly to the president.

Independent Expenditures Unregulated political expenditures by PACs, organizations, and individuals that are not coordinated with candidate campaigns or political parties.

Independent Regulatory Agencies An agency outside the major executive departments charged with making and implementing rules and regulations within a specific area.

Indirect Primary A primary election in which voters choose convention delegates, and the delegates determine the party's candidate in the general election.

Indirect Techniques An interest group technique that uses third parties to influence government officials.

Inflation A sustained rise in the general price level of goods and services.

Inherent Powers Powers of the president derived from the statements in the Constitution that "the executive Power shall be vested in a President" and that the president should "take Care that the Laws be faithfully executed."

Initiative A procedure by which voters can petition to vote on a law or a constitutional amendment.

Institution An ongoing organization that performs certain functions for society.

Instructed Delegates Legislators or convention delegates who are agents of the voters who elected them and who vote according to the views of constituents, regardless of personal beliefs.

Intelligence Community The government agencies that gather information about the capabilities and intentions of foreign governments or that engage in covert actions.

Interest Groups Organized groups of individuals sharing common objectives who actively attempt to influence policymakers.

Intermediate, or Exacting, Scrutiny A judicial standard used to determine whether a law or government action unconstitutionally discriminates against women.

Internet Service Provider (ISP) A corporation or service that sells access to the internet.

Interstate Compacts Agreements between two or more states.

Invisible Primary The preprimary campaign to win supporters among elected officials, fundraisers, interest groups, and opinion leaders.

Iron Triangle A three-way alliance among legislators in Congress, bureaucrats, and interest groups to make or preserve policies that benefit their respective interests.

Isolationist Foreign Policy A policy of abstaining from an active role in international affairs or alliances, which characterized U.S. foreign policy toward Europe during most of the 1800s.

Issue Advocacy Advertising Advertising paid for by interest groups that support or oppose a candidate's position on an issue without mentioning the candidate, voting, or elections.

Issue Network A group of individuals or organizations—which may consist of legislators and legislative staff members, interest group leaders, bureaucrats, scholars and other experts, and media representatives—that supports a particular policy position on a given issue.

J

Joint Committee A legislative committee composed of members from both chambers of Congress.

Judicial Activism A doctrine holding that the federal judiciary should take an active role by using its powers to check the activities of governmental bodies when those bodies exceed their authority.

Judicial Implementation The way in which court decisions are translated into action.

Judicial Restraint A doctrine holding that courts should defer to the decisions made by the elected representatives of the people in the legislative and executive branches when possible.

Judicial Review The power of the Supreme Court or any court to examine and possibly declare unconstitutional federal or state laws and other acts of government.

Jurisdiction The authority of a court to decide certain cases. Not all courts have the authority to decide all cases. When a case arises and what its subject matter is are two jurisdictional issues.

Justiciable Controversy A controversy that is real and substantial, as opposed to hypothetical or academic.

K

Keynesian Economics A school of economic thought that favors active federal government policy making to stabilize economy-wide fluctuations, including the use of discretionary fiscal policy.

Kitchen Cabinet The informal advisers to the president.

L

Labor Movement The economic and political expression of working-class interests.

Lawmaking The process of establishing the legal rules that govern society.

Legislature A governmental body primarily responsible for the making of laws.

Legitimacy Popular acceptance of the right and power of a government or other entity to exercise authority.

Libel A written defamation of a person's character or reputation. The defamatory statement must be observed by a third party.

Liberalism A set of beliefs that includes advocacy of positive government action to improve the welfare of individuals, support for civil rights, and tolerance for political and social change.

Libertarianism A political ideology based on skepticism or opposition toward most government activities.

Liberty The greatest freedom of the individual that is consistent with the freedom of other individuals in the society.

Limited Government A government with powers that are limited either through a written document or through widely shared beliefs.

Limited Jurisdiction A court's authority to hear cases that is restricted to certain types of claims, such as tax claims or bankruptcy petitions.

Line Organizations In the federal government, an administrative unit that is directly accountable to the president.

Literacy Test A test administered as a precondition for voting, often used to prevent African Americans from exercising their right to vote.

Litigate To engage in a legal proceeding or seek relief in a court of law. To carry on a lawsuit.

Lobbyists Organizations or individuals who attempt to influence the passage, defeat, or content of legislation and the government's administrative decisions.

Loopholes A legal method by which individuals and businesses are allowed to reduce the tax liabilities they owe to the government.

M

Madisonian Model A structure of government proposed by James Madison, in which the powers of the government are separated into three branches: executive, legislative, and judicial.

Majoritarianism A political theory holding that in a democracy, the government ought to do what the majority of the people want.

Majority Leader of the House A leader elected by the majority party in the House to assist the Speaker and foster party cohesion.

Majority Opinion A court opinion reflecting the views of the majority of the judges.

Majority Rule A basic principle of democracy asserting that the greatest number of citizens in any political unit should select officials and determine policies.

Markup In the U.S. Congress, the process by which committees and subcommittees amend or rewrite proposed legislation.

Media The channels of mass communication.

Medicaid A joint state-federal program that provides medical care to the poor (including indigent elderly persons in nursing homes). The program is funded out of general government revenues.

Medicare A federal health insurance program that covers U.S. residents over the age of sixty-five. The costs are met in part by a tax on wages and salaries.

Merit System The selection, retention, and promotion of government employees on the basis of competitive examinations.

Midterm Elections National elections in which candidates for president are not on the ballot. In midterm elections, voters choose all members of the U.S. House of Representatives and one-third of the members of the U.S. Senate.

Minority Leader of the House The party leader elected by members of the minority party in the House.

Monetary Policy The use of changes in the amount of money in circulation to alter credit markets, employment, and the rate of inflation.

Monroe Doctrine A policy statement made by President James Monroe in 1823. The United States would not accept any new European intervention in the Western Hemisphere. In return, the United States would not meddle in European affairs.

Moral Idealism A philosophy that views nations as normally willing to cooperate and to agree on moral standards for conduct.

N

National Committee A standing committee of a national political party established to direct and coordinate party activities between national party conventions.

National Convention The meeting held every four years by each major party to select presidential and vice-presidential candidates, write a platform, choose a national committee, and conduct party business.

National Security Council (NSC) An agency in the Executive Office of the President that advises the president on national security.

National Security Policy Foreign and domestic policy designed to protect the nation's independence and political integrity. Policy that is concerned with the safety and defense of the nation.

Natural Rights Rights held to be inherent in natural law, not dependent on governments.

Net Neutrality The principle that an ISP should treat all traffic equally.

O

Office of Management and Budget (OMB) A division of the Executive Office of the President. The OMB assists the president in preparing the annual budget, clearing and coordinating departmental agency budgets, and supervising the administration of the federal budget.

Open Primary A primary in which any voter can vote in either party primary (but must vote for candidates of only one party).

Opinion A statement by a judge or a court of the decision reached in a case. An opinion sets forth the applicable law and details the reasoning on which the ruling was based.

Opinion Leader One who is able to influence the opinions of others because of position, expertise, or personality.

Opinion Polls A method of systematically questioning a small, selected sample of respondents who are deemed representative of the total population.

Oral Arguments The arguments presented in person by attorneys to an appellate court.

Order A state of peace and security. Maintaining order by protecting members of society from violence and criminal activity is one of the oldest purposes of government.

Oversight In a legislature, the process by which it follows up on laws it has enacted to ensure that they are being enforced and administered as Congress intended.

P

Packing In gerrymandering, packing as many voters as possible of the opposing party into a single district.

Pardons A release from the punishment for, or legal consequences of, a crime. A pardon can be granted by the president before or after a conviction.

Party Identification Linking oneself to a particular political party.

Party Organization The formal structure and leadership of a political party, including election committees; local, state, and national executives; and paid professional staff.

Party Platform A document drawn up at each national convention, outlining the policies, positions, and principles of the party.

Patronage The practice of rewarding faithful party workers and followers with government employment and contracts.

Peer Groups Groups consisting of members who share common social characteristics. Such groups play an important part in the socialization process, helping to shape attitudes and beliefs.

Pendleton Act (Civil Service Reform Act) An act that established the principle of federal government employment based on merit and created the Civil Service Commission to administer the personnel service.

Pluralism A theory that views politics as a conflict among interest groups. Political decision making is characterized by bargaining and compromise.

Plurality A number of votes cast for a candidate that is greater than the number of votes for any other candidate but not necessarily a majority.

Plurality Opinion An opinion by a minority of the Court that decides a case because it is supported by one or more concurring opinions.

Pocket Veto A special veto exercised by the chief executive after a legislative body has adjourned. Bills not signed by the chief executive die after a specified period of time.

Police Power The authority to legislate for the protection of the health, morals, safety, and welfare of the people. In the United States, most police power is reserved to the states.

Policy Demanders Individuals or interest group members who participate in political parties with the intent to see that certain policies are adopted or specific groups favored.

Political Action Committees (PACs) Committees set up by and representing a corporation, labor union, or interest group. PACs raise campaign donations.

Political Consultant A paid professional hired to devise a campaign strategy and manage a campaign.

Political Culture A patterned set of ideas, values, and ways of thinking about government and politics that characterizes a people.

Political Party A group of political activists who organize to win elections, operate the government, and determine public policy.

Political Question An issue that a court believes should be decided by the executive or legislative branch, or both.

Political Realism A philosophy that views each nation as acting principally in its own interest.

Political Socialization The process by which people acquire political beliefs and values.

Politics The struggle over power or influence within organizations or informal groups that can grant or withhold benefits or privileges.

Poll Tax A special tax that had to be paid as a qualification for voting. The Twenty-fourth Amendment to the Constitution outlawed the poll tax in national elections, and in 1966, the Supreme Court declared it unconstitutional in state elections as well.

Popular Sovereignty The concept that ultimate political authority is based on the will of the people.

Precedent A court ruling bearing on subsequent legal decisions in similar cases. Judges rely on precedents in deciding cases.

President pro tempore The temporary presiding officer of the Senate in the absence of the vice president.

Presidential Primary A statewide primary election of delegates to a political party's national convention, held to determine a party's presidential nominee

Primary Election An election in which political parties choose their candidates for the general election.

Priming In a media report, using only certain facts to shape the public's response to an issue.

Prior Restraint Restraining an activity before it has actually occurred. When expression is involved, this means censorship.

Privatization The replacement of government services with services provided by private firms.

Progressive A popular alternative to the term *liberal*.

Progressive Tax A tax that rises in percentage terms as incomes rise.

Property Anything that is or may be subject to ownership.

Public Agenda Issues that are perceived by the political community as meriting public attention and governmental action.

Public Figure A public official, movie star, or other person known to the public because of their positions or activities.

Public Interest The best interests of the overall community. Also, the national good, rather than the narrow interests of a particular group.

Public Opinion The aggregate of individual attitudes or beliefs shared by some portion of the population.

Public, or National, Debt The total amount of debt carried by the federal government.

R

Ratification Formal approval.

Rational Basis Review A judicial standard for assessing a law or government action that is employed when neither strict nor intermediate scrutiny apply.

Realignment A large-scale, lasting change in the types of voters who support each of the major political parties.

Reapportionment The allocation of seats in the House of Representatives to each state after a census.

Recall A procedure allowing the people to vote to dismiss an elected official from office before his or her term has expired.

Recession An economic downturn, usually characterized by a fall in the GDP and rising unemployment.

Reconciliation In Congress, a special rule that can be applied to budget bills sent from the House of Representatives to the Senate. Reconciliation measures cannot be filibustered.

Redistricting The redrawing of the boundaries of the congressional districts within each state.

Referendum An electoral device whereby legislative or constitutional measures are referred by the legislature to the voters for approval or disapproval.

Registration The entry of a person's name onto the list of registered voters for elections. To register, a person must meet certain legal requirements of age, citizenship, and residency.

Regressive Tax A tax that falls in percentage terms as incomes rise.

Regular Order In Congress, channeling proposed legislation through committee and subcommittee hearings, with solicited testimony and votes on revised language.

Remanded To send a case back to the court that originally heard it.

Representation The function of members of Congress as elected officials representing the views of their constituents as well as larger national interests.

Representative Democracy A form of government in which leaders elected by the people make and enforce laws and policies, but in which the monarchy may be retained in a ceremonial role.

Reprieves Formal postponements of the execution of a sentence imposed by a court of law.

Republic A form of government in which sovereign power rests with the people, rather than with a king or a monarch.

Republican Party One of the two major American political parties. It emerged in the 1850s as an antislavery party and consisted of former northern Whigs and antislavery Democrats.

Reversed To annul or make void a court ruling on account of some error or irregularity.

Reverse Discrimination Discrimination against individuals who are not members of an underrepresented group.

Rule of Four A United States Supreme Court procedure by which four justices must vote to grant a petition for review if a case is to come before the full court.

Rules Committee A standing committee of the House of Representatives that provides special rules under which specific bills can be debated, amended, and considered by the House.

S

Sampling Error The difference between a sample result and the true result if the entire population had been interviewed.

Select Committee A temporary legislative committee established for a limited time period and for a special purpose.

Senate Majority Leader The chief spokesperson of the majority party in the Senate, who directs the legislative program and party strategy.

Senate Minority Leader The party officer in the Senate who commands the minority party's opposition to the policies of the majority party and directs the legislative program and strategy of his or her party.

Seniority System A custom followed in both chambers of Congress specifying that the member of the majority party with the longest term of continuous service will be given preference when a committee chairperson (or a holder of some other significant post) is selected.

Separate-but-Equal Doctrine The doctrine holding that separate-but-equal facilities do not violate the equal protection clause of the Fourteenth Amendment to the U.S. Constitution.

Separation of Powers The principle of dividing governmental powers among different branches of government.

Service Sector The sector of the economy that provides services—such as health care, banking, and education—in contrast to the sector that produces goods.

Sexual Harassment Unwanted physical or verbal conduct or abuse of a sexual nature that interferes with a recipient's job performance, creates a hostile work environment, or carries with it an implicit or explicit threat of adverse employment consequences.

Signing Statement A written declaration that the president may make when signing a bill into law. It may contain instructions to the bureaucracy on how to administer the law or point to sections of the law that the president considers unconstitutional or contrary to national security interests.

Slander The public uttering of a false statement that harms the good reputation of another. The statement must be made to, or within the hearing of, someone other than the defamed party.

Social Contract A voluntary agreement among individuals to secure their rights and welfare by creating a government and abiding by its rules.

Social Movements Movements that represent the demands of a large segment of the public for political, economic, or social change.

Socialism A political ideology based on strong support for economic and social equality. Socialists traditionally envisioned a society in which major businesses were taken over by the government or by employee cooperatives.

Socioeconomic Status The value assigned to a person due to occupation or income. A professional person with a substantial income, for example, has high socioeconomic status.

Soft Money Campaign contributions unregulated by federal or state law, usually given to parties and party committees to help fund general party activities.

Sound Bite A brief, memorable comment that can easily be fit into news broadcasts.

Soviet Bloc The Soviet Union and the Eastern European countries that installed Communist regimes after World War II and that were dominated by the Soviet Union.

Speaker of the House The presiding officer in the House of Representatives. The Speaker is chosen by the majority party and is the most powerful and influential member of the House.

Spin An interpretation of political events that is favorable to a candidate or officeholder.

Spin Doctors Political advisers who try to convince journalists of the truth of a particular interpretation of events.

Splinter Parties A new party formed by a dissident faction within a major political party. Often, splinter parties have emerged when a particular personality was at odds with the major party.

Spoils System The awarding of government jobs to political supporters and friends.

Standing Committees Permanent committees in the House or Senate that consider bills within a certain subject area.

Stare Decisis To stand on decided cases—the judicial policy of following precedents established by past decisions.

States A group of people occupying a specific area and organized under one government. It may be either a nation or a subunit of a nation.

State Central Committee The principal organized structure of each political party within each state. This committee is responsible for carrying out policy decisions of the party's state convention.

State of the Union Message An annual message to Congress in which the president proposes a legislative program. The message is addressed not only to Congress but also to the American people and to the world.

Statutory Powers Powers created for the president through laws enacted by Congress.

Straight-Ticket Voting Voting exclusively for the candidates of one party.

Strict Scrutiny A judicial standard for assessing the constitutionality of a law or government action when the law or action threatens to interfere with a fundamental right or potentially discriminates against members of a suspect classification.

Subpoenas An order by a court or legislative committee requiring that an individual appear and testify.

Suffrage The right to vote; the franchise.

Super PAC A political organization that aggregates unlimited contributions by individuals and organizations to be spent independently of candidate committees.

Superdelegates A party leader or elected official who is given the right to vote at the party's national convention. Superdelegates are not elected at the state level.

Supremacy Clause The constitutional provision that makes the Constitution and federal laws superior to all conflicting state and local laws.

Supremacy Doctrine A doctrine that asserts the priority of national law over state laws. This principle is stated in Article VI of the Constitution.

Suspect Classification A classification, such as race, religion, or national origin, that triggers strict scrutiny by the courts when a law or government action potentially discriminates against members of the class.

Symbolic Speech Expression made through articles of clothing, gestures, and other forms of nonverbal conduct.

T

Terrorism A systematic attempt to inspire fear to gain political ends, typically involving the indiscriminate use of violence against noncombatants.

Third Party A political party other than the two major political parties (Republican and Democratic).

Totalitarian Regime A form of government that controls all aspects of the political, social, and economic life of a nation.

Transgender Persons Persons whose gender identity, expression, and/or role does not conform to what is culturally associated with their sex assignment at birth.

Treasuries U.S. Treasury securities—bills, notes, and bonds. Debt issued by the federal government.

Trial Court The court in which most cases begin.

Truman Doctrine The policy adopted by President Harry Truman in 1947 to halt Communist expansion.

Trustees In a legislature, members who act according to their conscience and the broad interests of the entire society.

Twelfth Amendment An amendment to the Constitution, adopted in 1804, that specifies the separate election of the president and the vice president by the Electoral College.

Twenty-Fifth Amendment A 1967 amendment to the Constitution that establishes procedures for filling presidential and vice-presidential vacancies and makes provisions for presidential incapacity.

Two-Party System A political system in which only two parties have a reasonable chance of winning.

U

Unanimous Opinion A court opinion or determination on which all judges agree.

Unemployment The inability of those who are in the labor force to find a job.

Unicameral Legislatures A legislature with only one legislative chamber, as opposed to a bicameral (two-chamber) legislature, such as the U.S. Congress.

Unit Rule A rule by which all of a state's electoral votes are cast for the presidential candidate who receives a plurality of the votes in that state.

Unitary System A centralized governmental system in which ultimate governmental authority rests in the hands of the national, or central, government.

Universal Suffrage   The right of all adults to vote for their representatives.

V

Veto Message   The president's formal explanation of a veto, which accompanies the vetoed legislation when it is returned to Congress.

Vote-Eligible Population   The number of people who, at a given time, enjoy the right to vote in national elections.

Voter Turnout   The percentage of citizens taking part in the election process. Also, the number of eligible voters who actually "turn out" to cast their ballots.

Voting-Age Population   The number of people of voting age living in the country at a given time, regardless of whether they have the right to vote.

W

War Powers Resolution   A law passed in 1973 spelling out the conditions under which the president can commit troops without congressional approval.

Wave Election   An election in which voters display dissatisfaction with one of the major parties through a "wave" of support for the other. In contrast to a realigning election, the results of a wave election are not permanent.

Whig Party   A major party in the United States during the first half of the nineteenth century, formally established in 1836. The Whig Party was anti-Jackson and advocated spending on infrastructure.

Whips   A member of Congress who aids the majority or minority leader of the House or the Senate.

Whistleblower   In the context of government, someone who brings gross governmental inefficiency or an illegal action to the public's attention.

White House Office   The personal office of the president, which tends to presidential political needs and manages the media.

White Primary   A state primary election that restricted voting to whites only. Outlawed by the Supreme Court in 1944.

Working Class   Currently, those with no college education. Traditionally, individuals or families in which the head of household was employed in manual or unskilled labor.

Writ of *Certiorari*   An order issued by a higher court to a lower court to send up the record of a case for review.

Writ of *Habeas Corpus*   *Habeas corpus* means, literally, "you have the body." A writ of *habeas corpus* is an order that requires jailers to bring a prisoner before a court or judge and explain why the person is being held.

Subject Index

A

AARP (formerly American Association of
  Retired Persons), 329
    accomplishments of, 159
Abortion
    partial-birth, 84, 300
    privacy rights and, 82–84
    special interest groups and, 159
Absentee ballots, 196
Accuracy in Media, 148
Accused, rights of
    basic rights, 87–88
    exclusionary rule, 88–89
    Miranda warning, 88
Actual malice, 80
Adams, John, 25, 167
Adams, John Quincy, 24, 168, 195, 237
Adams, Samuel, 38
Adarand Constructors, Inc. v. Peña, 106
Administrative agency, as source of
    American law, 311
Administrative law tribunals, 288
Administrative Procedure Act, 247
Advertising
    campaigns ads by special interest
        groups, 186
    First Amendment protection and, 79
    issue advocacy, 186
    media's profit-making function and, 139
    political, 143
Advice and consent, 239–241
Affirmation of judgment, 292
Affirmative action, 105–107
    defined, 105
    end of, 106–107
    implementing, 105
    limits on, 106
Affordable Care Act (ACA), 9
    details of, 315
    legal challenges to, 314
    Obamacare, 314–316
    passage of, 315
    policymaking process, 310–312
    reconciliation used for, 214–215
    states and Medicare expansion, 62
Afghanistan
    al Qaeda and, 337
    American invasion of, 240
    federalization of National Guard, 53
    Northern Alliance, 337
    Taliban government in, 333, 337
AFL (American Federation of Labor), 155
AFL-CIO, 155
African Americans
    civil rights and, 96–104, 153
    consequences of slavery and, 96–104
    equality and, 9

extralegal methods of enforcing white
    supremacy, 98
importance of religion, 203
incarceration rate, 103
Jim Crow laws, 98
lynching and, 98
percentage of U.S. population, 9
political participation by, 102
as public officials, 182
school integration and, 99
separate-but-equal doctrine, 98–99
social and economic disparities, 102–104
support of Democratic Party, 169
voter behavior, 101–102, 130
voting rights of, 96, 98, 101, 201
Agency capture, 266
Agenda building, health care and, 310–311
Agenda setting
    by Congress, 211
    defined, 125
    by media, 126, 138
    priming and framing, 138
Aggregators, 140
Agriculture Department
    functions of, 267
    in iron triangle, 278
    subagencies of, 267
Agriculture interest groups, 154
al Qaeda
    in Afghanistan, 337
    goals of, 336
    insurgency in Iraq, 337
    in Pakistan, 338
    reasons for attack, 335
    rise of ISIS, 338
    September 11, 2001 terrorist attacks
        and, 336
al-Assad, Bashar, 2, 338, 341
Alien "removal" courts, 289–290
Alito, Samuel, 295, 299
Allende, Salvador, 348
American Bar Association (ABA), 157
American Civil Liberties Union, 152
American Dairy Association, 153
American Farm Bureau Federation, 155, 278
American Federation of Labor (AFL), 155
American Federation of Teachers, 156
American Friends Service Committee, 356
American Indians
    assimilation, 111
    demographic collapse of, 111
    gambling casinos, 112
American League of Lobbyists, 153
American Revolution, 5, 24
American Woman Suffrage Association, 112
Americans for Democratic Action, 159, 161
Americans for Tax Reform, 159

Amicus curiae brief, 286
Amnesty International, 355
AMTRAK, 269
Anthony, Susan B., 112
Anti-Federalists, 37, 38, 167
Anti-Ku Klux Klan Act (Civil Rights Act of
    1872), 97
Antiterrorism and Effective Death Penalty
    Act, 110, 111
Appellate court, 287, 288
Apple, government surveillance and, 91
Appointment power, 239
Appropriation, 231
Arab Spring, 335
Aristocracy, 4
Arraignment, 87
Articles of Confederation, 47
    accomplishments under, 30
    government established under, 30
    weaknesses of, 30–31
Asian Americans
    percentage of U.S. population, 10
    voting behavior, 127–128
Assembly, freedom of, 70
Association, freedom of limits on rights of,
    and deportees, 110–111
Association of Government Relations
    Professionals, 153
Astroturf lobbying, 162
Australia, federal system of government
    in, 48
Australian ballot, 196
Authoritarianism, 4
Authority, 3
Authorization, 231

B

Bad tendency rule, 77
Bagram Air Force Base, 290
Ballots
    absentee, 196
    Australian, 196
    voting by mail, 196
Banking industry
    bank bailout, 269
    banking crisis of 2008, 269
    government ownership of, 269
    national bank, 54
Bankruptcy, government control of private
    corporations and, 269
Bathroom Bill Issue, 118
Bear arms, right to, 70
Benghazi, Libya consulate attack, 210
Benton v. Maryland, 71
Bias, in media, 146–147
Bicameral legislature, 208
Bicameral (two-chamber) legislature, 33

Bicameralism, 208
Biden, Joe, 210, 235, 250
  cabinet of, 250
  candidate committees, 188
  and media, 147
  political participation, 102
  votes by groups, 128
  White House Office, 251
Biden Administration, 268
Big government, 13
  entitlement programs and, 309
  Great Recession and, 13
  liberals and, 16
  Obamacare and, 13
Bill, becomes a law, 228
Bill of attainder, 69
Bill of Rights. *See also individual*
    amendments
  adoption of, 39
  defined, 10
  extending to state government, 70
  freedom of expression (*See* Press,
    freedom of; Speech, freedom of)
  incorporating Fourteenth Amendment
    into, 70–71
  incorporation theory, 70–71
  ratification, 39
Bin Laden, Osama, 333
  death of, 254, 338
Bipartisan Campaign Reform Act, 186
Bisexuals. *See* Lesbian, Gay, Bisexual and
    Transgender (LGBT)
Blackburn, Marsha, 169
Blackmun, Harry A., 76
Blanket primary, 192
Block grants, 66
Blog, 143
Blogosphere politics, 145
Blue states, 170
Boehner, John, 215
Bork, Robert, 296
Bosnia, 347
  American troops sent to, 240
Boston Globe, 139
Boston Marathon bombing, 336
Boston Tea Party, 26
Boumediene v. Bush (2008), 290
Bowers v. Hardwick, 116
Bradford, William, 23
Brady Handgun Violence Prevention
    Act, 62
Branch Ministries, Inc., 74
Brandeis, Louis, 49
Brandenburg v. Ohio, 77
Brazil, federal system of government in, 48
Brexit, 346
Breyer, Stephen, 297
Broad construction, 299
Brown, John, 56
Brown, Linda Carol, 98
Brown, Oliver, 98
Brown v. Board of Education of Topeka,
    98–99
Bryan, Williams Jennings, 169, 171
Buckley v. Valeo, 185
Budget. *See* Federal budget
Budget deficit
  deficit spending and, 322
  defined, 321
  Great Recession and increase in, 61, 323

Keynes on, 321
  public debt and, 322–324
Budget surplus, 324
Bull Moose Progressive Party, 176
Bureau of the Budget, 252
  conservatives' view of, 16
Bureaucracy, 260–279
  congressional control of, 279
  defined, 260
  history of civil service, 270–272
  iron triangles, 278
  issue network, 278–279
  merit system, 271
  nature of, 260–263
  organization of federal, 263–269
    cabinet departments, 264–266
    chart of, 265
    government corporations, 268–269
    independent executive agencies, 266
    independent regulatory agencies, 266
  policymaking and, 278–279
  political appointees, 270
  private, 260
  privatization and, 273–274
  public, 260
  reform, modern attempts at, 272–275
  size of, 260–261
  spoils system, 271
  staffing, 270–272
  sunshine laws and, 273
  whistleblowers and, 274–275
Bureaucrats, as policymakers and
    politicians, 278–279
Burger, Warren, 77
Burr, Aaron, 237
Burwell v. Hobby Lobby, 301
Bush, George H. W.
  approval rating of, 136
  armed forces ordered by
    into combat without congressional
      approval, 349
    into Middle East, 240
    into Panama, 240
  Flag Protection Act, 76
  foreign policy and, 353
  judicial appointment and, 295
  reregulation and, 268
  Soviet Union and, 353
Bush, George W., 235
  approval rating of, 136
  armed forces ordered by
    invasion of Afghanistan, 240
    invasion of Iraq, 240
    in Iraq, 336, 347
  Cheney as vice president, 253
  election of 1992, 176
  election of 2000, 170, 176
    electoral college, 238
    Latino vote, 130–131
    Muslim American support for, 130
    Supreme Court decision and, 290–291
    winning without popular vote, 195
    without majority of vote, 238
  election of 2004, demographics and, 128
  federal government's reach expanded
    by, 59
  federalization of National Guard, 53
  financial crisis of 2008 and deregulation,
    268
  as fundraiser, 244

greenhouse gas emissions, 276
  inherent powers and fighting terrorism,
    246
  Iraq war and, 337, 347
  judicial appointment, 295
  No Child Left Behind Act, 59
  partial-birth abortions, 84
  public approval of, 245
  signing statements and, 248
  suspected terrorist detainees, 290
  tax cuts, 324
  use veto power, 243
  war on terrorism, 289, 336
  warrantless wiretaps, 90
Bush, Jeb, 86
Bush v. Gore (2000), 291
Business cycle, 321
Business interest groups, 154
Busing, 99–100

C
Cabinet
  defined, 250
  kitchen, 251
  members of, 250–251
  presidential use of, 251
Cabinet departments
  defined, 264
  listed, 267
  president and, 264
Cameron, David, 346
Campaign financing, 184–188
  Buckley v. Valeo, 185
  Citizens decision, 187–188
  current environment of, 186–187
  evolution of, 185–186
  Federal Election Campaign Act
    (FECA), 185
  501(c)4 organizations, 188
  527 organizations, 187–188
  interest groups and, 185
  issue advocacy advertising, 186
  political action committees (PACs), 185
  president as fundraiser, 244
  presidential candidate committees, 187
  public financing for primaries, 188
  regulating, 185–186
  soft money, 186
  super PACs, 187
Campaigns
  advertising, 144
  candidate-centered, 183
  changes in, from those earlier, 182
  coattail effect and, 217
  federal employees and, 272
  financing (*See* Campaign financing)
  focus groups and, 184
  goals of, 182–183
  interest groups and assistance with, 160
  Internet and, 144–145
  managing news coverage, 143–144
  media and, 142–147
  opinion polls and, 184
  political consultants and, 184
  power of incumbency, 218
  presidential debates, 142, 144
  professional, 183–184
  role of parties in, 183
  twenty-first century, 181

Canada
  federal system of government in, 48
  health care spending and, 309
  lobbying by, 159
  U.S. oil imports from, 317
Candidate(s), 180–181
  African Americans as, 182
  candidate-centered campaigns, 183
  coattail effect and, 217
  for congressional elections, 217
  power of incumbency, 218
  professionals as, 182
  recruiting, by political parties, 163
  women as, 182
Cantwell v. Connecticut, 71
Capital gains, 328
Capitalism
  defined, 12
  laissez-faire capitalism, 17
CARES Act
  agenda building, 310–311
  COVID-19 pandemic, 312
  impact of reforms, 312
  policy adoption, 311
  policy evaluation, 312
  policy formulation, 311
  policy implementation, 311–312
Caribbean, lobbying by, 159
Carter, Jimmy, 190
  China and, 353
  deregulation, 268
  election of 1980, 135
  as evangelical, 130
  judicial appointment and, 294
  Mondale and, 253
  People's Republic of China recognized
    by, 241
  public approval of, 245
Case citations, 52
Case law, 284–285
Casework, 210
Categorical grants, 60
Catholics
  Democratic Party and, 169
  voting behavior, 127, 128
Caucus, 191, 221
Caucus system, 192
Central Intelligence Agency (CIA)
  creation of, 348
  criticism of, 348
Certiorari, writ of, 291
Chamber of Commerce, U.S., 154
Change to Win Coalition, 155
Checks and balances, 35–36
  judicial review and, 298
Cheney, Dick, 348
Cheney, Liz, 207
Chicago Tribune, 139
Chief diplomat, 241–242
Chief executive, 239–240
Chief legislator, 242–244
Chief of staff, 252
Children
  child labor, 57–58
  political socialization of, 124
  pornography and, 78
Children's Health Insurance Program
    (CHIP), 313
Children's Internet Protection Act (CIPA),
    78

China
  aid provided to North Korea by, 351
  Communist Party of, 3
  current account surplus, 344
  cyberattacks on U.S. computers networks,
    345
  economic growth of, 346
  foreign policy and, 343–344
  formal diplomatic recognition of, 353
  Great Firewall of, 142
  nationalism, 345
  nuclear weapons and, 339
  ownership of U.S. public debt, 322
  President Carter's recognition of, 241
  relationship with North Korea, 341
  Taiwan and, 344–345
Christianity, nation's founders and, 25
CIO (Congress of Industrial Organizations),
    155
Circuit courts of appeals, U.S., 287
*Citizens United v. Federal Election
    Commission,* 43
Civil Aeronautics Board, 268
Civil contempt, 286
Civil disobedience, 100
Civil liberties, 68–92
  bill of attainder, 69
  Bill of Rights and, 69–71
  versus civil rights, 95
  defined, 10
  ex post facto law, 69
  freedom of expression, 75–81
  freedom of religion, 71–75
  freedom of speech, 75–81
  freedom of the press, 80
  privacy rights, 81–86
  protections in original
    Constitution, 69
  rights of accused *vs.* rights of society,
    86–91
  search and seizure, 92
  vs. security issues, 90
  writ of *habeas corpus,* 69
Civil right(s)
  African Americans and consequences of
    slavery, 96–104
  versus civil liberties, 95
  civil rights movement, 99–100
  courts and, 104–107
  defined, 95
  immigration and, 107–109
  King's philosophy of nonviolence, 100
  Latinos and, 107–109
  of LGBTQ+ rights movement, 116
  March on Washington, 100
  modern legislation regarding, 100–104
  Native Americans and, 111–112
  transgender individuals, 118
  women and, 112–115
Civil Rights Act
  of 1866, 97
  of 1872 (Anti-Ku Klux Klan Act), 97
  of 1875 (Second Civil Rights Act), 97
  of 1964, 100
  of 1968, 101
  ineffectiveness of early civil rights laws,
    97–98
  Title VII, 100, 115
Civil Rights Cases, 97
Civil rights movement, 96–104, 153, 170

Civil service
  defined, 239
  difficulty in firing, 270
  history of, 270–272
  merit system, 271
  political campaigns and, 272
  whistleblowers and, 274–275
Civil Service Commission, 271
Civil Service Reform Act
  of 1883, 271–272
  of 1978, 272
Civil War
  civil liberties suspended during, 246
  national government's growth and, 56–57
  political parties during, 168
  slavery and, 57
  states' rights and, 55–57
Class-action suits, 286
Clean Air Act, 319
Clean Power Plan (CPP), 277
Climate change
  addressing issue, 319
  debate over, 318–319
Clinton, Bill, 74
  appointments by, 117
  approval rating of, 136
  armed forces ordered by
    to bomb Serbia, 240
    to Bosnia, 240, 347
    into combat without congressional
      approval, 347
    to Haiti, 240, 347
  budget surplus during, 324
  deregulation, 268
  "don't ask, don't tell" policy, 117
  election of
    1992, 176
    without majority of vote, 237
  as evangelical, 130
  as fundraiser, 244
  judicial appointment and, 297
  welfare reform, 59
Clinton, Hillary Rodham, 11, 254
  Arab Spring and, 335
  debates, 144
  election of 2016
    campaign spending, 188
    faithless electors, 195
    as female candidate, 182
    national convention, 195
    perception of, and voting behavior, 202
    popular vote, 237
    winning popular vote but not electoral
      college, 195
  gender gap, 131
  media and, 144–145
  opinion poll predictions, 135
  private email server issue, 147
  as Secretary of State Benghazi
    attack, 210
Closed primary, 191
Cloture, 213–214
Coercive Acts, 26
Cohen, Bernard, 125
Cohen, Marty, 166
Cohort effect, 126
Cold War
  defined, 340
  superpower relations during, 351–354
Cole, Tom, 207

Colleges
  campus speech and behavior codes, 79
  political correctness on campus, 79
  segregation, 97
Colonial America
  British taxation of, 26
  Continental Congresses, 26
  Declaration of Independence, 28–29
  establishment of, 23
  Mayflower compact, 23–24
  rise of Republicanism, 29
Combat Exclusion Policy, 114
Comcast, 141
Comey, James, 249
Commander in chief, 240–241
Commerce
  defined, 55
  interstate, 55
  intrastate, 55
Commerce clause, 41
  defined, 55
  Gibbons v. Ogden, 55
  limiting national government's authority
    under, 63
Commerce Department
  functions of, 267
  subagencies of, 267
Commercial speech, 76
Common Cause, 158
Common law
  defined, 283
  tradition of, 283
Common Sense (Paine), 26
Concentrated benefits and dispersed costs,
  163
Concurrent powers, 52–53
Concurring opinions, 292
Confederal system
  defined, 47–48
  flow of power in, 48
Confederation, 30
Conference committee, 223–224
Conflict resolution, Congress and, 211
Congress, 207–232. *See also* House of
    Representatives, of the United
    States; Senate, of the United States
  apportionment and, 217–218
  bicameralism of, 208
  budget and, 228–232
  bureaucracy and control of by, 279
  checks and balances, 35–36
  checks on courts and, 303
  committees of
    members of, selection of, 224–225
    power of, 222
    structure of, 221–228
    types of, 223–224
  contacting representative, 232
  Democratic control of, 13, 170
  earmarks and, 209
  elections for, 209, 216–220
    voter turnout and, 196, 197–198
  foreign policy and balancing president, 349
  formal leadership in, 225
  functions of, 208–213
    conflict-resolution, 211
    lawmaking, 209
    oversight, 210
    public-education, 211
    representation function, 209
    service to constituents, 210

  health care reform, 299
  incumbency and power of, 217
  lawmaking, 209
    bill becomes a law, 228
    president as chief legislator and, 242
  logrolling, 209
  members of
    age of, 215
    compared to citizenry, 215–216
    income and wealth of, 216
    minorities, 215
    perks of, 216
    privileges and immunities of, 216
    professional staff, 216
    religion of, 215
    requirements for office, 181
    salary of, 216
    term of, 208
    women as, 112–114, 182, 215–216
  opposition to Obamacare, 316
  powers of
    constitutional amendments, 212
    to declare war, 42, 240
    enumerated, 50–51, 211–212
    inherent, 51
    necessary and proper clause, 51,
      212–213
    to override presidential veto, 243–244
    of the purse, 349
    regulate foreign and interstate
      commerce, 41
  president as chief legislator, 242–244
  public opinion regarding, 202
  Republican control of, 13, 170
  seniority system, 225
  separation of powers, 35
Congress of Confederation, 30
Congress of Industrial Organizations (CIO),
  155
Congressional Budget Office, 62
Congressional elections, 216–221
  candidates for, 217
  coattail effect, 217
  midterm gains and losses by party of
    president, 217
  power of incumbency, 217
  requirements for, 218
Congressional Union for Woman Suffrage,
  112
Connecticut Compromise, 208
The Conscience of a Liberal, 145
Consensus, 123
Consent of the people, 5
Conservative movement
  defined, 16
  modern, 16
Conservatives/conservatism
  Cuban Americans, 130–131
  defined, 16
  economic status and, 129
  entitlement spending, 309
  favoring state government, 63
  four-cornered ideological grid, 18, 129
  global warming and, 318
  judicial restraint and, 299
  modern, 16
  Muslim Americans, 130
  political blogs, 145
  Republican Party and, 16
  on traditional political spectrum, 17–18
  values of, 16

Constituent governments, 48
Constituents
  defined, 208
  as lobbyists, 161–162
  of president, 244
  service to, by members of Congress, 210
Constitution of United States, 22–43.
    See also Bill of Rights
  altering, 39–43
    formal amendment process of, 40–41
    informal means to, 41–42
  Amendment to
    Eighth, 71, 86
    Fifth, 71, 81, 86
    First (*See* First Amendment)
    Fourteenth, 70–71
    Fourth, 71, 81, 86, 88, 89
    Ninth, 71, 81, 82
    Second, 70, 71
    Sixth, 71, 86, 88
    Third, 70, 71, 81
  Amendments to
    to check courts, 303
    Fifteenth, 199
    Fifteenth, 96, 97, 98
    First (*See* First Amendment)
    Fourteenth (*See* Fourteenth
      Amendment)
    listed, 40
    Nineteenth, 199
    Nineteenth, 112
    Seventeenth, 208
    Sixteenth, 212, 303
    Tenth, 46, 51, 52
    Thirteenth, 96
    Twelfth, 212, 237
    Twentieth, 212
    Twenty-fifth, 212, 255
    Twenty-fourth, 98
    Twenty-second Amendment,
      248–249
    Twenty-sixth, 199
  Article I of, 208, 245
    Section 4 of, 216–217
    Section 6 of, 216
    Section 8 of, 41, 50, 51, 55, 211
    Section 10 of, 69
  Article II of, 42, 239
    Section 1, 194, 236, 254, 346
    Section 2, 239, 293
    Section 3, 242
  Article III of, Section 1, 285
  Article IV of
    Section 1, 53
    Section 2, 53
  Article V of, 39
  Article VI of
    Christianity and, 25
    Clause 2 of, 53
    drafting, 32–37
      checks and balances, 35–36
      Constitutional Convention, 32–37
      electoral college and, 37
      Great Compromise, 33–34
      Madisonian model, 35
      New Jersey Plan, 33
      separation of powers, 35
      slavery and, 34–35
      Supremacy doctrine, 33
      three-fifths compromise, 34
      Virginia Plan, 33

powers under
  of Congress, 40
  of president, 42
Preamble to, 23
ratification, 37–39
civil liberties protection in original, 69
commerce clause, 55
drafting, Constitutional Convention, 48
equal protection clause, 104, 113
necessary and proper clause, 51
powers under
  of Congress, 40
  of president, 42, 239
slavery under, 96
as source of American law, 283
supremacy clause and, 53
Constitutional Convention, 32–37, 48
Constitutional democracy, 6
Constitutional powers, 245
Consumer movement, 158
Consumer price index, 320
Consumer Reports, 158
Consumers Union, 158
Containment policy, 351
Contempt of court, 239
Content providers, 140
Continental Illinois, 269
Continuing resolution, 231
Contractionary monetary policy, 326
Convention delegates, 164–165
Cooperative federalism
  defined, 58
  methods of implementing, 60–62
  New Deal and, 58
Cornwallis, Charles, 29
Coronavirus, 8–9
Council of Economic Advisers, 251
Council on Environmental Quality, 251
Court of Appeals for the Thirteenth Circuit,
  287
Courts, 282–305
  appellate courts, 287
  civil rights and, 104–107
  common law tradition and, 283–285
  contempt of court, 239
  executive checks, 302–303
  federal (*See* Federal court system)
  impact of lower courts, 304
  judicial activism, 299
  judicial restraint, 299
  judicial traditions and doctrine, 304
  legislative checks, 303
  parties to lawsuits, 285–291
  policymaking function, 298–304
  political question, 304
  procedural rules, 286
  requirements to bring case before, 285
  sources of American law and, 283–285
  state (*See* State courts)
  Supreme Court (*See* Supreme Court of
    United States)
  trial courts, 286
Courts of appeal, U.S., 287
COVID-19, 8–9, 261
Cracking, in redistricting, 219
Crawford, William H., 237
Credentials committee, 194
Criminal contempt, 286
Cross burning, 76
Crossley, Archibald, 133

*Cruzan v. Director, Missouri Department of
  Health,* 85
Cuban Americans, 130–131
  voting behavior, 130–131
Cuban missile crisis, 352
Culture
  dominant, 9
  political, 9

D

Daesh, 338
The Daily Show, 138
Daley, Richard J., 165
De facto segregation, 99
De Jonge v. Oregon, 71
De jure segregation, 99
Death with dignity law, 63
Debs, Eugene V., 175
Debt ceiling, 231
Declaration of Independence
  natural rights and social
    contracts, 28–29
  significance of, 29
  universal truths, 28
Declaration of Sentiments, 112
Defamation of character, 78
Defendants, 285
  pretrial rights, 87
Defense Department, 333
  creation of, 348
  foreign policymaking and, 349
  functions of, 267
  size of, 349
  subagencies of, 267
Defense of Marriage Act, 117
Defense policy, 333
Defense spending, amount of federal budget,
  262
Deficit hawks, 264
Deficit spending
  Obama and stimulus package, 322
  public debt and, 322–324
Delegates
  caucus system for choosing, 192
  convention activities, 194
  to national convention, 193–194
  seating, 194
  selecting, 164–165
  superdelegates, 190
Democracy
  constitutional, 6
  defined, 4
  direct, 4–5
  elite theory and, 7
  for groups, 8
  majoritarianism and, 7
  pluralism and, 8
  principles of, 6
  in United States, 6–9
Democratic Party
  blue states and, 170–171
  Congress controlled by, 13, 171
  convention delegates, 164–165
  debt ceiling crisis, 231
  economic status, 129
  education and, 127
  formation of, 168
  gender gap and, 131
  geographic region and, 131–132
  health care reform, 299

history of, 167–172
liberalism and, 17
midterm elections of 2010 and, 171
midterm elections of 2014 and, 171
National Convention of, in 1968, 189
nuclear option and judicial appointments,
  215
Obama and young voters, 131
party identification and, 176
policy demanders in, 166
populism and, 169
in post-Civil War period, 168–169
race and ethnicity, 130
regaining control of presidential primary,
  193
today, 171–172
unauthorized immigrants and Obama's
  executive order, 144
voters who grew up in Great Depression,
  126
wave elections and, 171
Democratic republic
  compared to representative democracy, 6
  defined, 5–6
Democratic Republicans, 168
Depression, 324. *See also* Great Depression
Deregulation, 268
Desegregation, 100
Détente, 352–353
Devolution, 58
Dictators, 3
Diplomacy
  as aspect of foreign policy, 333
  defined, 333
Diplomatic recognition, 241
Direct democracy
  dangers of, 5
  defined, 4
Direct payments, 155
Direct techniques of interest groups,
  160–161
Discharge petition, 222
Discouraged workers, 320
Discretionary fiscal policy, 321
Discrimination
  affirmative action and, 105–107
  dealing with, 119
  employment, 105
  gender and, 113
  housing, 101
  against potential jurors, 286
  race and, 96–104
  reverse, 106
  sexual orientation and, 117
  wage, 115
Dissenting opinion, 292
District courts, United States, 286–287
Diversity of citizenship, 285
Divided government, 166
  era of, 170
Divided opinion, 123
Domestic policy, 308–329
  defined, 309
  energy and environment, 316–319
  health care and, 312–316
  promotional policy, 309
  redistributive policy, 309
  regulatory policy, 309
Dominant culture, 9
Double jeopardy, 71, 88
Douglas, William O., 81

Dropbox, 142
Dual federalism, 57–58
Due process, limits on rights of, and
    deportees, 110
Due process clause, 104, 116
Duterte, Rodrigo, 334

E

Earmarked expenditures, 209
Earth Day, 158
East Germany, 351
Economic aid, 333
Economic equality, 11–12
Economic interest groups, 154–158
Economic policy, 320–327
    deficit spending and public debt, 322–324
    entitlement reform, 329
    fiscal policy, 322
    monetary policy, 324–327
    politics of taxation, 327–329
Economic status
    liberalism and conservatism, 129
    voting behavior and, 129
Economy, health care's role in, 312
Education
    aid to church-related schools, 72
    busing, 99–100
    forbidding teaching of evolution, 73
    No Child Left Behind Act, 59
    political socialization and, 124
    school integration and, 99
    school prayer and, 73
    school vouchers, 72
    separate-but-equal doctrine, 98–99
    voting behavior and, 127
Education Department
    functions of, 267
    subagencies of, 267
Edwards, Natalie, 275
Egalitarianism, 12
Egypt
    Arab Spring, 335
    dictatorial rule in, 4
    unitary system of government in, 47
Eighth Amendment, 71, 86
Eisenhower, Dwight D., 170, 239, 240
    cabinet of, 251
    pact with vice president regarding
      incapacity of, 255
    school integration and, 99, 303
Elastic clause, 51
Elections. *See also* Primary elections
    economic issues influence on, 170
    general, 182
    organization and running of, by political
      parties, 163
    primary, 182
Electoral college
    choosing president, 236–237
    defined, 37, 173
    drafting Constitution and, 37
    election of 2000, 170, 244
    electors, 194
    problems with, 195
    unit rule, 173
    winner-take-all system, 173–174
Electors, 173
    choosing, 194
    defined, 194
    faithless, 194–195

Elite theory, 7
Emancipation Proclamation, 96
Emergency powers, 246
Employment discrimination
    Civil Rights Act and, 105
    gender-based, 114
Employment rates, Great Recession and, 13
Endangered Species Act, 260, 276
Energy Department
    functions of, 71
    subagencies of, 267
Energy policy, 316–318
    America's reliance on foreign oil,
      316–319
    fracking, 317
    higher fuel efficiency standards for
      vehicles, 317
    legislation to limit greenhouse gas
      emissions, 319
    new U.S. production, 317
    politics of expensive oil, 317
    Russia's invasion of Ukraine, 318
    subsidies for alternative fuels, 316
Enforcement Act of 1870, 97
Engel v. Vitale, 73
Enlightenment rationalism, 25
Entitlement programs
    controversy over value of, 309
    defined, 309, 313
    reform of, 329
    Social Security, Medicare and Medicaid
      as, 309, 313, 329
    spending on, 309
Enumerated powers, 50–51, 211–212
Environmental Defense Fund, 158
Environmental interest groups, 158
Environmental policy, 316–319
    America's reliance on foreign oil, 316
    climate change, 318–319
    legislation to limit greenhouse emission,
      319
Equal Employment Opportunity
    Commission (EEOC), 100, 105
Equal Pay Act, 115
Equal protection clause, 39, 97–98, 104, 220
    affirmative action and, 105
    gender discrimination and, 113
Equal Rights Amendment, 113
Equality
    African Americans and, 11
    defined, 11
    economic, 11–12
    liberty *versus*, 11–12
Eras
    of divided government, 170–171
    of good feelings, 168
    New Deal, 170
Espionage Act, 76, 275
Establishment clause, 71–74
Estate tax, 329
Ethanol, 317
Ethnicity, voting behavior and, 130
European Central Bank (ECB), 345
European Union (EU)
    Brexit, 346
    as confederal system of government, 48
    debt crisis, 345
    lobbying by, 159
Everson v. Board of Education, 71, 72
Evidence, exclusionary rule, 88

Evolution, teaching of, 73
Ex post facto law
    limits on rights of, and deportees, 111
    protection against, in Constitution, 69
Exacting scrutiny, 104–105
Exclusionary rule, 71, 88–89
    good faith exception, 89
    plain view doctrine, 89
Executive agencies
    agency capture, 266
    deregulation and reregulation, 268
    purpose and nature of, 266
Executive agreements, 42, 242, 347
Executive branch
    checks and balances, 35–36
    electoral college, 37
    separation of powers, 35
    structure of, 263–269
Executive Office of the President, 251–252
    agencies within, 251
    defined, 251
    National Security Council, 253
    Office of Management and Budget, 252
    White House Office, 252
Executive order, 247
    immigration reform, 109
Executive privilege, 247–248
Expansionary monetary policy, 326
Export taxes, 35
Expressed powers, 50, 245
Expression, freedom of. *See* Press, freedom
    of; Speech, freedom of

F

Facebook, 140–142, 145
    impact on public opinion, 125
Factions, among delegates to Constitutional
    Convention, 32–33
Fairness and Accuracy in Reporting, 148
Fairness Doctrine, 125
Faithless electors, 194–195
False Claims Act, 274
Family, political socialization and, 124
Fannie Mae, 269
Farm Bureau, 155
Faubus, Orval, 99, 303
Fed. *See* Federal Reserve System (Fed)
Federal budget, 228–232
    budget deficit and Keynes, 321
    budget resolutions and crisis, 231–232
    categories of spending, 269
    Congress and, 231
    continuing resolution, 231, 232
    debt ceiling and, 231
    defense spending, 262
    deficit (*See* Budget deficit)
    election-year budgets, 230–231
    executive budget, 230
    preparing budget, 230
    size of, 269
    social spending of, 262
Federal Circuit, 287
Federal Communications Commission
    (FCC), 266
    Fairness Doctrine, 125
    net neutrality and, 141–142
Federal court system, 285–293
    alien "removal" courts, 289–290
    basic judicial requirements for cases, 285
    constitutional authority for, 285

executive checks, 302–303
FISA court, 289
impact of lower courts on, 304
judicial activism, 299
judicial appointment, 293–295
judicial restraint, 299
judicial traditions and doctrine, 304
jurisdiction, 285
legislative checks, 303–304
parties to lawsuits, 285–286
policymaking function of, 298–304
procedural rules, 286
Supreme Court (*See* Supreme Court of United States)
suspected terrorist detainees, 290
types of courts
administrative law tribunals, 288
courts of appeals, 287
district courts, 286–287
Supreme Court, 288
as three-tiered system, 286–288
war on terrorism and, 289–290
Federal Deposit Insurance Corporation (FDIC), 269
Federal Election Campaign Act (FECA), 185
Federal Election Commission (FEC)
creation of, 185
501(c)4 organizations, 188
Federal Employees Political Activities Act, 272
Federal government. *See* National government
Federal grants
block, 60–61
categorical, 60
conditions attached to, 62
Federal Home Loan Mortgage Corporation, 269
Federal mandates, 62
Federal National Mortgage Association, 269
Federal Open Market Committee, 325
Federal question, 285, 288
Federal Register, 247, 276, 277
Federal Reserve System (Fed)
Board of Governors of, 325
defined, 325
functions of, 325
organization of, 325
Federal system, 48. *See also* Federalism
Federal Trade Commission (FTC), 160
Federalism, 46–65
arguments against, 50
benefit of, for United States, 49
characteristics of, 47
constitutional basis for, 50–54
cooperative, 58
devolution, 59
dispute over division of power, 57–62
dual, 57
fiscal federalism, 61
politics of, 58
Supreme Court and
early years, 54–57
today, 62–64
Federalist Papers, 35, 38, 50, 214
Federalists, 167–168
ratification of Constitution, 37–39
Feminine Mystique, The (Friedan), 113
Feminism, 113
Fertility rate, 108

Fifteenth Amendment, 57, 96, 97, 98, 199
Fifth Amendment, 71, 81, 86
Filibuster, 214
advantages and disadvantages of, 215–216
constitutionality of, 214
increased use of, 214
nuclear option, 215
reconciliation, 214–215
Films. *See* Movies
First Amendment
clear and present danger, 76
commercial speech, 76
cross burning, 76
establishment clause, 73
federal employees and, 272
flag burning, 76
free exercise clause, 74–75
freedom of press (*See* Press, freedom of)
freedom of religion (*See* Religion, freedom of)
freedom of speech (*See* Speech, freedom of)
hate speech, 69
imminent lawless action test, 77
incorporation theory, 70–71
interest groups and, 148
privacy rights and, 81
symbolic speech, 75
First Bank of the United States, 54
First budget resolution, 230
First Continental Congress, 26
First Gulf War, 337
FISA court, 289
Fiscal federalism, 61
Fiscal policy, 322
criticism of Keynes, 322
defined, 61, 321
discretionary fiscal policy, 321
government spending and borrowing, 321
timing problem of, 322
Fisher v. University of Texas, 106
501(c)4 organizations, 188
527 organizations, 187–188
Flag Protection Act, 76
Flynn, Michael, 250
Focus group, 184
Food stamps, 309
Ford, Gerald, armed forces ordered by into combat without congressional approval, 349
Foreign Affairs, 351
Foreign governments, lobbying by, 159
Foreign Intelligence Surveillance Act (FISA), 289
after September 11, 289
establishment of, 289
National Security Agency and, 289
Foreign policy, 332–356
Afghanistan and, 337–338
Arab Spring, 335
China and, 343–344
civil war in Syria and rise of ISIS, 338–339
Congressional powers and, 349
containment policy, 351
defense policy, 333
defined, 333
diplomacy, 333
economic troubles in Europe, 345–346
human rights and, 355

intelligence community and, 348
Iraq, wars in, 337
isolationist, 350
Israel and Palestinians, 342–343
moral idealism and, 334
National Security Council and, 347
national security policy and, 333
nuclear weapons, 339–342
political realism and, 334
presidential powers and, 346–348
process of, 333
September 11, 2001 and changed view of, 333
State Department and, 348
techniques and strategies of, 333
terrorism and, 335–336
themes in, 350–354
formative years, 350
internationalism, 350–351
superpower relations, 351–354
Truman Doctrine, 351
Forward guidance, 326
Four-cornered ideological grid, 18–19
Fourteenth Amendment, 57, 96, 109
affirmative action and, 105
due process clause of, 104, 110
equal protection clause, 39, 104, 113
gender discrimination and, 113
incorporating Bill of Rights into, 71
incorporation theory, 70–71
rights of deportees and, 110
Fourth Amendment, 71, 81, 86, 88, 89
special needs exception, 289
Fox News, 125, 146
conservative perspective, 141
Fracking, 52, 317
Framing, 138
France
domestic terrorism and, 336
nuclear weapons and, 340
unitary system of government in, 47
Franchise, 199
Francis, Pope, 127
Franken, Al, 203
Franklin, Benjamin, 33
Freddie Mac, 269
Free exercise clause, 74–75
Freedom
of press (*See* Press, freedom of)
of religion (*See* Religion, freedom of)
of speech (*See* Speech, freedom of)
Freedom House, 3
Freedom of Access to Clinic Entrances Act, 84
Freedom of Information Act (FOIA), 273
Free-rider problem, 153
French and Indian War, 26
Friedan, Betty, 113
Front-loading, 192–193
Front-runner, 193
Fulton, Robert, 55
Fundamental Orders of Connecticut, 25

G
Gaddafi, Muammar, 335
Gallup, George, 133
Gallup poll, 133, 176
Garland, Merrick, 297
Gates, Robert, 254
Gay Activist Alliance, 116

Gay Liberation Front, 116
Gay men. *See* Lesbian, Gay, Bisexual and
    Transgender (LGBT)
Gay men and lesbians, 117
Gender discrimination, 113
Gender gap, 131
General election, 182
General jurisdiction, 286
General Services Administration (GSA), 279
Generational effect, 126
Geographic region, public opinion and,
    131–132
George III, English King, 26, 29
Germany
    at close of World War II, 351
    current account surplus, 346
    East, 351
    EU debt crisis and, 346
    federal system of government in, 48
    West, 351
Gerry, Elbridge, 218
Gerrymandering, 64, 218–219
Ghana, unitary system of government in, 47
Ghettos, 99
Gibbons, Thomas, 55
Gibbons v. Ogden, 55
Gideon v. Wainwright, 71, 88
Ginsburg, Ruth Bader, 297
Gitlow v. New York, 70, 71, 77
Global warming
    debate over, 318
    interest groups and, 158
Goldwater, Barry, 16
Good faith exception, 89
Google, 140, 142
GOP (grand old party), 169
Gore, Al, 170
    demographics and, 170
    election of 2000, 170, 176
        electoral college, 238
        Supreme Court decision and, 291
Gorsuch, Neil, 297, 301, 302
Government
    authority and legitimacy of, 3–4
    based on consent of the people, 5
    big government, 13
    confederal system, 47–48
    defined, 2
    divided, 166
    limited, 6
    limiting power of, 3
    need for, 2–3
    as preeminent institution, 2
    public opinion about, 137
    security and order, 3
    size and scope of, 12–14
    types of, 4
    unitary system of, 47
Government corporations, 268–269
    bankruptcy and government control of
        private corporation, 269
    defined, 268
    government ownership of private
        enterprise, 269
Government in the Sunshine Act, 273
Government regulation. *See also* Regulation
    deregulation, 268
    reregulation, 268
Governors, popular election of, 176

Graber, Doris A., 125
Grandfather clause, 98
Granger, Kay, 207
Grants
    block, 60–61
    categorical, 60
Great Britain
    Brexit, 346
    colonization of America and, 24–27
    health care spending and, 312
    immigration of Syrian refugees, 346
    nuclear weapons and, 340
    representative democracy, 6
    unitary system of government in, 47
Great Compromise, 33–34
Great Depression
    cooperative federalism, 58
    election of 2008 and, 171
    generational effect and, 126
    Keynes and budget deficit, 322
    New Deal and, 170
    unemployment during, 320
Great Recession
    big government and, 13
    budget deficit and, 324
    deficit spending, 324
    impact on state budgets, 61
    public debt, 322
    unemployment during, 322
Greece, debt crisis, 346
Green Party, 175
Greenhouse gas emission, 318
Grenada, American invasion of, 240
Griswold v. Connecticut, 71, 81
Gross domestic product (GDP)
    defined, 312
    health care spending and, 312
    public debt as percentage of, 323
Grutter v. Bollinger, 106
Guantánamo Bay, Cuba, detainees held
    at, 290
Gun-Free School Zones Act, 63
Guns, right to bear arms, 70

H

Habeas corpus, writ of, 69, 87, 290
Haiti, 347
    American troops sent to, 240
Hamas, 342–343
Hamilton, Alexander, 5, 7, 32, 39, 314
    Constitutional Convention and, 32, 33
    elite theory and, 7
    Federalist Papers and, 38
Harding, Warren G., 350
Harris, Kamala, 171
Harrison, Benjamin, 195
Harrison, William Henry, 254
Hatch Act, 185, 272
Hate speech, 69
    colleges and campus speech, 79
Hayden, Michael, 91
Hayes, Rutherford B., 195
Head of state, 237
Health and Human Services, Department of
    functions of, 267
    subagencies of, 267
Health care, 312–316
    agenda building, 310
    high costs and, 314

individual mandate, 62, 315
Medicare and Medicaid costs, 313–314
opposition to implementation of
    Obamacare, 315–316
per capita spending on, 314
role in American economy, 312–313
uninsured and problem of, 314
universal coverage and, 314
Health Care and Education Reconciliation
    Act, 314
Hearst Television, 143
Henry, Patrick, 38
Heritage Foundation, 329
Hidden unemployment, 320
Highway construction, federal grants and,
    60
Hiroshima, 240
Hispanics
    incarceration rate, 103
    income, 103
    percentage of U.S. population, 10
    vs. Latino, 107
Hitler, Adolf, 4, 351
Ho Chi Minh, 352
Holmes, Oliver Wendell, 76
Homeland Security, Department of, 264
    functions of, 267
    subagencies of, 267
Honest Leadership and Open Government
    Act, 163
Hong Kong, 345
Hoover, Herbert, 170
Hostile-environment harassment, 115
House effect, 134–135
House of Representatives, of the United
        States. *See also* Congress
    budget and, 228–232
    committees of, 221–228
    contacting representative, 232
    debate in, 213–215
    differences between Senate and,
        213–216
    gerrymandering, 218–219
    incumbency and power of, 218
    leadership in, 225–226
    majority leader of, 226
    members of
        age of, 215
        election of, 208
        income and wealth of, 216
        perks of, 216
        privileges and immunities of, 216
        professional staff, 216
        religion of, 215
        term of, 208
        women as, 215–216
    minority leader of, 226
    minority-majority districts, 220
    reapportionment, 217
    redistricting, 217
    requirements for office, 181
    Rules Committee of, 224
    rules of, 213
    seniority system, 225
    size of, 213
    speaker of, 225
    whips in, 226
    winning seat in, cost of, 217
House Rules Committee, 224

Housing
    discrimination and, 101
    housing assistance and federal grants, 60
Housing and Urban Development,
        Department of
    functions of, 267
    subagencies of, 267
Hussein, Saddam
    First Gulf War and, 337
    Iraq War and, 337

I

Illegal immigrants
    countries of origin, 107
    deportation of, 109
    number of, 107
    Obama and executive action, 109
Immigrants/immigration
    change in U.S. ethnic distribution, 108
    civil rights of, 107–109
    deportation of illegal, 110
    due process and deportees, 110
    ex post facto laws and deportees, 111
    freedom of association and deportees,
        110–111
    Latino, 107
    limiting state government authority
        over, 62
    national security and civil liberties of,
        109–110
    Obama administration and, 109, 144
    political socialization and media,
        138–139
    Republican Party and Latino voters, 131
    unauthorized immigration issue, 108–109
Immigration Reform and Control Act, 108
Imminent lawless action test, 77
Impeachment, 248–249
Implied power, 54
Incarceration rate, race and, 103
Income, race and, 102–104
Income tax
    congressional power to impose, 212
    imposed during Civil War, 56
    as progressive tax, 328
    rates of, 327–328
Incorporation theory, 70
Independent executive agencies, 266
    agency capture, 266
    deregulation and reregulation, 268
    purpose and nature of, 266
Independent regulatory agencies, 266
Independents
    defined, 163
    rise of, 176
India
    federal system of government in, 48
    nuclear weapons and, 340
Indirect primary, 191
Indirect techniques of interest groups,
        160–162
Individual mandate, 315
Inflation
    defined, 320
    measuring, 320
    monetary policy and, 326
Information disclosure, 273
Inherent powers, 246
    of national government, 51

Initiatives, defined, 5
Institute of Electrical and Electronic
        Engineers, 157
Institutions, 2
Instructed delegate, 209
Intellectual property, 154
Intelligence community
    defined, 348
    foreign policymaking and, 348
    war on terrorism and, 348–349
Intelligent design, 73–74
Interest groups, 151–163
    campaign assistance by, 161
    campaign financing and, 185
    compared to political parties, 152
    constituents as lobbyists, 161–162
    defined, 151
    direct techniques, 160–161
    economic, 154–158
    527 organizations, 187–188
    free-rider problem, 153
    indirect techniques, 161–162
    iron triangles, 278
    issue advocacy advertising, 186
    issue network, 278–279
    lawsuits brought by, 285–286
    lobbying techniques, 160
    low incomes Individuals, 157–158
    number of, 152
    public pressure generated by, 161
    public-interest, 158
    ratings game, 161
    reasons to join, 153
    social movements and, 153
    strategies of, 160–163
    types of, 153–159
Intergovernmental Panel on Climate
        Change, 318
Interior Department
    functions of, 267
    subagencies of, 267
Intermediate scrutiny, 105
Internal Revenue Code, 327
International Telecommunication Union
        (ITU), 142
Internet
    campaigns and, 144–145
    net neutrality, 141–142
    as news source, 138–140
    pornography on, 78
    potential problems with foreign
        governments, 142
    unregulated, 141
Internet Corporation for Assigned Names
        and Numbers (ICANN), 142
Internet Service Provider (ISP), 141
Interstate commerce, 41, 55
Interstate Commerce Commission (ICC),
        266
Interstate compacts, 54
Interstate relations, 53–54
Intolerable Acts, 26
Intrastate commerce, 55
Invisible primary, 190
Iran
    nuclear weapons and, 339–342
    as oil exporter, 316–317
    as theocracy, 4
Iraq. *See also* Iraq War (Second Gulf War)

American invasion of, in 2003, 240, 337
    end game for war, 337
    federalization of National Guard, 53
    First Gulf War, 327
    insurgency, 337
    invasion of Kuwait, 337
    Kurdish community in, 337
    more troops sent to, by Obama, 240
    occupation of, 337
    rise of ISIS, 339
    Second Gulf War, 337
    Shiite community in, 337
    Sunni community in, 337
    three principal ethnic/religious groups
        in, 337
    UN weapons inspection, 337
Iraq War (Second Gulf War)
    Congress and power of the purse, 349
    cost of and deficit spending, 324
    end game for, 337
    insurgency, 337
    occupation, 337
    withdrawal of American troops, 338
Ireland
    debt crisis, 346
    IRA and, 335
Irish Republican Army, 335
Iron triangles, 278
Islamic State (ISIS), 2
    ground troops in Syria debate, 240
    rise of, 338
Isolationist foreign policy, 350
Israel
    attacking Iran's nuclear sites, 340
    conflict with Palestinians and, 342–343
    unitary system of government in, 47
    on U.S. nuclear negotiations with Iran, 340
Issue advocacy advertising, 186
Issue network, 278–279
Issue preference, voting behavior and,
        201–202

J

Jackson, Andrew, 168, 237, 302
    kitchen cabinet, 251
    spoils system, 271
Jamestown, colony at, 23
Japan
    attack on Pearl Harbor, 350
    lobbying by, 159
    ownership of U.S. public debt, 322
    unitary system of government in, 47
Japanese Americans, internment camps
        and, 11
Jay, John, 38
Jefferson, Thomas, 28, 195, 270
    Declaration of Independence, 28–29
    electoral college and, 237
    establishment clause, 71
    Republican Party of, 168
Jews, voting behavior, 129
Jim Crow laws, 98
Johnson, Andrew, 249
Johnson, Lyndon B.
    as chief legislator, 242
    Medicare, creation of, 313
    pact with president regarding incapacity
        of, 254
    Vietnam War and, 240

Joint committee, 223
Judges. *See also* Supreme Court justices
  election of state judges, 294
  federal, 293–298
  judicial traditions and doctrine, 304
  nuclear option and judicial appointments, 215
Judicial activism, 299
Judicial implementation, 303
Judicial powers
  checks and balances, 35–36
  separation of powers, 35
Judicial restraint, 299
Judicial review
  checks and balances and, 35–36, 298–299
  defined, 42
  Federalist Papers and, 38
  informal constitutional change and, 41–42
  rational basis review, 105
  standards for, 104–105
  strict or intermediate scrutiny, 105
Judiciary. *See* Courts
Judiciary Committee, 294
Jurisdiction
  defined, 285
  of federal court system, 286
  general, 286
  limited, 286
Jury
  prospective members of, discrimination against, 286
  right to impartial, 71
Justice Department, 264
  functions of, 267
  solicitor general and, 291
  subagencies of, 267
Justiciable controversy, 285
Justiciable question, 217

K

Kagan, Elena, 296
Kasich, John, 195
Kennan, George F., 335
Kennedy, Anthony, 300
Kennedy, John F., 236
  Cuban missile crisis, 352
  debate with Nixon, 144
  discretionary fiscal policy, 321
  election of, without majority of vote, 237
  federal forces sent to Mississippi by, 99
  Keynesian economics, 321
  pact with vice president regarding incapacity of, 254
Kerry, John F., election of 2004, demographics and, 128
Keynes, John Maynard, 321
  criticism of, 322
Keynesian economics, 321
  European debt crisis and, 346
Keystone XL pipeline, 318
Khamenei, Ayatollah Ali, 3
Kim Jong-un, 3
King, Martin Luther, Jr., 99–101
Kissinger, Henry A., 348, 353
Kitchen cabinet, 251
Klopfer v. North Carolina, 71
Koch, Charles
  contributions to Republican campaigns, 187
  as policy demander, 166

Koch, David
  contributions to Republican campaigns, 187
  as policy demander, 166
Korean War, 246, 351–352
Ku Klux Klan, 77
Kurds in Iraq, 337, 338
Kuwait, Iraq's invasion of, 327

L

Labor Department
  functions of, 267
  measuring unemployment, 320
  subagencies of, 267
Labor interest groups, 155
Labor movement, 155
Laissez-faire capitalism, 175
Landon, Alfred, 133
Lasswell, Harold, 2
Last Week Tonight, 138
Latino, 107. *See also* Hispanics
  immigration issue and Republican Party, 131
  voting behavior, 130–131
Lawmaking
  bureaucracy and policymaking, 275–279
  defined, 209
  as function of Congress, 209
  negotiated rulemaking, 277
  president as chief legislator and, 243
  president's veto power, 243–244
  waiting periods and court challenges, 276
Lawrence v. Texas, 116, 300
Laws
  bill becomes a law process, 228
  case, 284–285
  common law, 283
  Jim Crow, 98
  oversight, 210
  rewriting, as check on courts, 303
  sodomy, 116
  sources of American law, 283–285
  sunshine, 273
Lawsuits
  basic requirements to bring, 285
  class-action, 286
  diversity of citizenship, 285
  interest groups and, 286
  parties to, 285–286
  standing to sue, 285
League of Nations, 334
League of Women Voters, 159
Lebanon, American troops sent to, 240
Ledbetter v. Goodyear, 303
Legal Defense Fund, 286
Legislation
  enabling, 275–279
  negotiated rulemaking, 277
Legislature
  bicameral (two-chamber), 33
  checks and balances, 35–36
  defined, 5
  president and passing, 243
  president's veto power, 243–244
  separation of powers, 35
  unicameral (one-body), 29
Legitimacy, defined, 3
Lemon test, 72
Lemon v. Kurtzman, 72

Lesbian, Gay, Bisexual and Transgender (LGBT)
  "don't ask, don't tell," 117
  growth in rights movement of, 116
  in military, 117
  privacy rights and, 10
  rights and status of, 116–118
  same-sex marriage, 11, 117–118
  state and local laws targeting, 116–117
  transgender persons' rights, 118
Lesbians. *See* Gay men and lesbians
Lewinsky, Monica, 249
Libel, 78
  actual malice, 80
  defined, 80
  public figures and, 80
Liberals/liberalism
  big government and, 17
  defined, 16
  Democratic Party and, 17
  economic status and, 129
  four-cornered ideological grid, 18–19, 129
  judicial activism and, 299
  modern, 16
  political blogs, 145
  on traditional political spectrum, 17
  values of, 17
Libertarian Party, 175
Libertarianism
  defined, 17
  economic status and, 129
  four-cornered ideological grid, 18–19
  on traditional political spectrum, 17–18
Liberty. *See also* Civil liberties
  defined, 3
  equality *versus,* 11–12
  order *versus,* 10–11
Libya, 240
  air strikes, 335
  Arab Spring, 335
  dictatorial rule in, 4
Lilly Ledbetter Fair Pay Act, 303
Limbaugh, Rush, 146
  as policy demander, 166
Limited government, 6
Limited jurisdiction, 286
Lincoln, Abraham, 29, 347
  cabinet of, 251
  election of, without majority of vote, 237
  Emancipation Proclamation and, 96
  emergency power use, 246
  Republican Party of, 168
Linde, Hans A., 294
Line organization, 264
Literacy tests, 98
Literary Digest, 132
Litigate, 286
Living wills, 85–86
Livingston, Robert, 55
Lobbying
  Astroturf, 162
  concentrated benefits and dispersed costs, 163
  by foreign governments, 159
  impact of, 163
  origin of term, 160
  techniques used in, 160
Lobbying Disclosure Act (LDA), 162–163
Lobbyists
  activities of, 160
  constituents as, 161–162

defined, 152, 162
regulating, 162–163
Local government, voter turnout for, 197–198
Local legislative bodies, 18
Local party machinery, 165
Locke, John, 25, 28
Logrolling, 209
Loopholes, 328
Loose monetary policy, 325–326
Louisiana Purchase, 51
Lower courts, 304
Lynching, 98

M

Madison, James, 138, 152
    Bill of Rights, 39
    Constitutional Convention and, 32–33
    Federalist Papers and, 39, 50
    Madisonian model and, 35–36
    on problems of pure democracy, 5
    slavery and drafting Constitution, 34–35
Madisonian model, 35–36
Mail, voting by, 196
Majoritarianism, 7
Majority, 5
Majority leader of the House, 226
Majority opinion, 292
Majority rule, 6
Malloy v. Hogan, 71
Manning, Bradley, 275
Mapp v. Ohio, 71, 89
Marbury v. Madison, 42, 298
March on Washington, 100
Marginal tax rate, 327, 328
Marijuana
    legalizing, 49, 63
    medical, 63
Marriage, same-sex, 117
Marshall, John, 54–55, 62, 63, 302
Marshall, Thurgood, 90
Marshall Plan, 351
Mason-Dixon poll, 184
Massachusetts Bay Colony, 24
Massachusetts Body of Liberties, 25
Material incentives for joining interest groups, 153
Mayflower compact, 23–24
McCain, John, 128
McCain-Feingold Act, 186
McCarthy, Kevin, 207
McConnell, Mitch, 227
McCulloch, James William, 54
McCulloch v. Maryland, 51, 53, 54
McDaniel, Ronna Romney, 166
McDonald v. Chicago, 71
McGovern, George, 190
McGovern-Fraser Commission, 190
Media, 137–147
    agenda setting by, 126, 138
    bias in, 146–147
    Biden, Joe, 147
    consolidation trends in, 141
    continuing influence of television, 140–141
    defined, 125
    entertainment function, 138
    functions of, 137–140
    identifying public problems, 138
    impact of new media, 125

information disclosure and, 273
net neutrality, 141–142
new patterns of media consumption, 140
news reporting function, 138
political campaigns and, 142–147
popularity of, 125
profit function of, 139
providing political forum, 139
social networking, 125
socializing new generations, 138–139
spin, 143
spin doctors, 143
talk radio, 146
Trump and Clinton, 146–147
unregulated Internet, 141
Medicaid
    creation of, 159
    defined, 313
    described, 313
    as entitlement program, 313
    expansion of, by Obamacare, 62
    federal budget spent on, 262
    federal grants and, 60
    government spending on, 313
Medicare
    creation of, 159, 313
    defined, 313
    described, 313
    as entitlement program, 313
    entitlement reform, 329
    federal budget spent on, 262
    government spending on, 313
    prescription drug coverage, 313
    spending growth problem, 314
    taxes for, 327, 328
Medvedev, Dmitry, 353
Men, employment rates, 13
Meredith, James, 99
Merit system, 271
Merit Systems Protection Board (MSPB), 272
Metadata, 289
Mexican Americans, 109
Mexico
    federal system of government in, 48
    unauthorized immigration, 108
Microsoft, government surveillance and, 91
Mid-term elections
    of 2006, 171
    of 2010, 171
    of 2014, 171
    low voter turnout and, 171
    midterm gains and losses by party of president, 217
    voter turnout and, 198
Miers, Harriet, 297
Military
    Articles of Confederation and, 31
    federal budget spent on, 262
    gay men and lesbians in, 117
    president as commander in chief, 240–241
    service, 118
    women and military combat, 114
Miller v. California, 77–78
Minimum wage, 52–53
    states raising, 156
Minor parties
    ideological third parties, 175
    impact of, 176
    role in U.S. politics, 174–176

splinter parties, 175–176
state and federal laws favoring two parties, 174
Minority leader of the house, 226
Minority rights, 6
Minority-majority districts, 220
Miranda, Ernesto, 88
Miranda v. Arizona, 88
Mondale, Walter, 253
Monetary policy, 324–327
    defined, 324
    forward guidance, 326
    loose (expansionary), 325–326
    organization of Federal Reserve System, 324
    quantitative easing, 326
    during recession, 326
    tapering, 326
    tight (contractionary), 325–326
Monroe, James, 168, 350
Monroe Doctrine, 350
Montesquieu, Baron de, 38
Moral idealism, 334
Mossadegh, Mohammad, 348
Motion Picture Association of America, 78
Motor voter bill, 201
Mott, Lucretia, 112
Movies, prior restraint, 81
Mubarak, Hosni, Arab Spring and, 335
Mueller, Robert, 249
Muir, John, 158
Murder rate, 86, 87
Murdoch, Rupert, 141
Muslim Americans, voting behavior, 130

N

NAACP (National Association for the Advancement of Colored People), 98, 159, 286
Nader, Ralph, 158, 175, 176
Nagasaki, 240
NARAL Pro-Choice America, 159
National American Woman Suffrage Association, 112
National Association of Manufacturers, 154
National Audubon Society, 158
National Cattlemen's Beef Association, 278
National committee, 165
National Committee to Preserve Social Security and Medicare, 329
National convention
    convention activities, 164, 194
    defined, 164
    delegates to, 164–165, 177, 193
    as meeting of party elites, 189
    party platform, 164
    reform of, 189
    seating delegates, 194
    superdelegates to, 190
National Corn Growers Association, 278
National debt, 326. *See also* Budget deficit
National Education Association (NEA), 153, 156
National government
    aristocracy of, 270
    budget, 228–232
    bureaucracy of
        congressional control of, 279
        employment today, 260–261
        organization of, 263–269

National government (*continued*)
  policymaking and, 275–279
  reform of, modern attempts at, 272–275
  size of, 260–261
  staffing, 270–272
  cooperative federalism, 58
  devolution, 58
  dual federalism, 57–58
  powers of, 50–51
    commerce clause, 55, 63
    concurrent, 52–53
    division of, between state government
      and, continuing dispute over, 57–62
    enumerated powers, 50–51
    implied, 54
    inherent powers, 51
    to levy taxes, 52
    necessary and proper clause, 51, 54
    prohibited, 51, 52
    supremacy clause and, 53
National Guard, federalization of, and
    deployment to Afghanistan/Iraq, 53
National Organization for Women (NOW),
    113, 159
National Popular Vote movement, 238
National Public Radio, 139
National Review, 148
National Rifle Association, 159
National Right to Life Committee, 159
National security
  Apple and Microsoft *vs.* government
    surveillance, 91
  civil rights of immigrants and, 109–111
  privacy rights *versus,* 11, 90
National Security Act, 348
National Security Adviser, 348
National Security Agency (NSA)
  FISA court and, 289
  metadata collection, 90
  Snowden and, 90, 275
  surveillance by, 90
  warrantless wiretaps, 90
National Security Council (NSC), 252, 348
  foreign policymaking and, 348
  purpose of, 348
National security orders (NSOs), 91
National security policy, 333
National Wildlife Federation, 158
National Woman Suffrage Association, 112
NATO. *See* North Atlantic Treaty
    Organization (NATO)
Natural rights, 28–29
Navy SEALS, 338
Near v. Minnesota, 71
Necessary and proper clause, 51, 212–213
Negative advertising, 143
Negotiated rulemaking, 277
Negotiated Rulemaking Act, 277
Net neutrality, 141–142
Net public debt, 323
Netanyahu, Benjamin, 343
Netflix, 142
New Deal, 58, 170, 250, 272
New England town meetings, 5
New Jersey Plan, 33
New START Treaty, 353
New York Times, 147
New York Times Co. v. Sullivan, 80
New York Times v. United States, 75

News
  being critical consumer of, 148
  bias in, 146–147
  political campaigns and managing,
    144–145
  reporting of, as function of media, 138
Newspapers
  bias in, 146–147
  falling revenues and financial difficulty,
    139–140
  as news source, 138
  online, 139–140
Nineteenth Amendment, 112, 199
Ninth Amendment, 71, 81, 82
Nixon, Richard, 249
  Cambodia invasion and, 240
  China and, 353
  debate with Kennedy, 144
  devolution, 58
  election of, without majority of vote, 237
  impeachment and, 248
  Keynesian economics, 322
  pact with president regarding incapacity
    of, 252
  Strategic Arms Limitation Treaty
    (SALT I), 353
  veto of War Powers Resolution, 241, 349
  Vietnam War and, 349, 352
  Watergate break-in and, 248
No Child Left Behind Act, 59
Noah, Trevor, 138
Nonviolent public disobedience, 100
Norquist, Grover, 159
North Atlantic Treaty Organization (NATO),
    335, 351
North Korea
  dictatorial rule in, 3
  Kim Jong-un's leadership of, 3
  Korean war and, 351–352
  nuclear weapons and, 340
  South Korea invaded by, 351–352
  testing nuclear missiles, 341
Northern Alliance, 337
Northern Ireland, 336
Northwest Ordinance, 30
Nuclear energy, 318
Nuclear option, 215
Nuclear Regulatory Commission, 266
Nuclear weapons, 240, 340–342
  attacking Iran's nuclear sites, 340

O

Obama, Barack, 13, 245
  air strikes in Libya, 347
  appointments
    federal district court judges, 294–295
    to Supreme Court, 115, 295
  Arab Spring and, 335
  armed forces ordered by
    air strike in Libya, 240
    more troops to Afghanistan, 240,
      337–338
  Biden as vice president, 253
  birth certificate controversy, 236
  California air pollution regulations and,
    63
  deficit spending and, 324
  "don't ask, don't tell" policy, 117
  election of 2008, 102

  African American support for, 130
  demographics and, 127
  economic issue and, 171
  Latino vote, 130–131
  public financing and, 192, 188
  election of 2012, 171
  demographics and, 127
  geographic region and, 131–132
  Latino vote, 130–131
  executive agreements, 242
  executive orders by, 247
  federalization of National Guard, 53
  as fundraiser, 244
  higher fuel efficiency standards, 317
  immigration and, 107–109, 144
  ISIS and, 338
  Israeli-Palestinian negotiations, 343
  Keynesian economics, 321
  Libya air strikes, 335
  on Medicare, Medicaid and Social
    Security, 13
  monetary policy and, 326
  New START Treaty, 353
  public opinion and, 245
  reregulation, 268
  signing statements and, 248
  stimulus plan, 322
  use veto power, 243
  waterboarding, 348
  whistleblowers under, 275
  young voter to Democratic Party, 131
Obamacare
  big government and, 13
  individual mandate, 315
  policymaking process, 310–312
Obergefell v. Hodges, 286
Obscenity, 77–78
  definitional problem, 77
  Internet pornography, 78
  protecting children, 78
  remaining restrictions, 78
  rise and fall of *Miller v. California,* 77–78
Occupational Safety and Health Act, 275
Occupational Safety and Health
    Administration, 275
O'Connor, Sandra Day, 294, 295, 299
Office of Administration, 252
Office of Management and Budget (OMB),
    230, 252
Office of National Drug Control Policy, 252
Office of Personnel Management (OPM),
    272
Office of Science and Technology Policy,
    252
Office of Special Counsel (OSC), 274
Office of the Attorney General, 260
Office of the Vice President, 252
Office of United States Trade
    Representative, 252
Ogden, Aaron, 55
Oil industry
  fracking, 317
  new U.S. production and, 317
  politics of expensive oil, 317–318
  U.S. dependency on foreign oil, 317
Oklahoma City bombing, 289–290, 336
Oligarchy, 4
Oliver, In re, 71
Oliver, John, 138

Open primaries, 191
Opinion leaders
    influence of, 124–125
    as policy demander, 166
Opinion polls
    campaigns and use of, 184
    defined, 132
    history of, 132–133
    house effect, 134–135
    problems with, 135–136
    questions asked in, 135–136
    sampling errors, 133–134
    sampling techniques, 133
    statistical nature of, 133
    unscientific and fraudulent, 136
    weighting sample, 134
Opinion Research poll, 184
Opinions
    concurring, 292
    defined, 292
    dissenting, 292
    majority, 292
    oral arguments, 292
    per curiam, 292
    plurality, 292
    publishing, 293
    of Supreme Court of United States, 292
    unanimous, 292
Order
    defined, 3
    liberty *versus,* 10–11
Ordinances, 284
Oversight, 210

P

Packing, in redistricting, 219
Paine, Thomas, 26–27
Pakistan
    al Qaeda and Taliban in, 338
    nuclear weapons and, 340
    Osama bin Laden and, 340
Palestinian Authority, 342
Palestinian Liberation Organization (PLO),
    342
Palestinians, conflict with Israel and, 343
Panama, American troops sent to, 240
Pardon, 239–240
Paris, Treaty of, 29
Parker v. Gladden, 71
Parks, Rosa, 99
Partial birth abortions, 84, 300
Partisanship, judicial appointments and, 295
Party Decides, The (Cohen), 190
Party identification
    defined, 176
    independent voters and, 176
Party organization, 164–165
    defined, 164
    local party machinery, 165
    national, 164
    national chairperson, 165
    national committee, 165
    party-in-government, 166
    patronage, 165
    role in campaigns, 183
    state, 165
Party platform, 164
Party-in-the-electorate, 165–166
Paterson, William, 33

Patient Protection and Affordable Care Act.
    See Affordable Care Act
Patronage, 165, 244, 294
Paul, Alice, 112
Pearl Harbor, 11
Peer group, political socialization and, 124
Pelosi, Nancy, 19, 114, 211, 223
Pence, Mike, 253
Pendleton Act, 271–272
Peng Liyuan, 344
Pennsylvania Charter of Privileges, 25
Pennsylvania Frame of Government, 25
Pentagon Papers case, 75
People's Republic of China. *See* China
Per curiam, opinion, 292
Perot, Ross H., 176
Perpetual Union, 30
Peshmerga militia, 339
Petition, right to, 70
Pew Economic Mobility Project, 310
Philippines
    Spanish-American War and, 350
    unitary system of government in, 47
Physician-assisted suicide, 86
Plain view doctrine, 89
Plaintiff, 285, 286
Plessy, Homer, 97
Plessy v. Ferguson, 97–98
Plum Book, 270
Pluralism, 8
Plurality, 173
Plurality opinion, 292
Pocket veto, 243
Police
    limits on conduct of, 87
    searches and interacting with, 92
Police power
    defined, 51
    states and, 51–52, 57
Policy adoption, health care and, 311
Policy and Supporting Positions, 270
Policy demanders, 166
Policy evaluation, health care, 312
Policy formation, health care and, 311
Policy implementation, health care, 311–312
Policymaking. *See also* Domestic policy;
        Economic policy
    courts and, 298–304
    process of, 310–312
Political action committees (PACs), 184
    campaign financing and, 185
    defined, 185
    soft money, 186
    super PACs, 187
Political Activities Act, 185, 272
Political appointees, 270
Political consultant, 184
Political correctness, on campuses, 79
Political culture
    defined, 9
    public opinion and, 136–137
Political ideologies, 15–19
    conservatism, 15–16
    defined, 15
    four-cornered ideological grid, 18–19
    liberalism, 16–17
    traditional political spectrum, 17–18
Political parties, 167–177
    compared to interest groups, 152

    defined, 152
    functions of, 163–164
    history of, in U.S., 167–172
    major, influence of minor party on,
        175–176
    minor, role of, in U.S. politics, 174–176
    national chairperson of, 165
    national committee, 165
    national party organization, 164
    organization of, 164–165
    party platform, 164
    party-in-government, 166–167
    party-in-the-electorate, 165–166
    patronage, 165
    platform of, 164
    in power, opposition to, 164
    president as chief of, 244–245
    role in campaigns, 183
    splinter parties, 175–176
    state party organizations, 165
    today, 171–172
    voter behavior and, 201–202
Political question, 304
Political realism, 334–335
Political socialization, 9, 123–127
    defined, 123
    education and, 124
    family and, 124
    new generations and media, 138–139
    opinion leaders and, 124–125
    peers and peer groups, 124
    second chance at, 124
    two-party system and, 173
Politics, 2
Poll taxes, 99
Popular Front for the Liberation of Palestine
        (PFLP), 110
Popular sovereignty, 5, 24
Populist, on four-cornered ideological
        grid, 18
Populists, 169
Pornography
    child pornography, 78
    on Internet, 78
Postal Service, U. S., 260–261
    number of employees, 239
Poverty, race and, 96, 102–104, 103
Powell, Colin, 246
Powell, Lewis, 106
Powell v. Alabama, 71
Powers
    concurrent, 52–53
    enumerated, 50–51
    expressed, 50
    implied, 54
    inherent, 51
    limiting government power, 3
    of national government, 50–51
    prohibited, 52
    of state government, 51–52
Prayer, in schools, 73
Precedent, 283
Preclearance requirement, 197, 201
President, 235–256
    becoming
        age of, 236
        birth controversies, 236
        constitutional requirements for, 235–236
        process of, 236–237

President (*continued*)
  cabinet, 250–251
  cabinet departments and, 264–266
  checks and balances, 35, 36
  checks on courts and, 302–303
  as commander in chief, 42
  communicating with, 249
  constituencies of, 244
  creating congressional agenda, 242–243
  death or incapacitation of, 212
  diplomatic recognition, 241
  electoral college, 37
  executive agreement, 242
  executive agreements and, 42
  executive organization, 250–253
  foreign policy made by, 346–348
  going public, 245
  to grant reprieves and pardons, 239–240
  impeachment and, 248–250
  powers of
    appointment, 239, 270, 293–298
    constitutional, 245, 346–348
    emergency, 246
    executive agreement, 242, 347
    executive orders, 247
    executive privilege, 247–248
    expressed, 245
    to grant reprieves and pardons, 239–240
    inherent, 246
    patronage, 244
    signing statements, 248
    statutory, 245
    treaties, 347
    veto, 243–244
    war powers, 347
    wartime, 246
  proposal and ratification of treaties, 241–242
  public approval of, 244–245
  removal, 239
  requirements for office, 181
  roles of
    chief diplomat, 241–242
    chief executive, 239–240
    chief legislator, 242–244
    chief of party, 244–245
    commander in chief, 240–241
    head of state, 237–238
    wartime powers, 240–241
  salary of, 236
  separation of powers, 35
  State of the Union message, 242–243
  succession to, 254–255
Presidential elections
  of 1800, 168
  of 1824, 168
  of 1828, 168
  of 1896, 169
  of 1912, 169, 176
  of 1932, 170
  of 1936, opinion polls predicting, 133
  of 1980, opinion polls, 135
  of 1992, 176
  of 2000, 171
    demographics and, 128
    electoral college, 170, 238
    impact of minor party on, 176
    Supreme Court decision and, 290
  of 2004, 171
    demographics and, 128

  of 2008
    demographics and, 128
    economic issue and, 171
    political parties and, 171
  of 2012, 171
    campaign spending on, 188
    debates, 144
    demographics and, 128
    voting restrictions during, 197–198
  of 2016
    big government, 13
    campaign spending, 188
    debates, 144
    demographics and, 128
    electoral college, 173
    faithless electors, 194–195
    gender gap, 131
    opinion poll predictions, 135–136
    popular vote and, 171
    white working class, 14
  campaign financing, 184–188
  candidate committees and financing, 188
  candidates who run for, 181–182
  debates and, 144
  electoral college, 194, 236–238
  gender gap and, 131
  as longest campaign, 189
  national conventions, 193
  by other than direct popular vote,
    236–238
  popular election of, 173
  primaries, 189–193
  voter turnout, 197–198
  winner-take-all system, 173
  winning without popular vote, 195
Presidential memoranda, 247
Presidential primaries, 181
  as beauty contest, 189
  front-loading, 192–193
  historical perspective on, 189–190
  invisible primary, 190
  reforming, 189–190
  types of, 191
Presidential Succession Act, 255
Press, freedom of, 70, 80–81
  clear and present danger, 76
  libel, 80
  prior restraint, 75, 81
Primary elections (primaries)
  blanket, 192
  closed, 191
  defined, 182
  direct, 191
  early, and consequences of, 193
  historical perspective on, 188
  indirect, 191
  open, 191
  presidential (*See* Presidential primaries)
  proportional and winner-take-all, 191
  public financing for, 188
  run-off, 192
  top-two, 192
Priming, 138
Prior restraint, 75, 81
PRISM, 90
Privacy Act of 1974, 279
Privacy rights, 81–86
  abortion and, 82–85
  constitution and, 81
  national security *versus,* 11, 90

  right to die and, 85–86
  roving wiretaps, 90
  USA Patriot Act, 90
  warrantless wiretaps, 90
Privatization, 273–274
Probable cause
  arrest and, 87
  for search warrants, 88, 92
Professionals, interest groups of, 157
Profits, making, as media function, 139
Progressive tax, 328
Progressives, term of, 19
Progressivism, 169
Prohibition, 40
Promotional policy, 309
Property
  defined, 12
  right to, and capitalism, 12
Proportional primary, 191
Proportional representation, 173–174
Proposition, 7, 74
Prosecutors, limits on conduct of, 87
Protestants
  evangelical and fundamental, 129, 130
  Republican Party and, 169
  voting behavior, 128–130
Prurient interest, 77
Public agenda
  defined, 138
  setting by media, 138
Public debt
  deficit spending and, 322–324
  defined, 322
  historical perspective on, 323–324
  net, 323
  as percentage of gross domestic product,
    323
  perspectives on, 323–324
Public employee unions, 156
Public figure, libel and, 80
Public interest, 158
Public Interest Research Groups (PIRGs),
    158
Public opinion, 122–137
  about government, 138
  check on courts and, 303–304
  consensus, 123
  defined, 123
  demographic factors and, 127–132
  divided, 123
  economic status and, 129
  education and, 127
  formation of, 123–125
  gender gap and, 131
  generational effect, 126
  geographic region and, 131–132
  measuring, 132–136
  media and, 137–142
  policymaking and, 137
  political culture and, 136–137
  political process and, 136–137
  political socialization and, 123–127
  of president, 244–245
  race and ethnicity, 130
  religious influence on, 127, 129
  Supreme Court and, 304
Public pressure, 161
Public problems, identifying by media, 138
Public-interest groups, 158–159
Puerto Rico, 350

Punishment, cruel and unusual, 71, 88
Purposive incentives for joining interest
    groups, 153
Push poll, 136
Putin, Vladimir, 334, 353, 354

Q

Qaddafi, Muammar. *See* Gaddafi,
    Muammar
Quantitative easing, 326
Questions, in opinion polls, 135–136
Quinlan, In re, 85
Quinlan, Karen Ann, 85

R

Race
    affirmative action programs and, 105–106
    incarceration rate, 103
    income and, 102–104
    poverty rate and, 102–103
    redistricting based on, 220
    strict scrutiny and, 104
    voting behavior and, 130
Race riots, 170
Radio
    bias in, 146
    as entertainment source, 138
    Fairness Doctrine, 127
    First Amendment freedoms and, 81
    talk radio, 125
Randolph, A. Philip, 100
Randolph, Edmund, 33
Randomness, principle of, 133
Ranking committee member, 225
Ratification
    Bill of Rights, 39
    defined, 37
    of United States Constitution, 37–39
Ratings game, 161
Reagan, Ronald, 236
    approval rating of, 136
    armed forces ordered by
        into combat without congressional
            approval, 349
        to invade Grenada, 240
        into Lebanon, 240
    deregulation, 268
    devolution, 58
    economic prosperity under, 127
    election of 1980, 135
    on federalism, 50
    foreign policy and, 353
    gender gap, 131
    government employment under, 261
    judicial appointment and, 294, 295
    Soviet Union and, 353
RealClearPolitics, 145
Realignment
    of 1896, 167
    of 1932, 167
    defined, 169
Reapportionment, 217
Recall, 5
Recession
    in business cycle, 321
    defined, 320
    monetary policy during, 326
    unemployment and, 320
Reconciliation, 214–215

Red states, 170–171
Redistributive policy, 309
Redistricting
    after 2010 census, 220
    defined, 217
    gerrymandering, 218–220
    minority-majority districts, 220
    packing and cracking, 219
    race-based, 220
Referendum, 5
Reform Party, 176
Regents of the University of California v.
    Bakke, 106
Regulation
    campaign financing, 185–186
    of lobbyists, 162–163
    negotiated rulemaking, 277
    waiting periods and court challenges, 276
Regulatory agencies, 266
Regulatory policy, 309
Rehnquist, William, 295, 299
Rehnquist Court, 295
Religion
    aid to church-related schools, 72
    endorsement of candidate by religious
        organizations, 74
    establishment clause, 71–74
    forbidding teaching of evolution, 73
    free exercise clause, 74–75
    freedom of, 71–75
    importance of, to African Americans, 203
    nation's founders and, 25
    political attitudes and, 129
    religious displays on public property, 74
    separation of church and state, 71–74
Religious buildings, construction of, 75
Remandment of court case, 291
Removal power, 239
Representation
    defined, 209
    instructed-delegate view of, 209
    by members of Congress, 209
    trustee-view of, 209
Representative assembly, 23
Representative democracy
    compared to democratic republic, 6
    defined, 6
    principles of, 6
Reprieve, 239–240
Republic, 5
Republican Party
    of Abraham Lincoln, 168
    Congress controlled by, 13, 171
    conservatism and, 16
    convention delegates, 164–165, 177
    debt ceiling crisis, 231
    devolution, 58–59
    economic status and, 129
    education and, 127
    formation of, 168
    geographic region and, 131–132
    global warming disbelief, 318–319
    GOP nickname, 169
    Hastert Rule, 215
    history of, 167–172
    Latino vote and immigration issue, 131
    midterm elections of 2010 and, 171
    midterm elections of 2014 and, 171
    nuclear option and judicial appointments,
        215

    opposition to Obamacare, 315
    party identification and, 176
    policy demanders in, 166
    in post-Civil War period, 168–169
    race and ethnicity, 130
    red states and, 170–171
    regaining control of presidential primary,
        193
    of Thomas Jefferson (Democratic
        Republicans), 167
    today, 171–172
    unauthorized immigrants and Obama's
        executive order, 144
    wave elections and, 171
Republicanism, rise of, 29
Reregulation, 268
Reserved powers, 51
Resolution of Independence, 28
Reversal of judgment, 292
Reverse discrimination, 106
Right to censor, 92
Right to die, 85–86
Rights. *See also* Bill of Rights
    natural, 29
Rights of transgender
    Bathroom Bill issue, 118
    military service, 118
Right-to-work laws, 157
Roberts, John G. Jr., 219, 295, 298, 299,
    300, 301
Roberts Court, 299–302
Robinson v. California, 71
Robocalls, 134
Roe v. Wade, 85
Romney, Mitt
    demographics and, 128
    election of 2012, ministers endorsement
        of, 74
    Ryan as running mate, 253
Roosevelt, Franklin D., 16
    Bureau of the Budget and, 252
    as chief legislator, 242
    election of 1936, opinion polls predicting,
        133
    emergency power use, 246
    establishment of Executive Office of the
        President, 250
    generational effect, 126
    Great Depression and, 170
    inherent powers and internment camps,
        246
    New Deal and, 58, 130, 170, 250, 272
    Soviet Union recognized by, 241
    World War II and, 350
Roosevelt, Theodore
    election of 1912, 169, 176
    as progressive, 169, 176
Roper, Elmo, 133
Roper poll, 133
Rouhani, Hassan, 340, 341
Roving wiretaps, 90
Rule of four, 291
Rulemaking, environment of, 276–277
Rules Committee, 213
Run-off primary, 192
Russia
    dissolution of Soviet Union and, 353
    New START agreement, 353
    nuclear weapons and, 340, 353
    as oil exporter, 317

Russia (*continued*)
  population of, 354
  Syria and, 340
  Ukraine and, 353–354
Rustin, Bayard, 100
Ryan, Paul, 253

S

Safe seats, 225
Sales tax, 329
Salman bin Abdulaziz Al Saud, 3
Same-sex marriage, 11, 49, 74
  Defense of Marriage Act, 117
  state recognition of, 117–118
Sampling error, 133–134
Sampling techniques for opinion polls, 133
San Bernardino shooting, 336
Sanders, Bernie
  election of 2016
    as democratic socialist, 17, 175
    populist appeals by, 18
    superdelegate issue, 190
Saudi Arabia
  king's rule of, 3
  as oil exporter, 317
Scalia, Antonin, 297, 301, 302
Schiavo, Terry, 85, 86
School vouchers, 72
Schools
  busing, 99–100
  church-related, government aid to, 72
  forbidding teaching of evolution, 73
  freedom of speech and students, 79
  political socialization and, 124
  prayer in, 73
  school integration and, 99, 303
  vouchers and, 72
Schumer, Charles, 197
Search and seizure, unreasonable
  constitutional prohibition of, 86, 90, 91
  exclusionary rule, 88–89
  interacting with police, 92
  probable cause, 88, 92
Search warrants, probable cause and, 88–89
Second Bank of the United States, 54
Second budget resolution, 231
Second Civil Rights Act (Civil Rights Act of 1875), 97
Second Continental Congress, 26–27, 30
Security
  national security policy, 333
  vs. civil liberties, 90
Segregation
  buses, 99–100
  de facto, 99
  de jure, 99
  school integration and, 99
  separate-but-equal doctrine, 98–99
Select committee, 223
Senate, of the United States. *See also* Congress
  budget and, 228–232
  checks and balances, 35, 36
  cloture, 213–214
  committees of, 221–225
  contacting representative, 232
  debate in, 213–215
  differences between House of Representatives and, 213–216

elections for, 216–221
filibustering in, 214
incumbency and power of, 217
judicial appointment and, 293–298
leadership in, 227–228
lobbying rules, 163
majority leader of, 227–228
members of
  age of, 215
  election of, 208
  income and wealth of, 216
  minorities, 215
  perks of, 216
  privileges and immunities of, 216
  professional staff, 216
  religion of, 215
  term of, 208
  women as, 114, 215–216
minority leader of, 227
nuclear option, 215
powers of, 212
president pro tempore of, 227
ratification of treaties and, 241–242
reconciliation, 214–215
requirements for office, 181
rules of, 213
senatorial courtesy, 295
seniority system, 225
separation of powers, 35
size of, 213
vice president as president of, 227, 253
whips in, 227
winning seat in, cost of, 216
Senatorial courtesy, 295
Seniority system, 225
Separate-but-equal doctrine, 42, 98–99
Separation of church and state, 71–74
Separation of powers, 35
Separatists, 23–24
September 11, 2001 terrorist attacks, 336
  al Qaeda and, 333
  changed view of security and foreign policy afterwards, 333
  powers of FISA court expanded after, 289
  reasons for attack, 336
  security *vs.* privacy rights after, 11
  spending on security afterwards, 324
  sunshine laws after, 273
  suspected terrorist detainees, 290
  Taliban government in Afghanistan, 333
Serbia, American bombing of, 240
Service sector, 155
Seventeenth amendment, 208
Sexual harassment, 115
Sharon, Ariel, 342
Shays, Daniel, 31
Shays' Rebellion, 31
Shelby County v. Holder, 201
Shiites in Iraq, 337
Sierra Club, 158, 286
Signing statements, 248
Silver, Nate, 133
Sixteenth Amendment, 212, 303
Sixth Amendment, 71, 86, 88
Slander, 78
Slavery/slaves
  Civil War and, 56, 168
  Connecticut Compromise, 34
  consequences of, for African Americans, 96–104

drafting Constitution and, 33–37
  Emancipation Proclamation and, 96
  end of, 96
  three-fifths compromise, 34
  Whig Party and, 168
Smith, Adam, 25
Snowden, Edward, 90, 275, 289
Social contract, 28
Social movements
  civil rights movement, 153
  consumer, 158
  defined, 153
  labor movement, 155
Social networking, impact on public opinion, 141–142
Social Security
  annual cost-of-living increases and AARP, 159
  as entitlement program, 309
  entitlement reform, 329
  federal budget spent on, 262
  taxes for, 327, 328
Socialism
  defined, 17
  on traditional political spectrum, 17–18
Socialist Party, 175
Socioeconomic status
  defined, 202
  voter behavior and, 129, 202–203
Sodomy laws, 116
Soft money
  defined, 186
  restricted by Bipartisan Campaign Reform Act, 186
Solicitor general, 291
Solidarity incentives for joining interest groups, 153
Sotomayor, Sonia, 296
Sound bite, 140
Souter, David, 296
South Korea
  invaded by North Korea, 351–352
  Korean war and, 351–352
  lobbying by, 159
Southern Christian Leadership Conference (SCLC), 100, 153
Soviet Bloc, 351
Soviet Union
  beginning of Korean War, 351
  Cold War and, 351
  Cuban missile crisis, 352
  détente and, 352–353
  dissolution of, 353
  nuclear weapons and, 340
  Roosevelt's recognition of, 241
  Russia after, 352–353
  Strategic Arms Limitation Treaty (SALT I), 353
  superpower relations with United States and, 351–354
Spain, dept crisis, 346
Spanish-American War, 350
Speaker of the House, 225
Speech, freedom of, 10, 71
  clear and present danger, 76
  commercial speech, 76
  imminent lawless action test, 77
  obscenity, 77–78
  prior restraint, 75
  slander, 78–79

student speech, 79
symbolic speech, 75–76
Speech, hate, 69
Spin, 143
Spin doctor, 143
Splinter party, 175
Spoiler effect, 176
Spoils system, 271
Spring review, 230
Stalin, Joseph, 4
Stamp Act, 26
Standing committees, 223
Standing to sue, 285
Stanton, Elizabeth Cady, 112
Stare decisis, 283–284
State central committee, 165
State courts
    basic judicial requirements for
      cases, 285
    election of judges, 293
    procedural rules, 286
State Department, 260, 264, 333
    foreign policymaking and, 348
    functions of, 267
    subagencies of, 267
State government
    cooperative federalism, 58
    devolution, 58
    dual federalism, 57–58
    employee unions, 64
    extending Bill of Rights to, 68
    fiscal federalism, 61
    Great Recession and budgets of, 61
    interstate compacts, 54
    interstate relations, 53–54
    legislature, requirements of members
      of, 181
    Medicaid spending and, 313
    minimum wage, 52–53
    powers of, 39, 51–52
      Civil War and, 55–56
      concurrent, 52–53
      division of, between state government
        and, continuing dispute over, 57–62
      to levy taxes, 52
      police, 51–52, 57
      prohibited, 51, 52
      reserved, 51
      supremacy clause and, 53
    prohibited from entering into treaty
      and, 52
    raising minimum wage, 156
    same-sex marriage recognized by, 74,
      117–118
    states' rights
      recent Supreme Court trend toward, 63
      shift back to, before Civil War, 55
State of the Union message, 242
State party organization, 165
States
    constitutions of, 29, 284
    defined, 30
    red and blue states, 170–171
    statutes, 284
Statutes, as source of American law, 284
Statutory powers, 245
Stevens, John Paul, 296
Stewart, Jon, 138
Stewart, Potter, 77
Stimulus package

deficit spending and fiscal policy, 322
    unemployment rate and, 320
Stone, Lucy, 112
Stonewall Inn, 116
Straight-ticket voting, 176
Strict construction, 299
Strict scrutiny, 104
Suffrage
    defined, 96
    universal, 6
    women's, 112
Sugar Act, 26
Suicide, physician-assisted, 86
Sunnis in Iraq, 337
Sunshine laws, 273
Super PACs, 43, 187
Super Tuesday, 187
Superdelegates, 190
Supplemental Nutrition Assistance Program
    (SNAP), 157
Supremacy clause, 53
Supremacy doctrine, 33
Supreme Court justices
    appointments, 293–298
      partisanship and, 295–296
      Senate's role in confirmation, 296
    background of, 296
    photo of, 299
    strict or broad construction, 299
Supreme Court of United States, 287
    after Civil War, 57
    campaign ads, 187
    caseload of, 293
    cases that reach, 291
    checks and balances, 35, 36
    death with dignity law, 63
    decisions of, 292
    dual federalism and, 57–58
    executive checks over, 302–303
    federalism and, 54–55, 63
    gerrymandering, 64
    gun free zone, 63
    as highest court in land, 284, 287
    hypothetical and political questions, 304
    immigration, 62
    impact of lower courts on, 304
    judicial activism, 299
    judicial restraint, 299
    judicial review and, 42, 104–105
    judicial traditions and doctrine, 304
    legislative checks over, 303
    Marshall Court, 54
    medical marijuana, 63
    opinions of, 292–293
    political question, 304
    preclearance requirement, 201
    procedures of, 292
    public opinion, 303–304
    Rehnquist Court, 295
    Roberts Court, 299–302
    rule of four, 291
    rulings of
      abortion, 82–85
      affirmative action, 105–107
      Affordable Care Act, 301
      apportionment, 217
      candidates' financing of campaign, 185
      civil rights, 96–104
      civil service system, 271
      commercial speech, 76

emergency power, 246
    establishment clause, 71–72
    evolution, teaching of, 73
    executive privilege, 248
    free legal counsel, 88
    health care reform, 315
    incorporation theory, 70
    Miranda rule, exceptions to, 88
    Obamacare, 315
    obscenity, 77–78
    physician-assisted suicide, 86
    prior restraint, 75
    same-sex marriage, 117–118
    school prayer, 73
    school vouchers, 72
    separate-but-equal doctrine, 98–99
    sodomy laws, 116
    suspected terrorist detainees, 290
    symbolic speech, 75
    solicitor general and, 291
    state government employee unions, 64
    at work, 290–293
Surface Transportation Program, 61
Suspect classification, 104
Sweden, unitary system of government
    in, 47
Switzerland, direct democracy, 5
Symbolic speech, 75
Syria
    al-Assad's leadership of, 2
    al-Assad's leadership of, 338
    Arab Spring, 335
    chemical weapons in, 341–342
    civil war in, 340
    dictatorial rule in, 2
    lack of law and order, 2
    rise of ISIS, 338
    U.S. bombing of IS targets, 340

T

Taft, William Howard, 176, 295
Taiwan, 344–345
Taliban
    in Afghanistan, 338
    in Pakistan, 338
Talk radio, 125
Tapering, 326
Taxes, 327–329
    capital gains, 328
    estate, 329
    export, 35
    fiscal policy and, 326
    income (*See* Income tax)
    loopholes and, 328
    marginal tax rate, 327, 328
    Medicare, 327, 328
    progressive, 328
    regressive, 328
    sales, 329
    Social Security, 328, 329
    types of, 329
Tea Party movement, 26
    big government and, 13
Telecommunications Act, 81
Television
    bias in, 146–147
    continuing influence of, 140–141
    as entertainment source, 138
    First Amendment freedoms and, 81

Television (*continued*)
  influence on political process, 136
  as news source, 138
Temporary Assistance for Needy Families
  (TANF), 262
Tenth Amendment, 46, 51, 52
Terrorism. *See also* al Qaeda; War on
  terrorism
  death of bin Laden, 338
  domestic, 336
  emergence of, 335–336
  rise of ISIS, 338
  September 11, 2001, 336
Thailand, military rule of, 3
Theocracy, 4
Third Amendment, 70, 81
Third Parties
  defined, 174
  ideological, 175
  impact of, 176
  splinter parties, 175–176
  state and federal laws favoring two
    parties, 174
Thirteenth Amendment, 57, 96
Thomas, Clarence, 76, 293, 297
Tight monetary policy, 325–326
Tinker v. Des Moines School District, 75
Tocqueville, Alexis de, 152, 283
Top-two primary, 192
Totalitarian regime, 4
Totalitarianism, 4
Town meetings, 5
Tracking polls, 134, 184
Traditional political spectrum, 18
Transgender individuals. *See* Lesbian, Gay,
  Bisexual and Transgender (LGBT)
Transportation, Department of
  functions of, 267
  subagencies of, 267
Treasuries, 322, 324
Treasury, Department of, 250, 252
  functions of, 267
  subagencies of, 267
Treaties
  proposed by president, 241–242, 347
  ratification of, 241–242
Trial
  right to speedy, 71, 87
  rights and, 87–88
Trial courts, 286
Truman, Harry, 237
  decision to use atomic bomb against
    Japan and, 240, 351
  election of, without majority of vote, 237
  emergency power use, 246
  on German's trade surplus, 346
  troops sent to Korea, 240, 347
  Truman Doctrine and, 351
Truman Doctrine, 351
Trump, Donald, 13
  appointments to Supreme Court, 297
  election of 2016
    big government and, 13
    debates, 144
    educational achievement and voters, 127
    electoral college, 174
    faithless electors, 194–195
    invisible primary and, 190
    older voters and Make America Great
      Again, 127
    opinion poll predictions, 135–136

  perception of, and voting behavior, 202
  popular vote, 237
  religious commitment and voters,
    129–130
  white working class, 14
  winning without popular vote, 196
Pence as vice president, 253
political realism, 334
regulation under, 268
sanctuary cities and revoking grant
  money, 62
use of Twitter, 145
waterboarding and, 348
Trustee, 209
Tubman, Harriet, 96
Tunisia
  Arab spring, 335
  dictatorial rule in, 4
Twelfth Amendment, 212, 237
Twentieth Amendment, 212
Twenty-fifth Amendment, 212, 255
Twenty-fourth Amendments, 98
Twenty-second Amendment, 249
Twenty-sixth Amendment, 199
Twenty-third, 194
Twitter, Trump's use of, 145
Two Treatises of Government (Locke), 28
Two-party system
  defined, 167
  endurance of, reasons for, 172–177
  historical foundations of, 172–173
  state and federal laws favoring, 174
Tyler, John, 254

U

Ukraine, 353–354
UN. *See* United Nations (UN)
Unanimous opinion, 292
Unemployment
  defined, 320
  discouraged workers, 320
  during Great Recession, 323
  hidden, 320
  measuring, 320
  stimulus package and, 322
Unemployment benefits
  as entitlement program, 309
  federal grants, 59
Unfunded Mandates Reform Act, 62
Unicameral (one-body) legislature, 29
Unions
  affirmative action, 105
  membership in, declining, 155
  political environment today, 157
  public employees, 156
  right-to-work laws, 157
Unit rule, 173
Unitary system
  defined, 47
  flow of power in, 48
United Nations (UN)
  ection in Iraq, 337
  Intergovernmental Panel on Climate
    Change, 318
  weapons inspection in North Korea, 340
United States
  benefits of federalism for, 49
  democracy in, kind of, 6–8
  federal system of government in, 48
  health care spending in, 312

United States Constitution. *See* Constitution
  of United States
United States Reports, 293
*United States v. Curtiss-Wright Export
  Corp.,* 246
United States v. Windsor, 118, 301
Universal health insurance, 314
Universal suffrage, 6
Universal truths, 28
University. *See* Colleges
Urban League, 153
U.S. Treasury securities, 322
USA Freedom Act, 289
USA Patriot Act, 90, 289

V

Venezuela, as oil exporter, 316
Ventura, Jesse, 176
Verizon, 289
Versailles Treaty, 242
Veterans Affairs, Department of
  functions of, 267
  subagencies of, 267
Veto
  override of, 243–244
  pocket, 243
  president's power of, 243–244
  veto message, 243
Vice president, 253–255
  death or incapacity of, 254
  job of, 253
  as president of the Senate, 227
  presidential succession and, 254–255
Vietnam War, 16, 75, 170, 349, 352
  American involvement in, 349
  generational effect and, 126
Vietnamese Americans, voting behavior, 131
Virginia Company of London, 23
Virginia Plan, 33
Voltaire, 25
Vote-eligible population, 198
Voter turnout
  calculating, 199
  for congressional elections, 198
  defined, 198
  impact of restrictive voting laws on,
    197–198
  low, and effect of, 199
  for presidential elections, 198–201
  voter identification and, 196
Voting. *See also* Voting behavior
  African Americans and, 100
  ballots for, 196
  fraud in, 196–198
  legal restrictions on, 199
  by mail, 196
  preclearance requirement, 197
  registration for, 102, 201
    age requirements, 203
    motor voter bill, 201
    property requirements, 199
    requirements for, current eligibility
      and, 201
    residency requirements, 203
    time limits, 203
    universal suffrage, 6
    voter identification, 196
Voting behavior
  demographic influences, 127–132, 203
  economic status and, 129

education and, 127
gender and, 131
geographic regions and, 131–132
by groups for presidential elections 2004-2020, 128
issue preference, 202
party identification, 201–202
perception of candidate and, 202
race and ethnicity, 130
religion and, 129–130
straight-ticket voting, 176
women, 131
Voting fraud, 196–198
Voting rights
African Americans, 96, 98, 101, 199
age and, 199, 203
grandfather clause, 98
literacy tests, 98
poll taxes, 99
white primary, 98
women and, 112, 220
Voting Rights Act, 201, 301
preclearance for voting procedure changes, 196–197
Voting Rights Act of 1964, 100
Voting Rights Act of 1965, 101
Voting-age population, 199
Vox.com, 145

W

Wage discrimination, 115
Wages, minimum, 52–53
Walt Disney Company, 154
War on terrorism, 336
alien "removal courts," 289–290
federal courts and, 290
FISA court, 289
intelligence community and, 348–349
suspected terrorist detainees, 290
War Powers Resolution, 241, 349
Warren, Earl, 88, 99, 299
Warren, Elizabeth, 183
Wartime powers of president, 240–241

Washington, George, 167
as commander in chief, 240
Constitutional Convention and, 32
slavery and drafting Constitution, 34
Washington community, 244
Watergate break-in, 126, 249
Wave elections, 171
Welfare programs, federal grants for, 60
Welfare reform
block grants and, 60–61
control transferred to states, 58–59
West Germany, 351
Whig Party, 168
Whips, 226
Whistleblower
defined, 274
laws protecting, 274
under Obama, 275
and private data, 275
Whistle-Blower Protection Act, 274
White House, communicating with, 256
White House Military Office, 252
White House Office, 252
White primary, 98
White supremacy, 98
Whites
percentage of U.S. population, 10
working class and 2016 election, 14
William the Conqueror, 283
Wilson, James, 33
Wilson, Woodrow, 16, 42, 237, 242, 250
election of, without majority of vote, 237
election of 1912, 169, 176
League of Nations and, 334
Wind energy, 317
Winner-take-all electoral system, 173–174
Wiretaps
roving, 90
warrantless, 90
Wolf v. Colorado, 71
Women
as candidates, 182
civil rights of, 112–115

in Congress, 215–216
discrimination in workplace, 114–115
employment rates, 13
Equal Rights Amendment and, 113
gender gap and, 131
gender-based discrimination and, 114–115
intermediate scrutiny and, 105
in politics, 114
sexual harassment, 115
voting behavior, 131
voting right, 112, 199
wage discrimination, 115
women's movement, 112–113, 153
Working class
defined, 14
white working class and 2016 election, 14
Workplace discrimination. *See* Employment discrimination
World War I, isolationist foreign policy and, 350
World War II, 250
atomic bombs dropped on Japan and, 351
emergency power and fall of France, 246
Japanese attack on Pearl Harbor, 11
Yalta Conference and, 352
Writ
of certiorari, 291
of habeas corpus, 69, 87

X

Xi Jinping, 344

Y

Yalta Conference, 352
Yanukovych, Viktor, 353
Year Books, 283
Yeltsin, Boris, 353
Your Right to Federal Records, 279
YouTube, 138, 140, 142

Z

Zuckerberg, Mark, 141